Literacy in Ancient Everyday Life

Literacy in Ancient Everyday Life

Edited by Anne Kolb

DE GRUYTER

ISBN: 978-3-11-059188-0
e-ISBN (PDF): 978-3-11-059406-5
e-ISBN (EPUB): 978-3-11-059202-3

Library of Congress Cataloging-in-Publication Data
Names: Kolb, Anne, editor.
Title: Literacy in ancient everyday life / edited by Anne Kolb.
Description: Berlin ; Boston : Walter de Gruyter, [2018] | Includes index. | Text in English and German.
Identifiers: LCCN 2018007858| ISBN 9783110591880 (hardcover) | ISBN 9783110594065 (pdf) | ISBN 9783110592023 (EPUB)
Subjects: LCSH: Inscriptions, Ancient. | Literacy--History--To 1500. | Writing--History--To 1500. | Language and culture.
Classification: LCC CN120 .L58 2018 | DDC 411/.7--dc23 LC record available at https://lccn.loc.gov/2018007858

Bibliografische Information der Deutschen Nationalbibliothek
Die Deutsche Nationalbibliothek verzeichnet diese Publikation in der Deutschen Nationalbibliografie; detaillierte bibliografische Daten sind im Internet über http://dnb.dnb.de abrufbar.

©2018 Walter de Gruyter GmbH, Berlin/Boston
Einbandabbildung: ©Foto Benjamin Hartmann
Satz: Dörlemann Satz GmbH & Co. KG, Lemförde
Druck und Bindung: CPI Books GmbH, Leck
♾ Gedruckt auf säurefreiem Papier
Printed in Germany

www.degruyter.com

Contents

Preface —— IX

Anne Kolb
Literacy in Ancient Everyday Life – Problems and Results —— 1

I A Global Perspective

Li Feng
The Development of Literacy in Early China: With the Nature and Uses of Bronze Inscriptions in Context, and More —— 13

Harry Falk
The Creation and Spread of Scripts in Ancient India —— 43

Katharina Zinn
Literacy in Pharaonic Egypt: Orality and Literacy between Agency and Memory —— 67

Josef Wiesehöfer
Anmerkungen zu Literalität und Oralität im teispidisch-achaimenidischen Iran —— 99

Irene Madreiter
Der Raum alltäglicher weiblicher Literalität im Achaimeniden-Reich —— 113

William V. Harris
Literacy in Everyday Ancient Life: From Gabii to Gloucestershire —— 143

II Roman Empire

Social Groups

Sabine R. Hübner
Frauen und Schriftlichkeit im römischen Ägypten —— 163

Michael A. Speidel
Soldiers and Documents: Insights from Nubia. The Significance of Written Documents in Roman Soldiers' Everyday Lives —— 179

Roger Tomlin
Literacy in Roman Britain —— 201

Kai Ruffing
Schriftlichkeit und Wirtschaft im Römischen Reich —— 221

Religious Practice

Wolfgang Spickermann
Als die Götter lesen lernten: Keltisch-germanische Götternamen und lateinische Schriftlichkeit in Gallien und Germanien —— 239

Amina Kropp
Schriftlichkeit in der Schadenzauberpraxis am Beispiel der vulgärlateinischen *defixionum tabellae* —— 261

Administration

A. Caballos Rufino
Monumenta fatiscunt.
Meaning and Fate of Legal Inscriptions on Bronze: the Baetica —— 289

W. Graham Claytor
The Municipalization of Writing in Roman Egypt —— 319

Paul Schubert
Who Needed Writing in Graeco-Roman Egypt, and for What Purpose? Document Layout as a Tool of Literacy —— 335

Benjamin Hartmann
Schreiben im Dienste des Staates. Prolegomena zu einer Kulturgeschichte der römischen *scribae* —— 351

Education

Marietta Horster
Geschichte und Geschichten im Alltag —— 363

Winfried Schmitz
Bedrohte Latinitas. Sprachliche Veränderungen auf spätantik-frühmittelalterlichen Grabinschriften aus dem Rhein-Mosel-Gebiet —— 387

List of Authors —— 413
Fotograph of the Participants During the Conference —— 415
Index —— 417

Preface

This volume presents the papers delivered at the international conference held from the 10th to the 12th of November 2016 at the Historisches Seminar der Universität Zürich on the theme of „Literacy in Ancient Everyday Life – Schriftlichkeit im antiken Alltag".

The conference itself and the publication of these proceedings has been generously funded by various institutions, all of which are due the greatest gratitude: the Swiss National Fund, the Higher Education Fund of Zurich University, the Zurich University Society, as well as the University of Zurich itself.

My colleagues at Zurich provided invaluable support both in organising the conference and in editing the volume. I am particularly grateful to Monika Pfau, whose sheer omnipresence was remarkable. Gratitude is further due to Yannick Baldassarre, Dr. Jens Bartels, Miriam Bastian, Nikolas Hächler, Dr. Ursula Kunnert (all Zurich), Dr. Joachim Fugmann (Konstanz), as well as to the staff at De Gruyter (Berlin) for the productive collaboration.

Anne Kolb
Zurich, June 2018

Anne Kolb
Literacy in Ancient Everyday Life – Problems and Results

Admiror te paries non cecidisse, qui tot scriptorum taedia sustineas.

"I admire you, Wall, for not having collapsed, despite having been made to endure the tedium of so many writers."[1]

This statement, scratched into a wall of the amphitheatre at Pompeii by an anonymous writer, sheds an interesting light on the everyday use of writing in an Italian city of the 1st century AD. The writer does not reveal their name, though it was the name above all else that generated identity in society. As such, the great mass of graffiti are generally names.[2] What is truly interesting about these few words, however, is that its ironical author immortalised not only their own literacy but also that of numerous others, who apparently also left their scratched and drawn markings on the city's buildings. One can imagine a whole range of people among their number, casual passers-by of varying social and economic background, such as idle dalliers, business people, clients waiting on their patrons, and even magistrates and their entourages. The quip quoted here may have been popular in Pompeii, since it was inscribed not only in the amphitheatre, but also at the theatre and on the walls of the basilica – unless of course one wishes to assume that they all were left by the same person.[3]

Who in particular these spectral authors were who left their various, apparently unnecessary or pointless messages (*tot scriptorum taedia*) spattered across the city's wall-space, and what proportion of Pompeii's inhabitants partook in this pastime unfortunately largely eludes us today. Nevertheless, the so-called "graffiti habit" provides an important indicator for ancient literacy in its day to day practice, especially since it left individual and spontaneous messages not only in public space, but also in various locations inside houses.[4] Besides the ubiquitous names, one finds practice alphabets, accounts, obscenities, Virgilian verses, declarations of love, curses and many other forms of textual utterances. Graffiti thus neatly illustrate the breadth of textual content as well as the plethora of uses writing saw in everyday life in Antiquity.

To what degree ancient societies were literate and which groups possessed the ability to read and write is a matter of long-standing debate in scholarship. Older

---

[1] CIL IV 2487.
[2] That the majority of all graffiti are names and/or markers of identity has recently been emphasized with some justification by LOHMANN 2017a, 58; for a different view see e. g. MILNOR 2014, 14.
[3] CIL IV 1904. 1906. 2461. 2487.
[4] BENEFIEL 2011; BENEFIEL 2016; LOHMANN 2017b; for the concept of the "graffiti habit" see COOLEY 2012, 111.

research generally gave rather positive answers, especially regarding the degree of literacy in the Graeco-Roman period,[5] a trend that WILLIAM HARRIS prominently opposed in his seminal monograph on the subject, published in 1989. In his view, structural deficits of ancient societies prevented the acquisition of reading and writing skills by more than a fraction of the population: the lack of a public school system, of technical media and of an appreciation of the written word, among other factors, led HARRIS to postulate that little more than 10 % were literate.[6] Overall, he sees literacy being confined mainly to the privileged parts of society, though he does admit various forms of literacy, as well as different levels of skill, such as "scribal" or "craftsmen's literacy". This concept of diversified or "sectoral" literacy[7] has since been refined by other scholars and analysed in various contexts,[8] resulting in differentiated accounts of "monumental, military, commercial" or "elite literacy" (WOOLF 2002, WOOLF 2009), of "functional literacy" (KEEGAN 2014) and even "epigraphic literacy" (BODEL 2010; BODEL 2015).[9] The difficulties inherent in starkly dichotomising illiteracy and literacy, as well as the problem of accurately defining a person's actual ability to read, write and perform casual arithmetic or handle numbers, have recently been raised once more by GREG WOOLF (2015). He is justified in rejecting a portrayal of ancient societies as fundamentally illiterate and calls for a conceptual adjustment of literacy, which he would like to define as the ability to handle a complex system of graphical signs. According to WOOLF, this skill was commanded by a significant amount of people and rendered them literate in the sense that they were capable of utilizing signs from a complex system of signification for their specific needs.

The complex utilization of writing in ancient every-day life was also the subject of the conference held at Zürich in November of 2016. The papers presented were able to profit from the results of a number of recent studies that pursued similar interests and provided detailed assessments of the primary material, such as minor inscriptions,[10] or the various forms and uses of graffiti culture. These studies have not only

---

5 See e. g. MARQUARDT 1886, 96; for the older research cf. the overview by WERNER 2009.
6 For the estimates see HARRIS 1989, 327–332.
7 ASSMANN 2010, 17–10, defines it as script being limited to certain functional areas of the society; however he describes "sectoral literacy" as an earlier cultural stadium in opposition to a later, cultural literacy, which was used to fix and circulate cultural and identity building-texts.
8 See esp. the volume edited by JOHNSON/PARKER 2009.
9 Further research has elucidated various functions of literality by conducting case studies, some of which have been assembled in edited volumes. These touch, for instance, on the themes of politics and the exercise of power (BOWMAN/WOOLF 1994), on the diffusion of the Roman language as a medium of Romanisation (COOLEY 2002), on the culture of reading (JOHNSON/PARKER 2009) as well as on libraries and archives WOOLF/KÖNIG/OIKONOMOPOULOU 2013. BAGNALL 2011 has treated the writing culture of Graeco-Roman Egypt as a regional case study. Eckardt 2018 illuminates writing technology and practice on the basis of material evidence in the Roman world.
10 FUCHS/SYLVESTRE/SCHMIDT HEIDENREICH 2012.

provided new material for analysis, but also conducted useful case studies on specific themes.[11]

By contrast, this conference volume seeks primarily to offer an analysis of ancient literacy from a larger, historical vantage point. As such, the first part broadens the perspective beyond the Graeco-Roman Mediterranean to include early, non-European cultures and serves to establish the larger framework required for a global historical perspective. In the second part, the focus is on the specific value and use of written language in its everyday use in Roman Antiquity, traced in detail across all important aspects of life. Proceeding in this way allows the historically contingent use of writing to emerge from the comparative appreciation of societies from China, India, and Egypt to Persia, revealing differences and similarities in the materials employed, the kinds of texts produced, and the writing processes utilized. More specifically, religious practice, administration and education, as well as select social groups shall be studied for the Roman Empire. The contributions try to assess how exactly and for what purposes writing was used, while also being sensitive to the limits of our knowledge. Can different types of literacy be identified? Are regional differences visible? Does chronological differentiation reveal a historical development?

A Global Perspective

The first group of contributions provides an overview of the sources for and discussion of the uses made of writing in important cultures of the ancient world. The cultures selected here are early China, India under Ashoka, Pharaonic Egypt, Teispid-Achaemenid Persia, as well as the Graeco-Roman civilisation, all of which are presented at the bleeding edge of current research.

FENG LI uses the "oracle bone inscriptions" from the Shang dynasty (1554–1046 BC) to illustrate the first stage of literality in ancient China. He interprets these as documenting exclusively royal divination, with the result that the use of writing seems to have been restricted to the peak of society in this period. The younger, bronze inscriptions of the western Zhou dynasty (1045 – 771 BC) show that the use of writing has now spread to the majority of the elite that used precious votive vessels with inscriptions on their inner walls to document their status. In the following periods, writing on bamboo strips, silk and paper attests the growth of the bureaucracy in the time of the "warring states" and the establishment of imperial administration during the Qin and Han dynasties (221 BC–220 AD). This caused the use and proliferation of writing in the population to rise markedly. The key force in this development was thus the political trajectory of empire formation and interior administrative reform.

---

11 CORBIER/GUILHEMBET 2008; BAIRD/TAYLOR 2011; SCHOLZ/HORSTER 2015; see above n. 2 and 4; on graffiti in the ancient world see generally KEEGAN 2014.

HARRY FALK demonstrates that the oral culture of ancient India underwent a remarkable development during the reign of Ashoka (268–232 BC). After the end of Achaemenid rule in what is now northern Pakistan, Ashoka, who was in contact with the Hellenistic world through the Seleucids, introduced stone monuments (inscribed with Kharoshti script, derived from Aramaic) and further had the Brahmi script developed (which incorporated elements of Kharoshti and Greek). Although this benefitted cultural and religious developments, Brahmi was a short-lived and only regionally successful phenomenon, being used only under Ashoka and in the Ganges valley north of his capital. Due to its use in legal documents after the disappearance of Aramaic scribes, the older Kharoshti script, by contrast, was to remain significant for centuries.

For Pharaonic Egypt, KATHARINA ZINN stresses the great significance of the spoken word despite the existence of fully-fledged writing systems, which served to supplement orality in order to provide authoritative, fixed documentation. Literacy was mainly the prerogative of professional scribes who enjoyed high social status, as well as of the educated elite. The time-intensive training required to read and write Egyptian scripts meant that only a small section of the population, between 1–10 %, can be said to have possessed the requisite skills, depending on the definition of literacy used and the time period studied. Nevertheless, writing allowed Egyptian society to use texts and documents, and literacy was thus a central factor in producing its shared, elite culture and its specific culture of memory.

JOSEF WIESEHÖFER studies the role of literality and orality in Teispid-Achaemenid Iran. Overall, the pre-Islamic sources attest to the dominance of the spoken word, although one should not underestimate the impact of administrative documentation and of the royal edicts pronounced for purposes of political representation and legitimation. Besides the late emergence of a literary tradition, the great variety of languages and writing systems used also in official contexts emerge as especially notable features of Iranian literacy. In Achaemenid administration, native Old Persian speakers used Elamite, which they had learned as a second language and syntactically adapted to the rules of their primary language. To facilitate imperial communication throughout the multi-ethnic empire, the already traditional usage of Aramaic was further intensified. Although it served to link imperial communication with regional and local levels of administration, however, Aramaic was not the only "official" language of the empire. The elaborate procedures of dictation and translation in the Achaemenid Empire are clearly visible in the Persepolis archives. Furthermore, heralds, readers, singers and story-tellers will undoubtedly have been important in disseminating information about political or administrative developments to the mass of the illiterate population.

A complementary perspective is offered by IRENE MADREITER, who studies everyday female literacy in the Achaemenid Empire. Traces of such literacy are found mainly in private documents penned by members of lower social strata, which can be considered glimpses of everyday life. All extant evidence stems from the peripheral areas of the empire, such as Asia Minor, Egypt, Mesopotamia and Bactria. In the heartland of Fars, for which source material is generally more limited, any pertinent evidence is lacking. MADREITER emphasizes the predominantly oral culture of Fars, though she also sees the lack of female writing not as purely coincidental, but as a reflection of social differences between the conquered periphery and the imperial centre in Fars, for which she generally identifies a lower significance of writing.

Expanding upon the arguments put forward in his 1989 monograph, WILLIAM HARRIS reviews important recent contributions to the debate concerning the extent and social relevance of literacy in the Graeco-Roman period. In doing so, he emphasizes the impact of ideology on Greek education, but also investigates the factors that contributed to the decline in the use of writing observable in Late Antiquity. HARRIS argues that this question can only be adequately addressed if the plurality of languages in use in this period is taken into account. He further calls for a new synthesis, which would fully address the shifting functions of reading and writing, the teaching of these skills, as well as the impact of religious change.

Roman Empire

The bulk of the volume concentrates on literacy in the Roman Empire. The contributions address various important aspects of ancient everyday life, with the first section seeking to assess the specific literacies of various social groups.

Social Groups

SABINE HÜBNER studies the degrees of female literacy in Roman Egypt using the three levels of literacy defined by the ancient population itself. 1. Illiterates; 2. "Slow writers", who were capable of signing their names; 3. Skilled writers. The signatures on lease agreements reveal a rate of literacy (for "slow writers") of at least 0,32–1,2 % among land-owning women and 33–39 % among men. Applied to the total population of Egypt, that means that probably no more than 5 % of women were able to write. Although the mass of the population thus did not possess the ability to read and write, the sources nevertheless document the omnipresence of reading and writing in everyday life. Access to the information encoded in this form was provided by literate family members and professional helpers.

The central pillar of Roman power in the Empire, the Roman army, is the subject of MICHAEL SPEIDEL's article. As one of the most successful organisations of the Roman state, the army relied on written administration and communication, as has recently been affirmed once more by newly edited papyri from lower Nubia and other texts. But the soldiers wrote letters and used documents also for private purposes. In addition, the military diplomas serve to remind us of the great value the soldiers attached to the written materials documenting their service. As such, everyday life in the Roman army was clearly pervaded with reading and writing.

A regional case study is offered by ROGER TOMLIN, who studies the degree of literacy in Roman Britain. By contrast with WILLIAM HARRIS, he takes a slightly more positive view. Besides observing a generally higher level of literacy among the military than among urban civilians, TOMLIN also takes into account source material that provides new information on everyday uses of writing among the rural and urban populace. This includes the so-called "prayers for justice" on lead discovered in the temples at Bath and Uley, as well as the recently published accounts on wooden tablets from Roman London ("Bloomberg tablets").

Finally, KAI RUFFING discusses the significance of writing and literacy in imperial Roman economics by reviewing accounts preserved on various materials (stone, walls, wooden tablets, papyrus). His study reveals the omnipresence of such documents in everyday life throughout both the Empire's space and its social strata. Such documentation offered an important tool of control in all varieties of economic transactions and had thus clearly pervaded the economics of the Roman Empire.

Religious Practice

Writing and written communication had significance also in practical religion, as AMINA KROPP illustrates using the harmful spells inscribed on *defixionum tabellae*. Oral curses were preserved and intensified by being put into writing and encoded on lead tablets. The *defixio* ritual further involved "fixating" the target's name by piercing it. The written nature of this cult practice therefore had both a communicative and a metaphorical significance. Unfortunately, however, the practice allows few insights into the literacy of the ritual actors, since recurring formulae, pre-made tablets with blanks for names, and the practiced hands in evidence on the extant tablets all point to professional scribes or even specialized workshops.

WOLFGANG SPICKERMANN reviews the development of religious practices in Germany and large parts of Gaul after the Roman conquest, which brought the "epigraphic habit" to these areas and infused regional cult practices with a culture of writing. As the divine names attested in the epigraphic record of these areas show, the indigenous elites turned to new deities under Roman rule. Furthermore, the Celtic and Germanic divine names not only attest various new types of deities, but also that these were appealed to in order to protect Roman structures (*civitates, pagi, curiae*).

Administration

ANTONIO CABALLOS RUFINO highlights the typical Roman phenomenon of recording juridical texts on bronze tablets, many examples of which survive from Baetica.

Although the bronze material was intended to ensure the meaning and permanence of these documents, its value made recycling very attractive. New finds have allowed CABALLOS to further add to his 2009 catalogue of Baetican bronze inscriptions, bringing the total up to 128. Among their number are a wealth of different genres: city laws, *senatus consulta, acta senatus,* imperial letters, communal decrees including *tabulae patronatus* and *hospitalitatis,* military diplomas, as well as various unattributable fragments. The laws and decrees in particular were originally published to ensure monumental documentation in public space. Given the 176 communities of Baetica recorded by Pliny and the fact that these documents were produced for three hundred years, the catalogue surely contains but a tiny fraction of the originally extant bronze inscriptions.

GRAHAM CLAYTOR analyses from a cultural perspective the process of municipalization that transformed the administration and economics of Roman Egypt. In order to assess the role of literacy in everyday life, he picks out the public notaries as a case study. Offices of this kind existed not only in cities, but as *grapheia* also in villages, where they functioned as local institutions run by and for the inhabitants. From Karanis, more than 1000 contracts are attested from the local *grapheion* for the early 2nd century AD. This corpus shows that the people who made use of this institution possessed the kind of basic literacy that would place them in the category of "slow writers". This means that the use of writing was normal in official business and administration not only in the cities but also in rural areas. On the other hand, cases like that of Aurelius Isidorus caution us that even estate owners could be illiterate. Between the second and the fourth century AD, use of writing and literacy in general changed significantly in the Egyptian province, with the result that scribes and notaries came to be clustered in the metropoleis of the nomes.

A rather broader question is raised by PAUL SCHUBERT, who tries to reconstruct who wrote in Graeco-Roman Egypt and for what purposes. He is able to show that writing was important for officials and private individuals alike, who used it particularly for legal and tax affairs, business and communicating with relatives. A special range of documents specifically tailored for this purpose by professional scribes reveals that the organization of their sections and clauses was intended to help less skilled writers make use of them. The blanks left in these documents, which SCHUBERT calls "windows", allowed those of lesser skill to personalize them. Such windows can be identified in various types of documents, especially in the sacrifice certificates required after the edict of Decius in 250 AD. Overall, it becomes clear that in law and administration, a certain degree of written documentation and communication was unavoidable, but could of course be satisfied by paying a professional.

Finally, the article by BENJAMIN HARTMANN leads into the heart of imperial power, as it explains the central role of the *scribae* in the Roman state. As subaltern clerks of the magistrates they administered their written documentation (including *fasti* and *legis actiones*), checked account books and maintained the archives. As such, they were experts in the nexus of writing at the core of the Republican state. The world of the Roman *scribae* was the world of documentary scribality in the form of the *tabulae publicae*. Their position as dutiful and respected wardens of the state's records afforded the Roman *scribae* not only financial gain but also social advancement through connections.

Education

MARIETTA HORSTER attempts to assess the level of historical knowledge among the population of the Empire. To do so, she reviews various heuristic methods and sources capable of revealing such "everyday knowledge" and its significance in the daily lives of the educated. Among other things, she is able to show that inscriptions record not only elite communication, but can also serve as evidence for the appreciation of historiography and historians. Papyri can likewise occasionally provide relevant information, though they always need to be considered in their social, geographical and chronological contexts. The number of extant literary papyri containing historiographical texts is so small that already a small number of new finds could change what we believe to know about a period's preferences for specific authors or historical subjects.

WINFRIED SCHMITZ traces the development of the Latin language and its use in the late antique and early medieval funerary inscriptions (4th-7th century AD) from the area of Rhine and Mosel. Over the course of these four centuries, high Latin developed first into provincial Mosellian Latin and then into an early Romance language. The funerary texts further show changes in wording and content: the increasing predominance of single names and the disappearance of information about people's origins, offices and professions seem to suggest a focus on family and Christian values. In rural regions, SCHMITZ observes a significant decline in the use of Latin and of literacy in general: Latin words and clauses are used without coherent sentence structures, while other stones are entirely uninscribed or bear geometrical decorations and symbols instead of letters.

Results

Literacy, its precise definition and delineation, as well as its significance are an important field of historical research due to the relevance of writing and script for many areas of the ancient world and the lives lived in it. The concept of diversified or sectoral literacy, with different levels of competence in writing, reading and mathematics, allows scholars to differentiate the use of writing in everyday life by the types and areas of usage, as well as identify different functions of such literacy.

Various social groups developed different functional literacies tailored to their everyday needs – if these required some form of writing. This is particularly true of administrative and legal concerns, as well as various economic affairs. That notwithstanding, the great mass of the population of the Roman Empire could surely neither write nor read and comprehend longer texts – although being able to read *lapidariae litterae* was evidently not uncommon, as is revealed by Petronius' ribbing of social risers (Petron. Sat. 58,7) as well as the erasures in imperial inscriptions, milestones and local honorary inscriptions.

The evidence provided by papyrology in particular should further caution scholars against attributing widespread literacy to those wealthier groups below the ordines of senators, knights and decurions. Although they were often reliant on written documents, many landowners or local officials were clearly illiterate.

The higher rates of literacy observable in the army by contrast with the population at large are due to its tight organization and importance as an instrument of power. Similarly, the higher rates observable in urban contexts can be attributed to the plethora of options that hub communities – unlike rural areas – could offer, such as education, culture, administration, law, or employment. Nevertheless, the need for writing, as well as its everyday use, is also in evidence for rural areas.

Considering non-Mediterranean and, in part, older civilizations, especially in India or Pharaonic Egypt, reminds us how fundamental the spoken word was in Antiquity. Its codification in writing evolved to reinforce and consolidate this importance, and thus only ever constituted one component of both public and private communication. In principle, ancient societies were oral societies. The spread of writing culture was often spearheaded by political initiatives to develop fiscal and administrative structures. Trade routes and economic activities likewise helped spread the culture of writing, but only in the Roman Empire do people's everyday lives seem to have become more deeply affected by this development due to the sheer size, structural unity, stability and durability of this imperial construct. Wherever some form of writing was unavoidable and one unable to perform it oneself, it was always possible to use friends and relatives or to pay a specialist able to lend "secondhand literacy".[12] Last but not least, it is this phenomenon that drives home how important writing was as a cultural medium and that its impact upon everyday life in ancient societies should not be underestimated.

Bibliography

ASSMANN 2010 = J. ASSMANN, Der Raum der Schrift, in: M. LUMINATI et al. (ed.), Spielräume und Grenzen der Interpretation. Philosophie, Theologie und Rechtswissenschaft im Gespräch, Basel 2010, 9–28.
BAGNALL 2011 = R.S. BAGNALL, Everyday Writing in the Graeco-Roman East, Berkeley 2011.

---

12 HARRIS 1989, 35.

BAIRD/TAYLOR 2011 = J. BAIRD/C. TAYLOR (ed.), Ancient Graffiti in Context, London/New York 2011.
BENEFIEL 2011 = R.R. BENEFIEL, Dialogues of Graffiti in the House of the Four Styles at Pompeii (Casa dei Quattro Stili, I.8.17,11), in: BAIRD/TAYLOR 2011, 20–48.
BENEFIEL 2016 = R.R. BENEFIEL, The Culture of Writing Graffiti within Domestic Spaces at Pompeii, in: R.R. BENEFIEL/P. KEEGAN (ed.), Inscriptions in the Private Sphere in the Greco-Roman World, Leiden/Boston 2015, 80–110.
BODEL 2010 = J. BODEL, Epigraphy, in: A. BARCHIESI/W. SCHEIDEL (ed.), The Oxford Handbook of Roman Studies, Oxford 2010, 107–122.
BODEL 2015 = J. BODEL, Inscriptions and Literacy, in: C. BRUUN/J. EDMONDSON (ed.), The Oxford Handbook of Roman Epigraphy, Oxford/New York 2015, 745–763.
BOWMAN/WOOLF 1994 = A.K. BOWMAN/G. WOOLF (ed.), Literacy and Power in the Ancient World, Cambridge 1994.
COOLEY 2012 = A.E. COOLEY, The Cambridge Manual of Latin Epigraphy, Cambridge 2012.
CORBIER/GUILHEMBET 2008 = M. CORBIE/ J.-P. GUILHEMBET (ed.), L´écriture dans la maison romaine, Paris 2008.
ECKARDT 2018 = H. ECKARDT, Writing and Power in the Roman World: Literacies and Material Culture, Cambridge/New York 2018.
FUCHS/SYLVESTRE/SCHMIDT HEIDENREICH 2012 = M. FUCHS/R. SYLVESTRE/C. SCHMIDT HEIDENREICH (ed.), Inscriptions mineures – nouveautés et réflexions: Actes du premier Colloque Ductus 19–20 juin 2008, Université de Lausanne, Bern 2012.
HARRIS 1989 = W.V. HARRIS, Ancient Literacy, Cambridge/Mass. 1989.
JOHNSON/PARKER 2009 = W.A. JOHNSON/H.N. PARKER (ed.), Ancient Literacies. The Culture of Reading in Greece and Rome, Oxford 2009.
KEEGAN 2014 = P. KEEGAN, Graffiti in Antiquity, London 2014.
LOHMANN 2017a = P. LOHMANN, 2500 Jahre Graffitigeschichte im Überblick. Ein epochenübergreifender Vergleich einer unterschätzten Quellengattung, *AW* 4, 2017, 58–63.
LOHMANN 2017b = P. LOHMANN, Graffiti als Interaktionsform. Geritzte Inschriften in den Wohnhäusern Pompejis, Berlin 2017.
MARQUARDT 1886 = J. MARQUARDT, Das Privatleben der Römer 2, Leipzig 1886.
MILNOR 2014 = K. MILNOR, Graffiti and the Literary Landscape in Roman Pompeii, Oxford 2014.
SCHOLZ/HORSTER 2015 = M. SCHOLZ/M. HORSTER (ed.), Lesen und Schreiben in den römischen Provinzen. Schriftliche Kommunikation im Alltagsleben, Mainz 2015.
WERNER 2009 = S. WERNER, Literacy Studies in Classics, in: JOHNSON/PARKER 2009, 333–382.
WOOLF 2000 = G. WOOLF, Literacy, in: Cambridge Ancient History, vol. 11, Cambridge 2000², 875–897.
WOOLF 2002 = G. WOOLF, Afterword: How the Latin West was won, in: A.E. COOLEY (ed.), Becoming Roman, Writing Latin? Literacy and Epigraphy in the Roman West, JRA Suppl. 48, Portsmouth 2002, 181–188.
WOOLF 2009 = G. WOOLF, Literacy or Literacies in Rome?, in: JOHNSON/PARKER 2009, 46–68.
WOOLF 2015 = G. WOOLF, Ancient Illiteracy?, *BICS* 52.2, 2015, 31–42.
WOOLF/KÖNIG/OIKONOMOPOULOU 2013 = G. WOOLF/J. KÖNIG/K. OIKONOMOPOULOU, Ancient Libraries, Cambridge 2013.

I **A Global Perspective**

Li Feng

The Development of Literacy in Early China: With the Nature and Uses of Bronze Inscriptions in Context, and More

Abstract: In an effort to understand the significance of literacy in the everyday life of early China, the present paper identifies three stages in literacy's development before Empire: 1) An incipient stage (ca. 3000 BC–1250 BC) from the late Neolithic period when signs of writing (and reading) began to appear in the late Liangzhu culture in the south and Longshan culture in the north until the mid-Shang period when the condition for practicing full writing was ripe; 2) a stage marked by the use of a mature system of writing carved mainly on bones and shells for divination in the late Shang (ca. 1250–1046 BC), but the ability to do so was restricted to the group of professional scribes and some diviners; 3) during the Western Zhou period (1045–771 BC), writing moved beyond the hands of the specialized scribes to reach larger social circles, and the activity of reading and appreciation of the written words became widespread among the Zhou social elites. Particularly on the nature of the bronze inscriptions, this paper offers concrete evidence that inscribed bronzes were used in domestic as well as legal-economic contexts and so inscribed for documentary purposes, thus beyond the narrow religious perimeter. As the textual content of the inscriptions is usually independent of the function of the vessels that carried them, the bronzes were indeed *vehicles* for the written words to reach broad social contexts. In other words, the inscribed bronzes were not only very relevant to the everyday life of the Western Zhou elites, but they were also part of their effort to distill, celebrate, and interpret their life experience, and even to influence their future.

Zusammenfassung: Zum Verständnis der Bedeutung von Schriftlichkeit im Alltagsleben des vorkaiserzeitlichen China identifiziert und beleuchtet der Beitrag drei Phasen in der Entwicklung frühchinesischer Schriftlichkeit: 1) Eine Anfangsphase (ca. 3000–1250 v. Chr.) seit dem späten Neolithikum, die sich durch das erstmalige Auftreten der Technik des Schreibens (und Lesens) in der Späten Liangzhu-Kultur des Südens und der Longshan-Kultur des Nordens auszeichnet und bis in die Mittlere Shang-Zeit reicht, als die Voraussetzungen für die Entwicklung einer kompletten Schriftkultur gegeben waren. 2) Eine Periode in der Späten Shang-Zeit (ca. 1250–1046 v. Chr.), die durch die Benutzung eines voll entwickelten Schriftsystems auf Knochen und Muscheln zu Zwecken der Divination gekennzeichnet ist, wobei die Fähigkeit des Schreibens auf eine Gruppe professioneller Schreiber und einige Wahrsager

---

Article Note: I would like to express my gratitude to Professor Anne Kolb for inviting me to participate in the conference on "Literacy in Ancient Everyday Life," University of Zurich, November 10–12, 2016. I also thank Maxim Korolkov for his assistance to this paper.

beschränkt blieb. 3) Während der Zeit der Westlichen Zhou-Dynastie (1045–771 v. Chr.) dehnte sich die Benutzung von Schrift auf soziale Gruppen außerhalb der spezialisierten Schreiber aus, sodass sich Lesen und eine Wertschätzung für das Geschriebene unter den sozialen Eliten der Zhou ausbreitete. Der Beitrag beleuchtet insbesondere die Eigenheiten der Bronzeinschriften und zeigt auf, dass beschriftete Bronzen sowohl im häuslichen wie auch im rechtlich-ökonomischen Kontext zu dokumentarischen Zwecken verwendet wurden und damit auch außerhalb des religiösen Bereiches zum Einsatz kamen. Der Inhalt der Texte hatte üblicherweise keinen Zusammenhang mit der Funktion des Trägergefäßes. Die Bronzen waren damit regelrechte Vehikel für das Geschriebene, um breitere soziale Kontexte zu erreichen. Die beschrifteten Bronzen waren damit nicht nur relevant für das Alltagsleben der Eliten der Westlichen Zhou. Sie waren vielmehr Teil ihrer Bestrebungen, das eigene Leben festzuhalten, zu zelebrieren und zu interpretieren, ja sogar um die eigene Zukunft zu beeinflussen.

In an effort to understand the condition of literacy and its significance in the everyday life of the ancients, China may be ideally brought in for comparative reflections. This is necessary not only because China was one of the few world regions where an independent writing system composed of idiosyncratic graphs was invented and continued, but because very large quantities of such writing work have survived from very early times by random discovery or by archaeological excavation. However, there is little in previous scholarship, whether in its native tradition of historiography in China, or in Western Sinology, to draw on for a sensible comparison of literacy. In fact, literacy was almost never problematized as a subject of study for the early empires and before until a recent collective probe into the darkness.[1] Even for the middle and later empires in China from the sixth century to 1911, the issue of literacy was discussed only in the study of the civil service examination system or of education in general,[2] with perhaps only one exception.[3] In the near-absence of previous literature on literacy in early China, the historian who works to remedy this problem must always begin his course by analyzing the primary evidence of writing from the archaeologically informed period including excavated inscriptions and manuscripts, in addition to the sheer volume of the transmitted texts.

In our comparative analysis of literacy in the Mediterranean World and China, William HARRIS considered that pre-modern agrarian societies are highly unlikely to have achieved an overall adult literacy rate above 10 percent of the population;

---

[1] LI/BRANNER 2011.
[2] The literature on the Chinese civil examination system is large, but just to give a few: KRACKE 1953; MIYAZAKI 1981; LEE 1985; ELMAN 2000.
[3] RAWSKI 1979. A general discussion of literacy education in traditional China is found in LEE 2000, 431–544.

I agree that the same can be said of the Qin and Han Empires in China.[4] Taking this figure as a hypothetical cap, and assuming that the development of literacy in early China as in everywhere else was an incremental process, we can identify a number of stages in the development of literacy in early China: 1) An incipient stage from the time when signs of writing (and hence reading) began to appear until the mid-Shang period (ca. 1400–1250 BC) when the condition for practicing full writing was ripe; 2) a stage marked by the use of a mature system of writing carved on the bones and shells for divination in the late Shang period (ca. 1250–1046 BC); 3) during the Western Zhou period (1045–771 BC), writing moved beyond the hands of the specialized scribes to reach larger social circles, and the activity of reading was widespread among the elite population of the Western Zhou. Although the expansion of literacy and the maturity of the writing system are two different issues, they are parallel developments as far as we can tell from the evidence. Without the written words as basis, there can be no such thing as literacy, which is essentially "text-oriented events".[5] On the other hand, the development of the writing system can be seen as a process in which the utility value of the system is gradually enlarged as the inventory of the written words expanded and the system itself became structurally more complex and functionally more flexible. This, saving some very unusual circumstances, would necessarily lead to the expansion of literacy, understood both as an action of writing and that of reading. Therefore, it would seem important to begin with a brief discussion about the current evidence for the origin of the Chinese writing system.

1 The Problem of the Origin of Chinese Writing

It is agreed among scholars that the earliest "mature" form of writing in China was the oracle-bone inscriptions of the Shang Dynasty (1554 BC-1046 BC). By "mature," I mean a system of signs that were correlated in accordance with grammatical conventions of the spoken language and that could be used to express in the written form of statement "most" situations of the life experience of a person or a people. The oracle-bone inscriptions doubtless represent a system of writing of such quality.[6] But what had happened in China that led to the development of a mature system of writing like the Shang oracle-bones? There are two positions on this issue: The first is what I call the "Gradual Developmental School" which holds that because the oracle-bone scripts are a fully-functioning system of writing, it must have taken centuries for writing devel-

---

4 HARRIS/LI 2015, 14, 30. Earlier, HARRIS estimated that the literacy rate in Greece and the Roman Republic down to 100 BC is unlikely to have exceeded 10 %; as for the Roman Empire, he left it open as a large gap between cities in Italy and Greece and the distant provinces can make an overall estimate unrealistic. See HARRIS 1989, 114, 173, 328–330.
5 See JOHNSON/PARKER 2009, 3. On this point, see also LI/BRANNER 2011, 6.
6 For a general introduction to the oracle-bone inscriptions, see KEIGHTLEY 1978.

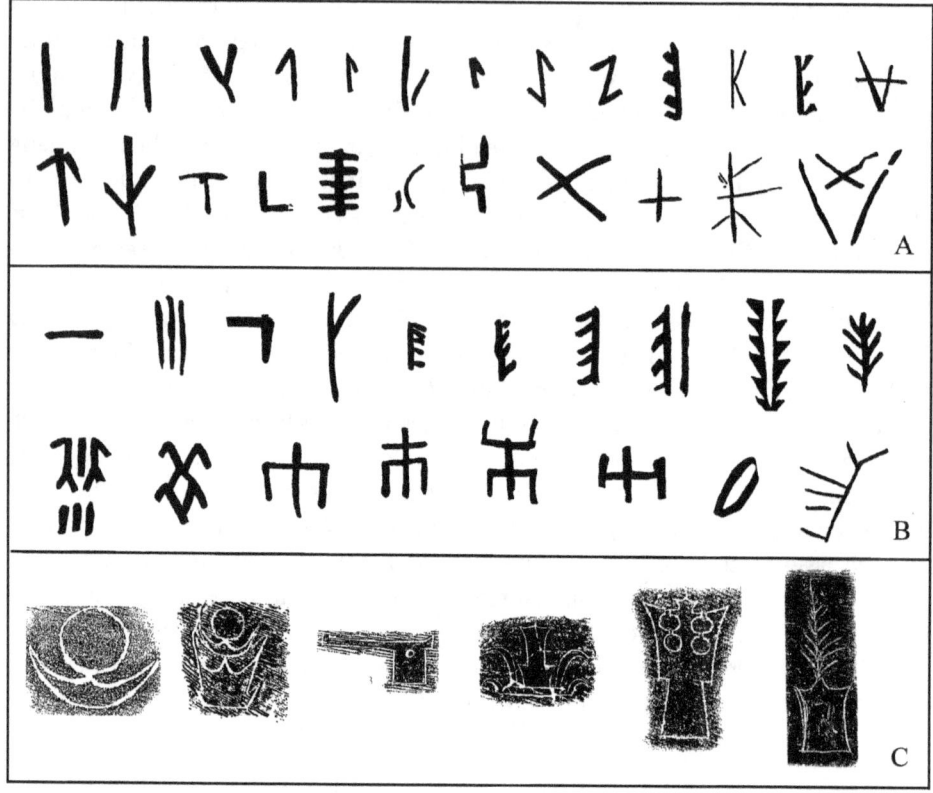

Fig. 1: Neolithic pottery marks: A. Yangshao Culture-Banpo site; B. Yangshao Culture-Jiangzhai site; C. Dawenkou Culture. Adopted with modification from ZHONGGUO SHEHUIKEXUEYUAN KAOGU YANJIUSUO 2010, 251, 303.

oping from its primitive stage to reach this level of maturity. This position has been widely shared by Chinese and Japanese scholars, and by still many in the West. Some scholars who endorsed this view looked for evidence of early writing in its pre-mature form in the preceding Neolithic period, such as marks on pottery sherds of the Yangshao-Dawenkou period (ca. 5000–3000 BC) (Figure 1).[7] Other scholars voiced considerable caution.[8] The weakness of this argument is quite obvious, for these are by and large isolated marks each engraved on a pottery vessel or a sherd as a single unit, gathered across a large geographic space, and there is no way to determine how widely a particular graph was accepted by a human community or communities or if it expressed a fixed meaning. Furthermore, there is no evidence that they are representations of any spoken language which if correlated should have given them phonetic values.

---

[7] TANG 1977; YU 1973, 32.
[8] For instance, GAO 1996, 29–31; QUI 2000, 31.

The second position is what I call the "Overnight School" that holds that as true for all systems of writing, the oracle-bone scripts are governed by certain formational rules. As soon as such rules are discovered and the principle of writing is learned, the whole system can be generated in a relatively short period of time, perhaps over a few generations. In other words, the oracle-bone inscriptions represent a system of writing that was posed still very close to its origin. This view, though of the minority, has been strongly advocated by some scholars in the West, for instance, William BOLTZ, who in fact places the time of the invention of the Chinese writing system in the middle of the Shang period.[9] To support this position, BOLTZ looks for evidence in the oracle-bones that a graph may stand for two different words that are related through a semantic value which remains static, in a construction that is called "Polyphony". There are such examples in the OBI (e.g. 月, 禾, 卜), which he considered as characteristic of the formative stage of a writing system.[10]

We are not yet able to bring this debate to a conclusion as to exactly when and where the Chinese writing system was first invented. However, recent archaeology has led us to a position to be more confident about the long history and perhaps the multiple origins of the Chinese writing system before Anyang. For instance, based on a few instances of consecutive "writing" on a pottery sherd from Dinggong in Shandong Province and another from Longqiu in Jiangsu Province, some scholars have argued for the emergence of a writing system millennia before the Shang.[11] More recently, pottery or stone objects that bear multiple graphs in contextualized formations have been found in large numbers from sites that belong to the Liangzhu culture (3200–2200 BC) in southern China.[12] These are evidence qualitatively different from the scattered marks on pottery previously known from the Neolithic period. They offer us meaningful new grounds to reevaluate previous assumptions about the process of as well as mechanisms in the rise of writing in China.

Among the "Graphic Narratives" found on the Liangzhu pottery and stone objects we can actually identify two levels of presentation: 1) a series of pictorial images that show direct links to real-world phenomena (Figure 2); 2) sequences of abstract linear graphs (some mixed with more realistic images) placed in specific spatial relationship to each other (Figure 3: lower). These are not isolated signs, but instead represent ideas connected to one another by an underlying logic or system to express complex and socially meaningful situations understandable to those who wrote and read them. Here, to borrow Boone's terms, "the syntax is fundamentally spatial, where meaning is created and directed by structure and by the principles of sequence, prox-

---

9 This would mean, sometime in the 14th century BC; BOLTZ 1994, 13.
10 BOLTZ 2011, 82–83. BOLTZ explains, the graph 月 stands equally for the word *yuè* 'moon' and *shuò* 'first day of the new month', the graph 禾 stands for *hé* 'grain, millet' and *nián* 'harvest', and the graph 卜 stands for *bǔ* 'prognosticate by cracking' and *wài* 'outside, outer'. See BOLTZ 2011, 76–78.
11 QIU 1993; MATSUMARU 1997.
12 ZHANG 2015, 592–613, 664–683.

Fig. 2: Graphical narrative on a pottery jar from Nanhu, Liangzhu Culture: from Zhang 2015, 600–602.

imity, inclusion, and exclusion."[13] Although it is always hard to detect the underlying system, particularly in the second case we simply cannot exclude the possibility that a language or languages came into play and gave these graphs phonetic values so that they could be read as sequential lines of statement. To broaden the context of this new evidence, some 600 incidences of pottery or stone objects inscribed with singular or the combination of two to three signs have been found at more than 30 archaeological sites, and most of them are dated to the later period (ca. 2800–2200 BC) of the same Liangzhu culture (Figure 3: upper).[14]

---

13 This is her characterization of the Aztec scripts; Boone 2004, 315.
14 Zhang 2015, 4. In fact, some of these combined signs are no less complex than the images on the U-j tags, considered earliest writing in Egypt. See Baines 2004, 155–156.

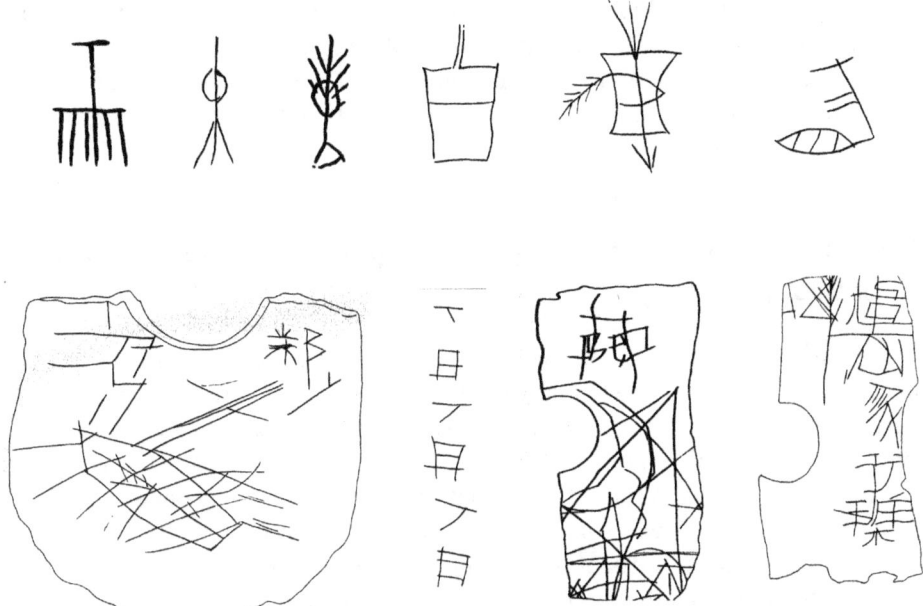

Fig. 3: Graphs on pottery and stone objects, Liangzhu Culture: Top row, marks on pottery sherds or vessels; bottom row, inscriptions on stone axes. Adopted with modifications from ZHANG 2015, 81, 89, 91, 94, 93, 117, 677, 674, 683.

Even in the case of such singular signs, the Liangzhu materials are significant in two ways: 1) the numerous signs can be indexed according to certain formational rules that seem to have remained quite constant; 2) sites that are located as far as 100 km from each other often yielded multiple numbers of identical signs, indicating that such signs were remotely shared among the Liangzhu communities.[15] The archaeological context suggests that these signs were products of a social-cultural system that encoded in them specific meanings widely understood and accepted in Liangzhu society.

Scholars have noted that, for instance, in Egypt and Mesopotamia, a notation system preceded the emergence of true writing and the transition to the latter was achieved once what had formed the notation system acquired phonetic values.[16] Although we are yet to fully understand the nature and significance of the above new evidence, it is very possible that the late Liangzhu culture indeed constituted one of the social-cultural contexts in which the conversion to true writing took place, though it might not have been the only place where writing was invented in China. As a matter of fact, the existence of similar materials in the north, for example, the sherd inscribed

---

15 ZHANG 2015, 798–811.
16 BOONE 2004, 313–317; WENGROW 2008, 864, 1133; BAINES 2004, 130–189; BOLTZ 2011, 51–52, 72–73; PANKENIER 2011, 21–28.

with eleven characters from Dinggong, dated to the Longshan period in Shandong Province (ca. 2600–2000 BC), suggests that a similar development might have taken place in other regions in China in the third millennium BC. If this is true as it is most likely, we will be able to talk about the "Neolithic origin" of the Chinese writing system or systems.

2 The Nature of the Oracle-Bone Inscriptions and the Implication for Shang Literacy

The oracle-bone inscriptions are records of divination engraved on turtle plastrons or on cattle scapula during the Shang period (1554–1046 BC). There are about 130,000 pieces of bone fragments as of 1989 that bear complete or partial inscriptions, and some were excavated in large quantities (Figure 4).[17] The Chinese writing system which made possible the carving of divinatory inscriptions on the bones and shells cannot be assumed to have been restricted to the divinatory context; in fact, a recent scholar has assumed a series of social contexts in which writing "might have been" used, but he concluded that we do not have evidence for it.[18] But evidence exists at least for the use of writing as self-referential inscriptions as marks and labels on bones and other media,[19] and by the end of the dynasty quite a few bronze vessels and zoomorphic objects had come to bear relatively long inscriptions. But inscriptions on the oracle-bones and shells are by far the most important work of writing left behind by the Shang. Therefore, the question for us is primarily: What do these bones or shells tell us about the development of literacy in the Shang dynasty? Who indeed wrote and read the words on these bones and shells?

It can be said at the outset that all divinations are the art of secrecy. The power of divination arises particularly from the closed process that limited access to the knowledge about the supernatural world of the spirits through a set of designated acts or words. This nature of divination in Shang has been retested by an important new discovery – some 1583 shells (689 inscribed) were excavated at Huayuanzhuang-East in Anyang in 1991, and published only in 2003.[20] Most of the oracle-bone inscriptions that we knew previously were records of royal divination, that is, they were conducted for the Shang king (particularly King Wu Ding, the first king for whom inscribed bones and shells were produced as far as we know) about subject matters that concerned him. But

---

17 SUN 2006, 24–47. Inscriptions on 632 such bones and shells have been recently translated into English, see TAKASHIMA 2010. For a general introduction to the oracle-bone inscriptions, see KEIGHTLEY 1978.
18 The contexts include the management of agriculture, muster rolls of troops, operation of bronze foundries, land survey, contracts, trade and other commerce, records of the king's activities, communication with outlaying polities and settlements, and so on; BAGLEY 2004, 190–261, esp. 223–224.
19 See KEIGHTLEY 2006, 184–185.
20 ZHONGGUO SHEHUI KEXUEYUAN KAOGU YANJIUSUO 2003.

Fig. 4: Discovery of Shang inscribed oracle shells in Huayuanzhuang-East, Anyang, 1991: from ZHONGGUO SHEHUI KEXUEYUAN KAOGU YANJIUSUO 2003, 40.

the Huayuanzhuang (as HYZ below) oracle-bone inscriptions were records of divinations conducted for/by a certain *Zi* 子, "Prince," whose real identity is still debated. The shells were found outside the royal palace zone in Anyang, but only 300 meters from it, probably from the residence of the hosting prince overlooking a moat that protected the settlement core of Anyang. Although questions on the HYZ shells were addressed to the same list of royal ancestors as in the royal divinatory inscriptions, the HYZ inscriptions were different from the royal inscriptions both at the level of the physical arrangement of inscriptions on the shells, and at the level of recoding conventions and vocabulary – they display a distinctive divinatory tradition, so much different from the royal oracle-bone inscriptions (Figure 5). After all, they were produced by fourteen diviners who were totally separate from the royal diviner groups of which we know as many as about 120 individuals.[21] And on the HYZ oracle shells the "Prince" sometimes played the role of a diviner, but in the royal inscriptions the Shang king never did.

The HYZ oracle-bone inscriptions teach us two important points: 1) divination (and the written records resulting from it) was not monopolized by the Shang king in the palace, but was conducted elsewhere by some of the Shang elites who resided

---

21 KEIGHTLEY 1978, 31, note 13.

Fig. 5: Inscribed oracle shells of Shang: left, royal divinatory inscription from Xiaotun; right, non-royal divinatory inscription from Huayuanzhuang-East. From ZHANG 1965–72, #96; ZHONGGUO SHEHUI KEXUEYUAN KAOGU YANJIUSUO 2003, #63.

in Anyang or perhaps also in some of the Shang outposts beyond it;²² 2) divination was ultimately a secret proceeding. It is likely that the HYZ diviners might not have ever been exposed to the standards for texts and vocabulary employed in the Shang royal divinatory institution, even they were using the same writing system to produce inscriptions only 300 meters away from the royal divinatory workshop. Since most of the written works from Anyang that we now have were products of the divinatory processes that were clearly demarcated by workshop lines, the observed uniqueness of the HYZ oracle shells is certainly important for us in understanding the spread as well as restrictions of the use of writing in Anyang.

In this regard, Adam SMITH's study of the practice inscriptions can also help us understand the nature and condition of literacy in Anyang. The oracle-bone inscriptions from Anyang include a quite large number of incompetently executed inscriptions produced by trainees in the divinatory workshops, with a concentration of such training down to reproducing the "60-Day Table" (Figure 6). It was not clear, however, whether these practice inscriptions were evidence of learning writing, or evidence for practicing engraving. Mainly on account of the fact that such inscriptions included many erroneous or inferior graphs, and also that the practicing was often done in textual units, but rarely in isolated characters, Smith argued that at least some of the practice inscriptions were produced by people who were just learning to write the Chinese scripts.²³ And this seems to indicate a situation that the transmission of literacy in Anyang was done "in-house" within the particular divinatory workshops. Previous studies by other scholars also show that a particular partnership existed in Anyang between the scribes (identified by the calligraphic features of their inscriptions) who actually executed the written records of divination and the diviners who presumably supervised the divinatory process and actually posed the charges on the bones and shells.²⁴

In a brief assessment of the condition of literacy in the Shang dynasty, it can be said that although it is possible, and even probable, that writing was brought in service of the Shang in other areas of the contemporaneous social life, it is above all a reasonable supposition that the religious use of writing in divination constituted the most prominent channel for the acquisition and transmission of literacy. The evidence analyzed by Adam SMITH on the learning of writing on bones and shells is important, and together with what we learn from the contrast between the royal inscriptions and the HYZ non-royal inscriptions, the evidence suggests strongly the important and yet confining role of the divinatory workshops as the hotbeds of Shang literacy. This is not solely because of the lack of evidence for literacy's appearance in other non-divinatory contexts, but because of the central role divination played in the Shang political-re-

---

22 On evidence of production of oracle-bone inscriptions outside Anyang, though of a very limited quantity, see TAKASHIMA 2011, 141–172.
23 SMITH 2011, 203–204.
24 MIHARA 1967, 34–52; 1968, 102–115; JIA 2009, 79–81.

Fig. 6: Practice inscription from Anyang: adopted from SMITH 2011, 184.

ligious structure. It is very likely that literacy remained a distinctive art of the professional groups of the scribes that worked in association with diviners in the various workshops both royal and non-royal in Anyang. The Shang could also have moved such professional groups of scribes to perform certain non-divinatory tasks when needed, rather than relying on the knowledge of writing on behalf of the Shang elites which, if any, is highly unlikely to have been commonly achieved. I think this condition of Shang literacy matches closely what William HARRIS once described as "scribal literacy," "a condition of society in which the ability to write is largely or wholly restricted to a class of specialists, typically working for the ruler or for a temple."[25]

3 The Multiple Social Uses of Writing in the Western Zhou

This very secrecy associated with the Shang oracle-bone inscriptions also provided a lens through which some scholars viewed the bronze inscriptions of the Western

---

[25] HARRIS/LI 2015, 7; earlier, HARRIS 1989, 7.

Zhou period (1045–771 BC). A total of 21,014 such inscriptions cast on bronze vessels or weapons have been recorded in various publications.²⁶ There are scholars, as most typically Lothar VON FALKENHAUSEN, who argued that the bronze vessels are religious objects donated to the ancestral temples of the elite families. The main purpose of the inscriptions on them was to convey messages to the ancestors, and not, or at least not primarily intended to deliver information to the later generations. Consequently, the nature of bronze inscriptions is such that they are religious documents with the ancestors in the heaven as their intended audience.²⁷ This argument was made compelling, mainly by reasoning, but it suffers badly from the test of evidence in broad consideration of the use of the bronze objects and the social contexts in which the written words appear. However, the concern here is not so much about the historical value of the inscriptions or about the functions of the bronze vessels, but about what this view may lead (or mislead) us to think about the condition of Western Zhou literacy. Since the bronze inscriptions are by far the most widely available sources of writing from the Western Zhou period, this is certainly an important question in the study of ancient literacies.

At the very least, this view categorically alienated the Zhou social elites from the readership of inscribed bronzes that they owned. It would only require the existence of a very small group of professional scribes who were able to handle the communication with the ancestors through the casting of inscriptions, bypassing members of the Zhou social elites who were the ones in daily contact with these inscriptions. By the extension of this logic, no matter how many or how few they are, the bronze inscriptions simply are not qualified as evidence of literacy in Western Zhou society because they were not intended to be read or understood by anyone there. So they are irrelevant to an assessment of Western Zhou literacy. But these are very wrong positions, and an assessment of Western Zhou literacy must rely on a clear and uncompromising understanding of the nature of the bronze inscriptions, the most important and widely available evidence of writing in Western Zhou society.

Over years, I have argued for a position that sees the nature of bronze inscriptions in a much broader social context or multiple social contexts.²⁸ Without rejecting the important role that bronze vessels played in Western Zhou religion, or in the political-religious construction of the Western Zhou state, I see rather a much larger spectrum of social roles that the bronze vessels played in the Western Zhou, both religious and non-religious. The bronze inscriptions, on the other hand, were not only relevant in content to the everyday life of the Western Zhou elites, but were part of their effort

---

26 See WU 2012, supplements 2015. The first recorded 19,505 inscriptions, to which were added 1,509 new inscriptions three years later. A total of 98 inscriptions have been recently translated into English, in addition to previously published translations, see COOK/GOLDIN 2016. For a general introduction to the study of the bronze inscriptions, see SHAUGHNESSY 1991.
27 FALKENHAUSEN 1993, 146–147, 167; LUO 2006, 343–374.
28 LI 2006, 8–10; LI 2008, 11–20; LI 2011, 293–300.

to distill, celebrate, and interpret their life experience, and even to influence their future. In other words, the written words on the bronzes mattered to the Zhou elites who owned, handled, and witnessed these bronzes, and they were intended to be read, understood, and appreciated in multiple social contexts which they served and in which they were held to be meaningful at all. This understanding of the nature (perhaps natures) and social roles of the bronze inscriptions leads to two general positions on the matter of Western Zhou literacy: 1) bronze inscriptions are evidence of writing and reading in Western Zhou society (instead of being religious propositions posed in the realm of the spirits), hence evidence of Western Zhou literacy; 2) they indicate that literacy as the activity of writing and reading in Western Zhou society could not have been restricted to the small groups of professional scribes ("professional" in the sense that their sole social role is tied to the knowledge of the written words), but could have involved the participation of the Zhou elite population as part of an educational system (to various degrees) maintained by the elite families that had the power and interests to cast bronzes and inscribed them. But there is still more to this.

While a fuller discussion of the inscriptions and their bronzes that suggest their broad social and political roles would require a book-long treatment, the space below allows for only a dense categorical summary of their contributions to understanding the condition of literacy in Western Zhou society for the purpose of the present volume:

a. Internal evidence suggests the "documentary" purpose of the bronze inscriptions. Cast on many bronzes, "to document" a royal command or will is the clearly stated purpose for which the relevant bronzes were produced and the way in which they were meaningful; the inscriptions as such were essentially to be read and reflected back upon by those who commissioned their birth as important guides to their lives and careers. The most significant among these inscriptions, for instance, is the Shi Tian *gui* 史話簋 (JC: 4031) that describes that the principal caster fixes the royal command onto the vessel so that he could "observe" (*jiàn* 監) the text every morning and night.[29] The Rong *gui* 榮簋 (JC: 4241) says literally that Rong, owner of the bronze, cast the vessel actually "to document" (*diǎn* 典) the royal command, presumably issued to him orally (Figure 7). The term "to document" in verbal form is also used in the inscription on the Pengsheng *gui* 倗生簋 (JC: 4262), but here it was an economic deal, the transaction of land between two elite families, that is to be documented and placed on the vessel. In any event, the archival or referential function (which would necessarily imply the action of reading and comprehension) of the inscriptions is clear. There are also inscriptions on bronzes, for instance, the Taibo *gui* 太保簋 (JC: 4140), that describe the need to respond to the Zhou king's orders as the primary purpose for which the bronzes were created and presented. Although in such

---

29 The numbering of inscriptions here follows Zhongguo Shehui Kexueyuan Kaogu Yanjiusuo 1984–94 as the standard recording system, which is the basis of the electronic database of bronze inscriptions from the Academia Sinica.

Fig. 7: The Rong *gui* and its inscription: image provided by the British Museum (1936,1118.2); © The Trustees of the British Museum). Inscription from ZHONGGUO SHEHUI KEXUEYUAN KAOGU YANJIUSUO 1984–94, #4241.

cases there is no direct reference to text-generated activities such as reading, the specific purpose of the inscribed words was certainly none other than recording the social event involving the king and his subject, the caster of the very bronze.

 b. Elite gatherings such as family banquets constituted one of the most important social contexts for the inscribed bronzes. Casting for aristocratic feasting or entertainment is the stated purpose on many bronzes, whether to celebrate the victory of war as on the Duoyou *ding* 多友鼎 (JC: 2835), or to solicit friendship among colleagues or family relatives as on vessels like the Mai *fangding* 麦方鼎 (JC: 2706), Ming *gui* 命簋 (JC: 4112), and Ling *ding* 令簋 (JC: 4300). Particularly, the second specifies the use of the vessel to "feast with the tureen" (*gǔi shí* 簋飤) the friends, and the third singles out colleagues in the same governmental bureau (*liáo rén* 寮人) among the guests to be entertained with the vessel. We also have a bronze, the Wu *gui* 敔簋 (JC: 3827), that states straightly that the purpose of the bronze was to serve food to the younger ones in a family. Whether these vessels could ever be used in religious contexts is a different question (there is no reason they could not); the primary purpose, and therefore their intended social value, were strictly defined by the context of the domestic life of the Western Zhou elites. Of an even larger number are bronzes cast as dowry vessels, including many inscribed for the inner chamber use by married women, for hair or facial washing. The use of bronzes in such contexts of family banquet or entertainment in the bronze inscriptions is well corroborated by the transmitted Zhou literature, for instance, the poem "Famu" 伐木 (Mao 165) in the *Book of Poetry*, that describes such family feasting in which sets of bronze vessels were deployed in front of the family's guests.[30]

 c. The fēn-vessels in a large number are essentially food-serving vessels. There are more than fifty bronzes vessels whose inscriptions clearly state that they were *fēn* 饋 vessels (followed by the typological name of the bronzes), and many indeed bear long and content-rich inscriptions. This graph *fēn* 饋 has been analyzed by paleographers and it means essentially the same as the character *fàn* 飯, 'meal', in classical Chinese.[31] While the nature of such bronzes described by the character *fēn* in their inscriptions as food-serving vessels has seemed no doubt to everyone, a very important point has often eluded scholarly eyes: in the more than fifty incidents, *none of them has a statement of dedication to any ancestor*. Although this is not a point that would exclude the possibility of some of these vessels being used for worship of the caster's ancestors under special circumstances, such use was ultimately peripheral and deviated from the main purpose of these bronzes to serve food to the living members of Zhou elite society. A typical case of such inscriptions is the Bo Kang *gui* 伯康簋 (JC: 4160), cast perhaps by a royal prince during the mid-Western Zhou period and inscribed: Bo Kang casts this treasured *gui*-tureen, using which he wishes to feast his friends, and to serve food to his royal father and royal mother (Figure 8). This situation corroborates so well

---

30 Li 2011, 298–299.
31 Chen 1955–56. 2.99–100; Zhou 1975, 3359–3364.

Fig. 8: The Bo Kang *gui* and its inscription: image provided by Zhou Ya; inscription from ZHONGGUO SHEHUI KEXUEYUAN KAOGU YANJIUSUO 1984–94, #4160.

the stated purpose of the bronze as a food-serving vessel. There is little doubt that these are the bronzes that were intended primarily for domestic use by the Zhou elites.

d. Inscriptions suggest that certain bronzes were cast to entertain the king. Of particular interest is a group of bronzes cast and inscribed for the sole purpose of feasting the Zhou king on his visit, as so described in the inscriptions of the Zhong Cheng *gui* 仲再簋 (JC: 3747) and Bo Zhefu *gui* 伯者父簋 (JC: 3748). There are about ten such bronzes that have special meaning for understanding the administrative activities of the Zhou king. As previously noted, different from the later Chinese emperors, the Zhou king made frequent tours out of his palace and sometimes to the residences or the administrative headquarters of his officials.[32] The existence of such bronzes seems to corroborates well this pattern in the Zhou king's conduct as they would be displayed on such occasions in the king's presence, pleasing the royal person with both the food they offered and the inscriptions they bore.

e. Some inscriptions preserve the genuine features of a written document used in legal or other contexts. A typical case is the Sanshi *pan* 散氏盤 (JC: 10176) (Figure 9). The inscription describes (more precisely, transmits) a treaty as the postwar settlement between the lineage of San and the state of Ze in western Shaanxi. But the information on the land features that the new border was determined to run through is very detailed and difficult to understand. Unlike other long inscriptions that have a half-line at the end of the text, on the Sanshi *pan*, the half-line begins half-way down, and is thus discontinued from the text of the treaty. This line says: "His Left Contract-Keeping Scribe verified: (signed) Zhong Nong." This is in fact the official verification of the treaty signed by the Ze king's secretary. This phenomenon implies, on one hand, a preexisting document (the treaty) possibly placed on a wooden or textile media that concluded the peace conference between the two polities existed; on the other hand, the reason for moving the documents onto bronze was precisely because of the durability of the metal to preserve the important document into the future. In this sense, the inscription truthfully preserves the textual features of the original treaty presented on perishable material, and the archival or referential nature of the inscription is beyond question.

f. Internal evidence from the inscriptions suggests a broad range of uses of writing. Though not themselves the carriers of the specific written works which they refer to, the bronze inscriptions testify to the use of writing documents/contracts in multiple social contexts, including royal edicts presented on bamboo or wooden media handed over to the officials during the official ceremony of appointment as, for example, described in the inscription of the Song *ding* 頌鼎 (JC: 2829). There are more than one hundred bronze inscriptions that include the whole or portions of a royal edict copied on to bronze from a bamboo or wooden document that the principal casters of the bronzes received at the Zhou court. Land contracts transferred as "paperwork" by the

---

32 Li 2001, 45.

Fig. 9: The Sanshi *pan* and its inscription: image provided by the Palace Museum, Taipei; inscription from Zhongguo Shehui Kexueyuan Kaogu Yanjiusuo 1984–94, #10176.

scribes to the beneficiaries of the transaction of the property is described, for instance, in the Wu Hu *ding* 吳虎鼎 (NA: 0709). Land registers passed from the royal court to the elite property-owning families are mentioned in the Sixth-year Zhousheng *gui* 六年琱生簋 (JC: 4293). Tallies used in the sale of horses for land is mentioned in the Pengsheng *gui* 倗生簋 (JC: 4262) that was cast precisely for the purpose of documenting this economic deal. Written records produced during military campaigns with regard to the punishment of soldiers also appear in Western Zhou inscriptions, for instance, Shi Qi *ding* 師旂鼎 (JC: 2809). The above bronzes provide an important stepping stone for an assessment of literacy beyond the bronze inscriptions in Western Zhou society, previously discussed at length by the author.[33]

The information presented above suggests that there were no restrictions to the purposes for which a bronze vessel could be cast and inscribed in the Western Zhou. Certainly, there was no such thing as the "religious nature" of bronze inscriptions that can explain the casting and inscribing of all bronze vessels and weapons. At the fundamental level, using a particular social context in which the inscribed bronzes served the need of the Western Zhou elites to determine the "nature" of the bronzes is epistemologically a very wrong bet. On the contrary, in most cases the textual content of the inscription is independent of (certainly not generated from) the function or functions of the vessel which carries it. The reason that they were placed on the bronze vessels was particularly because of the broad range of social contexts, both religious and non-religious, in which the Zhou elites needed the service of these treasured vessels, and because of their very durability that made them suitable for the better preservation of family prestige as well as information about personal merits of significant social values. Certainly, such information did not need to be limited to personal experience, but can also be extended to communal accomplishments that needed preservation for future reference such as in the case of the Sanshi *pan*. In other words, the bronze vessels were the vehicles for the written words to reach the broad society of the Western Zhou elites.

There is also the question of whether the bronze inscriptions can represent the full range of writing in the Western Zhou. Of course not; instead, they are the most prominent type of evidence of Western Zhou literacy only by their chances of survival. Given the existence of other types of writing work that they refer to (above *f*), and given also the fact that virtually all bronze inscriptions copied the texts initially written on perishable media and engraved on clay molds before casting,[34] there seems little doubt that a much larger volume of writing in the Western Zhou period must have been done on materials other than bronze. The remainders of such written works are preserved in a few transmitted texts including the *Book of Changes* (Yijing 易經), *Book of Documents* (Shang-

---

[33] Li 2011, 273–290.
[34] On the techniques of casting inscriptions on bronzes, see Li 2015.

shu 尚書), and *Book of Poetry* (Shijing 詩經), in addition to the bronze inscriptions.[35] Nevertheless, the bronze inscriptions still convey to us a distilled reality of writing activities during the Western Zhou. Based on what the bronze inscriptions represent, and what they refer to, writing must have fulfilled the need of the Western Zhou elites in at least fifteen different ways (Table 1).

This thus leads us to an assessment of Western Zhou literacy that was reasonably much broader than Shang literacy that was at the "scribal literacy" stage of development described by William HARRIS. Instead, the identification of the various social contexts in which the written works were created or used, known as or from the bronze inscriptions, suggests that a considerable number of Western Zhou elites must have been able to handle the relevant documents and appreciate the written words that were important to their lives, so to make their production or casting on the bronzes meaningful at all. By and large the Zhou kings were most likely literate, and the bronze inscriptions actually offer clear references that the king was reading commands written on bamboo media. Most members of the Zhou social elites who served in the central government and probably also in many local courts were likely literate. The various scribes that the inscriptions record counted for the largest category of officials in the Western Zhou government; they must have been literate members of the social elite. The bronze inscriptions are themselves indisputable displays of literacy of the contemporaneous Western Zhou society. Such a condition of literacy, I suggest, can be best termed "elite literacy," which by definition was meaningfully more extensive than "scribal literacy". In my view, "elite literacy" was a condition of literacy that a large number of the social elites, whose total size could still be very small when compared to the overall population, developed enough familiarity with, and appreciated, the art of writing and reading, and many were indeed able to employ such skills when needed. Moreover, it should also be noted, that while the discovery of Shang oracle-bone inscriptions was limited to Anyang and two or three sites outside the Shang capital, Western Zhou bronzes inscribed with texts have been found all over northern China and a part of southern China. Thus, literacy was not only expanded socially, it was widespread geographically, making the Western Zhou one of the most important periods of the expansion of literacy in China and the East Asian world.

4 Epilogue: Literacy and the Imperial Government

The fall of the Western Zhou state in 771 BC and the transition to the territorial states in the 6th-5th century BC created new social conditions that needed a large number of local officials as well as scribes to manage the counties as cells of the future empire.

---

35 For an introduction to the nature and dating of these texts, see LOEWE 1993, 216–238; 376–389; 415–423.

The process of transition to territorial states also created a massive number of free farmers in the fields and massive groups of craftsmen in the expanding cities that needed to be controlled directly by state bureaucracy. The new bureaucracies of the competing states were staffed with officials and clerks who were at least literate in order to manage revenues and to mobilize resources of the states to support wars to gain new territory. The total control of the population through the establishment of new social institutions such as taxation, household registration, and codification of law also offered impulses for literacy's expansion from members of the social elite to the non-elite members of society including the craftsmen, well-to-do farmers, as well as non-elite women. On the intellectual level, the prosperity of state-sponsored schools and academies as well as the rise of private education in an age of unprecedented philosophical debate and literary creation both helped foster an increasing literate population.

As the empire was emerging from one of the territorial states, Qin in the Wei River valley of Shaanxi Province, by victimizing all others, literacy as the necessary equipment of imperial bureaucracy was also expanded into areas in the south that were suitable for the preservation of written documents on bamboo slips or wooden tablets. From the wetlands of Hubei and Hunan Provinces in the middle-Yangzi village to the Yangzi River delta down to the east, large quantities of such wooden documents were excavated, dating to the Warring States period to the Han dynasty. Some of these documents, for instance the recently discovered wooden tablets in Liye in Hunan Province (Figure 10), offer tremendously detailed information about the local administration of the Qin Empire. To provide a quick capture of this new condition of expanded literacy, I have reproduced a table of classification of the various types of written documents on bamboo strips or wooden tablets excavated from tombs dating to the Qin-Han period (221 BC-AD 220), mostly from southern China (Appendix 2).

In general, it can be said that in the Han Dynasty the 130,285 officials in the year 5 BC were largely literate in a population of 59,594,978 men and women as recorded in the official history of Han. In addition, there were several other social groups such as the professional scribes, military officers, members of the Han aristocracy, merchants, landowners, and so on, who were likely literate. Hypothetically, if the people in these groups could mass a total number that is ten times greater than the recorded figure for Han civil officials, the literate people in the Han Empire all combined would still amount to less than 3 percent of the Han population. It is probably acceptable that, in line with Harris's hypothetical numbers for ancient Greece and Rome that China during the Warring States, Qin, and Han periods never exceeded a literacy rate of 10 percent of the total population.[36] Although this is still a relatively low figure, given the immense size of the Han Empire and the large population it controlled, there seems little doubt that literacy must have achieved tremendous growth under the Qin and Han Empires.

---

36 Harris/Li 2015, 30.

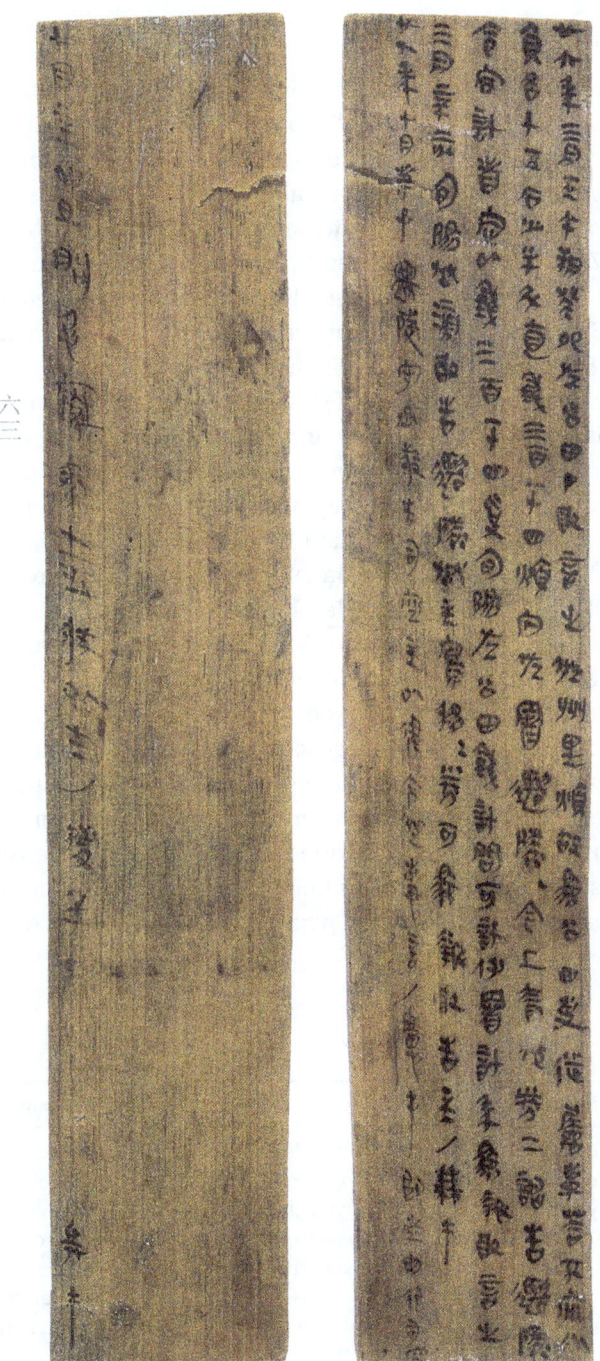

Fig. 10: The administrative wooden tablet from Liye, 2002:
from HUNAN SHENG WENWU KAOGU YANJIUSUO 2012, color pl. 4. V8-63

Conclusion

As far as the overall development of literacy in early China is concerned, we can actually identify two main periods in which literacy achieved the most significant expansion: The first period was the Western Zhou when literacy expanded both horizontally across a large geographical space and vertically across multiple social realms, helped by the founding of the Zhou regional states and the rise of the royal bureaucracy. The founding of the Zhou regional states was a process by which the Zhou elite population, a large part of which must have been literate, was translocated to a large area across northern China and the middle Yangtze region in the south, bringing along also the subjugated Shang scribes or diviners. These new locales in the centuries following the Zhou founding then became centers for the development of new cultures and literacy. The social expansion of literacy under the Western Zhou was helped by the bureaucratization of the Zhou government that was itself a result of the intensification of competition for more resources by the Zhou elite lineages in the royal domain in Shaanxi until 771 BC, the fall of the Western Zhou dynasty.

The second expansion of literacy paralleled the process of empire building under the Qin and Han Empires. On a general level, empire-building was itself a process of replication of the administrative unit called "county" (*xian* 縣) in regions that previously knew no-Chinese writing, nor even Chinese speaking, leading inevitably to the expansion of local bureaucracies. This was true for both the Qin and Han Empires. But this was possible only with the presence of a relatively large number of scribes and servants of various kinds who could perform literary tasks in the maintenance of the county as shown in the Liye documents. Quite different from the situation in Mesopotamia or in the Mediterranean world where commercial expansion effectively led to the expansion of literacy, in early China, it would seem, both waves of literacy's expansion was closely related to, or perhaps was driven by, the expansion of the political system.

Tab. 1: Functions of Literacy in the Western Zhou.

Cat.	Functions of Literacy	Transmission
1	Record keeping including records of merits, list of gifts, calendar, etc.	Royal court.
2	Copies of royal speeches or memorials of high officials.	Royal court.
3	Royal edicts of official appointment, some cast on bronzes.	Royal court to individual.
4	Royal command about land award or transaction.	Royal court to individual.
5	Official communications.	Officials to officials.
6	Land registers, as results of administrative decisions or legal settlements.	Royal court to elite family.
7	Military uses including records of awards or punishment.	Military headquarters or personnel.
8	Land tallies or contracts of sale of properties.	Between elite individuals.

9	Treaties to conclude wars.	Between lineages/local states.
10	Religious prayers addressed or dedicated to ancestors, cast on bronzes.	Elite lineages.
11	Records of divination, on bones or other media.	Royal or elite lineages.
12	Commemorations of individual merits, military or civil, cast on bronzes.	Elite lineages.
13	Appraisal of family history including genealogy.	Elite lineages.
14	Ownership of bronzes.	Elite lineages.
15	Works of literature such as poems or verses. Etc.	Elite individuals.

Tab. 2: Excavated Bamboo and Wooden Documents from the Qin and Han Empires*

1. Letters and Articles (*Shu-Xi*)	Imperial edicts, appointment letters, official memorials, official communications, dispositions of government policies, emergency announcements, reports of legal cases, statements of matters, official impeachments, and passports for official or private businesses, etc.
2. Statutes and Ordinances (*Lü-Ling*)	Statutes on murder, statutes on robbery, statutes on land, statutes on household, statutes on currency, statutes on market, statutes on postal service, statutes on scribes …..45 categories. Ordinance on ferries and passes, ordinance on merits, ordinance on awards, ordinance on guarding troops, etc. Rank list of awards to officials, rank list of frontier signals, etc. Modules of legal cases, question and answers about legal matters, etc.
3. Accounts and Registers (*Bu-Ji*)	General accounts, account on cash spending, account on inlet outlet grains, account on rations, account on weapons, account on funeral items, etc. Register of officials, register of foot soldiers, register of cavalrymen, list of recipients of rations, list of clothes, list of casualties of war, etc.
4. Records and evaluations (*Lu-Ke*)	Memorandum of official inspection, memorandum of official visits, memorandum of frontier signals, memorandum of postal arrivals, etc.
5. Tallies and Contracts (*Fu-Juan*)	Tallies for travelers, tallies of personal identity, tallies for soldiers on patrol, etc. Contracts for loan of cash, contracts for land and property, etc.
6. Labels and Tags (*Jian-Jie*)	Labels and tags for documents, labels and tags for goods, etc.

*Source: LI 2009, table of contents.

Appendix: Translation of Inscriptions

Figure 5-1 (Left):
This plastron carries as many as twenty-seven inscriptions as records of royal divination by the Shang king, with frequently two inscriptions paired and placed on the two sides of the shell. Starting at the upper-right edge, the first seventeen inscriptions read:
1 (*upper-right*). Crack-making on the *yichou*-day (#2), Que charged: "During the night between the *jiazi*-day (#1) and *yichou*-day (#2), the king dreamed of herding the *shi*-deer. Is it not misfortune? Or is it fortune?"
2 (*upper-left*). Charged: "During the night between the *jiazi*-day (#1) and *yichou*-day (#2), the king dreamed of herding the *shi*-deer. Is it not misfortune? Or is it fortune?" Third month.
3 (*middle-right*). Charged: "[The king had a] dream, will [he] call upon Yu to perform exorcism over his shoulder?"
4 (*middle-left*). Charged: "The king had a dream, will [he] not call upon Yu [to perform exorcism] over his shoulder?"
5 (*right-bridge*). Charged: "Will the king have a sick shoulder?"
6 (*middle-central*). "Will the king have something not agreeable?"
7 (*middle-central*). "Will the king not have something not agreeable?"
8 (*middle-right*). Charged: "Now Pan captured [victims] in Tun. If the king uses [them in sacrifice], will it be agreeable?"
9 (*on top of 8*). Charged: "Will we receive harvest of millets?"
10 (*middle-left*). "Will [we] not receive harvest of millets?"
11 (*upper-right*). Charged: "If the king cuts three Qiang (prisoners) on the sacrificial table, will it not be agreeable? [Will it be] agreeable?"
12 (*right-bridge*). Charged: "If the king cuts three Qiang (prisoners) on the sacrificial table, will it not be agreeable? [Will it be] agreeable?"
13 (*middle-right*). "Next *yihai*-day (#12), will it (weather) clear up?"
14 (*middle-left*). "Next *yihai*-day (#12), will it (weather) not clear up?"
15 (*middle-central*). "[On] coming *yiwei*-day (#32), will [we] not conduct entreatment ritual?"
16 (*central-right*). Crack-making on the *gengzi*-day (#37), Que charged: "When lady Guo gives birth to a child, [will she be] lucky?"
17 (*central-left*). Charged: "When Lady Guo gives birth to a child, [will she be] not lucky?"

Figure 5-2 (Right):
A total of seven inscriptions are engraved on this plastron, divided into upper and lower parts, each inscription is going around the edge of the noted crack(s):
1 (*right-bridge*). [Plastrons] from Ning, totaling three.
2 (*lower-left*). Crack-making on the *xinhai*-day (#48): "The Prince accompanied Lady Hao to enter Dai. The Prince called out to the many officials to have an audience with Lady Hao, and they presented her ten bundles of textile. [Will we] go to Xing?"
3 (*lower-right*). Crack-making on the *xinhai*-day (#48): "Tan presented Lady Hao three bundles of textile and Chang presented Lady Hao two bundles of textile; used. [Will we] go to Xing?"
4 (*lower-right edge*). Crack-making on the *xinhai*-day (#48): "Will it be that Tan has an audience with Lady Hao? Not used."
5 (*upper-right*). Crack-making on the *guichou*-day (#50): "[Will we] cut and offer cow to Father Jia? Used."
6 (*below 5*). Crack-making on the *yimao*-day (#52): "Will it be that we offer a white big to Father Jia? Not used."
7 (*upper-left*). [Crack-making on] the *yimao*-day (#52): "[Will we] cut [and offer] Father Yi a bull and a bottle of *you*-alcohol?"

Figure 7-2:
A total of 67 characters were cast on the interior bottom of the vessel:
It was the third month. The King commanded Rong and the Interior Scribe saying: "Replace the service of the Ruler of Xing. [I] award you three types of servants: the Zhou people, Dong people, and the Yong people." [Rong] bowed with his head touching the ground, and extols the Son of Heaven's granting him repeated fortune, with which he will be able to run [in service of] High God, who will not end his mandate to the Zhou state. [He] pursues filial piety in response and will not dare to fail, and he opens my blessing sacrifice. I be the servant of the Son of Heaven, and use [this vessel] to document the command of the king. [I] make for the Duke of Zhou this sacrificial vessel.

Figure 8-2:
39 characters were cast on the interior bottom of the tureen:
Bo Kang makes [this] treasured *gui*-tureen, using it to feast his friends, and using it to offer food to the Royal father and Royal mother, [so he will] extendedly receive this eternal mandate without boundaries and pure blessing. May Kang for ten thousand years [enjoy] abundant longevity, forever treasure this *gui*-tureen, using it morning and night without laxity.

Figure 9-2:
A total of 349 characters were cast on the flat bottom of this basin:
Because Ze attacked the settlements of San, [the officials of Ze] then arrived in San to use land [as compensation]. Surveying: Cross the Xian River to the south and arrive at the Great Pond, making the first tree-marker; ascend, making the second tree-marker; arrive at Bianliu, crossing the Xian River again. Climb the slope of Zha and Luo west, tree-marking near the paper mulberry tree of Bo Town, tree-marking at Zoulai, and tree-marking at Zou-Lane. Entering Zou and ascending, upon the Cliff-Spring, tree-mark at Zhu-Bank, Slope-Hill, and Ridge-Bank. Tree-marking at Shan-Road, tree-marking at Yuan-Road, and tree-marking at Zhou-Road; moving east, tree-marking to the right of the eastern border of Chuo. Returning, tree-marking at Li-Road. Moving south, tree-mark at Zhulai-Road; moving west, reach Weimo. Surveying the fields of the settlement of Jing: from the left of *Láng*-tree-Road to the Jing settlement, tree-marking. To the east of the Road, one tree-marker; returning to the west, one tree-marker; ascending the ridge, three tree-markers; descending to the south, tree-mark at Tong-Road; going up Zhou-Ridge, climbing the bank, and descending to the Yu-woods, two tree-markers. Those officials of the Ze people who have surveyed the land: Xian, Qie, Wei, Wufu, Xigong Xiang; Supervisor of Marshes of the Dou people Gai, Lu Zhen, Marshal You Sheng, Little Gate Official Yao; Supervisor of Marshes of the Yuan people Nai; Supervisor of Construction of Huai named Hu, Zi Lun, Fengfu; the officials of the Wei people Jing and Gai — in all, fifteen men. Those [from San] who have verified and surveyed the land transferred by Ze: Supervisor of Land Ni Yin, Supervisor of Horses Shan Kun; Supervisor of Construction of the Bang people Jing Jun, Superintendent Defu; the Young Boys of the San people who have participated in the survey, Rong, Weifu, and Yao Qufu; officials of the Xiang people, Tuo, Zhou Jing, You Cong Guo — in all, officials of San, ten men. It was the [Zhou] king's ninth month, the time was *yǐmǎo* (day 52), Ze had Xian, Qie, X, and Lü take the oath, saying: "We have already submitted the land and the utensils to the San-lineage, and if we overturn [the agreement], having the fact of plotting against the San-lineage, fine us a thousand *yuán* of metal, publicly denouncing us [throughout the Zhou state]." Xian, Qie, X, and Lü thus swore the oath. Then, asking Xigong Xiang and Wufu to swear the oath: "We have handed over to the San-lineage the marshy fields and the fields divided into grids and, if we overturn [the agreement], will be fined one thousand *yuán* of metal!" Xigong Xiang and Wufu thus took the oath. They made a map, in the Ze king's presence in the eastern court of the New Palace of Dou.
Its (his) Left Contract-Keeping Scribe verified; (signed) Zhong Nong.

Figure 10:
This documented wooden tablet has traveled from Xunyang County of the Qin Empire in present-day southern Shaanxi to Qianling County in western Hunan:
Obverse:
In the twenty-six year, third month of which the first day was *renwu* (#19), on the *guimao*-day (#40), Ding, officer of the left public land, dares to report this: Fan, the assistant from the Zhou district, was an officer of the public land; but he had since been transferred [to a new post]. [He] was in charge of red beans, but there was a shortage, for which he owed fifteen *shi* and one third of a *dou* [of red beans], which valued 314 coins. Fan is an adjunct officer in Qianling. Now [I] submit the two halves of the contract, petitioning to report to the accountant under the Magistrate of Qianling, that [he] must count on receiving 314 coins that is the money of the left public land of Xunyang. Asking for reply: what office handled this amount? What [fiscal] year this was counted in? [I] dare to report.

In the third month, on the *xinhai*-day (#48), the Assistant of Xunyang, Pang, dares to report to the Chief Assistant of Qianling: Copy it, transfer the contract, and [then you] can please reply. Daring to report to the Chief. Jian signed.

In the twenty-seventh year, tenth month, on the *gengzi*-day (#37), Jing, Assistant to the Governor of Qianling, reports to the chief supervisor of works: proceed in accordance with the statutes and ordinances. Lü signed. Promptly [dispatches] messenger Shen to deliver it to the supervisor of works.
Reverse:
In the tenth month, on the morning of the *xinmao*-day (#28), Zhuang, who is of the *shiwu* rank from the Suqin district of Quren [County], brought it to come. Qing opened. Bing signed.

Bibliography

BAGLEY 2004 = R. BAGLEY, Anyang Writing and the Origin of the Chinese Writing System, in: S.D. HOUSTON (ed.), The First Writing, Cambridge 2004, 190–249.
BAINES 2004 = J. BAINES, The Earliest Egyptian Writing: Development, Context, and Purpose, in: S.D. HOUSTON (ed.), The First Writing, Cambridge 2004, 130–189.
BOLTZ 1994 = W.G. BOLTZ, The Origin and Early Development of the Chinese Writing System, New Haven 1994.
BOLTZ 2011 = W.G. BOLTZ, Literacy and the Emergence of Writing in China, in: LI/BRANNER 2011, 51–84.
BOONE 2004 = E. HILL BOONE, Beyond Writing, in: S.D. HOUSTON (ed.), The First Writing, Cambridge 2004, 313–348.
CHEN 1955–56 = Chen Mengjia 陳夢家. Xi Zhou tongqi duandai I-VI 西周銅器斷代, *Kaogu xuebao* 考古學報 9, 1955, 137–75; 10, 1955, 69–142; 1956.1, 65–114; 1956.2, 85–94; 1956.3, 105–278; 1956.4, 85–122.
COOK/GOLDIN 2016 = C.A. COOK/P.R. GOLDIN (ed.), A Source Book of Ancient Chinese Bronze Inscriptions, Berkeley 2016.
ELMAN 2000 = B.A. ELMAN, A Cultural History of Civil Examinations in Late Imperial China, Berkeley 2000.
FALKENHAUSEN 1993 = L. VON FALKENHAUSEN, Issues in Western Zhou Studies: A Review Article. *Early China* 18, 1993, 139–226.
GAO 1996 = GAO MING 高明. Zhongguo guwenzi xue tonglun 中國古文字學通論 (A general introduction to Chinese paleography), Beijing, 1996.
HARRIS 1989 = W.V. HARRIS, Ancient Literacy, Cambridge MA 1989.

Harris/Li 2015 = W.V. Harris/F. Li, Ancient Literacy: Parallels and Divergences between the Mediterranean World and China. Manuscript, February 2015.
Hunan Sheng Wenwu Kaogu Yanjiusuo 2012 = Hunan Sheng wenwu kaogu yanjiusuo 湖南省文物考古研究所. Liye Qin jian 里耶秦简, vol. 1., Beijing 2012.
Jia 2009 = Jia Shuangxi 賈雙喜. Jiaguwen zhong zhenren bushi buci qikeren 甲骨文中貞人不是卜辭契刻人 (The diviner in the oracle bone inscriptions is not the engraver of the inscription), Tushuguan gongzuo yu yanjiu 图书馆工作与研究 2009.2, 79–81.
Johnson/Parker 2009 = W.A. Johnson/H.N. Parker (ed.), Ancient Literacies: The Culture of Reading in Greece and Rome, Oxford 2009.
Keightley 1978 = D.N. Keightley, Sources of Shang History: The Oracle-Bone Inscriptions of Bronze Age China, Berkeley 1978.
Keightley 2006 = D.N. Keightley, Marks and Labels: Early Writing in Neolithic and Shang China, in: M.T. Stark (ed.), Archaeology of Asian, Malden 2006, 177–202.
Kracke 1953 = E.A. Kracke, Civil Service in Early Sung China, Cambridge MA 1953.
Lee 1985 = Th.H.C. Lee, Government Education and Examinations in Sung China, Hong Kong 1985.
Lee 2000 = Th.H.C. Lee, Education in Traditional China, Leiden 2000.
Li 2001 = F. Li, 'Offices' in Bronze Inscriptions and Western Zhou Government Administration, Early China 26–27, 2001–2002, 1–72.
Li 2006 = F. Li, Landscape and Power in Early China: The Crisis and Fall of the Western Zhou, 1045–771 B.C., Cambridge 2006.
Li 2012 = F. Li, Bureaucracy and the State in Early China: Governing the Western Zhou, Cambridge 2012.
Li 2015 = F. Li, Solving Puzzles about the Method of Casting Inscriptions on Western Zhou Bronzes, Chinese Archaeology 15, 2015, 1–13.
Li /Branner 2011 = F. Li/D. Prager Branner (ed.), Writing and Literacy in Early China: Studies from the Columbia Early China Seminar, Seattle 2011.
Li 2009 = Li Junming 李均明, Qin Han jiandu wenshu fenlei jijie 秦漢簡牘文書分類輯解, Beijing 2009.
Loewe 1993 = M. Loewe (ed.), Early Chinese Texts: A Bibliographical Guide, Berkeley 1993.
Luo 2006 = Luo Tai 羅泰 (Lothar von Falkenhausen). Xi Zhou tongqi mingwen de xingzhi, 西周銅器銘文的性質 (The nature of the Western Zhou bronze inscriptions), in: Kaoguxue yanjiu 考古學研究 6, 2006, 343–374.
Matsumaru 1997 = Matsumaru Michio 松丸道雄. Kanji kigen mondai no shin tenkai 漢字起源問題の新展開 (New developments in the study of the origin of the Chinese characters), Shudū bijutsu shinbun 書道美術新聞, June 11-August 1, 1997.
Mihara 1968 = K. Mihara, 三原研田. Kōkotsu moji no shufū ni tsuite 甲骨文字の書風について (On the calligraphic styles of oracle bone inscriptions), Shiga daigaku kyōikubu kiyō 滋賀大学教育学部紀要 17, 1967, 34–52; (续编) 18, 1968, 102–115.
Miyazaki 1981 = Miyazaki Ichisada, China's Examination Hell: The Civil Service Examinations of Imperial China, translated by Conrad Schirokauer, New Haven 1981.
Pankenier 2011 = D.W. Pankenier, Getting "Right" with Heaven and the Origins of Writing in China, in: Li/Branner 2011, 19–50.
Qiu 1993 = Qiu Xigui 裘錫圭, Jiujing shi bus hi wenzi –tantan woguo xinshiqi shidai shiyong de fuhao 究竟是不是文字--谈谈我国新石器时代使用的符号 (Are they writing or not? On the marks used in the Neolithic period of China), Wenwu tiandi 文物天地 1993.2.
Qiu 2000 = Qiu Xigui, Chinese Writing, translated by Gilbert L. Mattos and Jerry Norman, Berkeley 2000.
Rawski 1979 = E.S. Rawski, Education and Popular Literacy in Ch'ing China, Ann Arbor 1979.

SHAUGHNESSAY 1991 = E.L. SHAUGHNESSY, Sources of Western Zhou History: Inscribed Bronze Vessels, Berkeley/Los Angeles 1991.

SMITH 2011 = A. SMITH, The Evidence for Scribal Training at Anyang, in: LI/BRANNER 2011, 173–205.

SUN 2006 = SUN YABING 孫亞冰, Bainian lai jiaguwen ziliao tongji 百年來甲骨文資料統計 (Statistic account of oracle bones discovered in the past one hundred years), *Gugong bowuyuan yuankan* 故宮博物院院刊 1, 2006, 24–47.

TAKASHIMA 2010 = KEN-ICHI TAKASHIMA 高嶋謙一, Studies of Fascicle Three of Inscriptions from the Yin Ruins, Volume 1: General Notes, Text and Translations (up to plastron #259 translated by Paul L-M. Serruys); Volume 2: New Palaeographical and Philological Commentaries, Taipei 2010.

TAKASHIMA 2011= KEN-ICHI TAKASHIMA. Literacy to the South and the East of Anyang in Shang China: Zhengzhou and Daxinzhuang, in: LI/BRANNER 2011, 141–172.

TANG 1977 = TANG LAN 唐蘭, Cong Dawenkou wenhua de ciqi wenzi kan woguo zuizao wenhua de niandai 從大汶口文化的瓷器文字看我國最早文化的年代 (The writing on the ceramics of the Dawenkou culture and the date of the earliest culture in China), *Guangming ribao* 光明日報, July 14, 1977.

WENGROW 2008 = D. WENGROW, Limits of Decipherment: Object Biographies and the Invention of Writing, in: B. MIDANT-REYNES (ed.), Egypt at Its Origins 2: Proceedings of the International Conference "Origin of the State, Predynastic and Early Dynastic Egypt", Toulouse (France), 5th-8th September 2005, Paris 2008, 1021–1032.

WU 2015 = WU ZHENFENG 吳鎮烽, Shang Zhou qingtongqi mingwen ji tuxiang jicheng 商周青銅器銘文暨圖像集成 (A compendium of inscriptions and images on bronzes from the Shang and Zhou period), 36 vols., Shanghai 2012; supplements, Shanghai 2015.

YU 1973 = YU SHENGWU 于省吾, Guanyu guwenzi yanjiu de ruogan wenti 關於古文字研究的若干問題 (Issues in the study of paleography), *Wenwu* 文物 1973.2, 32–35.

ZHANG 2015 = ZHANG BINGHUO 張炳火 (ed.), Liangzhu wenhua kehua fuhao 良渚文化刻畫符號 (Pictographs of the Liangzhu Culture), Shanghai 2015.

ZHANG 1965–72 = ZHANG BINGQUAN 張秉權, Xiaotun 2: Yinxu wenzi bingbian 小屯第二本：殷墟文字丙編, 3 vols., Taipei 1965–1972.

ZHONGGUO SHEHUI KEXUEYUAN KAOGU YANJIUSUO 1984–94 = ZHONGGUO SHEHUI KEXUEYUAN KAOGU YANJIUSUO 中國社會科學院考古研究所, Yin Zhou jinwen jicheng 殷周金文集成 (A compendium of Shang and Zhou bronze inscriptions), 18 vols., Beijing 1984–1994.

ZHONGGUO SHEHUI KEXUEYUAN KAOGU YANJIUSUO 2003 = ZHONGGUO SHEHUI KEXUEYUAN KAOGU YANJIUSUO 中國社會科學院考古研究所, Yinxu Huayuanzhuang dong di jiagu 殷墟花園莊東地甲骨 (Oracle Bones from Huayuanzhuang-East in Yinxu), 6 vols., Kunming 2003.

ZHONGGUO SHEHUI KEXUEYUAN KAOGU YANJIUSUO 2010 = ZHONGGUO SHEHUI KEXUEYUAN KAOGU YANJIUSUO 中國社會科學院考古研究所, Zhongguo kaoguxue: Xin shiqi shidai juan 中國考古學：新石器時代卷 (Chinese Archaeology: the Neolithic Period), Beijing 2010.

ZHOU 1975 = ZHOU FAGAO 周法高, Jinwen gulin 金文詁林, 14 vols., Hong Kong 1975.

Harry Falk
The Creation and Spread of Scripts in Ancient India

Abstract: Like his ancestors before him, King Aśoka (ca. 268–232 BC) was linked to the Seleucid dynasty in the West by family ties. Unlike his predecessors, however, he was the first to react to the immense cultural differences separating the two realms. One of the major deficits concerned the use of dressed stone for public monuments, the other was the lack of a script. India had produced a vast literature of a sacerdotal and secular nature, kept alive solely by oral means. Aśoka had a script designed for his country which amalgamated the best features of the two scripts current in his time, Greek and Kharoṣṭhī. The latter had been created only few years previously, 1600 km away in what is now northern Pakistan in an area formerly under Achaemenid rule, administrated with the help of Aramaic clerks. Although less suited to the language, Kharoṣṭhī script was not superseded by the new Brāhmī script from the East. This paper explains the perseverance of the western script on the basis of its function as a means for legal transactions. The need for documents had provided the incentive for the creation of a local script after the Aramaic clerks with their foreign script for a foreign language had started to disappear, rendering older documents illegible and thus worthless. Brāhmī, on the other hand, had little success as a script of administration, but served to demonstrate to the West the cultural and ethical standards of its homeland, and of its creator, Aśoka.

Zusammenfassung: Mit dem König Aśoka (ca. 268–232 v. Chr.) der Maurya-Dynastie begann eine neue Zeit in Indien, denn er war nicht nur familiär mit den Seleukiden im Nahen Osten verbunden, sondern er war auch der Erste, der die kulturellen Unterschiede begriff und Veränderungen in seinem Land herbeiführen wollte. Zwei Momente sind für uns besonders deutlich fassbar, einmal die Einführung einer Steintechnologie, die zu seinen monumentalen Säulen mit Tierkapitellen führte und zu den künstlichen Höhlen bei Bodh Gaya, zum zweiten ließ er für sein Land eine Schrift erschaffen und beendete damit eine Phase ausschließlicher Oralität, die von den vedischen Brahmanen zum Schutz ihrer Ritual-Literatur gepflegt wurde. Diese Schrift, Brāhmī genannt, übernahm innovative Züge der Kharoṣṭhī-Schrift. Diese war kurz zuvor im heutigen Nord-Pakistan entstanden, das bis zu Alexanders Eroberungen zum Reich der Achaemeniden gehörte. Trotz einiger struktureller Defizite ließ sich die Kharoṣṭhī nicht von der Brāhmī verdrängen. Die Zählebigkeit der Kharoṣṭhī wird hier mit ihrer Funktion als Medium der Rechtssicherheit in Verbindung gebracht: Mit dem allmählichen Verschwinden der aramäischen Schreiber-Kaste waren auf Aramäisch geschriebene Urkunden aller Art unlesbar und damit wertlos geworden. Nicht lange nach der Kharoṣṭhī wurde die Brāhmī entwickelt und verbreitet. Für sie ist eine frühe Verwendung in Handel oder privaten Verträgen nicht nachzuweisen. Für die Verwaltung wurde sie nur unter Aśoka und nur in der Ganges-Ebene nördlich der Hauptstadt eingesetzt. Die kultur- und religionsfördernden Aspekte, die den Ursprung der Brāhmī ausmachten, blieben auch weiterhin dominant.

Leaving the Harappan culture of the third millennium BC apart, scripts in ancient India did not develop out of simple beginnings in a gradual fashion, as in the literate cultures around the eastern Mediterranean, but pop out into view late, suddenly and almost fully developed in the early third century BC.[1]

After the fall of the Harappan culture of unknown linguistic affiliation, around 1900 BC, literature was produced in the so-called Vedic language for Vedic rituals, and to our advantage a great part of it was preserved to this very day by mainly oral means. Even after the Iranian Achaemenids occupied lands up to the banks of the Indus, the adjoining Vedic groups never thought of developing a script for their textual treasures. The mechanics of orality in those days are comparable to what Julius Caesar (*Caes. Gall.* 6,14) reported about the literature in Celtic France: the Druids knew an amazing amount of verses by heart. Their knowledge was the basis of their social standing and also of their livelihood, causing these specialists to have an unfavourable view of writing. Nobody in India east of the Iranian dominions challenged this attitude because India lived at the fringe of the known world, with very little contacts to the West and North, happy in its own sort of splendid isolation.

Things changed with Alexander the Great, coming from outside, and with the indigenous Maurya dynasty, willing to intensify contacts with the Hellenistic rulers of the West. Alexander left a network of newly founded towns from Mesopotamia up to the Indus, in part populated with Greek-speaking and -writing veterans. These urban centres were by definition interrelated through commerce and spread knowledge of Western material culture and also of actual political events. They also helped to introduce a range of cultural concepts concerning property rights, building in stone and dressing stone for artistic purposes, and also script as a means of administration and for private purposes, freely available for everyone.

Even before Alexander, people and rulers in India had certainly heard of the buildings of Persepolis, Babylon or Memphis, but without the secure roads and seaways from Mesopotamia and Egypt to the Indus needed for bulk trade in both directions, this had had little impact. The transformation effected by Alexander now allowed a greater number of people in India to become aware of the huge cultural differences concerning material culture, administration and other components of what we call civilization. Candragupta (ca. 321–297 BC) and Bimbisāra (ca. 297–273 BC), alias Amitraghāta, the first two rulers of the Mauryas, were in contact with Seleuceia, but they

---

1 An exposition of the facts was given by Max Müller as early as 1859; for a summary of all arguments proposed so far cf. Falk 1993.

seem to have been busy securing their enormous realm, without spending too much time on modernising their country.

The State of Stone Working before Aśoka

It pays to glance at what an archaeologist can find in Indian soil that dates from the time before Alexander opened the roads to the West. There are a number of old cities and commerce stations, and many of them are known from the itineraries of the Buddha in the decades prior to 400 BC, meaning that they definitely existed before the Macedonians reached the Indus. HÄRTEL has shown how little of their remnants can be dated to times earlier than the Mauryas,[2] and ERDOSY'S neat summary of the problem still remains valid: "To this day not a single house-plan is available for pre-Mauryan levels".[3] Arrian gives us a reason why and also explains why this state of affairs persists even into Mauryan levels: "... such cities as are situated on the banks of rivers or on the sea-coast are built of wood, for were they built of brick they would not last long–so destructive are the rains; (...) those cities, however, which stand on commanding situations and lofty eminences are built of brick and mud."[4] Brick and mud, but not stone was used.

When things change, non-humans seem to be at work, a topic of talk for centuries to come. The Chinese pilgrim Faxian was told shortly after AD 400 that "Pataliputra is where Asoka ruled. The royal palace was wholly built by ghosts who piled up stones for walls and towers, who incised letters, made inlays which cannot be done in this (human) world. It still exists as of old".[5]

A visitor soon realizes that many of the oldest cities are nestled inside a narrow ring of surrounding hills. The most famous such site is Rājagṛha, modern Rajgir. Similar sites are the old Shahbazgarhi in Gandhara, or the old Kopbal in Madhya Pradesh, in between the Aśokan Minor Rock Edicts (MRE) of Palkiguṇḍu and Gavīmath. Bairaṭ, near Jaipur, likewise falls into this category, as does Hathial, the oldest part of Taxila. This kind of settlement allows for only a limited number of inhabitants, who are supplied with water from the surrounding hills.

A second and younger type of city provides shelter inside huge, mostly square earthen wall constructions in places where there are no major hill formations. Famous examples are Śiśupālgarh near Bhubaneswar in Orissa, then the whole site of Jaugarh, also in Orissa, Sannati on the Bhīmā and Kauśāmbī on the Ganges, all sites famous for their vestiges of Aśoka. Without preserved traces of Aśoka are Adam, Mahāsthāngarh, or Candraketugarh in Bengal. In all cases, the huge earthen walls furnish remarkably

---

2 HÄRTEL 1991.
3 ERDOSY 1995, 110.
4 Arr. an. 10 = MAJUMDAR 1981, 223 f.
5 After DEEG 2005, 547.

few traces of habitation, recalling our Celtic oppida in size and construction, which served to shelter merchants until they were numerous enough to depart in a secure caravan.

What did houses look like in the "wooden" days of Pāṭaliputra? We should not project backwards the depictions on the gates of Sanchi. Those houses are 200 years younger and impress with their high bases, so that the inhabited part is elevated to the second floor. But we have the caves which Aśoka had cut into the boulders at Barabar, yet another old site surrounded by hills near Bodh Gaya. His most ingenious architects copied luxurious private dwellings into the rocks for the ascetics of the Ājīvika order. One cave has received an entrance front that copies in stone the wooden beams and rafters and carvings from a standard house. The most telling part is found inside: all caves without exception show slanting long-side walls, and upright end-walls. This slanting (about 10 cm inwards with a height of 180 cm) copies basic constructions of upright pillars along the sides of houses, topped by a close sequence of semi-circular ribs. This stable barrel-shaped roof construction then received vertical end-walls in the form of the entrance at the Lomas Rishi Cave at Barabar. A stunning example is provided by the Gopālī Cave at the Nagarjuni Hills, one km further east from Barabar,[6] with two circular ends on the narrow sides, under a rounded roof. A comparable design is also used for long-houses built on the ground at nearby Rajgir. Unfortunately, the documentation is very superficial, but one photograph (IA-R 1954–55, pl. XXIX) and two ground-plans (IA-R 1954–55, fig. 4; 1958–59, 13) leave no doubt that the Gopālī Cave copies constructions where the foundations, 1 m thick and more than 1 m high, were not made from burned bricks but from rubble and mud-mortar.[7] At the Gopālī cave with its two semi-circular ends as well as in most other Aśokan caves there is a sharp and straight line separating the slanting wall-sides from the vaulted ceiling, reminiscent of the line where in ordinary houses the wall met the ribs shaping the roof. Rubble and mud was in use, but bricks can be expected also for foundations, although so far they are mainly found inside stūpas. For this reason I characterize the pre-Aśokan housing culture in India as a "culture of wood and bricks", materials which seem to have dominated the public world, and I dwelt here on the simplicity of construction techniques at seemingly undue length in order to make clear how sharply the years before ca. 270 BC differ from the phase to follow.

---

[6] Cf. FALK 2006, 257; these caves have been "handed over" (niṣiṭha) to the Ājīvikas by Daśaratha, probably after the demise of Aśoka, who always uses "given" (dinna) for his personally effected donations.
[7] According to IA-R 1954–55, 16, the constructions are found immediately above the Northern Black Polished Ware and yielded copper coins. This looks like a Śuṅga time horizon, but without further evidence an occupation by monks not using luxury ceramics in Mauryan times should not be excluded. CHAKRABARTI 1976, 263 f. considers the site unimportant.

Towards the Transformation

After Alexander, and after the first two Mauryas who did not leave a single clear trace to the spade,[8] the third in line, Aśoka (268–232 BC), modified his country in a revolutionary manner. His realm reached from modern Calcutta to Kabul, from Pokhara in Nepal almost to Madras. He changed India from a "wood and bricks" country to a "stone and art" country. His impact cannot be exaggerated. He had people cut monolithic pillars and animal figures in stone, with huge dimensions, the pillars up to 14 m high[9], weighing up to 300 tons, the animal figures adding another 2 to 2.5 m. The animal capitals are chiselled in a very naturalistic way, the surface of the stone is polished to a glaze. One may imagine the reactions of the locals as they were first confronted with these works of art. Judging by what present-day rustics say, the people of old must likewise have believed that these pillars and the animals were made and transported by gods.

Besides introducing stone and art, Aśoka had a script designed and spread, carrying his messages. It seems that Aśoka's intention in doing so was not merely to guide his people, but also to communicate with visiting foreigners, as is suggested by the fact that many inscriptions are located on borders. Why? Indians returning from the Western countries must have told tales of all sorts of wonders they had encountered, be it the pillars of Persepolis or the obelisks of Egypt. At the Mauryan court, people must have realized that there was nothing in India that could impress foreigners in a similar way. The most glaring differences concerned building in stone, plastic art and the use of script, all of them absent in India. We can be sure that building in bricks, wood and bamboo was of a high quality and had its own aesthetic appeal, but anything only vaguely similar to the temples or palaces in Bactria, Persepolis, Seleuceia or Alexandria in Egypt was absolutely lacking. Every foreign visitor would sooner or later ask for the local temples. But there were no temples, there were no statues of gods. Aśoka was personally related to the Seleucid dynasty, he must have met Greek and Macedonian guests in the household of his family. He must have heard them talk about what they could not find in the capital: stone foundations of houses, stone-lined city walls, stone-paved roads, temples for stationary gods, statues of gods, and many things more.

Once Aśoka had installed edifices and artefacts made from stone, the new technology was spread everywhere and the traders and diplomats from the West returning about half a century after Candragupta had reason to speak with awe of the India created by Aśoka. In principle, Mauryan India was rich; it sold elephants, gems and spices to all parties in the West. Aśoka wanted more than riches, he wanted to be king

---

8 JACOBS 2016.
9 FALK 2006, 152.

of a country that stood culturally on par with the countries of the famous Macedonian kings following Alexander.

A country without any script certainly appeared backward to the people in the West, but Aśoka was about to fill this gap. However, before he could introduce a script of his own something happened at the western border of his own empire.

Script Was "in the Air"

Around 550 BC the Achaemenid dynasty in Iran made what is now Pakistan its tributary. Although writers came from the West an indigenous Indian writing system was still not in sight, although we can expect a general knowledge of writing as such. The grammar of Pāṇini from roughly the middle of the fourth century BC knows a term for script, to be spelled *lipi* or *libi*, but this grammar itself is a composition of such phonetic subtlety that it can only be preserved unchanged by oral means.[10] The mistakes innate in writing would have destroyed the text in a very short time. The admitted spelling variance shows that *lipi* or *libi* are foreign terms with no Sanskritic derivation and thus no dogmatic orthophony. In fact, both forms of pronunciation, *libi* and *lipi*, reproduce a term which is ultimately Sumerian, used by the Achaemenid administrators active in northern Pakistan from the 6th to the 3rd century BC. Pāṇini, who hailed from a site on the Indus in northern Pakistan, thus knew writing, but did not make use of it for his so-called grammar – which is rather a philosophy of sound and meaning. The reason is obvious: the sounds which can be reproduced by the Aramaic script used by the clerks in the service of the Achaemenid dynasty are not in the least suited to represent the range of sounds analysed by the Indian grammarians as phonetically relevant. The Aramaic alphabet knows of 22 letters, plus number signs, and whereas the sounds to be distinguished by a student of Sanskrit amount to about 50, the exact number varies depending on whether theoretically possible sounds are included or not. A simple adoption of a Semitic script without additions is thus impossible. Even if more letters were added to make good for the remaining Indian sounds, the system would still lack the ability to represent doubled consonants and vowels of different length. Realizing that there are incompatible languages (Aramaic and Sanskrit), different sound systems, and different purposes (administrative and sacerdotal) must have led to the logical conclusion that Aramaic writing, which appeared as writing as such, was of absolutely no use to Sanskrit speaking priests and philosophers.

A short time later, after the fall of the Achaemenids in the wake of the conquests of Alexander, the general situation changed completely. Although the Aramaic clerks continued to work for or under the Macedonian rulers, genuine Greek writing became

---

10 DESHPANDE 2011.

known to the public, a writing not shrouded in the garb of a Semitic language, but open to everyone interested and used for a language with a number of structural similarities to the local Indic idioms. Once the attitude towards writing had changed to the positive it must have been tempting to try writing also on the local vernaculars. For us, these vernaculars had clearly branched off from Sanskrit long ago, but the pandits maintaining pure Sanskrit were not part of the process of introducing literacy in the third century BC. On the other hand, those who finally tried to adapt the Aramaic writing system lacked even the basic knowledge of the Sanskrit grammar schools. There were at least two such attempts at adaptation, taking place almost simultaneously, one in northern Pakistan and another in the capital of the Mauryan empire, at Pāṭaliputra, modern Patna in Bihar.

The Invention of the Kharoṣṭhī Script

The first such attempt apparently took place in northern Pakistan and drew substantially on what people were used to seeing, and that was the Aramaic script. The Arameans, responsible for the term, had once installed some short-lived kingdoms in Mesopotamia, which were destroyed by the Assyrians, who distributed this people all over their Assyrian realm in the eighth century BC. The Aramaic clerks spoke a language closely related to Hebrew and served as a sort of postal system for their Mesopotamian oppressors, and continued to do so once the Iranian Achaemenids took over the Neo-Babylonian empire in 539 BCE. As the Achaemenid realm expanded, Aramaic clerks were dispatched "on duty" further east as well, up to sites on the Indus. After the fall of the Achaemenids brought about by Alexander the Great, Aramaic clerks continued to work for the local courts. We have two texts documenting the outcome of court cases, each one mentioning "Vasu the judge" (*w'šw dyn'* / *w'šw ŠHM dyn'br*), written in Aramaic and dated to the regnal years 16 and 17 of the third king of the Mauryan dynasty, Aśoka, showing us that the script of the Achaemenid administration survived the downfall of the empire by at least eighty years.

By their very nature, these documents in the old script help us to understand why a new script, named *kharoṣṭhī*, had to be invented. Both documents ("Laghman I and II") were found on vertical rock sides in the lower Laghman valley near Jalalabad.[11] Such documents are of high value when it comes to defending ownership positions once sanctioned by a local court. The preparation and interpretation of these documents naturally required the presence of Aramaic clerks. Without them the written verdict was useless. How difficult it is to understand the few pieces that have come down to us becomes obvious when comparing the various translations offered so far

---

11 FALK 2006, 247–250.

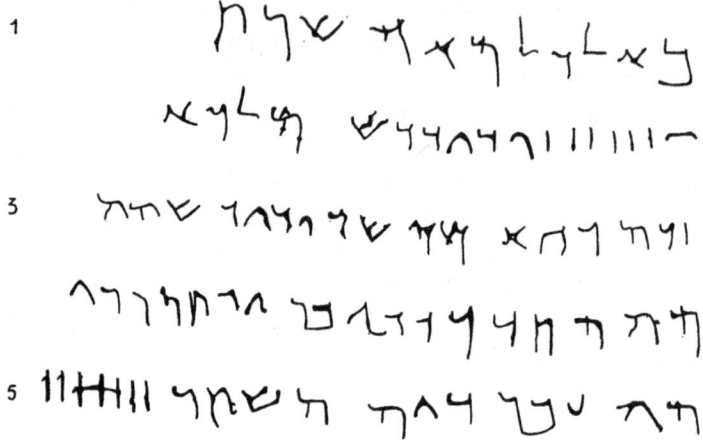

Abb. 1: Aramaic writing from the Laghman valley, Eastern Afghanistan, describing a plot of land and mentioning the year 16 of Aśoka; eye-copy DJELANI DAVARY, cf. FALK 2006, 250.

by modern scholars otherwise well versed in the Aramaic language as such. The texts seem to contain a number of juridical terms or their abbreviations, which to some extent still defy philological analysis.

A number of Aramaic documents on goat skins, mostly economic contracts and administrative accounts, written in Afghanistan under Greek rule soon after the conquest of Alexander have been published recently.[12] Amongst Macedonian families Greek idioms and script were certainly in use, but for local landlords and their juridical needs documents held in Greek would have been much under the same risk as those requiring readers of Aramaic. It must have been in this period when the Aramaic clerks were on their way out that some agencies dependent on court decisions realized the need for a new script, this time for reproducing the local language. Land was re-allotted in the wake of the Macedonian conquest, the new land-owners needed authoritative documents, legible, held in the local language, usable for generations to come, independent of clerks or rulers preferring foreign languages. Many of the new land-owners were Greek or Macedonian, but a number of collaborators to the foreign forces received rights as well, as we learn from the works describing Alexander's campaign in Pakistan. The last and most recent documents using the Aramaic language and script in Gandhara are the court decrees mentioned above, and the need for dependable and comprehensible court decrees and other business documents is proposed here as the reason behind the creation of a new script. Land-owners or traders in bulk, when they come in some numbers are a fraction of society economically strong enough and by nature politically close enough to a local sovereign to be able to promote the spread

---

[12] NAVEH & SHAKED 2012.

and use of a medium necessary for all sorts of business. The rulers may not even have needed much convincing – it only needed someone bold enough to start and others influential enough to implement the general use of the new form of writing.

As was explained above, it was impossible to adopt Aramaic directly for use with the local language, and so the foreign script was modified to suit its new purpose. First, a number of additional letters were designed, and then, most important, the vowels, which are not or only insufficiently represented in Aramaic writing, were given a definite shape for mandatory use in initial and in medial position alike, by adding short strokes to the basic character. Thus, the local language, nowadays generally termed Gāndhārī after the region of Gandhara in and around the Peshawar valley, could be reasonably well expressed in writing, and understood by all its speakers when read aloud.[13] The script looks like Aramaic at first glance, like Aramaic it runs from right to left, and it even has identical ciphers and a number of characters which express the same or closely similar sounds in both languages (yod/ya, waw,va, nun/na, reś/ra, bet/ba, dalet/da). So there can be no doubt that this new script, later called Kharoṣṭhī, had Aramaic script as an antetype with good reason: by retaining the script's traditional appearance, the documents looked as trustworthy as the purely Aramaic documents had done before.

Surprisingly, this new script has also a number of letters that look alike in Aramaic script and Kharoṣṭhī, but express completely different sounds in the Aramaic language and in Gāndhārī (peh/a, taw/pa). To add to the confusion, there are also sounds, used in both languages, which are represented by very differently shaped characters in the two scripts (gimel/ga, he/ha, kap/ka, lamed/la, mem/ma, peh/pa, taw/ta). In the 19th century it was Georg Bühler, an influential Indologist from Vienna, who tried to explain the genesis of Kharoṣṭhī. To explain the cases of "identical letters but different sound values", and "identical sounds but different shapes", he twisted and mirrored the Aramaic letters until they resembled some Kharoṣṭhī counterparts. The twisting and mirroring was regarded as a reconstruction of what he thought happened to the original letters through the centuries. Such gradual deformations are known in all scripts that have come of age, but then we have all or most stages of the changes documented. In the case of Kharoṣṭhī, not a single intermediate form of this kind was available for Bühler and so he tried to find help through the Aramaic papyrus documents from Elephantine, written in Achaemenid times in southern Egypt in the 8th century. Certainly, there are shapes differing from the prototypical Phoenician script used in the Levant, but all changes follow the standard principles of formal modifications. And no such change resulted in any of the letter-forms Bühler would have needed to prove that Kharoṣṭhī had locally and gradually emerged out of the Aramaic

---

13 An intermediate state is in evidence in a text of Aśoka found at Kandahar, which presents its content twice: first in Aramaic script and language, then in Aśoka's own language rendered in Aramaic letters (cf. FALK 2006, 246).

Abb. 2: Kharoṣṭhī writing, rubbing from Rock Edict 12 of Aśoka at Shahbazgarhi, Northern Pakistan. After Hultzsch 1925, 64.

script. Because of this flaw, other, and better models for the origin of Kharoṣṭhī were proposed already in his time, but for various reasons they were not well received.[14]

One of Bühler's basic assumptions was that all intermediate forms necessary for his hypothesis are undocumented because they were written on perishable material. The Indian termites, certainly fond of birch-bark and palm-leaves, are an indispensable element in all attempts at making Indian scripts older than they can demonstrably be. Fortunately, the Indian termites don't travel to Bactria and they may also shrink back from gnawing at animal skins, and so a number of documents were preserved, not from Elephantine but from northern Afghanistan, not from the time of Kyros, but from Alexander at the end of the fourth century BC.[15] These documents reveal what was to be expected, that the Aramaic script in Bactria had remained the same regarding shape and sounds, with only some minor modifications; and not a single one of those indicated a twisting or bending in the sense of Bühler. Even the letters which developed out of the Aramaic script in the 2nd century AD for the Parthian, Middle Persian and Sogdian scripts still continue the shapes of standard Aramaic,[16] as it is

---

14 Falk 1996, 127 ff.
15 Falk 1996, 127 ff.
16 Frye 2006, 60.

found i.a. in Gandhara, in the Aśokan texts in Laghman, in the 3rd century BC. To expect evidence of "twisting" in Elephantine Aramaic centuries earlier seems rather anachronistic. Although to my mind the "twisting technique" has nothing to its credit it produced a long-term model which still lives on and assumes an "adaptation of the Aramaic script" "developed sometime in or around the fifth century BCE",[17] i.e. in Achaemenid times, when all other Achaemenid provinces retained their Aramaic script as it was.[18]

With the twisting hypothesis eliminated, we have to reconsider how identically shaped letters can receive completely different sound values, and how identical sound values can have taken on a completely different graphical representation. The only solution, to my mind, is taking leave from a gradual change over centuries resulting in a script in use for centuries alongside Aramaic. Instead, I consider a spontaneous process more likely, involving an Aramaic clerk, who shows an interested person of definitely non-Aramaic stock how the letters work as a system, writing down parts or the whole alphabet on a medium – to take away. This supportive Aramaic clerk was not the one who invented Kharoṣṭhī, as then he would have had to allot some completely new sound-values to letters he had used for years for very different sounds. For such a radical break with traditional sound values to occur the creator must have been free from Aramaic cleric learning. Our unknown local Gandharan inventor to-be kept in mind correctly a number of sound-attributions from the instruction he received. However, he had forgotten a number of sounds attributions and thus combined the remaining sounds at random partly with characters he still had unused on his exemplar or he invented other forms freely for those sounds of Gāndhārī still remaining unrepresented, occasionally *enlarging* signs for related sounds.[19] This model can explain the similarities as well as all deviations, and it does away with the almost schizophrenic situation that a correct Aramaic script could be used in the time of Aśoka side by side with its own derivation wherein sounds and letter-shapes had received different and thus confusing realisations.

The assumed spontaneous creation must be considered against the political background. The Aramaic clerks lived in their own little world, with colleagues all over the Achaemenid realm. They, and only they, knew to listen to words in one language, e.g. Gāndhārī, write them down in Aramaic letters and language, and retranslate it for the recipient into Greek, or Babylonian or Egyptian, whatever needed. Imagine a clerk in Gandhara using any of the twisted or mirrored shapes for a document. The

---

17 SALOMON 2012, 175.
18 According to BAUMS (2014, 214), O. VON HINÜBER and myself are said to agree that Kharoṣṭhī "is a derivative of the Aramaic script used in the administration of the Achaemenid empire". I cannot find such a statement in the work of O. VON HINÜBER and my own view is diametrically opposed and has been repeated in print since 1993. A spontaneous idiosyncratic creation using Aramaic as a base model ("Vorbild") is far removed from a "derivative" that would have required centuries to take shape.
19 STRAUCH 2012, 147.

recipient in Babylon would have been at a loss. A popular version of writing could only be launched once the postal *lingua franca* had already started to become supplanted by Greek.

The inventory of letters of most writing societies is conventionally taught in a fixed sequence to make sure that the full range of letters is kept in memory. The Greek and Roman sequences are inherited from an age-old[20] North Semitic inventory and are thus free from any systematic ordering.[21] If Kharoṣṭhī had been developed out of Aramaic writing its sequence should also follow a North Semitic prototype. But it does so only in part, in that it has no logical sequence. With the exception of the starting letter /a/, its other half, the sequence of sounds, is completely different. The convergence and variance seen when comparing the North Semitic alphabet with the arapacana order are once more better explained by my spontaneous creation model than by Bühler's gradual change hypothesis and its variants. The sequence of Kharoṣṭhī has been found in literature and on writing pads alike,[22] all identical with only trifling deviations, starting with *a, ra, pa, ca, na, la, da, ba, ḍa, ṣa, va, ta* and 30 more letters,[23] showing that already at this point there is no internal phonetic system apart from a separation of the one initial vowel and all following consonants. From no. 19 onwards there is a mixture of simple consonants and biphonematic sounds, as in *tha, ja, śpa, dha, śa, kha, **kṣa, sta,** ña*, proving, to my mind, that no brahmin trained in phonetics can have had anything to do with this hotchpotch.

How then did the *arapacana* originate? The outcome reveals the mechanism behind its origin, happenstance. When did it originate? In the Gāndhārī used for the Aśokan texts, a considerable number of signs later in use are still missing. Biphonematic sounds are scarce, as we find only *kṣa, sta* and *spa* and their signs are not formed as ligatures of *ka* and *ṣa*, of *sa* and *ta* or *pa*, but single graphemes independent of the shapes of their constituents. This shows that *kṣa, sta* and *spa*[24] were not reduced to their constituents, probably out of ignorance, and not because original clusters had changed to monophonematics. On the other hand, a correct analysis of sound clusters had taken place before Aśoka in the case of pre-consonantal *r-* and post-consonantal *-ra, -va* and *–ya*.

The classical *arapacana* range of 42 letters represents a much larger number of sounds compared to those used for the edicts of Aśoka, indicating that this full list was not in existence at the beginning but is rather the product of a gradual improvement

---

20 SALOMON 2013, 9.
21 SALOMON 2013, 12.
22 SALOMON 2016.
23 STRAUCH 2012.
24 For *spa* this original state was later changed and a true ligature designed where a *śa*-head came to stand above a *pa*-hook.

of this script.²⁵ Once enlarged, the *arapacana* order had a long life, even surviving the change of script from Kharoṣṭhī to Brāhmī.²⁶

The Invention of Brāhmī

In principle, the Aramaic monopoly on writing in ancient India collapsed with the Macedonian conquest. With the new creation called Kharoṣṭhī in Gandhara, writing was ready to be taken up by anyone. Naturally, a script needs some time to spread, and we see that it was already sufficiently widespread when around 250 BC Aśoka, from his capital at Pāṭaliputra, 1600 km further east, sent his "edicts" to Gandhara in the West in another new script, which we call "Brāhmī". At the local level, the newly popularized Kharoṣṭhī was regarded to be firmly enough established to disregard the script in which the texts arrived. Replacing Kharoṣṭhī by yet another new script in such a short time was not attractive to those who just had managed to get Kharoṣṭhī accepted. In my model the invention and proliferation of Kharoṣṭhī occurred following the inroad of the Macedonian army around 330 BC with their gradual invalidation of the Aramaic clerks; the encounter between the first and the second new script happened when the Aśokan edicts were sent west around 250 BC.

The refusal in Gandhara to replace Kharoṣṭhī by Brāhmī was somewhat short-sighted, because the script from the East had a number of advantages over the local pioneer. In fact, the system of vowel strokes is basically the same as in Kharoṣṭhī and shows that clerks from the West were part of the developing team in the capital of the Mauryan empire, Pāṭaliputra, today Patna. One of Aśoka's clerks came from the West, he disseminated Aśokan edicts in Southern India in Brāhmī script, added an explanatory part which he signed with his name and function in Kharoṣṭhī, "made by Capaḍa the clerk".

Despite all attempts at constructing alternative models, the Aśokan texts are the earliest material evidence of the use of Brāhmī, and Kharoṣṭhī as well. Initially, this king must have planned for an illiterate population. The edicts prescribe at which date the words of Aśoka "have to be made to listen to", not "have to be read". The verve perceptible in the distribution of his texts from Orissa to Kandahar, from the Terai of Nepal down to just outside Tamil Nadu shows that he wanted to spread not only his words, but also the knowledge of and the capacity to use writing. Whoever starts using a script in a culture not based on writing will have to tackle the question: How to make people write and read? The answer is simple: You just have to start using it and continue teaching it, begin the impossible and stick to it. Fortunately he succeeded.

---

25 STRAUCH 2012, 147.
26 SALOMON 2016, 20.

Abb. 3: Government order in Brāhmī script on stone from Mahasthangarh, the old Puṇḍranagara, north of Calcutta, regulating the use of victuals in state-controlled store-houses. After SIRCAR 1941, pl. XXI.

What induced him to try the impossible? He had grown up in a capital with links to the West. Around 300 BC Megasthenes had come from the Seleucid court in Babylon as an ambassador, and was surprised to see the Indians go to court without any written evidence in hand.[27] There were more ambassadors in the decades after Megasthenes,[28] there was the transport of figs and grape juice from the Seleucid court in Mesopotamia[29] to Pāṭaliputra in the time of Aśoka's father Bimbisāra. Aśoka was well-informed about some rulers in the Hellenistic East. He knew that there were 600 *yojana*s (Rock Edict 13) to the West, that is equivalent to 6000 km, covering the distance between Pāṭaliputra and Alexandria as the crow flies, or over land to Seleuceia following the land roads. Naturally, he knew the dynasties of Antiochos I (r. 281–261 BC) or Antiochos II Theos (r. 262–246) at Seleuceia, whom he calls the *yonarāja*, "the king of the Greeks", here as in Rock Edict 2. In addition, he gives four simple "kings" (*rājā*) of

---

27 VON HINÜBER 1989, 20.
28 KARTTUNEN 1997, 99–100.
29 The source is Athenaios of Naukratis in his *Deipnosophistai* (ed. C.D. Yonge, Book 14, 67), preceded by an episode which shows how Xerxes was led to implant figs from Athens into Achaemenid soil, an import the Seleucids would later pass on to India.

descending importance, mentioned by name in Rock Edict 13, summarily called "his adjoining kings" (*ye ca tasa samaṃtā lājāne*) in Rock Edict 2. In Rock Edict 13(Q) the first "adjoining" king is Ptolemy II (*tulamaya*; r. 285–246 BC) in Egypt, follows Antigonos II (*antekina*) Gonatas (r. 283–239 BC) of mainland Greece. Of clearly less importance was Magas (*maga/maka*) with his short-lived (276–250 BC) kingdom in Libya, and the least important was governor of the western Seleucid dominions in Anatolia, Alexander of Sardis (MERKELBACH 2000).[30] With all the roads and seaways secured by the Seleucid administration, people, goods and news could spread at a pace unheard of before in this part of the world. Even one lady from Seleucos' family was married into the Mauryan family and vice versa, so that in principle there was sufficient reason to stay in contact.[31] The lady from Seleuceia certainly spoke much about the differences she had to witness. How did Aśoka communicate with his in-laws in the Near East? Did he send messengers who conveyed the texts from memory? Or did he supply them with letters in Aramaic or Greek? With all this correspondence recurring on a regular basis there was no way to go on without a script to express one's own cultural standing.

Why did Aśoka not venture to adopt the Greek script? Like Aramaic, the Greek script cannot be used unchanged to represent Aśoka's local vernacular, called Māgadhī after the region Magadha, now Bihar. Like the inventor in Gandhara who probably knew "script" only in the shape of the Aramaic letters, Aśoka may have known "script" primarily in the shape of Greek, in those days written in nothing but capital letters, but Kharoṣṭhī was definitely known to him and his advisors. The Brāhmī script resulting from a comparison of Greek and Kharoṣṭhī shows that all their advantages and shortcomings were discussed in order to perfect their own creation. The Greek script definitely won over Kharoṣṭhī with regard to its visual impression, with its broad, upright and symmetrical forms. Writing from left to right also seems natural for all right-handers who can thus avoid having to move the pen against the medium. From Greek came the inspiration to distinguish between short and long letters, as found in Greek (E-H, O-Ω). On the other hand, Kharoṣṭhī was better than the Greek script in that it features the short -*a* "inherent" to every consonant, inherited from Aramaic.

---

30 MERKELBACH's view has garnered little attention in Indological literature so far, even though his solution is the only one which includes Anatolia in the range of competing diadochs. Unfortunately we know only that Alexander of Sardis as a vicegerent was on the side of Antiochos Hierax and that he signed a decree in 246 BC. This has no bearing on Aśoka's personal chronology. – All four named persons after Antiochos played a role in Seleucid politics during the decades in question where three difficulties needed a solution, first the futile attack of Antigonos's father on Seleucid possessions in Anatolia, then the pincer attack of Antiochus II Theos along with Magas on Magas' stepbrother Ptolemy II Philadelphos, and then the possibly foreseeable difficulties over the succession of Antiochus II involving his stepbrother Hierax and his uncle Alexander of Sardis. A personal visit by Aśoka's emissaries to Egypt, Libya and Anatolia was not necessary to learn about the Who Is Who in ongoing and pending wars.
31 Strab. 15,2,9 = MAJUMDAR 1981, 98.

Brāhmī also copies the vowel strokes from Kharoṣṭhī. As a new achievement, it develops a consistent system of linking graphs vertically for two succeeding consonants, a system which was later incorporated into Kharoṣṭhī.

The history of the scripts of ancient India shows that both of them have Semitic ancestors. One line of descent runs from a Western Semitic prototype, such as Phoenician, to Aramaic, reaching northern Pakistan through Achaemenid administrators where it inspired the creator of Kharoṣṭhī. The second thread likewise starts with Western Semitic and, with Phoenician settlers, leads to Greece and from there, after centuries of standardization, to India through the Macedonian armies. At the court of Aśoka parts of Kharoṣṭhī were united with parts of the Greek script into a system which is capable of rendering Indian idioms almost perfectly. With very few additions it is still in use for most of the Indian languages, be they of Sanskritic or Dravidian origin.

In a very short time, two writing systems were designed for an India on the verge of writing. How to employ them? While we do not have the density of documentation required for a full picture, it seems that use of writing remained tied to specific purposes. In the West, writing was used for administration, and after its invention, Kharoṣṭhī may have served just this purpose, to document transactions and court decisions. In Gandhara no court verdicts written in Kharoṣṭhī have been discovered so far, but in the documents on wood from the Taklamakan desert, particularly from Niya, we have mainly court decisions written in Kharoṣṭhī. In addition, we also have one business transaction,[32] put to writing and kept in a monastery, probably as a duplicate, which shows that profane business also made use of the means of literacy as present in Buddhist monasteries.

In Gandhara and at other sites in Xinjiang, Buddhist texts are reproduced on the oldest manuscripts preserved in this script, proving that this "heretical" religion made use of writing unimpeded by a brahminical preference for oral transmission.

With Brāhmī the picture is different. Instantly, we find the edicts of Aśoka spreading across mainland India, on stone pillars and on natural rock faces. These texts have a decidedly religious background. Aśoka wanted people to understand his attitude towards Buddhist groups, which he personally preferred over other religious movements. He wanted to spread certain ethics for the public, hoping to improve the relations inside families as well as social interactions. He must have been deeply convinced of the importance of his mission, which led him to promote Buddhist communities and to meddle with popular, pre-"Hindu" rites, which he felt he could not recommend.[33] What inspired him to engage in this new activity? Public laws on dressed stones or rock-faces have a long history in the Near East, and Hammurapi (r. 1792–1750 BC) was not the first to erect stone pillars with laws in public places. The most obvious formal parallels for the Rock Edicts are the rock inscriptions installed by the Achae-

---

32 FALK & STRAUCH 2014, 72, § 3.2.4.2.
33 FALK 2006, 56 f.

menid kings at Naghsh-e Rustam and Persepolis, seen by every visitor to the capital, but illegible on account of the distance between the reader on the ground and the texts high up on the rock walls. The Achaemenids had a particular cuneiform script designed for their own language which demonstrated that they were not forced to use the script of subject (and older) cultures, but could command their own means of scriptual expression when necessary. The same urge to express cultural independence can be expected as one of the reasons behind Aśoka's insistence on using a script of his own. After Alexander, with all nations in close contact, and India important as the main exporter of war elephants, gold and spices, the Mauryan empire needed its own script to avoid being considered a cultural backwater amongst the educated nations.

Official documents in Brāhmī from the offices of state administration are extremely rare and seemingly confined to the time of Aśoka. Two such documents mention storing goods for public use for times of distress or famines, both issued by the high officials (*mahāmātra*) specified as *saṃvagiya*, probably for Skt. *saṃvargya* or *saṃvargīya*. One is a copper plate found in Sohgaura[34] the other a flat stone from Mahasthangarh (Fig. 3)[35] north of Calcutta, 630 km apart from one another. Both documents are small, the cast copperplate with nail-holes measures 6.5×5 cm, the flat stone with some parts missing about 6×9 cm, and both texts deal with depots of victuals in storehouses (*koṭhāgāla*) for times of distress (*atiyāyika*). The script is no different from the one used for Aśoka's religious edicts; on the Mahasthangarh stone vertical strokes are used in the way Aśoka's scribe at Sassaram[36] applied them to indicate rhetoric pauses between words or phrases. The Mahasthangarh stone shows us how official decrees were dispatched: on small flat stones; the Sohgaura plaque shows us that metal was also in use, and the occurrence of ideograms above the letters shows that the time of picture "writing" had not yet passed. These two singular pieces of evidence show that in the time of Aśoka official decrees were communicated in writing, and the pause of evidence after Aśoka shows that his efforts were not continued by his successors.

There is a manual of state administration, the *Arthaśāstra*, composed in the decades before Aśoka and enlarged in the four centuries after his time, in which writing plays no role at all, at least in its old parts. Even in the younger passages there is no term for "register", "index" or "file". The first text to mention written documents used as evidence in lawsuits is the law book of Yājñavalkya, dating to the second century AD.[37] Oral communication and memorization of texts was effective and more in line with common habits. Even the British used servants instead of registers in court offices to remember exactly in which of the hundreds of paper bundles a certain case was filed.

---

34 Near Gorakhpur; SIRCAR 1943, 85; FALK 1993, 177.
35 Cf. SIRCAR 1943, 82; FALK 1993, 180.
36 HULTZSCH 1925, 228 ff.
37 FALK 1993, 251.

The Didactics of Writing

Brāhmī, to my mind, owes its shape and logic to a combination of improvements which started with some of those which had already led to Kharoṣṭhī. The didactic means of an alphabet, by which I mean the sequence by which the pupil learns all existing letters of Brāhmī by heart, did not draw upon the *a-ra-pa-ca-na* hotchpotch of Kharoṣṭhī. Instead, we see on terracotta figurines from the first cent. BC of children holding small writing-pads[38] that the sequence of all vowels is followed by a sequence of well-sorted consonants, starting in the classical braminical fashion with the velar group, *ka, kha, ga, gha, ṅa*. Thus, the sequence of letters to be learned was independent of older prototypes, be that Kharoṣṭhī (*a-ra-pa-ca-n*a), Greek (α-β-γ-δ-ε-ζ), or Aramaic ('-b-g-d-h-w). This new and systematic sorting made learning the gamut of all defined sounds much easier, and this sorting certainly came about through the influence of brahmins with their age-old classification of vowels and consonants and their similarly mature didactic techniques. Combining the best features from all current systems led to an almost perfect script which needed only a few refinements (geminata, vowel-blocker and two rare vowels) to be usable even for Sanskrit, – and for all of its derivations to this very day.

Terms for Writing and Utensils

All terms used to describe the technical procedure of writing were introduced from foreign languages into Indian languages. The term for "script/written document" occurs first as *libi* and *lipi* in the 4th cent. BC in the sūtras of Pāṇini (3.2,21), as was said above. Aśoka uses *lipi* in his Rock Edicts, although in the places close to Pāṇini's home on the upper Indus the redactors preferred *dipi*, a derivation of an Iranian form.[39] With some nationalistic undertones, the Indian use of *lip(i)* for "writing" is often traced back to the notion of "smearing", innate to a truly Indian root *li(m)p*. However, the Iranian *lipi* was also adopted further west in East-Iranian languages[40] such as Bactrian, where the term was pronounced δipi, which later led to Bactrian *libo* for "document".[41] A further case of Iranian influence can be seen at Shahbazgarhi (RE 4,J, K) in the Peshawar valley where the redactor often used the Iranian *nipista/nipesita* instead of the Indian term *likhita/likhāpita*, "written". *Nipista/nipesita* can be "directly compared to *nipištā*, perfect participle from the root *paiθ*, found, e. g., on the so-called Daiva-inscription of Xerxes at Persepolis".[42] Already at Mansehra, however,

---

[38] SALOMON 2016, 8, fig. 1.
[39] WITZEL 2006, 460 fn. 7.
[40] HENNING 1957, 337 fn. 1.
[41] SIMS-WILLIAMS 2002, 227.
[42] FALK 2010, 209.

on the eastern side of the Indus, the plain Indian verb *likhati* was used in place of the loan word *nipista*.

Iran and Bactria also provided other loan words, such as *mudrā*, "seal", *pustaka*, "book", *divīra* "writer",[43] and from Greek-speaking groups India borrowed *melā*, μέλαν "ink", *kalama*, κάλαμος "pen", and *melanduka, meraṇḍu* etc. "ink-pot" μελανδόχιον.[44]

Apart from these initial loans, India was very productive in transferring meaning and coining new terms, foremost *likh*, "to scratch", for the incising of letter lines in wax tablets or leaves of plants. That being said, our original impression remains valid: modern writing and its terminology came from outside with (late) Achaemenid terms and Greek literacy.

Picture Symbols for Pots and Coins

Despite Aśoka's efforts to disseminate writing, one of the most common uses for script outside India was disregarded by his own officials: coins were issued without any written reference to the issuing agency. Instead, the officials continued to use various groups of five symbols for recognition, a pictorial program common from the fourth cent. BC onwards, with each symbol being punched separately into the silver flan. Although the meaning of these symbols is disputed, it seems clear that they carried some sort of significance. It could be that the technique used to create the coins prevented the use of letters as maintaining it would have meant using a much larger number of punches, one for each letter, to express all that can be read, for instance, on the coins of the Indo-Greeks. The idea of a single large die imprinting a greater number of letters was obviously not considered attractive. The dynasties succeeding the Mauryas, the Śuṅgas and a number of local rulers, did use script occasionally for coins. Their coinage is mainly made of copper, lead or potin and these softer metals facilitated using larger dies.

Brāhmī for Seals

There is a certain number of seals for personal uses found all over northern Pakistan and India which show one strange "mis-used" letter: instead of the common *sa*, in use since Aśoka for the only sibilant necessary for his local language Māgadhī, the die-cutters use a letter which was introduced for a second sibilant *śa* as required for languages outside Magadha. It seems that this wrong use is restricted to die-cutters, as

---

43 WITZEL 2006, 461.
44 FALK 2010, 211. It seems that the Aramaic clerks left no trace in the vocabulary, despite their centuries of clerical dominance.

Abb. 4: Seals, mirror-inverted as they appear in print: a) Brāhmī *śidhathaśa*, Kharoṣṭhī *sidhathasa* (Taxila; photo AMAN UR RAHMAN); b) Br. *aśaḍhaśa* (*ḍha* unmirrored for seal) Skt. *āṣāḍhasya* (unknown find-place; Collection Derek J. Content; c) Br. *śaghiyaśa*, Skt. *saṃghikasya* (Khao Sek, Thailand, 3rd/2nd cent. BC; private collection Chumphon province; CNRS – Silpakorn).

if this trade had some kind of clerical training of its own. The most famous example is a bilingually inscribed cubical die from Taxila, reading *sidhathasa* (Skt *siddhārthasya*) in Kharoṣṭhī and *śidhathaśa* in Brāhmī, which is not an East Indian dialect form, but a peculiar new interpretation of a letter,[45] – just one more piece of evidence that writing in Mauryan times had no century-old tradition but produced some *ad hoc* decisions, erratic forms, and short-lived misunderstandings. I add a few more seal and token legends all of which contain more than one sibilant, and all reduced to the one written *śa*, spelled /sa/: *aśāḍhaśa*, Skt *āṣāḍhasya* (collection Content), *śoradvaraśa*, Skt *sauradvārasya* (VERMA 1983, 26: Mathura Museum acc.no. 72.9), *haśikaśa*, Skt *haṃsikasya* (excavation Kumrahar), *śaghiyaśa*, Skt *saṃghikasya* (Khao Sek, Thailand, Mauryan times), *śunakhataśa*, Skt *sunakṣatrasya*, *śuviśakhaśa*, Skt. *suviśākhasya* (Ashmolean; trader's token probably from Erich). Much larger is the collection of seals showing no second sibilant but only the final genitive -*sa* written as -*śa*. Apart from seals, coins with such a legend are extremely rare and comparatively late; a curious case of a "double genitive" is found on coppers of Rāmadatta from Sonkh, reading *ramadatasaśa* (BALDWIN 2007, 670). Weighing the large number of seals with *śa*-genitive against other types of epigrams we are led to the suspicion that seal cutters had developed their own orthography which cannot be explained through differences in pronunciation.[46]

---

[45] STRAUCH 2012, 156.
[46] Skt. *madhyama*, "the middle one", was a common first name in ancient Sri Lanka. It is tempting to imagine a seal bought in northern India by a Ceylonese, reading *majhimasa*, "Of Madhyama", in the popular northern language, pronounced /majimasa/ on the island. This seal would convey the most glaring mistakes of *jha* for /ja/ and of *śa* for /sa/. The peculiar form of the *ma* could also have been included, twice.

Brāhmī in Sri Lanka

Sri Lanka shows inscriptions in Brāhmī from an early time, in fact from the time of Aśoka. This is not surprising as Aśoka's own son, Milinda (Skt. Mahendra), went south from Pāṭaliputra and propagated Buddhism on the island. We can assume that he or some of his immediate successors had an alphabet on board. Inscriptions from Mihintale, where Mahendra had his headquarters, have a rather Aśokan appeal, but at other places other letterforms prevail which seem again to be based on misunderstandings, including the seal-cutters' blunder, in that they use the pointed *śa* for spoken /sa/.

A similar misconception affected the signs for the soft palatals, *ja* and *jha*, in Sri Lanka. Since old Sinhalese – like its modern successor – did not use aspiration due to a close phonetic relationship to Dravidian idioms, the sign for *jha* had no local phonetic counterpart and could be used for *ja* without any loss in spoken realisation. As a result, *rājā*, the king, would be written *rājhā*, adding aspiration where none was required, and the Buddhist order, *saṃgha*, came in a graphical form which would be read as *śaga* at other places, dropping the aspiration where it was expected. The earliest evidence comes from dedicatory legends incised inside or above the entrance of caves, cut to divert the rains and financed by laypeople donors. Many legends give the impression that the stonemasons responsible for these dedicatory legends drew upon a standard set of phrases and used them mechanically, with lots of mistakes, as though to them this "literary" language was a foreign idiom, and writing an as of yet ill-known craft.

Monks kept on coming to Ceylon from all quarters of India, with the clerical skills acquired at home, and so this idiosyncratic local script system was supplemented by and corrected to standard Brāhmī again and again. By the first century AD the old and irritating misuses of letters had completely disappeared. Apart from cave dedications, we have a great number of ownership inscriptions on dining and drinking vessels, certainly incised by the owners themselves. They again display a wide range of letter-shapes and also demonstrate that female helpers at the Buddhist monasteries knew how to write at least to the same degree as their male colleagues.[47]

Once an illiterate is confronted with writing for the first time he may be surprised, stupefied or enthusiastic. He or she may think of uses the inventors at home had never thought of. In RAHMAN & FALK[48] I proposed that the so-called *nandivardhana* sign may in fact express nothing but the term *namo*, "veneration", being composed of the Brāhmī letters *na* and *mo*. A certain dissatisfaction arose because in India, even in the oldest evidence at Sanchi and Bharhut, the two arms of the *mo* only rarely show the required form with arms extending sideways,[49] while in almost all cases shallow crescents sit symmetrically on the raised arms of the *ma*. However, when we turn to

---

47 FALK 2014.
48 RAHMAN/FALK 2011, 26.
49 Cf. CUNNINGHAM 1854, pl. XXXII, 20.

Ceylon, we find exactly what I had in mind, a *ma* with arms outstretched sideways and not centrally. Evidence comes from saddle querns buried below the circumambulation path of a stūpa at Tissamaharama,[50] in the very South of the island, one of the earliest centres of Buddhism on the island. The idealised form is found in Bharhut panels usually added to veneration scenes with people kneeling in front of thrones or relic containers. Sri Lanka, however, preserves this prototypical form. I would interpret this as an act of give and take: Brāhmī was brought to Ceylon, and the combination of letters into a monogram seems to have been formed there and was then re-transferred back to India, where people knew its general meaning, and used the symbol for veneration scenes, but in a shape already removed from its monogrammatic origins.

Summary

In sum, the culture of writing in India shows several aspects that are unique by comparison with other ancient cultures:
- The introduction of writing for Indic languages was twofold, both arising from the same political conditions which exerted their influence on two places 1600 km apart:
- a) After the forced linkage with Achaemenid Iran had ceased to affect Gandhara and when the Seleucid dynasty had set new standards, financial transactions continued to require the juridical stability offered by written contracts. As the old and foreign speaking clerical caste was slowly disappearing, the economically influential groups needed a new script and had Kharoṣṭhī designed to express the local language for all future needs. For the new script the pre-existing Aramaic script was copied to a certain extent, but mis-allocations of signs show the non-Aramaic nature of the design-shaping agency.
- b) Until the time of the Seleucids the area of Magadha was devoid of any writing. The introduction of writing in the form of the Brāhmī script was not a process necessitated by legal procedures as in Gandhara, but was an act of cultural adaptation and was used mainly for cultural purposes. A single person, king Aśoka, appears as the dominating force behind an entire range of innovations, which turned the tide, transforming a self-content but illiterate society cultivating an incredible mass of orally preserved literature into a society with breath-taking new tokens of civilization. Aśoka, and he alone, effected the public proliferation of writing with his rock inscriptions, he had huge pillars and other monoliths cut from stone, and he dotted the whole wide realm with stūpas, visible evidence for the high morals of his subjects and himself. Despite these changes, business, administration, and coinage would go on without making large-scale use of

---

50 WEISSHAAR 2014, 123, fig. 4g, 4h.

writing. For the new script, inspiration was taken from familiar scripts, including Kharoṣṭhī, but the result surpassed all previous models in both aesthetics and usability.
– Both newly invented scripts were not meant to remain confined to political elites, ethnic groups or a particular sex. However, there were some groups that adopted the new technique faster than others. Buddhist monks were far more inclined to take up the skills for their sacerdotal literature, while brahmin priests withheld their consent for quite a while; Buddhist nuns were at least as interested and dexterous in writing as their male counterparts.
– As the art of writing spread fast and wide all over India, some particular groups developed idiosyncratic features: early North-Indian seal cutters used a "wrong" sibilant for the genitive ending, which Sri Lankan stone-masons seem to have imported along with one more misunderstanding. Some particular font styles of Brāhmī are found exclusively on seals or on coinage, while some Aśokan types lived on unaltered for two hundred years and more. That means that there were different strands of literacy in different professional groups for a long time, which seems to speak against a predominant agency intent on standardizing writing for all parts of society.

Bibliography

BALDWIN 2007 = BALDWIN'S LONDON AUCTION 50, April 2007.
BAUMS 2012 = S. BAUMS, Gandhāran Scrolls: Rediscovering an Ancient Manuscript Type, in: J.B.D. QUENZER/D. BONDAREV/J.-U. SOBISCH (ed.), Manuscript Cultures: Mapping the Field, Berlin 2012, 183–225.
CHAKRABARTI 1976 = D.K. CHAKRABARTI, Rājagṛiha: an Early Historic Site in East India, *World Archaeology* 7, 1976, 261–268.
CUNNINGHAM 1854 = A. CUNNINGHAM, The Bilsa Topes; or, Buddhist Monuments of Central India, London 1854.
DEEG 2005 = M. DEEG, Das Gaoseng-Faxian-Zhuan als religionsgeschichtliche Quelle, Wiesbaden 2005.
DESHPANDE 2011 = M.M. DESHPANDE, From Orality to Writing: Transmission and Interpretation of Pāṇini's Aṣṭādhyāyī, in: Travaux de Symposium International Le Livre. La Roumanie. L'Europe. Troisième édition – 20 à 24 Septembre 2010, Tome III: La troisième section – Études Euro- et Afro-Asiatiques, Bucarest 2011, 57–100.
ERDOSY 1995 = G. ERDOSY, City States of North India and Pakistan at the Time of the Buddha, in: F.R. ALLCHIN (ed.), The Archaeology of Early Historic South-Asia, Cambridge 1995, 99–122.
FALK 1993 = H. FALK, Schrift im alten Indien – Ein Forschungsbericht mit Anmerkungen, Tübingen 1993.
FALK 1996 = H. FALK, Aramaic Script and the Kharoṣṭhī – A Comparison, *Berliner Indologische Studien* 9/10, 1996, 151–156.
FALK 2006 = H. FALK, Aśokan Sites and Artefacts, Mainz 2006.
FALK 2010 = H. FALK, Foreign Terms in Sanskrit Pertaining to Writing, in: A. DE VOOGT/I. FINKEL (ed.), The Idea of Writing: Play and Complexity, Leiden 2010, 207–217.

Falk 2014 = H. Falk, Owners' Graffiti on Pottery from Tissamaharama, *Zeitschrift für Archäologie Außereuropäischer Kulturen* 6, 2014, 45–94.

Falk/Strauch 2014 = H. Falk/I. Strauch, The Bajaur and Split Collections of Kharoṣṭhī Manuscripts within the Context of Buddhist Gāndhārī Literature, in: P.M. Harrison/J.-U. Hartmann (Hg.), From Birch Bark to Digital Data: Recent Advances in Buddhist Manuscript Research: Papers Presented at the Conference Indic Buddhist Manuscripts: the State of the Field, Stanford, June 15 – 19, 2009, Wien 2014, 51–78.

Frye 2006 = R.N. Frye, The Aramaic Alphabet in the East, *Journal of Inner Asian Art and Archaeology* 1, 2006, 57–60.

Härtel 1991 = H. Härtel, Archaeological Research on Ancient Buddhist Sites, in: H. Bechert (ed.), The Dating of the Historical Buddha / Die Datierung des historischen Buddha. Symposien zur Buddhismusforschung, IV,1, Göttingen 1991, 61–89.

Henning 1957 = W.B. Henning, The Inscriptions of Tang-i Azao, *BSOAS* 20, 1957, 335–342.

Hinüber 1989 = O. von Hinüber, Der Beginn der Schrift und frühe Schriftlichkeit in Indien, Wiesbaden 1989.

Hultzsch 1925 = E. Hultzsch, The Inscriptions of Asoka, Oxford 1925.

IA-R Indian Archaeology – A Review.

Jacobs 2016 = B. Jacobs, Beschreibung von Palibothra und die Anfänge der Steinarchitektur unter der Maurya-Dynastie, in: J. Wiesehöfer/H. Brinkhaus/R. Bichler (ed.), Megasthenes und seine Zeit / Megasthenes and His Time, Wiesbaden 2016, 5–26.

Karttunen 1989 = K. Karttunen, India in Early Greek Literature, Helsinki 1989.

Majumdar 1981 = R.C. Majumdar, The Classical Accounts of India, Calcutta 1981.

Merkelbach 2000 = R. Merkelbach, Wer war der Alexandros, zu dem Aśoka eine Gesandtschaft geschickt hat?, *Epigraphia Anatolica* 32, 2000, 126–128.

Müller 1859 = M. Müller, On the Introduction of Writing into India, *Journal of the Asiatic Society of Bengal* 28, 1859, 136–155.

Naveh/Shaked 2012 = J. Naveh/Sh. Shaked, Ancient Aramaic Documents from Bactria (Fourth Century B.C.E.) from the Khalili Collections, London 2012.

Rahman/Falk 2011 = A.U. Rahman/H. Falk, Seals, Sealings and Tokens from Gandhāra, Wiesbaden 2011.

Salomon 2012 = R. Salomon, Gandharan Reliquary Inscriptions, in: D. Jongeward/E. Errington/R. Salomon/S. Baums (ed.), Gandharan Buddhist Reliquaries, Seattle/London 2012, 165–199.

Salomon 2013 = R. Salomon, On Alphabetic Ordering: Some Principles and Problems, *Scripta* 5, 2013, 1–20.

Salomon 2016 = R. Salomon, Siddham, Across Asia: How the Buddha Learned his ABC (23nd J. Gonda Lecture 2015), Amsterdam 2016.

Sims-Williams 2002 = N. Sims-Williams, Ancient Afghanistan and its Invaders: Linguistic Evidence from the Bactrian Documents and Inscriptions, in: id. (ed.), Indo-Iranian Languages and Peoples, *Proceedings of the British Academy* 116, 2002, 225–242.

Sircar 1942 = D.C. Sircar, Select Inscriptions I, Calcutta 1942.

Verma 1983 = T.P. Verma, A Catalogue of the Seals and Sealings in Government Museum Mathura, Mathura 1983.

Weisshaar 2014 = H.-J. Weisshaar, Legged Saddle Querns of South Asia, *Zeitschrift für Archäologie Außereuropäischer Kulturen* 6, 2014, 119–144.

Witzel 2006 = M. Witzel, Brahmanical Reactions to Foreign Influences and to Social and Religious Change, in: P. Olivelle (ed.), Between the Empires – Society in India 3000 bce. to 400 ce., Oxford 2006, 457–499.

Katharina Zinn
Literacy in Pharaonic Egypt: Orality and Literacy between Agency and Memory

Abstract: The article presents a new conceptual framework for understanding literacy in ancient civilisations in order to conceptualise 'literacy' more broadly as a cultural and social practice. For this it is necessary to focus on the complex relationship between orality and writing, accentuate the materiality of writing as well as questions of agency and acknowledge the social role of texts and writing as part of Egyptian memory culture.

Zusammenfassung: Der vorliegende Artikel schlägt einen erweiterten konzeptuellen Rahmen für das Verständnis von Schriftlichkeit vor. Das Konzept ‚Schriftlichkeit' wird darin als kulturelle und soziale Anwendung und Tätigkeit verstanden. Das wird möglich bei Beachtung der vielschichtigen Beziehung von Mündlichkeit und Schriftlichkeit/Schreiben. Des Weiteren wird die Materialität des erweiterten Schreibprozesses und die Handlungsfähigkeit aller am Prozess beteiligten Instanzen diskutiert. Die soziale Funktion von Texten und Schreiben im Allgemeinen als Teil des altägyptischen kulturellen Gedächtnisses ist der dritte Bereich der diskutiert werden muss, um Schriftlichkeit innerhalb der altägyptischen Gesellschaft vollständig erfassen zu können.

> Look, no scribe will ever be lacking in food or the things
> of the House of the King, may he live, prosper and be well![1]

When discussing *literacy in ancient everyday life*,[2] we need to define or at least to think about two points: What is literacy? and what is everyday life? An answer to these questions will not be easy, as both terms include many layers. Additionally, these definitions are very contemporaneously biased. When assessing literacy in ancient everyday lives, these modern layers need to be stripped away.

Ancient – in its narrower sense as levels of Greek and Roman – literacy was beautifully discussed by William V. Harris in 1989.[3] The perspective chosen here is the question often asked: "[h]ow many people could read, how many people could write in

---
1 Satire of Trade (Instruction of Dua-Khety), (Pap. Sallier II, column XI, lines 1–4)
2 This was the title of the conference in Zürich from 10–12 November 2016 where the paper forming the backbone of this article was given. I thank the organiser, Prof. Anne Kolb, for inviting me and all participants for their stimulating discussions. I also would like to thank Dr Thomas Jansen for reading drafts of this paper.
3 HARRIS 1989.

the Graeco-Roman world?"[4] To answer this, a distinction needs to be drawn between literacy and illiteracy. In the past, the discussion circled around the fact where this line should be set for individuals: is the ability to put one's autograph at the bottom of a document already a form of literacy, is reading capability needed or does the proficiency to understand short written statements make a literate person?[5]

In this paper, I would like to take the discussion beyond the Graeco-Roman world and widen the debate of what literacy means for the individual as well as society as a whole. The article aims to bring together three different dimensions, to provide a new conceptual framework for understanding literacy in ancient civilisations and to conceptualise 'literacy' more broadly as a cultural and social practice beyond the skill of an individual.

1. In order to understand *literacy* as a cultural practice, not only narrowly as a skill related to 'reading and writing', we need to focus on the complex relationship between orality and writing. The predominance of writing emerged only gradually, never really leaving the sphere of the oral. Both spheres remain intimately connected throughout all periods of Egyptian history.
2. A focus on the materiality of writing and questions of agency helps to extend the concept of literacy beyond the expression of ideas through reading and writing. Material expressions of writing cannot clearly be separated from the exchange of meaning; material aspects of writing culture are more than just the material carriers of meaning, they produce meaning themselves. One consequence is that everyone who is involved in the material side of the writing process, for example by producing, changing or reassembling objects that carry texts, is part of Egyptian literary culture.
3. The social role of texts and writing as part of Egyptian memory is the last piece towards a more comprehensive understanding of 'literacy' in ancient cultures. Memory culture exhibits all the different aspects discussed above—the intimate interplay between orality and writing, the materiality of writing, thus providing an overarching social vector for literacy without which the ability to read and write would lack its broader social dimension.

Networks around literacy start from the process of production of writing. Archaeologically, this can be revealed as a personal or even intimate process, being evident by a fingerprint left behind or the application of a specific ductus of text which characterises a certain writer, even we cannot name this author. However, usage of writing and text always goes beyond the individual. It can provide a stimulus for cultural change.[6] Different degrees of literacy complicate the overview on this topic, especially as lit-

---

4 HARRIS 1989, 3.
5 HARRIS 1989, 3–5.
6 BAINES 2007, 143–144.

eracy in ancient Egypt involves illiterate users who consumed written texts through oral performances and sensory experiences. I wish to postulate two different forms of literacy: specific – or individual – and collective. To follow this lead, we need to develop an anthropology of the past.

From the Present to the Past

Before we go to the past it is useful to look at present worlds. What does it mean today to be literate or illiterate? This seemingly straight forward question is difficult to answer even for our modern world with its wide compulsory education. Official definitions provide some guidance. The UN Literacy Decade (UNLD)[7] defines literacy as
- fundamental human right and foundation for lifelong learning,
- essential to social and human development,
- instrument of empowerment and
- exchange of knowledge.

This definition is not limited to a particular skill, but sees literacy much broader as an outcome of social activity. In doing so, this approach goes beyond the meaning of literacy established by the UNESCO in 1958 focussing on the individual and describing a person as literate when they can both read and write short simple statements on their everyday life and are able to understand them.[8]

According to UNESCO, four theoretical understandings of literacy can be differentiated: literacy as an autonomous set of skills, as applied, practised and situated, literacy as a learning process and finally, literacy as text.[9]

These four understandings can be applied to ancient Egypt. Here, literacy is mentioned and phrased as an important point to discuss, but until the recent past, there were relatively few ongoing fruitful debates. John Baines, together with Christopher Eyre, tried to (re-)define literacy.[10] There was only one immediate response,[11] whilst others came in sparsely and one at a time over the last 30 years.[12] Latest discussions attempt to track literacy from the archaeological[13] and anthropological[14] approach.

---

[7] Literacy for all [n.d.]
[8] UNESCO 1958.
[9] UNESCO 2005, 148. For further explanations see 148–152.
[10] BAINES 1983 (anthropological audience) and BAINES/EYRE 1983 (Egyptological audience; republished with additional footnotes in BAINES/EYRE 2007).
[11] BRYAN 1984 on female literacy (JANSSEN 1992, 81).
[12] Studies written by Baines collected in BAINES 2007. On the reconstruction of documentary practice see EYRE 2013a. Short summary including literature until 2012: ZINN 2013c.
[13] PINARELLO 2015, 3.
[14] ALLON/NAVRATILOVA 2017, 3.

Remembrance, Memory, Memories

> We are what we remember, which is another way of saying that we are nothing other than the stories we can tell about ourselves and our past.[15]

Archaeologies of memory contribute to the understanding of the past.[16] The way past societies observed, presented and interpreted their past reflected their own ideas and formed their memories in the same way we observe their evidence and let this influence our social memory. The constructed social and cultural memory is evident in the archaeological context. This can be inscribed or incorporated.[17] Like us, the ancient Egyptians built places with words, they put texts in contexts and with the help of the connotative and performative aspect of narratives reflected on what these ideas were doing in their world.[18] This formed memory and with it identity.

The ability to preserve wisdom and knowledge via writing is expressed in several texts for ancient Egypt. One often cited example is a passage from P. Beatty IV,[19] often called *Eulogy of Dead Writers*.[20] This segment shows how the authors of Middle Kingdom wisdom texts were remembered due to their words being written down. Writing therefore guaranteed the creation of cultural memory. Such texts also convey ways on how to communicate culturally significant ideas without revealing too much of their hierarchical knowledge, often also called restricted knowledge.[21] Visual display accompanied the written and spoken word and allowed usage of languages beyond the restrictions of ancient knowledge. The set of rules behind these displays consisting of texts and images (*decorum*)[22] defined what was communicated and kept within the cultural memory as demarcation between the divine world of the kings and gods and the non-divine world of humanity.[23] Who was able to see, read or understand was hierarchically determined.

Words – which could have been spoken, should be spoken or were intended to be spoken – were given authority in writing. This is nicely highlighted in the tomb of Rawer (Giza 5270, 5th dynasty, reign of Neferirkare): "*His Majesty decreed that (it will be) put in writing on his tomb which is in the necropolis. His Majesty caused that there should [be made for him] an authorisation in respect of it, written beside the king himself on the stone-workshop of the palace, to write what was said in his tomb in the necropolis.*"[24]

---

15 Assmann 2002, 9.
16 Van Dyke/Alcock 2003, 1.
17 Van Dyke/Alcock 2003, 4.
18 Smith 2008, 5–6.
19 P. Beatty IV = BM EA10684 verso 2.5–3.11 – translation: Parkinson 1991, 148–150.
20 Parkinson 2002, 30.
21 Baines 1990, esp. 6–10.
22 Baines 1990, 20.
23 Baines 1990, 21.
24 For translation and discussion see Eyre 2013a, 80.

Literature and Literacy

Literature in its practice is deeply rooted in literacy: It includes authorship, transmission and reception which are all bound to the text provided. However, literature also goes beyond that in its – oral – performance and – material – transmission.[25] Literature therefore provides an insight in the social relationships connected with literacy. It was not meant for private use or silent reading, but as oral performance (recitation) directed to listeners.[26] Even poetry was characterised by its visual appearance, using inherent attributes of hieroglyphs as a form of display, as well as being read.[27]

Without going into the definition and interpretation of *literature* within the ancient Egyptian society,[28] it seems that fictional literature and poetry addressed the literate elite from the 12th dynasty (Middle Kingdom) onwards.[29] As such, it had high cultural value for the self-representation of the elite[30] and the formation of cultural memory. Following a different style than commemorative texts, literature and poems can show a different side of the society with the kings being fallible, the administration corrupt, and functioning as a "countercultural voice"[31]. Literature was distributed throughout the whole country, but interestingly showed variations in the text. Poems especially reached beyond the elite as they were meant to be recited, and thereby, undocumented, as were other notable literary events.[32] The performative character widened the audience beyond the literate elite. Narrative texts and literature were set out in writing, but they included vestiges of the oral tradition. Therefore, elite and popular storytelling overlapped.[33]

This could already be seen at the beginning of literary texts in the *Pyramid Texts*. They likely stem from an oral narrative and preserved a special language for the cognitive flow of the text.[34] Even written literature was not composed orally, it was set out for oral and aural performance.[35] To do so, it included certain forms such as an additive style, patterned rhythm or parallel phrasing.[36]

---

25 EYRE 2013b, 101.
26 EYRE 2013b, 103–104.
27 EYRE 2013b, 105.
28 See LOPRIENO 1996, PARKINSON 2002, ENMARCH/LEPPER 2013, PARKINSON 2015.
29 PARKINSON 2015, 180.
30 PARKINSON 2015, 180.
31 PARKINSON 2015, 181.
32 PARKINSON 2015, 182. Parkinson applied experimental philology by performing modern recitals of poems to show the emotional power inherent to these texts – see YOUTUBE 2017, PARKINSON 2015, PARKINSON 2009.
33 JAY 2016, 19.
34 JAY 2016, 80–81. MORALES 2017 on the process of monumentalising former oral forms (recitation).
35 JAY 2016, 80.
36 JAY 2016, 80–96.

Literary works also had later impact, bridging not only literacy and orality,[37] but also did so over time. From the New Kingdom onwards, Middle Kingdom literary texts were ascribed on ostraca – pottery or stone sherds – being edited and adapted in the process.[38] Their importance for Egyptian identity seems to be indicated by the facts that they were no longer copied from the Roman Period[39] onwards. If this also meant that they were not read anymore, cannot be proven.

Ways of Remembering

Orality

As mentioned before, one of the flaws of previous discussion of literacy is the neglect of the role of orality, focusing mainly on reading and writing. This modern understanding is not supported by ancient Egyptian sources.

> Every plant perishes even as it exists – but not the spoken word.[40]

This sentence from Pap. Ramesseum II illustrates the importance the spoken word had in Egyptian society. In the theological treatise called *The Memphite Theology* preserved on the so-called Shabaka Stone,[41] the god Ptah – town god of Memphis – is described to have created the world by speaking out the name of things which then came into being:[42]

> (48) The gods who came into Ptah: (49) Ptah-on-the-great-throne ------. (50a) Ptah-Nun, the father who [made] Atum. (51a) Ptah-Naunet, the mother who bore Atum. (52a) Ptah-the-Great is heart and tongue of the Nine [Gods]. [...] (56) [...] As to the tongue, it repeats what the heart has devised. Thus, all the gods were born and his Ennead was completed. For every word of the god came about through what the heart devised and the tongue commanded.

High culture in ancient Egypt was not only characterised by writing, literacy and language. Orality stayed therefore important within the literate sphere as a parallel medium of communication. Additionally, written and spoken language were not on the same level. Monumental texts of the New Kingdom were written in Middle Egyptian while one already spoke Late Egyptian.[43] Written language was behind in compar-

---

37 JAY 2016, 19–78.
38 PARKINSON 2015, 182.
39 PARKINSON 2013, 182.
40 Pap. Ramesseum II, vso ii,5 – BM EA10755,2 (frame 2), transl. PARKINSON 2015, 180; EYRE 2013a, 0.
41 London British Museum EA498.8
42 LICHTHEIM 1975, 54.
43 BAINES 1983, 582–583, esp. table 3.

ison to the spoken. This meant that written texts presented the reader / listener with a nearly foreign language including a different grammar and diverse words.

With the 5th dynasty it became necessary to give words authority by placing them in writing to survive beyond the single moment of the speaking situation. It took so long that the primacy of the written word emerged over the spoken word, which we take for granted. Authorisation happened via a king's document – ꜥ.⁴⁴ Oral and written forms together established the potency of language. This is clearly evidenced in tomb inscriptions mirroring royal decrees as a method to convey royal authority. Rawer described in his tomb the favour he received by the king Neferirkare (5th dynasty):⁴⁵

> His Majesty decreed that (it will be) put in writing on his tomb which is in the necropolis. His Majesty caused that there should [be made for him] an authorisation (ꜥ) in respect of it, written beside the king himself on the stone-workshop of the palace, to write what was said in his tomb in the necropolis.

Even Ancient Egypt had very likely always a parallel oral tradition to the written material, it is difficult to trace this during the historic period⁴⁶ and nearly impossible for the time before the emergence of writing.⁴⁷

Writing

> "One will do all you say if you are versed in writings."⁴⁸

Literacy understood as the individual ability to read and write was the stimulus for and prerequisite of ancient Egyptians entering a profession, connected with high social status as stated in the entry quote from the *Instruction of Ani*. Being literate could help to rise socially.⁴⁹

In Egyptian hieroglyphic writing, hieroglyphs and images are overlapping and are fluent in their application.⁵⁰ Especially early forms of writing integrate art and writing to communicate their message. The meaning of texts is not only read, but

---

44 EYRE 2013a, 79 translates ꜥ with *authority*. It is however not so much authority per se than the document – a material object – which transfers the authority from the king to its recipient.
45 Tomb Giza G 5270 = Cairo JE 66682, lines 7–11 (Urk I,232) – see EYRE 2013a, 80 (further literature in fn 13).
46 Glimpses can be seen in some genres of texts: biographies written in the first-person-structure, enriched with fictionality (JAY 2016, 26). For the case study of letters, see below. Further examples: JAY 2016, 19–78.
47 JAY 2016, 23.
48 *Instruction of Ani* (LICHTHEIM 1976, 140).
49 ZINN 2013c, 4100.
50 ALLEN 2010, 655.

also displayed.[51] This ensures meaningful communication beyond the early problems of limited writing of non-continuous language and the continuous problem of the absence of wide-spread literacy. This might indicate the origin in picture writing, but the earliest evidence – labels found in the tomb U-j in Abydos[52] – shows already the formal structure of writing as seen throughout the application of hieroglyphs: ideograms, phonograms and determinatives. The Egyptians mainly used an inventory of about 500 signs, although much more existed.[53] Theoretically, texts could have been written using one-consonant-signs – unilateral phonograms which stand for each of the language's consonants, similar to modern alphabet.[54] However, the ancient Egyptians deliberately stayed close to the hieroglyph – image connection and used their writing playfully.[55] This opened up possibilities beyond the straight forward literacy as ability to read and write. Monumental inscriptions on temple or tomb walls functioned also on meta-linguistic levels and could therefore be understood without the need to be read. Monumentality acts therefore as clear indication for the social function of literacy. The same principle applied to small scale objects like scarabs and their decorations on their bases.

The monumental display of writing was part of *decorum*.[56] This ideologically important communication system[57] describes a set of rules defining what can and will be presented on display, in which context and what form. These representations are pictorially – sometimes with captions – as well as written down.[58] Writing and images form the language which will be understood. Both writing and decorum were introduced before or at the brink of the dynastic time.[59]

In addition to the monumental form of hieroglyphs, the ancient Egyptians used a cursive form, written with a brush using ink / pigment, called cursive hieroglyphs. This form was used contemporary to the earliest hieroglyphic inscriptions on pottery. The more cursive variation of this is Hieratic, known from the Old Kingdom onwards, developing into abnormal Hieratic in administrative papyri of the Ramesside Period. The final script used is Demotic which appeared in the mid-7th century.[60] None of these writing systems indicates vowels.

These were the scripts taught to scribes as part of their education.[61] Learning to write and then to read was restricted to a specific pool of people – the educated. The

---

51 Baines 1989.
52 Allen 2010, 641, 655.
53 Allen 2010, 656.
54 Allen 2010, 656.
55 Morenz 2004, 14–17.
56 Baines 1983, 576.
57 Assmann 2011, 149–154.
58 Baines 1990, 20.
59 Baines 1083, 576.
60 Allen 2010, 659.
61 Overview with further literature: Zinn 2013a.

number of literate people is estimated to 1–10 % of the population depending on the period and the definition of literacy.[62]

Writing transformed the spoken word into the written one which could overcome space and time, albeit based on strategies of expressing ideas orally. Orality as an important carrier of language and communication co-existed with literacy in different ways at all times. As mentioned before, the turn from speech to writing took place around 3300 BC. It then took nearly 600 years until the earliest known written sentence on an ancient Egyptian artefact was attested – a cylinder seal of Peribsen (2nd dynasty, c. 2690 BC): "the golden one has united the Two Lands for his son, the Dual King Peribsen".[63] The writing of the six centuries between the first appearance of writing and the first sentence are characterised by names, titles, place names and some markers of events on labels and stela. Despite being very short, these texts correlate with the then spoken language, Old Egyptian.[64]

Continuous texts appeared during the 3rd or 4th dynasty, very likely required by the advances in administration, law and religion.[65] Longer texts outside the administrative and legal sphere were introduced in the late Old Kingdom (religious text – Pyramid Texts), First Intermediate Period (biographical texts) and the Middle Kingdom (literary texts).

Not only took the transition from the spoken to the written word and from short to long literary texts very long, it is very difficult to draw a clear line between people being literate and illiterate throughout all phases of Egyptian history. Even already indicated by the large range of estimation regarding literacy, this not even shed light on the form of functional illiteracy or people being "semi-literate"[66]. Both terms describe Egyptians who had gone to school or learned to write by other means, but never had practiced it. Some recognised various signs still much later. The phenomenon of semi-literacy highlights another difficulty in assessing literacy in the past. As *scribe* is used as category within Egyptological research to describe a social class,[67] many officials use the title as main one in shorter texts. To assume this title in the first place, they needed to be educated in reading and writing. Using the title however does not necessarily indicate functional literacy.

It would also be interesting to know the level of active literacy among high officials. They presented themselves as scribes in statues, but in tomb reliefs they let others write and are depicted observing these agents. This indicates that they saw practicality of writing as a chore, but the status of being a scribe was kept as an indica-

---

[62] PARKINSON 2002, 66–67; BAINES / EYRE 1983; JANSSEN 1992, 81.
[63] ALLEN 2010, 646: *nb.wj d(m)d.n.f t3.wj n s3.f nswt-bjt pr-jb.snj*
[64] ALLEN 2010, 646.
[65] BAINES 1983, 577–578. REGULSKI 2015, 2.
[66] JANSSEN 1992, 81.
[67] PINARELLO 2015, 19 even speaks of an exclusive caste based on the assumed literacy of its members.

tor of being literate.⁶⁸ Had they become semi-literate by leaving the area of *functional literacy* due to lack of practice coming with their rank and standing? Another question results from the specific situation of the workmen of the royal tombs of the Egyptian New Kingdom at Deir el-Medina.⁶⁹ Here, literacy is assumed at a higher rate⁷⁰ and more people carried the title scribe than actually could have been employed as scribes by *the Tomb*, the institution responsible for the building of the tombs created by workforce in Deir el-Medina.⁷¹ We have evidence for local schooling.⁷² The two to four employed scribes were most likely practically literate as they not only wrote texts, but were responsible for the administration of the place. Therefore, literacy was a necessity. The case is not so clear cut for foremen and their deputies or the workforce cutting the hieroglyphs or writing hieratic texts to the walls.⁷³ They were in constant contact with writing, they might have recognised some signs, especially such for their own names and the name of the ruling king whose tomb they built.⁷⁴ Deir el-Medina also gives us – albeit very sparse – evidence for female literacy.⁷⁵ This seems to contrast with texts which mainly speak of male students / learners.⁷⁶

Fluent Boundaries between Orality and Literacy

Despite the low percentage of literacy, ancient Egypt was a *literate society* due to the enormous influence the word – written and spoken – had on culture.⁷⁷ To explain this phenomenon, we must discuss the different levels of literacy and the phenomenon *collective literacy* I would like to postulate for ancient Egypt.

Writing down texts does not always reiterate strict literacy. Some text forms were potent due to their writing, others were written down to be orally recited and many stand between orality and literacy. Genres which are predominantly transmitted in written form are magical texts as it was important to keep the spell working by an exact copy of the word which aided the performance. Oracles also needed to be written down.⁷⁸ The writing preserved the magical power inherent in the spell. Written

---

68 BAINES 1983, 580.
69 BAINES/EYRE 2007.
70 Supported by the high percentage of ostraca from Deir el-Medina (JANSSEN 1992, 84–87).
71 pA xr – BAINES/EYRE 2007, 90 ; JANSSEN 1992.
72 BAINES/EYRE 2007, 92.
73 BAINES/EYRE 2007, 90–94.
74 BAINES/EYRE 2007, 93.
75 JANSSEN 1992, 89–90.
76 ALLEN 2010, 661. Wisdom texts encourage young men to become scribes – see *Teaching of Khety*, also known as the *Satire of Trades* (HELCK 1970; FOSTER 1999).
77 JANSSEN 1992, 81; BAINES 1983.
78 BAINES 1983, 588.

texts show signs of orality through all times, starting already from the Pyramid Texts.[79] Letters form an interesting case study to discuss the flowing perimeters between orality and literacy. Many letters, especially some from Deir el-Medina, were not only written down as part of a literate world with allusions to known literary texts.[80] However, they are part of a dialogue or conversation between communicating actors.[81] Eyre calls them "self-consciously oral"[82]. As expressed in their grammatical form and structure, both communicants engaged in speech acts[83] by formulating requests,[84] asking questions[85] and convey information.[86] Letters acted as transcription of the spoken word which was sent (h3b): The sender said something (ḏd) or greeted the other party (nḏ ḥr qr swḏ3 jb), while the recipient heard the words (sḏm).[87] This correlates to polite oral behaviour.

The conversational character of letter writing is especially stressed by the fact that it was often referred to previous letters and therefore engaged in discussion as it is otherwise known from situations of oral communications. This could include third-party letters and opened the discussion beyond addressee and sender[88] Grammatically, two modes of reported speech were included: direct and indirect.[89] Ancient Egyptian letters, despite being a written genre, were therefore set out as direct speech,[90] which can already be seen in the greeting formula:[91]

> The overseer of cattle Bakenkhonsu, of the altar of Amun-Re, King of the Gods, greets the scribe of the offering table Iryaa, of the warehouse of deliveries. In life, prosperity and health! In the favour of Amun-Re, King of the Gods! I say to Pre-Horakhty, when he rises and sets, "Make you healthy! Make you live! Make you youthful!", every day.

Messengers were described to "bring a letter, saying ..."[92] using the verb Dd to express face-to-face contact.[93] Sometimes, short communications like face-to-face situations

---

[79] Jay 2016, 79–82.
[80] See Janssen 1992, 87, esp. fn. 35 and 36 for examples.
[81] See already the title of Deborah Sweeney's 2001 book *Correspondence and Dialogue: Pragmatic Factors in Late Ramesside Letter Writing* (Sweeney 2001).
[82] Eyre 2013a, 95.
[83] Sweeney 2001, 29–43.
[84] Sweeney 2001, 44–100.
[85] Sweeney 2001, 101–149.
[86] Sweeney 2001, 150–189.
[87] Eyre 2013a, 94.
[88] Sweeney 2001, 23.
[89] Sweeney 2001, 24–25.
[90] Eyre 2013a, 94; Janssen 1992, 87–88.
[91] Pap. Mallet = Pap. Louvre 1050 (E11006), V, 1–5. I follow the translation given by Eyre 2013a, 94.
[92] Pap. Bibliothèque Nationale 196, III. Černý 1939, 52, 5–6; Wente 1967, 67–68: "Statement for the scribe Butehamon, quote: Your father has sent me the letter saying, 'Cause them to take it to you.'"
[93] Sweeney 2001, 28.

without any greeting formulations or the names of sender and recipient are given. These otherwise often orally communicated messages were written down with the help of a scribe.[94] Some scholars argue against this and see such communications as examples of a widening of individual (semi-)literacy.[95]

This orality is bound to the written form and the medium it is written on. Letters were "purposeful communication" which conveyed a message beyond establishing social contact.[96] The composing milieu is that of the (wider) scribal class, but far more people were included as sender or recipient. We do not know if letters were dictated to scribes, if the recipients were reading them themselves or had the message read out to them like public communications.[97] We, however, know that scribal training started with the formulation of letters. The main textbook – the *Kemyt* – trained the pupils in key letter formulae.[98] Schooling and elementary education showed the closeness of orality and literacy by its methodology of memorising standard texts. The reading technique was also more geared towards orality: reading was done aloud, even though silent reading existed.[99] The written text was directly transformed back into speech. A similar phenomenon is captured by literature as ancient Egyptian literature is metric, performative and rhythmic.[100] These characteristics are criteria of oral forms.

Agency and Writing

The fluency between orality and literacy is also expressed in the material culture of ancient Egypt. The situation of direct communication as created in letters is also stated in objects. One example is the very impressive statue of the *Seated Scribe* (Fig. 1).[101]

The scribe, whose name and titles we do not know, is sitting in the usual writing pose where the stretched-out skirt over the crossed legs presents a good pad for the papyrus to rest on. This statue is an example for the group of *writing* scribe. The scribe's left hand holds the rolled-up papyrus while his right hands was once clutching a reed or a brush. This is now lost, but the act of writing with reeds is illustrated

---

94 BAINES/EYRE 2007, 75–78.
95 JANSSEN 1992, 88–89.
96 EYRE 2013a, 96.
97 BAINES/EYRE 2007, 73.
98 EYRE/BAINES 1989, 94–95; EYRE 2013a, 95 (esp. fn 88).
99 MORENZ 1996, 43–57; EYRE/BAINES 1989, 102–104.
100 EYRE/BAINES 1989, 110–112. For the discussion of Egyptian metrics see FECHT 1982, G. Burkard and W. Guglielmi in LOPRIENO 1996. Metric seems less important when we see the "material reality of the texts and their former contexts as a way to reconstruct [...] the literary space and the specific experience of these works" (PARKINSON 2009, xiii). For the form of speech and its social contexts see ENMARCH/LEPPER 2013.
101 Le "scribe accroupi," Paris Louvre E 3023; Old Kingdom, Forth Dynasty (Seated Scribe [n.d.]).

Literacy in Pharaonic Egypt: Orality and Literacy between Agency and Memory — 79

Fig. 1: The "writing scribe" – The Seated Scribe (Paris, Louvre E 3023) © Musée du Louvre, dist. RMN-Grand Palais/Christian Décamps

in many tombs, so in the scene of recording the harvest in the New Kingdom Theban tomb of Menna (TT69, Fig. 2).[102]

While the posture and body language of the Louvre scribe suggest an enclosed writing action, the position of the head and especially the mimic advocate a direct communication with an audience. The scribe faces towards an imaginary audience – see especially the design of the eyes (Fig. 3) – and does not look down to the papyrus. The eyes are carefully worked. The socket is white with red veins. In the middle sits a

---

102 Here is the pose translated from a 3-dimensional medium into the 2-dimensionality of a tomb painting. Tomb of Menna: Transverse Chamber, South wing, east entry wall: lower subregister of the upper register (Menna [n.d.]).

Fig. 2: The measurement of the grain. Tomb of Menna (TT69), Transverse Hall, South Wing, upper register, lower subregister © www.osirisnet.net

polished rock crystal which encloses an iris, altogether giving the impression of lifelike eyes, which even seem to follow the observer.[103]

Another type is the *reading* scribe as seen in the statue of Min-nakht (Fig. 4).[104] This scribe holds his right hand down on the papyrus on the open side while his left hand grasps the rolled papyrus. This compares to the modern gesture of reading a book. Again, the face looks towards an anticipated listener to whom the scribe reads the papyrus.[105] Here, facing the listener makes sense as reading is mostly reading out aloud, but it very likely is only one side of the medal. Comparing both types of scribal statues reveals that writing and reading are part of a wider direct communication situation which combines orality and literacy.

Important for the discussion is the approach of *material agency* which was inspired by Latour's *Actor-Network-Theory* as well as Gell's *Art and Agency*.[106] This methodology goes beyond the allocation of agency to humans alone and starts from premise that both humans and things can participate and initiate results. Following this interpretation, objects – i. e. writing and their materiality – are active in influencing the social sphere. Not only art, but also texts convey agency. The latter express both the what and how of agency.[107] This happens through the text plus the information conveyed by the (archaeological) object. It reveals the process of thoughts inherent of a society as opposed to the text which states what was thought.[108] This

---

[103] Seated Scribe [n.d.]
[104] Baltimore, Walters Art Museum 22.230, New Kingdom (Scribe Statue [n.d.]).
[105] MORENZ 1996, 43–52.
[106] LATOUR 2005; GELL 1998.
[107] MALAFOURIS 2011.
[108] MALAFOURIS 2011, 70.

Fig. 3: Eyes of Louvre scribe – The Seated Scribe (Paris, Louvre E 3023) © Musée du Louvre, dist. RMN-Grand Palais/Christian Décamps

information is discovered, if the wider context is taken into consideration: social and cultural predispositions, complex relationships between the actors, actors and materials as well as the materials themselves.[109]

Even ancient Egyptian writing is not so clearly connected with the idea of the individual author as modern writing is, it is nevertheless interesting that writing is very rarely discussed in connection with agency. We can trace some cases of individual agents – i. e. writers – in colophons,[110] as well as agents in history – i. e. people about whom is written. However, agency as archaeological concept goes beyond that.[111] Texts are outcomes of agency processes. They show their relationships as well as the materiality of the whole process. Following other areas of anthropological archaeology, such discussions involve ideas about intentional acts of individuals, personhood, identity, motivations and strategies of social actors, materiality of agency, cultural contact and much more.[112]

---

[109] ENGLEHARDT/NAKASSIS 2013, 2.
[110] LUISELLI 2003; ZINN 2013d (esp. ch. 2.2.3.).
[111] ENGLEHARDT/NAKASSIS 2013, 1–2.
[112] ENGLEHARDT/NAKASSIS 2013, 2–5 (with further literature).

Fig. 4: The "reading scribe" – Scribe Statue of Min-nakht (Baltimore, Walters Art Museum 22.230) © The Walters Art Museum

Agency of writing therefore goes beyond individual authorship. Due to its function as administrative device and part of monumental art, it was practiced by individual scribes, but benefited much more people directly and indirectly.[113]

Agency in ancient Egyptian reading and writing manifests itself in different ways:[114]

– Agency revealed in written documents

Texts describe agency in cultures, their daily life and offer information about this society. As such, textual evidence of ancient civilisations could partially substi-

---

[113] BAINES 1983, 579–580.
[114] WHITEHOUSE 2013, 249–253.

tute for areas, for which anthropologists can obtain information with different methods in modern societies (observation, recording of oral narratives, etc.).
– Agency needed to produce writing
First, it is necessary to develop a writing system which can be used to express cognitive and linguistic issues and reflects the language. This focuses on the cultural ability to write texts and transmit them by looking on abstract agency instead of specific agents. An important type of agency relates to the process of writing content, another focuses on the artefact itself and the actual production of the inscribed object including all steps (choice of material, decision on the content, application of the intended text).
– Agency of writing itself
The actions of the writer influence the end-product as does the written word itself. This includes the moment of the writing process and the extension of the direct communication beyond the time-space constraints of direct oral communication, describing both the agency of the writer and the writing itself.

Therefore, discussion of agency should include both anthropocentric as well as material agency.[115] Then we would be able to look at all aspects of *specific* and *collective* literacy. Agency beyond individual literacy is often discussed relating to the development of writing, focusing on the connection of origins and state formation,[116] even the term *agency* is not specifically stated. Writing in ancient Egypt started relatively late compared with other characteristics of a complex society with very short inscriptions. John Baines called this the "principle of scarcity."[117] The always inherent fluency between image/art and writing is then in time even stronger due to the representational characteristics of both.[118] It is not easy to state what is still iconography and what is already word. The meaning of many words is open for debate, the pool of signs is different to later times.[119]

Both the developmental process of the early writing system as well as the system itself show already characteristics which are typical for all agency processes connected with literacy in ancient Egypt. Writing and connected literacy allow communication across boundaries, especially time and space. For ancient Egypt we need to include the communication over the boundary of life and death, as writing mediates the relationship between the living and their ancestors and advocates a continued

---

115 For the non-anthropocentric approach and especially the neglect of the material networks see KNAPPETT/MALAFOURIS 2008 and MALAFOURIS 2013 (esp. 119–149). This also includes *writing as material practice* which looks at the physicality of texts and their relations to writers and users (PIQUETTE/WHITEHOUSE 2013).
116 REGULSKI 2015, 3; PINARELLO 2015, [1].
117 BAINES 2007, 42.
118 BESTOCK 2013, 98.
119 REGULSKI 2015 with further literature.

agency of the dead.[120] A good example are offering formulas, a standardised text which guarantees continued offerings of everything the deceased would need in the afterlife. When recited by the funerary priest, the relatives or simply by being written down in the tomb, this text corpus ensures provision of the tangible things mentioned. It also embeds the deceased into wider social structures as the offerings are given by the king on behalf of one of the funerary gods.[121]

The beginning of writing is well evidenced in connection with mortuary practices and projected power and relationships from this life to the afterlife.[122] We find the first ever known writing in the tomb U-j in Abydos dating to the Naqada IIIa period (c.3300 BC).[123] Already, different media are used: ivory or bone tags, pottery and mud seals.[124] All three material groups seem specifically linked to the type of inscription they contain and are differently distributed within the tomb.[125] This suggests an already sophisticated approach towards writing, its different usages and functions. Best known are the group of 150–175 tags.[126] They were produced by different writers maybe at point of one of the stages of collection of the jars/objects to whom they were attached.[127] Similar signs are on the above-mentioned pottery storage jars.[128] Seals are found on mud jar stoppers.[129] They seem to be the least advanced media, and might not yet be writing in the sense of expressing words.[130] These sealings were connected with jars whose types are interpreted as being of Canaanite origin.[131] The manifold media and their inclusion in the funerary sphere show that writing was beyond specific – individual – literacy and combined several areas for its application.

It would take another 2–300 years until the First Dynasty before writing presents more legible words,[132] while the material which was inscribed stayed the same.[133] During this period, the wish to stay connected with the king in the afterlife was expressed more clearly as seen in about 360 private stelae from Abydos which marked subsidiary graves around the royal tombs. Their inscriptions personified these graves,

---

[120] BESTOCK 2013, 95–96.
[121] BARTA 1963.
[122] BESTOCK 2013, 98.
[123] DREYER 1998; KAHL 2003. Even we do not know who the owner of U-j was, Dreyer assumes him to be a king. Against some arguments in Dreyer's discussion see WENGROW 2006, 202.
[124] BESTOCK 2013, 101.
[125] BESTOCK 2013, 99–101.
[126] DREYER 1998, 113–145; BESTOCK 2013, 104.
[127] KAHL 2001, 108–112; KAHL 2003, 111.
[128] DREYER 1998, 47–91.
[129] HARTUNG 1998.
[130] BESTOCK 2013, 105.
[131] DREYER 1998, 92.
[132] BESTOCK 2013, 98.
[133] BESTOCK 2013, 106.

Fig. 5: Stela of a Woman Named Niseret (New York, Metropolitan Museum of Art 1. 4. 93) © www.metmuseum.org

most of them recognise women.[134] The phonetic value of the hieroglyphs is not always clear as these signs still preceded standard hieroglyphic readings. So, the name of the owner of stela MMA 1. 4. 93 (Fig. 5) could be read differently: Senba, Niseret, and Nitkhnum. The female figure under the hieroglyphs which form the name serves as determinative for the word category *women*.[135] Being visualised in image and personified in writing established authority and displayed prestige in this life and after. Personhood and existing social relationships continued beyond the border of time, space and death.

The Materiality of Writing

Material culture and with it the materiality of writing is dependent on memory and also forms memory. The mentally stored human memory is prone to get lost, being forgotten and can only be described as fragile.[136] Every form of material culture used

---

[134] Stela [n.d.].
[135] Stela [n.d.].
[136] JONES 2007, 1.

to hold cultural memory is not only increasing capacity to create cultural memory, but especially allows us today to track the role memory played in the transmission of cultural ideas and specifics.[137]

Literacy is always connected with the materiality of texts and writing practice. Writing is essentially material practice which deals with substances, specific surfaces and acts as a medium.[138] This materiality connects the transmitted text with the social sphere. This grants agency to the materiality of writing. Artefacts are actants within the writing process.[139] All involved material can cause actions and reactions which influence the writing process including reading. Graphic media in this context is either concerned with the production of new content or the repetition of already stated one.[140] Choices were made regarding different materials and the forms of writing attached (hieroglyphs on stone walls, hieratic on papyrus to name only two). This determined not only the production of the actual text but also its reproductivity: using seals allowed reproductivity compared with the usage of reed or chisel where a text had to be written completely new every time.[141] Contexts are dependent from the materiality of writing and form it as well.[142]

The materiality of texts reveals agency in the first stage production of the text, its material form and forms of usage as well as any changes in the materiality of texts – transformation, reworks and de(con)structions.[143] After a first inscription is done, further text can be applied, (partially) erased, and maybe re-inscribed.[144] Materiality determines display, text forms, expression and appearance of the text attached. This means changes occurring here can alter the identity of the artefact[145] including the text. The materiality of ancient texts always also includes the archaeology of the texts understood as the entangled interplay of archaeological and textual characteristics. This forms the identity of texts, their visual and symbolic encoding of the language present at the time, the storage and transmission of ideas and therefore supporting the memory,[146] brought to light by archaeological investigation.[147] Writing practice is also based on datasets representing the technical side of writing: used scripts, tools to write and media containing script.[148]

---

[137] For different approaches towards interplay of memory and materiality of things involved see JONES 2007.
[138] PIQUETTE/WHITEHOUSE 2013.
[139] MALAFOURIS 2013, 130.
[140] PINARELLO 2015, 18.
[141] PINARELLO 2015, 18.
[142] PINARELLO 2015, 19.
[143] PIQUETTE 2013.
[144] PIQUETTE 2013, 217.
[145] PIQUETTE 2013, 222.
[146] RUTZ/KERSEL 2014.
[147] KERSEL/RUTZ 2014, 3.
[148] PINARELLO 2015, 26; ALLON/NAVRATILOVA 2017, 5–12; SCHLOTT 1989, 29–98.

Texts could be written in a monumental form (hieroglyphs), hieratic, demotic or Coptic.

Hieroglyphs are best known today, the implements shown as marker or status symbol for a scribe are forms of the scribal palette and the rolled papyrus which were used for the conception of the handwriting forms (hieratic, demotic).[149] People involved with these writing practices and especially their archaeologically presented implements do not necessarily possess specific / individual literacy.[150] The materiality of the writing process opens up a new horizon of engaging with texts that goes beyond a narrowly defined reading/writing skill. For example, the craftsmen involved in producing the material objects associated with writing have to be considered an essential part of ancient Egyptian literary culture.

Types of Literacy in Ancient Egypt

Specific Literacy – the Individual Ability to Read and Write

Even the concept of individually known authors as creators of a text is not typical for ancient Egypt, we distinguish some literate people. Certain names of wise men from the Middle Kingdom to whom instructions are allocated, are known from the *Eulogy of Dead Writers* from Pap. Chester Beatty IV.[151] Egyptologists can track known scribes beyond typical scribal careers.[152] The title scribe indicated high status, (some form of) literacy and gave access to elite experiences and high culture.[153] As such, being depicted as a scribe or holding scribal titles was often seen as a symbol for high culture, carrying the scribal palette was a sign of membership to the elite. Good examples are the three wooden panels from the mastaba of Hesire from Saqqara which show Hesire in different stages of his career, always carrying the traditional scribal palette.[154]

Privately owned book collections existed, but in contrast to private libraries of the more present past, they were less literary than magical or professional.[155] Often cited are the *Ramesseum Library* which was found with professional magical equipment,[156] the *Berlin Library* which has four literary papyri whose connection is not proven beyond being grouped together by the first collector in modern times[157] as well

---

149 ALLON/NAVRATILOVA 2017, 5.
150 ALLON/NAVRATILOVA 2017, 12.
151 See above.
152 For 10 famous New Kingdom scribes see ALLON/NAVRATILOVA 2017.
153 BAINES 2013, 40–41, see also fn.1
154 Cairo, Egyptian Museum, CG1426–1428; 3rd dynasty, reign Djoser (Netjerikhet).
155 QUIRKE 2004, 14–23; BLUMENTHAL 2011.
156 PARKINSON 2017; BLUMENTHAL 2011, 67–71.
157 BLUMENTHAL 2011, 72; MORENZ 1996, 135–141.

as the very heterogeneous *Collection Deir el-Medina* of the scribe Qenherkhepshef, Accountant of the Project for the King's Tomb.[158] They are also evidenced in literary texts. In the Pap. Westcar, the magician Djedi asks the king to call his children to bring his books.[159] Such a bringing of books is visually presented on the Stela of Jkj:[160] In the middle register a musician is accompanied by a helper carrying book chests.[161] Many of the papyri found in tombs might also have been evidence for privately owned books.[162]

Beyond this specific evidence, literacy rates for ancient Egypt are not known and need to be estimated. The number of literate people varies depending on used estimation model, period and place.[163] Literacy was practiced in administration – maybe to the fullest functional sense – as well as religion, especially within the ritual and temple sphere. Temples seem to have become the largest depositories of books and otherwise written knowledge.[164] The figure suggested by Baines and Eyre lies by about 1% of the population,[165] estimated based on Old Kingdom tomb inscriptions and reliefs. Literacy rates very likely rose already during the Old Kingdom and clearly from the New Kingdom to 5%[166] and is sometimes calculated even higher.[167] It is argued that the Intermediate Periods saw a decrease with a rise at the begin of each following period.[168] Evidence from the 4th century BC suggests that 7% of the whole population were literate. The proportion of the Egyptian population is slightly lower (6%) which suggests that the Greek and other foreign population at the time had a higher rate.[169] This might be related to the increase of semi-literate people who needed to be able to write their names under contracts.[170]

---

158 BLUMENTHAL 2011, 73–80; PESTMAN 1982.
159 Pap. Berlin 3033, 8,3–4 (Middle Kingdom). BLUMENTHAL 2011, 65; LICHTHEIM 1975, 218. For Djedi as *homme de lettres* see MORENZ 1996, 107–123.
160 Leiden, Rijksmuseum van Oudheden AP 25 (Middle Kingdom). Stèle van Iki [n.d.].
161 MORENZ 1996, 77 argues for book chests to be carried while YAMAMOTO 2015, 157 sees sandals being carried.
162 BLUMENTHAL 2011, 80–83.
163 ZINN 2013c with further literature. For Deir el-Medina see above.
164 ZINN 2013b; ZINN 2011; ZINN 2008.
165 BAINES/EYRE 2007, esp. 64–73. For special groups (royal sphere and women) and places (Deir el-Medina) see 78–94. BAINES 1983, 584. For a short overview on Greco-Roman Egypt, please see CLIVAZ 2012.
166 BAINES/EYRE 2007, 94.
167 LESKO 1994; JANSSEN 1992. This can go up to 15% in urban hotspots like Lahun (LITERACY 2003), which housed the workers and administrators associated with the Middle Kingdom pyramid complexes nearby.
168 BAINES 2007, 68.
169 RAY 1994, 65.
170 DEPAUW 2012, 499–500. As this paper focusses on pharaonic Egypt, specifics of Graeco-Roman Egypt will be deliberately left out.

Within this already very low number of literate people, different levels of literacy are included. Even it is often assumed that there are two nearly opposing groups – literate vs. illiterate – this is not the case.[171] The borders are fluid and literacy starts from limited reading ability of the people who carved the monuments and leads over several degrees of reading ability to extended forms of literacy which include the skill to compose texts for administrative, literary or religious purposes.[172] As discussed above, literacy could also be assumed for relief sculptors or painters who were able to carve signs despite having a limited reading ability.[173] Writing as part of monumental art could be practiced by craftsmen with limited or no literacy as they were controlled by a foremen or other literate person.[174] This is proven by corrections found on tomb and temple walls.[175]

Studies were conducted regarding the individual literacy of certain groups of people beyond that of scribes. Of special interest were literacy of women[176] and the personal ability to read and write by kings[177]. Even this could have promised an extension of the understanding of literacy beyond the individual case by looking at certain social groups, this last step was often not pursued.

Collective Literacy – Orality and Literacy as Tools to Express Shared Historical and Cultural Memories

Literacy understood as personal ability to read and write does not recognise the position of scribes[178] and other literati as social figures with an important place within society.[179] Both orality and literacy are able to create a shared identity via the cultural memory they transmit. Texts and images were kept re-usable as they carried the self-understanding of the culture and stabilised the society. Myths were orally performed, but preserved in writing. Literacy via the media text and image shaped the interest in "history" and renewed in this way identity. These patterns created a *collective literacy* beyond the practiced individual literacy mentioned above which con-

---

171 Lesko 2001.
172 Baines/Eyre 2007, 63–70; Baines 1983, 584.
173 Laboury 2016.
174 Baines 1983,
175 Tomb of pharaoh Horemheb (KV 57): hieroglyphs were outlined in red above which black corrections are applied (Strudwick/Strudwick 1999, 181).
176 Bryan 1985; Robins 1993, 111–114; Zinn 2013a, 2321 (with further literature).
177 Schlott 1989, 54–56, 165; Morenz 1996, 24–26; Eyre 2013, 280.
178 The category *scribe* is currently re-discussed and critiqued (Pinarello 2015; Allon/Navratilova 2017). Pinarello reasons that our view of ancient Egyptian scribes stems from the romanticised perception of ancient Egypt by the "modern educated men" (Pinarello 2015, 19, 23).
179 For the many – often contradictory – roles of scribes see the case studies in Allon/Navratilova 2017.

nected high and low culture spread over all levels of the whole society with the literal elite encoding the information and providing decoding tools for non-elites. History and identity were kept alive through the creation of a shared cultural memory via text transmitted in writing or orally as well as imagery.[180]

One specific example for this process can be found in the scene of *Pharaoh smiting his enemies*,[181] in which the king holds one or more prisoner and smites them with a mace, sword or axe.[182] This presented the longest-lasting iconographical motif and pictorial description of an ideal event which needed to be re-confirmed by every Pharaoh. The first example might already be depicted in Tomb 100 in Hierakonpolis (Naqada II, around 3300 BC), but the best known early example is on the Narmer Palette (ca. 3100 BC, transition from dynasty 0 to 1).[183] The motive is still used in the decoration programme of Graeco-Roman temples, such as Edfu. The collective remembrance in this mostly but not always monumental scene is knowledge about important events which formed Egyptian identity: The king who is doing his duty and upholds Ma'at, the right order, by being victorious. In the case of the Narmer Palette this is the first unification of Upper and Lower Egypt, a sacred event which needs to be re-enacted and confirmed by every king who followed. This scene is very often found on temple pylons and is directed towards the gods to whom the king proves his dutiful action. However, it is enacted for all members of the society and could therefore be understood as performed, acted and substitutional literacy. The latter conclusion can be drawn from a motive typical to the Amarna Period of the 18th dynasty which shows the *Smiting of the enemies* as an image-in-image decoration on the cabins of the royal barges of Akhenaten and Nefertiti, depicting both the king and the queen in the pose of smiting.[184] The audience of the scene is here much wider, extended beyond the divine world of the temple: Everybody who saw the ships passing by on the Nile could "read" it and remembered the mythical past without a written record had survived of the first happening as a quasi-historical event.[185]

The same mechanism was used depicting the account of the Battle of Megiddo fought by Thutmose III on the walls in the Hall of Annals of the Karnak Temple.[186] It mentions a second transcript: *jw=sn smn ḥr ꜥr.t n.t ḥw.t-nṯr n.t Jmn m hrw pn* – they were stored on a leather roll in the temple of Amun on this day.[187] The same text is adapted to different audiences which are supposed to use it even they do not read it personally as outlined in the more traditional definition of individual literacy. The monumental

---

180 ASSMANN 1992, 52–53.
181 LUISELLI 2011.
182 SCHOSKE 1994.
183 LUISELLI 2011, 13–14.
184 For the discussion of the unusual case of the queen as the protagonist see ZINN 2015, 43–46.
185 LUISELLI 2011, 20.
186 ZINN 2011, 188.
187 Urk. IV, 662.

version set in stone of the temple wall was directed to the gods and as such fixed the event in time, while the archival copy on a leather role was kept elsewhere in or nearby the temple, likely in a *pr-ꜥnḫ*, the *House of Life*.[188]

This shows the mythological function of the temple as part of an idealised place to store knowledge – a huge library in stone of important texts. Jan Assmann called this phenomenon *the temple as book*,[189] characterising the temple as a three-dimensional and monumental translation of a book into space. *Book* should be understood as an ideal text corpus comprised from all sorts of texts covering a wide knowledge in the sense of a monumental library. Here, texts are often only indicated by title or part of the text. This was enough to enable the agency of these text within the temple as image of the (ideal) world. These so presented and preserved texts act as *cultural texts*[190] and are outcome, part and originator of cultural memory. Two of the main functions of writing are storage and communication of ideas. As Assmann explains, the first function preserves knowledge and ideas from forgetting as an extended human memory while the second ensures an extended audience.[191] Even it is clear that the cultural memory is shaped by written and visual narratives which placed the literate elite in a special position, these narratives are closely connected to and influenced by parallel oral traditions. This was the case from the beginning of texts, but becomes more poignant from the New Kingdom onwards. Therefore, cultural memory is not only shaped by the literate elite but the Egyptian society in its entirety.[192] Such ability to use these texts was extended to all meaning that all were "literate" to use or consume them. This is a more comprehensive understanding of literacy which looks at the society in its entirety, instead of looking at literati only. Literacy in this sense is mediated literacy.

Collective literacy was institutionalised literacy: Texts to be used were stored as collections. That could be on temple walls as mentioned above or in libraries and archives.[193] Even only very few libraries are architecturally known,[194] their setup documents an interface between orality and literacy. The temple libraries in Edfu and Philae (both *pr-mḏꜣ.t*) were small special libraries used for the daily cult-ritual.[195] The small room – 2m² – in Edfu was inscribed with a book catalogue and decorated with scenes of offering book chests to Horus Behedeti – the main god of the temple. In the east and west wall of this room there were several niches, which might have contained

---

[188] SCHLOTT 1989, 218. For different institutions holding such documents see ZINN 2013d, esp. ch. 3.4 and 3.5.
[189] ASSMANN 1992, 177–185; ASSMANN 2011, 156–170.
[190] ASSMANN 1999, 7.
[191] ASSMANN 1999, 5–6.
[192] JAY 2016, 348–349.
[193] RYHOLT 2013; ASSMANN 2001; for libraries and archives as crucial institutions within the process of transmission of knowledge see ZINN 2008; 2011; 2013b; 2013d.
[194] ZINN 2008.
[195] ZINN 2011, 191–196.

wooden book chests as shown in the offering scenes in this room. Interestingly for the interplay between literacy and orality is the usage of these libraries being bound into the daily cult ritual. If we look on the performance of the ritual in the way of an organigramm, we can state that the priests cleansed and robed themselves as preparation for the ritual in the adjacent Morning House (*pr-dw3.t*), which in Edfu is situated as a mirror image over the central axis and in Philae next to the *pr-mḏ3.t*.[196] When proceeding into the temple inner, the priests picked up the books needed for the ritual in the *pr-mDA.t*. From the papyri, the incantations and recitations for the ritual were made while proceeding towards the sanctuary.

Summary

In order to re-conceptualise *literacy* for ancient Egypt, I focussed on three different areas: the relationship between orality and the written word; the materiality of writing and agency; and writing/literacy as constituent part of Egypt's memory culture.

Taken together, these three aspects underpin the role of writing/reading as the main criteria in the discussion of literacy. They help to re-focus the discussion with the aim of conceptualising 'literacy' more broadly as a cultural and social practice beyond the skill of an individual. Literacy should not be seen too simplistically as individual capacity to read and write or establishing the status of literate person within the society as a result of their literate skills. Literacy also reveals an overarching component which enables society to deal with texts and documents as well as the information contained. This is necessary to build up a social memory which creates a shared cultural identity and keeps the society alive. In this sense, a literate elite culture is working for and in the everyday life of all members of this society, be it consciously or subconsciously.

Bibliography

ALLEN 2010 = J.P. ALLEN, Language, Scripts, and Literacy, in: A. LLOYD (ed.), A Companion to Ancient Egypt II, Chichester 2010, 641–662.
ALLON/NAVRÁTILOVÁ 2017 = N. ALLON/H. NAVRÁTILOVÁ, Ancient Egyptian Scribes: A Cultural Exploration, London/New York 2017.
ASSMANN 1992 = J. ASSMANN, Das kulturelle Gedächtnis: Schrift, Erinnerung und politische Identität in frühen Hochkulturen, München 1992.
ASSMANN 1999= J. ASSMANN, Cultural and Literary Texts, in: G. MOERS (ed.), Definitely: Egyptian literature, Proceedings of the Symposion "Ancient Egyptian Literature – History and Forms", Los Angeles, March 24 – 26, 1995, Göttingen 1999, 1–15.

---

196 ZINN 2011, 194.

Assmann 2001 = J. Assmann, Libraries in the Ancient World – with Special Reference to Ancient Egypt, in: S. Bieri/W. Fuchs (ed.) Building for Books: Traditions and Visions, Basel 2001, 50–67.
Assmann 2002 = J. Assmann, The Mind of Egypt: History and Meaning in the Time of the Pharaohs, New York 2002.
Assmann 2011 = J. Assmann, Cultural Memory and Early Civilization: Writing, Remembrance, and Political Imagination, Cambridge 2011.
Baines 1983 = J. Baines, Literacy and Ancient Egyptian Society, *MAN* 18, 1983, 572–599.
Baines 1988 = J. Baines, Literacy, Social Organization, and the Archaeological Record: The Case of Early Egypt, in: J. Gledhill/B. Bender/M.T. Larsen (ed.), State and Society: The Emergence and Development of Social Hierarchy and Political Centralization, London 1988, 192–214.
Baines 1989 = J. Baines, Communication and Display: The Integration of Early Egyptian Art and Writing, *Antiquity* 63, 1989, 471–482.
Baines 1990 = J. Baines, Restricted Knowledge, Hierarchy, and Decorum: Modern Perceptions and Ancient Institutions, *JARCE* 27, 1990, 1–23.
Baines 2007 = J. Baines, Visual and Written Culture in Ancient Egypt, Oxford 2007.
Baines 2013 = J. Baines, High Culture and Experience in Ancient Egypt, Sheffield 2013.
Baines/Eyre 2007 = J. Baines/C. Eyre, Four Notes on Literacy, in: J. Baines, Visual and Written Culture in Ancient Egypt, Oxford 2007, 63–94.
Barta 1963 = W. Barta, Die altägyptische Opferliste von der Frühzeit bis zur griechisch–römischen Epoche, Berlin 1963.
Bestock 2013 = L. Bestock, Agency in Death: Early Egyptian Writing from Mortuary Contexts, in: J. Englehardt (ed.), Agency in Ancient Writing, Boulder 2013, 95–111.
Bleeker 1975 = C.J. Bleeker, Religious Tradition and Sacred Books in Ancient Egypt, in: C.J. Bleeker (ed.), The Rainbow: A Collection of Studies in the Science of Religion, Leiden 1975, 91–105.
Blumenthal 2011 = E. Blumenthal, Privater Buchbesitz im pharaonischen Ägypten, in: E. Blumenthal/W. Schmitz (ed.), Bibliotheken im Altertum, Wiesbaden 2011, 51–85.
Bryan 1984 = B. Bryan, Evidence for Female Literacy from Theban Tombs of the New Kingdom, *Bulletin of the Egyptological Seminar* 6, 1984, 17–32.
Burkard 1990 = G. Burkard, Frühgeschichte und Römerzeit: P. BERLIN 23071 vso, *Studien zur Altägyptischen Kultur* 7, 1990, 107–133.
Černý 1939 = J. Černý, Late Ramesside Letters, Bruxelles 1939.
Clivaz 2012 = C. Clivaz, Literacy, Greco-Roman Egypt, The Encyclopedia of Ancient History, 7, 2013, 4097–4098.
Depauw 2012 = M. Depauw, Language Use, Literacy, and Bilingualism, in: C. Riggs (ed.), The Oxford Handbook of Roman Egypt, Oxford 2012, 493–506.
Dreyer 1998 = G. Dreyer, Umm el-Qaab I: das prädynastische Königsgrab U-j und seine frühen Schriftzeugnisse, Mainz 1998.
Englehardt/Nakassis 2013 = J. Englehardt/D. Nakassis, Individual Intentionality, Social structure, and Material Agency in Early Writing and Emerging Script Technologies, in: J. Englehardt (ed.), Agency in Ancient Writing, Boulder 2013, 95–111.
Enmarch/Lepper 2013 = R. Enmarch/V.M. Lepper (ed.), Ancient Egyptian Literature: Theory and Practice, Oxford 2013.
Eyre 2013a = C. Eyre, The Use of Documents in Pharaonic Egypt, Oxford 2013.
Eyre 2013b = C. Eyre, The Practice of Literature: The Relationship between Content, Form, Audience, and Performance, in: R. Enmarch/V.M. Lepper (ed.), Ancient Egyptian Literature: Theory and Practice, Oxford 2013, 101–142.
Eyre/Baines 1989 = C. Eyre/J. Baines, Interactions between Orality and Literacy in Ancient Egypt, in: K. Schousboe/M.T. Larsen (ed.), Literacy and Society, Copenhagen 1989, 91–119.

FECHT 1982 = G. FECHT, Prosodie, in: W. HELCK/W. WESTENDORF, Lexikon der Ägyptologie 4, 1982, 1127–1154.
FOSTER 1999 = J.L. FOSTER, Some Comments on Khety's Instruction for Little Pepy on his Way to School (Satire of the Trades), in: E. TEETER/J.A. LARSON (ed.), Gold of Praise: Studies on Ancient Egypt in Honor of Edward F. Wente, Chicago 1999, 121–129.
GELL 1998 = A. GELL, Art and Agency: An Anthropological Theory, Oxford 1998.
GESTERMANN 1998= L. GESTERMANN, Die „Textschmiede" Theben – Der thebanische Beitrag zu Konzeption und Tradierung von Sargtexten und Totenbuch, *Studien zur Altägyptischen Kultur* 25, 1998, 83–99.
HARRIS 1989 = W.V. HARRIS, Ancient Literacy, Cambridge, Mass. 1989.
HARTUNG 1998 = U. HARTUNG, Prädynastische Siegelabrollungen aus dem Friedhof U in Abyds (Umm el-Qaab), *MDAIK* 54, 1998, 187–217.
HELCK 1970 = W. HELCK, Die Lehre des _wA-xtjj I, Wiesbaden 1970.
JANSSEN 1992 = J. JANSSEN, Literacy and Letters at Deir El-Medina, in: R. DEMAREE/A. EGBERTS (ed.), Village Voices: Proceedings of the Symposium "Texts from Deir El-Medina and their Interpretation" Leiden, May 31 – June 1, 1991, Leiden 1992, 81–94.
JAY 2016 = J.E. JAY, Orality and Literacy in the Demotic Tales, Leiden 2016.
JONES 2007 = A. JONES, Memory and Material Culture, Cambridge 2007.
KAHL 2001 = J. KAHL, Hieroglyphic Writing during the Fourth Millennium BC: An Analysis of Systems, *Archéo-Nil* 11, 2001, 103–135.
KAHL 2003 = J. KAHL, Die frühen Schriftzeugnisse aus dem Grab U-j in Umm el-Qaab, *Chronique d'Egypte* 78, 2003, 112–135.
KERSEL/RUTZ 2014 = M.M. KERSEL/M.T. RUTZ, Introduction: No Discipline is an Island, in: RUTZ/KERSEL 2014 = M.T. RUTZ/M.M. KERSEL (ed.), Archaeologies of Text: Archaeology, Technology and Ethics, Oxford 2014, 1–13.
KNAPPETT/MALAFOURIS 2008 = C. KNAPPETT/L. MALAFOURIS (ed.), Material Agency: Towards a Non-Anthropocentric Approach, New York 2008.
LABOURY 2016 = D. LABOURY, Le Scribe et le Peintre, in: P. COLLOMBERT et al. (ed.), Aere perennius: Mélange égyptologiques en l'honneur de Pascal Vernus, Leuven 2016, 371–396.
LATOUR 2005 = B. LATOUR, Reassembling the Social: An Introduction to Actor-Network-Theory, Oxford 2005.
LESKO 1994 = L. LESKO, Literature, Literacy, and Literati, in: L. LESKO (ed.), Pharaoh's Workers: The Villagers of Deir el Medina, Ithaca 1994, 131–144.
LESKO 2001 = L. LESKO, Literacy, in: The Oxford Encyclopedia of Ancient Egypt 2, 2001, 297–299.
LICHTHEIM 1975 = M LICHTHEIM, Ancient Egyptian Literature: A Book of Readings, Bd. 1: The Old and Middle Kingdom, Berkeley 1975.
Literacy 2003 = http://www.ucl.ac.uk/museums-static/digitalegypt//literature/literacy.html (available online, accessed 26/03/2017).
Literacy for all [n.d.] = http://www.unesco.org/new/en/education/themes/education-building-blocks/literacy/ (available online, accessed 02/01/2017).
LOPRIENO 1996 = A. LOPRIENO (ed.), Ancient Egyptian Literature: History and Form, Leiden/New York/Köln 1996.
LUISELLI 2003 = M.M. LUISELLI, The Colophone as an Indication of the Attitudes towards the Literary Tradition in Egypt and Mesopotamia, in: S. BICKEL/A. LOPRIENO (ed.), Basel Egyptology Prize: Junior Research in Egyptian History, Basel 2003, 343–360.
LUISELLI 2011 = M.M. LUISELLI, The Ancient Egyptian Scene of 'Pharaoh Smiting his Enemies': An Attempt to Visualize Cultural Memory?, in: M. BOMMAS (ed.) Cultural Memory and Identity in Ancient Societies, London 2011, 10–25.

LUISELLI [n.d.] = M.M. LUISELLI, Writing – Image – Material: On Media and Communication in Ancient Egypt. http://www.birmingham.ac.uk/research/activity/connections/Essays/MLuiselli.aspx (available online, accessed 24/04/2017)

MALAFOURIS 2011 = L. MALAFOURIS, Linear B as Distributed Cognition: Excavating a Mind Not Limited by the Skin, in: N. JOHANNSEN/M. JESSEN/H.J. JENSEN, Excavating the Mind: Cross-Sections through Culture, Cognition and Materiality, Aarhus 2011, 69–84.

MALAFOURIS 2013 = L. MALAFOURIS, How Things Shape the Mind: A Theory of Material Engagement, Cambridge, Mass. 2013.

Menna [n.d.] = https://www.osirisnet.net/popupImage.php?img=/tombes/nobles/menna69//photo/menna_c1_eastwall-s_16_bg.jpg&lang=en&sw=1366&sh=768 (available online, accessed 12/08/2017)

MORALES 2017 = A.J. MORALES, From Voice to Papyrus to Wall: Verschriftung and Verschriftlichung in the Old Kingdom Pyramid Texts, in: M. HILGERT (ed.), Understanding Material Text Cultures: A Multidisciplinary View, Berlin 2017, 69–130.

MORENZ 1996 = L. MORENZ, Beiträge zur Schriftlichkeitskultur im Mittleren Reich und in der 2. Zwischenzeit, Wiesbaden 1996.

MORENZ 2004 = L. MORENZ, Bild-Buchstaben und symbolische Zeichen: Die Herausbildung der Schrift in der hohen Kultur Altägyptens, Fribourg 2004.

PARKINSON 1991 = R.B. PARKINSON, Voices from Ancient Egypt: An Anthology of Middle Kingdom Writings, London 1991.

PARKINSON 2002 = R.B. PARKINSON, Poetry and Culture in Middle Kingdom Egypt, London/New York 2002.

PARKINSON 2009 = R.B. PARKINSON, Reading Ancient Egyptian Poetry: Among other Histories, Chichester 2009.

PARKINSON 2015 = R.B. PARKINSON, The Impact of Middle Kingdom Literature: Ancient and Modern, in: A. OPPENHEIM et al. (ed.), Ancient Egypt Transformed: The Middle Kingdom, New Haven/London 2015, 180–187.

PARKINSON 2017 = R.B. PARKINSON, The Ramesseum Papyri, http://www.britishmuseum.org/research/publications/online_research_catalogues/rp/the_ramesseum_papyri.aspx (available online, accessed 23/05/2017).

PESTMAN 1982 = P. PESTMAN, Who Were the Owners, in the 'Community of Workmen,' of the Chester Beatty Papyri, in: R. DEMAREE/J. JANSSEN (ed.), Gleanings from Deir el-Medina, Leiden 1982, 155–172.

PINARELLO 2015 = M.S. PINARELLO, An Archaeological Discussion of Writing Practice: Deconstruction of the Ancient Egyptian Scribe, London 2015.

PIQUETTE/WHITEHOUSE 2013 = K.E. PIQUETTE/R.D WHITEHOUSE, Writing as Material Practice: Substance, Surface and Medium, London 2013.

PIQUETTE 2013 = K.E PIQUETTE, "It is Written"?: Making, Remaking and Unmaking Early 'Writing' in the Lower Mile Valley, in: K.E. PIQUETTE/R.D WHITEHOUSE, Writing as Material Practice: Substance, Surface and Medium, London 2013, 213–238.

QUIRKE 2004 = S. QUIRKE, Egyptian Literature 1800BC: Questions and Readings, London 2004.

RAY 1994 = J. RAY, Literacy and Language in Egypt in the Late and Persian Periods, in: A.K. BOWMAN/G. WOOLF (ed.), Literacy and Power in the Ancient World, Cambridge, 51–66.

REGULSKI 2015 = I. REGULSKI, The Origins and Early Development of Writing in Egypt, http://www.oxfordhandbooks.com/view/10.1093/oxfordhb/9780199935413.001.0001/oxfordhb-9780199935413-e-61 (available online, accessed 13/04/2017).

ROBINS 1993 = G. ROBINS, Women in Ancient Egypt, London 1993.

RUTZ/KERSEL 2014 = M.T. RUTZ/M.M. KERSEL (ed.), Archaeologies of Text: Archaeology, Technology and Ethics, Oxford 2014.

Ryholt 2013 = K. Ryholt, Libraries in Ancient Egypt, in: J. König/K. Oikonomopoulou/G. Wolf (ed.), Ancient Libraries, Cambridge 2013, 23–37.

Schlott 1989 = A. Schlott, Schrift und Schreiber im Alten Ägypten, München 1989.

Schoske 1994 = S. Schoske, Das Erschlagen der Feinde: Ikonographie und Stilistik der Feindvernichtung im alten Ägypten, Ann Arbor 1994.

Scribe Statue [n.d.] = Scribe Statue of Min-nakht (Baltimore, Walters Art Museum 22.230), http://art.thewalters.org/detail/23346/scribe-statue-of-min-nakht/ (available online, accessed 12/08/2017).

Seated Scribe [n.d.] = The Seated Scribe (Paris, Louvre E 3023), http://www.louvre.fr/en/oeuvre-notices/seated-scribe (available online, accessed 24/03/2017).

Smith 2008 = M. Smith, Religion, Culture, and Sacred Space, New York 2008.

Stela [n.d.] = Stela of a Woman Named Niseret (New York, Metropolitan Museum of Art 1. 4. 93), http://www.metmuseum.org/art/collection/search/547441 (available online, accessed 24/03/2017).

Stèle van Iki [n.d.] = http://www.rmo.nl/collectie/zoeken?object=AP+25 (available online, accessed 12/09/2017).

Strudwick/Strudwick 1999 = N. Strudwick/H. Strudwick, Thebes in Egypt: A Guide to the Tombs and Temples of Ancient Luxor, Ithaca 1999.

Sweeney 2001 = D. Sweeney, Correspondence and Dialogue: Pragmatic Factors in Late Ramesside Letter-Writing, Wiesbaden 2001.

UNESCO 1958 = Recommendations Concerning the International Standardization of Educational Statistics, Paris 1958.

UNESCO 2005 = Education for All – Literacy for Life: EFA Global Monitoring Report 2006. Paris 2005. Available online http://unesdoc.unesco.org/images/0014/001416/141639e.pdf (accessed 11/07/2017).

Van Dyke/Alcock 2003 = R.M. Van Dyke/S.E. Alcock, Archaeologies of Memory: An Introduction, in: R.M. Van Dyke/S.E. Alcock (ed.), Archaeologies of Memory, Oxford 2003, 1–13.

Wengrow 2006 = D. Wengrow, The Archaeology of Early Egypt: Social Transformations in North-East Africa 10,000 to 2650 BC, Cambridge 2006.

Wente 1967 = E.F. Wente, Late Ramesside Letters, Chicago 1967.

Whitehouse 2013 = R.D. Whitehouse, Epilogue: Agency and Writing, in: J. Englehardt (ed.), Agency in Ancient Writing, Boulder 2013, 249–255.

Yamamoto 2015 = K. Yamamoto, Stela of the Overseer of Priests Iki, in: A. Oppenheim et al. (ed.), Ancient Egypt Transformed: The Middle Kingdom, New Haven 2015, 156–157.

Youtube 2017 = Ancient Egyptian Poetry: The Tale of Sinuhe, https://www.youtube.com/watch?v=SpxVxa0ex-Y (available online, accessed 23/03/2017)

Zinn 2008 = K. Zinn, Altägyptische Tempelbibliotheken, in: H. Froschauer/C.E. Römer (ed.), Die Bibliothek des Weissen Klosters: Leben und Lesen in frühchristlichen Ägypten, Wien 2008, 81–91.

Zinn 2011 = K. Zinn, Temples, Palaces and Libraries – a Search for their Alliance between Archaeological and Textual Evidence, in: K. Spence/R. Gundlach (ed.), Palace and Temple – Architecture, Decoration, Ritual, Wiesbaden, 181–202.

Zinn 2013a = K. Zinn, Education, Pharaonic Egypt, in: The Encyclopedia of Ancient History, 5, 2013, 2318–2323.

Zinn 2013b = K. Zinn, Libraries, Pharaonic Egypt, in: The Encyclopedia of Ancient History, 7, 2013, 4061–4063.

Zinn 2013c = K. Zinn, Literacy, Pharaonic Egypt, in: The Encyclopedia of Ancient History, 7, 2013, 4100–4104.

ZINN 2013d = K. ZINN, Bibliotheken, Archive und Erinnerungskultur im Alten Ägypten: eine kulturhistorische Rekonstruktion, Leipzig, Univ. Diss., 2013.
ZINN 2015 = K. ZINN, Nofretete – eine Königin ihrer Zeit?, in: M. ELDAMATY/F. HOFFMANN/M. MINAS-NERPEL (ed.), Königinnen in Ägypten, Vaterstetten 2015, 27–67.

Josef Wiesehöfer
Anmerkungen zu Literalität und Oralität im teispidisch-achaimenidischen Iran

Abstract: The contribution aims at pointing out the impact of language(s) and writing system(s), not least of Elamite, Old Persian and Aramaic, in Teispid-Achaemenid Iran in the context of royal pronouncements and administration, and at putting them in relation to those of the neighbouring cultures. In this context, it is also trying to find out which forms of language acquisition and communication can be proven and whether there has been such a thing as a Persian language policy. On the other hand, the fact that Iran has seen decidingly oral cultures up to Late Antiquity and even beyond, apart from the official contexts, raises the question of the media of communication and the afterlife of Teispids and Achaemenids in Iran's 'historical' traditions.

Zusammenfassung: Dem Beitrag geht es einerseits darum, die Bedeutung von Sprache(n) und Schrift(en), nicht zuletzt des Elamischen, Altpersischen und Aramäischen, im teispidisch-achaimenidischen Iran im Zusammenhang von Königsverlautbarung und Administration aufzuzeigen und ins Verhältnis zu jenen der Nachbarkulturen zu setzen. Er bemüht sich in diesem Zusammenhang auch darum zu ergründen, welche Formen des Spracherwerbs und der Kommunikation sich nachweisen lassen und ob es so etwas wie eine persische Sprachenpolitik gegeben hat. Aus der Tatsache, dass wir es im Iran bis in die Zeit der Spätantike und sogar darüber hinaus, abgesehen von den offiziellen Zusammenhängen, mit dezidert oralen Kulturen zu tun haben, erwächst andererseits die Frage nach den Medien der Kommunikation und nach dem Nachleben von Teispiden und Achaimeniden in den ‚historischen' Traditionen Irans.

I Einleitende Bemerkungen

Man hat schon vielfach überzeugend dargelegt, dass die iranische Welt der vorislamischen Zeit – trotz der nicht zu unterschätzenden Bedeutung des Verwaltungs- und königlichen Legitimationsschriftgutes – eine durch Oralität, den Vorrang des gesprochenen vor dem geschriebenen Wort, bestimmte Welt gewesen sei, dass eigentlich erst seit (spät)sasanidischer Zeit von iranischer ‚Literatur' gesprochen werden könne, die damals eben in Mittelpersisch abgefasst wurde. Dieser Vorrang lässt sich mit dem alt- und mitteliranischen Wortschatz belegen, der zahlreiche indigene Wörter für „sich erinnern", „memorieren", „vortragen", „hören" und „(den rezitierten Text) befragen" kennt, aber etwa auch dadurch, dass die altpersischen Termini für „Schrift" und „schreiben" aus den Nachbarsprachen entlehnt wurden (s. u.). Ähnlich Platons „Phaidros" (275c-279b) kennt die avestische Überlieferung zudem eine große Skepsis dem geschriebenen Text gegenüber und bevorzugt stattdessen den memorierten Text.[1]

Mit der langen Dominanz des gesprochenen Wortes im Iran liegen Probleme des Traditionszusammenhangs auf der Hand: Zum ersten enthalten viele der uns erhaltenen späten schriftlichen Texte und Kompositionen erheblich älteres Gedankengut, so dass das Alter einer bestimmten Schrift, d. h. das Alter ihrer Aufzeichnung, bedeutend weniger aussagekräftig ist, als es auf den ersten Blick erscheinen mag. Zum zweiten lassen sich, wie fast immer bei mündlich tradierter und erst später schriftlich fixierter Tradition, einzelne Phasen des Entstehungsprozesses dieser Literatur nur schwer voneinander scheiden. Zum dritten ist nur ein Teil dieser Tradition, zumeist religiös-didaktischen Charakters, direkt auf uns gekommen, obwohl feststeht, dass in sasanidischer Zeit (224–651 n. Chr.) die Hauptmasse iranischer Literatur eindeutig dem nichtreligiösen Bereich zuzuordnen war.[2] Viertens schließlich liefert die lange Dominanz der mündlichen Tradition und des mündlichen Vortrags auch die Erklärung dafür, dass – neben der inschriftlichen Hinterlassenschaft der historischen Könige Irans und dem Verwaltungsschriftgut – der Bilderwelt Irans, in Reliefs, auf Gemälden und Gefäßen, auf Teppichen, Münzen und anderen Bildträgern, so große Bedeutung für die Bewahrung der ‚historischen' Traditionen Irans zukommt. Methodisch-disziplinär bedeutet dies, dass für eine Auseinandersetzung mit dem Problem der Literalität im Iran die Aufwertung der Archäologie/der Bildwissenschaft zu einer auch ‚historischen' Disziplin angeraten ist.

Ein Letztes: Der Umstand, dass das durch Oralität bestimmte Hochland von Iran, abgesehen vom seleukidischen Intermezzo und von der durch das Zweistromland beeinflussten Susiane (Chusistan), das entscheidende politische Zentrum des Nahen Ostens zwischen 500 v. und 650 n. Chr. war (nicht etwa die Region des Fruchtbaren Halbmonds), ist vielfach noch nicht genügend ‚gewürdigt', ja oft genug durch die Griechenland- und (Ost)Rom- bzw. Babylonienzentriertheit des schriftlichen Überlieferungsbefundes verfälscht worden – so war etwa Ktesiphon zwar parthisch-sasanidischer Zentralort, aber nie war seine, übrigens mehrfach durch die Römer ins Werk gesetzte, Einnahme gleichzusetzen mit dem Ende des römischen Opponenten im Osten. Das war erst mit der Einnahme Ostirans durch die Muslime gekommen.

II Königsverlautbarungen und administratives Schriftgut

Es ist schon vielfach betont worden, dass im Achaimenidenreich eine Fülle von Sprachen (und Schriftsystemen), auch in offiziellen Zusammenhängen, genutzt wurde und dass die Koexistenz so vieler verschiedener Sprachen zu vielfältigen Formen des

---

[1] Zusammenfassend: HUYSE 2008.
[2] MACUCH 2009; MACUCH 2013.

Sprach- und Kulturkontaktes und der gegenseitigen linguistischen und andersartigen kulturellen Beeinflussung führte. Die letzten Jahrzehnte der Teispiden- bzw. Achaimenidenforschung haben dabei – auf Iran bezogen – den Beweis erbracht, dass die Anfänge des Perserreiches sich nicht einem iranisch-induzierten Bruch mit den Vorläuferkulturen Südwestirans und des südlichen Zweistromlandes verdanken, sondern das Ergebnis eines längeren Transformationsprozesses waren, in dem elamisch-iranische Akkulturation und persische Ethnogenese eine entscheidende Rolle spielten.[3] Neuelamische Einflüsse auf den Reichsbildungsprozess sind dabei nicht zuletzt auf den Feldern Religion, Herrschafts- und Herrscherideologie, Ikonographie, Administration und Bürokratie nachgewiesen worden.[4]

Was die Verwaltung angeht, so haben die neueren Forschungen zum einen ergeben, dass ein neuelamischer Staat bis ca. 540 (oder gar 520) v. Chr. existierte. Elamisch war in ihm die Sprache der königlichen Selbstverlautbarungen (Königsinschriften), aber auch der Verwaltung; daneben diente Akkadisch als Sprache der Diplomatie, in wirtschaftlichen Zusammenhängen und als Kontaktsprache mit den akkadischsprachigen Bewohnern Elams. Von den Verbindungen der Könige mit der iranischsprachigen Bevölkerung Südwestirans künden iranische Personennamen und Lehnwörter in elamischen Texten.[5] Zum anderen verweisen die bekannten achaimenidenzeitlichen elamischen Tontäfelchen des Persepolis Fortification- (erhalten aus den Jahren zwischen 509 und 493 v. Chr.) und des Persepolis Treasury-Archivs (erhalten aus den Jahren 492–458 v. Chr.) sowie von weiteren iranischen Plätzen wie Susa, Tschogha Misch und Kandahar nicht, wie früher angenommen, darauf, dass diese von elamischen Untertanen illiterater persischer ‚Herren' beschrieben wurden, sondern darauf, dass in der Regel altpersische bzw. altiranische Muttersprachler, die Elamisch als zweite Sprache erlernt hatten und seine Syntax nach den Regeln ihrer Erstsprache veränderten, in der Verwaltung tätig waren.[6] In der Forschung spricht man seitdem in der Regel von dieser Sprachform des Elamischen als dem *achaimenidischen Elamisch* (*Achaemenid Elamite*).[7] Aus dieser Erkenntnis ergeben sich aber noch weitere Konsequenzen als die Aufgabe des alten stereotypen – und in früheren Zeiten z. T. auch rassistisch gefärbten – Bildes einer strikten Trennung von Iranern (Ariern) und Elamern: Alle Fassungen der achaimenidischen Königsinschriften, nicht zuletzt die altpersischen und die elamischen, sind als „Worte des Königs" zu verstehen und nicht etwa als idiosynkratische Umsetzungen des königlichen Diktats durch die Schreiber.[8] Sie haben deshalb, auch in ihren Unterschieden, ihr je eigenes his-

---

3 HENKELMAN 2008, 56–57.
4 HENKELMAN 2008; ÁLVAREZ-MON/GARRISON 2011.
5 TAVERNIER 2017, 338–339.
6 HENKELMAN 2011, 587–588.
7 Zur jüngeren Forschungsgeschichte zum achaimenidischen Elamisch s. ROSSI 2017a.
8 HENKELMAN 2017.

torisches Gewicht. Ja, es spricht sogar viel dafür, dass die Inschriftentexte in allen Fassungen als Teil der Bildersprache mit numinoser Qualität aufzufassen sind.[9]

Im Gegensatz zum Avestischen mit seinen spezifischen Traditions- und Entwicklungsproblemen ist das Altpersische als "Sprache des achaimenidischen Königtums" räumlich und zeitlich exakt einzuordnen: Es ist in der Persis (Fārs) beheimatet, für das 6.–4. Jahrhundert v. Chr. nachgewiesen, in repräsentativen Inschriften (Königsinschriften) direkt überliefert und spielte in schriftlicher Form keine maßgebliche Rolle in administrativen Zusammenhängen. In dieser Form fasst man eine „'künstliche', stark stilisierte Sprache mit dialektfremden Wörtern und z. T. archaischen Formen."[10] Vom Inschriftenaltpersisch unterschied sich ganz offensichtlich das gesprochene bzw. diktierte Altpersisch, das, wie wir an den bilingualen Schreibern und an Umsetzungen altpersischer Ausdrücke und Formulierungen ins Elamische und Akkadische erkennen können, durchaus administrativ bedeutsam war[11], und dem man entsprechend mit Hilfe des Sprach- und Namenguts der verschiedenen Nebenüberlieferungen auf die Spur kommen kann.[12] Weiterhin gilt: Da wir auf der mitteliranischen Sprachstufe auch in anderen Teilen Irans iranische Sprachen nachweisen können, ist davon auszugehen, dass diese auch in altiranischer Zeit ihre Vorläufer besessen haben.[13] Letztere sind z. T. durch Wörter und Namen in anderssprachiger Überlieferung, nicht aber durch zusammenhängende Texte o. ä. bekannt, sodass, wie im Falle der nordwestiranischen Sprachen, nicht immer Einigkeit darüber besteht, um welche Sprache es sich genau handelt.[14]

Zur Erleichterung der administrativen Kommunikation griffen die Perserkönige, dabei ihren nahöstlichen imperialen Vorgängern folgend, auf das Aramäische zurück, das in vielen Teilen ihres Reiches verstanden wurde[15]; es hat allerdings, nach dem babylonischen Befund, den Anschein, als ob die Nutzung des Aramäischen als Kommunikationssprache nun noch intensiviert worden sei.[16] Es war nicht die einzige ‚offizielle' Sprache des Reiches, und es ersetzte auch nicht die anderen Sprachen als Verwaltungssprache[17], aber es war die einzige Sprache, die reichsweit kommunikativ genutzt wurde und in der Verwaltung auch vertikal die Reichs- mit der Regional- bzw. Lokalebene verband.[18] In der Regel wird die Variante des Aramäischen, die unter den Königen damals zur *lingua franca* des Reiches wurde, als „Reichsaramäisch" bzw.

---

9 GARRISON 2011, 58. Vgl. auch ROLLINGER 2011.
10 SCHMITT 1989a, 56.
11 TAVERNIER 2017, 343–347.
12 SCHMITT 1999, 59–118. Zur jüngeren Forschungsgeschichte zum Altpersischen s. ROSSI 2017a.
13 SCHMITT 1984; SCHMITT 1989b.
14 SCHMITT 2003; ROSSI 2017b.
15 Zur Rolle des Aramäischen (als Verwaltungssprache) unter den Achaimeniden s. zuletzt TAVERNIER 2017, *passim*; FOLMER 1995; FOLMER 2009; FOLMER 2011; FOLMER 2017.
16 JURSA 2012, 393.
17 FRYE 1955, 457; BRIANT 1996, 525–526.
18 TAVERNIER 2017, 382.

„Kanzleiaramäisch" (*Official Aramaic*) bezeichnet, doch ist besser vom „achaimenidischen Reichsaramäisch" (*Achaemenid Imperial Aramaic*) zu sprechen, von dem im Übrigen zu sagen ist, dass es aus Überlieferungsgründen nicht immer klar von lokalen bzw. Nichtstandarddialekten der Sprache zu scheiden ist.[19]

Was Iran angeht, so war seit längerem, nicht zuletzt durch die Funde aus den Tontafelarchiven in Persepolis, bekannt, dass Aramäisch – nach Elamisch – dort als zweite Sprache der Verwaltung diente: So fand man im Schatzhaus 163 aramäische Inschriften auf Mörsern, Stößeln und anderen Steinobjekten, und im Festungsarchiv kamen, neben aramäischen Beischriften (*dockets*) zu elamischen Täfelchen 700–800 einsprachig-aramäische Tontafeln ans Tageslicht; in den elamischen Texten ist zudem von aramäischen Kopien von Briefen und Dokumenten auf Leder die Rede. Heute geht man einerseits davon aus, dass ca. 6–7 % der (erhaltenen) Tontafeln in Aramäisch beschriftet sind und dass gegen Mitte des 5. Jahrhunderts die Verwaltung auf aramäische Dokumente auf Papyrus oder anderes verderbliches Schreibmaterial umgestellt wurde.[20] Vor allem aber haben die 2012 publizierten Briefe und Listen auf Leder und verwaltungstechnischen Vermerke auf Holzstäbchen aus Baktrien, vornehmlich aus dem ausgehenden 4. Jahrhundert v. Chr.[21], deutlich machen können, welche Bedeutung dem Aramäischen in achämenidischer Zeit auch auf dem Hochland von Iran zukam. Zugleich erkannte man, dass die Texte „exakt der Rechtschreibung, Grammatik, Idiomatik und inneren wie äußeren Form anderer offizieller aramäischer Dokumente aus der Zeit der achämenidischen Herrschaft entsprechen, ... daß in den örtlichen Kanzleien der östlichen Provinzen des Reiches dieselben sprachlichen Standards galten wie im Westen."[22] Ein soeben erfolgter genauer Vergleich der Brieftradition der in Babylon und Susa abgefassten, an Funktionäre in der Satrapie Ägypten gesandten und ebendort gefundenen aramäischen sog. Arschama-Korrespondenz vom Ausgang des 5. Jahrhunderts mit den mehr als ein halbes Jahrhundert später geschriebenen Briefen (eigentlich: Vorlagen der Briefe) des Achvamazda aus Baktrien an seinen hohen Funktionär Bagavant in Kulmi haben diese Fülle von Gemeinsamkeiten im Sprachlichen, im Briefstil und im Administrativ-Organisatorischen belegen können, allerdings auch Spezifika der beiden Korrespondenzen.[23]

---

19 FOLMER 2011, 578.
20 FOLMER 2011, 583.
21 Edition: NAVEH/SHAKED 2012.
22 GZELLA 2014, 817.
23 FOLMER 2017.

III Formen des Spracherwerbs und der Kommunikation

Die Identifikation von zweisprachigen Schreibern in der persepolitanischen Dokumentation führt uns zu den Problemen des Spracherwerbs, des Ausmaßes von Zwei- und Mehrsprachigkeit im teispidisch-achaimenidischen Iran und solchen der Übersetzungstechnik. Was den Spracherwerb angeht, soll es uns dabei weniger um die Ausbildung von Schreibern oder Übersetzern oder den Aspekt des Vorteils von Mehrsprachigkeit gehen als vielmehr um die Frage des Prestiges von Sprachen, die oben ja bereits mit der Rolle des Altpersischen aufgeworfen wurde. Hier helfen uns die griechischen Zeugnisse weiter: Wie die Beispiele des Themistokles (Thuk. 1,137,2. 138,1) und des Peukestas (Arr. an. 6,30,2f.) zeigen, die sich beide ernsthaft bemüht haben sollen, die Sprache des Großkönigs zu erlernen und mit den Sitten und Gebräuchen seiner persischen Untertanen vertraut zu werden, haben zumindest die Griechen dem Altpersischen ein besonderes Prestige und einen besonderen ‚ideologischen' Wert zugeschrieben. Thukydides und Arrian bzw. dessen Vorlagen hatten zweifelsohne ihren je spezifischen Grund, ihren Protagonisten ein solch außergewöhnliches Maß an kultureller Aufgeschlossenheit und Artaxerxes I. und Alexander eine solch positive Reaktion darauf zuzuschreiben; dennoch ist am Faktum des Spracherwerbs und des besonderen Prestiges des (gesprochenen) Altpersischen angesichts der ideologischen Stellung von Pārsa bzw. der Perser im Reichsganzen wohl nicht zu zweifeln. Die Frage, ob man sich Spracherwerb in einem Schul- oder in einem Lernen-durch-Handeln-Zusammenhang vorzustellen hat, ist demgegenüber zweitrangig und mit Hilfe des zur Verfügung stehenden Quellenmaterials im Moment wohl auch kaum zu beantworten.

Es sind vor allem griechisch-lateinische, aramäische und elamische Zeugnisse, die uns über Mehrsprachigkeit im teispidisch-achaimenidischen Iran informieren. Die westlichen Zeugnisse machen sie vor allem im Zusammenhang mit dem Alexanderzug zum Thema, wenn sie etwa einen lykischen Hirten an den Grenzen der Persis erwähnen, der in der Lage gewesen sein soll, sowohl Griechisch als auch Persisch zu sprechen (Curt. 5,4,4.10; Plut. Alex. 37,1), oder wenn von einem griechisch- und wohl auch baktrischsprachigen Abkömmling der Branchiden aus Didyma die Rede ist (Curt. 7,5,28 f.). Auch wenn die Historizität beider Episoden – zu Recht – bezweifelt wird, so wird es doch zahlreiche zweisprachige Untertanen des Großkönigs, auch außerhalb administrativer Zusammenhänge, gegeben haben, etwa unter den Nachfahren von Deportierten (vgl. etwa Diod. 17,109,3–5), in den ḫaṭru-Gemeinschaften in Mesopotamien, die oft nach ihrer linguistischen oder ethnischen Zugehörigkeit organisiert waren, in den kurtaš-Arbeitskollektiven, die in den Täfelchen aus Persepolis aufscheinen, oder unter den Angehörigen des Dienstpersonals am Königshof, an den Satrapenhöfen oder in den Haushalten des iranischen (Hoch-)Adels.[24]

---

[24] Zur Mehrsprachigkeit im Zusammenhang mit achaimenidischen Deportationen s. demnächst die Druckfassung der Kieler Dissertation von C. MATARESE.

In den letzten 10 Jahren hat die Forschung in den Persepolis-Texten nicht nur zwei Arten von Schreibern (und Übersetzern) identifizieren können – die hochgeschätzten zwei- oder mehrsprachigen ‚Schreiber (in Alphabetschrift) auf Pergament' (Akkadisch *sēpiru*, Elamisch *teppir*) und die ‚Schreiber auf Tontafeln (in Keilschrift)' (Akkadisch *ṭupšarru*, Elamisch **tallir*) –, sie ist auch in der Lage gewesen, uns einen genaueren Einblick in das elaborierte System des achaimenidischen Diktier- und Übersetzungssystems zu verschaffen:

> „1. A satrap or a high satrapal official gives an Old Persian order to the chancellor, who passes these instructions (**patigāma-*) orally to the *sēpiru/teppir*, perhaps after officially authorizing it.
> 2. The *sēpiru/teppir* translates it into Aramaic and produces a written Aramaic version of the order (Elamite *tumme*). In Persepolis, these Aramaic versions are not preserved.
> 3. If necessary (when a third language is involved), the *sēpiru/teppir* also produces a translation in a local language (Egyptian, Elamite) and lets a local scribe (**tallir*) make a copy in that local language."[25]

IV Sprachen und Sprachenpolitik: Ein Vergleich

Was die Antike betrifft, so gibt es, abgesehen vom Lateinischen bzw. vom Imperium Romanum, bislang noch keine zusammenfassenden Studien zur Sprachenpolitik. 2006 veröffentlichte der Sprachwissenschaftler Béla ADAMIK ein Buch mit dem Titel „Sprachenpolitik im Römischen Reich", unglücklicherweise allerdings auf Ungarisch.[26] In ihm wies er nach, dass es, anders als man früher angenommen hatte, in Rom keine gesetzgeberischen Versuche gegeben hat, Latein zur alleinigen ‚offiziellen' Sprache zu erklären. Allerdings erreichten nur das Lateinische und das Griechische den Rang von Sprachen, die als voll funktionsfähig und somit auch als im amtlichen Kontext verwendbar angesehen wurden.

> „Pārsa ist nach dem Rat der Götter dazu ausersehen, den Himmel selbst noch herrlicher zu machen, die zerstreuten Reiche zu einem Ganzen zu verbinden, die Sitten zu veredeln, die unterschiedlichen und ungeschliffenen Dialekte so vieler verschiedener Nationen durch die mächtigen Bande einer gemeinsamen Sprache zu vereinen, der Menschheit die Freude am Diskurs und an der höheren Bildung zu vermitteln, kurz das gemeinsame Vaterland sämtlicher Völker des Erdkreises zu werden."

Pārsa als *caput orbis*, seine Sprache als zivilisierendes und friedenstiftendes Band aller königlichen Untertanen – trotz allen Stolzes der achaimenidischen Könige auf ihre

---

25 TAVERNIER 2008; TAVERNIER 2017, bes. 378–383; Zitat S. 380. Zahlreich sind auch die Hinweise auf Übersetzer in den griechischen Quellen: Sie übersetzen königliche oder satrapale Anweisungen in die verschiedensten Idiome, übermitteln militärische Befehle oder begleiten diplomatische Gesandtschaften: Vgl. Thuk. 8,85,1 f.; Xen. an. 1,2,17. 8,12; 4,4,5; Xen. hell. 7,1,37; Plut. Them. 6,3.
26 ADAMIK 2006.

persische Abstammung und die Qualitäten ihrer Heimat, ihrer Bewohner, ihrer Pflanzen, Tiere und Götter haben weder Dareios noch Xerxes jemals zu einer solch übertriebenen Form des kulturellen Imperialismus Zuflucht genommen. Und so stammt dieses Zitat eben auch nicht aus dem antiken Iran, sondern aus dem antiken Italien, *Pārsa* muss durch *Italia* ersetzt werden, der Autor ist kein Großkönig oder iranischer Sänger (*gōsān*), sondern der römische Autor Plinius der Ältere (nat. 3,6,3 f.[27]). Kollegen betrachten dieses Zitat in der Regel als Beleg für das Ende der ersten Phase der Entwicklung des Latein zur Weltsprache. Plinius' Phrase: *et tot populorum discordes ferasque linguas sermonis commercio contraheret ad conloquia et humanitatem homini daret breviterque una cunctarum gentium in toto orbe patria fieret* ist die Fortsetzung und die Übersteigerung der ‚imperialistischen' Anweisung, die Vergil den Römern gegeben hatte (Aen. 6,851–853): *regere imperio populos ... parcere subiectis et debellare superbos* – „die Völker zu lenken ..., die Unterworfenen zu schonen, doch Hochmütige niederzuringen." Mit Plinius „wird (nun) daraus ein universaler Bildungsauftrag, der sich durch die globale Ausbreitung der lateinischen Sprache vollzieht." Durch diese sprachliche Form der Globalisierung „wird nicht nur ein Kommunikationsinstrument geschaffen, sondern sie macht die Barbaren aller Völker erst recht eigentlich zu gesitteten Menschen."[28] Eine solche Rolle haben die persischen Großkönige weder ihrer Muttersprache, noch ihrer Herrschaft zugedacht.

V Medien der Kommunikation

Die Bedeutung des gesprochenen Wortes im Iran, wie sie im diesbezüglichen altiranischen Wortschatz, in der späten Entwicklung von Literatur, aber etwa auch im achaimenidischen Diktier- und Übersetzungssystem und in der Bedeutung von Bildträgern als Kommunikationsmedien angedeutet wird, lässt die Frage stellen nach den Formen der Interaktion zwischen Königen und Untertanen sowie der Verbreitung von ‚Botschaften' und Berichten im teispidisch-achaimenidischen Iran.

> „Es kündet Dareios, der König: Nun soll dich überzeugen, was von mir getan (worden ist); so sage es dem Volk, verheimliche (es ihm) nicht (*avaθā kārahyā θādi, mā apagaudaya*)! Wenn du diesen Bericht (*imām handugām*) nicht verheimlichst, (sondern) dem Volk sagst (mitteilst), möge Ahuramazdā dir Freund sein und möge dir Nachkommenschaft (beschieden) sein in großer Zahl und sollst du lange leben!
> Es kündet Dareios, der König: Wenn du (aber) diesen Bericht verheimlichst (und ihn) dem Volk nicht sagst (mitteilst), möge Ahuramazdā dich ruinieren und möge dir Nachkommenschaft nicht (beschieden) sein!
> ...

---

27 *numine deum electa quae caelum ipsum clarius faceret, sparsa congregaret imperia ritusque molliret et tot populorum discordes ferasque linguas sermonis commercio contraheret ad conloquia et humanitatem homini daret breviterque una cunctarum gentium in toto orbe patria fieret.*
28 Zitate: STROH 2007, 99.

> Es kündet Dareios, der König: Nach dem Willen Ahuramazdās (ist) dies die Fassung der Inschrift (*dipiciçam*), die ich hinzugesetzt habe, (und zwar) auf Arisch. (Auch) auf Ton und auf Pergament wurde sie angebracht (*gr̥ftam āha*). ... und sie wurde niedergeschrieben und vor mir vorgelesen (*utā niyapaiθiya utā patiyafraθiya paišiyā mām*). Daraufhin habe ich diese Fassung der Inschrift ausgesandt überallhin in die Länder."

In seinem Tatenbericht aus Bisutun (hier: IV 52–57. 57–59. 88–92; Übers. R. Schmitt) unterscheidet Dareios, wie man zu Recht bemerkt hat[29], drei Formen der *res gestae*: die physische, schriftlich niedergelegte Inschrift selbst (Altpersisch *dipi-*, Elamisch *tup-pi*), die gesehen und vorgelesen, aber auch zerstört werden kann und deshalb bewahrt werden muss; eine Fassung bzw. Fassungen der Inschrift (Altpersisch *dipi-ciça-*, Elamisch *tup-pi-me*), die vervielfältigt, vorgelesen und in schriftlicher Form verbreitet werden kann (können); schließlich einen Bericht (Altpersisch *handugā-*), der (mündlich) kundgetan werden soll, aber auch verheimlicht werden kann. Es ist daraus der Schluss gezogen worden, dass die schriftliche(n) Version(en) der Inschrift, die, wie die Bilderwelt des Reliefs, tief in den Traditionen der Vorgängerreiche verankert ist (sind)[30], sich an ein Publikum im Zweistromland gerichtet habe (hätten), der mündliche Bericht dagegen, der sich in den griechischen Versionen der Ereignisse um die Thronbesteigung des Dareios gespiegelt finde und Anleihen bei Themen der iranischen Epik und iranisch-kosmologischen Konzepten erkennen lasse, an ein der Mündlichkeit verpflichtetes iranisches Publikum. Auf diese mündlichen Versionen gingen schließlich auch die meisten thematischen und linguistischen Parallelen zwischen den achaimenidischen und sasanidischen Inschriftencorpora zurück.[31]

Unabhängig von dieser – in meinen Augen ansprechenden – Theorie bleibt die Frage zu stellen, wie in einer oralen Kultur – aber nicht nur dort – einem illiteraten Publikum historisch-politische oder administrative Zusammenhänge haben erklärt und Anweisungen gegeben werden können. Personen wie Herolde, Ausrufer/Verkünder, Vorleser, Sänger, Geschichtenerzähler, sind im administrativ-politischen Zeugnisbefund aus dem teispidisch-achaimenidischen Iran leider nicht bezeugt, müssen damals aber auf jeden Fall im Iran eine bedeutsame Rolle gespielt haben.

VI Ausblick

Traditionsbestimmend für die iranische Sicht von Geschichte sind die an historischen Fakten orientierten, wiewohl vielfach ideologisch verbrämten und die funktionellen epigraphischen, numismatischen und archäologischen Zeugnisse aus dem Iran der Perserkönige, in unserem konkreten Fall vor allem die Inschriften der Achaimeniden

---

29 Shayegan 2012; Shayegan 2017, 442–444.
30 Zu den Vorbildern des Bisutunreliefs s. nun Rollinger 2016.
31 Shayegan 2012.

und das administrative Schriftgut aus Persepolis, Baktrien und von anderen Plätzen, nicht geworden. Auch dafür dürfte der Vorrang des gesprochenen vor dem geschriebenen Wort verantwortlich gewesen sein: Den frühen Sasaniden, obgleich, wie die Teispiden und die Achaimeniden, aus Fārs stammend, waren jedenfalls Kyros und seine Nachfolger namentlich und in ihrem konkreten Tun wohl nicht mehr bekannt, vermutlich, weil prestigeträchtige, möglicherweise religiös besonders aufgeladene ostiranische (kayānidische) Tradition die ‚historische' Überlieferung Südwestirans in eben diesen Teilen ersetzt hatte; und auch die *dramatis personae* der Reliefs von Dareios und seinen Nachfolgern dürften von den Einheimischen schon vor dem 3. Jahrhundert n. Chr. mit legendären Figuren und/oder Gestalten der iranischen Heldensage in Verbindung gebracht worden sein.

Die iranischen vorislamischen 'historischen' Traditionen, die lange Zeit den Regeln oraler Vermittlung unterworfen waren und erst in spät- oder gar nachsasanidischer Zeit schriftlich niedergelegt wurden, waren allerdings wohl viel weniger einförmig, als man lange Zeit angenommen hat – geprägt von der Vorstellung einer normativen und offiziösen "Herrenbuch-" (*Xwadāy-nāmag*)-Tradition. Und auch die Wege, auf denen diese Traditionen Eingang fanden in die frühislamische historiographische Tradition waren vermutlich deutlich vielfältiger und verwobener als früher angenommen. Immerhin lagen Jahrhunderte zwischen der Schöpfung des ersten *Xwadāy-nāmags* und der Edition von Firdausīs „Königsbuch" (*Šāhnāmeh*), von Werken, die man oft genug allzu leichtfertig aufeinander bezieht, ohne die Zwischenglieder, die unterschiedlichen Genreregeln aller dieser Werke, die Wirk- und Auftragsabsichten von Autoren und Auftraggebern genügend zu berücksichtigen. Manch anderes ‚historische' Material lief zudem im Iran der spätsasanidischen und frühislamischen Zeit um, Material, das der Fihrist mit seinen Titeln aufführt. Und auch die Formen der Bearbeitung dieses Materials durch die muslimischen Autoren und die Wege der Übermittlung von den ersten Übersetzungen mittelpersischer Stoffe ins Arabische zur frühabbasidischen Historiographie sind wohl komplizierter zu denken als bislang angenommen.[32]

Eine wachsende literarische Lesegesellschaft dürfen wir wohl erst für den Iran des 6./7. Jahrhunderts n. Chr. annehmen, eine elitäre Gesellschaft, die, in Nachahmung von und Konkurrenz zu der in Ostrom und in den christlichen Gemeinschaften, zunehmend daran interessiert war, religiöse, aber auch historische Überlieferung schriftlich niederzulegen. Allerdings wäre es falsch, eine vornehmlich orale Kultur an den Maßstäben einer literaten zu messen. Und die Einführung eines Schriftsystems, wie etwa das der weitgehend phonetischen, "ja fast phonematischen" avestischen Schrift[33] in spätsasanidischer Zeit, ist ja nicht gleichzusetzen mit dem Verschwinden

---

32 Zu all diesen Problemen erwarten wir inständig Jaakko Hämeen-Anttilas angekündigte Studie zum *Xwadāy-nāmag* und seinem Einfluss auf die arabische und persische Historiographie.
33 Durkin-Meisterernst 2013, 242.

oraler, in diesem Falle religiöser, Traditionen, genauso wie die Existenz einer schriftlichen, vom Zentrum bestimmten, ‚historischen' Sicht auf die Geschichte nicht das Aussterben oraler und literaler regionaler oder lokaler Traditionen bedeutet.

Was allerdings Sprache und Schrift in unmittelbarer postachaimenidischer Zeit angeht, so ist zu beobachten, dass einerseits die Keilschrift als Schriftsystem im Iran schon früh außer Gebrauch kam, dass andererseits die für die Verwaltung des Teispiden- und Achaimenidenreiches so bedeutsame aramäische Sprache und Schrift den Rahmen für die Verschriftung der meisten mitteliranischen Sprachen bildete: des Mittelpersischen, des Parthischen, des Sogdischen und des vorislamischen Choresmischen. Man hat diesen Prozess der Verschriftlichung dabei „als ein allmähliches Eindringen der jeweiligen iranischen Sprache in ein zunächst noch aramäisch gehaltenes Kommunikationsmittel" verstehen wollen.[34] Aber selbst mit Hilfe dieser gegenüber der Keilschrift deutlich leichter erlernbaren und im Alltag leichter handhabbaren Schriftsysteme gelang es dem geschriebenen Wort nicht, das gesprochene Wort, jenseits von Königsinschrift, Münzlegende und administrativem Schriftgut, aus seiner führenden Stellung im Iran zu verdrängen. Das Auswendiglernen von Gehörtem, das Rezitieren von erlernten, d. h. gehörten und nachgesprochenen Hymnen und Gebeten im Gottesdienst, aber auch das Hören auf mündliche Anweisungen und der Wunsch, den Darlegungen von Geschichtenerzählern oder Sängern lauschen zu können, bestimmten weiterhin den Alltag der meisten Menschen im Iran.

Bibliographie

ADAMIK 2006 = B. ADAMIK, Nyelvpolitika a római birodalomban (Language Policy in the Roman Empire), Budapest 2006.

ÁLVAREZ-MON/GARRISON 2011 = J. ÁLVAREZ-MON/M.B. GARRISON (ed.), Elam and Persia, Winona Lake 2010.

BRIANT 1996 = P. BRIANT, Histoire de l'Empire Perse. De Cyrus à Alexandre, Paris 1996.

DURKIN-MEISTERERNST 2013 = D. DURKIN-MEISTERERNST, Mitteliranisch, in: L. PAUL (ed.), Handbuch der Iranistik, Wiesbaden 2013, 239–257.

FOLMER 1995 = M.L. FOLMER, The Aramaic Language in the Achaemenid Period: A Study in Linguistic Variation, Leuven 1995.

FOLMER 2009 = M.L. FOLMER, Alt- und Reichsaramäisch, in: H. GZELLA (ed.), Sprachen aus der Welt des Alten Testaments, Darmstadt 2009, 104–131.

FOLMER 2011 = M.L. FOLMER, Imperial Aramaic as an Administrative Language of the Achaemenid Period, in: M.P. STRECK et al. (ed.), The Semitic Languages: An International Handbook, Berlin/New York 2011, 587–598.

FOLMER 2017 = M.L. FOLMER, Bactria and Egypt. Administration as Mirrored in the Aramaic Sources, in: B. JACOBS/W.F.M. HENKELMAN/M.W. STOLPER (ed.), Die Verwaltung im Achämenidenreich. Imperiale Muster und Strukturen / Administration in the Achaemenid Empire: Tracing the Imperial Signature. Akten des 6. Internationalen Kolloquiums zum Thema »Vorderasien im

---

34 DURKIN-MEISTERERNST 2013, 242.

Spannungsfeld klassischer und altorientalischer Überlieferungen« aus Anlass der 80-Jahr-Feier der Entdeckung des Festungsarchivs von Persepolis, Landgut Castelen bei Basel, 14.–17. Mai 2013, Wiesbaden 2017, 414–454.

Frye 1955 = R.N. Frye, Review of G.R. Driver, Aramaic Documents of the Fifth Century B.C., Oxford 1954, *Harvard Journal of Asiatic Studies* 18, 1955, 456–461.

Garrison 2011 = M.A. Garrison, By the Favor of Auramazdā: Kingship and the Divine in the Early Achaemenid Period, in: P.P. Iossif/A.S. Chankowski/C.C. Lorber (ed.), More than Men – Less than Gods. Studies on Royal Cult and Imperial Worship, Leuven 2011, 15–105.

Gzella 2014 = H. Gzella, Review of J. Naveh/S. Shaked (ed.), Aramaic Documents from Ancient Bactria, London 2012, *Bibliotheca Orientalis* 71, 2014, 816–823.

Henkelman 2008 = W.F.M. Henkelman, The Other Gods Who Are. Studies in Elamite-Iranian Acculturation Based on the Persepolis Fortification Texts (Achaemenid History XIV), Leiden 2008.

Henkelman 2011 = W.F.M. Henkelman, Cyrus the Persian and Darius the Elamite: a Case of Mistaken Identity, in: R. Rollinger/B. Truschnegg/R. Bichler (ed.), Herodot und das Persische Weltreich / Herodotus and the Persian Empire, Wiesbaden 2011, 577–634.

Henkelman 2017 = W.F.M. Henkelman, Humban and Auramazdā. Royal Gods in a Persian Landscape, in: W.F.M. Henkelman/C. Redard (ed.), Persian Religion in the Achaemenid Period / La religion perse à l'époque achéménide, Wiesbaden 2017, 273–345.

Huyse 2008 = Ph. Huyse, Late Sasanian Society between Orality and Literacy, in: V.S. Curtis/S. Stewart (ed.), The Sasanian Era (The Idea of Iran 3), London 2008, 140–157.

Jursa 2012 = M. Jursa, Ein Beamter flucht auf Aramäisch: Alphabetschreiber in der spätbabylonischen Epistolographie und die Rolle des Aramäischen in der babylonischen Verwaltung des sechsten Jahrhunderts v. Chr., in: G.B. Lanfranchi et al. (ed.), Leggo! Studies Presented to Frederick Mario Fales on the Occasion of his 65th Birthday, Wiesbaden 2012, 379–397.

Macuch 2009 = M. Macuch, Pahlavi Literature, in: R.E. Emmerick/M. Macuch (ed.), The Literature of Pre-Islamic Iran, London 2009, 116–196.

Macuch 2013 = M. Macuch, Iranische Literaturen in vorislamischer Zeit, in: L. Paul (ed.), Handbuch der Iranistik, Wiesbaden 2013, 281–311.

Naveh/Shaked 2012 = J. Naveh/S. Shaked (ed.), Aramaic Documents from Ancient Bactria (Fourth Century BCE.). From the Khalili Collections, London 2012.

Rollinger 2011 = R. Rollinger, Herrscherkult und Königsvergöttlichung bei Teispiden und Achaimeniden. Realität oder Fiktion?, in: L.-M. Günther/S. Plischke (ed.), Studien zum vorhellenistischen und hellenistischen Herrscherkult, Berlin 2011, 11–54.

Rollinger 2016 = R. Rollinger, The Relief at Bisitun and its Ancient Near Eastern Setting: Contextualizing the Visual Vocabulary of Darius' Triumph over Gaumata, in: C. Binder/H. Börm/A. Luther (ed.), Diwan. Untersuchungen zu Geschichte und Kultur des Nahen Ostens und des östlichen Mittelmeerraumes im Altertum. Festschrift für Josef Wiesehöfer zum 65. Geburtstag, Duisburg 2016, 5–51.

Rossi 2017a = A.V. Rossi, Ten Years of Achaemenid Philology: Old Persian & Achaemenid Elamite 2006–2016, in: E. Morano/E. Provasi/A.V. Rossi (ed.), Studia Philologica Iranica. Gherardo Gnoli Memorial Volume, Roma 2017, 359–394.

Rossi 2017b = A.V. Rossi, "… how Median the Medes were?" État d'une question longuement débattue, in: W.F.M. Henkelman/C. Redard (ed.), Persian Religion in the Achaemenid Period / La religion perse à l'époque achéménide (Classica et Orientalia 16), Wiesbaden 2017, 461–495.

Schmitt 1984 = R. Schmitt, Zur Ermittlung von Dialekten in altiranischer Zeit, *Sprachwissenschaft* 9, 1984, 183–207.

SCHMITT 1989a = R. SCHMITT, Altpersisch, in: R. SCHMITT (ed.), Compendium Linguarum Iranicarum, Wiesbaden 1989, 56–85.

SCHMITT 1989b = R. SCHMITT, Andere altiranische Dialekte, in: R. SCHMITT (ed.), Compendium Linguarum Iranicarum, Wiesbaden 1989, 86–94.

SCHMITT 1999 = R. SCHMITT, Beiträge zu altpersischen Inschriften, Wiesbaden 1999.

SCHMITT 2003 = R. SCHMITT, Die Sprache der Meder – eine große Unbekannte, in: G.B. LANFRANCHI/M. ROAF/R. ROLLINGER (ed.), Continuity of Empire (?): Assyria, Media, Persia, Padova 2003, 23–36.

SHAYEGAN 2012 = M.R. SHAYEGAN, Aspects of History and Epic in Ancient Iran. From Gaumāta to Wahnām, Cambridge, MA/London 2012.

SHAYEGAN 2017 = M.R. SHAYEGAN, Persianism: Or Achaemenid Reminiscences in the Iranian and Iranicate World(s) of Antiquity, in: R. STROOTMAN/M.J. VERSLUYS (ed.), Persianism in Antiquity, Stuttgart 2017, 401–455.

STROH 2007 = W. STROH, Latein ist tot, es lebe Latein! Kleine Geschichte einer großen Sprache, Berlin 2007.

TAVERNIER 2008 = J. TAVERNIER, Multilingualism in the Fortification and Treasury Archives, in: P. BRIANT/W.F.M. HENKELMAN/M.W. STOLPER (ed.), L'archive des Fortifications de Persépolis. État des questions et perspectives de recherches, Paris 2008, 59–86.

TAVERNIER 2017 = J. TAVERNIER, The Use of Languages on the Various Levels of Administration in the Achaemenid Empire, in: B. JACOBS/W.F.M. HENKELMAN/M.W. STOLPER (ed.), Die Verwaltung im Achämenidenreich. Imperiale Muster und Strukturen / Administration in the Achaemenid Empire: Tracing the Imperial Signature. Akten des 6. Internationalen Kolloquiums zum Thema »Vorderasien im Spannungsfeld klassischer und altorientalischer Überlieferungen« aus Anlass der 80-Jahr-Feier der Entdeckung des Festungsarchivs von Persepolis, Landgut Castelen bei Basel, 14.–17. Mai 2013, Wiesbaden 2017, 337–412.

Irene Madreiter
Der Raum alltäglicher weiblicher Literalität im Achaimeniden-Reich

Abstract: The article examines the place of female literacy within general everyday literacy in the Achaemenid period. Whereas the Achaemenid heartland lacks of sources written by women, we have abundant private correspondence from the other satrapies of the empire (Babylonia, Egypt, Bactria etc.). Therefore the lacuna from the Persis-region is not coincidental but resulting from the specific social structure of the empire with its dominant hegemonic manliness. This prevented a wider spread of literacy and the Achaemenid heartland remained an orally dominated culture with a functional literacy limited to the elite and higher levels of society.

Zusammenfassung: Der Beitrag geht der Frage nach, welchen Stellenwert alltägliche weibliche Literalität in einer oral geprägten Kultur wie jener des Achaimeniden-Reiches hatte. Im Gegensatz zu den Randzonen des Reiches, aus denen sich zahlreiche Belege für die private Verwendung von Schrift erhalten haben, fehlen solche Zeugnisse aus den Kernländern. Dies ist nicht auf die Verwendung vergänglichen Schriftmaterials zurückzuführen, sondern spiegelt typische Merkmale der Gesellschaftsstruktur, also die realen gesellschaftlichen Verhältnisse der achaimenidischen Kernländer wider, die weiblicher Literalität keinen Platz zumaß.

Einleitung

„… Ich zwar habe dich gerettet, und du wurdest durch mich gerettet, ich aber wurde durch dich vernichtet und habe selbst mich getötet; denn du wolltest mir keine Gunst erweisen …"[1]

Diese Zeilen schrieb ein General der achaimenidischen Armee laut Ktesias von Knidos auf ein Stück Leder, bevor er sich aus unerfüllter Liebe zur Saken-Königin das Leben nahm. Auch Herodot weiß, dass die achaimenidische Elite auf offizieller, aber hauptsächlich inoffizieller Ebene mittels Briefen verkehrte, die von Boten an die jeweiligen Adressaten übermittelt wurden. Etwas kurios mutet beispielsweise die Episode an, in der der medische Adelige Harpagos Kyros dem Älteren eine Geheim-

---

Anmerkung: Der Aufsatz entstand im Rahmen eines APART-Stipendiums der österreichischen Akademie der Wissenschaften. Ich danke Wouter Henkelman, John Hyland, Bruno Jacobs, Robert Rollinger, Christopher Tuplin und Josef Wiesehöfer für Anmerkungen und Diskussion.

---

[1] P. Oxy. XXII 2330 (BNJ 688 F 8b); s.a. Demetr. de eloc. 213–215, ausgebaut bei Nik. v. Damask. de virt. 1 p.335,20 (BNJ 90 F 5). Die fehlende Historizität der Episode ist in unserem Zusammenhang nicht relevant.

botschaft mit der Aufforderung zum Sturz des Meder-Königs zukommen ließ, indem er das Papier (βυβλίον) in den Bauch eines Hasen einnähte.² Es gibt also in den westlichen Quellen ein rudimentäres Wissen über Schriftlichkeit innerhalb der Eliten des Achaimeniden-Reiches. Aussagen über alltägliche Literalität jenseits der Eliten sind aus beiden Werken nicht zu gewinnen.

Im Vergleich dazu fließen die indigenen Schriftquellen zahlreicher, weisen jedoch eine andere Eigenheit auf: In achaimenidischer Zeit konnte die Verwendung von Schrift im Vorderen Orient auf eine bereits 2500-jährige Geschichte blicken, während der die Keilschrift zur Wiedergabe verschiedener Sprachen verwendet wurde. Dennoch scheint die Bedeutung von Schrift für den alltäglichen Gebrauch nun plötzlich geringer als in früheren Epochen gewesen zu sein, besonders in den achaimenidischen Kernländern, also der Persis, Elam und Medien. Dies ist umso erstaunlicher, als es die achaimenidische Verwaltung aufgrund der enormen Reichsausdehnung, – unter Dareios I. immerhin von Thrakien über Kleinasien, die Levante, Ägypten bis Indien, Afghanistan und Zentralasien–, mit unterschiedlichen Verwaltungssystemen³ und Sprachen zu tun hatte. Die ethnische Diversität war den achaimenidischen Königen durchaus bewusst. Sie drückten sie innerhalb ihrer Titulatur mit dem Terminus *paruzana-* "containing many (kinds) of men"⁴ aus. In der Praxis war es also eine große Herausforderung, Befehle zu kommunizieren, so dass sie auch von Nicht-Persern verstanden wurden.

Aus dem vordergründigen Fehlen von alltäglicher Literalität in den Kernländern ergeben sich folgende Fragen: Welchen gesellschaftlichen Raum nahm Literalität im Achaimeniden-Reich generell ein? Brauchte das Achaimeniden-Reich tatsächlich keine Schriftlichkeit auf gesellschaftlich unteren Ebenen? Ist dies im Vergleich zu früheren Reichsgebilden wie Assyrien, Babylonien, Ägypten und besonders auch Elam ein Rückschritt? Oder verstehen wir den Befund aufgrund der unvollständigen Quellenlage heute falsch? Welchen Raum konnte innerhalb dieses Befundes weibliche Literalität beanspruchen? Gerade dieser letzte Punkt verlangt Aufmerksamkeit und leitet zur These dieses Aufsatzes über. Trotz der unbefriedigenden Quellenlage ist besonders das Fehlen weiblicher Literalität (auf jeder sozialen Ebene!) in der Persis kein Zufall. Im Gegenteil legt der Vergleich mit den Randgebieten des Reiches nahe,

---

2 Hdt. 1,123,3–124,3. Bsp. für Briefe der Großkönige: Kyros an Kyaxares in Xen. Kyr. 4,5,26–34; Dareios an Megabazos in Hdt. 5,14,2; Xerxes an Pausanias in Thuk. 1,29,3; Artaxerxes an die Spartaner in Thuk. 4,15; Artaxerxes II. an die verfeindeten Griechen Xen. hell. 7,1,36–37; 5,1,31. Vgl. auch Esr 4,17–22; 6,6–12; 7,12–26 oder Est 3,12.
3 Die komplexe Struktur der Verwaltung hat zuletzt HENKELMAN 2017, 45–256 dargelegt.
4 TAVERNIER 2008, 59 ff.; TAVERNIER (im Druck) 2; *paruzana-* in der Formel *xšāyaθiya dahyunām paruzanānām* "king of countries containing many kinds of men" (DE 15–16, XE 15–16, A¹Pa 11–12); akkadisch übersetzt als *ša naphar lišānu* "of all tongues" (XPa 7, XPc 10, XPd 11, XPh 6; XV 15). Zu den Länder-Listen siehe JACOBS 2017, 3 ff.; zur dahinter stehenden Herrscherideologie siehe zuletzt ROLLINGER 2017, 189–215.

dass dieser Befund typische Merkmale der Gesellschaftsstruktur, also die realen gesellschaftlichen Verhältnisse der achaimenidischen Kernländer widerspiegelt.

Als hier zu untersuchende Alltagsdokumente kommen Verträge im privaten Umfeld, wie Schuldscheine, Verkäufe oder andere wirtschaftliche Transaktionen, zu privaten Zwecken erstellte Listen oder beschriftete Gegenstände in Frage. Besondere Aufmerksamkeit wird im Folgenden den Privat-Briefen gewidmet, da sie Rückschlüsse auf Literalität in den unteren Schichten zulassen. All diese Dokumente sind zahlenmäßig und geographisch unterschiedlich verteilt, stammen aber vor allem aus den Randzonen des Reiches wie Kleinasien, Ägypten, Mesopotamien oder Baktrien.[5]

Die heute geringe Anzahl an schriftlichen Zeugnissen ist bis zu einem gewissen Grad mit dem leicht vergänglichen Schreibmaterial in kausale Verbindung zu bringen: Die Tontafeln aus dem Persepolis-Archiv verdanken ihre relativ gute Erhaltung dem Faktum, dass sie bei der Zerstörung des Ortes unabsichtlich gebrannt wurden und dadurch die Jahrhunderte teilweise besser überdauerten. Die Bisutun-Inschrift wurde laut Paragraph 70 sowohl auf Ton als auch Leder verbreitet, wobei Leder den Ton mit den Jahren ersetzt haben dürfte.[6] Auf höchster Verwaltungsebene fand nach Ausweis der Persepolis-Täfelchen auch Pergament häufig Einsatz.[7] Dieses hat sich, abgesehen von ein paar Fragmenten aus Ägypten und Baktrien, ebenso selten erhalten wie Holz. Nach Informationen von Kolophonen der Tontafeln dürfte das Verhältnis zwischen Ton und Holztafeln ursprünglich 1 zu 3 betragen haben. Keinerlei Spuren gibt es hingegen von Wachs, das in griechischen Quellen genannt wird.[8] Umso bedeutender sind die aus Ägypten erhaltenen Papyri und Ostraka.

Auch wenn das vorhandene Quellenmaterial in den letzten Jahrzehnten durch Neufunde angewachsen ist, lässt es sich in Bezug auf die Frage nach der generellen Literalität nur begrenzt auswerten. Häufig sind auf den Tafeln oder Papyri keine Namen der Verfasser/innen erhalten, zudem mangelt es an Informationen zum sozialen Status der genannten Personen, wenn z. B. Berufsangaben fehlen. Dadurch lässt sich der endgültige Beweis, ob es sich bei den Schreibenden um Mitglieder der Elite oder sozial unterer Schichten handelte, oft nicht erbringen. Die Frage, ob die

---

5 Zahlenmäßig am häufigsten sind Dokumente in aramäischer Sprache, siehe die generellen Zusammenstellungen von NAVEH 1970; FOLMER 1995; GZELLA (im Druck); MILLARD 2003; LEMAIRE 2017, 469 ff.; SILJANEN 2017. Die alttestamentlichen Bücher Ester, Judit oder Daniel wurden bewusst nicht miteinbezogen, da sie keine Aussagen zu alltäglicher Schriftlichkeit zulassen.
6 Leder als Schreibmaterial: PF 323, PF 1986. Schreiber: PF 1808, PF 1810, PF 1947, PFa 27, PFNN 0061, PFNN 1040, PFNN 1255, PFNN 1369, PFNN 1511, PFNN 1752, PFNN 1775, PFNN 2394, PFNN 2486, PFNN 2493, PFNN 2529.
7 PFNN 1747; die meisten Schreiber auf Pergament waren von Parnakka oder Ziššawiš beauftragt, d. h. sie waren Mitarbeiter der höchsten Administration.
8 Demaratos schrieb am persischen Hof eine geheime Botschaft auf das Holz einer Wachstafel, die er danach wieder mit Wachs bedeckte und nach Sparta sandte, Hdt. 7,239. Wachstafeln mit Elfenbein-Fassungen aus neuassyrischer Zeit stammen bspw. aus Ninive und Kalḫu, vgl. WISEMAN 1955, 3–13; CHARPIN 2010, 73, 75.

Absender/innen von Briefen auch tatsächlich schreibkundig waren oder ihre Briefe in Auftrag gaben, ist aus heutiger Sicht ebenso nur mehr schwer zu beantworten. Einiges deutet darauf hin, dass sich illiterate Personen oft naher Verwandter als Substitute zum Schreiben oder Lesen von Nachrichten bedienten.[9] Schwierig abzuschätzen ist auch die alltägliche Bedeutung des Vorlesens von Briefen durch Boten, wie sie auf offizieller Ebene häufig und gut bezeugt ist.[10] Wenngleich aufgrund dieser Probleme einige Aussagen spekulativ bleiben müssen, soll im Folgenden doch eine vorsichtige Einschätzung der gesellschaftlichen Einbettung von Literalität erfolgen. Chronologisch behandelt die Untersuchung vor allem die ersten Jahrhunderte der achaimenidischen Herrschaft, jedoch sind aufgrund der spezifischen Quellenlage zum Vergleich auch Rückblicke in frühere Jahrhunderte nötig.

1 War das Achaimeniden-Reich eine Schriftkultur?

Den Ausgangspunkt für die Frage nach dem Grad der Literalität im Achaimeniden-Reich bilden Studien zu anderen antiken Kulturen, in denen aus den Quellen konkretes Zahlenmaterial zur Literalität abgeleitet wurde. W. HARRIS versuchte dies bereits 1989 für das antike Griechenland.[11] Er kam zu dem Schluss, dass die generelle Literalitätsrate in Griechenland und Rom bis 100 v. Chr. kaum 10 % der männlichen Gesamtbevölkerung überschritten habe. Auch wenn generelle Zahlenangaben das Bild verzerren, weil sie lokale Besonderheiten und zeitliche Unterschiede außer Acht lassen[12], scheinen sie für Griechenland und Rom realistisch, da sie prämodernen agrarischen Gesellschaften entsprechen. Von einer ähnlichen Literalitätsrate geht daher auch F. LI für die chinesischen Qin und Han-Dynastien aus.[13] Wenn man in diese Berechnungen Frauen inkludiert, dann vermindert sich der Prozentsatz an Schreibkundigen um mindestens die Hälfte, das heißt, auf 5–7 % der Gesamtbevölkerung.[14]

---

9 Dies konnte YOUTIE 1971, 239–261 oder 1975, 201–211 für das ptolemäische Ägypten nachweisen. HARRIS 1989, 33–35 spricht daher von einer „second-hand literacy".
10 Die angeblich riesige Anzahl von Boten und Gesandten, wird mehrfach im Zusammenhang mit dem ausgefeilten achaimenidischen Postsystem erwähnt, vgl. Aristot. mund. 398a, 30–35; Hdt. 8,8,1–2; Xen. Kyr. 8,6,17–18. BRIANT 2002, 91 f., 101 f., 369 ff, 376 f.; zu den Medien der Kommunikation s. a. WIESEHÖFER (in diesem Band) und JACOBS 2015.
11 HARRIS 1989, 114, 173, 328–330; auch in HARRIS/LI 2015, 14, 30.
12 So nimmt HARRIS 1989, 328 f. höhere Prozentzahlen für das klassische Athen (15 % der erwachsenen Männer) oder für die hellenistische Zeit (regional bis zu 30 oder 40 % der freigeborenen Männer) an. In diesem Punkt folgt ihm auch THOMAS 2009, 357.
13 Siehe den Beitrag von LI in diesem Band, und in HARRIS/LI 2015, 30. Dennoch ist ihre Schätzung für die Han Dynastie alleine deutlich geringer: "…the literate people in the Han Empire all combined would still amount to less than 3 percent of the Han population."
14 COLE 1981, 219 ff.; HARRIS 1989, 106, 142 f., 264, 268, 328, 330; THOMAS 2009, 358.

P. MICHALOWSKI konstatiert für den Vorderen Orient hingegen, dass "in Western Asia and Egypt no more than 2–5 % of the population could read and write.[15]" Speziell für das alte Ägypten nehmen einige Forscher eine noch geringere Zahl an, konkret 1 % der Bevölkerung. Dies entspräche je nach Periode der ägyptischen Geschichte zwischen 10.000 und 50.000 Menschen.[16] Die Hauptschwäche der genannten Studien ist, dass unklar bleibt, welche Arten von Literalität den Prozentangaben zugrunde liegen. Gilt jemand auch als literat, der nur seine Unterschrift unter ein Dokument setzen konnte? Daher vermeiden jüngere Arbeiten konkrete Prozentsätze. D. CHARPIN geht aufgrund eigener Studien, sowie ähnlicher Ergebnisse von Kollegen[17] davon aus, dass die Literalitätsrate in Mesopotamien höher als ursprünglich angenommen war. Für das Achaimeniden-Reich gibt es vor allem eine recht pessimistische Einschätzung M. DANDAMAYEVs, die Ausgangspunkt für die weiteren Ausführungen sein soll: „Even nobles and highly placed Persian civil servants were illiterate, and writing played no part in standard Persian education.[18]" Da die Quellenlage für die achaimenidische Zeit fragmentierter als für andere antike Kulturen ist, werden im Folgenden keine weiteren Zahlenspekulationen getätigt. Stattdessen ist zu fragen, welche Arten von Literalität sich unter den gegebenen Voraussetzungen entwickeln konnten.

Moderne Studien aus den Bereichen der Kognitionsforschung, oder der Sprachwissenschaft machten deutlich, dass es diverse Typen von Literalität innerhalb einer untersuchten Kultur gibt und nicht jede Person jedes Level erreicht. Für die klassische Antike differenzierte der bereits genannte W. HARRIS zwischen einer „scribal literacy", die in den frühen Hochkulturen des Vorderen Orients dominierend gewesen sei, und einer „craftsman's literacy" als Zustand, bei dem die Mehrheit der ausgebildeten Handwerker literat gewesen sei, – dies jedoch im Gegensatz zu Frauen und Bauern.[19] Eine solche Unterteilung greift für den Vorderen Orient allgemein zu kurz, da es (mit Ausnahme der achaimenidenzeitlichen Persis) genügend Zeugnisse für schreibende Frauen und Bauern gibt. LI erweitert den Begriff der „scribal literacy", indem er für das frühe China von einer „elite literacy" spricht. Damit verortet er Schreib- und Lesefähigkeit nicht nur innerhalb der Berufsgruppe der Schreiber, sondern generell innerhalb der politischen, militärischen oder landbesitzenden Eliten, sowie der Händler.[20]

---

15 MICHALOWSKI 1992, 57; VANSTIPHOUT 1995, 2187, folgt ihm in dieser sehr vorsichtigen Schätzung.
16 BAINES 1983, 584: „In most periods not more than one percent of the population were literate".
17 CHARPIN 2010, 53 ff., CHARPIN 2004, 489–491 bezugnehmend auf PARPOLA 1997 und WILCKE 2000.
18 DANDAMAYEV 1997, 178.
19 HARRIS 1989, 8–9: (Scribal literacy) „predominated in the ancient Near Eastern cultures, …, (and was) restricted to a specialized social group which used it for such purposes as maintaining palace records." Dagegen sei die craftman's literacy "a condition, in which the majority or a near majority of skilled craftsmen are literate, while women and unskilled labourers and peasants are mainly not." Wieder aufgenommen in HARRIS/LI 2015, 7.
20 Definition von LI in diesem Band: "…"elite literacy" was a condition of literacy that a large number of the social elites, whose total size could still be very small when compared to the overall population,

Niek VELDHUIS verfolgt einen anderen Ansatz, indem er nicht die sozialen Schichten der Träger von Literalität ins Auge nimmt, sondern von den erhaltenen Textsorten ausgeht. Er unterscheidet für Mesopotamien je nach orthographischer Komplexität der Inhalte eine funktionale, technische und wissenschaftliche Literalität.[21] Die beiden letztgenannten Kategorien bezeichnen zwei professionelle Level, wobei sich die technische Literalität auf die spezialisierte Sprache von Omina oder mathematischen Texten[22] bezieht und die „gelehrte Literalität" jene der ausgebildeten Schreibprofis bezeichnet, die seltene Lesungen verwendeten und alle *do's and don'ts* der Keilschrift beherrschten.[23] Für unsere Fragestellung ist die „functional literacy" am interessantesten, unter der VELDHUIS jenes nicht-professionelle Level der Kenntnis von Keilschrift versteht, das ausreichend ist, um private Dokumente selbst lesen oder schreiben zu können. Dass dies jedoch nicht die unterste mögliche Stufe an Literalität darstellt, ist auch klar. Die sogenannte „signature-literacy" beschreibt, wenn eine Person wenigstens ihren eigenen Namen schreiben und lesen kann.[24] Damit einher geht jedoch kein weiteres Lese- oder Schreibverständnis. Zumindest diese Stufe ist für weite Teile des Achaimeniden-Reiches wahrscheinlich zu machen, wogegen die Verbreitung einer „functional" und einer „craftmen's literacy" unterhalb der Eliten nur in bestimmten Regionen zu belegen ist.

Welche Funktionen hatte das geschriebene Wort nun innerhalb der achaimenidisch-altpersischen Kultur, in der Schriftlichkeit noch keine jahrhundertlange Tradition hatte? Jan ASSMANN hat für die Frühgeschichte Ägyptens und Mesopotamiens mehrere Funktionsbereiche der Schrift definiert: Wirtschaft, Religion, Kult und Divination, politische Repräsentation und in Ägypten auch monumentale Grabarchitektur.[25] Hingegen beschränken sich die Funktionen von Schrift in den achaimenidischen Kernländern auf ihre Buchhalterfunktion und auf einige wenige Monumental- und Prestigeinschriften[26], also eine offizielle, im weitesten Sinne politische Funktion. Es gibt beispielsweise keine indigenen literarischen Texte, keine religiösen Aufzeichnun-

---

developed enough familiarity with, and appreciated, the art of writing and reading, and many were indeed able to employ such ability when needed".
21 VELDHUIS 2011, 71–74.
22 Also Texte, die sich einer gewissen Fachsprache bedienen, aber mit relativ wenigen Lesungen und Zeichen auskommen. VELDHUIS 2011, 73 f.
23 Als typische Charakteristika nennt er die Verwendung seltener Lesungen, Kenntnisse in Paläographie, oder das Verfassen komplexer Textsorten wie Königsinschriften, vgl. VELDHUIS 2011, 74.
24 THOMAS (2009, 357) nennt dort auch weitere Subtypen, die es im antiken Griechenland in unterschiedlicher Ausprägung gegeben habe, wie die „list-literacy", die „commercial literacy" oder die „banking literacy".
25 ASSMANN 2010, 14.
26 Vgl. die in Susa gefundenen Alabastergefäße aus Ägypten mit einer viersprachigen Königsinschrift, vgl. WESTENHOLZ/STOLPER 2002; zur Bedeutung der Gefäße siehe HENKELMAN 2017, 104.

gen, keine Rechtstexte oder Verträge, und in der Persis keine beschrifteten Münzen[27] oder Namen als Besitzanzeiger[28] auf alltäglichen Gegenständen. Gänzlich fehlen aus den Kernländern auch Grafitti und Ostraka. Dieser Befund kann nicht allein mit der schwierigen Quellenlage erklärt werden, sondern entspricht dem, was Jan ASSMANN als „sektorale Schriftlichkeit" bezeichnet. Seiner Definition zufolge wird Schrift hier zwar in einzelnen kulturellen Bereichen eingesetzt (wie Wirtschaft und Verwaltung, Kult und Divination, Gräber und Grabausstattung) und kann gerade im Bereich der Wirtschaft auch durchaus in untersten Schichten Verwendung finden, aber es handelt sich um keine volle Schriftkultur.[29] Eine solche sieht er erst in der „kulturellen Schriftlichkeit" vollzogen, in der Schrift „zur Fixierung und Zirkulation der kulturellen, Bildung vermittelnden und identitätsstiftenden Texte" eingesetzt wird.[30] Um eine solche Stufe zu erreichen, muss der Zugang zu Schriftlichkeit durch positive Faktoren, ökonomischer, politischer, sozialer oder ideologischer Natur, begünstigt werden. Beim Fehlen dieser Kräfte bleibt Literalität selbst in jenen Kulturen gering, in denen das geschriebene Wort allgegenwärtig zu sein scheint.[31] Im Achaimeniden-Reich fehlte das Bedürfnis, generelle Literalität durch Technik oder Erziehung zu fördern, da man darin offenbar keinen praktischen Vorteil oder generellen Nutzen sah. Eine „kulturelle Schriftlichkeit" konnte sich daher nicht ausprägen.

2 Alltägliche (männliche) Schriftlichkeit im Achaimeniden-Reich

Alltägliche Schriftlichkeit in den achaimenidischen Kernländern

Im sogenannten Schrifterfindungsparagraph der Bisutun-Inschrift lässt Dareios verlauten:

> „Es kündet Dareios, der König: / Nach dem Willen Ahuramazdas / (ist) dies die Fassung der Inschrift, / die ich hinzugesetzt habe / (und zwar) auf Arisch. / (Auch) auf Ton und auf Pergament wurde sie angebracht .../ Und sie wurde niedergeschrieben / und vor mir vorgelesen./ Daraufhin habe ich diese Fassung der Inschrift ausgesandt / überall in die Länder. / Das Volk kooperierte (dabei)".[32]

---

27 Beschriftete Münzen aus dem späten 5./fr. 4. Jh. v. Chr. haben sich jedoch aus Kilikien und Juda erhalten, s. den Überblick bei NAVEH 1970, 49 ff.
28 Die beschrifteten Siegel von Mitgliedern der Achaimeniden-Familie oder hoher Beamter bilden hier natürlich eine Ausnahme, vgl. z. B. ROOT 2008 oder BROSIUS 2010.
29 ASSMANN 2010, 17.
30 ASSMANN 2010, 20 sieht den Übergang von sektoraler zu kultureller Schriftlichkeit in Ägypten erst am Übergang vom 3. zum 2. Jahrtausend bzw. vom Alten zum Mittleren Reich vollzogen.
31 HARRIS 1989, 11 f.
32 DB § 70 (Kol. IV 87–92), ed. Schmitt. In Sprachen und Schriften aller Länder übersetzt: Est 1,22; 3,12; 8,9.

Die genauen Beweggründe, warum Dareios die altpersische Keilschrift entwickeln ließ, sind nicht gänzlich geklärt.[33] Klar scheint nur, dass es sich um eine Kunstsprache handelt, die vor Dareios nicht verwendet wurde.[34] Die altpersische Schrift war weniger komplex, sie kam mit 34 Zeichen aus und war damit einfacher als die Keilschriften der Elamer (ca. 200 Zeichen) und Babylonier (bis zu 600 Zeichen). Zudem hatte sie zur besseren Lesbarkeit Wort-Trenner, womit sie leichter zu erlernen war. Dass er selbst schreiben konnte, behauptet Dareios ebenfalls in der Bisutun-Inschrift.[35] Damit setzt er sich in eine Reihe berühmter Vorgänger wie Assurbanipal und Nabonid, die sich beide brüsteten, dass sie der Schriftlichkeit mächtig wären.[36] Im Falle des Dareios ist jedoch eher davon auszugehen, dass man an ein Niederschreiben-Lassen der Inschrift denken sollte und weniger an ein aktives Schreiben des Königs.

Die Schrifterfindung kann im Sinne H. SANCISI-WEERDENBURGS[37] als ideologisches Statement der Achaimeniden interpretiert werden, weil die Sprache der neuen Elite damit auf die Ebene der alten Keilschrift-Kulturen gehoben wurde. Damit war sie Symbol der politischen und wirtschaftlichen Macht der persischen Elite, das heißt zugleich, Symbol sozialer Hierarchie und Kontrolle. Die Häufigkeit von Inschriften an Gebäuden oder an hoch gelegenen Felsen legt nahe, dass es bedeutender war, dass diese Schrift gesehen als gelesen wurde.[38] Mittlerweile kennt man aus den Persepolis-Texten auch ein singuläres Beispiel einer altpersisch beschriebenen Verwaltungstafel[39], sodass frühere Annahmen, das Altpersische sei eine reine Monumentalschrift ohne alltäglichen Bezug, revidiert werden müssen. In vier elamischen Tafeln aus der Regierungszeit des Dareios (um 499 v. Chr.) werden „persische Pagen (*puhu*), die Text kopieren[40]" genannt. Sie arbeiteten in Gruppen zu 16 oder 29 Personen und bekamen hohe Zuteilungen von Getreide und Wein. W. HENKELMAN bezeichnet die Gruppe der *puhu* als „elite servant taskforce"[41], die einen Teil der professionellen Gefolgschaft des Reichsadels oder der Königinnen bildeten. Bei den oben genannten 29 *puhu* ist daher

---

33 SANCISI-WEERDENBURG 1999, 91–112; WIESEHÖFER 1998, 27 ff., 33 ff.; BRIANT 2002, 63 ff; 76 f., 126 f.
34 ROSSI (im Druck) 1.
35 DB § 65 (Kol. IV) ed. Schmitt: „Du, wo immer, der du später diese Inschrift siehst, / die ich geschrieben habe (*tayām adam niyapinθam*) / oder diese Abbildungen, / zerstöre sie nicht!"
36 Assurbanipal beschreibt seine Ausbildung in den Einleitungen der Prismen A und F (A I 23–34/F I 18–32, BORGER 1996, 16), und lässt sich mit einem Schreibgriffel darstellen (z. B. auf dem Jagdrelief im Nord-Palast in Niniveh, Raum S). LIVINGSTONE 2007, 100; CHARPIN 2010, 55, 59. Auch die weiblichen Mitglieder seiner Familien konnten schreiben und lesen, s. 130 f.
37 SANCISI-WEERDENBURG 1999, 109.
38 MICHALOSWKI 1992, 58 beobachtet ähnliches für das frühe Mesopotamien: „This was writing intended to be more visible than read." Auch WIESEHÖFER (in diesem Band) betont, dass die Inschriften (wie Münzen oder Teppiche) als Teil der Bilderwelt gesehen werden müssen.
39 STOLPER/TAVERNIER 2007, 5–21; STOLPER (im Druck).
40 *puhu Paršipe tuppime sapi(man)pa*, PF 0871: 4–5; PF 1137: 5–6; PFNN 1485: 5–6; PFNN 1588: 4; TAVERNIER 2008, 64; HENKELMAN 2003, 136.
41 HENKELMAN 2003, 133 ff.

an eine solche unabhängige Arbeitseinheit zu denken, die der höchsten administrativen Ebene zugeteilt war.[42] Ihre Rationen übertrafen mit ca. 45 Liter bei weitem jene der professionellen Schreiber, die zumeist zwischen ca. 20 und 30 Liter Mehl pro Monat erhielten.[43] Es ist durchaus möglich, dass es sich bei den *puhu* um jene spezialisierten Schreiber handelte, die die altpersische Keilschrift lernten, um Repräsentationstexte umsetzen zu können.

Im alltäglichen Gebrauch waren jedoch das Elamische in seiner achaimenidischen Variante sowie das Aramäische als Verwaltungssprachen wesentlich bedeutender als das Altpersische.[44] Wenngleich die Unterschiede in der Funktion der verschiedenen Sprachen und Schriften noch unklar sind, muss von einem Multilingualismus auf allen Ebenen der persischen Verwaltung ausgegangen werden.[45] Aus dem Persepolis-Archiv stammen etwa 30.000[46] elamische und mehr als 800 rein aramäisch geschriebene Tafeln aus der Zeit zwischen 509 und 493 v. Chr.[47] Außerdem wurden in Persepolis 750 nach ihrem Fundort als „Treasury Texts" bezeichnete Tafeln ausgegraben, die Silberzahlungen vom Schatzhaus erfassen.[48] In dieser relativ großen Menge an Texten gibt es keine Hinweise auf die alltägliche Bedeutung von Schrift außerhalb des Verwaltungsbereichs. Für das Aramäische[49] sieht der Befund (zumindest für die Kernländer) ähnlich aus. Aramäisch wurde während der achaimenidischen Herrschaft standardisiert[50] und für die überregionale Kommunikation und lokale Aufzeichnungen verwendet. Es gab also bei den Achaimeniden Bestrebungen, die Verbreitung bestimmter Sprachen in Form einer aktiven Sprachpolitik zu forcieren[51], aber keine Absicht, eine einzelne Schriftart für alle Untertanen zugänglich zu machen. Aramäische Dokumente jenseits der Verwaltungstäfelchen wie Stelen, Grabinschriften oder Graffiti, die Aussagen über den alltäglichen Gebrauch von Schrift zulassen würden,

---

42 Im konkreten Fall unterstanden sie dem Schatzmeister Šuddayanda.
43 Rationen für (babylonische) Schreiber, die als *kurtaš* (d. h. als Abhängige) organisiert waren: PF 1810; PF 1828; PF 1947: 17–18, 21–26, 29–30; PFNN 2394; PFNN 2529; HENKELMAN 2003, 136 mit Fn. 60.
44 Aktuellster Überblick bei STOLPER (im Druck); s. a. den Beitrag von WIESEHÖFER in diesem Band.
45 ROSSI (im Druck) 4 nimmt an, dass man beim Persepolis-Archiv von einem "simultaneous use of several languages and asymmetric interference among them" ausgehen müsse. Zum komplexen Verwaltungsablauf s. TAVERNIER 2008, sowie ders. (im Druck); s. a. den Beitrag von WIESEHÖFER in diesem Band.
46 Zahlenangaben in JONES/STOLPER 2008, 27–50; STOLPER (im Druck). Neben den elamischen fand man auch jeweils eine neubabylonische, griechische und phrygische Tafel.
47 JONES/STOLPER 2008, 30.
48 Die Fortification Texts datieren zwischen 492 und 458/7 v. Chr. Hunderte dieser Tafeln tragen aramäische Zusätze aus Tinte, vgl. STOLPER (im Druck).
49 ROSSI (im Druck) 1 bezeichnet Aramäisch im Anschluss an FOLMER (1995, 13) als „vehicular language", im Unterschied zu einer „official language."
50 Sogenanntes „Imperial Aramaic" oder Reichsaramäisch, s. GZELLA (im Druck).
51 WIESEHÖFER (in diesem Band) sieht die gesetzgeberisch verankerte Durchsetzung in Art eines universellen Bildungsauftrages zu Recht erst im römischen Reich verwirklicht.

fehlen aus den Kernländern jedoch. Sie stammen vor allem aus den Randzonen des Achaimeniden-Reiches.

Die bereits zu Beginn zitierte Einschätzung Muhammad DANDAMAYEVS[52], dass selbst edle Perser und hochrangige Beamte illiterat waren, ist wohl zu pessimistisch. Auch wenn die Historizität der eingangs zitierten Episoden aus Herodot und Ktesias über schreibkundige Perser gering ist, muss man von einem bestimmten Prozentsatz an schreib- und lesekundigen Mitgliedern der Elite ausgehen. Die Literalität der Eliten war nicht zuletzt zur Kontrolle der großen Zahl an Dolmetschern[53] und professionellen Schreibern[54] nötig, um ihnen nicht hilflos ausgeliefert zu sein.[55] M. JURSA bringt beispielsweise die ab Kambyses vermehrte Verwendung des Aramäischen in Babylonien überzeugend mit dem achaimenidischen Bedürfnis nach Kontrolle der (keilschriftlichen) Tempelverwaltungen in Verbindung.[56]

Archive auf lokaler Ebene wie in Baktrien, Arachosien[57] oder Ägypten belegen die Notwendigkeit von Literalität auf Provinzebene.[58] Ein jüngst ediertes Archiv der Regierungszeit Artaxerxes III. aus Baktrien[59] enthält Briefe des baktrischen Satrapen Achvamazda an den ihm untergeordneten Provinzbeamten Bagavant.[60] In der aramäisch geschriebenen Korrespondenz geht es hauptsächlich um die Übermittlung von Befehlen an Bagavant oder um Tadel wegen nicht korrekt ausgeführter Aufträge. Die Schreiber dieser Briefe tragen iranische Namen, d. h., sie wurden wohl in Schreiber-Schulen in Aramäisch ausgebildet, weil Aramäisch keine lebende Sprache in Baktrien war, sondern als Schreibsystem zur Übertragung iranischer Sprachen diente. Daher

---

52 DANDAMAYEV 1997, 178 (online 2011, eingesehen April 2017).
53 Dolmetscher: BRIANT 2002, 508–9; TAVERNIER 2008, 60–63; TAVERNIER 2017, 348–356; Thuk. 8,85,1–2; Xen. an. 1,2,17; 4,4,5; Plut. Them. 6,3; Curt. 5,13,6–7. Der akkadische Terminus sepīru (JURSA 2012, 381 f.) bezeichnet entweder einen Alphabetschreiber, einen Beamten oder einen schreibkundigen Dolmetscher, siehe CAD S 225–226: „scribe writing alphabet script", „administrative functionary", „interpreter".
54 TAVERNIER 2008, 60–63; z. B. „Schreiber des Schatzhauses" (aram. spry 'wṣr' in TAD B 4.4:12), akkad. ^{LÚ}ṭupšarru ša bīt kāṣirānu (Kamb. 384: 15–16), elam. teppir kapniškima (PF 1947: 17; PFNN 2356: 12–15); „Schreiber des Distrikts" (aram. spry mdynt' in TAD A 6.1:1, 6); „Schreiber der Armee" (akkad. sepīru ša ūqu BE 10, 102: 7; PBS 2/1 34: 4, 9 etc.).
55 Ein auf einer Großteils illiteraten Oberschicht basierendes System konnte nur funktionieren, so lange die (schriftkundigen) Untertanen loyal waren und Botschaften nicht zu ihren Gunsten veränderten; diese Loyalität scheint im Achaimeniden-Reich gegeben gewesen zu sein. Die zahlreichen herodoteischen Anekdoten über gefälschte oder veränderte Briefe verkürzen daher wohl die Realität.
56 JURSA 2012, 393.
57 Siehe zuletzt HENKELMAN 2017, 151–174. Von dem ursprünglich anzunehmenden Archiv haben sich nur zwei elamische Tafeln aus dem Satrapensitz Qandahār (SF 1399, SF 1400) erhalten.
58 Herodot (3,128) beschreibt durchaus korrekt, dass alle Statthalter königliche Schreiber hatten.
59 Edition SHAKED/NAVEH 2012; s. a. SHAKED 2004; FOLMER 2017, 413–416: das Archiv umfasst 30 Dokumente auf Leder und 18 beschriebene Holzstöcke. Sie datieren zwischen 353–324 v. Chr.
60 SHAKED/NAVEH 2012, 16: Bagavant residierte in der Stadt Khulmi (heute Khulm in N-Afghanistan), wo er zwischen 353 und 348 v. Chr. aktiv war. Sein aramäischer Amtstitel lautete pḥt', „governor", ein Terminus, der akkadisch pāḫatu/pīḫatu (CAD P 365–369) entspricht.

weisen die Texte viele altpersische Wörter und Schreibfehler auf. Für letzteres gibt es mehrere Erklärungen: Entweder stammten die Schreiber aus Baktrien, und/oder sie waren relativ ungeübt, oder es handelte sich bei den Briefen um *drafts*.[61] Das Archiv zeigt auch die alltägliche Seite dieser bedeutenden Satrapie: So ersuchen in einem Text Soldaten um die zeitweise Befreiung vom Militärdienst, weil eine Heuschrecken-Plage ihre Ernte bedroht.[62] Ebenso privaten Charakter hat ein Schild, auf dem eine Lieferung Kräuter verzeichnet ist, die Bagavants Frau ihm gesandt hatte.[63] Aus dem Archiv ist zu schließen, dass auch an den Randzonen des Reiches Schreiben und Lesen zur alltäglichen Routine innerhalb der Verwaltung gehörte. Funktionale Literalität ist für die Elite somit reichsweit nachweisbar, darüber hinausgehend allerdings unwahrscheinlich.

Dass Schreiben keinen prominenten Platz in der persischen Erziehung einnahm, wie DANDAMAYEV[64] auch behauptet, findet in den indigenen Quellen indes implizit Bestätigung. Die altpersischen Inschriften betonen andere Tugenden (ap. *ūnara*)[65], vor allem Jagd, Reitkunst, Bogen-Schießen, Speerwurf, die Wahrheit zu sprechen sowie Gehorsam, Besonnenheit[66] und Weisheit/*sophrosyne*.[67] Schreiben oder Lesen waren kein Teil des Curriculums, bzw. waren so unbedeutend, dass sie nicht genannt wurden. Die gesellschaftliche Einbindung von Schrift ist daher zumindest für die Kernländer als gering zu bezeichnen.

Auch wenn es mit dem Aramäischen und Altpersischen relativ einfach zu erlernende Schriftsysteme gab, fanden diese kaum alltägliche Verwender, abgesehen von professionellen Schreibern und Verwaltungspersonal. Die Annahme, dass die komplexe Verwaltung des Achaimeniden-Reiches auch unterhalb der höchsten Ebenen/außerhalb der Verwaltungsebene Schreibkundige brauchte, findet in den Quellen keine Unterstützung. Im Gegenteil scheint deren Anwesenheit auf unteren Gesellschaftsebenen nicht zwingend erforderlich.[68] Daraus ist zu schließen, dass es in den Kernländern keinen strukturellen Bedarf an ausgedehnterer Literalität gab. Um das

---

61 SHAKED/NAVEH 2012, 17, 50 ff.
62 SHAKED/NAVEH 2012, 94–99, Text A 4 (= Khalili IA 1), datiert 348/47 v. Chr.; vgl. Z.3: "There is locust, heavy and numerous, and the crop is ripe(?) for reaping …" Z.6: "Those troops that are appointed in your presence, set them free to go about their work. That locust let them [smash?], and let them reap the crop."
63 SHAKED/NAVEH 2012, 30, 122–125, Text A 9 (= Khalili IA 15); "label attached to a jar or a basket".
64 DANDAMAYEV 1997, 178.
65 Siehe dazu ausführlich zuletzt ROLLINGER 2017, 189 ff.
66 ROLLINGER 2017, 207 f.
67 Der König betont diese Fähigkeiten in DNb § A–G = XPl § 9 A–J (ed. Schmitt): „…als Reiter bin ich ein guter Reiter; als Bogenschütze bin ich ein guter Bogenschütze; sowohl zu Fuß wie auch zu Pferd; als Lanzenkämpfer bin ich ein guter Lanzenkämpfer; sowohl zu Fuß wie auch zu Pferd." S. a. sie Grab-Inschrift des Dareios in Naqš-i Rustam: DNb 40–45; in griechischen Quellen rezipiert bei: Hdt. 1,136; Xen. Kyr. 1,2,2–12; 7,5,86; 8,6,10; vgl. Xen. an. 1,9,2–6; Strab. 15,3,18.
68 Zu den verschiedenen Arten der Kommunikation innerhalb des Reiches vgl. JACOBS 2015, siehe: ://www.iranicaonline.org/articles/achaemenid-royal-communication (eingesehen am 19. 12. 2017).

System im Alltag aber trotzdem aufrecht zu erhalten, musste es Substitute gegeben haben, die lesen und/oder schreiben konnten, d. h. die fehlende Literalität wurde durch „second-hand literacy" kompensiert.[69]

Alltägliche Literalität im achaimenidenzeitlichen Babylonien

Im gesamten steht der Befund der Persis, Elams und Mediens jedoch in scharfem Gegensatz zu zeitgleichen anderen Reichsteilen, wie Babylonien oder Ägypten: In den alten Keilschriftkulturen wurden bereits in altassyrischer Zeit (2500 v. Chr.) ein vereinfachtes Syllabar, ein reduzierter Zeichensatz[70], sowie einfachere Schreibungen für den Alltag benützt, der es auch Laien ermöglichte, eigene Korrespondenzen und Aufzeichnungen zu führen. Oft sind diese Privatbriefe der altassyrischen Händler aus Kaneš/Kültepe und ihrer Frauen jedoch sehr amateurhaft.[71] Auch für die altbabylonische Zeit legen Untersuchungen nahe, dass in privatem Kontext eigenhändig gelesen und geschrieben wurde, was beispielsweise an Fehlern in den Texten ersichtlich ist.[72] Die in dieser Zeit entwickelte Kursive deutet darauf hin, dass die funktionale Schriftlichkeit seither weiter verbreitet war als in früheren Epochen.[73] In den Keilschriftkulturen Mesopotamiens gab es zudem ein höheres Bewusstsein um die Bedeutung von Schrift. Knaben wurden in Schreib-Schulen unterrichtet, wo sie neben der Schrift auch Grammatik, Mathematik und Astronomie lernten.[74] Dies war Ausgangspunkt für eine professionelle Karriere. Funktionale und technische Literalität wurden zumeist außerhalb der Schulen, als Lehre bzw. innerhalb der Familien weitertradiert. Der Übergang zur achaimenidischen Herrschaft markiert hier keinen sichtbaren Bruch.

Im achaimenidenzeitlichen Babylonien ist Schriftlichkeit auch weiterhin bis in niedere Gesellschaftsschichten, seien es nun Bauern, Sklaven, Ochsenhirten oder ähnliches nachweisbar. Einen gewissen Einschnitt gab es jedoch: Dareios und Xerxes griffen die nord-babylonische Elite, als Reaktion auf deren Revolten von 521 und 484 v. Chr. bewusst an, wodurch weite Teile der literaten Population aus den Schriftquellen verschwanden.[75] Dies könnte eine Erklärung dafür sein, dass der Anteil an Briefen aus Privatarchiven deutlich geringer als beispielsweise aus der gut belegten altbaby-

---

69 Zu dieser sogenannten „second-hand literacy" s. YOUTIE 1971, 239 ff. und HARRIS 1989, 33 ff.
70 CHARPIN 2004, 501 wies für das altbabylonische Mari nach, dass die Schreiber mit nur 112 Syllabogrammen und 57 Logogrammen auskamen, um akkadisch schreiben zu können. Dies entspricht in etwa einem Viertel der gesamt vorhandenen Zeichen; s. a. CHARPIN 2010, 10, 59–62.
71 CHARPIN 2004, 501; CHARPIN 2010, 59; LION 2011, 102–103.
72 WILCKE 2000, 34–49, 66–80; LION 2011, 102 f.
73 VELDHUIS 2011, 71; CHARPIN 2010, 59 ff.
74 S. u. a. CHARPIN 2010, 19 ff., 25 ff. mit einem Überblick über die jeweiligen Curricula.
75 WAERZEGGERS 2003/4, 150 ff.; BEAULIEU 2007, 205 ff. Welcher Art die Folgen der Revolten tatsächlich waren, ist nicht gänzlich geklärt. Archäologisch lässt sich die Schließung einiger der bedeutendsten Tempel samt deren Archiven nachweisen, traditionelle Stadtviertel der städtischen Elite Babylons

lonischen Zeit ist. Von 8.000 untersuchten Texten aus Privatarchiven des sogenannten „langen" sechsten Jahrhunderts v. Chr.[76] sind plötzlich nur mehr 3.5 % Briefe, im Vergleich zu früheren 13.3 %.[77] Trotz des Fehlens expliziter Hinweise auf einen parallelen Schriftverkehr auf Aramäisch, erklärt M. JURSA diesen Befund monokausal mit den verlorenen aramäischen Quellen. Ein Zusammenhang mit der Ausdünnung literater Schichten durch die Achaimeniden-Herrscher scheint aber durchaus ebenso erwägenswert. Zugleich darf man jedoch nicht von einem kontinuierlichen Wachsen von Schriftlichkeit im privaten Umfeld des ersten Jahrtausends ausgehen, weil es in achaimenidischer Zeit keine großartigen technologischen oder gesellschaftlichen Veränderungen im Vergleich zu früheren Jahrhunderten gab, die die Literalität befördert hätten, sondern nur mehr oder weniger Gründe um zu schreiben.

Beispiele für alltägliche Schriftlichkeit sind Privatarchive der spätbabylonischen Zeit, in denen es neben Briefen zwischen Haushaltsmitgliedern und Sklaven, auch Korrespondenzen der Archivinhaber/innen mit sozial höher gestellten Adressaten gibt.[78] Inhaltlich befassen sich diese Briefe mit einer breiten Palette von Themen: von wirtschaftlichen Transaktionen und deren Problemen, Spannungen bei der Eintreibung von Abgaben, vom Umgang mit gewalttätigen Bauern oder Gärtnern, Bitten von Sklavenfamilien um Freilassungsdokumente bis hin zu familieninternen Angelegenheiten, wie der Sorge um Verwandte.[79] So drückt beispielsweise ein Absender die Freude über die Schwangerschaft seiner Frau aus.[80] Bedrohlicher wirkt der Brief eines Mannes an seine Gattin und zwei seiner Söhne(?), in dem er Anweisungen für seine Abwesenheit gibt: „Ich bin wohlauf. Ich hoffe, euch geht es gut. Die Aufsicht über das Haus und die Arbeiter dürft ihr nicht vernachlässigen, (oder) ihr werdet sterben![81]" Literate Sklaven sind ebenso mehrfach bezeugt. So soll ein Tempelsklave aus Uruk Schreibtafeln bringen und sie auch lesen.[82]

M. JURSA kommt zu folgender Einschätzung: „Nichts an der erhaltenen Korrespondenz deutet darauf hin, dass der Austausch von in Babylonisch und Keilschrift geschriebenen Briefen in dem Umfeld, aus dem unsere Texte stammen, ein unüblicher

---

verarmten. Klar ist, dass es keinen vollständigen Bruch gab, sondern einen Austausch der alten Elite durch loyale *homines novi*.

76 Das „lange" sechste Jahrhundert dauert bis in das zweite Regierungsjahr des Xerxes (484 v. Chr.), das in mehrerlei Hinsicht einen Einschnitt im Verhältnis zwischen Babylonien und den Achaimeniden markiert.

77 HACKL/JURSA/SCHMIDL 2014, 78; s. a. FRAHM/JURSA 2011, 3.

78 Im Corpus von HACKL/JURSA/SCHMIDL 2014 gibt es zahlreiche Belege, in denen Sklaven an ihre Herren schreiben, z. B. Nr. 7, 31, 39, 77, 235.

79 HACKL/JURSA/SCHMIDL 2014, 80–93, 101–105.

80 HACKL/JURSA/SCHMIDL 2014, Nr. 210 (= CT 22, 40, BM 64781) aus Sippar.

81 HACKL/JURSA/SCHMIDL 2014, 333–334, Nr. 224 (= PSBA 31, 169 ff., pl. 19), Z.5, bes. 7–9: *ana maṣṣarti ša bīti u ṣābi lā tašuṭṭā tammuttā*.

82 FRAHM/JURSA 2011, 47 Nr. 140 (YBC 11330) pl. LXXVII. Weitere Briefe von Sklaven im Corpus von HACKL/JURSA/SCHMIDL 2014: z. B. Nr. 7, 31, 39, 77, 235.

Vorgang war.⁸³" Die Archivinhaber schreiben ihre Briefe nachweislich selbst. Interessanterweise verwenden sie weiterhin Keilschrift, anstelle des Aramäischen. Das ist möglicherweise ein Indiz, dass die schreibende Mittelschicht Babyloniens sehr traditionsbewusst war. Obwohl der Bote eine Alternative zum Brief bleibt, ist ein eindeutiges Primat der schriftlichen Nachricht sichtbar. Insgesamt deutet die babylonische Evidenz darauf hin, dass der Grad an Literalität in Babylonien auf jeden Fall höher als jener in den Kernländern war, mithin der Raum von Literalität größer.

Alltägliche Literalität im achaimenidenzeitlichen Ägypten

Ähnlich verhält es sich mit Ägypten, wo mit dem Einzug des Aramäischen neben der demotischen Schrift eine weitere Kursive vorhanden war, die leichter als die Hieroglyphen zu erlernen war. So haben sich aus Ägypten nicht zufällig, das heißt, nicht nur aufgrund besserer klimatischer Verhältnisse, mehr Schriftfunde (Ostraka, Papyri, Lederdokumente) erhalten als aus den Kernländern. Die Zahl an aramäischen Inschriften auf privaten Grabstelen[84], Gefäßen[85], Holzpaletten[86], Anhängern, oder auf Stein (Grafitti) wächst immer noch kontinuierlich. Allein aus Elephantine stammen insgesamt 583 aller derzeit bekannten aramäischen Dokumente.[87] Davon sind 52 Papyri, die etwas mehr als die ersten hundert Jahre der achaimenidischen Herrschaft umspannen.[88] Besonders wertvoll sind Kopien der Ahiqar-Geschichte und Auszüge einer adaptierten Form der Bisutun-Inschrift.[89]

Die erhaltenen Texte belegen Literalität von der Ebene der Provinzverwaltung bis in unterste Schichten. In den Bereich der lokalen Verwaltung fällt die semi-private Korrespondenz des Satrapen von Ägypten, Aršama (dat. 410/408 v. Chr.). Es handelt sich um dreizehn Briefe auf Leder, die aus einer achaimenidischen Kanzlei, –vermutlich Babylonien–, nach Ägypten gesandt wurden.[90] Die Orthographie der Briefe zeigt eine standardisierte Form des Aramäischen und damit den offiziellen Charakter der

---

83 HACKL/JURSA/SCHMIDL 2014, 76.
84 Zu den 33 aramäischen Grabinschriften auf Stelen oder Grabmonumenten: vgl. SILJANEN 2017, 320–329.
85 Vier Silbergefäße aus Tel el-Maskhuṭa: TAD D 15.1, TAD D 15.2, TAD D 15.3, TAD D 15.4.
86 Palette eines Schreibers aus Assuan: TAD D 13.1.
87 Das sind 56 % aller Dokumente, vgl. SILJANEN 2017, 68, 73 f.
88 PORTEN/YARDENI 1986–1999; s. a. die kommentierten englischen Übersetzungen in PORTEN 1996.
89 Ahiqar: TAD C 1.1; Bisutun-Kopie: TAD C 2.1. Vermutlich wurde der Text anlässlich der 100-Jahr-Feier des Achaimeniden-Reiches, in der Regierungszeit Dareios II., geschrieben, er basiert aber möglicherweise auf älteren Kopien der Inschrift. Ausführlichere Analyse bei WIESEHÖFER 1998, 40 f.; ROLLINGER 2016, 122 f. und 125 f.
90 TAD A 6.1–15; s. a. SHAKED/NAVEH 2012, 39 f.; FOLMER 2017, 413 ff. Fotographien der Siegel und Briefe, sowie die kommentierte englische Online-Edition (s. TUPLIN/MA 2013), finden sich auf: „Thus speaks Arshama. Letters of a fifth century Persian prince": https://arshama.bodleian.ox.ac.uk/

Texte. Zugleich ist der Inhalt privater Natur, da der Satrap den ägyptischen Verwaltern seiner dortigen Ländereien Anweisungen erteilt.

Hierarchisch unter die satrapale Ebene gehört das Gemeinde-Archiv des Jedaniah, des Vorstehers der jüdischen Gemeinde von Elephantine mit einigen historisch interessanten Dokumenten,[91] wie beispielsweise einer Anweisung für die korrekte Ausführung des Passah-Festes[92], oder einem *draft* der Petition der Juden von Elephantine an den persischen Gouverneur von Juda, betreffend den Wiederaufbau ihres Tempels.[93] Privateren Charakter hat das Archiv seiner Tante Mibtahiah[94], einer wohlhabenden Dame im Besitz mehrerer Häuser, die sie an ihre Kinder weitergab. In keinem der Dokumente gibt es Hinweise, dass sie Verträge selbst geschrieben hätte, oder zumindest als Zeugin unterschrieben hätte. Ob sie die in ihrem Haus archivierten Schriftstücke lesen konnte, bleibt ebenso ungewiss. W. HARRIS nimmt für das ptolemäische Ägypten an, dass selbst in dieser Zeit die Mitglieder der höheren Mittelschicht kaum schreib- und lesekundig waren, außer jene spezialisierten Berufsgruppen, wie Priester, Steuereintreiber oder Bankiers, die Schrift zur Ausübung ihres Berufes benötigten[95]. Das Familien-Archiv des Ananiah[96], eines niederen Tempelbediensteten führt endgültig auf die Ebene der unteren Mittelschicht. Auch er tätigte wirtschaftliche Transaktionen, verkaufte Hausanteile an Familienmitglieder, verhandelte über Mitgift oder verlieh Geld in kleinen Summen.[97]

Von besonderer Bedeutung für unsere Fragestellung sind Briefe von „aramäischen"[98] Soldaten in achaimenidischen Diensten, die zeitweilig in Memphis stationiert waren. Die Mehrzahl der nach ihrem Fundort benannten Hermopolis-Briefe ist an die weiblichen Mitglieder (Ehegattin und/oder Schwester[99]) der Familien in

---

91 Jedaniah-Archiv, bestehend aus 11 Dokumenten ab 419 v. Chr.: PORTEN 1996, 77f., Texte B 13–22; MILLARD 2003, 233f.
92 PORTEN 1996, 125ff. zu Text B 13 (= TAD A 4.1), dat. 419/18 v. Chr.
93 PORTEN 1996, Texte B 19–20 (= TAD A 4.7–8).
94 Mibtahiah-Archiv PORTEN 1996, 79ff., Texte B 23–33: Die 11 Dokumente decken einen Zeitraum von drei Generationen (über 60 Jahre, ab 471 v. Chr.) ab. Paläographisch konnten vier bis fünf unterschiedliche Schreiber unterschieden werden.
95 HARRIS 1989, 142f. Er nimmt für diese Zeit eine Literalitätsrate von 20–30 % an.
96 Das Archiv umfasst 13 Dokumente ab 456 v. Chr.; PORTEN 1996, 80; Texte B 34–46 (= TAD B 3.1–13); hier wurden fünf von 13 Dokumenten vom gleichen Schreiber geschrieben. Die Frau des Ananiah war eine ägyptische Sklavin namens Tamet, was einmal mehr die ethnische Durchmischung der Militär-Kolonie von Elephantine zeigt.
97 PORTEN 1996, Text B 34.
98 Die Absender bezeichnen sich selbst als „Aramäer". Die Hermopolis-Briefe wurden 1945 intakt (und noch nicht zugestellt) im Ibieion der Nekropole von Hermopolis (Tuna el-Gebel) in einem Krug mit Ibis-Mumien gefunden. Eventuell wurden sie vom Boten nur auf Zeit in dem Topf abgelegt und gingen dann verloren, so SILJANEN 2017, 76; Edition und Übersetzung der Briefe bei PORTEN 1996, 75f., Texte B 1–7 (= TAD A 2.1–7).
99 Die Differenzierung ist heute schwierig, da die Bezeichnung „Schwester" auch für „Gattin" verwendet wurde.

Luxor und Syene[100]adressiert, doch dazu genaueres unten. Thematisch befassen sich die Papyri mit alltäglichen Belangen: Die Soldaten benötigten bestimmte Dinge (Öl, Getreide, Gewand), und beklagten sich häufig[101], wenn diese Dinge nicht sofort geliefert wurden. Die Absender gaben Anweisungen an jene zu Hause, was in ihrer Abwesenheit zu tun sei und wollten über alle Belange im Haus informiert werden.[102] Am häufigsten sind jedoch Fragen nach dem Wohlbefinden der Familien: Jeder Brief des Makkibanit oder seines Bruders endet mit einer ähnlichen Formel: „(Um) nach deinem Wohlbefinden (zu fragen), schickte ich diesen Brief.[103]" In einem Brief erkundigt sich der Absender kurz nach dem Wohlergehen des Vaters und der Familie, um danach gleich die Bitte um Leder anzuschließen: „Schicke mir Häute, genug für ein Ledergewand." Der Absender selbst habe einen gestreiften Stoff und parfümiertes Öl gekauft, aber „noch keinen Boten gefunden, der die Waren nach Hause liefert."[104] Der Brief eines Vaters anlässlich der Entlassung seines Sohnes aus dem Militärdienst reflektiert die Sorge der Eltern um ihren Sohn, der sich noch auf Kampagne in Oberägypten aufhielt. Der Vater ermahnte ihn, er solle sich wie ein Mann verhalten und beklagte, dass die Eltern keine Zuwendungen der achaimenidischen Verwaltung erhalten hätten, seit der Sohn in Oberägypten sei.[105]

Für eilige Privatmitteilungen zwischen nahe gelegenen Orten wurden anstelle von Papyri häufig Ostraka verwendet, die per Schiff von Syene/Assuan nach Elephantine und wieder zurück gebracht wurden.[106] J. NAVEH erkannte, dass allein 32 der Ostraka von einer einzigen Person geschrieben wurden und schloss daraus, dass es sich um einen Schreiber der Werft von Syene gehandelt haben könnte, der für jene schrieb, die selbst nicht schreiben konnten.[107] Ein Absender eines Ostrakons forderte beispielsweise den Adressaten auf, dass er „morgen" kommen solle,[108] andere enthielten religiöse Anweisungen, wie ein Schaf für das Passah-Fest zu scheren.[109] Mehrmals wurden

---

100 Luxor: PORTEN 1996, Texte B 5–6 (= TAD A 2.5–6); Syene: PORTEN 1996, Texte B 1–4 (= TAD A.2.1–4); andere Elephantine-Papyri nennen auch Memphis oder Migdol als Adressen.
101 z. B. PORTEN 1996, Text B 5,2–3 (= TAD A 2.5,2–3).
102 PORTEN 1996, 96–98, Text B 3,11–12 (= TAD A 2.2).
103 z. B. PORTEN 1996, Texte B 1,12–13; B 2,17; B 3,12–13; B 4,13; B 5,14–15 etc. Häufig liest man auch die Phrase „mache dir keine Sorgen um mich, ich sorge mich um dich", z. B. PORTEN 1996, Text B 4,13.
104 PORTEN 1996, 99–101, Text B 4,7–8 (= TAD A 2.4).
105 PORTEN 1996, 107ff., Text B 8 (= TAD A 3.3), dat. 1. H. 5. Jh. v. Chr., bes. Z.2: „seit dem Tag, an dem du dich auf den Weg machtest (i. e. den Kriegszug), ist mein Herz nicht gut. Ebenso (ergeht es) deiner Mutter."...Z.7: „sei ein Mann, weine nicht bis du wieder..."
106 Die Mehrheit der über 300 Ostraka stammt aus der ersten Hälfte des 5. Jhs. v. Chr. (um 475 v. Chr.), vgl. TAD D 7-10; NAVEH 1970, 37; MILLARD 2003, 234.
107 NAVEH 1970, 37. Völlig spekulativ ist seine Ansicht, dass nach dem Tod des Werft-Schreibers keine Ostraka mehr geschrieben wurden und daher keine jüngeren Ostraka mehr vorhanden sind.
108 z. B. Ostrakon aus Elephantine (BM 45035); s. a. TAD D 7.3. Daneben gibt es auch Aufforderungen, Waren noch am selben Tag zu liefern, z. B. TAD D 7.1; 7.2; 7.48.
109 TAD D 7.8; siehe auch die Anweisungen in TAD 7.20 und 7.24..

Frauen instruiert, die Kinder zu füttern, den Ochsen einzuspannen oder altes Brot zu essen.[110] Ostraka wurden überdies auch für Aufzählungen von Gütern oder Namenslisten verwendet.[111]

J. NAVEH unterschied aufgrund paläographischer Unterschiede (und der gehobenen Sprache) professionelle Schreiber von jenen, die zufällig schrieben oder nur ihre Namen signierten. In diesen alltäglichen Bereich der „signature-literacy" gehören auch die aramäischen Graffiti an Tempelwänden aus verschiedenen Orten in Ägypten, wenngleich ihre genaue Datierung oft unsicher ist.[112] Aufgrund der Häufigkeit von eigenhändigen (aramäischen) Unterschriften hält M. DANDAMAYEV den Grad an Literalität der Militär-Kolonisten in Elephantine für höher als jenen der Bevölkerung im achaimenidischen Kernland.[113] Seine Annahme wird dadurch gestützt, dass die Schreiber der Hermopolis-Briefe eine relativ grobe aramäische Kursive verwendeten.[114] Dieser Befund kann einerseits Zufall der Überlieferung sein, weil aus anderen Regionen keine verwertbaren Zeugnisse mehr erhalten sind,[115] oder er ist der Beweis für verbreitete „signature-literacy" bzw. sogar funktionale Literalität bis in die untere Mittelschicht Ägyptens.

Der Überblick über alltägliche (männliche) Literalität im Achaimeniden-Reich lässt folgende Schlussfolgerungen zu: Nicht die jeweiligen Technologien, also die Schreibtechnik oder Schreibmaterialien, auch nicht die Art und Anzahl der Zeichen oder die Schwierigkeit des Erlernens der Schrift sind ausschlaggebend für den Grad der Literalität einer Gesellschaft, sondern die soziale Konstruktion von Literalität, das heißt die Art, in der Schreiben und Schrift in einer Kultur verwendet wurden: als Mittel der Kommunikation für alle oder Instrument sozialer Kontrolle.[116] Letzteres ist für das Achaimeniden-Reich zutreffend.

Ein zentralisierter Staat wie das Achaimeniden-Reich hätte Schrift aktiv verbreiten können, da Schrift die Ausübung von Macht durch geschriebene Gesetze oder Tatenberichte erleichtert und damit politische und religiöse Autorität verleiht. Die tatsächlichen Verwendungen von Schrift waren in den Kernländern indes auf männliche Mitglieder der Eliten (zur Repräsentation) und die oberste Verwaltung eingeschränkt. Die Illiteralität der Masse trug zur Stabilität der politischen Ordnung[117] bei, da die Abhängigkeit zwischen Schreibkundigen und Illiteraten ein kohäsiver Faktor der Gesellschaft war (und ist). Damit hatte Schrift zugleich einen „socially conserva-

---

110 NAVEH 1970, 38 zu den Ostraka Nr. 1, 4, 30, siehe TAD D 7.6.
111 TAD D 8.1-2 und TAD D 9.1-2.
112 49 aramäische Graffiti datieren in achaimenidische Zeit, vgl. SILJANEN 2017, 320 ff., Appendix 1.
113 NAVEH 1970, 22.
114 NAVEH 1970, 6, 22 ff.; FOLMER 1995, 40, 41; SILJANEN 2017, 113.
115 DANDAMAYEV 1997, 178.
116 MICHALOWSKI 1994, 64.
117 HARRIS 1989, 329 f.

tive effect[118]", weil sie die bestehende Klassen-Hegemonie[119], in unserem Fall jene der Achaimeniden-Dynastie und des persischen Reichsadels, bewahrte.

3 Der Raum weiblicher Literalität im Achaimeniden-Reich

Vor dem Hintergrund der offensichtlich generell geringeren Bedeutung von Literalität im Achaimeniden-Reich ist im Folgenden zu fragen, wie der Grad weiblicher Literalität einzuschätzen ist. Umgekehrt zum vorherigen Kapitel wird nun der Befund aus den anderen Reichsteilen vorangestellt, die – um es vorweg zu nehmen–, ein völlig anderes Bild als für die Persis, Elam und Medien zeichnen. Die aussagekräftigsten Zeugnisse weiblicher Literalität stammen dabei erneut aus den Regionen Ägypten und Babylonien.

Literate Frauen in Meopotamien?

Professionelle weibliche Schreiberinnen (*tupšarritu*) sind in Mesopotamien keineswegs ungewöhnlich und bereits seit der Akkad-Zeit (Ende des 3. Jahrtausends) sicher belegt. Aus Texten der frühen altbabylonischen Zeit (ab etwa 1800 v. Chr.) wird klar, dass Schreiberinnen kein hohes soziales Prestige, sondern einen servilen Status innehatten. Ihr Aufgabenfeld lag z. T. auch in kultischem Umfeld. Daraus ist zu schließen, dass es ein Interesse der Männer gab, die Präsenz von anderen Männern in weiblichem Umfeld (Palast, Tempel) zu limitieren.[120] In neuassyrischer Zeit werden Schreiberinnen mehrfach im administrativen Management des Haushaltes der Königin[121] oder als „Schreiberin der Königin"[122] genannt. Neben diesen (wenigen) professionellen Schreiberinnen, gibt es auch literate Mitglieder der königlichen Familien, wie die Frau und die Schwester des Assurbanipal. In einem Brief tadelt die Prinzessin ihre Schwägerin (die Gattin des Assurbanipal), dass diese zu wenig Schreiben und Lesen übe.[123] Die weiblichen Mitglieder des Königshauses bewirtschafteten wenigstens nominell Ländereien und beaufsichtigten Arbeiter, es gibt aber keine Indizien, dass sie daraus resultierende schriftliche Transaktionen selbst durchgeführt hätten.[124] Es ist jedoch

---

118 HARRIS 1989, 334.
119 BRIANT 2002, 77, 82, 10–183 prägte hierfür den Begriff der „éthno-classe dominante".
120 CHARPIN 2010, 63 f.; LION 2011, 98 f.
121 z. B. sechs aramäische Schreiberinnen in einer Liste von Personal aus Niniveh, (SAA 7,24); CHARPIN 2010, 64; SVÄRD 2016, 132.
122 Attar-palṭi, Schreiberin des königlichen Haushaltes von Kalḫu (CTN 3,39;40, beide 615 v. Chr.); SVÄRD 2016, 132 nennt auch noch Saraia (SAA 16,49), die an den Palast-Schreiber, „ihren Herrn", schreibt.
123 SAA 16,28; LIVINGSTONE 2010, 104; CHARPIN 2010, 64; LION 2011, 102.
124 LION 2011, 104.

festzuhalten, dass es in Assyrien keine auf Geschlecht basierenden Einschränkungen von Literalität gab. Weibliche Literalität ist dennoch eher die Ausnahme als die Regel und nur unter besonderen Umständen nachzuweisen, aber sie ist existent.

Im Babylonien des 1. Jahrtausends ist in den vorhandenen Quellen ein genereller Rückgang der Nennung von Frauen beobachtet worden[125], der mit einer gesellschaftlichen Zurückdrängung der Frau aus der Öffentlichkeit verbunden wurde. Es werden auch keine Schreiberinnen mehr genannt. Dass dies eher Zufall der Überlieferung ist, belegen unter anderem Archive von Frauen der städtischen Mittelschicht, wie jenes der Inṣabtu, dem Mitglied einer Schreiner-Familie aus Borsippa.[126] Von besonderer Bedeutung sind die bereits genannten 300 Privatbriefe[127] aus dem achaimenidenzeitlichen Babylonien: In dem von J. HACKL, M. JURSA und M. SCHMIDL zusammengestellten Corpus wurden zumindest 27 Briefe (ca. 9 %) von Frauen gesendet oder waren an Frauen gerichtet. Zwölf Briefe wurden von Frauen geschrieben.[128] Die Absenderinnen und Adressatinnen gehörten der schreibkundigen Mittelschicht innerhalb der städtischen Elite Babyloniens an. Inhaltlich handelt es sich um Alltagstexte im engeren Sinn mit stark informellem Charakter, wie beispielsweise Dankesschreiben, Anweisungen an Töchter[129] oder die Sorge um Verwandte.[130] Bittere Beschwerde über die mangelnde Fürsorge des Sohnes führt eine Mutter: „Wie wirst du (wenn) ich sterbe, an meiner Stelle (meinen) Kindern Gutes tun und sie, (wenn) du sie in Gefangenschaft siehst, gegen Silber auslösen – du erweist mir (ja sogar) schon jetzt zu meinen Lebzeiten keinen Gefallen."[131]

Interne Verweise auf frühere Schreiben von / an Frauen deuten darauf hin, dass private Literalität weiter verbreitet war, als es die Zahl an erhaltenen Briefen nahelegt. Konkrete Prozentzahlen sind kaum abschätzbar, realistisch ist die Hälfte der Gesamtzahl an literaten Männern. Wichtiger als ihre exakte Zahl ist jedoch ihre pure Existenz.

---

125 KÜMMEL 1979, 155 stellte fest, dass in den Archiven von Uruk Frauennamen „ganz ungewöhnlich selten ... belegt" sind und dies „kein Zufall der Überlieferung (sei), da eine auffällige Zurückdrängung der zuvor günstigeren rechtlichen und gesellschaftlichen Stellung der Frau zu den wesentlichen neuen Elementen der neu- und spätbabylonischen Zeit gehört." Auch BEAULIEU 1993, 13 konstatiert eine Zurückdrängung der Frau auf ihre häusliche Rolle im Vergleich zu früheren Jahrhunderten.
126 WAERZEGGERS 1999–2000, 183–200. Das Archiv stammt aus dem frühen 5. Jh. v. Chr. Inṣabtu ließ ihre Dokumente von einem Schreiber aufsetzen, weshalb man bei ihr eher von reiner Lesefähigkeit ausgehen sollte.
127 HACKL/JURSA/SCHMIDL 2014.
128 HACKL/JURSA/SCHMIDL 2014, 53 ff.
129 HACKL/JURSA/SCHMIDL 2014, 348–9, Nr. 240 (= PTS 2357): Aufforderung einer Mutter an ihre Tochter, beim Verkauf eines Feldes (das offenbar der Mutter gehörte) als Zeugin zu fungieren.
130 HACKL/JURSA/SCHMIDL 2014, 326–327, Nr. 216, 8–9 (= CT 22, 225, BM 84943) aus Sippar: Eine Frau erkundigt sich nach dem Zustand ihrer kranken Schwägerin: „Hast du dir eine Salbe mit Wachs für deine Augen genommen?" Wenige Zeilen zuvor gibt die Absenderin auch ihrer Sorge um den Bruder Ausdruck.
131 HACKL/JURSA/SCHMIDL 2014, 349–351, Nr. 241, 4–11 (= TCL 9, 141, AO 8821).

Literate Frauen in Ägypten?

Im Kapitel zu männlicher alltäglicher Literalität wurde bereits auf M. DANDAMAYEVS Behauptung hingewiesen, dass die Literalitätsrate der Militär-Kolonisten in Elephantine höher als jene in den persischen Kernländern gewesen sei. Überblickt man die erhaltenen Texte, kann man diese Behauptung auch auf die weiblichen Familienmitglieder der Kolonisten sowie der jüdischen Gemeinde ausdehnen. Im edierten Material befinden sich nicht nur Papyrus-Archive von hochgestellten Frauen und deren Rechtsgeschäften, sondern vor allem auch ganz private Briefe, die an Frauen, Schwestern oder Mütter von Soldaten gerichtet sind. Einige der bereits genannten Hermopolis-Briefe geben zudem Anweisung, dass eine Frau einer anderen etwas schreiben solle.[132] Wie oben bereits angesprochen, handelt es sich um vorwiegend alltägliche Inhalte, wie die Sorge um das Wohlbefinden der Familie und der Kinder[133] oder die Aufforderung, bestimmte Waren zu senden.

Ein eindrucksvolles Beispiel aus dem Hermopolis-Corpus ist der gemeinsame Brief der Brüder Nabusha und Makkibanit an ihre Schwestern Tarou und Tabi (die Hauptadressatin)[134], in der sich die Brüder beschweren, dass ihnen die Familie seit ihrer Abreise aus Syene nichts geschickt habe.[135] Sie verlangen eine Truhe, *bynbn*[136] und Rizinus-Öl. Nabusha tadelt Tarou außerdem, dass sie ihm nicht geschrieben (Z.7–8)[137] und sich nicht nach seiner Gesundheit erkundigt habe, obwohl er von einer Schlange gebissen worden war (Z.8–9): „(7) And what is this that a letter you have not dispatched (8) to me?! And I, a snake bit me and I was dying and you did not send (to inquire) (9) if alive I was or if dead I was.[138]" In diesem Fall hat man ebenso von einer literaten Adressatin auszugehen, wie in anderen Fällen, in denen der Absender klagt, dass die Adressatin nicht geschrieben hätte.[139] Auch die bereits genannten Ostraka aus Syene richten sich häufig an Frauen mit Anweisungen, Ochsen einzuspannen,

---

132 PORTEN 1996, Text B 2 (= TAD A 2.2:4–7), sp. 6./fr. 5.Jh.: Makkibanit instruiert seine Schwester Tashai, sie solle der Tabi wegen 1 Shekels Wolle schreiben. In Text B 3,6–8 (= TAD A 2.5) nimmt er erneut auf diesen Brief an Tashai Bezug.
133 PORTEN 1996, Text B 7,2–3 (= TAD A 2.7): Ein gewisser Ami bittet seine Mutter, sich um seine drei Kinder zu kümmern.
134 PORTEN 1996, 102–3, Text B 3,2–3 (= TAD A 2.5); beide Frauen tragen ägyptische Namen, siehe Porten 1996, 75.
135 PORTEN 1996, 102, Text B 3 (= TAD A 2.5).
136 Es ist unklar, worum es sich bei dem Terminus gehandelt haben könnte, evtl. einen Gegenstand aus Holz.
137 PORTEN 1996, 102, Text B 5,7–8 (= TAD A 2.5); ähnlich TAD 3.5.5; in demotischen Texten sind solche Beschwerden häufig (vgl. z. B. PORTEN 1996, Texte C 10 und C 20).
138 Übersetzung von PORTEN 1996, 102–3, Text B 5,7–9 (= TAD A 2.5).
139 PORTEN 1996, 102–3 (= TAD A 2.5) Text B 3,4–5, 6–8: Klage des Makkibanit an seine "Schwester" Reia.

sich um die Kinder zu kümmern oder Brot sofort aufzuessen. Leider sind keine Antwortschreiben der Frauen erhalten.¹⁴⁰

Die Frage, ob die Absenderinnen auch tatsächlich immer die Schreiberinnen von Briefen waren, kann nicht mit Sicherheit beantwortet werden. Im Hermopolis-Material gibt es Briefe, die in der externen Adresszeile an Väter oder Männer gerichtet waren, intern aber an Frauen. Dies könnte darauf hindeuten, dass die angeschriebene Frau illiterat war und ihr der Brief vorgelesen werden musste.¹⁴¹ Von den insgesamt acht Briefen aus Hermopolis waren sechs an Frauen adressiert, was einem Prozentsatz von etwa 75 % entspräche. Als Absenderinnen von Briefen können sie aus dem erhaltenen Material nur indirekt erschlossen werden, da in manchen Briefen Bezug auf frühere Schreiben dieser Frauen genommen wird.¹⁴² Nun bietet das Hermopolis-Corpus keine repräsentative Größe an Texten, die eine Generalisierung zulassen würde, aber es bleibt festzuhalten, dass es doch eindeutige Hinweise auf schreibende und/oder lesende Frauen während der achaimenidischen Herrschaft gibt. Der Grad an Literalität in den Randzonen dürfte somit im gesamten höher gewesen sein, als bislang angenommen. Die allzu pessimistischen Zahlen bedürfen daher der Revision.

Literate Frauen in den achaimenidischen Kernländern?

Wie sieht nun der Befund für das iranische Hochland aus? Beginnen wir mit den griechischen Autoren, die spärliche Informationen zur Literalität der weiblichen achaimenidischen Elite überliefern. Laut Hellanikos von Lesbos sei Atossa, die Mutter des Xerxes, die erste gewesen, die einen Brief „komponiert" (συντάσσειν) habe.¹⁴³ Das kurze bei Klemens von Alexandria überlieferte Statement lässt offen, ob Hellanikos sich dabei auf die „Erfindung" offizieller Briefe oder die erstmalige private Korrespondenz bezog. Bemerkenswert ist, dass Hellanikos diese Errungenschaft einer fremden Frau zuwies. Als Frau Briefe zu schreiben galt, wie jüngere Belege¹⁴⁴ bestätigen, im griechischen gesellschaftlichen Umfeld als exotisch, verweichlicht und gefährlich.

Auch bei Herodot werden Briefe hauptsächlich als Mittel der geheimen Kommunikation sowie der Konspiration eingesetzt und sind typisch für die orientalische Monarchie.¹⁴⁵ Nur in seltenen Fällen verfassen oder erhalten Frauen des Königshauses in

---

140 NAVEH 1970, 38 f. (Ostraka Nr. 1, 4, 30), siehe TAD D 7.6.
141 PORTEN 1996, 96 Anm. 2, Text B 3 (= TAD A 2.3), sp. 6. Jh. v. Chr.; Brief des Makkibanit an seine Schwester Reia, außen an ihren Vater Psami adressiert.
142 z. B. PORTEN 1996, Texte B 3 (= TAD A 2.3) und B 5 (= TAD A 2.5).
143 BNJ 4 F 178b; Clem. Strom. 1,16,76,10; s. a. Anon. De mul. 7; auf Semiramis projiziert bei Iust. 1,2,1 ff.; CECCARELLI 2013, 88.
144 Menander F 702 (Körte); s. a. Theophrast in Stob. 4,193 no. 31; zur negativen Einstellung gegenüber literaten Frauen in Griechenland siehe COLE 1981, 227 f.
145 Die Verbindung von Verrat und Brief bei Herodot untersucht ausführlich ROSENMEYER 2004, 45–60.

den Historien Briefe. Beispielsweise korrespondiert Phaidyme mit ihrem Vater Otanes, bezüglich der wahren Identität ihres Gatten, des Magers Smerdis[146] und die Frau des Intaphernes schickt Botschaften an Dareios.[147] Beide Episoden weisen deutlich topischen Charakter auf und sind der Erzählstruktur Herodots untergeordnet. Sie sind Teil seines Perser-Stereotyps und reflektieren griechische Ansichten. Sowohl Hellanikos als auch Herodot können zur Frage der generellen Literalität achaimenidischer Frauen nichts beitragen.

Leider verschlechtert sich das Bild in den indigen achaimenidischen Quellen noch mehr. In Maria BROSIUS' „Women in Ancient Persia (559–331 BC)" gibt es keine Belege, die auf die Schriftlichkeit von Frauen hindeuten würden. Auch im von ihr noch nicht bearbeiteten bzw. im noch nicht edierten Text-Material aus der Persis gibt es bislang keine Belege für Schreiberinnen oder weibliche Autorschaft.[148] Die wenigen Belege aus dem Persepolis-Material, die von Frauen in Auftrag gegeben wurden, sind schnell aufgezählt. Irtašduna (Artystone), eine Frau des Dareios, ist als Senderin eines Briefes bezeugt.[149] Er trägt eine einzigartige Siegelung, die wie eine Tapete den ganzen unbeschrifteten Teil des Briefes bedeckt, sodass kein Text mehr hinzugefügt werden konnte. Das Siegel ist damit deutlich als Symbol der Macht des/der Siegelnden zu sehen – der/die jegliche weitere Veränderung des Textes verhindert. Die bildliche Repräsentation durch das Siegel ist wenigstens in diesem Fall wichtiger als die Schrift. Auch von Irdabama ist ein *letter order* mit Siegel[150] erhalten, der von ihr in Auftrag gegeben, aber auf jeden Fall von professionellen Schreibern geschrieben wurde. In den höchsten sozialen Schichten des Achaimeniden-Reiches gab es also Frauen, wie Irdabama, oder Parysatis[151], die eigene Siegel besaßen und ökonomisch unabhängig (auf eigenen Landgütern und mit eigenen Arbeitern) agierten, aber nicht selbst schrieben. Dass es mit ihrer Lesefähigkeit besser aussah, ist zu bezweifeln.

Die Absenz von schreibkundigen Frauen korrespondiert mit ihrer eingeschränkten gesellschaftlichen Rolle innerhalb der achaimenidischen Kultur. Die Gesellschaftsstruktur der persischen Kernländer war durch die hegemoniale Männlichkeit der dominanten Ethno-Klasse, der Achaimeniden-Dynastie sowie des persischen Reichsadels[152], gekennzeichnet. Sie nahm besonders Elite-Frauen aus dem Blickpunkt der Öffentlichkeit.[153] Daher fehlen sie in offiziellen Quellen und werden auch nicht

---

146 Hdt. 3,68,4–5.
147 Hdt. 3,119,3–5; CECCARELLI 2013, 124; allerdings wird hier nicht explizit von einem Brief gesprochen, sondern nur von der Übermittlung von Botschaften via Boten.
148 Ich danke WOUTER HENKELMAN für diese Auskunft.
149 PFS 0038; ROOT 2008, 108 und 137 f., Fig. 19a; s. a. Fig. 19b (PF 2035); 20a (PFS 0732); Fig. 20b (PF 1838).
150 PFa 27, ohne Datum, HALLOCK 1978, 113; HALLOCK 1977, 128; Irdabama war evtl. eine Gattin Dareios I.: BROSIUS 1996, 127; 129–144; BROSIUS 2016, 160–162.
151 Parysatis, Gattin des Dareios II.: BROSIUS 1996, 127–129; BROSIUS 2016, 162–163.
152 BRIANT 2002, 77, 82, 180–183, 350; ROLLINGER 2017, 200 ff. spricht von „Reichsadel".
153 Dazu im Detail MADREITER/SCHNEGG (im Druck); dem widerspricht nicht, dass Frauen soziales

bildlich auf Reliefs dargestellt. Dies steht in Kontrast zur elamischen Zeit, in der die weiblichen Mitglieder der Königsfamilie und der Elite seit dem 23. Jahrhundert v. Chr. auf verschiedensten Medien abgebildet wurden. Man kennt sowohl Inschriften als auch Siegel, Gemmen, Reliefs und lebensgroße Statuen von Frauen.[154] Daraus kann jedoch nicht geschlossen werden, dass die Literalitätsrate von Frauen in elamischer Zeit höher gewesen wäre als in achaimenidischer. Lediglich die gesellschaftlichen Rahmenbedingungen zur Ausbildung weiblicher Schriftlichkeit wären in elamischer Zeit vorteilhafter gewesen.

Zusammenfassend lässt sich zu weiblicher Literalität festhalten: Im Achaimeniden-Reich fehlten die positiven Rahmenbedingungen, die den Grad an Literalität erhöhen hätten können, weil man Literalität keinen alltäglichen, praktischen Zweck zumaß. Positiv festzuhalten ist, dass es keine Restriktionen für Frauen in Reichsteilen wie Ägypten oder Babylonien gab, in denen es eine lange Tradition weiblicher Literalität gab. Die Achaimeniden griffen nicht aktiv in bestehende Traditionen ein, förderten Literalität aber auch nicht, – weder von Männern und noch weniger von Frauen. Der Hauptgrund liegt, wie bereits öfters betont, in der geringeren Bedeutung von Schrift innerhalb der achaimenidischen Gesellschaft. Dies unterscheidet das Achaimeniden-Reich von Mesopotamien: Dort waren die Auftraggeber von Inschriften auf Weihegeschenken oder überhaupt beschrifteten Objekten häufig Frauen, die – ob nun selbst literat oder nicht–, der Schrift(lichkeit) Bedeutung zumaßen.[155] Das Fehlen solcher Zeugnisse aus dem Achaimeniden-Reich ist also nicht zufällig, sondern zeigt einen anderen Bedeutungsgehalt von Schrift. Für den Großteil der Frauen in der agrarisch geprägten Gesellschaft war sie im Alltag schlichtweg nicht nötig. Der Zugang zu Schriftlichkeit war im Gesamten weniger vom Geschlecht abhängig, als von der Zugehörigkeit in einen beruflichen oder kulturellen Kontext und von sozialem Status.

Prestige durch Imitation der Männer erlangen konnten, indem sie eigene Bankette und Audienzen (vgl. die Siegelabbildung PFS 77*) hielten, siehe BROSIUS 2010 (eingesehen September 2017). Auch Grabstelen wie jene aus Kleinasien (Bakir) oder Statuen aus den Randzonen wie Ägypten bilden Ausnahmen.
154 CARTER 2014, 49 konstatiert eine "remarkable presence of women in Elamite royal iconography"; MATSUSHIMA 2016, 416 f. weist auf die ungewöhnliche Häufigkeit der Nennung von Frauen als "my beloved wife" hin; BROSIUS 2016, 156 ff. und 159 kommt zum Schluss: "Women at the Elamite court were neither hidden in the palace nor restricted to a life of passive existence, but publicly visible, active, and most likely enjoyed independent economic wealth."
155 LION 2011, 92.

Fazit: Ein Reich zwischen fehlender und relativ hoher alltäglicher Literalität

Ausgangspunkt dieses Aufsatzes war die Beobachtung, dass Literalität im Achaimeniden-Reich weniger Bedeutung zu haben scheint als in früheren vorderorientalischen Reichen. Die Kombination von schwieriger Quellenlage und dem generellen Fehlen von aussagekräftigen Texten, erschwerte a priori endgültige Aussagen.

Die Iraner hatten keine eigenständige Schrifttradition, sondern ihre dominante Ethno-Klasse, – im besonderen das Haus der Achaimeniden –, übernahm sie im Zuge der Expansion von den eroberten Kulturen. Mit der Ausdehnung des Reiches wuchs die Herausforderung, Befehle zu kommunizieren, sodass sie von allen Untertanen verstanden wurden. Die Lösung lag in der Etablierung einer Verwaltungssprache in Form des Aramäischen und dem extensiven Einsatz von Dolmetschern auf offizieller Ebene. Die Umwelt im Achaimeniden-Reich war jedoch auch weiterhin nicht schriftlich geprägt, da außerhalb der größeren Zentren kaum jemand Zugang zu Schrift hatte. Dies ist nicht als Rückschritt im Vergleich zu anderen Kulturen des Vorderen Orients zu verstehen, sondern liegt in einem anderen Verständnis der Bedeutung von Schrift begründet.

Die Bedeutung von Literalität in einer Gesellschaft wird von der Ideologie, d. h. von den jeweilgen Machtstrukturen, definiert, die sie umgibt.[156] Gerade beim Altpersischen wird deutlich, dass es den Mechanismen von Repression und Kontrolle untergeordnet war. Schrift war ein Symbol der Macht des Herrschers, visualisiert an den zum Teil mehrsprachigen Inschriften auf wichtigen Bauprojekten in der Persis, Elam und Medien und in Ägypten[157]. Auch das Aramäische hatte eine eindeutige Kontrollfunktion, beispielsweise, wenn es um die korrekte Ausführung von Befehlen ging, die ursprünglich in Altpersisch oder Elamisch gegeben worden waren. Schriftlichkeit war für die wirtschaftliche Ausbeutung des Reiches wichtig, wie sich an den vorhandenen Listen, Steuerabgaben und der ausgefeilten Redistribution von Gütern zeigt. Der Ausbeutungscharakter von Schrift alleine ist jedoch zu wenig, war sie doch auch ein kohäsiver Faktor der Gesellschaft: Sie hielt nicht nur die Gruppe aller Schriftkundigen zusammen, sondern band auch die Nicht-Schriftkundigen an diese mächtige Gruppe. Insofern stabilisierte das Altpersische die Hegemonie der dominierenden Ethno-Klasse, des persischen Reichsadels. Über diesen Bereich hinaus bestand keine Notwendigkeit, Literalität innerhalb der Gesellschaft weiter zu fördern. Die Fähigkeit Schreiben und Lesen zu können, war kein Wert innerhalb der persischen Erziehung. Dies spiegelt sich in den Funktionen von Schrift im Kernland wieder, die auf ihre Buchhalterfunktion und eine im weitesten Sinne politische oder repräsentative Funktion beschränkt blieb. Die konkrete Verwendung von Schrift unterscheidet sich also deutlich von den potentiellen Möglichkeiten einer Schriftart: Aramäisch und selbst

---

156 BROCKMEIER/OLSON 2009, 18.
157 Siehe zuletzt ROLLINGER 2016, 118 ff. (z. B. Suez Kanal, Hibis Tempel in der Oase Khargah).

Altpersisch wären einfach zu erlernen gewesen, wurden aber im Alltag gar nicht oder nur selten verwendet.

Dies leitet zur Frage über, ob das Achaimeniden-Reich überhaupt als Schriftkultur bezeichnet werden kann. Die gesellschaftliche Einbettung der Schrift ist am Anteil und sozialen Rang der Schriftkundigen in einer Gesellschaft, sowie den Funktionen des Schreibens sichtbar.[158] Der soziale Rang der Schreibkundigen war den Rationen-Listen zufolge nicht sehr hoch[159], und sie verfügten über ein niedrigeres Sozialprestige im Vergleich zu Schreibern am assyrischen Hof oder im frühen Ägypten. Bei Frauen ist es kein Zufall, dass sie von alltäglicher Literalität ausgeschlossen waren, sondern Resultat der Gesellschaftsstruktur der Kernländer, die dies nicht vorsah. Änderungen oder gar Restriktionen für Frauen in Regionen mit langer Schrifttradition (Ägypten und Babylonien), wurden von den Achaimeniden allerdings nicht gesetzt, d. h., sie griffen nicht in Bestehendes ein. Der gesellschaftliche Raum der Schrift war im Achaimeniden-Reich generell nicht groß, jener von Frauen noch kleiner bzw. im Kernland nicht existent. Die Zugänglichkeit zu Schrift war hier nicht gegeben, daher blieb ihre Verbreitung gering. Dies überrascht umso mehr, als mit dem Aramäischen eine einfach zu erlernende Kursive zur Hand gewesen wäre. Wenngleich die Bedeutung des Aramäischen als Alltagssprache nicht unterschätzt werden darf, scheint es doch mehr und mehr klar zu werden, dass die heute geringe Zahl an Schriftfunden weniger die Folge schlechter klimatischer Bedingungen oder mutwilliger Zerstörung ist, sondern dass auch im 6./5. Jahrhundert nicht substantiell mehr Texte geschrieben wurden. Ein Indiz, dass die Bedeutung von Schrift in der Persis, Elam und Medien geringer war, ist, dass es im Gegensatz zu Ägypten keine Ostraka privaten Inhalts oder Grafitti auf unvergänglichem Material gibt. Neue Textfunde dürften also wenig am Gesamteindruck ändern, dass die schriftliche Ausdrucksweise von der herrschenden Ethno-Klasse als nur bedingt notwendig erachtet wurde.

Wenn also die täglichen Verwaltungsabläufe in der Persis keine Literalität benötigten, die über jene der hohen Beamten und der Berufs-Schreiber hinausging, ergibt sich die Frage, wie Privatleute im achaimenidischen Kernland Geschäfte regelten, die in anderen Gebieten traditionell schriftlich fixiert wurden, wie beispielsweise Eheverträge, Schuldscheine, Darlehen, Verkäufe etc. Wären solche Transaktionen auch in der Persis schriftlich niedergelegt worden, müsste an mit einem hohen Grad an „second-hand literacy[160]" ausgehen, das heißt, man hätte für solche Zwecke Schriftkundige anheuern müssen. Da es allerdings im Gesamten weniger schriftliche Dokumente gibt, ist es eher wahrscheinlich, dass der Grad an Oralität in der Persis weiter-

---

158 Assmann 2010, 13.
159 Die Rationen von Schreibern beliefen sich bspw. auf ca. 20 bis 30 Liter Mehl pro Monat, was einer durchschnittlichen Höhe für *kurtaš*-Arbeiter entsprach, s. Henkelman 2003, 129 ff.; 136 mit Fn.40. Wesentlich höhere Rationen bekamen jene unabhängigen Schreiber, die der Gruppe der *puhu* zugeordnet waren, s. 120 f.
160 Definition nach Harris 1989, 33–35.

hin sehr hoch war und blieb. Die in klassischen Quellen häufig genannten Boten, die innerhalb des Achaimeniden-Reiches unterwegs waren, können daher im Kontext der Weitergabe von Befehlen und Informationen in mündlicher Form gesehen werden.[161]

Zu pessimistische Interpretationen des Grades an Literalität verkürzen indes die Realität. Alltagstexte aus den Randzonen belegen eindrücklich, dass prinzipiell auch mit weiblicher Literalität zu rechnen ist. Dort existierte selbst in unteren Schichten funktionale Literalität, die deutlich über eine reine „signature-literacy" hinausging. Für Mesopotamien, Ägypten und auch Kleinasien kann man von kultureller Schriftlichkeit sprechen, in der zeitgleichen Persis oder Baktrien hingegen nur von sektoraler. Die Situation in den achaimenidischen Kernländern ist also ein bemerkenswertes Spezifikum. Den Schritt von einer sektoralen zu einer vollständigen kulturellen Schriftlichkeit vollzog das Achaimeniden-Reich nicht. Diese war kurzfristig in den hellenistischen Reichen verwirklicht, doch selbst danach blieben das Parther- und Sasaniden-Reich bis in die Spätantike weitgehend orale Kulturen.

Bibliographie

ASSMANN 2010 = J. ASSMANN, Der Raum der Schrift, in: M. LUMINATI et al. (Hg.), Spielräume und Grenzen der Interpretation. Philosophie, Theologie und Rechtswissenschaft im Gespräch, Basel 2010, 9–28.

BAINES 1983 = J. BAINES, Literacy and Ancient Egyptian Society, *Man* (New Series) 18.3, 1983, 572–599.

BEAULIEU 1993 = P.-A. BEAULIEU, Women in Neo-Babylonian Society, *Bulletin of the Canadian Society for Mesopotamian Studies* 26, 1993, 7–14.

BEAULIEU 2007 = P.-A. BEAULIEU, Official and Vernacular Languages: The Shifting Sands of Imperial and Cultural Identities in First-Millennium B.C. Mesopotamia, in: S.L. SANDERS (Hg.), Margins of Writing. Origins of Cultures (Oriental Institute Seminars 2), Chicago 2007, 191–220.

BRIANT 2002 = P. BRIANT, From Cyrus to Alexander. A History of the Persian Empire, Winona Lake, Ind. 2002.

BROSIUS 1996 = M. BROSIUS, Women in Ancient Persia, 559–331 BC, Oxford 1996.

BROSIUS 2010 = M. BROSIUS, Women. in Pre-Islamic Persia, *Encycloaedia Iranica*, online edition, http://www.iranicaonline.org/articles/women-i, eingesehen September 2017.

BROSIUS 2016 = M. BROSIUS, No Reason to Hide: Women in the Neo-Elamite and Persian Periods, in: S.L. BUDIN/J. MACINTOSH TURFA (Hg.), Women in Antiquity. Real Women across the Ancient World, London/New York 2016, 156–174.

CARTER 2014 = E. CARTER, Royal Women in Elamite Art, in: M. KOZUH et al. (Hg.), Extraction and Control: Studies in Honor of Matthew W. Stolper, Chicago 2014, 41–61.

---

[161] Zu den Medien der Kommunikation s. a. JACOBS 2015 und WIESEHÖFER (in diesem Band). BRIANT 2002, 127, 267 f., 330 weist wiederholt auf die Rolle der Mager (und Sänger) bei der mündlichen Weitergabe offizieller Traditionen hin, vgl. auch Hdt. 1,132; Strab. 15,3,14; Xen. Kyr. 8,1,23; Curt. 3,3,9; 5,1,22; Paus. 5,27,5–6; Athen. 633d-e. Ihre Bedeutung in der alltäglichen Informationsübermittlung dürfte allerdings gering gewesen sein.

CECCARELLI 2013 = P. CECCARELLI, Ancient Greek Letter-Writing: A Cultural History (600 BC-150 BC), Oxford 2013.
CHARPIN 2004 = D. CHARPIN, Lire et écrire en Mésopotamie: une affaire de spécialistes?, *Comptes rendus de l'Académie des Inscriptions et Belles Lettres*, 2004, 481–508.
CHARPIN 2010 = D. CHARPIN, Reading and Writing in Babylon, Cambridge Ma. 2010.
COLE 1981 = S.G. COLE, Could Greek Women Read and Write?, in: H. FOLEY (Hg.), Reflections of Women in Antiquity, New York 1981, 219–245.
DANDAMAYEV 1997 = M.A. DANDAMAYEV, Education i. In the Achaemenid Period, *Encyclopaedia Iranica* 8.2, 1997, 178–179, siehe: http://www.iranicaonline.org/articles/education-i, eingesehen September 2017.
FOLMER 1995 = M.L. FOLMER, The Aramaic Language in the Achaemenid Period, Leuven 1995.
FOLMER 2017 = M.L. FOLMER, Bactria and Egypt. Administration as Mirrored in the Aramaic Sources, in: B. JACOBS et al. (Hg.), Die Verwaltung im Achämenidenreich – Imperiale Muster und Strukturen. Administration in the Achaemenid Empire – Tracing the Imperial Signature, Wiesbaden 2017, 413–454.
FRAHM/JURSA 2011 = E. FRAHM/M. JURSA, Neo-Babylonian Letters and contracts from the Eanna Archive (Yale Oriental Series, Babylonian Texts 21), New Haven and London 2011.
GZELLA (im Druck) = H. GZELLA, Aramaic Sources, in: B. JACOBS/R. ROLLINGER (Hg.), A Companion to the Achaemenid Empire (Blackwell Companions to the Ancient World), Oxford (im Druck).
HACKL/JURSA/SCHMIDL 2014 = J. HACKL/M. JURSA/M. SCHMIDL (Hg.), Spätbabylonische Privatbriefe Bd. 1, Münster 2014.
HARRIS 1989 = W.V. HARRIS, Ancient Literacy, Cambridge Ma., London 1989.
HARRIS/LI 2015 = W.V. HARRIS/F. LI, Ancient Literacy: Parallels and Divergences between the Mediterranean World and China, unpubl. Manuskript 2015.
HENKELMAN 2003 = W.F.M. HENKELMAN, An Elamite Memorial: The *Šumar* of Cambyses and Hystaspes, in: W. HENKELMAN/A. KUHRT (Hg.), A Persian Perspective. Essays in Memory of Heleen Sancisi-Weerdenburg, Leiden 2003, 101–172.
HENKELMAN 2017 = W.F.M. HENKELMAN, Imperial Signature and Imperial Paradigm: Achaemenid Administrative, Structure and System across and beyond the Iranian Plateau, in: B. JACOBS et al. (Hg.), Die Verwaltung im Achämenidenreich – Imperiale Muster und Strukturen. Administration in the Achaemenid Empire – Tracing the Imperial Signature, Wiesbaden 2017, 45–256.
JACOBS 2015 = B. JACOBS, Achaemenid Royal Communication, *Encycloaedia Iranica*, online edition, http://www.iranicaonline.org/articles/achaemenid-royal-communication, eingesehen Dezember 2017.
JACOBS 2017 = B. JACOBS, Kontinuität oder kontinuierlicher Wandel in der achämenidischen Reichsverwaltung? Eine Synopse von PFT, *dahyāva*-Listen und den Satrapienlisten der Alexanderhistoriographen, in: B. JACOBS et al. (Hg.), Die Verwaltung im Achämenidenreich – Imperiale Muster und Strukturen. Administration in the Achaemenid Empire – Tracing the Imperial Signature, Wiesbaden 2017, 3–44.
JONES/STOLPER 2008 = C.E. JONES/M.W. STOLPER, How Many Persepolis Fortification Tablets Are There? in: P. BRIANT et al. (Hg.), L'archive des Fortifications de Persépolis: État des questions et perspectives de recherches: Actes du colloque organisé au Collége de France, 3–4 novembre 2006, Paris 2008, 27–50.
JURSA 2012 = M. JURSA, Ein Beamter flucht auf Aramäisch: Alphabetschreiber in der spätbabylonischen Epistolographie und die Rolle des Aramäischen in der babylonischen Verwaltung des sechsten Jahrhunderts v. Chr., in: G.B. LANFRANCHI et al. (Hg.), Leggo! Studies Presented to Frederick Mario Fales on the Occasion of his 65th Birthday, Wiesbaden 2012, 379–397.
KÜMMEL 1979 = H.-M. KÜMMEL, Familie, Beruf und Amt im spätbabylonischen Uruk, Berlin 1979.

LEMAIRE 2017 = A. LEMAIRE, The Idumaean Ostraca as Evidence of Local Imperial Administration, in: B. JACOBS et al. (Hg.), Die Verwaltung im Achämenidenreich – Imperiale Muster und Strukturen. Administration in the Achaemenid Empire – Tracing the Imperial Signature, Wiesbaden 2017, 469–488.

LION 2011 = B. LION, Literacy and Gender, in: K. RADNER/E. ROBSON (Hg.), Oxford Handbook of Cuneiform Culture, Oxford 2010, 90–112.

LIVINGSTONE 2007 = A. LIVINGSTONE, Ashurbanipal: Literate or Not? *Zeitschrift für Assyriologie* 97, 2007, 98–118.

MADREITER/SCHNEGG (im Druck) = I. MADREITER/K. SCHNEGG, Sex and Gender in Achaemenid Persia, in: B. JACOBS/R. ROLLINGER (Hg.), A Companion to the Achaemenid Empire, Oxford (im Druck).

MATSUSHIMA 2016 = E. MATSUSHIMA, Women in Elamite Royal Inscriptions: Some Observations, in: B. LION/C. MICHEL (Hg.), The Role of Women in Work and Society in the Ancient Near East, Boston/Berlin 2016, 416–428.

MICHALOWSKI 1994 = P. MICHALOWSKI, Writing and Literacy in Early States, in: D. KELLER-COHEN (Hg.), Literacy: Interdisciplinary Conversations, Cresskill N.J. 1994, 9–70.

MILLARD 2003 = A. MILLARD, Aramaic Documents of the Assyrian and Achaemenid Periods, in: M. BROSIUS (Hg.), Ancient Archives and Archival Traditions. Concepts of Record-Keeping in the Ancient World, Oxford 2003, 230–240.

NAVEH 1970 = J. NAVEH, The Development of the Aramaic Script, Jerusalem 1970.

PARPOLA 1997 = S. PARPOLA, The Man without a Scribe and the Question of Literacy in the Assyrian Empire, in: B. PONGRATZ-LEISTEN (Hg.), *Ana šadî Labnāni lū allik*: Festschrift für Wolfgang Röllig, Neukirchen-Vluyn 1997, 315–324.

PORTEN/YARDENI 1986–1999 = B. PORTEN/A. YARDENI, A. (Hg.), Textbook of Aramaic Documents from Ancient Egypt, 4 Bde., Jerusalem 1986–1999.

PORTEN 1996 = B. PORTEN et al. (Hg.), The Elephantine Papyri in English. Three Millenia of Cross-Cultural Continuity and Change, Leiden/New York/Köln 1996.

ROLLINGER 2016 = R. ROLLINGER, Royal Strategies of Representation and the Language(s) of Power: Some Considerations on the Audience and the Dissemination of the Achaemenid Royal Inscriptions, in: S. PROCHÁZKA et al. (Hg.), Official Epistolography and the Language(s) of Power, Wien 2016, 117–130.

ROLLINGER 2017 = R. ROLLINGER, Monarchische Herrschaft am Beispiel des teispidisch-achaimenidischen Großreichs, in: S. REBENICH (Hg.), Monarchische Herrschaft im Altertum, Berlin 2017, 189–215.

ROOT 2008 = M.C. ROOT, The Legible Image: How Did Seals and Sealing Matter in Persepolis?, in: P. BRIANT et al. (Hg.), L'archive des Fortifications de Persépolis, Paris 2008, 87–148.

ROSENMEYER 2004 = P.A. ROSENMEYER, Ancient Epistolary Fictions: The Letter in Greek Literature, Cambridge 2004.

ROSSI (im Druck) = A.V. ROSSI, Languages and Script, in: B. JACOBS/R. ROLLINGER (Hg.), A Companion to the Achaemenid Empire (Blackwell Companions to the Ancient World), Oxford (im Druck).

SANCISI-WEERDENBURG 1999 = H. SANCISI-WEERDENBURG, The Persian King and History, in: C.S. KRAUSS (Hg.), The Limits of Historiography: Genre and Narrative in Ancient Historical Texts, Leiden 1999, 91–112.

SHAKED 2004 = S. SHAKED, Le satrape de Bactriane et son gouverneur. Documents araméens du IVe s. avant notre ère provenant de Bactriane, Paris 2004.

SHAKED/NAVEH 2012 = S. SHAKED/J. NAVEH (Hg.), Aramaic Documents from Ancient Bactria (Fourth Century B.C.E.) from the Khalili Collections, London 2012.

SILJANEN 2017 = E. SILJANEN, Judeans of Egypt in the Persian Period (539–332 BCE) in Light of the Aramaic Documents, unpubl. Diss. Univ. Helsinki 2017.

STOLPER (im Druck) = M.W. STOLPER, Elamite Sources, in: B. JACOBS/R. ROLLINGER (Hg.), A Companion to the Achaemenid Empire (Blackwell Companions to the Ancient World), Oxford (im Druck).

SVÄRD 2016 = S. SVÄRD, Neo-Assyrian Elite Women, in: S.L. BUDIN/J. MACINTOSH TURFA (Hg.), Women in Antiquity. Real Women Across the Ancient World, London/New York 2016, 126–137.

TAVERNIER 2008 = J. TAVERNIER, Multilingualism in the Fortification and Treasury Archives, in: P. BRIANT et al. (Hg.), L'archive des Fortifications de Persépolis, Paris 2008, 59–86.

TAVERNIER 2017 = J. TAVERNIER, The Use of Languages on the Various Levels of Administration in the Achaemenid Empire, in: B. JACOBS et al. (Hg.), Die Verwaltung im Achämenidenreich – Imperiale Muster und Strukturen. Administration in the Achaemenid Empire – Tracing the Imperial Signature (Classica et Orientalia 17), Wiesbaden 2017, 337–412.

TAVERNIER (im Druck) = J. TAVERNIER, Peoples and Languages, in: B. JACOBS/R. ROLLINGER (Hg.), A Companion to the Achaemenid Empire (Blackwell Companions to the Ancient World), Oxford (im Druck).

THOMAS 2009 = R. THOMAS, The Origins of Western Literacy: Literacy in Ancient Greece and Rome, in: D.R. OLSON/N. TORRACE (Hg.), The Cambridge Handbook of Literacy, Cambridge 2009, 346–361.

TUPLIN/MA 2013 = C.J. TUPLIN/J. MA (Hg.), The Arshama Letters from the Bodleian Library, pdf 2013; siehe: https://arshama.bodleian.ox.ac.uk/, eingesehen September 2017.

VANSTIPHOUT 1995 = H. VANSTIPHOUT, Memory and Literacy in Ancient Western Asia, in: J.M. SASSON et al. (Hg.), Civilizations of the Ancient Near East, Bd. 4, New York et al. 1995, 2181–2196.

VELDHUIS 2011 = N. VELDHUIS, Levels of Literacy, in: K. RADNER/E. ROBSON (Hg.), Handbook of Cuneiform Literature, Oxford 2011, 68–89.

WAERZEGGERS 1999–2000 = C. WAERZEGGERS, The Records of Inṣabtu from the Naggāru Family, *Archiv für Orientforschung* 46/47, 1999–2000, 183–200.

WAERZEGGERS 2003–2004 = C. WAERZEGGERS, The Babylonian Revolts against Xerxes and the "End of Archives", *Archiv für Orientforschung* 50, 2003–2004, 150–173.

WESTENHOLZ/STOLPER 2002 = J.G. WESTENHOLZ/M.W. STOLPER, A Stone Jar with Inscriptions of Darius I in four Languages, *ARTA* 2002.005.

WIESEHÖFER 1998 = J. WIESEHÖFER, Das antike Persien. Von 550 v. Chr. bis 650 n. Chr., Düsseldorf, Zürich 1998.

WISEMAN 1955 = D.J. WISEMAN, Assyrian Writing-Boards, *Iraq* 17.1, 1955, 3–13.

YOUTIE 1971 = H.C. YOUTIE, *Bradeos graphon*: Between Literacy and Illiteracy, *GRBS* 12, 1971, 239–261.

YOUTIE 1975 = H.C. YOUTIE, *Hypographeus*: The Impact of Illiteracy in Graeco-Roman Egypt, *ZPE* 17, 1975, 201–221.

William V. Harris
Literacy in Everyday Ancient Life: From Gabii to Gloucestershire

Abstract: This paper offers a partial survey of recent publications that bear on our understanding of literacy and illiteracy in the classical world. But its central purpose is to re-frame two major and difficult problems in the history of ancient literacy: (1) did ideology have a large role in changing the educational practices of the late classical and Hellenistic Greeks? and (2) how should we balance the various factors at work in the history of late-antique literacy, 284–641 AD? The article also advocates greater precision on the part of scholars who write about ancient literacy with regard to social classes and milieux.

Zusammenfassung: Der Beitrag bietet eine Übersicht über ausgewählte neue Publikationen, die zu unserem Verständnis von Schriftlichkeit und Schriftlosigkeit in der Antike beitragen. Die Hauptabsicht liegt darin, zwei zentrale Problemstellungen der antiken Schriftlichkeitsforschung neu zu beleuchten: 1) Spielten ideologische Überlegungen eine gewichtige Rolle in der Erziehung im spätklassischen und hellenistischen Griechenland? 2) Wie sind die unterschiedlichen Faktoren, welche die Geschichte der spätantiken Schriftlichkeit (284 – 641 n. Chr.) beeinflussen, zu gewichten? Der Beitrag plädiert zudem für einen präziseren Umgang mit den Konzepten der sozialen Klasse und des sozialen Milieus in ihrer Anwendung auf antike Schriftlichkeit.

It might be useful to write a review of the literature about literacy that ancient historians have produced in recent years, but its bulk is enormous, and furthermore such a review would have to take account of every ill-informed *esternazione* as well as of the most useful contributions, and for that life is too short. In this paper I will start and end with some pertinent documents, keeping in mind that the theme of this volume is "everyday life" (slippery phrase). In between I shall raise – but not answer – two larger historical questions and consider in some detail two relevant recent books.

Two Small Puzzles

1. Let's consider to begin with (Fig. 1) an expensive mosaic of the late second or early third century from the palace at Nea Paphos known as the Villa of Theseus. The subject is the first bath of Achilles, with the three *Moirai* (Fates) in attendance. The *Moirai* were of course named Atropos, Clotho and not ΔΑΧΕΣΙΟ but ΛΑΧΕΣΙΣ, Lachesis, the

Fig. 1: The First Bath of Achilles, with the Fates in attendance. Villa of Theseus, Paphos, in situ.

Distributor.¹ The master mosaicist, that is to say, made two mistakes in a single word, presumably because he was not able to read properly, let alone write (unlike Lachesis herself, who carries a diptych). That should not surprise us, even in this relatively literate part of the Roman Empire. What is more striking, in fact, is that the wealthy owner who commissioned the work, while he wished writing to be included, did not take the trouble to have a correction made – signs of illiteracy, in other words, did not bother him much. He was not alone in this: "typographical" errors are in fact quite common in mosaics.²

2. Now let us consider an interesting case of the opposite, literacy. An unusually high-quality funerary relief from the city of Rome, this too quite well-known now, shows us a scene from a butcher's shop, with a well-coiffed women writing in a codex of wooden tablets in a somewhat separate space on one side (Fig. 2).³ She might be the *patrona* of a freedman butcher, but more likely she is his wife. In that case, the family of a prosperous butcher in the imperial capital was evidently pleased that she was able to keep written accounts; whether she had learned to write at school, like a

---

1 The mosaic is discussed in Daszewski/Michaelides 1988, 60–63, who suggest (53) that the building was the residence of the provincial governor.
2 See Donderer 1989, 43, 62, 97, and Donderer 2008, 54. But there is a lot more evidence.
3 The relief is discussed by Zimmer 1982, 94–95 (with the older literature), Zanker 1992, 352, D'Ambra 1995, 679.

Fig. 2: A funerary relief from Rome now in the Staatliche Kunstsammlungen Dresden (inv. Hm 415). By permission.

baker's wife in Apuleius (Apul. met. 9,17), or in some other way, we cannot tell (probably at school). The skill had everyday value for her. How many other butchers' wives were literate, in this period or any other, in or far away from the sophisticated capital, we also cannot tell with much confidence, but Rome was probably different from any provincial town in the western empire.

Two Big Questions

1. *The possible effects of ideology on late-classical and Hellenistic literacy*.[4] The circumstances in which the Greek alphabet was invented, and initially caught on, remain obscure, and it is unlikely that any new "earliest known" inscription – a single word from Gabii, now dated c. 825 BC, currently holds the title[5] – will settle the matter. But what caused the subsequent spread of Greek literacy down to the fourth century BC is in general terms reasonably clear. It was a fairly simple technology that offered multiple practical advantages to certain kinds of people, most of all, we may suppose, in economic and political life but also for fulfilling specific religious and military pur-

---

[4] To be explicit: these are the two of the three large questions about ancient literacy that seem to me to be most worth discussing in the present state of research; the third one concerns the use of languages other than Greek and Latin within what is considered to be the Greek and Roman world and the effects of these changing language patterns on the functions and extent of literacy.
[5] BIETTI SESTRIERI et al. 1989–90; cf. in particular RIDGWAY 1995, 328.

poses, for commemoration, and for the writing down of poetic texts.[6] Writing gained prestige, as the nonsense inscriptions familiar from so many vases demonstrate,[7] but also gained, with some people at least, a somewhat sinister reputation[8] (both processes deserve still further study).

But in Hellenistic times something quite different happened. Previously, no Greek community, as far as we know, had ever subsidized basic education or attempted to spread literacy to all of its citizens, unless we are to believe what Diodorus the Sicilian (Diod. 12,12,4) wrote (patriotically?) about the lawgiver Charondas of Catana, to the effect that all the sons of the citizens should "learn letters", with the *polis* providing the pay of the teachers. All scholars except one, as far as I know, consider this claim to be no more than a projection of fourth-century BC or later ideas.[9] In any case public financing of quite a number of schools was a Hellenistic phenomenon, unfortunately known to us only from fragmentary evidence. The principal relevant texts – so often cited – concern Teos, Miletus, Delphi and Rhodes, inscriptions in the first three cases, a passage of Polybius (Pol. 31,31) in the case of Rhodes. The period in question runs from the late third century to 159 BC. The Teos inscription is the most remarkable of these texts, since it aims at both the universal education of the sons of the citizens and at the education of (some of) their daughters. In reality Polythrous, the benefactor of Teos, probably had well-to-do sympathizers in some other Greek cities, particularly perhaps along the Aegean coast of Asia Minor (although one notes that the epigraphical record of, for instance, Ephesus is very abundant and, like the similarly abundant inscriptions of Athens, gives no hint of publicly financed education).

What gave such ideas to Polythrous, to Eudemus of Miletus, and to Attalus II and Eumenes II, and to others who thought as they did? The sources do not tell us. It may well be that the practical advantages of literacy in civic and economic life were uppermost in their minds. In Ptolemaic Egypt, the interests of the government were served by the increased use of the written word. But the question of ideology also arises. This is not simply a matter of prestige. As already noted, writing acquired a certain kind and measure of prestige at an early date, but that does not by any means explain the quasi-democratic urge to spread education to all or very many of the sons and even daughters of the citizens.[10]

---

6 Among recent writers who have discussed the utility of writing in archaic Greece see especially HAWKE 2011, CECCARELLI 2013, JANKO 2015.
7 See IMMERWAHR 2010.
8 HARTOG 1980, 282–291, STEINER 1994.
9 Cf. HARRIS 1989, 98, HÖLKESKAMP 1999, 139–142. The exception is GREEN 2006, 199, who suggests that the colonial environment may have made the Greeks in the West foster their Hellenism by means of universal public education – which is not at all probable (the silence of Plato and Aristotle about such already-existing laws is in itself telling). But this passage is very valuable as an indication of Greek thinking in Diodorus' time, even though one might read it as a *cri de coeur*. See further below.
10 For the Hellenistic period, at least down to the mid-second century, as a relatively democratic period of Greek history see CARLSSON 2010.

We lack information about the contents of the fairly numerous books that philosophers had written about education[11] – none is known to have made any radical proposal on the subject –, but we do know what Plato and Aristotle had to say. In the *Laws* Plato certainly seems to say (Plat. leg. 7,804c-e) – as he had not said in the *Republic* – that all the sons and daughters of the citizens are to learn to read and write, this in three years beginning at the age of ten and in schools built by the state. Three words of his, however, make me doubt that we should take this injunction altogether literally. "No father shall either have his son go to school or not take part in education (*paideia*) according to his own wishes, but the boys are to be compelled to take part, every last one of them (as the expression has it), *as far as is possible* (*kata to dunaton*). The same goes for females as well..." (Plat. leg. 7,804d).[12] This doctrine is in any case radical, but commentators have not given enough weight to *kata to dunaton*. Plato explains his proposal by saying that children belong to the *polis*, but he is never explicit about the advantages that the *polis* will receive from universal or widespread literacy, and I do not believe that he aimed at universality.

Aristotle leaves the practical details even more obscure, and though he states his reasons for holding that education (*paideia* once again) should be communal (*koine*), by which he must mean that it should be widespread – but may not mean strictly that it should be universal –, he is content with generalities ("letters" are useful for many purposes) (Aristot. pol. 1337a33–34; 1337b24–26).[13]

In Crete, according to Ephorus, "the boys" are made to learn letters (FGrHist 70 F149),[14] and this admonitory fantasy is perhaps a story that he picked up in Athens. But the most explicit text is the passage in Diodorus the Sicilian mentioned above, a somewhat strange passage because the author, who, as a Sicilian scholar, presumably knew better, transferred the early lawgiver Charondas of Catana to fifth-century Thurii.[15] The point, however, is that Diodorus' lengthy encomium of "letters", though it reads as an expression of passionate personal conviction, undoubtedly reflects the explicit view of a good number of the educated Greeks of recent generations. (According to a very common view of Diodorus' sources it should go back to Ephorus.[16]) And

---

[11] The prime source is Diogenes Laertius; see the references gathered by MARROU 1965 = 1971, 158.
[12] When I previously wrote (HARRIS 1989, 100) that Plato does not consider how to put such a doctrine into practice I was less than fair. It is probably true that the great majority of ten-year-old Greek farm-boys already worked in Plato's time and that he does not consider how to dispense with child labour; but he does appear to recognize, though not explicitly, that the "Magnesian" state will have to pay the teachers (ibid.).
[13] For some useful discussion of Aristotle's thinking on this subject see NIGHTINGALE 2001, 154–166. KRAUT 1997, 171, supposes that Aristotle thought that "wealthy individuals [could] be persuaded to fund the teachers and schools" according to the liturgical system.
[14] P. 88, lines 18–19 (from Strab. 10,4,20).
[15] As to who actually wrote the laws of Thurii cf. GREEN 2006, 196.
[16] But see SCHOLZ 2004, 108 n. 22.

the high value that many – though not all – Hellenistic Greeks assigned to *paideia* is well attested in inscriptions.[17]

But a proper answer to the question of ideological influence will have to pay further attention both to the material basis of that ideology and, very importantly, to the role that ideologies of various kinds have played in promoting widespread literacy in other societies. Protestant Christianity was a major influence in spreading at least one kind of literacy in early modern Europe and New England[18] – just in case anyone needs proof that ideology can have large practical effects in this area. But that was an ideology that spread across all social classes and concerned personal salvation. The Hellenistic world was very different, but no discussion of ancient literacy is worth attending to unless its author shows evidence of having studied the development of literacy, and of ideologies of education, in other societies too. One can argue that the classical Greeks were a *Sonderfall* with respect to literacy, but only if one takes a good look at other societies, especially early-modern ones.

2. *Another even larger question that begs for further attention is the decline of literacy in late antiquity, 235–641 AD.* The "explosion of late antiquity" has not so far contributed very much to this question; indeed it has arguably obscured the question by injecting a kind of partisanship into assessments of late-antique culture. A whole volume of *L'Antiquité Tardive* (9, 2002) devoted to the so-called "democratization of culture" failed to throw any light on the subject of literacy. The Centro di Studi sull'alto medioevo at Spoleto also lost an opportunity.[19] The series Utrecht Studies in Medieval Literacy has scarcely contributed. Eva WIPSZYCKA has remained unconvinced by my analysis, to say the least, but as far as the social contours of literacy are concerned she has not presented a proper analysis of her own even for Egypt, let alone the rest of the late Roman Empire.[20]

While it may seem obvious that in the territories that formed the Latin part of the Roman Empire as of 235 AD the incidence of literacy declined notably in the next two centuries, the causes, extent and effects of this decline are to a considerable extent obscure. In the East, the problem is even more severe, since some evidence points to a certain decline, at least in Egypt (for reasons that presumably had some effect elsewhere too), as early as the reign of the Tetrarchs,[21] while other considerations might lead us to think that the real decline did not occur until after the reign of Justinian. My only contribution to the debate, in *Ancient Literacy*, did not take account of developments in the eastern empire between the fifth century and the seventh, an

---

17 See the texts, mainly epigraphical, assembled by THOMPSON 2007, 126. For the special case of Teos see ibid. 121–123. The claim that Epicurus was hostile to *paideia* (Diog. Laert. 10,6, cf. Quint. inst. 12,2,24) is not perhaps to be taken seriously (but see ASMIS 2001, 215).
18 HARRIS 1989, 20, etc.
19 SETTIMANE DI STUDIO 2012. But the paper by MOSTERT was very useful (MOSTERT 2012).
20 WIPSZYCKA 1996.
21 See HARRIS 1989, 316.

omission for which I hope to have made some slight amends in *Roman Power: a Thousand Years of Empire*,[22] where, however, the question of late-antique literacy was not addressed.

It should be said at once that this question can only be addressed profitably if one takes proper account of the varieties of language in use in the areas in question, a pattern that was in constant flux. We know much more about this topic than we used to, thanks above all to the labours of Jim ADAMS and Fergus MILLAR,[23] but expressions of opinion about late-antique literacy seldom take any notice, even in Egypt where the rise of Coptic is relatively well-documented. The question is a pressing one in the majority of the whole area that had made up the empire of Constantine.

In the western part of the Roman Empire, "the numerous stamps, seals, and painted or scratched inscriptions that had characterized the commercial and military life of the Roman world seem to disappear almost completely".[24] The decline of the towns, the simplification of both economic and military life, and the breakdown of the traditional education were certainly not compensated for before the seventh century by the initial rise of monasticism. But we lack, as far as I know, a good discussion of overall effects of religious change on literacy in the West down to say the age of Pope Gregory.[25] And even in the West, there were probably differences: it can be argued, for instance, that prior to the Vandal invasion the north-African provinces held up better both economically and educationally than the European ones.[26]

Yet in the eastern part of the empire the story is still more complicated, if only because it was much more drawn out. I set out the considerations and the evidence known to me in 1989, as far as the third, fourth and fifth centuries were concerned.[27] Since then there have been some useful discussions, and a certain amount of new evidence has appeared. Roger BAGNALL gave an accurate account of the Egyptian evidence, with appropriate attention to social class.[28] Harry GAMBLE's book *Books and Readers in the Early Church* attempted to combine some good sense about literacy with the usual Christian partisanship, but in any case he scarcely goes beyond the lifetime

---

22 HARRIS 2016.
23 Especially in ADAMS 2002, MILLAR 1998a, and MILLAR 1998b.
24 WARD-PERKINS 2005, 165, q.v. See further SCHMITZ 2015, 101–102 and his paper below in this volume. It has been entertaining to see that some other mediaevalists, like some classicists, have patriotically exaggerated historical levels of literacy. BRIGGS 2000, 407–409, for instance, argued that neither illiteracy nor semi-literacy was "substantially greater among the masses in the Frankish kingdoms than it had been during the Roman Empire", referring for evidence solely to McKITTERICK 1989 and HARRIS 1989, who do not help him.
25 Many questions arise. Do the new magical properties of writing (MOSTERT 2012, 71–73) result from the increase in illiteracy or simply from greater credulity? On holy ignorance one should not forget SAWARD 1980.
26 Cf. HARRIS 1989, 286–287, etc.
27 HARRIS 1989, 285–322.
28 BAGNALL 1993, esp. 255–60.

of Augustine.²⁹ Konrad Vössing contributed an important paper about late-antique schools.³⁰ Raffaella Cribiore's collection of Egyptian school-exercises has no relevance for the peasants or the poor, but its chronological distribution suggests at least that the literacy of the more prosperous Egyptians held up fairly well until the seventh century.³¹ The late Robert Browning provided an admirable survey of fifth- and sixth-century education.³² Kim Haines-Eitzen published another valuable but very brief survey.³³ Christophe Schmidt Heidenreich has pointed out, interestingly and relevantly, that Roman soldiers, once great enthusiasts for labelling things, ceased to do so as early as the third century.³⁴

But we need a new synthesis that will consider the changing functions of writing and reading, changing ways of transmitting literacy, and of course the impact of religious change. We need an empire-wide view, and one which will take in the whole period down to at least the death of Heraclius. And above all we need an account that is attentive to distinctions of social class.

Two Recent Books

1. Rebecca Benefiel and Peter Keegan recently brought out an edited volume under the title *Inscriptions in the Private Sphere in the Greco-Roman World*,³⁵ optimistically supposing that a clear meaning can be given to the term "private" in the world of antiquity. The collection as a whole ignores questions about who could write and who could read, but there may be something to be gleaned. J. A. Baird, in a study of the graffiti of Dura, brings out very well the differences in the functions of graffiti between their world and ours, and also between their world and Pompeii; graffiti in the rich houses of Dura often serve religious purposes.³⁶ Mantha Zarmakoupi, in the footsteps of Philippe Bruneau, makes a somewhat similar point about the graffiti of Delos, where in some cases were clearly seen as decorative in well-to-do houses (some of

---

29 Gamble 1995.
30 Vössing 2002.
31 Cribiore 1996. Approximately 171 of these texts are dated between 100 and 400 AD, 126 between 400 and 700 (I omit all those to which Cribiore assigns a 'IV/V' date). Numerous factors may have distorted this record.
32 Browning 2000. But his assertion that "many children were taught to read and write at home, either by their parents or by private tutors", though it is to be understood in the context of his recognition of widespread illiteracy, is not supported by sufficient evidence.
33 Haines-Eitzen 2009, 247–250.
34 Schmidt Heidenreich 2016, 519. I return to this essay later.
35 Leiden 2016.
36 Baird 2016.

the ship graffiti).³⁷ BENEFIEL herself is rather bolder, and asks who was involved in writing and reading graffiti at Pompeii, which she unfortunately seems to regard as a typical ancient city.³⁸ Students of literacy have usually contented themselves with pointing out that Pompeii's graffiti are very numerous (as noted by the writers of a famous Pompeian graffito, CIL IV 1904; 2487).³⁹ BENEFIEL goes considerably further, closely examining two *insulae* (I.ix and VI.xv) and concluding that "the numbers of graffiti… are modest".⁴⁰ She also shows, in accord with the two other studies just mentioned, that in wealthy Pompeian houses graffiti strongly tend to be most numerous in the most visible areas, the vestibule and the peristyle, though without damaging the wall-paintings. As to who wrote, she is markedly restrained (I still hope that someone will systematically examine the graffiti in Pompeian kitchens). Nothing is said about Pompeian schools or the Pompeian countryside.

Other contributions to this book offer interesting tidbits of epigraphical information without telling us anything about literacy. Peter KEEGAN, however, reveals a problem of some importance when he tells us that at Pompeii "persons… of likely sub-elite social status could read and write at a level of education beyond the purely functional".⁴¹ The problem here is terminological. I have always avoided the expression "functional literacy" because no one, as far as I know, has ever given it a clear meaning. Was it "functional" to be able to write a letter to a lover, to write out a curse, to keep written accounts? "Sub-elite" is even harder to parse. Some people use this expression to refer to people who were a little bit outside the elite, others to refer to all who were outside. Who in any case made up the elite at Pompeii – ten families, a hundred, five hundred? The term "sub-elite" should be quarantined.

2. Another recent book from which something might be expected is *Instrumenta Inscripta* VI, edited by Maurizio BUORA and Stefano MAGNANI as part of the series *Antichità Altoadriatiche*.⁴² Some forty scholars contributed, most of them favouring antiquarian investigations and no one asking large historical questions. But a number of the papers are thought-provoking. One point, for instance, that many papers bring out is that most of the categories of writing known conventionally in modern times as *instrumentum domesticum* are not domestic in any narrow sense at all, they are commercial or production-related documents, and indeed, as Angela DONATI remarks in

---

37 ZARMAKOUPI 2016, 60. These claims call for some modification, if not outright rejection, of the argument of Kruschwitz (esp. KRUSCHWITZ 2010) that graffito-writing was regarded as vandalism in Roman Italy.
38 BENEFIEL 2016, 80.
39 On which see further KRUSCHWITZ 2010, 211.
40 BENEFIEL 2016, 94.
41 KEEGAN 2016, 254.
42 VECCHIO 2016. For a fuller discussion see HARRIS 2018 forthcoming.

her brief conclusion to this volume, the expression *instrumentum domesticum* seems to be disappearing, unmourned.⁴³

This volume will be indispensable for the future study of inscriptions on portable objects of all kinds, most of all because it contains some useful if highly specialized lists. One of them catalogues Italian wine-amphorae with consular dates on them, 161 items, almost all dating from the period from 129 BC (they suddenly became popular in that decade, which gives a context to *Opimianum*) down to the 80s AD, with a handful of outliers before and afterwards.⁴⁴ Why this pattern, one wonders. Another list catalogues weights, more specifically *pondera exacta ad Castoris*, forty-four items from many parts of the western empire but not all of it.⁴⁵ Again, one would like to understand the pattern. José REMESAL RODRÍGUEZ at least tries to make sense of stamps on Dressel 20 amphorae even if his answers have to be controversial. Other papers are historically interesting for diverse reasons: Silvia BRAITO puts together the dossier of the first-century AD Italian businesswoman (if that is the right concept) Annia Arescusa, producer of architectural terracottas, bricks and tiles, and Cristina GIRARDI throws light on the regionality of some of the gods of the high Roman Empire.⁴⁶

Coming nearer to the subject of literacy, SCHMIDT HEIDENREICH attempts to sort out what he simply calls *militaria*, by which he means words written on military objects of all kinds. He claims that the material suggests "a relatively high degree of *alphabétisation* among soldiers",⁴⁷ and I agree as far as the high-imperial legionaries are concerned. But "relatively high degree" requires some more thought: on the one hand, the names of units and individuals written on *militaria* do not by any means entitle us to suppose that the ordinary legionary was literate in any proper sense of that term; on the other hand, as in 1989, I am only aware of a single illiterate legionary attested in the existing evidence, and in my view the legions were a privileged environment in this respect, for reasons that are easy to understand. More controversially SCHMIDT HEIDENREICH suggests – paradoxically – that the auxiliaries wrote more *militaria* than the legionaries, but since he seems unfamiliar with the extensive evidence that suggests the opposite,⁴⁸ this can hardly be treated as a significant conclusion.

Finally, two papers present an intriguing contrast: Luigi VECCHIO, known to scholars for his work on ancient Velia, publishes here a group of ten inscribed loom weights (*pesi da telaio*), from that city that are datable to the third or second century BC;⁴⁹ they carry single-word names incised before the weights were baked – which suggests large-scale operations. In any case, these are examples of functional writing in a Hel-

---

43 DONATI 2016, 573. On the relevance of *instrumentum domesticum* to literacy cf. Harris 1995.
44 RIGATO/MONGARDI 2016.
45 LUCIANI/LUCCHELLI 2016.
46 REMESAL RODRÍGUEZ 2016; BRAITO 2016; GIRARDI 2016.
47 SCHMIDT HEIDENREICH 2016, 519.
48 Cf. HARRIS 1989, 253–254.
49 VECCHIO 2016.

lenistic city; unfortunately we are not told how many uninscribed loom-weights Velia has produced. They are in any case a nice contrast with the loom weights from early-imperial Vicenza that are also published in this volume, by Stefania MAZZOCCHIN: these were never inscribed with anything more complicated than an X.[50] One can compare the weights from Aquileia, here described by Maria SUTTO (the majority of them previously unpublished), where the inscribed texts are mostly numbers.[51] But inscribed loom weights are more relevant, because they sometimes have real words on them; these inscribed cases mostly seem to be concentrated on Greek colonial sites[52] and in Hellenistic times – one kind of milieu that was likely to enjoy relatively extensive literacy by the standards of the classical world. The practice goes back to the fifth century,[53] and its popularity would be worth tracing. I note that there are certainly some inscribed loom weights from Roman Venetia.[54]

Two Dossiers of Documents[55]

1. *The Bloomberg tablets.* One of the great pleasures of the Zurich conference was learning about the new writing tablets from London's so-called Bloomberg site, texts now efficiently published by Roger TOMLIN.[56] At Zurich, the editor spoke of "widespread" literacy in Roman Britain, without indicating what that would mean (see further below), but he disclaimed any controversial conclusions about literacy that might be drawn from these new documents. I trust that that will continue to be the case, because the documents in question, though fascinating and indeed very important in at least two respects, do not tell us anything at all new about the use of writing in the first-century Roman Empire, though they remind us that conquering "barbarians" meant exporting writing skills into territories where such skills were rare indeed. The new London texts are business documents of Roman or Romanized businessmen who trailed along behind the legions (though some such people were undoubtedly there *before* the legions too) and profited from Roman imperialism at its most brutal. Needless to say – or almost – no literate Britons are known to have been involved; though some certainly existed.

---

50 MAZZOCCHIN 2016.
51 SUTTO 2016.
52 SOFRONIEW 2011, 200.
53 HARRIS 1989, 68 n.14.
54 BASSO et al. 2015.
55 The fact that both these dossiers are British should not be taken to mean that I consider Britain to have been a typical part of the Roman Empire. Elsewhere I have recently discussed, from the point of view of literacy, dossiers from Siscia (HARRIS 2017a), from Cerrione (in the territory of Roman Eporedia) (HARRIS 2014), and from Karanis (HARRIS forthcoming).
56 TOMLIN 2016.

The historical importance of these documents obviously consists in part of what they suggest about the decision of Claudius and his court to subjugate Britain after three generations of Roman rulers had declined to do so, presumably for the reasons that had been lucidly set out by Strabo (Strab. 2,5,8; 4,5,3).[57] The other, more esoteric, significance of these documents is their use of a legal formula, "eive ad quem ea res pertinebit",[58] which shows that the merchants in question made use of a sophisticated Roman method of making payments that, in my opinion, has not so far received quite the recognition from historians that it deserves.[59]

2. *Uley and Bath*. I apologize to non-British readers for turning now to another dossier from the same frontier province. One of the most interesting but at the same time most misguided critiques of my opinions about Roman literacy came from a scholar who joined to miscellaneous fantasies the claim that Britain's curse tablets showed that my views about the social range of literacy were quite mistaken. But his argumentation is feeble.[60]

Two west-country sites, Uley in Gloucestershire and Bath, have produced large numbers of *defixiones*. The total originally deposited at Bath must have been roughly 780, according to Tomlin, covering the approximate period 175 AD to 400.[61] That is to say, an average of slightly more than three a year at what was arguably Roman Britain's most important cult centre. Some of the curse tablets originated with people of modest social standing, as is the case with curse tablets all over the Greek and Roman worlds (curse tablets go back to at least 500 BC). But the point of contention is who actually wrote the Bath and Uley tablets, and about that we of course lack direct information. Most of the Bath curses were written by practised and habitual writers (a few by illiterates who were not really writing at all); they tend to use legalistic terminology,[62] which favours specialist writers. A number of other considerations point in the direction of specialists (specialists rather than professionals, since it is hard to imagine that anyone made a living from such an activity): these were cult centres, where local scribes had every incentive to gather and offer their services; and a magical spell is formulaic and requires precise language, best left to experts. There is absolutely no justification for saying that "those who made a petition to a god had to do it [i. e. write it] themselves".[63] Tomlin's careful discussion sets out the arguments for individual

---

57 Cf. Harris 2016, 130.
58 See tablets 44, 54 and 55, with Tomlin 2016, 155.
59 Cf. Harris 2011, 241–242. I hope to return to this matter elsewhere.
60 Ingemark 2000–2001. He starts from a crudely false dichotomy: "whether literacy in the Roman world, and Roman Britain in particular, was limited to a small part of society or whether individuals of different social standings could have been literate" (19). What lends this critique some interest is that its author does briefly address my comparative argument about the extent of Graeco-Roman literacy – though he misdescribes it.
61 Tomlin 1988, 100: six times the number of those recovered; for the chronology see ibid. 73.
62 Tomlin 71.
63 Ingemark 2000–2001, 23.

and specialist authorship[64] – except crucially the more general arguments that apply to literacy in Roman Britain –, but somewhat obscures their relative importance.

Envoi

Since this paper has to some extent, in spite of the disclaimer at the beginning, the function of a *Forschungsbericht*, I will mention one rather strange recent publication, this one owed to Hendrik MOURITSEN.[65] The subject is Pompeii once again, this time some new graffiti from a *taberna* attached to the Domus Postumiorum. Having set out some banal graffiti, MOURITSEN sets up a straw man, who contends that Pompeian literacy was restricted to the "upper echelons", and sidesteps that fact that the Postumii were a wealthy family who presumably had an adequate supply of literate dependants.

This is a technically competent study which goes outrageously wrong. MOURITSEN writes that my monograph claimed "that literacy inevitably must have been restricted to the upper echelons of society".[66] Never said anything of the kind![67] That such a sound scholar as MOURITSEN can write thus underlines yet again how careful one should be about describing social classes in the ancient world. The social structures of the classical world were not simple, and we can debate the appropriate terminology – the word "class" itself is notoriously problematic.[68] Now, fortunately, ancient historians are getting used to the idea that there may really have been something in antiquity that we can properly call a "middle class" – but more analysis is still needed. Let us at least remember that in traditional societies the daughters of peasants somewhat outnumbered the rentier intellectuals.

Bibliography

ADAMS 2002 = J.N. ADAMS, Bilingualism and the Latin Language, Cambridge 2002.
ASMIS 2001 = E. ASMIS, Basic Education in Epicureanism, in: Y.L. TOO (ed.), Education in Greek and Roman Antiquity, Leiden 2001, 209–239.
BAGNALL 1993 = R.S. BAGNALL, Egypt in Late Antiquity, Princeton 1993.
BAIRD 2016 = J.A. BAIRD, Private Graffiti? Scratching the Walls of Houses at Dura-Europos, in: R. BENEFIEL/P. KEEGAN (ed.), Inscriptions in the Private Sphere in the Greco-Roman World, Leiden 2016, 13–31.

---

64 TOMLIN 1988, 98–101.
65 MOURITSEN 2015.
66 MOURITSEN 2015, 201.
67 See HARRIS 1989, 255–259, and *passim*.
68 Cf. HARRIS 2011, chapter 1.

Basso/Busana/Bonato/Maritan/Mazzoli 2015 = P. Basso/M.S. Busana/E. Bonato/L. Maritan/ C. Mazzoli, Pesi da telaio romani dalla Venetia fra archeologia, epigrafia e archeometria, *SEBarc* 13, 2015, 163–194.

Benefiel 2016 = R. Benefiel, The Culture of Writing Graffiti within Domestic Spaces at Pompeii, in: R. Benefiel/P. Keegan (ed.), Inscriptions in the Private Sphere in the Greco-Roman World, Leiden 2016, 80–110.

Bietti Sestieri/De Santis/La Regina 1989–1990 = A.M. Bietti Sestieri/A. De Santis/A. La Regina, Elementi di tipo cultuale e doni personali nella necropoli laziale di Osteria dell'Osa, *Scienze dell' Antichità* 3–4, 1989–1990, 83–88.

Braito 2016 = S. Braito, Iscrizioni di produzione sulle Lastre Campane: il caso di Annia Arescusa, in: M. Buora/S. Magnani (ed.), Instrumenta Inscripta vol. 6, Trieste 2016, 465–477.

Browning 2000 = R. Browning, Education in the Roman Empire, in: A. Cameron et al. (ed.), Cambridge Ancient History, vol 14. Late Antiquity: Empire and Successors, A. D. 425–600, Cambridge 2000², 855–883.

Carlsson 2010 = S. Carlsson, Hellenistic Democracies. Freedom, Independence and Political Procedure in some East Greek City-States, Stuttgart 2010.

Ceccarelli 2013 = P. Ceccarelli, Ancient Greek Letter Writing, A Cultural History (600 BC-150 BC), Oxford 2013.

Cribiore 1996 = R. Cribiore, Writing, Teachers, and Students in Graeco-Roman Egypt, Atlanta 1996.

D'Ambra 1995 = E. D'Ambra, Mourning and the Making of Ancestors in the Testamentum Relief, *AJA* 99.4, 1995, 667–681.

Daszewski/Michaelides 1988 = W.A. Daszewski/D. Michaelides, Guide to the Paphos Mosaics, Nicosia 1988.

Donati 2016 = A. Donati, Conclusioni, in: M. Buora/S. Magnani (ed.), Instrumenta Inscripta vol. 6, Trieste 2016, 573–576.

Donderer 1989 = M. Donderer, Die Mosaizisten der Antike und ihre wirtschaftliche und soziale Stellung: eine Quellenstudie, vol. 1, Erlangen 1989.

Donderer 2008 = M. Donderer, Die Mosaizisten der Antike und ihre wirtschaftliche und soziale Stellung: eine Quellenstudie, vol. 2, Erlangen 2008.

Gamble 1995 = H.Y. Gamble, Books and Readers in the Early Church, New Haven 1995.

Girardi 2016 = C. Girardi, Le raffigurazioni di divinità con didascalia su terra sigillata. Alcune considerazioni, in: M. Buora/S. Magnani (ed.), Instrumenta Inscripta vol. 6, Trieste 2016, 439–452.

Green 2006 = P. Green, Diodorus Siculus, Books 11–12,37,1. Greek History 480–431 B.C. The Alternative Version, Austin, TX 2006.

Haines-Eitzen 2009 = K. Haines-Eitzen, Textual Communities in Late Antique Christianity, in: P. Rousseau (ed.), A Companion to Late Antiquity, Chichester 2009, 246–257.

Harris 1989 = W.V. Harris, Ancient Literacy, Cambridge, MA 1989.

Harris 1995 = W.V. Harris, Instrumentum domesticum and Literacy, in: H. Solin et al. (ed.), Acta Colloquii Epigraphici Latini, Helsinki 1995, 19–27.

Harris 2011 = W.V. Harris, Rome's Imperial Economy. Twelve Essays, Oxford 2001.

Harris 2014 = W.V. Harris, Literacy and Epigraphy II, in: C. Apicella/M.-L. Haack/F. Lerouxel (ed.), Les Affaires de Monsieur Andreau: économie et société du monde romain, Bordeaux 2014, 280–289.

Harris 2016 = W.V. Harris, Roman Power. A Thousand Years of Empire, Cambridge 2016.

Harris 2017a = W.V. Harris, Literacy Muddles, *Athenaeum* 105.2, 2017, 720–724.

Harris 2017b = W.V. Harris, Afterword, in: K. Hopkins, Sociological Studies in Roman History, Cambridge 2017, 391-397.

Harris forthcoming = W.V. Harris, Review of M. Buora/S. Magnani (ed.), Instrumenta Inscripta VI, *JRA* 31, 2018.
Hartog 1980 = F. Hartog, Le miroir d'Hérodote, Paris 1980.
Hawke 2011 = J.G. Hawke, Writing Authority. Elite Competition and Written Law in Early Greece, De Kalb, IL 2011.
Hölkeskamp 1999 = K.-J. Hölkeskamp, Schiedsrichter, Gesetzgeber und Gesetzgebung im archaischen Griechenland, Stuttgart 1999.
Immerwahr 2010 = H. Immerwahr, Observations on Writing Practices in the Athenian Ceramicus, in Studies in Greek Epigraphy and History in Honor of Stephen V. Tracy, Bordeaux 2010, 107–122.
Ingemark 2000–2001 = D. Ingemark, Literacy in Roman Britain. The Epigraphical Evidence, *ORom* 25–26, 2000–2001, 19–30.
Janko 2015 = R. Janko, From Gabii and Gordion to Eretria and Methone: The Rise of the Greek Alphabet, *BICS* 58.1, 2015, 1–32.
Keegan 2016 = P. Keegan, Graffiti as Monumenta and Verba: Marking Territories, Creating Discourses in Roman Pompeii, in: R. Benefiel/P. Keegan (ed.), Inscriptions in the Private Sphere in the Greco-Roman World, Leiden 2016, 248–264.
Kraut 1997 = R. Kraut, Aristotle, Politics. Books VII and VIII, Oxford 1997.
Kruschwitz 2010 = P. Kruschwitz, Attitudes towards Wall Inscriptions in the Roman Empire, *ZPE* 174, 2010, 207–218.
Luciani/Lucchelli 2016 = F. Luciani/T. Lucchelli, Pondera exacta ad Castoris, in: M. Buora/ S. Magnani (ed.), Instrumenta Inscripta vol. 6, Trieste 2016, 265–289.
Marrou 1965/1971 = H.-I. Marrou, Histoire de l'éducation dans l'antiquité, Paris 1965/1971.
Mazzocchin 2016 = S. Mazzocchin, Pesi da telaio da Vicenza romana, in: M. Buora/S. Magnani (ed.), Instrumenta Inscripta vol. 6, Trieste 2016.
McKitterick 1989 = R. McKitterick, The Carolingians and the Written Word, Cambridge 1989.
Millar 1998a = F. Millar, Language, Religion, and Culture: Ethnic Identity in the Roman Near East, *JMA* 11, 1998, 159–176; 325–450.
Millar 1998b = F. Millar, Il ruolo delle lingue semitiche nel vicino oriente tardo-romano (V-VI secolo), *MediterrAnt* 1.1, 1998, 71–94.
Mostert 2012 = M. Mostert, Using and Keeping Written Texts. Reading and Writing as Forms of Communication in the Early Middle Ages, in: Settimane di studio, Spoleto 2012, 71–96,
Mouritsen 2015 = H. Mouritsen, New Pompeian Graffiti and the Limits of Roman Literacy, in: Antike. Kultur. Geschichte: Festschrift für Inge Nielsen zum 65. Geburtstag, Aachen 2015, 201–214.
Nightingale 2001 = A.W. Nightingale, Liberal Education in Plato's Republic and Aristotle's Politics, in: Y.L. Too (ed.), Education in Greek and Roman Antiquity, Leiden 2001, 133–173.
Remesal Rodríguez 2016 = J. Remesal Rodríguez, Sellar para qué?, in: M. Buora/S. Magnani (ed.), Instrumenta Inscripta VI, Trieste 2016, 73–90.
Ridgway 1995 = D. Ridgway, The Cemetery at Osteria dell'Osa (Gabii). New Light on Early Latium, *JRA* 8, 1995, 320–329.
Rigato/Mongardi 2016 = D. Rigato/M. Mongardi, Tituli picti con datazione consolare su anfore vinarie italiche: indagini preliminari, in: M. Buora/S. Magnani (ed.), Instrumenta Inscripta vol. 6, Trieste 2016, 101–129.
Saward 1980 = J. Saward, Perfect Fools, Oxford 1980.
Schmidt Heidenreich 2016 = C. Schmidt Heidenreich, Un cas particular des inscriptions à fonction explicative et didactique: les inscriptions sur militaria, in: M. Buora/S. Magnani (ed.), Instrumenta Inscripta vol. 6, Trieste 2016, 511–520.
Schmitz 2015 = W. Schmitz, Neue spätantike-frühmittelalterliche Grabinschriften in der Provinz Germania secunda, in: L. Clemens/H. Merten/C. Schäfer (ed.), Frühchristliche

Grabinschriften im Westen des Römischen Reiches. Beiträge zur internationalen Konferenz "Frühchristliche Grabinschriften im Westen des Römischen Reiches", Trier, 13.-15. Juni 2013, vol. 3: Interdisziplinärer Dialog zwischen Archäologie und Geschichte, Trier 2015, 87–102.

SCHOLZ 2004 = P. SCHOLZ, Elementarunterricht und intellektuelle Bildung im hellenistischen Gymnasion, in: D. KAH/P. SCHOLZ (ed.), Das hellenistiche Gymnasion, Berlin 2004, 103–128.

SETTIMANE DI STUDIO 2012 = FONDAZIONE CENTRO ITALIANO DI STUDI SULL'ALTO MEDIOEVO, Scivere e leggere nell'alto Medioevo, Settimane di studio della Fondazione Centro italiano di studi sull'alto Medioevo 59, Spoleto, 28 aprile – 4 maggio 2011, Spoleto 2012.

SOFRONIEW 2011 = A. SOFRONIEW, Women's Work. The Dedication of Loom Weights in the Sanctuaries of Southern Italy, *Pallas* 86, 2011, 191–209.

STEINER 1994 = D.T. STEINER, The Tyrant's Writ. Myths and Images of Writing in Ancient Greece, Princeton 1994.

SUTTO 2016 = M. SUTTO, I pesi parlano: i pondera metallici e lapidei iscritti del Museo Archeologico Nazionale di Aquileia, in: M. BUORA/S. MAGNANI (ed.), Instrumenta Inscripta VI, Trieste 2016, 291–314.

THOMPSON 2007 = D.J. THOMPSON, Education and Culture in Hellenistic Egypt and Beyond, in: J.A. FERNÁNDEZ DELGADO/F. PORDOMINGO/A. STRAMAGLIA (ed.), Escuela y Literatura en Grecia Antigua, Cassino 2007, 121–140.

TOMLIN 1988 = R.S.O. TOMLIN, The Curse Tablets, in: B. CUNLIFFE (ed.), The Temple of Sulis Minerva at Bath vol. 2: The Finds from the Sacred Spring, Oxford 1988, 59–105.

TOMLIN 2016 = R.S.O. TOMLIN, Roman London's First Voices. Writing Tablets from the Bloomberg Excavations 2010–14, London 2016.

VECCHIO 2016 = L. VECCHIO, Un gruppo di 'pesi da telaio' iscritti da Velia, in: M. BUORA/S. MAGNANI (ed.), Instrumenta Inscripta vol. 6, Trieste 2016, 227–247.

VÖSSING 2002 = K. VÖSSING, Staat und Schule in der Spätantike, *AncSoc* 32, 2002, 243–262.

WARD-PERKINS 2005 = B. WARD-PERKINS, The Fall of Rome: and the End of Civilization, Oxford 2005.

WIPSZYCKA 1996 = E. WIPSZYCKA, Encore sur la question de la literacy après l'étude de W.V. Harris, in: E. WIPSZYCKA, Études sur le christianisme dans l'Égypte de l'antiquité tardive, Rome 1996, 127–135.

ZANKER 1992 = P. ZANKER, Bürgerliche Selbstdarstellung am Grab im römischen Kaiserreich, in: H.-J. SCHALLES/H. VON HESBERG/P. ZANKER (ed.), Die römische Stadt im 2. Jahrhundert n. Chr. Der Funktionswandel des öffentlichen Raumes, Cologne 1992, 339–358.

ZARMAKOUPI 2016 = M. ZARMAKOUPI, The Spatial Environment of Inscriptions and Graffiti in Domestic Spaces: The Case of Delos, in: R. BENEFIEL/P. KEEGAN (ed.), Inscriptions in the Private Sphere in the Greco-Roman World, Leiden 2016, 50–79.

ZIMMER 1982 = G. ZIMMER, Römische Berufsdarstellungen, Berlin 1982.

II Roman Empire

Social Groups

Sabine R. Hübner
Frauen und Schriftlichkeit im römischen Ägypten

Abstract: This chapter shows that writing and the use of writing were ubiquitous, even for the majority Roman-Egyptian society who could neither read nor write. The percentage of women who could write was still far below that of men, even though we have evidence for highly-educated women from Roman Egypt who could not only read and write, but were also closely familiar with classical literature. It is also clear, however, that even in a society that was mostly illiterate, writing meant power and access to information, even in everyday family life.

Zusammenfassung: Der Beitrag zeigt, dass selbst für die grosse Mehrheit der Gesellschaft des römischen Ägyptens, die weder lesen noch schreiben konnte, Schrift und Schriftlichkeit allgegenwärtig waren. Der Anteil der Frauen, die schreiben konnten, lag noch weit unter dem der Männer, auch wenn wir aus dem römischen Ägypten auch Zeugnissen von hochgebildeten Frauen besitzen, die nicht nur lesen und schreiben konnten, sondern auch mit der klassischen Literatur eng vertraut waren. Es wird jedoch ebenfalls deutlich, dass selbst in einer Gesellschaft, die weitestgehend aus Analphabeten bestand, selbst im Familienalltag Schriftlichkeit Macht und Zugang zu Informationen bedeutete.

Frauen und Schriftlichkeit in komparativer Perspektive

Man schätzt, dass zwei Drittel der rund 900 Millionen Analphabeten der Weltbevölkerung Mädchen und Frauen sind. Die Hälfte der Analphabeten lebt in Süd- und Westasien, ein weiteres Viertel in Afrika südlich der Sahara. Alphabetisierung ist hier gemäß der OECD definiert als eine kurze, einfache Aussage zum alltäglichen Leben mit Verständnis sowohl lesen als auch schreiben zu können. Selbst in solchen Staaten, in denen in den letzten Jahrzehnten enorme Fortschritte gemacht wurden, den Prozentsatz der Analphabeten zu senken, besteht immer noch ein substantieller Gender Gap. Vor allem in ländlichen Gebieten ist der Anteil der weiblichen Analphabeten enorm.

Gründe für diese Geschlechterkluft sind vielfältig. Unterschiede im Prozentsatz an schreibkundigen Mädchen und Frauen in der Stadt und auf dem Land lassen sich vor allem mit Zugang zu Bildung erklären. In ländlichen Siedlungen ist die nächste Schule oft viele Kilometer weit entfernt. Den Familien fehlt es an Geld für den Schulbus, wenn denn überhaupt einer fährt. Hitze im Sommer und unpassierbare Straßen durch Schnee oder Überschwemmung im Winter erschweren den Weg zusätzlich. Für viele Familien ist es zudem schlicht weg nicht akzeptabel, dass ihre Töchter alleine den langen Schulweg zurücklegen. Bei Söhnen hat man hier weit weniger Bedenken.¹

Im heutigen Westeuropa und den USA müssen wir einen entgegengesetzten Gender Gap feststellen, allgemein als ‚boy crisis' bezeichnet.² Jungen sind hier die Under-achiever, Mädchen erzielen durchweg durch alle Schulstufen und Schichten bessere Leistungen im Lesen und Schreiben, ein Phänomen, das oft durch die Feminisierung des Lehrkörpers, d. h. den wachsenden Anteil an weiblichen Lehrkräften, in den letzten Jahrzehnten erklärt wird.

Für Deutschland wird geschätzt, dass 14,5 Prozent (7,5 Mio.) der erwerbsfähigen Bevölkerung nicht oder nur unzureichend lesen und schreiben können und dass dieser Analphabetismus überwiegend männlich geprägt ist: Über 60 Prozent aller deutschen Analphabeten sollen Männer sein.

Auf den folgenden Seiten befasse ich mich mit den Unterschieden zwischen den Geschlechtern im Hinblick auf Schriftlichkeit in der römischen Bevölkerung, ein Thema, das erstaunlicherweise trotz der Fülle an Literatur, die in den letzten 25 Jahren zum Thema Schriftlichkeit erschienen ist, wenig Beachtung gefunden hat. Da die papyrologische Überlieferung wie so oft unsere beste Quellenbasis für derartige Fragen bildet, wende ich mich dem römischen Ägypten zu.

Schrift und Schriftlichkeit im römischen Ägypten

Gerade durch die erhaltenen Papyri Ägyptens wird deutlich, welche Rolle in römischer Zeit Schriftlichkeit im alltäglichen Leben spielte. Die gesamte römische Verwaltung bis hin zum Funktionieren der kleinsten Einheit der Gesellschaft, dem Familienhaushalt, beruhte auf dem Geschriebenen.³ Alan BOWMAN betont in seinem Aufsatz von 1991,⁴ dass selbst die Analphabeten der antiken Gesellschaft in bedeutender Weise an der Schriftlichkeit teilnahmen. Die erforderliche Registrierung im Provinzialzensus, die Verpflichtung, Geburten und Todesfälle innerhalb der Familie registrieren zu lassen, schriftliche Verträge bei Kauf oder Pacht auszustellen, die Abfassung eines Ehevertrags bei einer Heirat, eine Scheidungsvereinbarung, falls sich das Paar wieder trennte, die Abfassung eines Testaments, die Kenntnis römischen Rechts, um seine Ansprüche gegenüber einem Kontrahenten geltend zu machen, die Ausstellung von Quittungen, machte den Kontakt mit Schrift zu einer beinahe alltäglichen Erfahrung

---

1 UNESCO EATLAS OF LITERACY: Gender disparities in literacy rates for 2015 http://tellmaps.com/uis/literacy/#!/tellmap/-1082895961 (accessed 1 August 2016).
2 POLLACK 2006; DAMMASCH 2007.
3 Vgl. e. g., KELLY 1994, 164–165; auch die entsprechenden Kapitel von HANSON 1991 und HOPKINS 1991.
4 BOWMAN 1991, 121–123. Er akzentuiert dabei vielleicht zu stark die Sonderstellung Ägyptens, auf dessen Zeugnisse er sich weitestgehend stützt.

für alle bis auf vielleicht die Ärmsten. Zum anderen machte die hohe gesellschaftliche Mobilität, die Arbeitsmigration in die größeren Städte und die Rekrutierung von jungen Männern aus der lokalen Bevölkerung für die römischen Hilfstruppen es wünschenswert, dass man mit abwesenden Familienmitgliedern durch regelmäßige Briefwechsel in Kontakt bleiben konnte.

BAGNALL/CRIBIORE unterscheiden drei verschiedene Arten der Abfassung von Privatbriefen: 1) Briefe, die von einem professionellen Schreiber oder einem schreibkundigen Familienmitglied entlang inhaltlicher Richtlinien eigenständig komponiert wurden – hierbei wurde der gewünschte Inhalt dem Schreiber mitgeteilt, 2) einem Schreiber oder schreibkundigen Familienmitglied Wort für Wort diktierte Briefe und 3) eigenständig verfasste und niedergeschriebene Briefe.[5] Sowohl Männer als auch Frauen bedienten sich je nach Schreibkompetenz und finanziellen Mitteln eines dieser drei Szenarien und ihrer Mischformen.[6] Für offizielle Eingaben bediente man sich wohl in jedem Fall eines Schreibers, der mit dem offiziellen Formular vertraut war.

Drei Stufen von Schriftlichkeit werden dabei von der Bevölkerung des römischen Ägypten selbst unterschieden: 1) gar nicht schreiben zu können, nicht einmal seinen eigenen Namen, also ἀγράμματος zu sein bzw. γράμματα μὴ εἰδῶν. Hierzu gehörte, wie wir noch sehen werden, ein Großteil der männlichen und fast die gesamte weibliche Bevölkerung. 2) ein langsamer Schreiber zu sein – *βραδέως γράφων* oder βραδέως γράφουσα.[7] YOUTIE beschreibt die langsamen Schreiber folgendermaßen: „*The slow writers are persons of very limited education. They may as children have spent a year or two with a teacher. Some of them may have learned to read, but most would have lost this acquisition through the many subsequent years in which they read nothing. None stayed at school long enough to develop firm habits of writing, and what little progress they may have made was dimmed through lack of use.*"[8] Ein langsamer Schreiber war aber zumindest in der Lage, seinen eigenen Namen mit Mühe und Anstrengung in ungelenken Buchstaben unter eine Urkunde zu setzen. Wir werden aber gleich noch sehen, dass ein „langsamer Schreiber" jedoch oft nicht einmal verstand, was er da kopierte, also nach heutiger Definition als Analphabet eingestuft würde. 3) Die dritte Gruppe in den Papyri, ein nur kleiner Prozentsatz der Bevölkerung, in den dokumentarischen Papyri aber naturgemäß weit überrepräsentiert, waren die wirklich Schreibkundigen, wobei man auch hier unterscheiden muss, ob jemand unbeholfen, aber eigenständig einen Brief in Umgangssprache an seinen Bruder verfassen oder elegante Prosa mit literarischen Anspielungen komponieren konnte.[9] CRIBIORE betont, dass gerade der geläufige Gebrauch von *ostraca*, Tonscherben, die jederzeit kostenlos zur Verfügung

---

5 BAGNALL/CRIBIORE 2006, 59–67.
6 BAGNALL/CRIBIORE 2006, 60.
7 z. B. Sentia Asklatarion P.Sot. 19–21.
8 YOUTIE 1971, 252.
9 ROWLANDSON 1998, 301.

standen, selbst den untersten bildungsfernen Schichten einen informellen Weg zum Schreiben öffnete, während im Ägypten früherer Jahrhunderte und Jahrtausende das Schreiben auf die Priesterkaste, professionelle Schreiber und hohe Verwaltungsbeamte beschränkt geblieben war.[10] Für die Elite und aufstrebende Schichten war die Fähigkeit, lesen und schreiben zu können und mehr noch, sich gewandt und fehlerfrei auch schriftlich ausdrücken zu können, eine Grundvoraussetzung für eine Karriere im gehobenen Staatsdienst. Für Handwerker, Händler, Verwalter und sonstige Dienstleister reichte vermutlich eine funktionale Schriftlichkeit.

Generell galten Lesen und Schreiben als Fähigkeiten, die zwar als nützlich, aber nicht als absolut notwendig betrachtet wurden. Man konnte also auch ohne lesen und schreiben zu können, am öffentlichen Leben teilhaben und sogar öffentliche Ämter bekleiden. Der Dorfschreiber Petaus im Fayum am Ende des 2. Jhs. war bekanntermaßen Analphabet. Ein nicht des Schreibens kundiger Dorfschreiber scheint zwar kurios, doch nur auf den ersten Blick: YOUTIE argumentiert, dass die römische Verwaltung in einer weitestgehend analphabetischen Gesellschaft Schwierigkeiten gehabt hätte, alle drei Jahre einen neuen Kandidaten für das Amt des Dorfschreibers zu finden, hätte sie nur schriftkundige Männer akzeptiert.[11] Doch ganz so einfach scheint es nicht gewesen zu sein. Denn Petaus gab nach Außen vor, lesen und schreiben zu können, andernfalls hätte ihm wie seinem analphabeten Kollegen Ischyrion die Absetzung gedroht. Petaus konnte dieses Schauspiel jedoch nur aufgrund seines Bruders Theon aufrecht erhalten, der die Schreibarbeit für ihn übernahm. Viele Analphabeten konnten sich daher wohl hinter der Maske des langsamen Schreibers verbergen, auch weil schreibkundige Familienmitglieder oder Freunde für sie einsprangen. Schwieriger zu erklären ist es, warum wir selbst in den urbanen Mittelklasse Männer finden, die nicht schreiben konnten; warum ein Bruder schreiben konnte, der andere aber nicht; warum manche Eltern der Elite ihren Töchtern eine höheren Bildung angedeihen ließen, andere aber nicht einmal ihren Namen schreiben konnten. WIPSZYCKA erklärt sich diese Unterschiede mit den Neigungen und Fähigkeiten des Einzelnen.[12]

---

10 CRIBIORE 2001, 159: „*The extemporaneous and casual quality of Greek and Roman writing technology successfully counterbalanced the limiting and intimidating factor that strongly characterized it in ancient Egyptian and medieval times and that created definite problems of access to writing.*"
11 YOUTIE 1966.
12 WIPSZYCKA 1996, 108: „*Les individus appartenant à une même couche, à une même groupe social, peuvent savoir écrire ou non, phénomène que l'on ne saurait expliquer autrement que par les inclinations ou facultés personnelles de tel ou tel.*" Ebenda: „*La société répond nettement a un modèle demandant une connaissance très généralisée de l'écriture; elle comprend de nombreux groupes de fonctionnaires et d'employés qui produisent au jour une surabondante documentation des toutes leurs activités, et pourtant le nombre de gens sachant lire et écrire reste limite, il ne suffit pas à créer ce climat de pression psychologique qui obligerait tous les membres des élites locales à apprendre.*"

Schreibkundige Frauen im römischen Ägypten

Nach HARRIS lag der Anteil der schreibkundigen Frauen in den antiken Gesellschaften allerorts noch weit unter dem der Männer. „*The general presumption must be that in a world of craftsman's literacy, and certainly in a world of scribal literacy, notably fewer women than men will have been literate.*"[13] Vergleiche mit anderen vormodernen oder frühmodernen Gesellschaften erhärten für HARRIS diese Vermutungen: „*The majority, or a near-majority of skilled craftsmen are literate, while women and unskilled laborers and peasants are mainly not, this being the situation which prevailed in most of the educationally more advanced regions of Europe and North America from the sixteenth to the eighteenth century*".[14] Es finden sich zwar für alle Epochen der antiken Welt Beispiele für des Lesens und Schreibens kundige Frauen. So finden wir durchaus eine ganze Reihe an schreibkundigen Frauen in den Papyri des griechisch-römischen Ägypten, die sich zudem durchaus gewählt ausdrücken konnten. Manche dieser gebildeten Frauen unterrichteten gar selbst als Lehrerinnen Lesen und Schreiben.[15] Frauen bestritten auch als Schreiberinnen ihren Lebensunterhalt. Eusebius berichtet beispielsweise, dass sich Origenes bei der Publikation seiner Schriften mehrerer weiblicher Kalligraphen bediente.[16] HARRIS hat aber wohl Recht, wenn er diese konsequent alle zu Ausnahmen erklärt.

ROWLANDSON und CRIBIORE/BAGNALL folgen HARRIS in der Annahme, dass die große Mehrheit der römisch-ägyptischen Frauen nicht lesen und schreiben konnte und dass ihr Prozentsatz an der schreibkundigen Gesamtbevölkerung noch weit unter dem der Männer lag.[17] AST hat zudem erst kürzlich in seinem 2015 erschienenen Aufsatz "Writing and the City in Later Roman Egypt. Towards a Social History of the Ancient 'Scribe'" als Beispielfall ein Mitglied des Stadtrats von Arsinoe namens

---

13 HARRIS 1989, 24. Was das Geschlechterverhältnis im römischen Ägypten angeht, statuiert HARRIS 1989, 279: „It is certain that the women of Roman Egypt were less literate than the men." Vor HARRIS haben schon CALDERINI 1950 und COLE 1981 für weitverbreiteten Analphabetismus bei den Frauen argumentiert. Vgl. CRIBIORE 2002; ILAN 2005, 177–180; BAGNALL/CRIBIORE 2006, 48–55; YIFTACH 2016.
14 HARRIS 1989, 8.
15 Wenn auch wohl nur auf der Elementarstufe, wie Cribiore argumentiert (CRIBIORE 2001, 51, 78).
16 Eus. HE 6,23: „1. At that time Origen began his commentaries on the Divine Scriptures, being urged thereto by Ambrose, who employed innumerable incentives, not only exhorting him by word, but also furnishing abundant means. 2. For he dictated to more than seven amanuenses, who relieved each other at appointed times. And he employed no fewer copyists, besides girls who were skilled in elegant writing." Siehe auch CRIBIORE 2001, 182.
17 Ob die von Frauen versandten Briefe, die sich zahlreich unter den Papyri befinden, nun von den Frauen selbst geschrieben oder einem Schreiber oder schreibkundigen Familienmitglied diktiert wurden, kann nicht so leicht beurteilt werden. Die Chance, dass die Frauen die Briefe selbst niederschrieben, waren nach BAGNALL/CRIBIORE in den höheren gesellschaftlichen Schichten zumindest wesentlich grösser als in den Unterschichten. BAGNALL/CRIBIORE 2006, 6.

Aurelius Zoilos vorgestellt, der selbst eine gründliche Bildung genossen hatte, dessen Schwester jedoch nicht einmal ihren eigenen Namen schreiben konnte.[18]

Die schreibkundigen Frauen des römischen Ägypten sind ohne Zweifel der im zahlenmäßigen Verhältnis sehr kleinen städtischen Elite zuzurechnen. Schulbildung war nicht kostenlos, es gab kein öffentliches Schulsystem.[19] Die günstigste Variante war sicherlich, sein Kind zu einem Lehrer auf das Forum zu schicken, der dort gleich mehrere Kinder in der Vorhalle eines Tempels im Frontalunterricht in den Grundzügen des Lesens, Schreibens und Rechnens unterwies. Waren Söhne vorhanden, gab man diesen zweifellos den Vorzug vor den Töchtern, wenn Mittel begrenzt waren. Familien der lokalen Oberschichten konnten sich vielleicht auch einen Privatlehrer leisten, der alle Kinder des Haushalts gemeinsam unterrichtete.[20] Allein aus diesem Grund konnten wohl Mädchen der Oberschicht eher lesen und schreiben, denn diese Mädchen konnten in der Sicherheit ihres Heims den Schulunterricht mit ihren Brüdern besuchen. Eltern hatten wohl weit mehr Bedenken, ihre Tochter allein zu einem öffentlichen Lehrer auf den Marktplatz oder gar in die nächstgrössere Stadt zu schicken.

In Amheida in der Daklah Oase wurde vor einigen Jahren vom Grabungsprojekt der Columbia bzw. New York University der vielleicht erste Schulraum dieser Art neben einem Privathaus der lokalen Elite entdeckt.[21] Der Schulraum mit Bänken an den Wänden stammt aus den 30er Jahren des 4. Jhs. An den verputzten Wänden der Räume haben sich bis heute die vermutlich vom Lehrer selbst in roter Farbe angeschriebenen Verse erhalten.

In den Papyri des römischen Ägypten sind auch weibliche Lehrerinnen belegt.[22] So schreibt eine Frau aus dem Dorf Karanis im Fayum an ihren Mann, der auf Reisen war: *„Mach Dir keine Sorgen um die Kinder. Sie sind bei bester Gesundheit und gut beschäftigt mit ihrer Lehrerin."*[23] Vielleicht vertraute man Mädchen sogar lieber dem Unterricht von Frauen an, wenn man die Wahl hatte.

Mühe habe ich jedoch mit dem wiederholt vorgebrachten Argument, dass ein frühes Heiratsalter von 12–14 Jahren ein Mädchen am Erlernen von Lesen und Schreiben gehindert hätte und sie „no better than semi-literate" zurückgelassen hätte.[24] Auch in der römischen Welt begann der Schulunterricht mit 6–7 Jahren.[25] Fließend

---

18 Ast 2015, 6 § 1.
19 Harris stellt daher die Bildung von Frauen allgemein wiederholt mit der generellen Bildung der Landbevölkerung auf eine Stufe: „if we include women and country people", Harris 1989, 22.
20 Zum Schulwesen im griechisch-römischen Ägypten vgl. Wilcken 1912, 136–138; Pomeroy 1990; Morgan 1998, 48–49; Cribiore 2001; Parca 2013, 474–476.
21 Cribiore/Davoli/Ratzan 2008.
22 z. B. P.Mich. VIII 464 von 99 n. Chr.; P.Oxy. L 3555 vom 1./2. Jh. n. Chr.
23 P.Mich. VIII 464 von 99 n. Chr.
24 Harris 1989, 253.
25 Cribiore 1996; Cribiore 2001.

Lesen und Schreiben lernt man innerhalb von 2–3 Jahren; beim Übertritt in die Sekundarstufe, also schon in einem Alter von 10 Jahren, kann man Kinder wohl kaum noch als „semi-literate" bezeichnen. Heiratete dann ein Mädchen in einem Alter von 12–14 Jahren, sollte es, wenn es bis dahin die Schule regelmäßig besucht hatte, zweifellos flüssig lesen und schreiben können, mit Zahlen umgehen und sogar mit den wichtigsten Werken klassischer Literatur vertraut gewesen sein. Die meisten Mädchen des römischen Ägypten heirateten sogar erst einige Jahre später zwischen ihrem 15.–18. Geburtstag. Bei einem derart hohen Anteil an weiblichen Analphabeten dürfen wir also davon ausgehen, dass nicht die frühe Heirat eine Mitschuld trug, sondern vielmehr dass die meisten Mädchen entweder nie eine Schule besucht hatten oder schon lange vor ihrem Übertritt in den Ehestand den Unterricht verlassen hatten.

Keine der bislang erschienenen Studien wagt jedoch auch nur eine grobe Schätzung zur Alphabetisierungsrate bzw. Analphabetenquote in der römischen weiblichen Bevölkerung. Hier kommt eine kürzlich erschienene Studie von YIFTACH-FIRANKO gelegen, die auf den *Hypographai* in den Pachtverträgen von Land im Gau von Arsinoe in den ersten drei Jahrhunderten römischer Herrschaft fußt. Hypographe meint die Unterschrift unter einen Vertrag. Die vertragschließenden Parteien mussten in eigener Hand diese Unterschrift leisten. D.h. man musste zumindest ein βραδέως γράφων sein, um seinen Namen und einige weitere Worte der Kenntnisnahme unter die Urkunde setzen zu können. Ein Stellvertreter durfte nur unterschreiben, wenn explizit in der Urkunde statuiert wurde, dass die vertragschließende Partei nicht des Schreibens mächtig war. YIFTACH kommt nach den Auswertungen dieser Urkunden zu folgendem Ergebnis: 80 % der belegten Frauen, die Land verpachteten, setzten einige Zeilen der Kenntnisnahme mit eigener Hand unter den Schuldschein. Bei den männlichen Landbesitzern waren es sogar 96 %.[26] Anders sah der Prozentsatz bei den Landpächtern aus: der Anteil deren, die schreiben konnten, lag weit darunter: nur 1/3 der männlichen Pächter unterschrieb selbst. Weibliche Pächter, die selbst unterschrieben, sind überhaupt nicht belegt. Unterschiede lassen sich wohl wiederum auf die gesellschaftliche Schicht zurückführen: Die Landbesitzer gehörten wohl zur städtischen landbesitzenden Elite, die Pächter zur arbeitenden Landbevölkerung. Die Rate an Analphabeten hing damit von der sozialen Schicht, vom Wohnort Stadt oder Land und schlussendlich vom Geschlecht ab.

Basierend auf diesen Überlegungen möchte ich es sogar wagen, mich rechnerisch dem Prozentsatz der schreibkundigen Frauen an der römisch-ägyptischen Gesamtbevölkerung anzunähern. TACOMA kommt in seiner 2008 erschienenen Studie zu dem Schluss, dass im römischen Ägypten des 2.–4. Jhs. je nach Region rund 10–20 % des Landes in weiblicher Hand war. Frauen besaßen dabei weniger große Flächen Land

---

26 YIFTACH 2016.

als Männer, was erklärt, dass sie je nach Region 20–30 % der Landbesitzer stellten.[27] Land wiederum konzentrierte sich in den Händen einiger weniger. TACOMA legt dar, dass in den größeren Städten nur 2 %, in den kleineren Dörfern des Fayum wohl max. 5 % der Bevölkerung Land besaßen.[28] 95–98 % der Bevölkerung waren also landlos. Wenn 80 % der landbesitzenden Frauen schreiben konnten und Frauen zwischen 20–30 % der Landbesitzer stellten, gleichzeitig aber das Land sich in den Händen von nur 2 %-5 % der Bevölkerung konzentrierte, kommt man zu folgenden Zahlen: 0,32 % – 1,2 % der weiblichen Bevölkerung waren zumindest βραδέως γράφουσαι, d. h. sie konnten zumindest einige Zeilen in eigener Hand, vielleicht langsam und mit unsicherer Hand kopierend schreiben. Es handelt sich hier wohlgemerkt um Mindestwerte, denn über schreibkundige Frauen aus dem städtischen Milieu, die kein Land besaßen, sagen diese Zahlen natürlich nichts aus. Dies heißt jedoch wiederum, dass der Anteil der Frauen, die schreiben konnten, wohl insgesamt kaum über 5 % hinausreichte.[29]

Da bei den Männern 98 % der landbesitzenden Schicht selbst in eigener Hand die *hypographe* leisteten und von den landpachtenden Männern immerhin noch 32 %, kommen wir auf wesentlich höhere Prozentzahlen, was den Anteil der schreibkundigen Männer angeht. 33–39 % der gesamten männlichen Bevölkerung war offensichtlich in der Lage, den eigenen Namen sowie einige weitere Worte zu schreiben. Nach HARRIS waren 90 % der Bevölkerung des römischen Ägypten Analphabeten, d. h. sie konnten überhaupt nicht lesen und schreiben, nicht einmal ihren eigenen Namen.[30] Wenige haben diese These angezweifelt, und sie darf auch heute noch als *opinio communis* gelten. Die Auswertung der *hypographai* revidiert diese Annahme. Ein gutes Drittel der männlichen Bevölkerung selbst auf dem Land konnte offensichtlich doch den eigenen Namen schreiben.

Bestätigung finden diese Zahlen in weiteren von YIFTACH untersuchten 316 *hypographai* aus dem öffentlichen Archiv für Rechtsurkunden, dem römischen grapheion. Beinahe ¾ dieser schriftlichen Kenntnisnahmen, 235 von insgesamt 316, wurden nicht von den Vertragspartnern selbst geschrieben, sondern von einem Stellvertreter, der des Schreibens mächtig war. Nur 81 von 316 Individuen verfassten diese Unterschriften selbst. 34 % der Männer unterschrieb in eigener Hand, jedoch nur 6.7 % der Frauen.[31]

---

[27] TACOMA 2006, 107–111. Vgl. ROWLANDSON 1998, 220, die wohl fälschlicherweise von einem weitaus höheren Anteil von 1/3 an weiblichen Landbesitzern ausgeht.
[28] TACOMA 2006, 92–96.
[29] Für die männliche Bevölkerung kommen wir dementsprechend auf höhere Zahlen (cf. YIFTACH 2016). 34–41 % waren hier zumindest ‚functional literate'. Hinzurechnen müssen wir die Angehörigen der städtischen Handwerkerschicht, Dienstleister, Sklaven, die alle kein Land besaßen oder pachteten, aber vielleicht oft schreiben konnten.
[30] HARRIS 1989, 276–279.
[31] YIFTACH 2016.

Jedoch bedeutet dies nicht, dass ein Drittel der männlichen Gesamtbevölkerung wirklich schriftkundig war. An den Unterschriften sieht man, dass viele nur langsam, in wackeliger Schrift mühsam Buchstaben für Buchstaben kopieren konnten. Meine vierjährige Tochter kann das. Erhalten ist eine Schreibübung des bereits erwähnten Dorfschreibers Petaus. Er übt hier seine Unterschrift, Πεταῦς ἐπιδέδωκα «Ich, Petaus, habe eingereicht», indem er immer wieder die gleich darüber stehende Zeile kopiert. Er merkt nicht einmal, als er in Z. 5 einen Buchstaben vergisst und kopiert den Fehler über die nächsten Zeilen immer wieder. Um eine Unterschrift zu leisten, musste man nicht schreiben können. Man musste in der Tat nicht einmal Griechisch können, um diese eine gleiche Formel unter seine Dokumente zu setzen.

Denn hinzu kommt, dass wir es größtenteils mit einer zweisprachigen Gesellschaft zu tun haben – ein Aspekt, dessen Bedeutung kaum überschätzt werden kann. Die indigene Bevölkerung des römischen Ägypten sprach zumindest im Familienverband weiterhin Ägyptisch. Ägyptisch blieb durch die gesamte hellenistische und römische Epoche die Umgangssprache der einfachen Bevölkerung. Vor der Geburt des Koptischen erforderte jedoch jeder Kontext, der das geschriebene Wort verlangte, die Kenntnis des Griechischen als einzig zur Verfügung stehende Schriftsprache.[32] Manch einer unserer griechischen Briefe an Familienmitglieder mag daher zunächst aus dem Ägyptischen übersetzt worden sein, bevor er von einem Schreiber niedergeschrieben werden konnte. Männer und Frauen, die eine Hypographe in eigener Hand unter einen Vertrag setzen konnten, mögen vielleicht nur ihren eigenen Namen und einige weitere formelhafte Wendungen in Griechisch verstanden und schreiben gekonnt haben. Die Tatsache, dass für einen sehr großen Teil der Bevölkerung Schreiben und Lesen lernen zunächst erst einmal das Erlernen einer Fremdsprache erforderte, drückte zweifellos den Anteil derer, die wirklich diese Fähigkeit erwarben und diese auch dann als Erwachsener im Alltag einsetzen konnten. Es scheint zudem, dass Mädchen und Frauen weit öfter nur ägyptisch sprachen, allein weil sie weitaus seltener im öffentlichen griechischsprachigen Raum auftraten. Allein aus diesem Grund mögen sie sich mit dem Schreiben lernen umso schwerer getan haben.[33]

Eudaimonis vs. Saturnila

Man gewinnt aus den erhaltenen Papyri zweifellos den Eindruck, dass mehr Männer als Frauen des Schreibens und Lesens mächtig waren. Die Papyri, vor allem Unter-

---

32 Koptisch wurde erst ab der byzantinischen Zeit auch für die Privatkorrespondenz und Privatverträge üblich. Im Jahr 719 lässt eine gewisse Elizabeth, die selbst wohl nicht lesen und schreiben konnte, ihr Testament mit den Worten enden: „Ich, Elizabeth, Tochter des verstorbenen Epiphanios und der Maria, habe dieses verfügt. Sie lasen es mir auf ägyptisch vor. Ich habe es gehört und bin damit einverstanden." (P.KRU 68,95–99, eigene Übersetzung basierend auf WILFONG 2002, 61).
33 Siehe dazu FEWSTER 2002.

suchungen der Hypographai liefern zwar statistisch auswertbares Material, durch welches sich die Unterschiede annähernd in Prozentzahlen ausdrücken lassen, jedoch stellt sich letztendlich immer die gewichtige Frage der Repräsentativität der Daten. Bedeutende Unterschiede bestanden wohl zwischen Dorf-Stadt, der griechischen und indigenen Bevölkerung, Alexandria und den übrigen Gauen sowie den Gauen untereinander, den Epochen und Jahrhunderten, den sozialen Schichten, und so weiter. Endgültige Antworten erlauben unsere Papyri nicht.

Ich möchte abschließend zwei Fallbeispiele vorstellen, um das Spektrum von Schriftlichkeit im römischen Ägypten zu veranschaulichen. Wir haben hier zwei verwitwete Damen mittleren Alters, die eine mit Namen Eudaimonis, die andere Saturnila. Beide Frauen lebten im 2. Jahrhundert nach Christus in Mittelägypten. Eudaimonis war eine verwitwete Mutter und Großmutter aus der Metropolis Hermopolis, Saturnila eine ebenfalls verwitwete Mutter und Großmutter aus dem Dorf Karanis im Gau von Arsinoe. Beide Frauen lebten zusammen mit ihren Kindern und Enkelkindern und beide gehörten zur lokalen Oberschicht.

Eudaimonis

Beginnen wir mit Eudaimonis, die uns durch das Archiv ihres Sohnes, des Strategen Apollonios aus dem frühen 2. Jh. n. Chr., bekannt ist. Das Archiv des Strategen Apollonios wurde an der Stelle des antiken Hermopolis in Mittelägypten gefunden, vermutlich sogar in dem Haus, das die Familie einst bewohnte. Eudaimonis' Familie gehörte zur griechischen Oberschicht ihrer Stadt. Ihr Sohn Apollonios war im frühen 2. Jh. zum Strategos, also zum Oberhaupt der römischen Zivilverwaltung, von Heptakomia in Oberägypten ernannt worden, das rund 100 km weiter südlich von Hermopolis lag. Seine Frau Aline und seine jüngere Tochter folgten ihm an seinen neue Arbeitsstätte, seine Mutter blieb jedoch in Hermopolis zurück. Bei Eudaimonis verblieb auch deren Enkelin, Apollonios' ältere Tochter, Heraidous, ein Mädchen von vielleicht 10 Jahren, die in Hermopolis den Schulunterricht besuchte.[34] Dieser temporären Trennung der Familienmitglieder verdanken wir eine interessante Korrespondenz zwischen der in Hermopolis zurückgebliebenen Eudaimonis und Apollonios in Heptakomia und ebenso Aline, dessen Frau, die sich mal in Hermopolis, dann wieder einmal bei ihrem Mann in Heptakomia aufhielt.[35]

In diesen Briefen lernen wir Eudaimonis als eine gebildete, resolute Frau kennen, die unbestrittene Matriarchin dieser Grossfamilie, die mit ihrem Sohn und dessen Frau Aline in regem Briefkontakt stand.[36] Elf ihrer Briefe sind überliefert, die sie größ-

---

34 P.Alex.Giss. 59 = SB X 10652C.
35 CRIBIORE 2002, 152.
36 Zu den Frauen der Familie des Strategen Apollonios vgl. ROWLANDSON 1998, 118–124; BAGNALL/CRIBIORE 2006, 139–163.

tenteils einem Sekretär diktierte. Sie fügt ihren diktierten Briefen jedoch Grüße[37] oder ein Postskriptum in eigener Hand hinzu.[38]

Drei ihrer elf erhaltenen Briefe hat sie vermutlich selbst verfasst – in ungelenker Handschrift – wie die Editoren es bezeichnen.[39] Die von Eudaimonis vermutlich selbst verfassten Briefe enthalten keine Syntaxfehler, obwohl es selbst nicht einmal selbstverständlich war, dass professionelle Schreiber fehlerfrei schrieben, und nur einer der drei Briefe offenbart einige wenige, der Aussprache geschuldete Rechtschreibfehler.

Die Schwiegertochter der Eudaimonis, Aline, war ebenfalls eine gebildete Frau, die eine rege Briefkorrespondenz mit ihrer Schwiegermutter, ihrem Ehemann Apollonios und weiteren Familienmitgliedern und Bediensteten der Familie führte. Ihre drei erhaltenen Briefe sind zwar diktiert, aber ihre in einem Schreiben selbst hinzugefügten Grußworte am Briefende verraten, dass sie mühelos und flüssig schreiben konnte.[40]

In den Briefen der Eudaimonis begegnet uns auch die bereits erwähnte Enkelin Heraidous. Mehrere der erhaltenen Briefe des Familienarchivs befassen sich mit der Schulbildung der Heraidous, die deren Großmutter Eudaimonis und deren Eltern Apollonios und Aline sehr ernst nahmen. Vor allem ihre Fortschritte im Lesen kommen wiederholt zur Sprache.[41] Es war vielleicht sogar Heraidous' Schulausbildung, die schon über den Elementarunterricht hinaus war, die die Eltern veranlasst hatte, Heraidous bei ihrer Großmutter in der Hauptstadt zurückzulassen. In jedem Fall haben wir dem Umstand der Trennung des Mädchens von ihren Eltern zu verdanken, dass wir über die Schulbildung Heraidous' überhaupt informiert sind. Dem Lehrer wurden Speisereste geschickt, die vom Besuch des Strategen zu Hause bei seiner Mutter übriggeblieben waren, damit er sich besonders um Heraidous bemühte: „*Die Tauben und die Hühner, die ich nicht zu essen pflege, schick dem Lehrer von Heraidous. (...) Was ich bei meinem Besuch bei Dir nicht gegessen habe, schick dem Lehrer meiner Tochter, damit er sich besonders um sie bemüht.*"[42] Man besorgte Heraidous ein Buch, damit sie das Lesen übe.[43] Großmutter Eudaimonis versichert den Eltern, dass Heraidous fleißig lerne: „*Das kleine Mädchen grüsst Dich und lernt eifrig für die Schule.*"[44] Die Fürsorge, die der Ausbildung dieses Mädchens aus der Oberschicht der hellenisierten Gau-

---

37 z. B. P.Brem. 63; siehe auch dazu BAGNAL/CRIBIORE 2006, 143–144; P.Giss. 21; siehe auch dazu BAGNALL/CRIBIORE 2006, 154–155.
38 P.Flor. III 332; siehe auch dazu BAGNALL/CRIBIORE 2006, 147: „The personal greetings of Eudaimonis are also fast and fluent."
39 P.Giss. 22; P.Giss. 23; P.Giss. 24; siehe auch dazu BAGNALL/CRIBIORE 2006, 155–158. Evtl. stammt auch P.Giss. 79 von Aline (BAGNALL/CRIBIORE 2006, 139–40; 162–163).
40 P.Giss. 78; siehe auch dazu BAGNALL/CRIBIORE 2006, 161–162. Für Alines übrige bekannte Briefe siehe P.Giss. 19 und P.Giss. 20.
41 P.Giss. 78; P.Giss. 80; P.Giss. 85.
42 P.Giss. 80.
43 P.Giss. 85.
44 P.Brem. 63. Siehe auch dazu ROWLANDSON 1998, 94; BAGNALL/CRIBIORE 2006, 143–144.

metropole Hermopolis zukam, scheint zwar außerordentlich, ist aber dennoch nicht verwunderlich, schaut man auf die erwachsenen Frauen der Familie. Hinzu kommt, dass Apollonios und Aline bislang keinen Sohn hatten,[45] vielleicht investierten sie auch aus diesem Grund mehr Aufmerksamkeit in die Bildung ihrer älteren Tochter.

Saturnila

Kommen wir zum zweiten Fallbeispiel, der Saturnila. Saturnila lebte im späten 2. Jh. im Fayum in Mittelägypten und war eine römische Bürgerin, vielleicht die Tochter eines Veteranen der römischen Hilfstruppen. Saturnila lebte zusammen mit ihren fünf Söhnen, ihren Schwiegertöchtern, Enkelkindern und weiteren Familienmitgliedern im Dorf Karanis. Die Familie hatte Landbesitz in der Gegend und gehörte zweifellos zur wohlhabenden lokalen Oberschicht. Saturnilas ältester Sohn Sempronius hatte des Öfteren geschäftlich in Alexandria zu tun, unterhielt Geschäftsbeziehungen mit dem in der Nähe stationierten römischen Heer und schrieb von dort aus Briefe nach Hause an seine Mutter und Brüder.

Zum Archiv der Familie gehören bislang 8 Papyrusdokumente. Da manche der Papyrusblätter mehrere Briefe enthalten, zählt man insgesamt 12 Briefe.[46] Der Fundort der Papyri ist nicht bekannt. Sie tauchten im frühen 20. Jh. auf dem Antikenmarkt auf und das einstmals zusammengehörende Familienarchiv ist heute verstreut auf verschiedene Sammlungen auf der ganzen Welt.[47] Da Mitglieder dieser Familie in ihren Briefen auffallend liebenswert und zartfühlend miteinander sprechen, wurde dieses Archiv von Bell das „Happy-Family–Archiv" getauft.[48]

Die verwitwete Mutter Saturnila ist diejenige, an die die meisten Briefe der Sammlung gerichtet sind. Ähnlich der Eudaimonis ist auch Saturnila der Dreh- und Angelpunkt der Familie und der Familienkorrespondenz – oder wird zumindest von ihren erwachsenen Söhnen in dem Glauben gelassen. Denn Saturnila konnte offensichtlich gar nicht lesen, sondern musste sich die an sie gerichteten Briefe von ihren Söhnen vorlesen lassen.

Wir wollen uns einen der an sie gerichteten Briefe, einen sogenannten Doppelbrief, näher anschauen.[49] Er wurde 1919 vom British Museum in Ägypten zusammen mit Dokumenten aus dem Zenon-Archiv angekauft und befindet sich heute in

---

45 P.Brem. 63.
46 P.Heid.Gr. VII 400; P.Mich. III 206, 209; P.Mich. XV 751–752; P.Wisc. II 84; SB III 6263; SB XXVI 16578; SB III 6263 und P.Mich. XV 752 enthalten jeweils zwei Briefe, P.Wisc. II 84 enthält sogar drei Briefe.
47 Dokumente des Archives befinden sich heute in der Sammlung der University of Michigan in Ann Arbor, der Universität Heidelberg, der British Library in London, der Wisconsin State University in Madison und der Columbia University in New York.
48 BELL 1950, 206.
49 SB III 6263.

der British Library in London. Das Papyrusblatt enthält zwei Briefe des Sempronius, ältester Sohn der Saturnila, der sich auf Reisen in Alexandria befand. Der erste Brief richtet sich an die Mutter; der zweite Brief auf dem gleichen Blatt gleich darunter gesetzt ist nur für die Ohren seines Bruders gedacht. Der Hinweis für den Briefboten auf der Rückseite des Blattes bzw. der Aussenseite des Briefes lautet: „Übergib an seinen Bruder Maximus von Sempronius." Sempronius schreibt an seine Mutter in der Erwartung, dass sein Bruder Maximus ihr den Brief vorliest:

„*Sempronius an seine Mutter und Herrin Saturnila, sehr viele Grüsse. Ich hoffe vor allem, dass es dir und meinen süssesten Brüdern gut geht, dass der böse Blick euch keinen Schaden zufügt. Und gleichzeitig bete ich täglich zu Gott Sarapis für euer aller Wohlergehen. So viele Briefe habe ich euch geschickt, und nicht einen hast Du mir zurückgeschickt, obwohl so viele Leute flussabwärts gereist sind. Bitte schreib mir, Herrin, so bald als möglich über Dein Wohlergehen, so dass ich weniger beunruhigt bin; denn es ist Dein Wohlergehen, für das ich beständig bete. Grüsse an Maximus und seine Frau und Saturninus und Gemellus und Helena und deren Familie. Richte ihr aus, dass ich einen Brief von Sempronios aus Kappadokien erhalten habe. Grüsse an Julius und jeden einzelnen seiner Familie und Skythikus und Thermuthis und deren Kinder. Gemellus schickt euch ebenfalls Grüsse. Lebe immer wohl, meine Herrin.*"[50]

Nach diesem überaus liebevollem Schreiben an seine Mutter, in der er die geehrte Mutter seiner Liebe und Fürsorge versichert, fügt Sempronius eine Notiz für seinen Bruder Maximus an, die nur für dessen Augen bestimmt ist:

„*Sempronius seinem Bruder Maximus recht viel Freude. Vor allem wünsche ich Dir Gesundheit. Ich erfuhr, dass ihr unsere Frau Mutter wie eine Magd behandelt. Lass dich bitten, süssester Bruder, betrübe sie nicht im Geringsten. Widerspricht ihr einer der Brüder, so solltest du ihnen Ohrfeigen geben, denn du solltest jetzt ihr Vater heissen. Ich weiss, dass du auch ohne meinen Brief ihr zu verhelfen vermagst. Also nimm meinen Mahnbrief nicht übel, denn wir sollen sie wie Gott ehren, die uns gebar, vor allem wenn sie so gut ist. Dies hab ich dir geschrieben, mein Bruder, weil ich weiss, wie süss es ist, Eltern zu haben. Du wirst gut tun, mir von eurem Befinden zu schreiben. Bleib gesund, mein Bruder.*" (Übers. SCHUBART 1923, 104, Nr. 75).

Sempronius und seine vier Brüder ehren ihre Mutter hoch, das ehrerbietige Auftreten der Söhne hat ganze Papyrologengenerationen beeindruckt, doch sie bevormunden sie gleichermassen. Die Brüder regelten untereinander, was die Mutter erfahren sollte und was eben nicht. Der Antrieb des ältesten Sohnes, Sempronius, ist ehrenhaft, er will die Mutter im Glauben lassen, dass sie das Familienoberhaupt ist, das alle Zügel in der Hand hält. Die Mutter soll glauben, dass ihre Söhne, wenn sie auf Reisen sind, ihre Briefe an sie als Familienoberhaupt richten. Man schreibt der verehrten Mutter und richtet durch sie Grüsse auch an alle übrigen daheim gebliebenen Bewohner des Haushalts aus. Sogar an Maximus lässt Sempronius seine Mutter Grüsse

---

50 Vgl. P.Wisc. II 84 (eigene Übersetzung).

ausrichten, obwohl er doch einen weiteren Brief an seinen Bruder selbst richtet, der sogar auf dem gleichen Blatt steht. Saturnila, die nicht lesen kann, weiss dies natürlich nicht. Und sie weiss auch nicht, was der Brief an Maximus enthält, dass es um sie selbst geht, dass Sempronius gewahr ist, dass die Brüder die Mutter nicht immer mit dem gebührenden Respekt behandeln.[51]

Conclusio

Schrift war zweifellos allgegenwärtig im römischen Ägypten. Schriftliche und nichtschriftliche Teile der Bevölkerung lebten dabei keineswegs in Parallelwelten, die abgehobene literarische städtische Elite und die nicht schriftkundige Landbevölkerung beispielsweise, sondern überschnitten sich über Familien, Generationen, Schichten und Berufsgruppen hinweg durchweg in allen möglichen Alltagsgeschäften, die Schriftlichkeit voraussetzten. Sicher spielte Schriftlichkeit eine geringere Rolle für Menschen der Unterschichten und landarbeitende Familien auf den Dörfern, doch heißt dies nicht, dass sie nicht auf Schritt und Tritt dem geschriebenen Wort begegneten.

Lesen und Schreiben zu können war wünschenswert, um als vollwertiges Mitglied in der Gesellschaft des römischen Ägypten operieren zu können. Das bedeutete jedoch keineswegs den Ausschluss derjenigen, die diese Fähigkeit nicht besaßen. Denn es ließ sich offenbar immer jemand im nahen Verwandten- oder Bekanntenkreis auftun, der des Schreibens kundig war und einem bei Vertragsabschlüssen oder beim Abfassen privater Briefe zur Seite stehen konnte. Die meisten langsamen Schreiber, wie sie sich selbst nannten, die lediglich ihre eigene Unterschrift schreiben konnten, würde man nach der heutigen Definition der OECD als Analphabeten bezeichnen müssen.

Dies galt offensichtlich besonders für den weiblichen Teil der Bevölkerung, der weitaus seltener in den Genuss einer Schulbildung kam. Auch wenn wir aus dem römischen Ägypten mehrfach Zeugnisse von hochgebildeten Frauen besitzen, die nicht nur lesen und schreiben konnten, sondern auch mit der klassischen Literatur eng vertraut waren, stellten sie doch die absolute Minderheit dar. Das heißt jedoch nicht, dass die übrigen Frauen sich beispielsweise nicht an der Brief- und Grußkultur im römischen Ägypten beteiligten. Sie baten schreibkundige Familienmitglieder, erhaltene Grüße vorzulesen, oder diktierten ihrerseits einige Zeilen an abwesende Familienmitglieder, um um Neuigkeiten zu bitten, und um zu versichern, dass zu Hause alle gesund seien. Es wird jedoch ebenfalls deutlich, dass selbst in einer Gesellschaft,

---

51 Es sind noch zwei weitere Briefe des Sempronius erhalten, in dem er zwei Briefe, einen an seine Mutter und einen an den Bruder direkt untereinander setzt (P.Mich. XV 752, 27–42 ebenfalls an Maximus und P.Wisc. II 84a an Saturnilus). Als Adressat auf der Aussenseite des gefalteten Papyrusblattes ist für den Briefboten, soweit das Verso erhalten ist, niemals Saturnila, sondern entweder ihr Sohn Maximus oder Saturnilus angegeben.

die weitestgehend aus Analphabeten bestand, selbst im Familienalltag Schriftlichkeit Macht und Zugang zu Informationen bedeutete. Wer selbst nicht lesen konnte, fand zwar leicht andere, die vorlasen, doch ob dies immer alles korrekt oder vollständig war, was man zu hören bekam, stand – wie wir im Fall der Saturnila gesehen haben – auf einem anderen Blatt.

Bibliography

AST 2015 = R. AST, Writing and the City in Later Roman Egypt. Towards a Social History of the Ancient 'Scribe', *Center for Hellenic Studies Research Bulletin* 4, 2015. http://nrs.harvard.edu/urn-3:hlnc.essay:AstR.Writing_in_the_City_in_Later_Roman_Egypt.2016

BAGNALL/CRIBIORE 2006 = R.S. BAGNALL/R. CRIBIORE, Women's Letters from Ancient Egypt 300 BC–AD 800, Ann Arbor, MI 2006.

BARRENECHEA 2001 = F. BARRENECHEA, A New Document from the Sempronius Dossier: A Letter from Maximus, *Bulletin of the American Society of Papyrologists* 38, 2001, 21–34.

BELL 1950 = H.I. BELL, A Happy Family, in: S. MORENZ (Hg.), Aus Antike und Orient. Festschrift Wilhelm Schubart zum 75. Geburtstag, Leipzig 1950, 38–47.

BOWMAN 1971 = A.K. BOWMAN, The Town Councils of Roman Egypt, Toronto 1971.

BOWMAN 1991 = A.K. BOWMAN, Literacy in the Roman Empire: Mass and Mode, in: J.H. HUMPHREY (Hg.), Literacy in the Roman World, Journal of Roman Archaeology Supplementary Series 3, Ann Arbor, MI 1991, 119–131.

CALDERINI 1950 = R. CALDERINI, Gli agrammatoi nell'Egitto greco-romano, *Aegyptus* 31, 1950, 14–41.

COLE 1981 = S.G. COLE, Could Greek Women Read and Write?, in: H.P. FOLEY (Hg.), Reflections of Women in Antiquity, New York/London 1981, 219–245.

CRIBIORE 1996 = R. CRIBIORE, Writing, Teachers, and Students in Graeco-Roman Egypt, Atlanta 1996.

Cribiore 2001 = R. Cribiore, Gymnastics of the Mind: Greek Education in Hellenistic and Roman Egypt, Princeton 2001.

CRIBIORE 2002 = R. CRIBIORE, The Women in the Apollonios Archive and their Use of Literacy, in: H. MELAERTS/L. MOOREN (Hg.), Le rôle et le statut de la femme en Egypte hellénistique, romaine et byzantine, Leuven 2002, 149–166.

CRIBIORE 2007 = R. CRIBIORE, The Schools, in: A.K. BOWMAN et al. (Hg.), *Oxyrhynchus*: A City and its Texts, London 2007, 287–295.

CRIBIORE/DAVOLI/RATZAN 2008 = R. CRIBIORE/P. DAVOLI/D. RATZAN, A Teacher's Dipinto from Trimithis (Dakhleh Oasis), *Journal of Roman Archaeology* 21, 2008, 170–191.

FEWSTER 2002 = P. FEWSTER, Bilingualism in Roman Egypt, in: J.N. ADAMS/M. JANSE/S. SWAIN (Hg.), Bilingualism in Ancient Society: Language Contact and the Written Text, Oxford 2002, 220–245.

HANSON 1991 = A. HANSON, Ancient Illiteracy, in: J.H. HUMPHREY (Hg.), Literacy in the Roman World, Ann Arbor MI 1991, 159–198.

HARRIS 1989 = W.V. HARRIS, Ancient Literacy, Cambridge MA 1989.

HOPKINS 1991 = K. HOPKINS, Conquest by Books, in: J.H. HUMPHREY (Hg.), Literacy in the Roman World, Ann Arbor MI 1991, 133–158.

HORSTER 2011 = M. HORSTER, Primary Education, in: M. PEACHIN (Hg.), The Oxford Handbook of Social Relations in the Roman World, Oxford 2011, 84–99.

ILAN 2005 = T. ILAN, Learned Jewish Women in Antiquity, in: B. EGO/H. MERKEL (Hg.), Religiöses Lernen in der biblischen, frühjüdischen und frühchristlichen Überlieferung, Tübingen 2005, 175–190.

Kraus 2000 = T.J. Kraus, (Il)literacy in Non-Literary Papyri from Greco-Roman Egypt: Further Aspects of the Educational Ideal in Ancient Literary Sources and Modern Times, *Mnemosyne* 53, 2000, 322–342.
Luijendijk 2008 = A.M. Luijendijk, Greetings in the Lord: Early Christians and the Oxyrhynchus Papyri, Cambridge MA 2008.
Morgan 1998 = T. Morgan, Literate Education in the Hellenistic and Roman Worlds, Cambridge 1998, 48–9.
Parca 2013 = M. Parca, Children in Ptolemaic Egypt: What the Papyri Say, in: J. Evans Grubbs/T. Parkin (Hg.), The Oxford Handbook of Childhood and Education in the Classical World, Oxford 2013, 465–483.
Parsons 2007 = P. Parsons, Copyists of Oxyrhynchus, in: A.K. Bowman et al. (Hg.), *Oxyrhynchus*: A City and its Texts, London 2007, 262–270.
Pomeroy 1990 = S.B. Pomeroy, Women in Hellenistic Egypt: from Alexander to Cleopatra, revised edition, Detroit MI 1990.
Rowlandson 1998 = J. Rowlandson (Hg.), Women and Society in Greek and Roman Egypt. A Sourcebook, Cambridge 1998.
Schubart 1923 = W. Schubart, Ein Jahrtausend am Nil. Briefe aus dem Altertum verdeutscht und erklärt, Berlin 1923.
Sijpesteijn 1976 = P.J. Sijpesteijn, A Happy Family?, *ZPE* 21, 1976, 169–181.
Tacoma 2006 = L.E. Tacoma, Fragile Hierarchies: The Urban Elites of Third Century Roman Egypt, Leiden und Boston 2006.
Thompson 1994 = D.J. Thompson, Literacy and Power in Ptolemaic Egypt, in: A.K. Bowman/G. Woolf (Hg.), Literacy and Power in the Ancient World, Cambridge 1994, 67–83.
Wilcken 1912 = U. Wilcken, Grundzüge und Chrestomathie der Papyruskunde, Leipzig 1912.
Wilfong 2002 = T. Wilfong, Women of Jeme: Lives in a Coptic Town in Late Antique Egypt, Ann Arbor 2002.
Wipszycka 1996 = E. Wipszycka, Le degré d'alphabétisation en Egypte byzantine, in: E. Wipszycka, Etudes sur le Christianisme dans l'Egypte de l'antiquité tardive, Rome 1996, 107–126.
Yiftach 2016 = U. Yiftach, Quantifying Literacy in the Early Roman Arsinoitês: the Case of the *Grapheion* Document, in: D.M. Schaps/U. Yiftach/D. Dueck (Hg.), When West Met East. The Encounter of Greece and Rome with the Jews, Egyptians, and Others. Studies Presented to Ranon Katzoff in Honor of his 75th Birthday, Triest 2016, 269–284.
Youtie 1966 = H. Youtie, Pétaus, fils de Pétaus, ou le scribe qui ne savait pas écrire, *CE* 41, 1966, 127–143.
Youtie 1971 = H. Youtie, Βραδέως γράφων: Between Literacy and Illiteracy, *GRBS* 12, *1971*, 239–261.

Michael A. Speidel
Soldiers and Documents: Insights from Nubia. The Significance of Written Documents in Roman Soldiers' Everyday Lives

Abstract: The Roman army as an institution and the Roman soldier as an individual could not have functioned without the written word. A few newly published finds from Primis / Qasr Ibrim in Lower Nubia as well as a number of other documents discussed in this paper illustrate the extent to which administrative paperwork and the soldiers' (semi-)private correspondence contributed to the army's functioning and governed the soldiers' everyday lives already in the first decades of the new imperial army. Other evidence shows how the formal and symbolic qualities of imperial and official texts, and administrative documents served Roman soldiers from all types of units in their private documents and monuments as a means to demonstrate military identity.

Zusammenfassung: Sowohl das römische Heer als Organisation als auch der römische Soldat als Person waren in ihrem Alltag auf das geschriebene Wort in mannigfacher Weise entscheidend angewiesen. Einige jüngst veröffentlichte Papyri aus Primis / Qasr Ibrim in Unternubien und weitere Texte, die hier besprochen sind, veranschaulichen besonders deutlich, wie sehr administrative Urkunden und die (halb)private Korrespondenz der Soldaten zum Erfolg des römischen Heeres beitrugen und den Alltag der Soldaten schon in den frühesten Tagen der kaiserzeitlichen Armee prägten. Weitere Zeugnisse beleuchten den Wert, den Soldaten aller Truppengattungen den formalen und symbolischen Eigenschaften kaiserlicher und offizieller Text und administrativer Urkunden beimaßen, um in ihren privaten Denkmälern und Dokumenten ihre Heereszugehörigkeit zu zeigen.

In winter 25/4 BCE, Gaius Petronius, the third Roman prefect of Egypt, received orders from Augustus to launch a military campaign into Lower Nubia. The expedition was officially declared to occur in retaliation of an alleged Meroitic attack on Roman territory. In the course of the successful Roman campaign, Petronius' troops occupied Primis, an important Meroitic settlement in Lower Nubia now called Qasr Ibrim. The site lies some 200 km south of Egypt's traditional southern border on the first Cataract of the Nile. The Roman garrison of Primis initially consisted of 400 soldiers which Petronius left behind with supplies for two years. In 22 BCE it was strengthened in anticipation of another Meroitic attack. Yet, less than two years later, in 21/20 BCE, Rome and Meroë concluded a lasting peace treaty, and Rome withdrew its garrison from Lower Nubia.[1]

---

1 Strab. 17,1,54; Plin. nat. 6,35,181–182; Cass. Dio 54,5,4–5; SB V, 7944; SEG 8, 1937, 860. Cf. FHN 2,

In the 1970s and 1980s, the Egypt Exploration Society carried out archaeological excavations at Qasr Ibrim. These excavations recovered an important lot of Greek and Latin Papyri from the roughly four years of Roman military occupation.[2] It includes 185 items, of which 181 are fragments of papyri and 4 are inscriptions on pottery. 131 papyri and 2 inscriptions on pottery are in Greek, whereas 50 papyri and 2 inscriptions on pottery are in Latin. The Greek papyri include fragments of book rolls with literary texts such as the Iliad and the Odyssey, and one Latin papyrus contains the now famous verses that have been ascribed to Egypt's notorious first Roman governor Cornelius Gallus. Such texts remind us that the commanders of Roman army units belonged to the well-educated equestrian and senatorial élite of the Empire.[3] Other texts are school exercises and lists, including lists of deliveries and lists of soldiers. The majority of the texts, however, are letters written by soldiers in Egypt to their comrades of the Qasr Ibrim garrison. Only a relatively small number of papyri from Qasr Ibrim have so far been published, the remainder, however, is currently being prepared for publication by a team from the University of Warsaw.[4]

I Document Production and Survival

There is nothing unusual about the categories and types of texts that were recovered at Qasr Ibrim, nor about the composition of the lot as a whole. As elsewhere, documents and accounts from the military administration accompany private and semi-private letters as well as literary and subliterary texts. What is truly remarkable about the written records from Qasr Ibrim, however, is their early date and the short period in which they were produced and in use at Primis.[5] These traits underline the close relation officers and soldiers of the Roman army had with the written word in their everyday lives, and thereby shed important light on the extent to which writing characterized the Roman military from the earliest days of imperial rule.[6] Moreover, they

---

168; FHN 3, 190; 204–205. For chronology see JAMESON 1968. On Roman Qasr Ibrim: ADAMS 1983; ADAMS 1985. Cf. BOWMAN 2006, 76–77. On Rome's military presence in Lower Nubia in general see e. g. DEMICHELI 1976; KIRWAN 1977; BURSTEIN 1979; SPEIDEL 1992, 240–274; LOCHER 2002. On Augustus' Red Sea politics see R. Gest. div. Aug. 26,5 and Strab. 16,4,22–24, and cf. SPEIDEL 2015 and SPEIDEL forthcoming A.
2 The following figures are from DERDA/ŁAJTAR 2013, 101–102; DERDA/ŁAJTAR/PŁÓCIENNIK 2014/15; DERDA/ŁAJTAR/PŁÓCIENNIK 2015.
3 For fragments of Virgil's works found in Roman military contexts see the material collected in SCAPPATICCIO 2009; SCAPPATICCIO 2013; BOWMAN/THOMAS/TOMLIN 2010, 191–196.
4 WEINSTEIN/TURNER 1976; ANDERSON/PARSONS/NISBIT 1979; P.Rain.Cent. 164 (P.Parsons). For the work of the Polish team see DERDA/ŁAJTAR 2012a; DERDA/ŁAJTAR 2012b; DERDA/ŁAJTAR 2013; DERDA/ŁAJTAR/PŁÓCIENNIK 2014/15; DERDA/ŁAJTAR/PŁÓCIENNIK 2015.
5 For the Roman army keeping 'files' on individual soldiers since the Late Republic see COSME 1993.
6 Scholarly discussions of the degrees of literacy in the Roman army are now abundant: see only the literature in PHANG 2007 and HAYNES 2013, 313–336.

serve to remind us of the nearly total loss of texts on perishable materials from other military sites. Texts from the army's daily routine and the soldiers' everyday life have, of course, also been recovered elsewhere, including, for instance, Dura Europos on the Middle Euphrates, Bu Njem in North Africa, many sites in Egypt and its Eastern desert, Vindolanda on Hadrian's Wall, Vindonissa in what is now Northern Switzerland, and others. Together with many stray finds, these sites yielded a large number of documents on bronze, papyrus, parchment, ceramic, wood, leather and other materials.[7] Still, it is important to keep in mind that all these texts are no more than a tiny fraction of the everyday writing that was once part and parcel of life in the Roman army.

Moreover, not all categories of texts have received the same degree of scholarly interest. Soldiers' private letters and documents, for instance, have not yet been systematically collected, studied and analysed by historians of ancient Rome.[8] Documents from the army's administration have attracted more attention.[9] The most influential work in this respect was no doubt the ground-breaking collection and re-edition, by ROBERT ORWILL FINK in 1971, of all 'Roman military records on papyrus' ranging from Augustus to Diocletian known to him until 1968. Contrary to what the title suggests, however, not all of the many documents of FINK's collection were written on papyrus. Six of his documents were parchments (nos. 16. 17. 19. 42. 65. 128) and one entry (78) consists of seventy seven individual *ostraca*. His catalogue includes one hundred and thirty four entries which he divided into thirteen individual categories and several sub-categories. FINK's corpus also includes a substantial number of Greek documents, which are receipts for money or foodstuffs given within a unit to an under-officer or clerk by or for individual soldiers. In the light of the many new and important discoveries, however, FINK's volume needs to be revised and brought up to date.[10]

Nevertheless, FINK's collection immediately betrays the extent to which the very functioning of the Roman army depended on written documents, as these contained, for instance, commands, instructions, reports, and passwords for the night watch or countless lists of personnel, matériel, provisions and resources in greater or smaller quantities. Information from such lists could be extracted from one type of document and entered in another, re-organised and condensed, up-dated and amended. Topical lists were produced, with each different category designed to answer specific questions. Depending on the hierarchy of a camp and the importance of a document,

---

[7] Dura: Ch.L.A. VI-IX. Bu Njem: MARICHAL 1992. Eastern Desert: CUVIGNY 2006. Vindolanda: T.Vindol.I-III; BOWMAN/THOMAS/TOMLIN 2010 and 2011. Vindonissa: SPEIDEL 1996.
[8] For a comparison between letters of soldiers from the First World War and those of Roman soldiers see ZERBINI 2015. Cf. also COSME 2016, 86–88.
[9] Cf. e.g. DARIS 1964; FINK 1971; MITTHOF 2001; STAUNER 2004; CUVIGNY 2006.
[10] For a re-assessment of some of FINK's categories see SPEIDEL 2009, 283–304. Cf. also SPEIDEL 2009, 213–234 for a category unknown to FINK. For recent general overviews of Roman military documents see also STAUNER 2004 and PHANG 2007.

such records were either sent on, archived, or thrown away on the very day they had been produced. The impression all this material conveys is one of an extremely busy bureaucracy that aimed to register everyone and everything at practically every place and point in time, in order to achieve as complete control as possible of the extent, the condition, and whereabouts of the Roman army's men and resources, as well as to control and coordinate actions in the present, or to record past activities. It has repeatedly and no doubt rightfully been said that the pen may have been more crucial to the success of the Roman Empire's army even than the sword.[11] At any rate, regardless of how we choose to interpret the surviving scraps from the offices and archives of Roman military units, and from the desks of its officers and soldiers, we must surely admit that the vital processes that kept this institution functioning depended fundamentally on written documents.

FINK's collection of Roman military records includes "records and correspondence concerned solely with the internal administration of the army".[12] To an extent this narrow definition makes sense as the majority of FINK's documents conceivably belong to such groups that could be subjected to audits or were shared with superior military authorities. But that, for instance, can hardly be true for the substantial number of Greek *ostraca* that he also included, which therefore raises a number of important questions about what we should term 'military documents' and about the use of Greek in the army. In his recent book on the *auxilia* of the Roman army, IAN HAYNES concluded that Latin was in fact not the Roman imperial army's official language.[13] Yet, that hypothesis is not tenable, despite the well-documented fact that countless soldiers in the Roman army knew (and used in their daily lives) various languages other than Latin. For on the one hand, military documents written in Greek were only of minor, short-lived significance compared to those composed in Latin (*pridiana* and related documents, for instance, are known only in Latin), and on the other hand tactical commands in Latin are known to have still been in use in the Byzantine army of the 6th and 7th centuries.[14] The army of the Roman emperors was, politically, still the *exercitus populi Romani*, and Latin, obviously, was the language of the Romans.[15]

Other aspects may appear to be even more uncomforting. Thus, for instance, no single site has produced the full range of FINK's 13 types of documents. In this respect, Qasr Ibrim is again typical. In fact, some categories are known from only one single

---

11 Cf. most recently HAYNES 2013, 314–318.
12 FINK 1971, 1.
13 HAYNES 2013, 315.
14 See, for instance, Ps.-Maurik. strat. praef.; 1,8; 12 B 7; 12 B 24.
15 See e. g. CIL VI 32323 = ILS 5050 = AE 2002, 192; AE 1984, 508 = AE 1999, 891; CIL II²/5, 1022; AE 1919, 60; CIL XIV 4301 and 4303. Cf. also Cass. Dio 57,2,3. For the emphasis in Roman military doctrine on the army being Roman see SPEIDEL 2010. For the importance of Latin in the provinces as the language of Rome see e. g. ECK 2003 and ECK 2009.

find spot, and recently discovered documents have added new categories (e.g. the *renuntia* from Vindolanda) to those known from elsewhere. Attempts to make sense of the surviving documentation as a whole have been surprisingly few and are often somewhat sweeping. The traditional view that emphasises the uniformity of the surviving records over space and time has repeatedly been challenged in recent years.[16] It has, for instance, been proposed that "the evidence suggests much less uniformity than FINK's classification implies," and that "we should perhaps be prepared to admit more decentralization and room for local initiative and variation than we have hitherto imagined".[17] Moreover, the nature of the Roman military bureaucracy is said to have been fundamentally different from modern bureaucracies, allegedly because it was less anonymous.[18]

Such criticism does not easily withstand close scrutiny.[19] Yet it cannot be denied that the there is a true problem at the bottom of such issues which lies with the extremely small size of the sample available to work from. Unfortunately, FINK's collection cannot be used as a guide to reliably establish the significance of military records in the Roman soldier's daily life, partly because so many new documents and types of records have been found since its publication, but also because of FINK's narrow definition of 'military documents', which excludes all transactions between the army and civilians, the army and other state institutions, the soldiers' semi-private (or semi-official) correspondence, as well as the entire documentation concerning military diplomas. Moreover, it is not enough to consider the material that has survived. In order to make sense of the surviving evidence we must also develop a notion of the extent to which written records have perished. FINK was aware of this. He pointed out that in the roughly 300 years between Augustus and Diocletian at least around 225 million individual pay accounts for Roman soldiers must have been produced. Only about 50 of these are currently known which equals a survival rate of *c.* 0.000025 %![20] Moreover, these 50 texts have survived on only five documents, all of which are from Egypt. ROGER TOMLIN identified another type of document, which is as yet only known from Carlisle and presumably survived at a local rate of 0.00015 %.[21] By way of comparison, it might be worth mentioning that the survival rate of military diplomas has been calculated very much higher, at between *c.* 0.15 and 0.5 %![22] Where the writing material itself has disintegrated, *stili* often survive. Unfortunately,

---

[16] Traditional view: cf. most recently STAUNER 2004. The methods employed in this book, and the use of selective samples have, however, been criticised: HOFFMANN 2010. Cf. SPEIDEL 2009, 286 f. n. 9.
[17] BOWMAN/THOMAS 1991, 65, repeated, for instance, in: BOWMAN 2006, 80–81. See also PHANG 2007, 293–294.
[18] PHANG 2007, esp. 293.
[19] See e.g. SPEIDEL 2009, 283–304; COSME 2017.
[20] FINK 1971, 242. Cf. SPEIDEL 2009, 283–284 with n. 1.
[21] TOMLIN 2003. SPEIDEL 2009, 283 n. 1.
[22] ECK 2010, 57–58.

however, finds of *stili* are not generally included in discussions of ancient literacy, although they have been recovered in great numbers and from many different sites.[23] In the case of the legionary fortress at Vindonissa, 560 *stili* have been excavated and recorded, and Vindolanda has produced over 200.[24] Metal *stili*, of course, had the potential of being reused countless times. Thus, although their numbers are of no help in establishing even the approximate volume of lost documents, they, too, serve to remind us of the infinite loss of records, official and private, from the Roman soldiers' everyday lives.[25]

II Communicating in Writing

Any attempt to understand the significance of reading and writing in the army must include all types of written evidence. When looking at the written records produced by Roman soldiers, most scholars distinguish between private documents and official records or documents from the army's administrative services. Administrative records as well as official letters containing commands or orders of foodstuffs, matériel or personnel etc. were obviously crucial to the daily running of the Roman army as an institution and fighting force. Private letters, on the other hand, are generally thought of as having provided the means to keep contact with family members, friends, and fellow soldiers.[26] Yet the spheres of private and administrative records often overlapped and interacted to a surprising degree. Thus, to name just one well-known category, many candidates from the Empire's senatorial and equestrian élite for junior officer or staff positions procured letters of recommendation.[27] Although they not always achieved their purpose, *litterae commendaticiae* were also deemed useful at much lower echelons, for instance, if one sought promotion or relocation.[28] Such letters were essentially private in nature, as they were written on someone's own initiative for non-official purposes, but they nevertheless played an important role in the process of appointing individuals.

Most surviving private and semi-private letters of Roman soldiers are known from Egypt, but examples from Vindolanda and elsewhere confirm that they were common throughout the army. Many of them deal with minor personal affairs. Even a short invitation for someone nearby could be extended in writing rather than being deliv-

---

23 But cf. SPEIDEL 1996, 16 and now HAYNES 2013, 319. On *stili* see SCHALTENBRAND OBRECHT 2012.
24 Vindonissa: SCHALTENBRAND OBRECHT 2012, 18. Vindolanda: TOMLIN 2016, 58. http://vindolanda.csad.ox.ac.uk/exhibition/docs-2.shtml.
25 SPEIDEL 2009, 533.
26 Cf. e. g. ZERBINI 2015.
27 Cf. e. g. BIRLEY 1992, 16–29; COTTON 2014.
28 Cf. e. g. T.Vindol. II 250. P.Mich. VIII 468. Cf. BOWMAN/THOMAS 1983, 105–106.

ered orally by a messenger.[29] The following two recently published letters suffice to illustrate the point. The first letter was written between c. 25 and 21 BCE by a man named Licinius, stationed at Koptos on the Nile (possibly the garrison place of Egypt's third legion in those years),[30] to a fellow soldier called Caesius at Primis / Qasr Ibrim:[31]

      Λικίνιος Καισίῳ τῷ ἀδελφῷ πλεῖστα
      χαίρειν καὶ ὑγιαίνε[ι]ν· εἰ ἔρρωσαι, ἔρρωμ-
      αι δὲ καὶ αὐτός σου τὴν ἀρίστην μνή-
4   αν ποιούμενος διὰ παντὸς ἐπ' ἀγ{γ}α-
      θῷ παρὰ τοῖς θεοῖς τοῖς ἐν Κόπτῳ·
      ἐρωτῶ σοὶ μή με [μν]ῄσθῃς ὅτι πυ-
      κνά σοι οὐ γράφω ἀλ[λὰ] ἐλπίζω ὅ-
8   τι κοσοτε . ονες̣ .. [. .]α πυκνότε-
      ρά σοι γράψω· καὶ επιε . . . . ος εἰς
      Ἀλεξάνδρεαν ἀπ[ῆλθ]ον πε-
      ρὶ τοῦ κώδωνος ὅν μοι ἐνετείλου·
12 σύσκηνος [   ] πειράσο̣-
      μαί πω εγε[   ]εται σὺ κώδω-
      να. καὶ ἀπέ[στ]ειλά σοι ἐπιστό-
      λιον. πρῶτο[ν] διασάφησόν μο̣ι̣
16 εἰ σὺ ἠνέχθη[ς]. καὶ γράψον μοι πῶς
      ἔχεις καὶ ἄν [τι] χρέαν{ν} ἔχεις. ἀσπά-
      ζου Νίχρον [σα]λπιστὴν λίαν. ἐπιμε-
      λῶς ἔσται εἰ ἔ[χῃς] παρὰ Ἔρωτος τοῦ
20 σαλπιστοῦ, [δι]ασάφησόν μοι. ἀσπά-
      ζου σὺ δὴ [κ]αὶ πάντες τοὺς σαλ-
      πιστάς. ἔρρω[σ( )].

Verso

      Λικίν̣ι̣ος Καισί βουκινάτωρι
      εἰ<ς> Πρῖμα

3–4. μνείαν. ‖ 17. χρείαν ἔχῃς. ‖ 17–18. ἀσπάζου. ‖ 18. Νίγρον . ‖ 21. πάντας . ‖ 21–22. σαλπιστάς.

"Licinius to Caesius, brother, many greetings and wishes of health. If you keep your health, I am well too, and am doing best remembrance of you in everything for the good before the gods that are in Koptos. I am asking you do not remember of me that I have not written to you often, but I am hoping to write to you more often [- - -]. And [- - -] I came to Alexandria because of a trumpet that you asked me about. [- - -] a tent-companion [- - -] I will try [- - -] you the trumpet. And I sent you a letter [- - -

---

29 Cf. T.Vindon. 45; T.Vindol. II 291.
30 Thus Derda/Łajtar/Płociennik 2014/15.
31 Derda/Łajtar/Płociennik 2014/15 offer a preliminary publication with the text and a translation of the letter, which is reproduced above. A full publication by the same authors is forthcoming.

]. Let me know first if you succeeded. Write me about how you are and if you need anything [---]. Greet Niger, trumpeter, very much. It would be interesting (to know) if you have (this) from Eros the trumpeter. Let me know. Greet all trumpeters. Remain in health".

Verso:
"Licinius to Caesius, trumpeter, to Prima" (i. e. Primis / Qasr Ibrim).

We are clearly dealing with a private letter that contains issues pertaining to aspects of the military profession. The term 'brother' (*frater* / ἀδελφός) was a frequent address among Roman soldiers, and no doubt intended to convey a sentiment of close relationship.[32] Apart from Caesius, to whom Licinius addressed his letter, he also mentions two other trumpeters (*bucinatores*) by name (Niger and Eros). In his final line, he even sends his greetings to all trumpeters at Primis. The apparently substantial number of trumpeters suggests that we are dealing with members of a legion.[33] The letter concerns some business about a trumpet at Alexandria, of which Caesius had told his 'brother' Licinius. Licinius may therefore have been a trumpeter himself. At any rate, he was probably a legionary soldier at Koptos. Although his letter is of private nature, it comes from within a network of military trumpeters that was active at Koptos, Alexandria and Primis (and perhaps elsewhere) and concerns a small aspect of their professional lives. It also reveals that their communication extended over great distances and was based, in part, on letters. That goes well with what is known from other cases, in which soldiers exchanged private letters and notes even over very short distances.[34]

It seems unlikely that private letters were exclusively exchanged between a small and privileged group of literate soldiers, if only because illiterate soldiers no doubt also wanted to hear from friends and dear ones, to be able to conduct their businesses from afar, or address petitions and requests to their superiors.[35] The difficulties of illiterate soldiers in such respects were similar to those who needed to overcome language barriers. Both might have found help from fellow soldiers with the relevant skills.[36] A recently published example for such a case comes from Didymoi, one of the outposts in Egypt's eastern desert. It dates to the first half of the second c. CE.[37]

---

[32] SPEIDEL 1996, 35 and 104.
[33] Thus convincingly DERDA/ŁAJTAR/PŁÓCIENNIK 2014/15.
[34] SPEIDEL 1996, 83–85.
[35] Cf. e. g. SPEIDEL 2009, 526; 530; 532.
[36] Thus e. g. HAYNES 2013, 315, yet without examples.
[37] O.Did. 417 (dumped ca. 125–140 CE). Cf. also O.Did. 418–420. For commentaries see BÜLOW-JACOBSEN 2012, 352–356 and STAUNER 2016, 805–808.

Convex side:

> *Demeteru Claudio salute.*
> *Scire te volo conia non acc-*
> *epi a quratori esopera co-*
> 4 *ntubernio. Sicot abui*
> *frumentum omnia pa-*
> *ne feci. Nuc oc te rogo*
> *serva te ab omnes*
> 8 *donico ego at te ven-*
> *io ne qui te inponant.*
> *Numosis Claudio frat-*
> *eri et magisteri suo*
> 12 *salute. Comodo vis ve-*
> *nire contubernio*
> *sciribe mi ut ego* [[s ...]]
> [[..]] *pose vendere.*

Concave side:

> *Saluta Cerescenti*
> *conterane meum.*
> *Interroga si acepit*
> 4 *esaborio(!). Saluta / Diu[[r]]rponain.*
> *Vale.*

Convex: 1. Demetrus. salutem. ‖ 2. quoniam. ‖ 3. curatore. supra. ‖ 4. sicut. habui. ‖ 5. omnes. ‖ 5/6. pa/nem. ‖ 6. nunc. hoc. ‖ 7. omnibus. ‖ 8. donec. ad. ‖ 9. imponant. ‖ 10/11. frat/ri. ‖ 11. magistro. ‖ 12. salutem. quomodo. ‖ 12/13. ve/ndere. ‖ 14. scribe. ‖ 15. possem (i. e. possim). — Concave: 1. Crescentem. ‖ 2. conterraneum. ‖ 3. accepit.

Convex side:
"Demetrous to Claudius, greetings. I want you to know that I have not received (anything) from the *curator* concerning your *contubernium*. When I received the wheat, I made it all into bread. Now I ask you this: protect yourself from everyone until I come to you, lest anyone deceive you".
"Numosis to Claudius, his brother and master, greetings. Write to me how you want your living quarters to be sold so that I can sell it".
Concave side:
"Greet Crescens, my countryman. Ask if he received the little sandal(?). Greet Diurponais. Farewell".

The text is written by one hand onto both sides of a single ostracon and consists of two Latin letters addressed to one Claudius by two different people, Demetrous and Numosis (= Numisius?).[38] Both letters appear to concern Claudius' *contubernium* (his former military living quarters, probably in the outpost from where the letters were written). The Latin language, the Latin and Dacian names (Diurponais) as well as the technical military terms *contubernium* and *curator* (a military officer in charge of a *praesidium*-outpost) leave no doubt that the men named in this letter were soldiers and suggest that they probably served in the same auxiliary unit. Demetrous, a woman with a Greek name (and, it seems, with Greek reading skills),[39] wanted to send Claudius a message but was apparently unable to write Latin, the language in which Claudius evidently preferred to receive and write his letters.[40] Numosis helped out, despite his own defective knowledge of Latin spelling, grammar and word usage. He wrote Demetrous' letter and added a message of his own as well as greetings to two male acquaintances of his. All four men are likely to have been fellow soldiers. The first greeting went to a fellow countryman of Numosis named Crescens (not necessarily a native from Egypt) and the second to a man with a Dacian name (Diurponais). According to a suggestion by ADAM BÜLOW-JACOBSEN, Numosis may have used the help of a phrase-book or glossary to compose his translation.[41] At any rate, Numosis' shaky Latin is likely to have been superior to Claudius' knowledge of Greek.

The two auxiliaries appear to have served together in Egypt's Eastern Desert, and to have developed close bonds, for Numosis called Claudius *frater et magister* (O.Did. 417, ll.10–11) while Claudius called Numosis his *filius* (O.Did. 419, l.1). Claudius probably needed some Greek in order to perform routine duties in the Eastern desert or elsewhere in Egypt. Nevertheless, he and Numosis communicated in Latin, perhaps because Claudius was the senior partner and had a rather poor command of Greek. At any rate, Claudius surely appreciated the company of a junior Greek-speaking comrade with some knowledge of Latin, like Numosis. Perhaps Demetrous even worried about someone deceiving Claudius because she feared that without the help of trusted friends, Claudius' poor Greek might make him easy prey for crooks. Together, Numosis and Claudius would probably have made a linguistically sufficiently competent team, with the ability to read and write at least short messages in both Latin and Greek.[42] Perhaps, therefore, such pairings occurred fairly often (or even routinely) throughout the Roman army, for language barriers were hardly limited to the Greek East. As a model, such teams may have served as an alternative solution to Latin lessons from the

---

38 For more than one letter written on a single piece of writing material see O.Did. 383; T.Vindol. III 643; P.Tebt. II 416; SB III 6263 = P.Select. 121.
39 O.Did. 418 (in Greek) leaves no doubt that the female name Demetrous was meant, and suggests that Demetrous was able to read Greek.
40 Cf. O.Did. 419 (dumped ca. 115–120 CE).
41 BÜLOW-JACOBSEN 2012, 352–356.
42 Cf. STAUNER 2016, 806.

army's *librarii, qui docere possint*.⁴³ Yet in either case, soldiers experienced in teaching others Latin or Greek must have contributed significantly to the everyday running of the Roman army, and some may even have continued to teach after their discharge.⁴⁴

By facilitating the handling of minor private business affairs, such letters impacted directly on a soldier's well-being and, potentially, his readiness for duty.⁴⁵ Unfortunately, the mere number of surviving letters written by soldiers on papyrus, ostraca and wooden tablets is of no help in trying to estimate the volume of those lost over the centuries. Their often trifling contents, however, suggests that soldiers were rather quick at writing short notes, which implies that the occurrence of such letters was probably high in soldiers' everyday lives.⁴⁶ Illiteracy, at any rate, can hardly be said to have been an obstacle to written communicating. Short notes and letters will therefore have had a considerable impact on the morale of all soldiers and on the everyday functioning of the Roman military. They therefore surely contributed considerably to the Roman army's overall success and thus deserve particular consideration when trying to assess the significance of writing in the Roman army.

III The Attraction of Administrative Documents

Yet private and semi-private letters are not the only ancient texts that shed light on the significance of the written word in the Roman soldier's and veteran's everyday life. For, surprisingly perhaps, the innumerable administrative documents that enabled and regulated the operation of the Roman army also had a noteworthy influence on soldiers' writing behaviour. For individuals and groups of soldiers occasionally made use of copies of extracts from administrative military records for their own private documents and monuments.⁴⁷ In 240, for instance, a group of veterans from the legions *VIII Augusta* and *XXII Primigenia p(ia) f(idelis)* in Upper Germany individually petitioned the governor L. Silius Amicus Haterianus for the permission to copy, onto a bronze tablet, parts of a letter which the emperor Gordian III had addressed to the governor concerning the soldiers' discharge. They also asked for permission to add the governor's own discharge declaration, including its date by year and day. Two fragmentary copies survive, both produced by Thracians.⁴⁸ In one case, the veteran included the text of his petition to the governor onto his bronze tablet:

---

43 Dig. 50,6,7 (Tarrutienus Paternus). Cf. STAUNER 2016, 807.
44 Cf. e. g. RIU 185 (Scarbantia). Cf. HARRIS 2014, 293.
45 T.Vindol. II 346 and O.Krok. 94 sufficiently illustrate the point.
46 Cf. SPEIDEL 1996, 82–85.
47 For copies of decrees and official letters on private monuments of Roman soldiers see SPEIDEL 2014, 335–337 with further examples.
48 For the texts and excellent commentary see WEISS 2015. For the governor's permission to produce copies see also CIL XVI, app. 12 = ILS 9059 (a wooden tablet from 94 CE).

> *Commoda mea, quae mihi ob aemerita mili-*
> *[tia s]acratissimus Imp(erator) Gordianus Augustus dari prae-*
> *[stitit, ut etiam?] secundum sacram indulgentiam eius*
> *[veteranus? dem]ostrem, permittas mihi aeream ta-*
> *[bulam facere et] descriptum et recognitum pars ex*
> *[litteris Imp(eratoris) Gordian]i Augusti et consulem et diem*
> *[missionis ex tabu]lario legionis supra scriptae.*

"In order to enable me to demonstrate my privileges which the most sacred emperor Gordianus Augustus, according to his sacred graciousness, conceded that should be given because of the fulfilled military service, may you permit me to produce a bronze tablet and a certified copy in part of the letter by Imperator Gordianus Augustus and of the year and day of the discharge from the above mentioned legion's archive."

The veteran thus explicitly states that he intended to use the text on his new bronze document at home (i. e. in Thrace) to prove that he had received privileges upon his discharge from the emperor. In principle, therefore, this document served him much the same purpose as the military diplomas of the first and second centuries CE had done for Thracian and other veterans of the *auxilia* and fleets. PETER WEISS may be right in assuming that special circumstances facilitated the production of these specific bronze documents in 240 CE.[49] WEISS suggested that the emperor may have instigated the procedure with the governor preparing the texts and composing something like a master document for those who wished to produce a personalised copy on a bronze tablet. The permission to do so, granted by the governor, may therefore have amounted to an extraordinary imperial gift, which was intended to reward a group of soldiers for their loyal behaviour in 238 when Gordian rose to power. However, as there is nothing in the text itself to encourage such a conclusion, it must remain hypothetical.

In any case, we can recognise the owner's influence on the design of the document, as only the veteran of *legio VIII Augusta* included his petition on the tablet. Nor can a very similar bronze document from 248 / 249 CE have served as a reward for outstanding loyalty.[50] This tablet was produced by one M. Aurelius Mucianus, a soldier from Thrace who had served in *cohors II vigilum Philippiana*. His bronze tablet also contains an extract from an imperial letter which the emperor Philippus addressed to a high-ranking official (no doubt the prefect of the *vigiles*) asking for Mucianus to be discharged before the completion of his military service on account of ill health (*propter adversam corporis valetudinem*). Thus, the emperor's letter concerns Mucianus alone, and there is no notion in the imperial letter (and no reason to believe) that the tablet or the permission to produce it was extended to anyone else or

---

49 WEISS 2015, 56–58.
50 RMM 75 = AE 2003, 2040. Cf. SPEIDEL 2009, 300–302 and 344–346. VON SALDERN 2006.

that it served as an extraordinary imperial reward of any kind. The imperial words are followed by three further sections of text (engraved without separation), all of which evidently quote from administrative documents relating to this soldier.⁵¹ The second section lists data from Mucianus' 'personnel file' (unit, name, rank, origin, date of recruitment). It is followed by a list of his external missions and a declaration of his right to receive free monthly rations of wheat. A small number of original recordings of individual soldiers' external missions survive on an Egyptian papyrus of the later first century CE, which is now kept in Geneva. These registers illustrate that Mucianus' list is indeed a faithful copy of a real administrative document from the archives of his unit.⁵² Mucianus even reproduced minute technical details from the original such as the letter R with a cross bar through it which scribes in the military administrative services used to abbreviate the term *reversus* ('returned').⁵³

Mucianus' selection of texts for his private bronze document thus clearly reflects his personal choices and preferences. It illustrates the importance he seems to have attached to owning a shining bronze tablet with Latin texts from the imperial chancellery bearing his name as well as official documents referring to his military service. The same expression of pride is also apparent from several other phenomena on similar bronze documents. Thus, since 177 CE, the names (and initially also the personal data) of the recipients on the front faces of military diplomas were engraved in much larger letters than those of the surrounding text. Evidently, this new layout was designed to attract the reader's eye to the name of the owner of the tablet.⁵⁴ Also, not long after the reign of Commodus, when large scale production of bronze military diplomas for auxiliary soldiers was discontinued, some veterans (including legionaries) began to privately produce bronze copies of their wooden discharge documents.⁵⁵ Also, praetorians, curiously, continued to receive military diplomas until the 260s. This has recently been convincingly explained as a consequence of soldiers (Thracians above all others) wishing to own a shiny bronze document attesting to their superior status and their special relationship with the emperor.⁵⁶

Unfortunately, the overall survival rate of bronze tablets is very low.⁵⁷ It is nearly impossible, therefore, to tell with any degree of certainty, how many soldiers acquired a shiny bronze tablet commemorating their military service (military diploma or other) after their honourable discharge in the first half of the third century CE, even though we can be fairly certain that the majority of praetorians was among them. But the large percentage of soldiers from the Middle and Lower Danube known to have

---

51 The document thus contains four different sections, not three as VON SALDERN 2006, 294 assumes.
52 RMR 10. SPEIDEL 2009, 300–302 and 344–346.
53 SPEIDEL 2009, 301–302.
54 WEISS 2002, 527; WEISS 2017, 144–145; SPEIDEL 2009, 344–345; SPEIDEL 2015a, 57–58.
55 RMD 4, app. 1, 1–3 (all from the first half of the 3rd c.). SPEIDEL 2009, 333–346.
56 Thus ECK 2012.
57 Cf. above at n. 22.

owned such documents in the second and third centuries is conspicuous and hardly coincidental, and indeed somewhat puzzling. For the majority of soldiers from these parts were born peregrines before 212 CE and mostly hailed from rural backgrounds.[58] Especially in the case of rural Thrace, one wonders whether returning veterans found a satisfying number of people to impress with their newly acquired documents and the Latin texts incised on them, as there is little to suggest that Latin literacy was particularly wide spread in those parts.[59] Nevertheless, Thracian soldiers, whether serving as peregrines in the *auxilia*, the fleets or the imperial horse guard before 212 or in the legions and the praetorian guard thereafter, appear to have been particularly keen on owning bronze tablets with official texts commemorating their military service for Rome. There can be little doubt, therefore, that the symbolic qualities such as the shiny metal, the imperial source of the inscribed words, the Latin language, the elegant lettering and layout as well as the presence of the owner's name (especially if in large Roman letters and somewhere close to that of the emperor's) mattered as much to veterans from Thrace (but no doubt also from elsewhere) as the actual contents of the incised text.

Ordinary soldiers also often appear to have been impressed by the language of military records, as they seem to have quickly adopted certain trivial formulations for their own monuments, and thereby contributed to their dissemination within close and comparable communities. The army's administrative services, for instance, are not only known to have renamed recruits upon enlistment whenever they thought it was necessary, but they also kept extensive documents recording the (new) names and the origins of each and every soldier.[60] In the case of legionaries that meant: *nomina cum tribus et patriis*, as two inscriptions from the 240s univocally ascertain.[61] Remarkably, the army's recording practises appear to have standardised, to some extent, the ways in which soldiers inscribed their names and homes on their private monuments, for many soldiers adopted a military style nomenclature.[62] The habit is most strikingly apparent when groups of soldiers set up and dedicated a monument together, and chose to add their names and origins in the style of military lists as kept by their unit's administrative offices.[63]

---

58 Cf. e. g. Eck 2012; Speidel 2016, 341–342.
59 Sharankov 2011, 145–153. esp. 149–151. For the use of Latin by veterans in Thrace see also Slawisch 2007, 169.
60 New or standardized names, and military recording traditions: e. g. BGU II 423; P.Mich. IX 549; P.Oxy. XXII 2349 and XXXXI 2978. Cf. Mócsy 1992, 188–217; Waebens 2012, 18–19; Yon 2017; Speidel forthcoming.
61 AE 1981, 134 = AE 1989, 63 (Rom, 242 CE); CIL VI 793 = 14, 2258 = ILS 505 (Albanum, 244 CE).
62 Cf. e. g. Speidel 1992, 321; Speidel 1994, 86; Speidel forthcoming. For an exception: CIL III 10307. For an inappropriate military style indication of a Roman senator's geographical origins by a centurion see Eck 2017.
63 For such lists from various types of units on papyrus see e. g. BGU IV 1083 = RMR 36 (32 / 38 CE); P. Dura 122 = RMR 32 (242–249 CE?); P.Oslo III 122 = RMR 24 (238–242 CE); P.Ryl. II 79 = RMR 28 (144–151 CE).

The oldest lists of soldiers on papyrus currently known come from Qasr Ibrim (Primis) and have only recently been published by T. DERDA, A. ŁAJTAR, and T. PŁÓCIENNIK. All three lists are drawn up as a single column of names. Two of these lists contain single Greek and Latin names, and probably concern auxiliaries.[64] The third list reads (fig. 1):

Fig. 1: list of soldiers on papyrus from Qasr Ibrim (Primis), Qasr Ibrim Archive courtesy Trustees of the British Museum

---

64 DERDA/ŁAJTAR/PŁÓCIENNIK 2015, 49–55. On the standardization of the *auxilia* after the conquest of Egypt in 30 BCE cf. SPEIDEL 2017. The men with Roman *gentilicia* in the first two lists were not necessarily all from other provinces, as the editors suggested, but (some?) may have been re-named Egyptians. Cf. P.Oxy. XXII 2349 (70CE) and n. 60 above.

	P. Tibellius	P. [f.]	Fal(erna)
	P. Iunius	P. f.	Vet(uria)
	M. Helvius	M. f.	Pol(lia)
	M. Saufeius	M. f.	Fal(erna)
5	L. Publilius	L. [f.]	Gal(eria)
	M. Salasius	M. f.	Pol(lia)
	C. Cattius	C. f.	Gal(eria)
	P. Cornelius	P. f.	Pol(lia)
	L. [Pe]tronius	L. f.	Vet(uria)
10	L. Catillius	L. f.	Cor(nelia)
	L. Arruntius	L. f.	Pol(lia)
	P. Paconius	P. f.	Ser(gia)
	L. Granius	L f.	Sub(urana)
	L. Livius	L. f.	Pol(ia)
15	C. Rutilius	C. f.	Vet(uria)
	C. Oc[t]avius	[C.] f.	Vel(ina)
	C. Aurel[ius	C. f. - - -]	

The Latin language of this papyrus and its find spot at Primis betray its nature as a military document. All names are registered by *praenomen, nomen gentile*, filiation and *tribus*. *Cognomina* appear to be missing throughout, which goes well with the early date of the papyrus (the 20s BCE). According to the editors, the list of names survives in full, but there seems to be no trace of a heading or of the soldiers' origins, which later such documents usually include. The editors maintain that the lines are complete both at the left and the right. If true, this might suggest that recording soldiers' homes had not yet become standard practice in the army or that the intended purpose of the list did not require such an indication.

Be that as it may, the *tribus* indications betray the citizen status of those registered in this document and therefore that we are surely dealing with legionary soldiers. Remarkably, all soldiers in this list bear the same *praenomina* as their fathers. This surely indicates that these were not their original names but ones the military authorities had given them upon enrolment.[65] If true, this document provides solid proof for the enfranchisement of peregrine recruits (most probably Egyptians) upon their enrolment into a legion.[66] Moreover, it is the first document to attest this procedure in the earliest years of Roman rule in Egypt and may reflect normal recruiting practises. This unimposing scrap of papyrus from beyond the empire's southern frontier thus provides a number of important new aspects to our image of the relations between Rome and provincial societies. In the present context it is worth to maintain that the

---

[65] Thus, no doubt correctly, DERDA/ŁAJTAR/PŁÓCIENNIK 2014/15, 54.
[66] The editors have not discussed the great importance of the document in this specific context. Before its publication, WAEBENS 2012 argued for enfranchisement upon discharge, whereas HAENSCH 2010, 119–120 and HAENSCH 2012, 72–73 favoured enrolment. Both authors offer further literature on the subject.

new list from Qasr Ibrim strongly encourages to rethink at least in part the formerly emphasised distinctions between citizen units and the *auxilia* in terms of their soldiers' literacy.⁶⁷

Another very remarkable feature of the new list is its arrangement of the onomastic elements in a vertical, justified column. This is a well-known feature of military documents of later date, but the names of thirty peregrine Spanish horsemen of the *turma Sallvitana* were also listed in justified columns of similar design on a famous bronze tablet in 89 BCE.⁶⁸ By contrast, the list of fifty-nine Roman citizens who served in the council (*in consilio*) of Gnaeus Pompeius Strabo, the Roman commander in the field, were recorded in continuing lines on the same tablet. It therefore appears that listing soldiers individually in justified columns was a characteristic trait of military records since at least the early first century BCE. Yet on the bronze tablet of 89 BCE, the soldiers' homes were recorded in centred lines within the columns, thereby grouping soldiers of common origin. Around ca. 32 / 38 CE a list of legionary soldiers (of *legio III Cyrenaica* or *legio XXII Deiotariana*?) was drawn up on papyrus in Egypt in very much the same style, but now with the origins added to the soldiers' names on the same line, just like in all documents of later date (fig. 2):⁶⁹

	[- G]enucius ·	C(ai) · f(ilius) ·	Aem(ilia) ·	Pesinuntem [·]
	[- C]anidius ·	C(ai) · f(ilius) ·	Pol(lia) ·	Ancyra ·
	[-] Ḅaebius ·	Q(uinti) · f(ilius) ·	[Po]l(lia) ·	Ancyra ·
	[-] Cornelius ·	Sex(ti) · f(ilius) ·	Pol(lia) ·	Ancyra ·
5	〚- Sulpicius ·	L(uci) · f(ilius) ·	Aem(ilia) ·	Pesinuntem ·〛
	[- I]ụlius · 〚m〛	L(uci) · f(ilius) ·	Cla(udia) ·	Cremona ·
	[- A]franius ·	L(uci) · f(ilius) ·	Cor(nelia) ·	[·] . . . . . . ·
	[-ca.?-]bius ·	Q(uinti) · f(ilius) ·	Pol(lia) ·	Apam[ea ·]
	[- O]ctauius ·	A(uli) · f(ilius) ·	Pol(lia) ·	Adrymeto ·
10	[-ca.?-] ̣ius ·	C(ai) · f(ilius) ·	. . .	Philomedia ·
	[- Sal]lustius ·	C(ai) · f(ilius) ·	Fab(ia) ·	Utica ·
	[- Ar]runtius ·	Ḷ(uci) · f(ilius) ·	Cor(nelia) ·	Laudicia ·
	[- A]ṇtonius ·	L(uci) · f(ilius) ·	Cor(nelia) ·	Laudicia ·
	[-ca.?-]tọrius ·	[.] f(ilius) ·	Faḅ(ia)	Altino ·
15	[-ca.?-] ̣ṣ[– ? –	] f(ilius)	Po[l(lia)]	Ṇicopoli b(ene)f(iciarius) ·
				Flacc[i – ? –]

-- -- -- -- -- -- -- --

---

67 HARRIS 1989, 253–254; BOWMAN 1994a, 96. Cf. SPEIDEL 1996, 64.
68 CIL I² 709 = CIL VI 37045 = ILS 8888. Photos and a drawing of the inscription are, for instance, available on the website of the Epigraphik-Datenbank CLAUSS / SLABY.
69 BGU IV 1083 = Ch.L.A. X 426 = RMR 36 (Arsinoïtes).

Fig. 2: list of legionary soldiers (of *legio III Cyrenaica* or *legio XXII Deiotariana*?) on papyrus from Egypt, Staatliche Museen zu Berlin – Ägyptisches Museum und Papyrussammlung, P 13319.

In this case the column with the *praenomina* is torn away, but the list is complete on the right side. Several lists of similar design have also survived on stone monuments dated to the first three centuries CE in Rome and the provinces.[70] These lists (often inscribed on the sides of altars) contain the names of the soldiers who dedicated the monuments. Remarkably, although such lists on stone were organised and designed precisely like those, which the army's administration produced on papyrus, most were not copies of existing administrative records but drawn up specifically to record the dedicants of a particular monument. Among the inscriptions from Egypt, two monumental dedications illustrate this phenomenon. The first one is a dedication from Koptos and was set up in the first century CE by soldiers of various types of units after they had completed construction works in the Eastern Desert.[71] The second list is inscribed on an altar from Nicopolis near Alexandria that was erected by veterans

---

[70] E. g. CIL III 6178–6179; 6580; 6627; 8110; 14214; 14507; VI, 1057 = 31234 = ILS 2157; 31140–31147; 31149–31152; 32515–32523; 32525–32531; 32533; 32536; 32542–32544; 32547; 32623–32640; VIII, 18065; 18067–18068; 18084; XIII, 6681; 6801; AE 1930, 57; AE 1940, 82; AE 1955, 238; AE 1969/70, 633; AE 2001, 555; AE 2004, 1223; Kayser 114.
[71] CIL III 6627 = 14147 = ILS 2483 (Koptos).

of *legio II Traiana* on the occasion of their discharge in 157 CE.[72] In both cases, the legionary soldiers are recorded with their *tria nomina* and their homes, and grouped by cohorts and *centuriae*, but only the earlier list from Koptos also mentions the soldiers' voting tribes (*tribus*). Such lists are not only known from Egypt. Many can also be found in Rome, on the Rhine and Danube as well as in North Africa. Their effect on the viewer is one in which the individual elements serve to make up an organised whole by forming a well-structured pattern. Perhaps, therefore, this particular design was chosen to promote or reinforce the notion that those named in such lists were more than loosely connected individuals but that they belonged to and acted as a tight-knit community that was the Roman army.

It is a long way from Lower Nubia of the late first c. BCE to Thrace in the first half of the third c. CE. Yet, as far as the role of reading and writing in the military sphere is concerned, significant common traits are recognisable. The evidence discussed above strongly suggests that the written word was not only an essential tool to keep the administration and the communication in the Roman army functioning. Various types of texts and documents also served many purposes in, and had several effects on, the everyday lives of Roman soldiers and officers. To a greater degree than generally assumed, the written word appears both to have governed the daily life of Roman soldiers and conveyed, not least through symbolic elements, military identity.

Bibliography

ADAMS 1983 = W.Y. ADAMS, Primis and the "Aethiopian" Frontier, *JARCE* 20, 1983, 93–104.
ADAMS 1985 = W.Y. ADAMS, Ptolemaic and Roman Occupation at Qasr Ibrim, in: F. GUES/F. THILL (ed.), Mélanges offerts à Jean Vercoutter, Paris 1985, 9–17.
ANDERSON/PARSONS/NISBIT 1979 = R.D. ANDERSON/P.J. PARSONS/G.M. NISBIT, Elegiacs by Gallus from Qasr Ibrim, *JRS* 69, 1979, 125–155.
BENEFIEL 2001 = R. BENEFIEL, A New Praetorian Laterculus From Rome, *ZPE* 134, 2001, 221–232.
BIRLEY 1992 = A.R. BIRLEY, Locus virtutibus patefactus?, Opladen 1992.
BOWMAN 1994 = A.K. BOWMAN, The Roman Imperial Army: Letters and Literacy on the Northern Frontier, in: A.K. BOWMAN/G. WOOLF (ed.), Literacy and Power in the Ancient World, Cambridge 1994, 109–125.
BOWMAN 1994a = A.K. BOWMAN, Life and Letters on the Roman Frontier, London 1994.
BOWMAN 2006 = A.K. BOWMAN, Outposts of Empire: Vindolanda, Egypt, and the Empire of Rome, *JRA* 19, 2006, 75–93.
BOWMAN/THOMAS 1983 = A.K. BOWMAN/J.D. THOMAS, Vindolanda: The Latin Writing-Tablets, London 1983.
BOWMAN/THOMAS 1991 = A.K. BOWMAN/J.D. THOMAS, A Military Strength Report from Vindolanda. *JRS* 81, 1991, 63–73.
BOWMAN/THOMAS/TOMLIN 2010 = A.K. BOWMAN/J.D. THOMAS/R.S.O. TOMLIN, The Vindolanda Writing-Tablets (Tabulae Vindolandenses IV, Part 1), *Britannia* 41, 2010, 187–224

---

72 AE 1955, 238; AE 1969/70, 633 = KAYSER 102 (Nicopolis).

Bowman/Thomas/Tomlin 2011 = A.K. Bowman/J.D. Thomas/R.S.O. Tomlin The Vindolanda Writing-Tablets (Tabulae Vindolandenses IV, Part 2), *Britannia* 42, 2011, 113–144.
Bülow-Jacobsen 2012 = A. Bülow-Jacobsen, Private Letters, in: Cuvigny 2012, 234–384.
Burstein 1979 = S. Burstein, The Nubian campaigns of C. Petronius and George Reisner's Second Meroitic Kingdom of Napata, *ZÄS* 106, 1979, 95–105.
Cosme 1993 = P. Cosme, Le livret militaire du soldat romain, *Cahiers du Centre Gustave Glotz* 4, 1993, 67–80.
Cosme 2016 = P. Cosme, Le prestige des enseignes, in: R. Baudry/F. Hurlet/I. Rivoal (ed.), Le Prestige à Rome à la fin de la République et au début du Principat, Paris 2016, 81–90.
Cosme 2017 = P. Cosme, Les archives de la cavalerie auxiliaire, in: C. Wolff/P. Faure (ed.), Les auxiliaires de l'armée romaine. Des allies aux fédérés, Lyon 2017, 309–315.
Cotton 2014 = H. Cotton, The Evolution of the so-called Provincial Law, or: Cicero's Letters of Recommandation and Private International Law in the Roman World, in: G. de Klijn/S. Benoist (ed.), Integration in Rome and in the Roman World, Leiden 2014, 43–56.
Cuvigny 2005 = H. Cuvigny, Ostraca de Krokodilô. La correspondence militaire et sa circulation, Cairo 2005.
Cuvigny 2006 = H. Cuvigny, La Route de Myos Hormos. L'armée romaine dans le desert Oriental, Cairo 2006.
Cuvigny 2012 = H. Cuvigny (ed.), Didymoi: une garnison romaine dans le désert oriental d'Égypte. II – les textes, Cairo 2012.
Demicheli 1976 = A.M. Demicheli, Rapporti di pace e di guerra dell' Egitto romano con le popolazioni dei deserti africani, Milano 1976.
Daris 1964 =S. Daris, Documenti per la storia dell'esercito romano in Egitto, Milano 1964.
Derda/Łajtar 2012a = T. Derda/A. Łajtar, P.Qasr Ibrim inv. 80/11: A Testimony to the Zenodotos' Edition of the Iliad?, in: R. Ast et al. (ed.), Papyrological Texts in Honor of Roger S. Bagnall, Durham 2012, 75–78.
Derda/Łajtar 2012b = T. Derda/A. Łajtar, Greek and Latin Papyri from the Egypt Exploration Society Excavations at Qasr Ibrim: A Testimony to the Roman Army in Upper Egypt and Lower Nubia in the First Years of Augustus', in: P. Schubert (ed.), Actes du 26e Congrès international de papyrologie, Genève, 16–21 août 2010, Geneva 2012, 183–186.
Derda/Łajtar 2013 = T. Derda/A. Łajtar, Roman Occupation of Qasr Ibrim as Reflected in Greek Papyri from the Site, in: J. Hagen/J. van der Vliet (ed.), Qasr Ibrim, between Egypt and Africa. Proceedings of the Leiden Conference, December 2009, Leuven 2013, 105–110.
Derda/Łajtar/Płóciennik 2014/15 = T. Derda/A. Łajtar/T. Płóciennik, Where Did the Third Legion of Augustan Egypt Have its Base?, *Palamedes* 9/10, 2014–2015, 99–105.
Derda/Łajtar/Płóciennik 2015 = T. Derda/A. Łajtar/T. Płóciennik, Three Lists of Soldiers on Papyrus Found in Qasr Ibrim, in: A. Tomas (ed.), Ad fines imperii Romani. Studia Thaddaeo Sarnowski septuagenario ab amicis, collegis discipulisque dedicata, Warsaw 2015, 47–57.
Eck 2003 = W. Eck, The Language of Power: Latin Reflected in the Inscriptions of Judaea / Syria Palaestina, in: L.H. Schiffman (ed.), Semitic Papyrology in Context: A Climate of Creativity. Papers from a New York University conference marking the retirement of Baruch A. Levine, Boston 2003, 125–144.
Eck 2009 = W. Eck, Presence, Role and Significance of Latin in the Epigraphy and Culture of the Roman Near East, in: H.M. Cotton/R.G. Hoyland/J.J. Price/D.J. Wasserstein (ed.), From Hellenism to Islam: Cultural and Linguistic Change in the Roman Near East, Cambridge 2009, 15–42.
Eck 2010 = W. Eck, Der Kaiser als Herr des Heeres. Militärdiplome und die kaiserliche Reichsregierung, in: J.J. Wilkes (ed.), Documenting the Roman Army. Essays in Honor of Margaret Roxan, London 2010, 55–87.
FHN = T. Eide/T. Hägg/R.H. Pierce/L. Török (ed.), Fontes Historiae Nubiorum, vol. III, Bergen 1998.

FINK 1971 = R.O. FINK, Roman Military Records on Papyrus, Cleveland 1971.
HAENSCH 2008 = R. HAENSCH, Der *exercitus Aegyptiacus* – ein provinzialer Heeresverband wie andere auch?, in: K. LEMBKE/M. MINAS-NERPEL/S. PFEIFFER (ed.), Tradition and Transformation: Egypt und Roman Rule, Leiden 2010, 111–132.
HAENSCH 2012 = R. HAENSCH, The Roman Army in Egypt, in: C. RIGGS (ed.), The Oxford Handbook of Roman Egypt, Oxford 2012, 68–82.
HARRIS 1989 = W.V. HARRIS, Ancient Literacy, Harvard 1989.
HARRIS 2014 = W.V. HARRIS, Literacy and Epigraphy II, in: C. APICELLA/M.-L. HAACK/F. LEROUXEL (ed.), Les affaires de Monsieur Andreau: économie et société du monde romain, Bordeaux 2014, 289–300.
HAYNES 2013 = I. HAYNES, Blood of the Provinces. The Roman Auxilia and the Making of Provincial Society from Augustus to the Severans, Oxford 2013.
HOFFMANN 2010 = B. HOFFMANN, Army Documents, in: K. STAUNER (ed.), Das offizielle Schriftwesen des römischen Heeres von Augustus bis Gallienus (27 v. Chr. – 268 n. Chr.), *CR* 60, 2010, 249–250.
JAMESON 1968 = S. JAMESON, Chronology of the Campaigns of Aelius Gallus and C. Petronius, *JRA* 58, 1968, 71–84.
KIRWAN 1977 = L.P. KIRWAN, Rome beyond the Southern Egyptian Frontier, *PBA* 63, 1977, 13–31.
LOCHER 2002 = J. LOCHER, Die Anfänge der römischen Herrschaft in Nubien und der Konflikt zwischen Rom und Meroe, *AncSoc* 32, 2002, 73–133.
MARICHAL 1992 = R. MARICHAL, Les Ostraca de Bu Njem, Tripoli 1992.
MITTHOF 2001 = F. MITTHOF, Annona militaris. Ein Beitrag zur Verwaltungs- und Heeresgeschichte des Römischen Reiches im 3.–6. Jh. n. Chr., Florenz 2001.
MÓCSY 1992 = A. MÓCSY, Pannonien und das römische Heer. Ausgewählte Aufsätze, Stuttgart 1992.
PHANG 2007 = S.E. PHANG, Military Documents, Languages, and Literacy, in: P. ERDKAMP (ed.), A Companion to the Roman Army, Oxford 2007, 286–304.
RMR = R.O. FINK, Roman Military Records on Papyrus, Cleveland 1971.
SCAPPATICCIO 2009 = M.C. SCAPPATICCIO, Virgilio, allievi e maestri a Vindolanda: per un'edizione di nuovi documenti dal forte britannico, *ZPE* 169, 2009, 59–70.
SCAPPATICCIO 2013 = M.C. SCAPPATICCIO, Papyri Vergilianae. L'apporto della Papirologia alla Storia della Tradizione virgiliana (I- VI d.C), Liège 2013.
SCHALTENBRAND OBRECHT 2012 = V. SCHALTENBRAND OBRECHT, Stilus. Kulturhistorische, typologisch-chronologische und technologische Untersuchungen an römischen Schreibgriffeln von Augusta Raurica und weiteren Fundorten, Augst 2012.
SHARANKOV 2011 = N. SHARANKOV, Language and Society in Roman Thrace, in: I.P. HAYNES (ed.), Early Roman Thrace. New Evidence from Bulgaria, Portsmouth R. I. 2011, 135–155.
SLAWISCH 2007 = A. SLAWISCH, Die Grabsteine der römischen Provinz Thracia. Aufnahme, Verarbeitung und Weitergabe überregionaler Ausdrucksmittel am Beispiel der Grabsteine einer Binnenprovinz zwischen Ost und West, Langenweißbach 2007.
SPEIDEL 1992 = M.P. SPEIDEL, Roman Army Studies II, Stuttgart 1992.
SPEIDEL 1994 = M.P. SPEIDEL, Die Denkmäler der Kaiserreiter. Equites singulares Augusti, Köln 1994.
SPEIDEL 1996 = M.A. SPEIDEL, Die römischen Schreibtafeln von Vindonissa. Lateinische Texte des militärischen Alltags und ihre geschichtliche Bedeutung, Baden-Dättwil 1996.
SPEIDEL 2009 = M.A. SPEIDEL, Heer und Herrschaft im Römischen Reich der Hohen Kaiserzeit, Stuttgart 2009.
SPEIDEL 2010 = M.A. SPEIDEL, *Pro patria mori…* La doctrine du patriotisme romain dans l'armée impériale, *Cahiers du Centre Gustave Glotz* 21, 2010, 139–154.
SPEIDEL 2014 = M.A. SPEIDEL, The Roman Army, in: C. BRUUN/J. EDMONDSON (ed.), The Oxford Handbook of Roman Epigraphy, Oxford 2014, 319–344.

SPEIDEL 2015 = M.A. SPEIDEL, 'Almaqah in Rom? Epigraphisches zu den römisch-sabäischen Beziehungen in der Hohen Kaiserzeit. *ZPE* 194, 2015, 241–258.

SPEIDEL 2015a = M.A. SPEIDEL, Kaiserliche Privilegien, Urkunden und die „Anarchie" des 3. Jahrhunderts n. Chr. Einige Beobachtungen, in: U. BABUSIAUX/A. KOLB (ed.), Das Recht der Soldatenkaiser – rechtliche Stabilität in Zeiten politischen Umbruchs?, Berlin 2015, 46–64.

SPEIDEL 2016 = M.A. SPEIDEL, Maximinus and the Thracians – Herodian on the Coup of 235, and Ethnic Networks in the Roman Army of the Third Century CE, in: V. COJOCARU/A. RUBEL (ed.), Mobility in Research on the Black Sea Region. The Proceedings of the International Symposium, Iaşi, July 5–10, 2015, Cluj-Napoca 2016, 335–361.

SPEIDEL 2017 = M.A. SPEIDEL, Actium, Allies, and the Augustan Auxilia: Reconsidering the Transformation of Military Structures and Foreign Relations in the Reign of Augustus, in: C. WOLFF/ P. FAURE (ed.), Les auxiliaires de l'armée romaine: des alliés aux fédérés, Lyon 2017, 79–95.

SPEIDEL forthcoming = M.A. SPEIDEL, Recruitment and Identity. Exploring the Meanings of Roman Soldiers' Homes, in: D. DANA (ed.), Entrer dans l'armée romaine: bassins de recrutement des unités auxiliaires (Ier-IIe s. ap. J.-C.), *HiMA*.

SPEIDEL forthcoming A = M.A. SPEIDEL, Roman Red Sea Politics from Augustus to Justinian I, in: C. ROBIN/M. WYSSA (ed.), Aksum, Himyar and Egypt. Merchants, Trade, Religion and the Changing World of the Cities in the Age of Justinian.

STAUNER 2004 = K. STAUNER, Das offizielle Schriftwesen des römischen Heeres von Augustus bis Gallienus (27 v. Chr.-268 n. Chr.): Eine Untersuchung zu Struktur, Funktion und Bedeutung der offiziellen militärischen Verwaltungsdokumentation und zu deren Schreibern, Bonn 2004.

STAUNER 2016 = K. STAUNER, New Documents from the Roman Military Administration in Egypt's Eastern Desert: the Ostraca from the Praesidium of Didymoi, in: B TAKMER/E.N. AKDOĞU ARCA/N. GÖKALP ÖZDIL (ed.), Vir Doctus Anatolicus. Studies in Memory of Sencer Şahin, Istanbul 2016, 796–815.

TOMLIN 2003 = R.S.O. TOMLIN, Documenting the Roman Army at Carlisle, in: J.J. WILKES (ed.), Documenting the Roman Army. Essays in Honor of Margaret Roxan, London 2003, 157–187.

TOMLIN 2016 = R.S.O. TOMLIN, Roman London's First Voices: Writing Tablets from the Bloomberg Excavations, 2010–14, London 2016.

TÖRÖK 1989/1990 = L. TÖRÖK, Augustus and Meroe, *Orientalia Suecana* 38/39, 1989–1990, 171–190.

VON SALDERN 2006 = F. VON SALDERN, Ein kaiserliches Reskript zur Entlassung eines Angehörigen der vigiles, *ZPE* 156, 2006, 293–307.

WAEBENS 2012 = S. WAEBENS, Imperial Policy and Changed Composition of the Auxilia: The "Change in AD 140" Revisited, *Chiron* 42, 2012, 1–23.

WEINSTEIN/TURNER 1976 = M.E. WEINSTEIN/E.G. TURNER, Greek and Latin Papyri from Qasr Ibrim. *JEA* 62, 1976, 115–130.

WEISS 2002 = P. WEISS, Ausgewählte neue Militärdiplome. Seltene Provinzen (Africa, Mauretania Caesariensis), und späte Urkunden für Prätorianer (Caracalla, Philippus), *Chiron* 32, 2002, 491–543.

WEISS 2015 = P. WEISS, Eine honesta missio in Sonderformat. Neuartige Bronzeurkunden für Veteranen der Legionen in Germania Superior unter Gordian III, *Chiron* 45, 2015, 23–75.

WEISS 2017 = P. WEISS, Die Militärdiplome unter Marc Aurel und Commodus. Kontinuitäten und Brüche, in: V. GRIEB (ed.), Mark Aurel – Wege zu seiner Herrschaft, Gutenberg 2017, 135–154.

YON 2017 = J.-B. YON, L'onomastique de la garnison «palmyrénienne» de Doura Europos: la cohors XX Palmyrenorum et l'origine des recrues, in: D. DANA (ed.), Entrer dans l'armée romaine: bassins de recrutement des unités auxiliaires (Ier-IIe s. ap. J.-C.), *HiMA* 6, 143–153.

ZERBINI 2015 = A. ZERBINI, Greetings from the Camp. Memories and Preoccupations in the Papyrus Correspondence of Roman Soldiers with their Families, in: E. FRANCHI/G. PROIETTI (ed.), Guerra e memoria nel mondo antico, Trento 2015, 287–342.

Roger Tomlin
Literacy in Roman Britain

Abstract: Literacy in Roman Britain can only be illustrated, not quantified, but the low assessment in *Ancient Literacy* can be nudged cautiously upward. Inscriptions on stone largely reflect the army's literacy, which was higher than that of civilians in the towns, let alone the countryside. Literacy in the army extended beyond officers and clerical staff to common soldiers. Civilian literacy in town and countryside can be demonstrated from manuscript sources like the Bloomberg writing-tablets on wood from London and the 'prayers for justice' on lead from temples at Bath and Uley.

Zusammenfassung: Das Ausmaß der Schriftlichkeit im römischen Britannien kann lediglich veranschaulicht, nicht aber quantifiziert werden. Die pessimistische Einschätzung in Harris' "Ancient Literacy" kann dennoch vorsichtig nach oben korrigiert werden. Inschriften auf Stein widerspiegeln im Grossen und Ganzen das Schriftlichkeitsniveau der Armee, welches höher war als dasjenige der Zivilisten in den Städten, von der Landbevölkerung ganz zu schweigen. Die Schriftlichkeit erstreckte sich in der Armee über die Offiziere hinaus zum administrativen Personal und zum einfachen Soldaten. Die zivile Schriftlichkeit in Städten und auf dem Lande zeigt sich in kursiven Kleininschriften, etwa den hölzernen Schreibtafeln aus London (Bloomberg) oder den sogenannten "prayers for justice" auf Blei aus den Tempeln in Bath und Uley.

When studying the literacy of Roman Britain, as in "1066 and All That", there are two memorable dates. The first is the day on which it all began, 25 September 54 BC, when Julius Caesar wrote a letter to Cicero 'from the shores of Nearest Britain.'[1] Despite this auspicious beginning, the island remained almost entirely illiterate for another century, until the Claudian invasion. The second date is January 1988, when William HARRIS completed the manuscript of his "Ancient Literacy."[2] He famously concludes that literacy in Britain did not extend beyond 'representatives of the imperial power and those soldiers who were literate', and 'in every city some of the more ambitious merchants and artisans.' Any impression to the contrary is due to 'the remarkable care with which the most inconsequential-seeming pieces of writing from Britannia have been recorded.'[3] As one of the editors of "Roman Inscriptions of Britain", I have long

---

[1] Cicero notes its receipt a month later, on 24 October (Cic. Att. 4,18,5), *litteras datas a litoribus Britanniae proximae a(nte) d(iem) VI Kal(endas) Oct(obres)* (with Shackleton Bailey's emendation of *proximo* to *proximae*).
[2] HARRIS 1989, Preface.
[3] HARRIS 1989, 268–269. Compare BIRÓ 1975, 13: 'The epigraphic material of Roman Britain is strikingly small, which fact [...] cannot be explained with the backwardness of research.'

treasured this back-handed compliment, adding only that 1988, by coincidence, was also the year in which I published the Bath curse tablets, a trove of manuscripts not written by soldiers like the Vindolanda Tablets nor even by merchants and artisans, however ambitious, but by aggrieved visitors to the Sacred Spring of the goddess Sulis Minerva.[4] So if I were allowed a third memorable date, it would be 25 June 2014, when the Bath Tablets joined the plays of Shakespeare in UNESCO's Memory of the World UK register. A more objective choice, however, would be the day in March 1973 when Robin BIRLEY discovered the first ink writing-tablet at Vindolanda, the first of almost nine hundred.

In thanking HARRIS for his seminal book, I do not depart from his conclusion that literate persons in Roman Britain – those who could read and write at least to some degree – were quite a small minority; but I do believe that literacy was wider spread and extended further downward than he does, without claiming this to be more than my impression. I cannot answer the question 'How many people could read and write in Roman Britain, and what proportion of the population were they?' It is not really possible to quantify literacy in Roman Britain, although Jeremy EVANS, by carefully tabulating the numbers and proportion of graffiti against the type of site and vessel, has shown that literacy was wider spread than the distribution of stone inscriptions would suggest. This is an interesting statistical approach, but he concedes that 'around 75 per cent of all graffiti are personal names' (and no more than this).[5] I would certainly agree with HARRIS that literacy was low by modern standards, that the proportion of literates was higher within first the army and then the urban population, than it was in the countryside; and that it declined as one went down the social and economic scale. Nor can I answer questions about the degree of literacy: whether, for instance, someone who could write his name could also read Virgil. A box-tile from Silchester (FIG. 1) and a bowl from St Albans both make this claim, but the craftsmen's names are accompanied by that most banal of quotations, *conticuere omnes*.[6] Silence may be our portion also if we pursue this particular line of inquiry, but there is ample evidence that civilian tilemakers were at least able to write dates and batch-totals.[7]

The question of literacy in Roman Britain has traditionally begun with its stone inscriptions. "An Atlas of Roman Britain" shows their distribution very clearly.[8] The

---

4 TOMLIN 1988.
5 EVANS 1987, 202.
6 RIB II.5, 2491.148 (Silchester), *Pertacus perfidus / Campester Lucilianus / Campanus conticuere omnes*. RIB II.8, 2502.51 with *Britannia* 46, 2015, 419, add. (i) (St Albans), also quoting Aeneid 2,1. For the literary classics in Britain and the reading of books, see BARRETT 1978 and TOMLIN 2012.
7 RIB II.5, 2491.
8 JONES/MATTINGLY 1990, 152, Map. 5:10 (from RIB I, but noting that RIB III would not change the overall pattern greatly). Their distribution was treated in greater detail by BIRÓ 1975, who reached the same conclusion.

Fig. 1: Silchester: box-tile (Museum of Reading)

great majority are associated with the army – along the Antonine Wall, along Hadrian's Wall with its hinterland and outpost forts, and at the three legionary fortresses of Caerleon, Chester and York. Other concentrations occur at Colchester, Lincoln, Gloucester and Wroxeter, which all originated as legionary fortresses. Even London, which retained a military presence in the governor's staff and bodyguard, had some military beginnings: an early fort has now been discovered, and the recently published Bloomberg Tablets reveal the presence of three auxiliary cohorts which arrived shortly after the defeat of Boudica in AD 61.[9] But these tablets are more important for demonstrating that literacy was essential to business and commerce.

It is a fort in northern Britain which, paradoxically, reveals literacy among civilians and at the humblest level. A stone inscription from Malton (FIG. 2) carries this exhortation within a recessed ansate panel:

> 'Good luck to the *genius* of this place. Little slave (*servule*, vocative), use and enjoy this goldsmith's shop.'[10]

---

9 TOMLIN 2016, 56: cohors I Vangionum, cohors VI Nerviorum and one of the cohortes Lingonum.
10 *feliciter sit | genio loci | servule utere | felix tabern|am aurefi|cinam* (RIB I 712).

Fig. 2: Malton: stone plaque (Malton Museum)

By addressing the *servulus*, it implies that he can read. One of the Bloomberg tablets is expressly written by a slave. After giving the date in the consulship of AD 64, it begins:

'I, Florentinus, the slave of Sextus Cassius [...]tus, have written by order of my master that he has received the two payments in respect of the farm [name lost] ...'[11]

The phrase he uses, *scripsi iussu domini mei*, is almost the same as that used by two slave-secretaries in the archive of the Sulpicii at Pompeii. Other Bloomberg tablets also attest slaves and freedmen acting as agents. Here is the most important:

'I, Tibullus, the freedman of Venustus, have written and say that I owe Gratus, the freedman of Spurius, 105 denarii from the price of the merchandise which has been sold and delivered. This money I am due to repay him or the person whom the matter will concern ...'[12]

It is dated 8 January AD 57, and appropriately – since it was found on the site of Bloomberg's European headquarters – it is the City of London's first dated financial

---

11 Tab. Lond. Bloomberg 50: *Florentinus Sex(ti) Cassi [...]ti ser(v)us scrips[i] iussu domini mei eum accepisse pensiones duas ex fundo [...]*.
12 Tab. Lond. Bloomberg 44: *Tibullus Venusti l(ibertus) scripsi et dico me | debere Grato <S>puri l(iberto) (denarios) cu ex{s} pretio | mercis quae uendita et tradita <est> | quam pecuniam ei reddere debeo | eiue ad quem ea res pertinebit*.

document. It is a striking illustration of Tacitus' comment that London in AD 60 or 61, just before it was destroyed by Boudica, was 'full of businessmen and commerce.'[13] In all, fragments were found of some four hundred stylus writing-tablets; in north-western Europe beyond Italy, they are second only to the Vindonissa Tablets from Switzerland.[14] But these derive from a legionary fortress: by contrast, most of the writers of the Bloomberg tablets are civilians. About eighty carry some sort of legible text, now published as "Roman London's First Voices", since they belong by content and archaeological context to its first half-century or so, c. AD 50–90.[15] Another tablet, a contract between two Roman citizens, not only illustrates commercial activity in early London but is historically important:

> 'In the consulship of Publius Marius Celsus and Lucius Afinius Gallus, on the 12th day before the Kalends of November [21 October AD 62]. I, Marcus Rennius Venustus, (have written and say that) I have contracted with Gaius Valerius Proculus that he bring from Verulamium by the Ides of November [13 November] twenty loads of provisions at a transport charge of one-quarter denarius for each, on condition that …'[16]

The (now lost) condition probably reserved full payment until the deliveries had been completed. The date and place are important: Venustus was writing less than two years after the cities of Verulamium (now St Albans) and London were destroyed by Boudica, with the loss of 70,000 lives according to Tacitus.[17] This contract is evidence of a rapid recovery, surprisingly rapid, but a tribute to the resilience of the immigrant entrepreneurs who brought literacy to London. The tablets name some 92 persons, none of them a woman or child, and no one necessarily British by birth, but giving a little support to Tacitus' rhetorical claim that Agricola encouraged the natives to seek higher education.[18] True, there is no stone anywhere which attests a schoolmaster, but two of the tablets now show that literacy was being practised if not taught. One is a capital-letter alphabet ordered like the address on the outer face of a letter.[19] The other (FIG. 3), which at first sight resembles stylised flowerheads, is two columns of numerals increasing regularly by 1000s and then by 10,000s.[20] The same excavation recovered no fewer than two hundred writing-styluses (*stili*), including one as yet unpublished which itself is a startling assertion of imported literacy: octagonal in section, its alternate faces carry a four-line poem of 26 words incised in tiny letters 2 mm high, calling it 'a welcome gift to you' (*munus tibi gratum*).

---

13 Tac. ann. 14,33: *copia negotiatorum et commeatuum maxime celebre*.
14 SPEIDEL 1996, a model publication of such material.
15 TOMLIN 2016.
16 Tab. Lond. Bloomberg 45.
17 Tac. ann. 14,33. Tacitus dates the whole episode to AD 61, but a longer chronology is more likely.
18 Tac. Agr. 21,1.
19 Tab. Lond. Bloomberg 79.
20 Tab. Lond. Bloomberg 78.

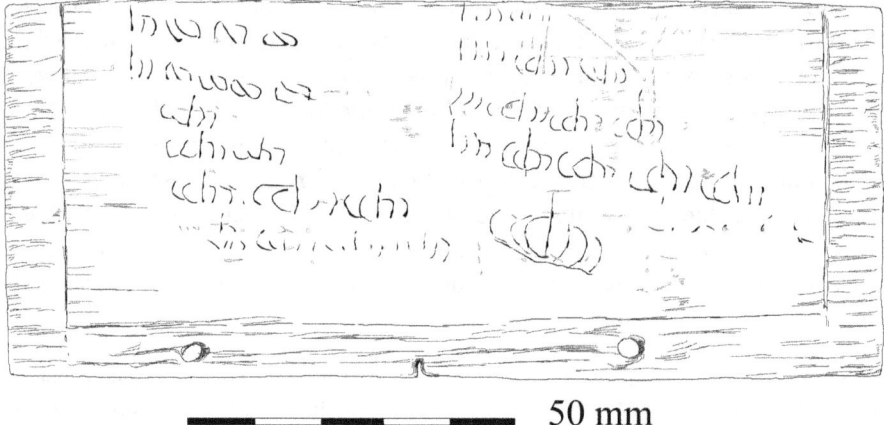

Fig. 3: London: writing-tablet (Museum of London Archaeology)

The Bloomberg tablets, which include letters addressed to a merchant (*negotiator*), a brewer or maltster (*bracearius*) and a cooper (*cuparius*), a cost-account of successive deliveries of beer (*cervesa*) written by different hands, a letter complaining of transport animals (*iumenta*) being taken without permission, an allusion to the ill-judged loan which has become a laughing-stock 'through the whole market' and a plea 'by bread and salt' for money to be sent as soon as possible, offer casual glimpses of the city's more ambitious merchants and artisans.[21] But there are soldiers among them, notably the prefect of the Sixth Cohort of Nervians, Classicus, who is surely the future leader of the Batavian Revolt.[22] So let us return to the army, seen within the context of its informal inscriptions. There is no need to emphasise the importance of literacy to the army. Reading and writing were essential to its economy of force, a point best made by Alan BOWMAN:

> 'The need to record and tabulate unit strengths, movement of troops, acquisition and dispensation of supplies, is part of the logic of an organisation which depended, for its efficiency and effectiveness, on economy of numbers.'[23]

BOWMAN's magisterial publication of the Vindolanda Tablets with David THOMAS[24] has shown that literacy was widespread within the community formed by a frontier garrison and the civilians in contact with it. 'What is truly astonishing […] is the

---

21 Respectively Tab. Lond. Bloomberg 7 (*Optato neg(otiatori)*), 12 (*Tertio braceario*), 14 (*Iunio cupario*), 72 (beer), 29 (Taurus' *iumenta*), 30 (*per forum totum*), 31 (*per panem et salem*).
22 Tab. Lond. Bloomberg 33.
23 BOWMAN 1994, 96. See also WILKES 2001.
24 T. Vindol. I-IV.

immense number of individual hands represented', several hundred in fact.[25] This evidence, although overwhelming in quantity and range, is not unique: similar ink tablets have been found in the Flavian fort of Carlisle, including this letter:

> 'Docilis to his prefect Augurinus, greetings. As you ordered, we have attached below all the names of lancers who were missing lances, either who did not have fighting lances, or who (did not have) the smaller *subarmales*, or who (did not have) regulation swords …'[26]

Docilis is a troop-commander (*decurio*) in the cavalry regiment (*ala*) based in Carlisle. He goes through the sixteen sub-units (*turmae*) one by one, itemising what weapons are missing. Another document lists the bushels of wheat and barley issued to all these sub-units.[27] These minutely detailed documents find an echo at the legionary fortress of Caerleon, where a fragmentary work-sheet also written on wood in ink was found in the well of an officer's house, raising the hope that other British military sites, given the right conditions of preservation, will produce further documents in manuscript form.[28] But for the moment, if we revert to the graffiti and informal stone inscriptions which were our portion in pre-Vindolanda days, we still find that literacy extended downwards, that it was not confined to officers and clerical staff: some common soldiers and military craftsmen, at least, could read and write. This impression cannot be quantified, it is true, but to argue that each instance is exceptional – that a literate craftsman was only showing off his literacy to his illiterate mates – would be special pleading; and sometimes it can be shown that sub-units like an infantry century or a cavalry troop (*turma*) contained more than one member who was literate.

Little need be said of the hundreds of graffiti scratched on samian and coarseware vessels after firing: they are mostly ownership-inscriptions and, strictly speaking, no more than evidence that someone could write his own name. It is not surprising that capital letters (often laboured) are much more common than cursive writing, but a pictorial graffito from Carlisle (FIG. 4) is irresistible. Underneath a samian dish is the economical drawing of a tufted bird, and in capital letters MΛRICΛII, *Maricae*; '(the property) of Marica'. This is probably a woman's name; but if only we knew it was also the name of a bird, a lapwing perhaps, we could see it as a sophisticated visual pun like the tile from the naval base of Dover decorated by its maker with a horned animal and his signature TΛVRI, *Tauri*; '(the work) of Taurus', punning on the word for 'bull' (*taurus*).[29]

---

25 Bowman 1994, 88.
26 Tab. Luguval. 14 *Docilis Augurino praefecto / suo salu[tem] ita ut praecepisti lanciaror[um] / quibus lanciae deessent om/nia nomina subiecimus aut / qui lancias pugnatorias aut / qui minores subarmales aut / qui gladia [i]nst[i]tuta non / hab[e]bant …*
27 Tab. Luguval. 1.
28 *Britannia* 17, 1986, 450, No. 84. Pearce 2004.
29 *Britannia* 28, 1997, 461, No. 20 (Carlisle); RIB II.5, 2491.124 (Dover). Compare RIB I 1821, the centurial stone of Sorio with the figure of a shrew-mouse (*sorex*).

Fig. 4: Carlisle: samian graffito (Tullie House, Carlisle)

Like this tilemaker, who was probably a soldier or sailor, military craftsmen signed their work. The grandest example was once discreetly displayed high above the east gate of Carpow, a very large fort in north-east Scotland beyond the Antonine Wall. The building-inscription, its well-cut letters 150 mm high, is now almost entirely lost; but to the left of them survives an elaborate *pelta* in high relief decorated with figures, Victory, capricorns and winged horses (*pegasi*), which symbolised the Second Legion Augusta. Below this *pelta*, in letters only 35 mm high which would have been unreadable from ground-level, is the end of the sculptor's signature: [...]P FE[CIT], '[...] made (this).'[30]

Quarry-face inscriptions are quite common. Some are found still *in situ* at the quarry, like those from a rock-face above the River Gelt south of Hadrian's Wall which because of their date can be added to the formal inscriptions which credit Septimius Severus' governor Alfenus Senecio (*c.* AD 205–07) with extensive rebuilding of Hadrian's Wall and its associated forts.[31] In clumsy letters:

> Apro et Maximo | consulibus | of(f)icina Mercati

'In the consulship of Aper and Maximus [AD 207], the working-face of Mercatius.' Close nearby is Mercatius' own signature, and the record of two legionary detachments,

---

[30] RIB III 3512. The name was abbreviated, perhaps to the initial letters of *tria nomina*.
[31] RIB I 1007–1015.

to one of which he must have belonged.³² Other quarry-face inscriptions survive on stones later incorporated into buildings, for example this block from Corbridge:

AVRELIVS
M

Aurelius M(...) has begun to peck out the letters of his name with a mason's point, but never finished it.³³ And at Brecon in Wales there is this appealing caricature (FIG. 5), also unfinished:

head in profile   GENI(ALIS)

Fig. 5: Brecon: quarry-face graffito (National Museum of Wales)

The lettering again is pecked with a mason's point. The letter-forms are ambiguous, making it uncertain whether this is a self-caricature by Genialis, the solution preferred by RIB III, or a caricature of *cent(urio)*, the centurion in charge.³⁴

Such stones can be difficult to distinguish from squared building stones which masons 'signed' by cutting their name on the face, as Civilis did at Hadrian's Wall: CIVILIS. The old caption in Chesters Museum calls it a centurial stone, but this is unlikely. There is no sign of a centurial symbol.³⁵ However, 'centurial stones' are very

---

32 RIB I 1009 (AD 207); 1010 (*Mercatius Ferni*); 1008 (*vex(illatio) leg(ionis) II Aug(ustae)*); 1014 (*vexil(l) atio leg(ionis) XX V(aleriae) V(ictricis)*).
33 RIB III 3294, rejecting Wright's suggestion that it is an unfinished tombstone.
34 RIB III 3113. G is almost indistinguishable from C, and I from T, but to judge by E, the writer would surely have barred his T.
35 RIB I 1640.

common: they are the facing-stones on which a century recorded the beginning or the end of the walling it had built, and 'about 150 centurions' are thus recorded from Hadrian's Wall.[36] Some twenty of them are recorded more than once, the most prolific being Lousius Suavis, with six stones to his credit.[37] This raises the question that if a centurion is named more than once, is the 'handwriting' always the same, with the implication that only one soldier inscribed the stones for his century? Cocceius Regulus' three stones, for example, look as if they were all cut by the same hand, and this can be said of others.[38] But some centurions are clearly recorded by more than one hand, to judge by the differences in formulation and layout, the differences in letter-form, for example whether A is 'open' (without cross-bar) or has a cross-bar either horizontal or vertical, whether E is 'E' or 'II', whether the second stroke of L is horizontal or diagonal, and so forth. Such differences can be seen in the stones of Avidius, Caecilius Clemens, Caledonius Secundus, Claudius Augustanus, Gellius Philippus, Helenus, Pompeius Rufus and Valerius Verus.[39] As an illustration, consider these two stones of Julius Candidus:

> 'The century of Julius Candidus made (this).'[40]

The lettering (FIG. 6) is coarsely incised with a mason's point, and the letters V, L and A are influenced by lower-case, handwritten (cursive) forms.

Fig. 6: Hadrian's Wall: centurial stone (Housesteads Museum)

---

36 BREEZE 2006, 150.
37 RIB III 3401 (with note).
38 RIB I 1860, 1862 and III 3402. Note also Arrius (RIB I 1345, 1346 and 1402), Claudius Priscus (RIB I 1972 and 1973), Maximus (RIB I 1669 and 1758), Valerius Flavus (RIB I 1362 and 1363, adjoining).
39 Respectively RIB I 1564 and 1565 (Avidius); 1440 and 2081 (Clemens); 1679, III 3379, I 1854 and III 3385 (Secundus, three hands); I 1770, 1855 and III 3297 (Augustanus, three hands); I 1572, 1668 and III 3297 (Philippus, three hands); I 1515 and III 3296 (Helenus); I 1447 and III 3308 (Rufus, but do not add I 1649); I 1761, 1853 and 2083 (Valerius Verus).
40 RIB I 1632 *(centuria) Iuli | Candidi | f(ecit)*.

Then compare:

'Of the First Cohort, the century of Julius Candidus.'[41]

Fig. 7: Hadrian's Wall: centurial stone (Chesters Museum)

This lettering (FIG. 7) is much neater, with conventional capitals contained within a rectangular outline. It must be admitted, however, that the issue is not clear-cut. Centurions might change their centuries by being promoted from one cohort to another: this is explicit of Claudius Augustanus and Olc(…) Libo, and may be true of Caledonius Secundus, Gellius Philippus, Julius Candidus (quoted above), Pompeius Rufus and Valerius Verus, since they are sometimes, but not always, attributed to a specific cohort. Thus the four stones which attribute Olc(…) Libo to the First Cohort all look as if they were cut by the same hand, but a fifth, which attributes him to the Second Cohort and calls him OBC Libo by mistake, is cut by another hand.[42] However, the three stones which attribute Caledonius Secundus to the Sixth Cohort are cut by two different hands, whereas a third hand is responsible for the stone which does not name his cohort.[43] Two stones attribute Caecilius Clemens

---

41 RIB I 1646, *coh(ortis) I (centuria) Iu/li Candid(i)*. The third stone of this century (RIB I 1674) is an elaboration of the second, with ansation and OH ligatured), but probably by the same hand.
42 RIB I 1647, 1849, 1857 and III 3382 (all COH I with OH ligatured, but only I 1647 specifies OLC); III 3411 (COH II, with OBC).
43 Respectively RIB I 1854 and III 3379 (first hand); I 1679 (second hand); III 3385 (no cohort, third hand).

to the Eighth Cohort, but despite some similarity, they seem to be cut by different hands.[44]

The issue is thus too complex to be resolved here, but a minimal conclusion is possible: a century 80-strong would surely have had more than one mason who was literate. There is economical confirmation of this from the Twentieth Legion's brickworks at Holt (Clwyd), a brick (FIG. 8) which was inscribed before firing with a note of expenses, *sum(p)tuaria*:

'Expenses:
Junius ...
4 (denarii)
Maternus ...
expenses:
Bellettus ...'[45]

Fig. 8: Holt: inscribed brick (courtesy of the finder)

---

44 RIB I 1440 (CHO, barred A, L with diagonal stroke, II for E); 2081 (COH, open A, L with straight stroke, E).
45 *Britannia* 26, 1995, 387, No. 28 (each line incomplete to the right): *sum(p)tu[aria ...] | Iuniu[s ...] | (denarios) iiii [...] | Maternu[s ...] | sum(p)tuaria [...] | Bellettus [...]*.

Since it was inscribed before firing, the writers must have been tilemakers; and the plural must be stressed. There are three names, each written in a different hand: evidently the signatures of different members of a sub-unit, a working-party (*officina*) if not a century. There is a nice parallel among the Bloomberg tablets, this fragmentary list of witnesses to a legal document:

> . . .
> 'Longinus, troop of Mar[...]
> Agrippa, troop of Silvanus
> Verecundus, troop of Silvanus'[46]

Each line is written by a different hand – the difference between the two instances of *tur(ma) Silvani*) is diagnostic – which means that Longinus, Agrippa and Verecundus each signed his own name against his seal, and identified himself by his sub-unit, a cavalry troop (*turma*) whether in an *ala* or a part-mounted cohort. They were following the procedure implied by another tablet, in which Atticus acknowledges his debt to Narcissus, slave of Rogatus, 'in the presence of those who have been written in (their own) hand above.'[47] Rogatus is identified as 'the Lingonian', which surely means that he belonged to a cohort of Lingones: four such cohorts are later attested in the British garrison. Like Rogatus himself, the witnesses are likely to have been soldiers; at all events, Atticus takes it for granted that they were literate enough to sign their own names.

This is not the place for a full collection of military signatures, but three more examples of soldiers signing their work may be added by way of illustration. The first comes again from the legionary brickworks at Holt, a jar made of the same clay as the bricks and tiles. Underneath, inscribed in fluent capitals before firing:

> 'Gaius Valerius Pudens, son of Gaius, of the *Maecia* voting-tribe.'[48]

This is the formal signature of the legionary who made the jar: he even added his voting-tribe to emphasise that he was a full Roman citizen – but he mis-spelled *Maecia* as *Maceia*. Also from Holt comes this roof-tile stamped by the Twentieth Legion, which however was inscribed by an auxiliary soldier:

> 'Julius Aventinus, soldier of the First Cohort of Sunici.'[49]

---

[46] Tab. Lond. Bloomberg 62 *Longinus tur(ma) Mar[...] | Agrippa tur(ma) Silvani | Verecundus tur(ma) Silvani.*
[47] Tab. Lond. Bloomberg 55 *eosque [m]anu q(ui) s(upra) s(cripti) s(unt) coram.*
[48] *Britannia* 40, 2009, 321, No. 14, *G(aius) V[al(erius) G(ai) f(ilius)] | Pud[ens] | Maceia*(!) *(tribu).*
[49] RIB II.5, 2491.96 *Iulius Aventinus milis | co(ho)rtis p[r]ima(e) Sunicor(um).*

His capital letters are fluent and accomplished, but he wrote his Latin as he pronounced it: *miles* for *milis*, *cortis* for *co(ho)rtis* and *prima* for *primae*. Such 'Vugarisms' are also found in the third example, an incense-burner made of clay slabs, dedicated in the shrine of the goddess Coventina at the fort of Carrawburgh on Hadrian's Wall:

> 'A votive offering for August Coventina (which) Gabinius Saturninus has made with his own hands.'[50]

Saturninus emphasizes that this is all his own work (*manibus suis*), but his text like that of Aventinus echoes spoken Latin: he confused the dative termination and wrote *Covetina* for *Coventina*, *Agusta* for *Augusta* and *votu* for *votum*. His Latin may have been colloquial, but obviously he composed his own inscription as well as cutting it.

The extent of literacy within the garrison of Roman Britain cannot be quantified, of course, but it should come as no surprise that some common soldiers could read and write. This is not to say that they spent their evenings reading Caesar and Virgil, but a significant minority must have possessed a basic literacy. But what about civilians in Roman Britain? And did their literacy extend from the towns to the countryside?

In the last thirty years a new source has become available to address these questions, the manuscripts loosely known as 'curse tablets', for which a better term would be 'prayers for justice'.[51] They are petitions to the gods inscribed on sheets of lead deposited in temples or running water. As the result of two major excavations and sporadic metal-detector finds, their total has increased since the publication of RIB I in 1965 from seven to more than two hundred.[52] Their distribution contrasts neatly with that of stone inscriptions: they are confined to the 'Civil Zone' in the south-east, the Severn estuary in particular. With only two exceptions (Caerleon and Leintwardine), they all come from non-military sites. They are quite widely distributed, but the great majority come from just two temple-sites, Bath and Uley. The Roman town of Bath (Aquae Sulis) is now a city still focused on its hot spring and bathing spa, but West Hill, Uley, is open farmland on the Cotswold escarpment overlooking the river Severn, altogether rural.

Like the Vindolanda Tablets, the Bath Tablets are inscribed in many hands, ranging from the very accomplished to the illiterate; from the beautiful Rustic Capitals in which Docilianus complains that his hooded cloak (*caracalla*) has been stolen, from the list of names inscribed on a pewter plate in cursive letters of calligraphic quality, to an enigmatic sequence of crudely inscribed capitals: ABCDEFX. This may only be an incomplete alphabet, but perhaps there is a hint of 'cursing' (*defixio*) here.[53]

---

50 RIB II.4, 2457.2 *Cove(n)|tina(e) A(u)|gusta(e) | votu(m) | man|ibus suis | Satu|rni|nus | fecit | Gabi|nius*.
51 VERSNEL 2010: not outright curses like RIB I 6 and 7 (London), which are very rare in Britain.
52 TOMLIN 1999 and 2002. Conveniently collected by KROPP 2008, 3. Britannien with 232 entries.
53 Respectively Tab. Sulis 10, 30 and 1.

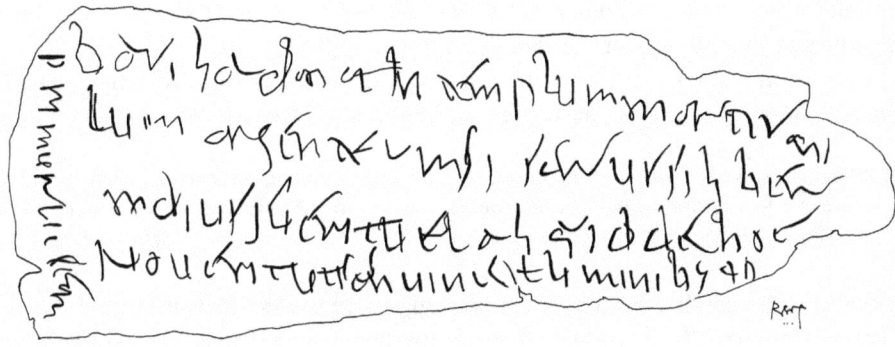

Fig. 9: Bath: inscribed lead tablet (Bath Roman Museum)

More likely it is a pretence at literacy, like the handful of tablets inscribed with regular, repeated scratches to look like writing. There are five such 'pseudo-texts' – and six blank tablets – among the 122 tablets. This wide variety of hands should be stressed: there is no sign of duplication, which would show professional scribes at work. It looks as if petitioners were expected to write their own tablets; and if they were illiterate, they could recite their complaint before tossing into the Sacred Spring a piece of scribble or even a blank.[54]

Two fourth-century tablets may be quoted as evidence of just how sophisticated literacy had become on occasion, despite being prompted by quite small losses. The first (FIG. 9) is also remarkable for being written by a woman, like the justly famous birthday invitation of Severa to Sulpicia Lepidina at Vindolanda.[55]

In New Roman Cursive, Basilia writes:

> 'Basilia gives into the temple of Mars a silver ring. May the person involved (*medius*) or who knows anything about it, whether slave or free, be accursed in his blood and eyes and every limb, or even have his intestines utterly eaten away, if he has stolen the ring or been involved.'[56]

She uses the rare term *medius* for anyone who is complicit or even an accomplice; but her bold phrase about his intestines, *intestinis excomesis*, is still more striking, since it is only paralleled in a moralising treatise composed by a British clergyman in the post-Roman period, who speaks of hunger for the Gospels eating away the bowels of the soul, *animae viscera excomedens*.[57] Surely their language betrays, not just liter-

---

54 TOMLIN 1988, 98–100, with 91–94 (tabulation of letter-forms).
55 T. Vindol. II 291, noted by the editors as 'evidence for correspondence between literate women of the equestrian class'.
56 Tab. Sulis 97 (emended) *Basilia donat in templum Martis anilum argenteum si ser(v)us si liber m(e) dius fuerit vel aliquid de hoc noverit ut sanguine et liminibus(!) et omnibus membris configatur vel etiam intestinis excomesis (om)nibus habe(at) is qui anilum involavit vel qui medius fuerit.*
57 Gildas, De Excidio 85,2.

acy, but the higher education in rhetoric of which St Patrick complains he was robbed when he was kidnapped from Britain as a schoolboy.⁵⁸

The second tablet is is also written in New Roman Cursive, but with the letters in reverse sequence, beginning at the bottom right-hand corner:

> 'Whether pagan or Christian, whosoever, whether man or woman, whether boy or girl, whether slave or free, has stolen from me, Annianus son of Matutina(?), six silver coins from my purse, you, lady Goddess, are to exact them from him ...'⁵⁹

Mutually exclusive clauses are typical of such texts, but the first is unique: 'whether pagan or Christian.'⁶⁰ Not only does the writer balance paganism against Christianity – despite knowing that Sulis Minerva is superior to Jesus Christ – but he also seems to parody the words of St Paul: '... there is neither slave nor free, there is neither male nor female, for ye are all one in Christ Jesus.'⁶¹ Surely he has read the New Testament, even if he does not accept it.

Finally if we turn from Bath to Uley, we find another wealth of documents, but this time in the countryside.⁶² It was probably not unique: there are tantalising hints to the contrary. When a rural settlement at Claydon Pike near Lechlade (Glos.) was excavated in the early 1980s, tiny scraps were found of Vindolanda-type wooden leaf tablets inscribed in ink in fluent Roman cursive. There are a few elongated letters in 'address script' and a diagonal annotation, both typical of correspondence, but unfortunately no complete words.⁶³ Fragments were also found of stylus tablets, which recalls the important survey by William HANSON and Richard CONOLLY. Stylus tablets are seldom found at rural sites, but this is due to the lack of anaerobic conditions like those at Vindolanda and London Bloomberg. In the Roman town of Silchester, George BOON was able to claim 'evidence of literacy is profuse' by pointing to stone inscriptions, graffiti and about 150 *stili*, but only one writing-tablet fragment.⁶⁴ This imbalance between pen and paper, so to speak, is emphasised by HANSON and CONOLLY, who contrast the near-total absence of stylus tablets – a notable exception being the fragment of a

---

58 Patricius, Confessio 9–12.
59 Tab. Sulis 98 *seu gens seu Ch(r)istianus quaecumque*(!) *utrum vir [u]trum mulier utrum puer utrum puella utrum s[er]vus utrum liber mihi Annia[n]o ma<n>tuten(a)e de bursa mea s(e)x argente[o]s furaverit tu d[o]mina dea ab ipso perexi[g]e ...*
60 *seu gens seu Ch(r)istianus*, understanding *gens* as the singular of *gentes* ('pagans') rather than an error for *gentilis*.
61 Gal 3,28.
62 TOMLIN 1993, supplemented by the annual 'Roman Britain: Inscriptions' surveys in *Britannia* (KROPP 2008, 3.22/1–39). He is currently preparing a full edition.
63 For this reason they were omitted from the annual 'Roman Britain' survey, except for the brief note of the excavation in *Britannia* 11, 1980, 384 and 13, 1982, 377–8.
64 BOON 1974, 62–64; a total increased by more recent excavations to about 160 (HANSON/CONOLLY 2002, 155 n. 35).

Fig. 10: Uley: inscribed lead tablet (British Museum)

deed of sale from the villa at Chew Stoke – with about 250 *stili* from 74 villa-sites, and another 90 from fifty non-villa rural sites.⁶⁵

Like Basilia at Bath, let another woman at Uley demonstrate the wealth of documents at this rural shrine of Mercury (FIG. 10):

> 'A memorandum (*commonitorium*) to the god Mercury [written over Mars Silvanus] from Saturnina a woman, concerning the linen cloth which she has lost. May he who stole it have no rest before / unless / until he brings the aforesaid property to the aforesaid temple, whether man or woman, whether slave or free ...'⁶⁶

The tablet continues overleaf with the offer of one-third of the goods recovered to the god Silvanus (again), whose name this time is not corrected to 'Mercury'. Saturnina's language is formal and legalistic: *commonitorium* and *s(upra)s(criptum)* for example. This is an extraordinary letter to find in a rural shrine, addressed to a god of whose identity she seems to be unsure. But the god's postbag is full of such letters which

---

65 HANSON/CONOLLY 2002, esp. 157–159 (tabulated). The Chew Stoke tablet is RIB II.4, 2443.13, a stylus tablet but inscribed (most unusually) in ink.
66 TOMLIN 1993, 121 (Tablet 2, with minor corrections): *commonitorium deo | Mercurio a Satur/nina muliere de lintia/mine quod amisit ut il/le qui hoc circumvenit non | ante laxetur nissi quando | res s(upra)s(criptas) dictas ad | fanum s(upra)s(criptum) attul[e]rit si vir si mu/lier si servus si liber ...*

artlessly reveal a rural community and its concerns: not only theft (cows, sheep, a draught-animal, a beehive, wool and linen cloth, clothes including gloves and gaiters, finger-rings, gold and silver coin, pewter plates) but 'those who think ill of me and do me harm' and the (named) persons 'who have brought evil harm on my beast.'[67] One text, inscribed in a peculiar cursive, even turns out to be Latin transliterated into Greek letters.[68] The handwritings have not yet been tabulated, so it is not possible to tell whether professional scribes were at work, but at the very least, this was a community aware of the written word. Uley leaves us with another disquieting question. 140 tablets were excavated, but only 86 are inscribed; the other 50 or so are blank. Were they simply unused stock – or did they accompany *verbal* petitions by illiterates, like the 'pseudo-texts' at Bath? Does the ratio between inscribed tablets and uninscribed even reflect the proportion of literates to illiterates among the countryfolk who petitioned Mercury? It would have been 9 to 5, a preponderance difficult to accept.

Bibliography

BARRETT 1978 = A.A. BARRETT, Knowledge of the Literary Classics in Roman Britain, *Britannia* 9, 1978, 307–313.
BIRÓ 1975 = M. BIRÓ, The Inscriptions of Roman Britain, *Acta Archaeologica Academiae Scientiarum Hungaricae* 27, 1975, 13–58.
BOON 1974 = G.C. BOON, Silchester: The Roman Town of Calleva, London 1974.
BOWMAN 1994 = A.K. BOWMAN, Life and Letters on the Roman Frontier: Vindolanda and its People, London 1994.
BREEZE 2006 = D.J. BREEZE (ed.), J. COLLINGWOOD BRUCE, Handbook to the Roman Wall, Newcastle upon Tyne 2006[14].
COOLEY 2002 = A.E. COOLEY (ed.), Becoming Roman, Writing Latin? Literacy and Epigraphy in the Roman West, Portsmouth RI 2002.
EVANS 1987 = J. EVANS, Graffiti and the Evidence of Literacy and Pottery Use in Roman Britain, *Archaeological Journal* 144, 1987, 191–204.
HANSON/CONOLLY 2002 = W.S. HANSON/ R. CONOLLY, Language and Literacy in Roman Britain: Some Archaeological Considerations, in: COOLEY 2002, 151–164.
HARRIS 1989 = W.V. HARRIS, Ancient Literacy, Cambridge Mass.1989.
JONES/MATTINGLY 1990 = B. JONES/D. MATTINGLY, An Atlas of Roman Britain, Oxford 1990.
KROPP 2008 = A. KROPP, *defixiones*: Ein aktuelles Corpus lateinischer Fluchtafeln, Speyer 2008.
PEARCE 2004 = J. PEARCE, Archaeology, Writing Tablets and Literacy in Roman Britain, *Gallia* 61, 2004, 43–51.
RIB I = R.G. COLLINGWOOD/R.P. WRIGHT, The Roman Inscriptions of Britain, I: Inscriptions on Stone, Oxford 1965, New Edition with Addenda and Corrigenda by R.S.O. TOMLIN, Stroud 1995.

---

[67] Summarising published texts and working-notes. The phrases quoted are *qui mihi male cogitant et male faciunt* (Tablet 76, unpublished) and *qu[i] pecori meo dolum malum intulerunt* (Tablet 43, *Britannia* 20, 1989, 329, No. 3).
[68] TOMLIN 1993, 129 (Tablet 52).

RIB II = R.G. COLLINGWOOD/R.P. WRIGHT, The Roman Inscriptions of Britain, II: Instrumentum Domesticum (in eight fascicules, edited by S.S. FRERE/R.S.O. TOMLIN, Stroud 1990–1995.
RIB III = R.S.O.TOMLIN/R.P. WRIGHT/M.W.C. HASSALL, The Roman Inscriptions of Britain, III: Inscriptions on Stone found or notified between 1 January 1955 and 31 December 2006, Oxford 2009.
SPEIDEL 1996 = M.A. SPEIDEL, Die römischen Schreibtafeln von Vindonissa, Brugg 1996.
Tab. Lond. Bloomberg = TOMLIN 2016
Tab. Luguval. = TOMLIN 1998 = R.S.O. TOMLIN, Roman Manuscripts from Carlisle: the Ink-Written Tablets, *Britannia* 29, 1998, 32–84.
Tab. Sulis = TOMLIN 1988
T. Vindol. II = A.K. BOWMAN/J.D. THOMAS, The Vindolanda Writing-Tablets (Tabulae Vindolandenses vol. 2), London 1994.
T. Vindol. III = A.K. BOWMAN/J.D. THOMAS, The Vindolanda Writing-Tablets (Tabulae Vindolandenses vol. 3), London 2003.
T. Vindol. IV.1 = A.K. BOWMAN/J.D. THOMAS/ R.S.O. TOMLIN, The Vindolanda Writing-Tablets (Tabulae Vindolandenses vol. 4, Part 1), *Britannia* 41, 2010, 87–224
T. Vindol. IV.2 = A.K. BOWMAN/J.D. THOMAS/ R.S.O. TOMLIN, The Vindolanda Writing-Tablets (Tabulae Vindolandenses vol. 4, Part 2), *Britannia* 42, 2011, 113–144.
TOMLIN 1988 = R.S.O. TOMLIN, Tabellae Sulis: Roman Inscribed Tablets of Tin and Lead from the Sacred Spring at Bath (Oxford) = Part 4 (The Curse Tablets) of B. CUNLIFFE (ed.), The Temple of Sulis Minerva at Bath vol. 2: Finds from the Sacred Spring, Oxford 1988.
TOMLIN 1993 = R.S.O. TOMLIN, Votive Objects: The Inscribed Lead Tablets, in: A. WOODWARD/P. LEACH, The Uley Shrines: Excavation of a Ritual Complex on West Hill, Uley, Gloucestershire: 1977–9, London 1993, 113–130.
TOMLIN 1999 = R.S.O. TOMLIN, Curse Tablets from Roman Britain, in: XI Congresso Internazionale di Epigrafia Greca e Latina, Rome 1999, 553–565.
TOMLIN 2002 = R.S.O. TOMLIN, Writing to the Gods in Britain, in: COOLEY 2002, 165–179.
TOMLIN 2012 = R.S.O. TOMLIN, The book in Roman Britain, in: R. GAMESON (ed.), The Cambridge History of the Book in Britain, Cambridge 2012, 375–388.
TOMLIN 2016 = R.S.O. TOMLIN, Roman London's First Voices: Writing Tablets from the Bloomberg Excavations 2010–14, London 2016.
VERSNEL 2010 = H.S. VERSNEL, Prayers for Justice in East and West: Recent Finds and Publications', in: R. GORDON/F. MARCO SIMÓN (ed.), Magical Practice in the Latin West, Leiden 2010, 275–354.
WILKES 2001 = J. WILKES, The Pen behind the Sword: Power, Literacy and the Roman army, *Archaeology International* 5, 2001, 32–35.

Figures

The Figures are drawings or photographs by the author, made or taken by courtesy of the museum concerned, except for Fig. 5, which the National Museum of Wales provided for RIB III.

Kai Ruffing
Schriftlichkeit und Wirtschaft im Römischen Reich

Abstract: Even though contemporary research drew the conclusion that writing as well as literacy were a common feature in the economy of the Roman Empire, there are different positions regarding their importance for the ecomomic life. Whereas one part of modern scholarship is rather sceptical and judges the lack of literacy as a constraint for the development of the Roman economy, the other one is pretty optimistic and sees literacy as being of high importance for everyday life in the Roman Empire. Thus the impact of writing on the Roman economy is discussed here by means of having a look at accounts, which are recorded on different materials (stone, walls, wooden tablets, papyri). The examples mentioned here at least hint at the omnipresence of accounts in the everyday life of the Roman Empire. It can be demonstrated that accounts were used also by individuals from the lower stratum of the Roman population in order to control their economic behaviour. All in all it can be concluded that writing as well as literacy were of highest importance for the economic life of the Roman Empire.

Zusammenfassung: Auch wenn die Forschung einen verbreiteten Gebrauch der Schrift bzw. von Schriftstücken in der Wirtschaft des Römischen Reiches als gegeben ansieht, werden doch in Hinsicht auf die Bedeutung desselben für die Wirtschaft unterschiedliche Positionen formuliert, die auf der einen Seite eine gewisse Skepsis verraten oder gar ihr angenommenes Fehlen als eine negative Rahmenbedingung für die Entwicklung und Performanz der Wirtschaft sehen; dem stehen überaus positive Einschätzungen der Reichweite der Alphabetisierung in der römischen Gesellschaft und damit auch des alltäglichen Gebrauchs der Schrift gegenüber, der damit auch im Bereich der Wirtschaft gegeben war. Dementsprechend wird die Frage nach der Bedeutung von Schrift und Schriftlichkeit in der reichsrömischen Wirtschaft am Beispiel der Textgattung der Abrechnung schlaglichtartig betrachtet. Dabei werden Texte auf unterschiedlichen Schriftträgern (Stein, Wand, Holztäfelchen, Papyrus) vorgestellt, die jedenfalls Hinweise darauf liefern, daß Schriftlichkeit und in diesem Falle Abrechnungen nicht nur allgegenwärtig im Römischen Reich waren, sondern auch von Individuen jenseits der imperialen Führungs- und Oberschicht alltäglich genutzt wurden und denselben zur Kontrolle des eigenen ökonomischen Handelns dienten. Dementsprechend darf der Schrift und Schriftlichkeit auch eine hohe Bedeutung für die Performanz der Wirtschaft des Römischen Reiches zugesprochen werden.

In seiner im Jahr 1989 vorgelegten, verdienstvollen Monographie zur Schriftlichkeit in der antiken Welt hat WILLIAM V. HARRIS bereits die grundlegende Funktion derselben für die Wirtschaft im Römischen Reich in der späten Republik und der hohen

Kaiserzeit betont. Die Führung von Haushalten der in ökonomisch behaglichen Verhältnissen lebenden Römer habe starken Gebrauch von elaborierten Abrechnungen gemacht. Dabei seien aber auch die Grenzen der Schriftlichkeit zu beachten: Abrechnungen seien offensichtlich nicht in allen größeren Geschäftsaktivitäten geführt worden. Aber ein genereller Trend zur Ausweitung des Gebrauchs von Schriftstücken sei in der hohen Kaiserzeit feststellbar. Die Frage, inwieweit Schrift und Schriftlichkeit eine Rolle in alltäglichen Transaktionen spielte, könne nur durch das Referieren von Eindrücken, die man aufgrund der einschlägigen Überlieferung erlange, beantwortet werden, die dazu führten, daß offenkundig Schriftlichkeit in eher geringem Umfange genutzt worden sei. Freilich konstatiert Harris ebenso das Vorhandensein vieler einfacher Menschen insbesondere in den deutlich hellenisierten und romanisierten Teilen des Reiches, die gelernt hätten, für spezifische Zwecke Gebrauch von Schriftstücken zu machen; dies bedeute freilich im Umkehrschluß nicht, daß sie selbst fähig gewesen seien, solche Dokumente zu verfassen. Freilich sei der Befund an Texten, die den Gebrauch von Schrift in den alltäglichen, nicht höherwertige Transaktionen betreffenden Geschäften, sowohl in Pompeji als auch im 'äußerst bürokratischen Umfeld' Ägyptens belegen, insgesamt eher überschaubar, auch wenn man im allgemeinen eine Steigerung des Gebrauchs von Urkunden nachvollziehen könne. Ferner konstatiert Harris umgekehrt aber auch allgemein einen reichsweit zu beobachtenden Gebrauch von Schrift und Schriftlichkeit in wirtschaftlichen Transaktionen.[1]

Roger Bagnall hingegen unterstrich in einer im Jahr 2011 publizierten Monographie die Alltäglichkeit des Schreibens und des Gebrauchs von Schriftstücken im griechisch-römischen Osten der mediterranen Welt von der Alexander-Zeit bis in die Spätantike. Dies betrachtete er freilich nicht als ein Spezifikum einer griechisch oder lateinisch schreibenden Bevölkerung, sondern auch als ein solches für diejenigen Individuen, die sich des Aramäischen befleißigten. Vielmehr, so Bagnall, habe der weite Gebrauch der Schrift in diesen zentralen Sprachen den Anlaß für einen vermehrten Gebrauch der Schrift in anderen Sprachen gegeben.[2] Diese globale Feststellung gilt selbstverständlich auch für den Bereich der Wirtschaft.

Gemeinsam ist den Arbeiten Bagnalls und Harris', daß sie grundsätzlich der Frage nach dem Ausmaß von Alphabetisierung und dem funktionalen Gebrauch von Schrift in der antiken Welt und hier insbesondere der griechisch-römischen Welt nachgehen. Demgegenüber fokussierte Neville Morley die Frage nach der Bildung und der Alphabetisierung sowie nach dem Gebrauch von Schrift auf die Bedeutung derselben für den Handel bzw. den Händler. Auch Morley konstatierte eine Ausweitung des Gebrauchs schriftlicher Verträge seit dem vierten vorchristlichen Jahrhundert, betonte aber in Gefolge von Harris, daß nicht jeder Händler des Lesens und des

---

1 Vgl. Harris 1989, 196–206. Vgl. dazu Bowman 1991 mit einer kritischen Auseinandersetzung zu den Positionen von Harris, die nicht zuletzt auf der Einbeziehung der papyrologischen Evidenz sowie derjenigen aus Vindolanda beruht.
2 Vgl. Bagnall 2011, 140–142.

Schreibens mächtig sein mußte, sondern sich auch der Dienste entsprechender Personen bedienen konnte. In der Fähigkeit, sich des Lesens und Schreibens im Handel zu bedienen, sieht MORLEY denn auch die Scheidelinie zwischen den Groß- und Kleinhändlern. Schließlich unterstreicht er die besondere Bedeutung dieser Fähigkeiten, indem er folgendes ausführt: „However, the absence of them (i. e. institutions like literacy, company organisation, money, wheights, measures, legal contracts and procedures) increased the risks of transporting large and/or valuable cargoes, of lending and borrowing money to finance trade, of delegating authority to agents or travelling someone else's boat, or it increased the time, effort and money involved in making an exchange."[3]

Ist sowohl bei HARRIS als auch bei MORLEY eine gewisse Skepsis gegenüber der Alltäglichkeit von Schriftlichkeit im Milieu von Kleinhändlern und Kleinhandwerkern erkennbar, so gewinnt man bei der Betrachtung von Kleininschriften einen deutlich anderen Eindruck, wie ein jüngst von MARKUS SCHOLZ und MARIETTA HORSTER herausgegebener Tagungsband anschaulich demonstriert: „Die Einwohner des Römischen Reiches waren im täglichen Leben mit vielfältigen schriftlichen Äußerungen konfrontiert. Weit mehr noch als durch öffentliche Monumentalinschriften auf Stein und Bronze [...] geschah dies durch schriftliche Informationen auf Wandflächen, mobilen Schriftträgern [...] sowie auf nahezu allen denkbaren Arten beweglicher Objekte und Alltagsgegenständen [...], die an sich nicht als Schriftträger gedacht waren."[4] Diese Kleininschriften beleuchten aber eben auch den Bereich der Wirtschaft und die Alltäglichkeit des Gebrauchs der Schrift in diesem Bereich, so etwa auf dem Felde der römischen Kleingeldrechnungen.[5] Des weiteren liefern die Kleininschriften und die mit ihnen verbundene Forschung in beeindruckender Art und Weise ein Bild vom weiten Gebrauch der Schrift in wirtschaftlichen Kontexten auf dem Lande in den germanischen Provinzen und Raetien.[6] In der aktuellen Forschung ist damit ein optimistischeres Bild hinsichtlich des Gebrauchs von Schrift und Schriftlichkeit in wirtschaftlichen Abläufen zu konstatieren, als dies in den 80er und 90er Jahren der Fall war.

In der einschlägigen wirtschaftsgeschichtlichen Forschung genießt diese Frage freilich keine größere Aufmerksamkeit. Zwar finden sich vereinzelte diesbezügliche Einlassungen, doch diese sind – soweit ich sehe – insbesondere der Frage nach der Rolle von vertraglichen Regelungen und dem Gebrauch von Verträgen im juristischen Umfeld gewidmet.[7] Nun wird aus dem oben Gesagten eine gewisse Alltäglichkeit des Gebrauchs der Schrift deutlich und in der Tat wäre es ein lohnendes Unterfangen, die Rolle der Schriftlichkeit im Bereich der Wirtschaft einer näheren Betrachtung zuzu-

---

3 Vgl. MORLEY 2007, 77–78 mit dem Zitat ebd.
4 Vgl. SCHOLZ 2015a, VII.
5 Vgl. GRASSL 2015. Zu den dort thematisierten Bleietiketten vgl. ferner FREI-STOLBA 2011.
6 Vgl. SCHOLZ 2015b, bes. 72–79.
7 Vgl. schon HARRIS 1989, 203–206; MORLEY 2007, 77.

führen. Solches kann hier freilich nicht geleistet werden, nähme ein solches Vorhaben doch ohne jeden Zweifel monographische Dimensionen an. Aus diesem Grund erscheint es angebracht, sich im folgenden in Gestalt der Abrechnung auf einen Typus von Dokument zu beschränken.[8] So stehen im Mittelpunkt der folgenden *tour d'horizon* Abrechnungen auf verschiedenen Schriftträgern, die die Ubiquität dieser Urkundenart zu demonstrieren und einen Einblick in die Wichtigkeit der Schriftlichkeit für wirtschaftliche Abläufe im Imperium Romanum zu geben vermögen. Hierzu sollen in einem ersten Schritt die Belange des römischen Staates im Mittelpunkt der Aufmerksamkeit stehen, um dann in einem zweiten Schritt die privatwirtschaftlichen Dimensionen in den Fokus zu rücken. Dabei werden lediglich einige Schlaglichter auf das Phänomen zu werfen sein, denn angesichts des Umfangs des zur Verfügung stehenden Quellenmaterials würde allein die Präsentation desselben gleichfalls monographische Züge annehmen.

Aus der Sicht des römischen Staates stellten die Abrechnungen über Einnahmen und Ausgaben generell ein Instrument der Kontrolle finanzieller Verhältnisse dar, um mit der offenkundigsten Funktion von Abrechnungen zu beginnen. Dieser Zugriff auf die finanziellen Gegebenheiten diente dann auch als Entscheidungsgrundlage für die Kaiser bzw. kaiserliche Funktionsträger. Ein in dieser Hinsicht besonders bemerkenswertes Dokument stellt eine umfängliche Inschrift Hadrians dar, die aus dem kleinasiatischen Alexandria Troas stammt. Der Text beinhaltet ein Dossier von drei Briefen, mittels derer Hadrian auf eine Eingabe der Dionysischen Techniten reagierte und im Zuge dessen er unter anderem die Periodos der Agone neu ordnete. Wie so oft, ging es nicht zuletzt um das liebe Geld. Im ersten Brief geht Hadrian auf Klagen über die Korinther ein, die offenkundig bei ihnen vorstellig werdenden Hieroniken keine oder Zahlungen in ungenügender Höhe geleistet haben.[9] Hadrian beschied nun, er wolle die Kalkulationen der Korinther, die dieselben dem Kaiser vorgelegt hatten, durch den Prokonsul überprüfen lassen. Das Prozedere sollte offenkundig dazu dienen, die Zahlungsfähigkeit festzustellen, denn die von den Korinthern vorgelegten Zahlen hatten wohl dazu gedient, den Kaiser von der nicht in vollem Ausmaß gegebenen Möglichkeit, die Beträge zu zahlen, zu überzeugen. Nun mußten die Korinther dem Prokonsul ihre Abrechnungen vorlegen, nach deren Prüfung dann eine endgültige Regelung erfolgen sollte.[10] Die Abrechnungen der Korinther sollten damit die Entscheidungsgrundlage für den Kaiser im Streit zwischen den Dionysischen Techniten und der Kolonie Korinth bilden.

Freilich bildeten Abrechnungen oder zumindest die Aufzeichnung von Preisen auch eine Entscheidungsgrundlage für staatliches Handeln in der Römischen Kaiserzeit. Solches wird etwa in dem von Mark Aurel und Commodus erwirkten *Senatus con-*

---

[8] Zur Abrechnung und ihrer Rolle in der Buchhaltung vgl. MINAUD 2005.
[9] Vgl. PETZL/SCHWERTHEIM 2006, 47–48.
[10] SEG 56, 2006, 1359, 32–34. Ed. pr.: PETZL/SCHWERTHEIM 2006. Zum Text dieser bemerkenswerten Inschrift vgl. JONES 2007; SLATER 2008; STRASSER 2010.

sultum de sumptibus ludorum gladiatoriorum minuendis deutlich.[11] Die sowohl durch ein Textzeugnis aus Hispanien (Italica) als auch durch ein solches aus Kleinasien (Sardeis) überlieferte Urkunde hat unter anderem die Festsetzung von Höchstpreisen für die Durchführung von Spielen und weitere damit verbundene Ausgaben zum Gegenstand.[12] Diese Preissetzung soll nach dem Text auf der Inaugenscheinnahme der Abrechnungen der letzten 10 Jahre basieren: „*Atque ita rationibus decem retroversum annorum inspectis…*"[13].

Die Funktion der Kontrolle von Einnahmen und Ausgaben von Institutionen läßt sich freilich auch und gerade im so quellenreichen Ägypten auf das Trefflichste zeigen. Eine in dieser Hinsicht überaus bemerkenswerte Urkunde ist eine auf das Jahr 113 n. Chr. datierender Text aus dem römischen Ägypten, der die Abrechnung einer Wasserversorgung der Gaumetropole des Arsinoites Ptolemais Euergetis beinhaltet.[14] In Ptolemaios Euergetis wurde seitens der Metropole ein Aquaeduct betrieben, der durch Wasserhebeinstrumente mit dem köstlichen Naß versorgt wurde. Der Text bildet nun eine von vier Verwaltern (φροντισταὶ εἰσαγωγῆς ὑδάτων καστέλλων καὶ κρηνῶν) verfaßte Abrechnung, die an einen ehemaligen Gymnasiarchen der Metropole namens Demetrios eingereicht wurde, der wiederum seiner Funktion als Prüfer (ἐξεταστής) nachzukommen hatte.[15] Jener tat nun solches mit äußerster Gewissenhaftigkeit. Mehrfach finden sich Randnotizen des Demetrios, die Anweisungen wie „kümmert euch darum" (Z. 32 in marg.) oder andere Aufforderungen beinhalten. Ihm unverständliche Posten kennzeichnete er demnach mit einer Randnotiz bzw. an anderen Stellen der Urkunde mit einem einfachen Querstrich. Damit nicht genug, vermerkte Demetrios jeden von ihm geprüften Betrag und offenkundig für gerechtfertigt erachteten Eintrag mit zwei kurzen Querstrichen.[16] Diese außergewöhnliche Urkunde demonstriert eindrücklich, welch hohe Bedeutung die metropolitane Oberschicht dem Rechnungswesen beimaß. Selbiges resultierte wohl nicht zuletzt aus der Tatsache, daß der Betrieb der Wasserversorgung für die Gaumetropole des Arsinoites eine defizitäre Angelegenheit war. So standen – bei allen Unwägbarkeiten, die aus dem Erhaltungszustand von Teilen des Papyrus resultieren – offenkundig Einnahmen in Höhe von 11.900 Drachmen Ausgaben in Höhe 16.142 Drachmen gegenüber. Mit anderen Worten: Innerhalb der Abrechnungszeitraums von sechs Monaten produzierte die Wasserversorgung von Ptolemais Euergetis ein Defizit von mehr als 4.000 Drachmen, das die Metropole auf

---

11 Vgl. MOMMSEN 1913.
12 ILS 9340 und 5163. Italica: CIL II 6278. Sardeis: Sardeis VII.1 Nr. 16 = CIL III 7106. Zur *reconstructio textus* siehe OLIVER/PALMER 1955. Zu den dort getroffenen Regelungen vgl. CARTER 2003; DUNKLE 2008, 59–65.
13 CIL II 6278 = ILS 5163 = OLIVER/PALMER 1955, p. 333, 46–55, Z. 51.
14 SB XXVI 16652. Der Text ist eine Reedition von P. Lond. III 1177, die von HABERMANN 2000 vorgelegt und ausführlich sowie grundlegend kommentiert wurde.
15 Vgl. HABERMANN 2000, 103 sowie 103–111 zum Amt des ἐξεταστής.
16 Vgl. HABERMANN 2000, 36–37 sowie 111–112.

anderem Wege ausgleichen mußte.[17] Die hohe Bedeutung der schriftlichen Dokumentation wirtschaftlicher Abläufe ist damit hier wie in den oben genannten Beispielen offenkundig.

Solches wird auch in einem anderen Lebensbereich in Gestalt der Religion deutlich. Hierzu seien wiederum zwei Beispiele aus dem römischen Ägypten angeführt, die dies zu illustrieren vermögen. Eines dieser Beispiele führt wiederum in das metropolitane Milieu des Landes am Nil. Es handelt sich um eine längere Abrechnung der Einnahmen und Ausgaben des Tempels des Iuppiter Capitolinus auf dem Kapitol von Ptolemais Euergetis aus dem Jahr 215/216 n. Chr.[18] In diesem Tempel spielten nun die Verehrung des Kaisers sowie der Kaiserkult nach Auskunft der besagten Abrechnung eine wesentliche Rolle.[19] Auch in diesem Fall werden die Ausgaben und Einnahmen des Tempels sorgfältigst aufgeführt. Interessanterweise wird in der Abrechnung auch das Bestellungsschreiben derjenigen Charge, die sich um die Administration des Tempels zu kümmern hatte, angeführt:[20] Die Verwaltung des Tempels und damit auch diejenige seiner Finanzen lag in den Händen eines Epimeleten namens Aurelios Serenos. Jener wiederum war Mitglied der metropolitanen Oberschicht, wie die frühere Bekleidung des Amtes des Kosmeten und seine Mitgliedschaft in der Boule zeigen. Diese war denn auch die Institution, die den Verwalter des Tempels bestellte. Letzterer unterlag offensichtlich aber auch einer gewissen, wenn nicht der Kontrolle der Provinzialverwaltung, wird der genannte Aurelios Serenos doch in dem besagten Schreiben aufgefordert, in Übereinstimmung mit den Befehlen des *procurator ousiacus* und diensttuenden ἀρχιερεύς namens Aurelios Italikos zu handeln. Interesse verdienen im hier behandelten die Kontext die Einnahmen des Tempels, die in der Urkunde angeführt werden. Neben Verpachtungen von Immobilien, die offenkundig Eigentum des Tempels waren, generierte man Einnahmen durch die Vergabe von Krediten, die mit einem Satz von 6 % p.a. verzinst wurden. Diese Kredite wurden wiederum von Mitgliedern der metropolitanen Oberschicht in Anspruch genommen.[21] Eine Erklärung für das Finanzierungsmodell des Tempels wird man sowohl im sozialen als auch im ökonomischen Bereich zu suchen haben, bot die Kreditaufnahme beim Tempel des Iuppiter Capitolinus den Mitgliedern der metropolitanen Oberschicht einerseits die Möglichkeit, ihrer Romanisation wie auch ihrer Kaisertreue beredten Ausdruck zu verleihen; andererseits konnte man aus der Kreditaufnahme auch selbst wirtschaftliche Vorteile schlagen: Der übliche Zinssatz betrug nämlich 12 % und trotz dieser Regelung wurden bisweilen deutlich höhere Sätze verlangt, wie die Urkunden

---

17 Vgl. Habermann 2000, 268–273.
18 BGU II 362. Zum Auftauchen der Kapitolia im römischen Ägypten vgl. Wilcken 1912, 116; Rübsam 1974, 48 sowie Pfeiffer 2010, 259; Ruffing 2014, 287.
19 Vgl. Ruffing 2014, 288.
20 BGU II 362 pag. V 1–17.
21 Vgl. Ruffing 2014, 290–291.

aus dem römischen Ägypten zeigen.²² Angesichts dessen sowie des Sachverhalts, daß gerade für die betreffende soziale Schicht der Verleih von Geld eine wesentliche Einnahmequelle darstellte,²³ wird man die begründete Vermutung wagen können, daß die besagten Kredite nicht etwa Konsumkredite waren, sondern zumindest bisweilen schlicht dazu dienten, Kapital aufzunehmen, um es gewinnbringend weiter zu verleihen.²⁴ Angesichts des bislang Gesagten verwundert die penible Rechnungsführung durch die Verwaltung des Tempels nicht, ging es doch hier gleichsam um das Geld der metropolitanen Oberschicht selbst. Freilich dürfte die Kontrolle durch den römischen Staat in Gestalt der Provinzverwaltung eine ausschlaggebendere Rolle gespielt haben, wie der bereits erwähnte Hinweis auf die Anordnungen des diensttuenden ἀρχιερεύς zeigt, denen der Verwalter des Tempels zu folgen hatte.

Die intensive Kontrolle von Tempelfinanzen durch die Provinzialverwaltung der *Aegyptus* läßt sich anhand eines anderen Beispiels – des Tempels des Krokodilgottes in Soknopaiu Nesos – trefflich zeigen, dessen wirtschaftlichen Verhältnisse sowohl durch griechische als auch durch demotische Urkunden illustriert werden.²⁵ Gerade die ägyptischen Kulte wurden durch die römische Provinzverwaltung in finanzieller Hinsicht straff kontrolliert. Dementsprechend löste das Auftauchen römischer Funktionsträger nachhaltige Unruhe auf Seiten der Priesterschaft aus, wie ein Brief aus Tebtynis zeigt, in dem ein Priester seinen Kollegen vom Auftauchen des Buchprüfers (ἐξεταστής) in Kenntnis setzt und ihm Furcht vor demselben einzujagen sucht.²⁶ Jedenfalls hatten die Tempel gegenüber der römischen Verwaltung Rechnung zu legen und taten dies in Form von Haushaltsbüchern.²⁷ Ein solches Haushaltsbuch bzw. ein Teil eines solchen ist aus Soknopaiu Nesos überliefert.²⁸ Die Kontrolle der Finanzen des besagten Tempels (wie auch anderer Tempel) durch den Staat dürfte aus zwei verschiedenen Motivlagen heraus erfolgt sein. Zum einen hob der Tempel für den römischen Staat Steuern und konnte hieraus Einkünfte generieren, zum anderen hatte – zumindest im Falle des Tempels von Soknopaiu Nesos – derselbe seine gesamten erwirtschafteten Überschüsse an den Staat abzuführen.²⁹

Auf der institutionellen Ebene zeigt sich mithin deutlich die besondere Bedeutung der Schriftlichkeit sowohl auf dem Gebiet der Kontrolle von Akteuren als auch – und das gilt es besonders zu betonen – auf der Ebene der Beschaffung von wirtschaftlichen Informationen, auf deren Grundlage gehandelt wird. Nun wurde die besondere Bedeutung der Schrift bzw. des Gebrauchs von Schrift auf dieser Ebene in der For-

---

22 Vgl. TENGER 1993, 23–27, 43–47, 59–60.
23 Vgl. TENGER 1993, 158–159.
24 Vgl. RUFFING 2014, 292.
25 Vgl. JÖRDENS 2005; LIPPERT/SCHENTULEIT 2005.
26 P.Tebt. II 315 = W.Chr. 71 (2. Jh. n. Chr.).
27 Zu diesem Urkundentyp vgl. OTTO 1905, 145–149.
28 P.Louvre I 4 (vor 166 n. Chr.).
29 P.Louvre I 4, 38–42; vgl. dazu P.Louvre I 4, Anm. zu Z. 41 f. Vgl. dazu RUFFING 2008, 577–578.

schung einhellig anerkannt. Etwas anderes stellt sich die Frage freilich im privaten Bereich dar. Wiederum ist es das römische Ägypten, das in diesem Kontext herausragende Beispiele liefert. Dies gilt etwa für die Gutsverwaltung, wie das Vorhandensein verschiedener Archive zeigt, die seit langem die Aufmerksamkeit der einschlägigen Forschung gefunden haben. Als Beispiele seien hier lediglich das Heroninos-Archiv mit seinem auch hinsichtlich der Masse der überlieferten Urkunden überaus beeindruckenden Informationen sowie das Archiv der Nachfahren des Patron – auch Laches-Archiv – genannt.[30] Handelt es sich bei den im Heroninos-Archiv nachzuweisenden Landeigentümern im wesentlichen um Alexandriner, die man mit Fug und Recht als Mitglieder der dortigen Oberschicht bezeichnen kann, und im Falle des Laches-Archivs um Angehörige der metropolitanen Oberschicht, so läßt sich die Wichtigkeit von Abrechnungen und damit von Schriftlichkeit auch auf der dörflichen Ebene in der Chora Ägyptens nachvollziehen. Einen Einblick in diese Ebene liefert etwa das Pakysis-Archiv, das aus dem bereits genannten Soknopaiu Nesos stammt. Dessen Bedeutung liegt zunächst darin, daß hier ein hellenisierter Ägypter und Priester des lokalen Heilgtums, der sowohl starke orthographische als auch sprachliche Schwierigkeiten mit dem Griechischen hat, darüber hinaus auch offensichtlich seine Mühen hatte, das Griechische zu verschriftlichen,[31] sich dennoch dieses Idioms befleißigte, um Abrechnungen zu erstellen. ANDREA JÖRDENS, die einen größeren Teil der Urkunden dieses Archivs ediert hat, kommt bei der Betrachtung derselben zu dem Ergebnis, daß die Abrechnungen „…schon aufgrund ihrer fragwürdigen äußeren Form…" keinen offiziellen Charakter besessen haben und in keiner Weise mit den Urkunden des genannten Heroninos-Archivs vergleichbar sind.[32] Offenkundig agierte Pakysis aber als ein Verwalter für eine oder mehrere nicht näher bekannte Personen und erhielt dafür einen monatlichen Lohn von 40 bzw. 48 Drachmen und steht damit auf einem Lohnniveau mit dem Gutsverwalter Heroninos.[33] WALTER OTTO rechnet in seinem immer noch maßgeblichen Werk zu Priestern und Tempeln die ersteren zu Personen, die schon durch ihre Amtseinnahmen wirtschaftlich günstig gestellt waren, ohne daß man diese freilich genauer beziffern könnte.[34] Offenbar suchte Pakysis dennoch seine Einkünfte durch Verwaltungstätigkeiten zu steigern. Wie dem auch sei, die Personen, für die Pakysis tätig war, scheinen jedenfalls nicht auf dem sozio-ökonomischen Niveau der alexandrinischen Oberschicht gewesen zu sein. So bleibt denn die Tatsache festzuhalten, daß eine wenn auch nicht wohlgeordnete, so doch eifrige Buchführung auch durch Personen betrieben wurden, denen Sprache und Schrift Schwierigkeiten

---

30 Zum Archivbegriff vgl. JÖRDENS 1997. – Zum Heroninos-Archiv vgl. grundlegend RATHBONE 1991; RATHBONE 2005. Vgl. ferner KEHOE 1992, 92–117. – Zum Laches-Archiv vgl. BAGNALL 1974.
31 Vgl. P.Louvre I, S. 223.
32 Vgl. P.Louvre I, S. 224.
33 Vgl. P.Louvre I, S. 224.
34 Vgl. OTTO 1908, 184.

machten. Selbiges demonstriert aber ohne jeden Zweifel die hohe Bedeutung von Schriftlichkeit für Alltäglichkeiten des Wirtschaftslebens.

Dies zeigt sich nicht zuletzt auch in der Nutzung der Wand als Schriftträger für Abrechnungen. In der Tat sind zahlreiche Graffiti aus verschiedenen Teilen des Römischen Reiches überliefert, die die Alltäglichkeit der Nutzung der Schrift für einfache Abrechnungen, aber auch für komplexere Geschäfte aufzeigen. Besonderer Bekanntheit erfreut sich dabei eine Abrechnung aus Pompeji,[35] die Preise für verschiedene Waren des alltäglichen Bedarfs nennt: Lebensmittel, d. h. Brot, Wein, Öl, Käse, Zwiebeln, Grieß, Wurstwaren, Datteln, Lauch und Fisch sind ebenso angeführt wie Weihrauch; darüber hinaus werden einfache handwerkliche Erzeugnisse in Gestalt von einem Eimer, einem Teller und einer Lampe genannt. Die Abrechnung läuft über einen Zeitraum von acht Tagen, alle Zahlungen erfolgen in *asses* (CIL IV 5380). Insgesamt belaufen sich die Ausgaben für den besagten Zeitraum auf 225 As oder rund 56,25 HS bzw. 14 Den., die zum größten Teil für Lebensmittel aufgewendet werden.[36] In der Tat sind die zur Debatte stehenden Beträge also äußerst überschaubar, zumal nach Abzug der Käufe von handwerklichen Produkten – 1 As für einen Breitopf, 1 As für einen Teller, 1 As für eine Lampe, 9 As für einen Eimer – und Weihrauch für 1 As sowie der Zahlung an eine Person in Höhe von 17 As im Schnitt nur ca. 24,3 As oder ca. 6 HS bzw. 1,5 Den. pro Tag für Lebensmittel verausgabt wurden. Auch wenn im Text keine Quantitäten angegeben werden, deuten die Höhe der Beträge und die täglich erfolgten Ausgaben darauf hin, daß es sich um eher überschaubare Mengen gehandelt haben wird. Gleichwohl verspürte man aber offensichtlich die Notwendigkeit, auch über diese bescheidenen Aufwendungen für das alltägliche Leben Buch zu führen. Anders gewendet: Selbst Konsumenten, die lediglich bescheidene Beträge verausgabten, nutzten Abrechnungen und damit die Schrift für die Alltäglichkeiten wirtschaftlichen Handelns.

In eine ähnliche Richtung deuten Befunde aus einem anderen Teil des Reiches, nämlich die Graffiti aus den Hanghäusern in Ephesos, die zum Teil in das fortgeschrittene dritte nachchristliche Jahrhundert datieren (SEG 49, 1999, 1481–1485). Eine der längeren Abrechnungen aus dem Hanghaus mit Preisangaben in ἀσσάρια verzeichnet ähnlich wie der bereits genannte Graffito aus Pompeji Ausgaben für verschiedene Lebensmittel. Im einzelnen werden Brot, Gemüse, Pökelfisch, gekochter Hahn, Tintenfisch und Garum genannt, darüber hinaus eine Zahlung für Ringe, eine für den Eintritt in die Thermen sowie eine Zahlung an einen Sklaven. Die Höhe der Zahlungen bewegt sich zwischen 2 Assaria und 9 Den., mithin auch in einem überschaubaren Rahmen (SEG 49, 1999, 1485 = TAEUBER 2016, GR 357). Auch in diesem Fall legte also ein Konsument Wert darauf, auch bescheidenste Transaktionen auf

---

35 Neben der klassischen, primitivistisch orientierten Studie zur Wirtschaft Pompejis von JONGMAN 1991 vgl. nun FLOHR/WILSON 2017 zu derselben.
36 Vgl. DREXHAGE/KONEN/RUFFING 2002, 297–298.

einer Wand schriftlich festzuhalten. Mit einer gewissen Berechtigung wird man daher folgern können, daß Schriftlichkeit im ökonomischen Handeln breiter Bevölkerungsschichten eine wichtige und konstitutive Rolle spielten, ein Eindruck, der durch die zahlreichen Abrechnungen aus dem römischen Ägypten bestätigt wird.

Daß auch komplexere Geschäfte mit Hilfe von Graffiti erfaßt wurden, zeigt das Beispiel Dura-Europos, dessen wirtschaftliches Leben dank einer günstigen Überlieferungslage, die nicht zuletzt einer vergleichsweise breiten Überlieferung von Graffiti geschuldet ist, relativ detailliert eruiert werden kann.[37] Von besonderem Interesse ist in diesem Kontext das Nebuchelos-Archiv, eine Gruppe von Graffiti, die aus dem am Schnittpunkt von *cardo* und *decumanus maximus* liegenden 'Haus der Archive' oder auch 'Haus des Nebuchelos' stammen und die Geschäfte des besagten Nebuchelos illustrieren (SEG 7, 1934, 381–430).[38] Die rund 50 Graffiti zeigen die offenkundige Sorgfalt, mit der Nebuchelos seine Rechnungen für seine eigenen Belange führte. Der Großteil der Texte stammt aus zwei am Innenhof des Gebäudes liegenden Räumen.[39] Daß die Graffiti sich auf die Geschäfte des Aurelios Nebuchelos beziehen, wird durch die Ich-Form deutlich, die in manchen Urkunden auftaucht (z. B. SEG 7, 1934, 382, 1: εἰσήνικα ἐγὼ Νεβουχηλος (δηνάραια) βρκ'). Aus demselben Grund wird das an so prominenter Stelle in Dura-Europos liegende Haus der Archive als Eigentum des Nebuchelos identifiziert.[40] Das Spektrum der Texte reicht von nicht näher zu kontextualisierenden Geldzahlungen bzw. der Feststellung des Vorhandenseins von Beträgen bis hin zu Aufstellungen, die den Handel mit verschiedenen landwirtschaftlichen sowie Textilerzeugnissen erkennen lassen. Auch ist er offensichtlich im Geldverleih tätig gewesen.[41] Einen besonderen Schwerpunkt seiner Aktivitäten dürfte jedoch der Handel mit Textilien eingenommen haben, da diesem eine große Anzahl der Texte gewidmet ist und er offenkundig mit einer größeren Menge verschiedener Textilien handelte, deren Preise nicht allzu gering waren und bemerkenswerterweise eine gewisse Vergleichbarkeit mit den Preisen im römischen Ägypten aufweisen.[42] In der Tat scheinen die ökonomischen Interessen des Nebuchelos, soweit es die Graffiti erkennen lassen, sowohl in bezug auf die diversen Geschäftsfelder als auch in Hinsicht der geographischen Reichweite seiner Geschäfte weitgespannt gewesen zu sein, reichten doch seine Geschäftsbeziehungen über die gesamte Region des mittleren Euphrat.[43]

---

37 Vgl. dazu allgemein KAIZER 2017, 74–75 und 77 zu den wirtschaftlichen Verbindungen am mittleren Euphrat sowie 83–87 zu den wirtschaftlichen Belangen der Beziehungen zwischen Dura-Europos und Palmyra. Zum wirtschaftlichen Leben in Dura und Umgebung vgl. ferner RUFFING 2007; RUFFING 2010; RUFFING 2016.
38 Die Texte wurden in WELLES 1933, 79–145 veröffentlicht und bereits zum Teil in ROSTOVTZEFF/WELLES 1931 vorab publiziert und kommentiert.
39 Vgl. ROSTOVTZEFF/WELLES 1931, 163 sowie Tafel XVI zu WELLES 1933.
40 Vgl. RUFFING 2000, 73.
41 Vgl. RUFFING 2000, 73–92 zu den einzelnen Geschäften des Aurelios Nebuchelos.
42 Vgl. RUFFING 2000, 82–89. Vgl. ferner BAIRD 2016, 36–37.
43 Vgl. RUFFING 2000, 103–104.

Umso größere Aufmerksamkeit verdient der Sachverhalt, daß Nebuchelos die Wand als Medium für seine Abrechnungen wählte und seine Transaktionen in einer Vielzahl einzelner, vergleichsweise kurzer Texte festhielt. Mit einer gewissen Dringlichkeit stellt sich hier die Frage, ob die überlieferten Abrechnungen die alleinige schriftliche Niederlegung bildeten, mit deren Hilfe sich Nebuchelos einen Überblick über seine Geschäfte verschaffte, oder ob die Graffiti gleichsam nur einen Zwischenschritt darstellten, der dazu diente, einzelne geschäftliche Operationen festzuhalten und später in einer Abrechnung auf einem anderen Schriftträger wie Papyrus oder Pergament niederzulegen. Wie dem auch sei, durch die Texte des Nebuchelos-Archivs gewinnt man nicht nur einen Einblick in die Geschäfte und die Buchführung eines Mitglieds der lokalen Oberschicht von Dura-Europos, sondern auch einen Eindruck von der Wichtigkeit des Gebrauchs der Schrift für auch alltägliche geschäftliche Transaktionen. Gerade in seinem Falle scheint es schwierig, wenn nicht unmöglich gewesen zu sein, den Überblick über alle seine geschäftlichen Transaktionen zu behalten. Schwierig zu beurteilen ist im Falle des Nebuchelos die Frage, ob es sich bei seinen Aktivitäten, wie sie in den Graffiti aus dem Haus der Archive evident werden, um Groß- oder Kleinhandel handelte. Nebuchelos war offenkundig Grundeigentümer und kümmerte sich dementsprechend auch selbst um die Monetarisierung seiner Erträge.[44] Im Falle der Textilien betätigte er sich jedenfalls als Händler. Wie aus einer der längeren Abrechnungen des Archivs deutlich wird, verschickte er in einer Lieferung 49 Textilien an einen Ort namens Apadana. Freilich ist die Stückzahl für einen Typus von Textilien mit sieben σουδάρια gegeben, während im Falle anderen im Text genannten Typen von Textilien in der Regel jeweils zwei oder vier Stück der Lieferung beigegeben wurden (SEG 7, 1934, 417 I). Auch hier wüßte man gerne mehr Details über die Herstellung der Kleidungsstücke, insbesondere in welcher Weise Nebuchelos mit Spinnern, Webern und Walkern interagierte, deren Tätigkeit ja für die Produktion von Textilien unabdingbar war, und wie sich die Arbeit derselben auf die Preisbildung für die einzelnen Stücke niederschlug.[45] Angesichts der eingangs referierten Positionen der Forschungsliteratur stellt sich hier darüber hinaus die Frage, ob man seine Bemühungen im Handel mit Textilien als Groß- oder Kleinhandel betrachten möchte und ob man aufgrund des Gebrauchs der Schrift ihn dann eben als Großhändler zu qualifizieren hat. Die Anzahl von 49 Textilien ist sicher nicht allzu gering, aber doch wohl kaum als Großhandel zu betrachten, weswegen den Gebrauch von Schriftlichkeit als Trennlinie zwischen Groß- und Kleinhändlern jedenfalls nicht ohne Probleme möglich erscheint.

Als ein letztes Beispiel für die Alltäglichkeit des Schriftgebrauchs in wirtschaftlichen Belangen und der hohen alltäglichen Bedeutung von Abrechnungen mag Britannien und hier zunächst Vindolanda dienen. Auch hier, an der nördlichen Peripherie

---

44 Vgl. RUFFING 2000, 79–81.
45 Zur Textilproduktion in Dura-Europos vgl. BAIRD 2016, 35–37.

des Reiches ist wie an der eben behandelten östlichen Peripherie dieser Texttypus allgegenwärtig.[46] Gerade die Abrechnungen sind es im Verbund mit den Geschäftsbriefen, die zahlreiche wirtschaftsgeschichtliche Informationen zu Vindolanda bieten.[47] Wiederum ist das Spektrum dessen, was mit Hilfe der auch ausführlicheren Abrechnungen erfaßt wird, eher breit. Darunter befindet sich etwa eine Abrechnung aus dem Haushalt des Präfekten Flavius Cerialis, die der Geflügelhaltung bzw. der Abgabe von Geflügel gewidmet ist (T. Vindol. III 581).[48] Ist die vermutliche Geflügelhaltung im Haushalt des Präfekten ein treffliches Beispiel dafür, daß sich Offiziere nicht ausschließlich dem grimmigen Kriegshandwerk widmen mochten, zeigen andere Abrechnungen, daß auch Erwerb und Abgabe von Waren des alltäglichen Bedarfs mittels Buchführung erfaßt wurden. So etwa im Falle eines hier willkürlich herausgegriffenen Textes, der den Erwerb von Schuhnägeln, Salz, Bier und Schweinefleisch illustriert (T. Vindol. II 186). Damit zeigt sich, eine wie hohe Bedeutung die schriftliche Niederlegung von Erwerb und Abgabe von Waren auch im äußersten Norden des Reiches in einem zwar durch das Militär stark romanisierten, aber eben durch die Herkunft der in Vindolanda stationierten Hilfstruppen eben auch stark 'germanisch' geprägten Umfeld besaß. Ein Indiz für letzteres ist übrigens der intensive Bierkonsum, dem sich die Herren in Vindolanda hingaben, wofür nicht nur die eben genannte Abrechnung einen Hinweis liefert, sondern auch ein Brief, in dem der Decurio Masclus seinem Kommandeur und König Cerialis den Vollzug von Befehlen sowie auch einen Mangel an Bier meldet, dem er abzuhelfen bat (T. Vindol. III 628).[49]

Die Allgegenwärtigkeit der Abrechnung zeigt sich schließlich auch in den jüngst veröffentlichten Schreibtafeln aus London. Unter diesen, überwiegend sehr fragmentarischen Texten, befindet sich eine Urkunde, die den Transfer verschiedener Beträge, darunter auch einer erheblichen Summe von 2065 Den., an verschiedene Sklaven belegt (Tab. Lond. Bloomberg 70), wie auch eine Abrechnung über Bier, für das Beträge zwischen 2 As und 7 den. genannt werden (Tab. Lond. Bloomberg 72). Offensichtlich reicht also hier in einem städtischen Kontext das Spektrum des Gebrauchs von Schriftlichkeit wiederum von eher alltäglichen Transaktionen – so dem Verkauf von Bier für 2 As – bis hin zu Geschäften in größeren Dimensionen, wie die besagte Zahlung in Höhe von 2065 den. an einen Sklaven zeigt, der wohl im Auftrag seines Herrn Geschäfte in Londinium tätigte.[50]

---

46 Laut Vindolanda Tablets Online 2 sind 62 der veröffentlichten Texte Abrechnungen: siehe http://vto2.classics.ox.ac.uk/index.php/tablets/view-all-tablets?sort=&row=category&value=Accounts [06. 07. 17].
47 Zur Wirtschaft Vindolandas vgl. ONKEN 2003; GRØNLUND EVERS 2011. Zu den Preisangaben aus Vindolanda vgl. auch DREXHAGE 1997, 20–25.
48 Zu dieser Abrechnung vgl. ONKEN 2003, 141; GRØNLUND EVERS 2011, 38–39.
49 Zum Bierkonsum in Vindolanda vgl. ONKEN 2003, 125–130.
50 Zu britannischen Preisangaben außerhalb Vindolandas vgl. DREXHAGE 1997, 16–19.

Die bislang gemachten Ausführungen dürften zeigen, daß der in der gegenwärtigen Forschung anzutreffende Optimismus hinsichtlich des Gebrauchs von Schriftlichkeit auch für den Lebensbereich der Wirtschaft berechtigt ist. Allein die schlaglichtartige Betrachtung von Abrechnungen auf verschiedenen Schriftträgern und aus verschiedenen Regionen des Imperium Romanum demonstrieren nicht nur ihre Allgegenwärtigkeit in regionaler Hinsicht, sondern auch in bezug auf die soziale Verortung der ökonomischen Akteure. In der Tat darf man mit großem Recht davon ausgehen, daß – um das von Karl Christ vorgeschlagene Modell für die soziale Gliederung des Reiches zu gebrauchen –[51] von der imperialen Führungs- und Oberschicht bis in den Bereich der Unterschichten in Gestalt der *plebs urbana* und *plebs rustica* die Schrift genutzt wurde, um Transaktionen – welcher Art auch sie auch immer gewesen sein mögen – zu erfassen. Wie zumindest das oben erwähnte Handeln des römischen Staates zeigt, beschränkte sich die Erstellung von Abrechnungen dabei nicht nur auf die Kontrolle des wirtschaftlichen Agierens von Personen und Institutionen. Abrechnungen bzw. die schriftliche Erfassung von Preisen wurden seitens der kaiserlichen Zentrale auch zur Grundlage weiteren Handelns gemacht, was zumindest auf diesem Level die überaus wichtige Funktion der Schrift für das wirtschaftliche Leben im Römischen Reich unterstreicht. Die eben genannte Kontrolle von Personen, insbesondere von Verwaltern, stellt darüber hinaus ein wesentliches Motiv für die Verschriftlichung von wirtschaftlichen Abläufen dar. Dies gilt – wie die papyrologische Überlieferung eindrücklich demonstriert – für die Verwaltung des Eigentums von Großgrundbesitzern, wie sie beispielsweise im Heroninos-Archiv zu fassen sind, wie auch für solche Individuen, die über eher bescheidenes Grundeigentum verfügten und sich daher der Dienste eines Verwalters bedienten, dem der Gebrauch der Schrift nicht immer leicht von der Hand ging, wie das oben erwähnte Pakysis-Archiv zeigt. Daß man sich auch des Gebrauchs der Schrift befleißigte, um den Überblick über das eigene Handeln in Hinsicht auf Eingänge und Aufwendungen zu bewahren und zwar selbst im Falle des Fehlens von transportablen Schriftträgern, zeigen die Abrechnungen, die sich als Graffito erhalten haben. Ist allein das schon eine bemerkenswerte Tatsache, wird die Nutzung von Wänden als Schriftträger für Abrechnungen, die die Geschäfte eines zumindest auf regionalem Niveau agierenden Händlers dokumentieren, besonders interessant. Es sind aber eben auch die Graffiti, die die Nutzung von Schrift auch für kleinste Transaktionen bzw. zu rechnerischen Erfassung derselben in einem vermutlich privaten, also nicht dem Erwerbsleben geschuldeten Kontext dokumentieren. Damit zeigt allein hier angestellte Umschau schon, daß eine Trennung von Groß- und Kleinhandel durch den Gebrauch der Schrift an sich nicht unproblematisch ist. Nähme man noch andere Urkundentypen hinzu, würde die Allgegenwart der Schrift auch und gerade auf eher niedrigen sozialen Niveaus noch offenkundiger. Dabei ist nicht nur an die Vielzahl der epigraphisch und papyrologisch überlieferten Verträge

---

51 Vgl. CHRIST 1983.

oder die zu Tausenden überlieferten Quittungen zu denken. Eine jüngst angestellte Analyse der Privatbriefe demonstriert ebenso anschaulich, daß der Briefverkehr nicht nur auf einer Vielzahl sozialer Niveaus als eine Alltäglichkeit zu gelten hat, sondern derselbe auch und gerade ökonomische Belange zum Inhalt hatte.[52] Alles in allem wird man sich daher der Einsicht nicht verschließen können, daß die Schriftlichkeit in der Wirtschaft des Römischen Reiches nicht nur allgegenwärtig war, sondern auch ganz wesentlich das Funktionieren derselben gewährleistete. Interessant wäre eine Betrachtung der Frage, welche Rolle Schrift und Schriftlichkeit für die Performanz derselben spielte. Eine solche muß freilich Aufgabe der zukünftigen Forschung bleiben.

Literaturverzeichnis

BAGNALL 1974 = W.S. BAGNALL, The Archive of Laches: Prosperous Farmers of the Fayum in the Second Century, Phil. Diss. Duke University 1974.

BAGNALL 2011 = R. BAGNALL, Everyday Writing in the Graeco-Roman East, Berkeley/Los Angeles/London 2011.

BAIRD 2016 = J.A. BAIRD, Everyday Life in Roman Dura-Europos. The Evidence of Dress Practices, in: T. KAIZER (Hg.), Religion, Society and Culture at Dura-Europos, Cambridge 2016, 30–56.

BOWMAN 1991 = A. BOWMAN, Literacy in the Roman Empire: Mass and Mode, in: J.H. HUMPHREY (Hg.), Literacy in the Roman World, Ann Arbor 1991, 119–131.

CARTER 2003 = M. CARTER, Gladitorial Ranking and the SC de pretiis gladiatorum minuendis (CIL II 6278 = ILS 5163), *Phoenix* 57, 2003, 83–111.

CHRIST 1983 = K. CHRIST, Grundfragen der römischen Sozialstruktur, in: DERS., Römische Geschichte und Wissenschaftsgeschichte Bd. 2, Geschichte und Geschichtsschreibung der römischen Kaiserzeit, Darmstadt 1983, 152–176.

DUNKLE 2008 = R. DUNKLE, Gladiators. Violence and Spectacle in Ancient Rome, London u. a. 2008.

DREXHAGE 1997 = H.-J. DREXHAGE, Preise im römischen Britannien (1.–3. Jh. n. Chr.), in: K. RUFFING/B. TENGER (Hg.), Miscellanea oeconomica. Studien zur antiken Wirtschaftsgeschichte. Harald Winkel zum 65. Geburtstag, St. Katharinen 1997, 13–25.

DREXHAGE/KONEN/RUFFING 2002 = H.-J. DREXHAGE/H. KONEN/K. RUFFING, Die Wirtschaft des Römischen Reiches (1.–3. Jahrhundert). Eine Einführung, Berlin 2002.

FREI-STOLBA 2011 = R. FREI-STOLBA, Les étiquettes en plomb: des documents de l'écriture au quotidien, in: M. CORBIER/J.-P. GUILHEMBET (Hg.), L'écriture dans la maison romaine, Paris 2011, 331–344.

GRASSL 2011 = H. GRASSL, Epigraphisches Kleingeld, in: M. SCHOLZ/M. HORSTER (Hg.), Lesen und Schreiben in den römischen Provinzen. Schriftliche Kommunikation im Alltagsleben. Akten des 2. Internationalen Kolloquiums von DUCTUS – Association internationale pour l'étude des inscriptions mineures, RGZM Mainz, 15.–17. Juni 2011, Mainz 2015, 141–148.

GRØNLUND EVERS 2011 = K. GRØNLUND EVERS, The Vindolanda Tablets and the Ancient Economy, Oxford 2011.

FLOHR, WILSON 2017 = M. FLOHR/A. WILSON (Hg.), The Economy of Pompeii, Oxford 2017.

HABERMANN 2000 = W. HABERMANN, Zur Wasserversorgung einer Metropole im kaiserzeitlichen Ägypten. Neuedition von P. Lond. III 1177. Text – Übersetzung – Kommentar, München 2000.

---

52 Vgl. REINARD 2016.

HARRIS 1989 = W.V. HARRIS, Ancient Literacy, Cambridge Mass./London 1989.
JÖRDENS 1997 = A. JÖRDENS, Papyri und private Archive. Ein Diskussionsbeitrag zur papyrologischen Terminologie, in: E. CANTARELLA/G. THÜR (Hg.), Symposion 1997: Vorträge zur griechischen und hellenistischen Rechtsgeschichte, Köln u. a. 2001, 253–268.
JÖRDENS 2005 = A. JÖRDENS, Griechische Papyri in Soknopaiu Nesos, in: S. LIPPERT/M. SCHENTULEIT (Hg.), Tebtynis und Soknopaiu Nesos. Leben im römerzeitlichen Fajum. Akten des Internationalen Symposions vom 11. bis 13. Dezember 2003 in Sommerhausen bei Würzburg, Wiesbaden 2005, 41–56.
JONES 2007 = C.P. JONES, Three New Letters of the Emperor Hadrian, *ZPE* 161, 2007, 145–156.
JONGMAN 1991 = W. JONGMAN, The Economy and Society of Pompeii, Amsterdam 1991².
KAIZER 2017 = T. KAIZER, Empire, Community, and Culture on the Middle Euphrates. Durenes, Palmyrenes, Villagers, and Soldiers, *BICS* 60, 2017, 62–95.
KEHOE 1992 = D.P. KEHOE, Management and Investments on Estates in Roman Egypt during the Early Empire, Bonn 1992.
LIPPERT/SCHENTULEIT 2005 = S. LIPPERT/M. SCHENTULEIT, Die Tempelökonomie nach den demotischen Texten aus Soknopaiu Nesos, in: DIES. (Hg.), Tebtynis und Soknopaiu Nesos. Leben im römerzeitlichen Fajum. Akten des Internationalen Symposions vom 11. bis 13. Dezember 2003 in Sommerhausen bei Würzburg, Wiesbaden 2005, 71–78.
MINAUD 2005 = G. MINAUD, La compatibilité à Rome. Essai d'histoire économique sur la pensée comptable commerciale et privée dans le monde antique romain, Lausanne 2005.
MOMMSEN 1913 = T. MOMMSEN, Senatus Consultum de sumptibus ludorum gladiatoriorum minuendis factum a.p.c. 176/177, in: DERS., Gesammelte Schriften Bd. 8. Epigraphische und numismatische Schriften Bd. 1, Berlin 1913, 499–531 (= Eph. epigr. VII, 1890, 388–428).
MORLEY 2007 = N. MORLEY, Trade in Classical Antiquity, Cambridge 2007.
OLIVER/PALMER 1955 = J.H. OLIVER/R.E.A. PALMER, Minutes of an Act of the Roman Senate, *Hesperia* 24, 1955, 320–349.
ONKEN 2003 = B. ONKEN, Wirtschaft an der Grenze. Studien zum Wirtschaftsleben in den römischen Militärlagern im Norden Britanniens, Phil. Diss. Kassel 2003 (http://nbn-resolving.de/urn:nbn:de:hebis:34–1061).
OTTO 1905 = W. OTTO, Priester und Tempel im hellenistischen Ägypten. Ein Beitrag zur Kulturgeschichte des Hellenismus Bd. 1, Leipzig/Berlin 1905.
OTTO 1908 = W. OTTO, Priester und Tempel im hellenistischen Ägypten. Ein Beitrag zur Kulturgeschichte des Hellenismus Bd. 2, Leipzig/Berlin 1908.
PFEIFFER 2010 = S. PFEIFFER, Der römische Kaiser und das Land am Nil. Kaiserverehrung und Kaiserkult in Alexandria und Ägypten von Augustus und Caracalla (30 v. Chr. – 217 n. Chr.), Stuttgart 2010.
PETZL/SCHWERTHEIM 2006 = G. PETZL/E. SCHWERTHEIM, Hadrian und die dionysischen Künstler. Drei in Alexandria Troas neugefundene Briefe des Kaisers an die Künstler-Vereinigung, Bonn 2006.
RATHBONE 1991 = D. RATHBONE, Economic Rationalism and Rural Society in Third Century AD Egypt. The Heroninos-Archive and the Appianus Estate, Cambridge 1991.
RATHBONE 2005 = D. RATHBONE, Economic Rationalism and the Heroninos Archive, *Topoi* 12–13, 2005, 261–269.
REINARD 2016 = P. REINARD, Kommunikation und Ökonomie. Untersuchungen zu den privaten Papyrusbriefen aus dem kaiserzeitlichen Ägypten, Rahden in Westf. 2016.
ROSTOVTZEFF/WELLES 1931 = M.I. ROSTOVTZEFF/C.B. WELLES, La «Maison des Archives» à Doura Europos, *CRAI* 1931, 162–188.
RÜBSAM 1974 = W.J.R. RÜBSAM, Götter und Kulte im Faijum während der griechisch-römisch-byzantinischen Zeit, Phil. Diss. Marburg 1974.

Ruffing 2000 = K. Ruffing, Die Geschäfte des Aurelios Nebuchelos, *Laverna* 11, 2000, 71–105.

Ruffing 2007 = K. Ruffing, Dura Europos: A City on the Euphrates and Her Economic Importance in the Roman Era, in: M. Sartre (Hg.), Productions et échanges dans la Syrie grecque et romaine. Actes du colloque de Tours, juin 2003, Lyon 2007, 399–411.

Ruffing 2008 = K. Ruffing, Heiligtum und Staat in der römischen Kaiserzeit – ein Vergleich zwischen Asia Minor und Ägypten, *Gymnasium* 115, 2008, 573–586.

Ruffing 2010 = K. Ruffing, Dura Europos und seine Rolle im Fernhandel der Römischen Kaiserzeit, in: R. Rollinger/B. Gufler/M. Lang/I. Madreiter (Hg.), Interkulturalität in der Alten Welt. Vorderasien, Hellas, Ägypten und die vielfältigen Ebenen des Kontakts, Wiesbaden 2010, 151–160.

Ruffing 2014 = K. Ruffing, Living Gods – State Gods. Social and Economic Conditions of Imperial Cult and of Emperor Worship in the Capitol of Ptolemais Euergetis, in: T. Gnoli/F. Muccioli (Hg.), Divinizzazione, culto del sovrano e apoteosi. Tra antichità e medioevo, Bologna 2014, 281–293.

Ruffing 2016 = K. Ruffing, Economic Life in Roman Dura-Europos, in: T. Kaizer (Hg.), Religion, Society and Culture at Dura-Europos, Cambridge 2016, 190–198.

Scholz 2015a = M. Scholz, Vorwort und Einleitung, in: M. Scholz/M. Horster (Hg.), Lesen und Schreiben in den römischen Provinzen. Schriftliche Kommunikation im Alltagsleben. Akten des 2. Internationalen Kolloquiums von DUCTUS – Association internationale pour l'étude des inscriptions mineures, RGZM Mainz, 15.–17. Juni 2011, Mainz 2015, VII-XVII.

Scholz 2015b = M. Scholz, Tumbe Bauern? Zur Schriftlichkeit in ländlichen Siedlungen in den germanischen Provinzen und Raetien, in: M. Scholz/M. Horster (Hg.), Lesen und Schreiben in den römischen Provinzen. Schriftliche Kommunikation im Alltagsleben. Akten des 2. Internationalen Kolloquiums von DUCTUS – Association internationale pour l'étude des inscriptions mineures, RGZM Mainz, 15.–17. Juni 2011, Mainz 2015, 67–90.

Slater 2008 = W.J. Slater, Hadrian's Letters to Athletes and Dionysic Artists Concerning Arrangements for the "Circuit" of Games, *JRA* 21, 2008, 610–620.

Strasser 2010 = J.-Y. Strasser, «Qu'on fouette les concurrents…». À propos des lettres d'Hadrien retrouvées à Alexandrie de Troade, *REG* 123, 2010, 585–622.

Taeuber 2016 = H. Taeuber, Graffiti und Inschriften, in: E. Rathmayr (Hg.), Hanghaus 2 in Ephesos. Die Wohneinheit 7. Baubefund, Ausstattung, Funde. Textband 1, Wien 2016, 233–257.

Tenger 1993 = B. Tenger, Die Verschuldung im römischen Ägypten (1.–2. Jh. n. Chr.), St. Katharinen 1993.

Tomlin 2016 = R.S.O. Tomlin, Roman London's First Voices: Writing Tablets from the Bloomberg Excavations, 2010–14, London 2016.

Welles 1933 = C.B. Welles, Graffiti, in: P.V.C. Baur/M.I. Rostovtzeff/A.R. Bellinger (Hg.), The Excavations at Dura-Europos Conducted by Yale University and the French Academy of Inscriptions and Letters. Preliminary Report of Fourth Season of Work October 1930-March 1931, New Haven 1933, 79–178.

Wilcken 1912 = U. Wilcken, Grundzüge und Chrestomathie der Papyruskunde. Erster Band: Historischer Teil. Erste Hälfte: Grundzüge, Berlin/Leipzig 1912.

Religious Practice

Wolfgang Spickermann
Als die Götter lesen lernten: Keltisch-germanische Götternamen und lateinische Schriftlichkeit in Gallien und Germanien

Abstract: After the conquest of Gaul and parts of Germany under Caesar and Augustus the strong settlement of Italians, the expansion of standing armies, the establishment of a new Roman administration and a new social system had serious consequences for all parts of daily life. This led to the fact that in many parts of these frontier provinces it was no longer possible to fall back on pre-Roman traditions. Basically, the soldiers and the urbanization by the army in the Rhine region were the determining factors with regard to population development, the integration of local elites, emigration, Latinization, economic development and ultimately Romanization. The formulated language introduced by the military in funeral monuments, structural ornamentation and the introduction of writing also in the private sphere had an enormous impact on the provincials. Particularly this is remarkable because the Germanies and large parts of Gaul were territories without literacy. Since votive inscriptions were almost unknown before the Roman conquest, the local elites now needed divinities that could "read", in contrast to the former Celtic gods. This resulted in completely new types of gods with Celtic, Germanic and / or Roman names, which first arose as protection deities of the newly founded *civitates* or local communities. So, most of the traditional Celtic and Germanic names of gods on votive inscriptions have emerged from a written culture initiated by the Roman conquest and thus document the religious conditions of the Roman Empire by means of their protective functions for Roman territorial authorities when those gods were able to understood and read Latin and also Celtic or Germanic dialects.

Zusammenfassung: Nach der Eroberung Galliens und von Teilen von Germanien unter Caesar und Augustus hatten die massenhafte Ansiedlung von Italikern, der Ausbau stehender Heere, die Errichtung einer neuen Reichsverwaltung und eines neuen sozialen Systems Folgen für alle Lebensbereiche. Dies führte dazu, dass man in großen Teilen dieser Grenzprovinzen nicht mehr auf vorrömische Traditionen zurückgreifen konnte oder wollte. Grundsätzlich waren das Militär und die Urbanisierung durch das Militär im Rheingebiet die bestimmenden Faktoren in Bezug auf die Bevölkerungsentwicklung, die Integration der lokalen Eliten, die Emigration, die Latinisierung, die ökonomische Entwicklung und letztlich die Romanisation überhaupt. Die vom Militär eingeführte Formensprache in der Sepulkralplastik, der Bauornamentik und die Einführung der Schriftlichkeit auch im privaten Bereich hatten einen enormen Einfluss auf die Provinzialen. Dies ist umso bemerkenswerter, als es sich bei Germanien und großen Teilen von Gallien um Gebiete ohne eigene Schriftkultur handelte. Da die inschriftliche Götterweihung vor der römischen Eroberung unbekannt war, brauchten die einheimischen Eliten nun Gottheiten, die anders als ihre Vorgänger „lesen konnten". Daraus entstanden völlig neue Göttertypen mit keltischen und/oder römischen Namen, die sich zunächst zu Schutzgottheiten der neu gegründeten in römischer Form verfassten *civitates* oder Ortsgemeinden aufschwangen. Daraus folgt, dass ein großer Teil der uns inschriftlich überlieferten keltischen und germanischen Götternamen aus einer durch die römische Eroberung initiierten Schriftkultur hervorgegangen sind und damit die religiösen Verhältnisse der römischen Kaiserzeit dokumentieren, als die Götter Latein sowie keltische und germanische Dialekte nicht nur verstanden, sondern auch lesen konnten.

Mit der Herrschaft des Augustus ist in allen Provinzen eine etwa gleichzeitig einsetzende „formative Periode" anzusetzen.[1] Insbesondere in Gallien und Germanien ist dabei ein gemeinsames Muster erkennbar. Der kulturelle Wandel in diesen Provinzen erfolgte damit gleichzeitig mit dem in Rom und Italien und kann nicht allein als Imitation der hauptstädtischen Kultur gefasst werden. Er muss vielmehr im Rahmen der politischen und sozialen Veränderungen begriffen werden, welche die Bürgerkriege und die Errichtung des augusteischen Principats mit sich brachten. Die massenhafte Ansiedlung von Italikern in den Provinzen, der Ausbau stehender Heere, die Errichtung einer neuen Reichsverwaltung und eines neuen sozialen Systems unter Augustus hatten damit Folgen für alle Lebensbereiche.[2]

In den germanischen Provinzen nimmt diese formative Periode jedoch einen längeren Zeitraum in Anspruch als etwa in Zentralgallien, da sich erst nach dem Bataveraufstand 69/70 n. Chr. eine dauerhafte Binnengliederung herausbildete.[3] Diese Grenzprovinzen waren eine Mischzone aus keltischen und germanischen Kultureinflüssen, wobei sie durch die starke römische Militärpräsenz, Umsiedlungsaktionen ganzer Stämme in der frühen Kaiserzeit und den Zuzug aus anderen Gegenden des Reiches eine sehr heterogene Bevölkerung besaßen, die mit Ausnahme einiger weniger Gebiete keineswegs auf eine einheitliche Kultur zurückgreifen konnte. Dabei sind drei Hauptphasen der Entwicklung einer Provinzkultur zu erkennen: 1. die formative Periode von der Eroberung bis ca. 70 n. Chr.; 2. die Phase der Konsolidierung bis ca. 150 n. Chr. und 3. die Blütezeit und Phase der intensiven ‚Eigen-Romanisierung' (Romanisation) bis zum Fall des Limes 230/260 n. Chr.[4] Die Eroberungsphase verlief in den einzelnen Teilen Germaniens höchst unterschiedlich. Bei den Kelten ist durch Kulturkontakte mit Griechen, Etruskern und Römern vor allem im religiösen Bereich schon gegen

---

1 GALINSKY 1998, 363–370.
2 Vgl. dazu grundlegend DERKS 1998, 1–19.
3 SPICKERMANN 2001, 36.
4 SPICKERMANN 2001, 35 ff.

Ende des 2. Jahrhunderts v. Chr. ein Veränderungsprozess sichtbar, in dessen Verlauf die alte druidische Religion mit ihren Menschenopfern und ihrer Trophäenpraxis zugunsten von anthropomorphen Götterbildern und kleineren Votivgaben verdrängt wurde.[5] Nach Verschwinden der Druiden und mit der römischen Eroberung bot sich den lokalen Eliten die Möglichkeit, sich durch monumentale Stiftungen einen Namen zu machen, welche die neu entstehenden Städte zierten, wobei die alten Oppida weitgehend aufgegeben wurden. Während Kontinentalgallien und die gallischen Teile der späteren Provinz Germania Superior ‚Binnenprovinzcharakter' zeigen und sich im Gebiet der Lingonen, Sequaner, Helvetier sowie z. T. auch der Treverer schon im frühen 1. Jahrhunderts die römische Gebietsverwaltung, Architektur (besonders in der Monumentalisierung von Heiligtümern) und auch die Urbanisierung mit monumentalen städtischen Zentren weitgehend durchgesetzt hatte, setzte dieser Prozess im Bereich des späteren Limes in größerem Maße erst in spätneronisch-flavischer Zeit ein.

Grundsätzlich bedeutet das, dass man in großen Teilen dieser Grenzprovinzen nicht mehr auf vorrömische Traditionen zurückgreifen konnte oder wollte. Wenn man zudem ernst nimmt, dass Druidenwissen mündlich weitergegeben wurde, so muss das konsequente Vorgehen der Römer gegen diese spätestens seit der Herrschaft des Claudius dahingehend Konsequenzen gehabt haben, dass große Teile der druidischen Religion nicht mehr oder nur noch eingeschränkt verbreitet werden konnte. Die Traditionen der Zeit vor der römischen Herrschaft bzw. vor der Umsiedlung konnten jedenfalls bei einem großen Teil der sich romanisierenden Stammeseliten keine Rolle mehr spielen, was auch für den religiösen Bereich Geltung beanspruchen muss. Hier ist WILLIAM VAN ANDRINGA beizupflichten, dass es eben keine direkte Linie einer ehemals keltischen Religion zu einer gallo-römischen Religion gab.[6] Die gallo-römische Provinzialreligion ist ein *tertium sui generis*.[7]

Mit Ausnahme der romtreuen Ubier, die bekanntlich schon 50 n. Chr. eine Colonia erhielten, und dem Südwesten der obergermanischen Provinz, wurde auch der größte Teil der germanischen Stammesverbände erst nach dem Bataveraufstand 69/70 n. Chr. endgültig als *civitates* verfasst.[8] Erst ab diesem Zeitpunkt setzt eine Phase der Konsolidierung ein, in der es weder größere Gebietsveränderungen in Bezug auf die schon bestehenden *civitates* noch militärische Unternehmungen mit direkten Auswirkungen auf die Infrastruktur der germanischen Heeresbezirke gab, die dann ja bekanntlich um 85 n. Chr. zu eigenen Provinzen wurden. So kann man die formative Periode und die mit ihr verbundenen Entwicklungen in einen Zeitraum von etwa 13 v. Chr. bis 70 n. Chr. fassen. Grundsätzlich waren das Militär und die Urbanisierung durch das Militär im Rheingebiet die bestimmenden Faktoren in Bezug auf die Bevölkerungs-

---

5 BRUNAUX 1995, 74.
6 VAN ANDRINGA 2002.
7 SPICKERMANN/STEENKEN 2003.
8 Dazu grundlegend: WOLFF 1976.

entwicklung, die Integration der lokalen Eliten, die Emigration, die Latinisierung, die ökonomische Entwicklung und letztlich die Romanisation überhaupt.[9] Die vom Militär eingeführte Formensprache in der Sepulkralplastik und der Bauornamentik hatte einen nicht zu unterschätzenden Einfluss auf die Provinzialen. Charakteristikum der Bevölkerung am Rhein war ihr kosmopolitisches Gepräge. Die ländlichen Strukturen waren hier weniger fest verwurzelt als etwa in den ostgallischen Gebieten. Außerdem verfügten die neu angesiedelten *civitates* nicht über den gesamten Boden ihres Territoriums, da es auch kaiserliche Domänen und Territorien der Armee beinhaltete.[10] Während große Teile der früh übergesiedelten bzw. der ansässigen Stämme schon unter der iulisch-claudischen Dynastie das Bürgerrecht erhalten hatte,[11] setzten sich auch in anderen (zugewanderten) Bevölkerungsgruppen das römische Namensystem weitgehend durch.[12]

Die Latinisierung durch das Militär und die damit verbundene Einführung der Schriftlichkeit auch in den privaten Bereich hatte weitgehende Folgen für den Alltag der Provinzialbevölkerung. Die griechische Sprache und Schrift, die sich in Südgallien vereinzelt findet, hatte nachweislich auf Kontinentalgallien keinen Einfluss. Die römische Verwaltung machte aber schriftliche Kommunikation unbedingt notwendig. Damit wurde Latein zur öffentlichen Sprache. Dagegen handelt es sich bei den vereinzelt gefundenen gallo-lateinischen Texten meist um private Schriftzeugnisse oder Defixiones.

Das öffentliche Setzen einer Inschrift war eine Demonstration der Literalität ihres Urhebers. Die Motive wie auch die Akteure können dabei höchst unterschiedlich sein, in jedem Fall setzt eine Inschrift voraus, dass sie auch wahrgenommen, also gelesen wird. Sie soll dem Leser verdeutlichen, dass derjenige, der die Inschrift setzte, in der Lage ist, etwas schriftlich mitzuteilen, auch wenn dies nicht immer ganz der Wahrheit entsprach. Jedenfalls wurde die Lese- und Schreibfähigkeit als ein Gut angesehen, dessen man sich rühmen konnte. Dies ist umso bemerkenswerter, als es sich bei Germanien und große Teile von Gallien um Gebiete ohne eigene Schriftkultur handelte. So stammen auch die ersten schriftlichen Zeugnisse auch mehrheitlich von italischen Soldaten oder deren Angehörigen, die, dem Brauch ihrer Heimat folgend, Kameraden oder Familienmitgliedern, die in der Fremde gestorben waren, Grabsteine setzten. Das immer noch älteste Beispiel aus Germanien ist der bei Xanten gefundene Gedenkstein für den *centurio* der 18. Legion M. Caelius und seine beiden Freigelassenen, die in der *clades Variana* 9 n. Chr. fielen.[13] In der Folge wurden dann insbesondere an den Statthaltersitzen und Truppenstandorten (besonders Köln, Bonn und Mainz) aufwändige Grabsteine gesetzt, welche den Toten in Rüstung mit seinen Rangabzeichen oder als

---

9 RAEPSAET-CHARLIER 1998, 161–162
10 FRÉZOULS 1990, 495.
11 CHASTAGNOL 1995, 181–185.
12 ALFÖLDY 1968, 45.
13 CIL XIII 8646.

einen Feind niederwerfenden Reiter darstellen. Die Inschriften nennen Namen (mit *Tribus*), Dienstgrad, Alter und Dienstjahre. Die Typen der Grabstelen sind oberitalischen Vorbildern entlehnt und wurden von den Bildhauern am Rhein weiterentwickelt.[14]

Völlig anders stellt sich die Situation bei den Weihinschriften dar. Aus der Zeit bis 70 n. Chr. sind insgesamt für beide germanische Heeresbezirke nur 24 Inschriften bekannt.[15] Die sieben nieder- und siebzehn obergermanischen Weihinschriften stammen zur Hälfte von Angehörigen des Militärs. Dieser Anteil erscheint niedrig, da eigentlich zu erwarten wäre, dass zu diesem frühen Zeitpunkt zunächst überwiegend Soldaten die ihnen aus der Heimat geläufige schriftliche Dokumentation eines Votums in Form von Weihesteinen realisierten. Ihnen folgten bald Kaufleute, Funktionsträger und Mitglieder der einheimischen Eliten, die ebenfalls über die dazu notwendigen finanziellen Mittel verfügten. So kommt auch der überwiegende Teil dieser Weihungen aus der Umgebung von Militärlagern, die als Wirtschaftszentren in dieser frühen Zeit die technischen, finanziellen und personellen Ressourcen zur Herstellung von Dedikationen besaßen. Da die inschriftliche Götterweihung vor der römischen Eroberung unbekannt war, brauchten die einheimischen Eliten nun Gottheiten, die anders als ihre Vorgänger „lesen konnten". Daraus entstanden völlig neue Göttertypen mit keltischen und/oder römischen Namen, die sich zunächst zu Schutzgottheiten der neu gegründeten in römischer Form verfassten *civitates* oder Ortsgemeinden aufschwangen. Ich will dies im Folgenden an einigen aussagekräftigen Beispielen zeigen.

1 Mars Cicollos

Weihinschriften an den lingonischen Hauptgott Mars Cicollos sind insbesondere aus dem Bereich von *Mediolanum*/Mâlain (teilweise zusammen mit seiner Paredra Litavis oder Bellona) bekannt.[16] Der keltische Göttername erscheint im Dativ als *Cicollui*, woraus die Sprachwissenschaft den Nominativ Cicollos ableitet. „Cicollo" ist im Sinne von „muskelstark" zu interpretieren.[17] Ein bedeutender, in seinem Grundriss nicht ganz geklärter, gallo-römischer Umgangstempel für Mars Cicollos und Litavis/Bellona liegt unter dem heutigen Friedhof von Mâlain und seiner Kapelle. Er hing offenbar mit einem Kulttheater von 70 m Durchmesser zusammen.[18] Bisher waren insgesamt zwölf inschriftliche Erwähnungen des Cicollos bekannt, darunter nur vier außerhalb von Mâlain: eine aus *Dibio*/Dijon,[19] die nerozeitliche Inschrift der Lingonen aus *Vetera*/

---

14 Grundlegend: GABELMANN 1972; vgl. BOPPERT 1992, 47–55.
15 SPICKERMANN 2003, 122–124; vgl. SPICKERMANN 2008, 52.
16 CIL XIII 5597–5604; vgl. dazu SPICKERMANN 2003, 69.
17 SPICKERMANN/DE BERNARDO STEMPEL 2005, 139.
18 ROUSSEL 1994, 28; vgl. SPICKERMANN 2003, 69–70.
19 CIL XIII 5479.

Xanten,[20] die Weihung eines unbekannten Dedikanten aus *Vindonissa*[21] und eine an den Kaiser sowie Mars Cicollos und Litavis aus Aignay-le-Duc im benachbarten Mandubiergebiet.[22]

300 m vom römischen *vicus Mediolanum*/Mâlain entfernt befand sich außerdem ein kleines Heiligtum im Bereich einer Quelle am Ort ‚Les Froidefonds', welches nach Ausweis der Funde schon in vorrömischer Zeit genutzt wurde. Hier wurden Mars Cicollos und Litavis/Bellona verehrt. Der 23 × 15 m große Kultkomplex bestand aus einem gallo-römischen Umgangstempel und einem im Osten angrenzenden Peristylhof, an den sich im Süden zwei kleine Räume anschlossen. Der Tempel datiert in das frühe 1. Jahrhundert n. Chr., der Hof wurde später, vielleicht im späten 1. Jahrhundert n. Chr. angebaut. Schon im späten 2. Jahrhundert n. Chr. ist der Kultplatz aufgegeben worden.[23] Unter dem römischen Niveau fanden sich Gruben und Pfostenlöcher eines vorrömischen Bauwerks des frühen 1. Jahrhunderts v. Chr. in Holz. Hier konnten zahlreiche keltische Münzen, Tierknochen und Keramik geborgen werden.[24] Offenbar handelt es sich um ein latènezeitliches Heiligtum.[25] Aus der römischen Phase sind die Funde von Resten einer überlebensgroßen Statue, einer Kalksteinstatuette und einer bronzenen Marsstatuette erwähnenswert.[26]

Hervorgehoben werden sollen zwei epigraphische Zeugnisse, welche die Bedeutung und Funktion des Mars Cicollos und ähnlicher „Stammesgottheiten" besonders deutlich machen. Hierzu gehört die erwähnte Weihung einer Gruppe von Lingonen aus *Vetera*/Xanten an den Hauptgott ihrer *civitas*, Mars Cicollos, zum Heile Neros. Im benachbarten Ort Rindern wurde der Altar einer Gruppe von Remern an ihren Hauptgott Mars Camulus gefunden, der ebenfalls zum Heile Neros geweiht war. Das keltische Wort Camulos heißt „Sorge bringend".[27] Die Remer versprechen gleichzeitig die Errichtung eines Tempels. Nach C.B. Rüger ist dieser Altar aus Xanten verschleppt worden, da eine Aufstellung in Rindern wenige Erklärungsmöglichkeiten biete, und er aus derselben Werkstatt stamme, wie derjenige der Lingonen an Mars Cicollos.[28] Demnach seien beide Altäre von Händlergruppen in den Wirren um den Vindex-Aufstand vor Neros Tod im Jahre 68 n. Chr. geweiht worden, die zu dieser Ehrenerklärung für den Kaiser von den Xantener Truppen gezwungen worden seien.[29] Der Name Neros

---

20 Rüger 1981, 44 = AE 1981, 690 und AE 1984, 650.
21 N/L 54.
22 CIL XIII 2887.
23 Vgl. Spickermann 2003, 67–69.
24 Roussel 1969, 183–184.
25 So Horne/King 1980, 375; anders Roussel 1969, 190, der die Befunde aus dieser Schicht als profan interpretiert.
26 Roussel 1969, 185 f.; Horne/King 1980, 375.
27 Spickermann/De Bernardo Stempel 2005, 139.
28 CIL XIII 8701 u. AE 1981, 690 vgl. 1984, 650; vgl. Rüger 1981; ferner Spickermann/De Bernardo Stempel 2005, 131–133 u. 139 u. Spickermann 2008, 53–55.
29 Rüger 1981, vgl. Rüger 1987, 628–629 u. van Andringa 2002, 146.

muss bei beiden Altären kurz nach seinem Tod und der damit verbundenen *damnatio memoriae* eradiert worden sein. Außerdem enthält der Altar auf seiner Rückseite die in eine *corona civica* eingefassten Buchstaben *OCS*, was zu ‚*ob cives servatos*' aufgelöst werden kann.[30]

Die Inschriften zeigen deutlich, dass sich ortsfremde Zuwanderer als exklusive Gruppe über ihre Stammesgottheiten identifizierten und von anderen Gruppen abgrenzten.[31] Gerade aufgrund dieser beiden Dedikationen, die ja sicherlich ihren Platz auf einem Kultplatz fanden, ist für die vorcoloniazeitliche Siedlung in Xanten ein Marsheiligtum im Bereich des späteren Hafentempels angenommen worden.[32] Es gibt aber weder für die Lage noch für die tatsächliche Existenz eines solchen Heiligtums Anhaltspunkte. Das Formular der Dedikationen legt vielmehr Wert auf ihren Anlass, nämlich das Heil des Kaisers. Der Lingonenstein unterstreicht dies noch zusätzlich durch die Darstellung der Lorbeerbäume vor dem Hause des Augustus auf den Seitenflächen.[33] Zusammen mit der Großen Mainzer Iupitersäule sind dies die beiden frühesten germanischen Belege für die Verwendung der *pro salute imperatoris*-Formel überhaupt.[34] Damit handelt es sich auch um originäre Zeugnisse des Kaiserkultes.[35] Dies wird unter anderem auch dadurch unterstrichen, dass dem Stammesgott der Remer, welcher den Kaiser beschützen soll, dafür zusätzlich noch ein eigener Tempel versprochen wird. Der Gegenstand des Gelübdes der Lingoneninschrift ist verloren. Möglicherweise bezog er sich nur auf die Aufstellung des Altars. Man kann hieraus folgern, dass die Weihungen in einer dem Kaiserkult gewidmeten Anlage vollzogen wurden. Diese dürfen wir in der militärisch geprägten vorcoloniazeitlichen Siedlung Xantens angesichts der Bedeutung des Kaiserkultes für die Heeresreligion durchaus voraussetzen,[36] auch wenn es sich dabei nicht um einen eigentlichen Tempel gehandelt haben muss. Der ursprüngliche Aufstellungsort des Lingonenaltars wird übrigens aufgrund der Fundumstände an einer platzartigen Anlage oder einer Straße vermutet.[37]

Im Dezember 2000 ist aus dem Lingonengebiet ein weiteres Zeugnis des gallorömischen Gottes hinzugekommen: So wurde auf der Gemarkung von Chassey (commune de Mutigney; dep. Jura) im Randbereich der römischen Straße von *Vesontio*/Besançon nach Pontailler-sur-Saone, also im Sequanergebiet, durch Zufall eine

---

30 INSTINSKY 1959, 141 bezieht dies auf die *civitas Remorum* im Ganzen.
31 Die identitätsstiftende Funktion solcher Gottheiten in der Fremde betont treffend SCHÄFER 2001, 262–265.
32 RÜGER 1981, 333; vgl. RÜGER 1987, 632
33 RÜGER 1981, 331.
34 INSTINSKY 1959; vgl. LIERTZ 1998, 159.
35 Vgl. BAUCHHENSS 1992, 327. Zur Funktion des Mars als *deus patrius* der Remer und Lingonen: VAN ANDRINGA 2002, 147.
36 Vgl. z. B. die zahlreichen Kaiserfeste im *Feriale Duranum* bei HELGELAND 1978, 1481–1495; ferner HERZ 1978, 1193–1194 u. HERZ 2001.
37 RÜGER 1981, 331.

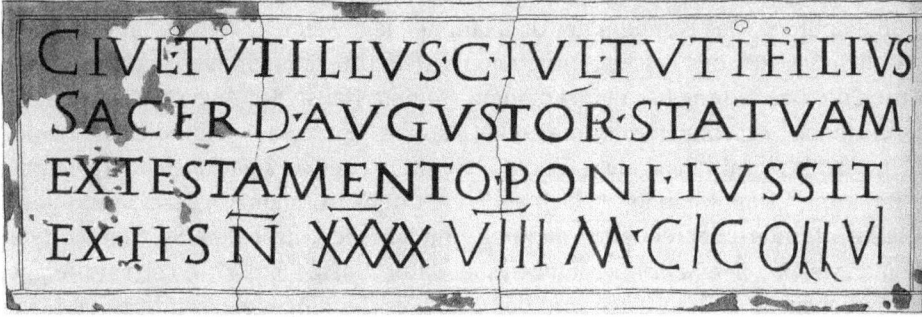

Abb. 1: Bronzeplatte mit eingravierter Weihinschrift aus Chassey
(nach BARBET/BILLEY 2004, 284 fig. 4)

68 cm breite versilberte Bronzeplatte mit eingravierter Weihinschrift gefunden, die ursprünglich wohl zu einer wertvollen Statue gehört haben muss. Es ist zu vermuten, dass diese in einem der umliegenden Heiligtümer stand. Später muss die Platte entfernt, in drei Teile gebrochen und verborgen worden sein.[38]

Die beiden letzten Wörter wurden offensichtlich von zweiter Hand zu späterer Zeit ergänzt.[39] Es handelt sich demnach um eine auch im Vergleich sehr wertvolle Statue eines wahrscheinlich lokalen oder regionalen Kaiserpriesters.[40] Aus *Andemantunnum*/Langres, dem Hauptort der lingonischen *civitas*, ist ein *sacerdos Augusti* Q. Sedulius Si[lanus] bekannt.[41] Es dürfte sich hier um ein Mitglied einer romanisierten Familie der lingonischen, vielleicht sequanischen Oberschicht gehandelt haben, das auch noch Ende des 2., Anfang des 3. Jahrhunderts stolz auf seine Romanitas war und dies durch Nennung der *tria nomina* ausdrückte.[42]

---

38 BARBET/BILLEREY 2004, 284–287; vgl. zuletzt SPICKERMANN 2014: *C(aius) Iul(ius) Tutillus C(ai) Iul(ii) Tuti filius / sacerd(os) Augustor(um) statuam / ex testamento poni iussit / ex (sestertium) n(ummum) XXXXVIII (milibus) M(arti) Cicollui*.
39 BARBET/BILLEREY 2004, 284–285; vgl. AE 2004, 998.
40 Vgl. die Zusammenstellung der Wertangaben von Statuen bei BARBET/BILLEREY 2004, 286.
41 CIL XIII 5688; vgl. SPICKERMANN 2003, 93; ferner SPICKERMANN 2014, 150.
42 Anders BARBET/BILLEREY 2004, 284–286.

Angesichts der Prominenz des Gottes im Lingonengebiet und seiner frühen Verbindung mit dem Kaiserkult, ist die Weihung eines Kaiserpriesters an Cicollos nicht ungewöhnlich, jedoch kann nicht mit Sicherheit behauptet werden, ob dies tatsächlich auch so war. Denn die Widmung an den Gott ist – wie gesagt – mit großer Wahrscheinlichkeit später angefügt worden, was die Editoren der Inschrift nicht groß beachten, wohl aber die Bearbeiter der *Année Epigraphique*. Wir dürfen daher vermuten, dass die zugehörige Statue des Gottes mit Stifterinschrift in seinem Heiligtum stand und sich dessen Name durch den Aufstellungsort ergab oder – weniger wahrscheinlich – dass die Weihung später umgewidmet wurde. Da die Tafel von weither verschleppt worden sein kann, können wir nur vermuten, dass sie ursprünglich aus dem Lingonengebiet stammte, möglicherweise aus dem Heiligtum in Mâlain. Jedenfalls ist davon auszugehen, dass die Verehrung dieses Gottes insbesondere durch Mitglieder der romanisierten Stammeseliten gefördert wurde.

2 Mars Loucetius und (Victoria) Nemetona

Die früheste bisher bekannt gewordene Weihinschrift aus Germanien, ist diejenige eines Reiters der *ala Petriana* aus Strasbourg. Seine Datierung ist umstritten. J. KRIER hat jedoch mit überzeugenden Argumenten nachgewiesen, dass der Aufenthalt der Truppe in Strasbourg nach der Neuordnung der germanischen Heere 17 n. Chr. und vor ihrem Abzug nach Britannien 43 n. Chr. anzusetzen sei, und die Inschrift wohl noch in tiberische Zeit fällt.[43] Die Weihung gilt einem Mars Loucetius und der Stifter, Fittio, kam wahrscheinlich aus dem linksrheinischen Grenzgebiet der Treverer, also dem *pagus* der Aresaces.[44] Loucetius „der Leuchtende" ist ein qualifizierendes Epitheton und kein originär keltischer Göttername.[45]

Ein Kultplatz des Mars Loucetius und seiner Paredra Nemetona ist aus Ober-Olm, 7,5 km südwestlich von Mainz in der Flur ‚Im Füllkeller' durch Streufunde bekannt. Eine im Jahr 1983 durchgeführte Grabung brachte nur geringe Baubefunde. Offenbar hat man bisher nur Randgebiete des eigentlichen Tempelbezirks erfasst.[46] Dennoch zeigen die zahlreichen Streufunde, dass der Kultplatz von großer Bedeutung gewesen sein muss und ebenfalls schon in vorrömischer Zeit genutzt wurde. Zu den Funden gehören zahlreiche Silber-, Gold- und Bronzebleche, Votivwaffen, mehr als 500 Münzen, darunter auch keltische Silbermünzen, und Keramik der späten Latènezeit sowie Architekturfragmente.[47] Die bisherigen Untersuchungen zeigen einen aufwändigen Ausbau des Heiligtums. Wände und Fußboden des Tempels waren mit

---

43 CIL XIII 11605; vgl. KRIER 1981, 74 f.; ferner SPICKERMANN 2003, 127.
44 Vgl. KRIER 1981, 74; zum *pagus* KLUMBACH 1959, 72 f.
45 MAIER 1994, 206.
46 FRENZ 1992, 16; vgl. RUPPRECHT. 1990, 511–512; ROYMANS 1990, 67 u. SPICKERMANN 2003, 83–85.
47 Insbesondere zu den Blechen und Votivlanzen: BEHRENS 1941, 18–21; vgl. KLEIN 1999.

orientalischen Schlangenmustern und Marmor aus Italien verziert.⁴⁸ Einer monumentalen Brunneninschrift aus der Mitte des 1. Jahrhunderts n. Chr. zufolge stellte ein Ehepaar, dessen Besitz an den Kultbezirk grenzte, seine Quelle zur Verfügung und baute eine Wasserleitung *(iter)*, die in den Brunnen am Tempel mündete. Die Aresaces stellten dafür die Inschrift öffentlich am Brunnen des Heiligtums auf.⁴⁹ Damit sind die Aresaces Träger des Kultplatzes, die ihren Hauptgottheiten, Mars Loucetius und Nemetona, geweiht war.⁵⁰ Problematisch ist die Einordnung dieser Gruppe, die offenbar eine Untereinheit der Treverer war, da sie wohl in keiner eigenen *civitas* verfasst war, aber dennoch Hilfstruppen stellte.⁵¹ In Ober-Olm scheint jedenfalls der wohl schon vorrömisch genutzte, zentrale Kultplatz dieses *pagus*? gelegen zu haben. N. ROYMANS vermutet jedenfalls aufgrund zahlreicher keltischer Münzen, latènezeitlicher Keramik und vorrömischer Lanzenspitzen einen eisenzeitlichen Kultplatz.⁵² Dass dieser auch noch in der zweiten Hälfte des 1. Jahrhunderts n. Chr. von eminenter Bedeutung war, zeigt die Weihung des Konsulars A. Didius Gallus Fabricius Veiento und seiner Frau Attica an Nemetona, die sich zwischen 83 und 85 n. Chr. anlässlich der Chattenkriege des Domitian in *Mogontiacum*/Mainz aufhielten.⁵³ Nemetona ist dem Wort *nemeton* entlehnt bedeutet so viel wie „Heiliger Hain".⁵⁴ Jedenfalls war der Kultplatz schon im 1. Jahrhundert n. Chr. so bekannt, dass eines der prominentesten Mitglieder der Reichsaristokratie dort weiht. Insgesamt kennen wir für die Zeit bis ca. 70 n. Chr. Kultplätze für gallo-römische Götterpaare nur aus dem Lingonen- Sequaner- und dem ehemaligen Trevererebiet, also nur aus den Gebieten, die traditionell keltisch besiedelt waren.

Eine schon lange bekannte, aber erst jüngst publizierte Weihung erweitert unser Bild in Bezug auf die Benennung gallo-römischer Götterpaare. Es handelt sich um eine bronzene Weihetafel an Mars Loucetius und Victoria Nemetona, die in Eisenberg in der Pfalz gefunden wurde (Abb. 2).⁵⁵ Die ca. 17 cm breite Tafel war ursprünglich in Form einer *tabula ansata* gearbeitet. Die Inschrift belegt die Dedikation eines Topfes mit Podest und Schale für das Götterpaar am 23. April 223. Sie lautet:

> [In h(onorem) d(omus)] d(ivinae) Marti Lou/[cetio et] Victoriae Neme/[tonae] M(arcus) A(urelius) Senillus Seve/[rus b(ene)f(iciarius)] l]egati urnam cum / [sortib]us et phiala(m) ex / [vo]to posuit l(ibens) l(aetus) m(erito) / [Grat]o et Seleuco co(n)s(ulibus) / X Kal(endas) Maias

---

48 DERKS 1998, 202.
49 CIL XIII 7252; vgl. dazu KLUMBACH 1959; BERNHARD 1990, 61 Abb. 27. u. SPICKERMANN 1994, 280–283.
50 Zu den inschriftlichen Belegen für diese Gottheiten SPICKERMANN 1989/90, 205–206.
51 Zu den Aresaces: KLUMBACH 1959, 74. und WILMANNS 1981, 98.
52 ROYMANS 1990, 67.
53 CIL XIII 7253 = ILS 1010; vgl. SPICKERMANN 1994, 280–281.
54 MAIER 1994, 249.
55 KRECKEL /BERNHARD 2007 = AE 2007, 1044.

Abb. 2: Bronzene Weihetafel an Mars Loucetius und Victoria Nemetona, Eisenberg in der Pfalz (nach KRECKEL/BERNHARD 2007, 5)

Ganz ungewöhnlicherweise ist die Paredra des Mars Loucetius mit einem Doppelnamen versehen, da Victoria direkt mit Nemetona verbunden ist. Dies weicht von den üblichen Dedikationen an gallo-römische Götterpaare ab, bei denen der Gott häufig mit römischem und keltischem Doppelnamen auftritt, die Göttin aber nur ihren einheimischen Beinamen trägt.[56] Die Identifikation von Victoria und Nemetona dürfte auch bedeuten, dass verschiedene Weihungen im Verbreitungsgebiet, die nur Mars und Victoria nennen,[57] an Loucetius und Nemetona gerichtet waren. Das gilt auch für die Inschriften, die Mars und Nemetona nennen.[58] Insgesamt sind bisher 15 Dedikationen an Mars Loucetius mit und ohne Paredra bekannt geworden.[59]

3 Mars Caturix

Mars Caturix trägt zwar den Stammesnamen der gallischen Caturiges, ist aber nahezu ausschließlich im obergermanischen Helvetiergebiet bezeugt.[60] Auffallend ist, dass zwei Weihungen an Caturix im Bereich des helvetischen Ortes Yverdon gefunden wurden, der wie der caturigische Vorort *Eburodunum* (heute Embrun) hieß.[61]

Mars Caturix war offenbar der „Stammesgott" der Helvetier, wobei sein Kult vor allem durch sein Heiligtum in Riaz/Tronche-Bélon (Marsens),[62] den nur inschriftlich bezeugten Tempel in Nonfoux bei Essertin nicht weit von Yverdon[63] und die genannten

---

56 SCHLEIERMACHER 1933, 110–111; vgl. SPICKERMANN 2007a, 243.
57 Etwa CIL XIII 6145 (Eisenberg).
58 CIL XIII 6131 (Altrip).
59 KRECKEL/BERNHARD 2007, 3; vgl. zuletzt vgl. SPICKERMANN 2014.
60 SPICKERMANN 2003, 109–110 u. 163–165.
61 CIL XIII 5054 u. 11473.
62 SPICKERMANN 2003, 109–110.
63 CIL XIII 5046 = ILS 4552 = WALSER 1979–1980, Nr. 58: *Marti Caturigi / L(ucius) Camill(ius) Aetolus / templum a novo / in[st]ituit.*

Dedikationen aus *Eburodunum*/Yverdon bezeugt ist.⁶⁴ In Yverdon ging er eine Verbindung mit dem dort an den Schwefelquellen wohl als Heilgott verehrten Apollo ein. Eine weitere inschriftliche Dedikation fand sich im Cigognier-Tempel in Avenches.⁶⁵ Weitere Dedikationen an den Gott außerhalb des Helvetiergebietes sind aus dem Heiligtum von Villards d'Héria im benachbarten Sequanergebiet und aus Böckingen (zusammen mit I(upiter) O(ptimus) M(aximus) und dem Genius loci) bekannt.⁶⁶ Beim Dedikanten der letzteren Weihung handelt es sich um einen *beneficiarius consularis*, der seine Einheit nicht nennt, und möglicherweise aus dem Helvetiergebiet stammte.⁶⁷ Der Name Caturix bedeutet ‚Schlachtenkönig' von irisch *cath* ‚Schlacht' und *ri* ‚König'.⁶⁸

Das bisher am besten bekannte Heiligtum des Mars Caturix und der Victoria ist das aus Riaz/Tronche-Bélon (Marsens) oberhalb des Lac de Gruyère. Eine vorrömische Nutzung ist nicht nachgewiesen, das Münzspektrum reicht bis in augusteische Zeit zurück. Der erste, wohl claudische Tempel bestand aus Holz. Er wurde wahrscheinlich in flavischer Zeit durch einen Massivbau in Form eines gallo-römischen Umgangstempels ersetzt. Es fanden sich zahlreiche Kleinfragmente von Votivinschriften an Mars Caturix und Mars Augustus⁶⁹ sowie Votivbeilchen, Reste von Bronzestatuetten, darunter diejenige einer gehörnten Gottheit, und sechs Bronzeglöckchen. Der Kultplatz, der an der Straße von Vevey nach Avenches lag, nahm etwa 10 ha ein.⁷⁰ Das wichtigste epigraphische Zeugnis ist eine in viele Teile zerbrochene Inschrift, die eine Liste von Personen und einen Geldbetrag von stereotyp jeweils 75 Denaren enthält. Es wird vermutet, dass es sich hier um einen Kultverein handelt, dessen Mitglieder diese Geldsumme für den Bau des Tempels gestiftet haben.⁷¹

4 Hercules Magusanus

Auch in Niedergermanien sind doppelnamige „Stammesgötter" nachweisbar. Zu nennen ist der wohl batavische Hercules Magusanus (auch Magusenus), der einen germanisierten, ursprünglich vielleicht keltischen ebenfalls qualifizierenden Beinamen trägt, der auf einem wohl aus dem Heiligtum von Elst verschleppten Altar aus Ruimel bezogen ist. Weihinschriften für diesen Gott sind auch in Empel und Neerij-

---

64 CIL XIII 5054 u. 11473 (mit Apollo).
65 N/L. 40.
66 MOREL 1976, 426 (Villards d'Héria) und CIL XIII 6474 = SCHALLMAYER et al. 1990, 100–101 Nr. 110.
67 SCHALLMAYER et al. 1990, 101 datieren aufgrund der Paläographie in die erste Hälfte des 2. Jh. n. Chr. und begründen damit eine Herkunft aus dem Mittelmeerraum. Neben der allenthalben unsicheren Datierung nach der Paläographie stünde dem entgegen, dass bis in die Zeit des Marcus Aurelius durchweg noch der Name des Statthalters genannt wird.
68 MAIER 1994, 73 s.v. Caturix; vgl. BIRKHAN 1999, 637–638.
69 CIL XIII 5035–5037.
70 Vgl. zuletzt SPICKERMANN 2003, 109–110. Inschriften: CIL XIII 5035–5041.
71 FREI-STOLBA 1985, 101; vgl. FELLMANN 1988, 243 u. BOSSERT 2001, 80 Anm. 149.

nen-Waardenburg belegt.⁷² Mehrere Dedikationen für Hercules Magusanus fanden sich ferner im benachbarten Gebiet der *Colonia Ulpia Traiana*, einmal ist er zusammen mit seiner Paredra, Haeva, genannt. Weitere Zeugnisse stammen aus Köln, Bonn, Neuss-Grimlinghausen, Tongeren, Houten und Westkapelle (Gebiet Domburg). Außerdem ist er auf einem Weihestein aus Mumrills am Hadrianswall und auf denen batavischer und thrakischer Gardereiter aus Rom genannt.⁷³ Der Gott wurde damit in nahezu allen Gegenden der Provinz verehrt.⁷⁴ Die Namensetymologie des Gottes ist nicht vollständig zu klären, vielleicht handelt es sich um einen germanisierten, ursprünglich keltischen Namen von Mogusenos „der mächtige Alte".⁷⁵ Nach einer anderen Interpretation geht er auf *Maguz/s -naz ‚der zur Kraft Gehörige' zurück, Haeva ist vielleicht auf germanisch *hiwan ‚heiraten' zu beziehen.⁷⁶ Auf Bilddenkmälern erscheint der Gott ausschließlich wie der römische Hercules.⁷⁷ Da insgesamt fünf Armringe mit Weihinschriften für den Gott bekannt geworden sind, scheint dies neben Waffen und Kleininschriften einer seiner bevorzugten Weihegaben gewesen zu sein, was vielleicht erklärt, warum in seinem Kernland so wenig inschriftliche Dedikationen gefunden wurden. Die repräsentativste und auch früheste Weihegabe stellt der in Ruimel gefundene Altar des *summus magistratus civitatis Batavorum* dar. Er diente der Selbstrepräsentation eines batavischen Adligen, der dem ‚Stammesgott' Hercules Magusanus wahrscheinlich im Heiligtum in Empel weihte, dessen Ausbau auf jene batavische Eliten zurückging.⁷⁸

N. ROYMANS und T. DERKS konnten herausarbeiten, dass der germanische Hercules Magusanus die Funktion einer ‚Stammesgottheit' der Bataver hatte und wohl vor allem in Empel und wahrscheinlich auch in Elst verehrt wurde.⁷⁹ Der Kultplatz in Elst

---

72 CIL XIII 8771, AE 1990, 740 (Bronzetäfelchen) u. AE 1994, 1282 (silberner Armring); vgl. BOGAERS/ HAALEBOS 1993.
73 CIL VIII 1090 u. CIL VI 31162 = SPEIDEL 1994, 87–88 Nr. 62 (29. 9.219 n. Chr.).
74 Bonn: CIL XIII 8010, 10027.212b (Armring), S-H. 161, 167 (?); Neuss-Grimlinghausen: CIL XIII 100027.212d (Armring); Köln: CIL XIII 100027.212d (Armring), 8492 (Deutz); Tongeren: CIL XIII 100027.212a (Armring); Xanten: CIL XIII 8610; CLAUSS 1976 Nr. 60 (Wardt-Lüttingen); Huissen: CIL XIII 8705 (mit Haeva); Houten AE 1994, 1284; Westkapelle (Gebiet Domburg): CIL XIII 8777.
75 SPICKERMANN/ DE BERNARDO STEMPEL 2005, 146; vgl. ähnlich TOORIANS 2003.
76 WAGNER 1977; vgl. STOLTE 1986, 626–629 u. 650–651; vgl. SIMEK 2006, 155 s.v. Haeva u. 172 s.v. Hercules Magusanus.
77 S-H. 161 u. 167.
78 CIL XIII 8771: *Magusa/no Hercul(i) / sacru(m) Flav(u)s / Vihirmatis fil(ius) / [s]ummus magistra(tus) / [c]ivitatis Batavor(um) / v(otum) s(olvit) l(ibens) m(erito)*.
79 ROYMANS/DERKS 1993; DERKS/ROYMANS 1994 u. zuletzt bes. DERKS 1998, 94–98, der den Gott als Exponenten einer Gesellschaft von Hirten und Viehzüchtern, von den Ackerbauern im Lößbereich der südlichen Provinz mit ihren Matronenkulten sowie von den gallischen Martes unterscheidet. Sein Verdienst liegt u. a in dem Nachweis, dass mit der Ausbreitung von Ackerbau, Viehzucht und Metallverarbeitung nicht nur eine Technologie, sondern auch eine Ausbreitung religiöser Vorstellungen verbunden ist, die einen unmittelbaren Zusammenhang mit diesen Techniken zeigen, vgl. DERKS 1998, 27–29. Skeptisch dazu, allerdings ohne Kenntnis von DERKS 1998 ist MOITRIEUX 2002, 183–187.

(Prov. Gelderland, Niederlande) wurde 1947 unter der gotischen Sint Maartenskerk entdeckt. Eine eisenzeitliche Nutzung konnte bisher angesichts der eingeschränkten Ausgrabungsfläche nicht nachgewiesen werden. Es ist aber wegen der Funde von kultisch deponierten Tierknochen anzunehmen, dass sich hier – ähnlich wie in Empel – vorher ein offener Kultplatz befand.[80] Das Heiligtum lag wahrscheinlich ohne direkte Siedlungsanbindung 9 km nördlich von *Ulpia Noviomagus*/Nijmegen entfernt an einer verkehrsgeographisch wichtigen Straßenkreuzung im dicht besiedelten batavischen Kernland. Um 50 n. Chr. wurde hier ein erster einfacher steinerner Tempel in Form eines Rechteckraums von 11,57 × 8,70 m mit Satteldach errichtet; das erste nachgewiesene Steingebäude und auch das größte seiner Art im Bereich der Niederlande vor den Funden von Lith-Kessel.[81] Der Fußboden dieses Gebäudes bestand aus *opus signinum* in dekorierter Marmorimitation. Dieser erste Bau wurde wahrscheinlich im Verlauf des Bataveraufstandes zerstört und dann in flavischer Zeit durch einen monumentalen Neubau ersetzt.[82] Der Ausgräber, J.E.A.T. Bogaers, vermutete schon 1955, dass hier der batavische Stammesgott Hercules Magusanus verehrt wurde.[83]

2002 konnte bei Bauarbeiten in Elst-Westeraam nur 560 m entfernt ein weiterer Umgangstempel lokalisiert werden, dem zwei Holzbauphasen vorausgingen. Die erste ist dendrochronologisch zwischen 36 und 41 n. Chr. (+- 6) zu datieren, um diese Zeit müssen jedenfalls die Holzpfosten in den Boden gekommen sein. Sie wäre damit in etwa zeitgleich mit der ersten Phase des Tempels unter der Sint Maartenskerk. Die zweite Holzbauphase ist ein paar Jahrzehnte jünger. Um 100 n. Chr. wurde das Gebäude dann in Stein monumentalisiert.[84]

Das 1986 entdeckte Heiligtum in Empel bei 's-Hertogenbosch in den Niederlanden ist ein eindrucksvolles Zeugnis der Vermischung der um 12 v. Chr. mit der römischen Eroberung zugewanderten Bataver und den Resten einer ursprünglich dort ansässigen Bevölkerung. Der Platz liegt auf einer deutlich sichtbaren Sanddüne aus dem Pleistozän etwa 500 m südlich der Maas. Die früheste Phase des Kultplatzes ist nach den Funden von 125 v. Chr. bis 15 v. Chr. zu datieren. Eine älteste Umfassung umgab die gesamte Düne. In frührömischer Zeit war der Platz mit Flechtwerk abgegrenzt und mit Kultpfählen versehen, bei denen sich Gruben mit Resten von Opfertieren und metallenen Votivgegenständen befanden. Eine Bebauung ist nicht nachzuweisen, es handelte sich offenbar um ein „Freilichtheiligtum". Die meisten Weihegaben sind aus Metall, darunter 700 keltische und 250 römische Münzen, 500 Fibeln, Armreifen, Landbaugeräte und vor allem 100 Teile römischer Militärausrüstung, vorwiegend aus der frühen Kaiserzeit. An Knochenmaterial fanden sich die Reste von Rind, Schaf/Ziege und Schwein. Die Tiere wurden innerhalb der Kultstätte geschlachtet und konsumiert.

---

80 Derks 1998, 177; vgl. zuletzt ausführlich Derks/van Kerckhove/Baetsen 2008.
81 Bogaers 1955, 254; vgl. Spickermann 2008, 32.
82 Bogaers 1955, 255–256.
83 Bogaers 1955, 173–201 u. 255.
84 Vgl. van Enckevort/Thijssen/Mols 2005.

Offenbar wurde ein ursprünglich lokaler Kult im römischen Sinne transformiert und umgewandelt, wobei offen bleiben muss, ob batavische Soldaten und Veteranen – etwa nach Beendigung des Dienstes in einer Auxiliarformation – oder auch Zivilbevölkerung die Waffen dedizierten.[85] Die Dedikation von Waffen ist für den Untersuchungsraum auch inschriftlich bezeugt. So stiftete ein Centurio der *legio III Cyrenaica* in Tongeren der sonst nicht mehr bezeugten Göttin Vihansa wohl noch im 1. Jahrhundert n. Chr. Schild und Lanze.[86] Der Kultplatz von Empel scheint so bedeutend gewesen zu sein, dass er durch die Errichtung des großen Tempels für den Stammesgott Magusanus offenbar durch Angehörige der batavischen Eliten monumentalisiert und häufig durch wohl batavische Soldaten frequentiert wurde.[87]

Ob Hercules Magusanus in den beiden Tempelbezirken von Empel und Elst tatsächlich die Hauptgottheit war, lässt sich nicht mit vollständiger Sicherheit behaupten, da er insbesondere in Elst inschriftlich eher durch Kleinfunde belegt ist. Kein Zweifel kann aber daran bestehen, dass er in einem Austauschprozess zwischen rechtsrheinischen Zuwanderern, lokalen Bevölkerungsresten und römischen Eroberern die Hauptgottheit der neu formierten Batavercivitas wurde und aller Wahrscheinlichkeit erst in der römischen Eroberungsphase zum ersten Mal auftaucht.

Die Liste dieser „Stammesgottheiten" ließe sich noch deutlich verlängern, z. B. durch die Schutzgottheit der Civitas der Sequaner, Mars Segomo („der Siegreiche"),[88] und vor allem den treverischen Lenus Mars mit seinen großen, auf vorrömische Anlagen zurückgehende Heiligtümer auf dem Titelberg und dem Martberg bei Pommern an der Mosel.[89] Ungewöhnlich ist, dass der keltische Beiname Lenos, der vielleicht „Hain" bedeutet,[90] vor dem römischen Namen des Gottes steht und er auf dem Martberg auch als Heilgott angerufen wurde. In Trier besaß er sogar einen eigenen Flamen.[91] Aufgrund der archäologischen und epigraphischen Funde und Befunde wird diese Gottheit am ehesten keltische Wurzeln gehabt haben, fügt sich dann aber nahtlos in das neue römische System ein.

---

85 Vgl. ROYMANS/DERKS 1993; ferner HAYNES 1997, 116–120.
86 CIL XIII 3592 = ILB 29.
87 Zum Heiligtum zuletzt SPICKERMANN 2008, 32–34.
88 SPICKERMANN 2003, 72–74 u. 180–184 mit weiterer Lit.
89 Zum Titelberg zuletzt: KREMER/METZLER/GAENG 2016; zum Martberg zuletzt zusammenfassend: SPICKERMANN 2016, 197–200.
90 HAINZMANN 2005, 7.
91 SPICKERMANN 2003, 79–83 mit weiterer Lit.

5 Früh bezeugte regionale und lokale Gottheiten

Neben den sogenannten „Stammesgottheiten" existierten eine Vielzahl von zum Teil toponymischen Lokalgottheiten wie z. B. Varneno und Sunuxal in Aachen Kornelimünster[92], für die aber in den wenigsten Fällen eine vorrömischen Verehrung eindeutig nachzuweisen ist. Dies gilt auch für überregional verehrte Gottheiten wie die Suleviae und Apollo Grannus. Das Paar Apollo Grannus und Sirona steht für Heilfunktionen. Wichtige Heiligtümer finden sich in Rätien mit Faimingen und Belgica mit dem „Pilgerheiligtum" von Hochscheid im Hunsrück. Sirona erscheint in Obergermanien inschriftlich aber stets mit Apollo, nicht mit Apollo Grannus, der einzeln aber in Horbourg, Neuenstadt am Kocher, Speyer und Alzey nachgewiesen ist.[93] Es scheint zwar naheliegend, Grannos als vorrömischen keltischen Heilgott zu interpretieren, doch lässt sich dies weder archäologisch noch epigraphisch zweifelsfrei nachweisen. Wirklich keltische Wurzeln scheinen auf den ersten Blick nur der für Mâlain Ancey im Lingonengebiet bezeugte Sucellus sowie Borvo und Damona aus dem ebenfalls im Lingonengebiet befindlichen Bourbonne-les-Bains zu haben. Ersterer ist der im gallischen Raum weit verbreitete Schlägelgott (der gute Schläger), der sich aber vor allem auf Bildzeugnissen findet. Im 1./2. Jahrhundert n. Chr. kommen auch die ersten Sucellus-Statuetten auf, von denen in Augst zwei sicher bezeugt sind, eine weitere stammt aus Besançon.[94] Borvo (der Kochende[95]) und Damona (Kuh[96]) sind das Götterpaar der heißen Quellen von Bourbonne-les-Bains, an denen sich auch ein Heiligtum befand, welches vor allem von Frauen frequentiert worden zu sein scheint.[97]

6 Schluss

Mit der römischen Eroberung Galliens und Germaniens wurden die Karten neu gemischt und auch im religiösen Bereich entstanden völlig neue Strukturen, welche die unter römischer Herrschaft neu formierten gesellschaftlichen und politischen Strukturen widerspiegelten. Dazu gehörte auch die Verbreitung einer Schriftlichkeit in der Öffentlichkeit, die insbesondere über das römische Militär und seine einheimischen Hilfstruppen Verbreitung im Totenkult und dann auch in der Götterverehrung fand. Dies förderte die Herausbildung neuer Göttertypen, die den neuen Verhältnissen

---

92 Vgl. dazu SPICKERMANN 2007b.
93 CIL XIII 5315, 6562, N. 71 u. 88; vgl. dazu SPICKERMANN 2007a, 249.
94 Augst: KAUFMANN-HEINIMANN 1998, 77 S 2 (2. Jahrhundert) u. 88 S 6 (1./2. Jahrhundert); vgl. auch das Bein ebd. S. 77 S 82, welches evtl. zu Sucellus gehört. Besançon: ebd. 44 f. mit Lit., wohl eine Replik von S 6.
95 MAIER 1994, 47–48.
96 MAIER 1994, 95.
97 Dazu zusammenfassend SPICKERMANN 2013, 132–133 u. SPICKERMANN 1994, 290–293.

gewachsen waren, also sich in die römische Bildersprache übersetzen ließen, zum Teil römische Namen (Mars, Hercules Mercurius etc.) annahmen und vor allem auch schriftliche Votive akzeptierten. Diese neuen „romanisierten" Gottheiten mussten als Exponenten einer neuen gallo-römischen Religion lesen können. Das schließt natürlich nicht aus, dass die vorrömischen analphabetischen keltischen und germanischen Götter weiter verehrt wurden, doch vermochte es die gallo-römische Religion insbesondere über die Schutzgottheiten größerer Gruppen wie die aus den Stämmen hervorgegangenen *civitates* oder die besonders in der Belgica und am Niederrhein bezeugten Kurien ein neues religiöses System zu schaffen, welches einer romanisierten Lebensweise entsprach und diese auch in der religiösen Bilder- und Symbolsprache widerspiegelte. Die Erforschung der auf römischen Inschriften überlieferten Götternamen vermittelt daher in den meisten Fällen weniger Informationen über vorrömische und daher vorschriftliche Verhältnisse, sondern dokumentiert vielmehr ein *tertium sui generis* aus dem Kontakt verschiedener religiöser Traditionen, bei der sich die römische Schriftlichkeit, Bildsprache und Opferpraxis weitgehend durchsetzte. Dies liegt insbesondere auch daran, dass die keltischen oder germanischen Beinamen – wie gezeigt – in der Regel qualifizierende Epitheta sind „der Mächtige", „der Starke", „der Siegreiche" etc., die einem römischen Mars, Hercules oder Mercurius dann im Zuge einer *Interpretatio Celtica* oder *Germanica* erklärend beigefügt wurden. Auch Grannos als Sonnengott[98] und Sirona „Stern"[99] scheinen eher einem graeco-romanen Astralkult entlehnt, als einem originär keltischem, wobei hier frühe Kulturkontakte natürlich nicht ausgeschlossen werden können.

Einen Sonderfall bilden die Matronen, die als maternale Trinität dargestellt sind, die von Orange und Marseille bis nach Ostgallien, aber auch in Oberitalien verbreitet war und am Niederrhein nur in der Darstellung der mittleren Matrone als Mädchen mit offenem Haar abgewandelt wurde.[100] Durch ihr häufiges Vorkommen im Ubiergebiet stellen sie die meist verehrten Gottheiten Niedergermaniens dar.[101] P. HERZ weist darauf hin, dass es unmöglich ist, alle Epiklesen, die man nach M. HAINZMANN besser als Kultnamen bezeichnen sollte,[102] mit einem einzigen Ansatz zu erklären.[103] Er verweist auf Matronen mit Ortsnamen-Epiklese wie die Matronae Iulianahenae für *Iuliacum*/Jülich, die kaum göttliche Ahnfrauen einer Sippe bezeichnen und in anderen Gegenden als Ortsgenien erscheinen würden. Matronen, deren Beinamen von Gewässern oder Flüssen abgeleitet seien, würde man auch als Nymphae bezeichnen können, daneben gebe es singuläre Epiklesen wie etwa die Ollogabiae; während die Matronae *paternae* oder *maternae* eher ein persönliches Verhältnis zwischen den

---

98 SPICKERMANN/DE BERNARDO STEMPEL 2005, 140–141.
99 MAIER 1994, 292–293.
100 BIRKHAN 1999, 519–520; ferner SCHEID 1999, 411 und SPICKERMANN 2009, 354.
101 Vgl. die Zahlen bei SPICKERMANN 2008, 183–184.
102 HAINZMANN 2005, 5.
103 In der Germania Inferior zähle ich 81 verschiedene Kultnamen: SPICKERMANN 2008, Anhang 2.

Weihenden und den Gottheiten ausdrückten.[104] Hier wird m. E. der Entwicklungsaspekt nicht berücksichtigt. Waren die frühen Matronen Schutzgottheiten und „Ahnfrauen" von in kleineren Gruppen übergesiedelten Personenverbänden, deren Namen sich oft aus eisenzeitlichen rechtsrheinischen Orts- oder Landschaftsbezeichnungen ableiten lassen, entwickelte sich mit der Übersiedlung über den Rhein unter römisch-italisch-gallischen Einfluss die für das Rheinland typische kleinteilige Matronenverehrung. Im Vordergrund steht hierbei die Schutzfunktion dieser Gottheiten, die sich auf alle Lebensbereiche und auch auf die politische Neuordnung des Lebensraumes unter römischer Herrschaft auswirkte. Das heißt, die Schutz- und lebensspendende Funktion der göttlichen Ahnfrauen konnte durch neue Gruppenbildungen von der ursprünglichen Trägergruppe abstrahiert und auf römische *vici*, auf Flüsse und Gewässer, an denen man nunmehr siedelt oder auch auf größere Personenverbände bezogen werden. Epiklesen der Matres dagegen gehen insbesondere auf Ethnonyme zurück, z. B. Matres Suebae, die allerdings zumeist in der Fremde angerufen wurden.[105]

Damit sollte deutlich geworden sein, dass der allergrößte Teil der uns inschriftlich überlieferten keltischen und germanischen Götternamen aus einer durch die römische Eroberung initiierten Schriftkultur hervorgegangen sind und damit die religiösen und – durch ihre Schutzfunktionen für römisch verfasste Gruppen (*civitates*, *pagi*, *curiae*) Verhältnisse der römischen Kaiserzeit dokumentieren, als die Götter Latein sowie keltische und germanische Dialekte nicht nur verstanden, sondern auch lesen konnten. Dass inschriftliche Weihungen in Ost- und Innergallien nicht so verbreitet waren, wie im Rheingebiet, mag einerseits am fehlenden Militär liegen, andererseits scheinen dort zumindest noch für eine Übergangszeit auch mehr vorrömische religiöse Traditionen weiter existiert zu haben, in denen die Schriftlichkeit und/oder das Setzen eines steinernen und damit dauerhaften Votivdenkmals keine oder eine sehr untergeordnete Rolle gespielt haben.

Abkürzungen

AE = *L'année épigraphique*, Paris.
CIL XIII = *Corpus Inscriptionum Latinarum*.
F. = H. Finke 1927. Neue Inschriften, *Bericht der Römisch-Germanischen Kommission* 17, 1927 (1929), 1–107 u. 198–231.
ILB = A. Deman/M.-Th. Raepsaet-Charlier, *Les Inscriptions Latines de Belgique* (ILB), Université Libre de Bruxelles. Faculté de Philosophie et Lettres. Sources et Instruments VII, Bruxelles 1985.
ILS = H. Dessau, *Inscriptiones Latinae Selectae*, 3 Bde. in 5 Teilen, Berlin 1862–1916 (NDr. 1962³).
N. = H. Nesselhauf, Neue Inschriften aus dem römischen Germanien und den angrenzenden Gebieten, *Bericht der Römisch-Germanischen Kommission* 27, 1937 (1939), 51–134.

---

104 Herz 2003, 144.
105 Zur Genese der Matronenkulte Spickermann 2008, 61–77; vgl. Spickermann 2009, 357.

N/L. = H. NESSELHAUF/H. LIEB, Dritter Nachtrag zu CIL XIII. Inschriften aus den germanischen Provinzen und dem Treverergebiet, *Bericht der Römisch-Germanischen Kommission* 40, 1959, 120–229.

S-H. = U. SCHILLINGER-HÄFELE, Vierter Nachtrag zu CIL XIII und zweiter Nachtrag zu FR. VOLLMER, Inscriptiones Baivariae Romanae. Inschriften aus dem deutschen Anteil der germanischen Provinzen und des Treverergebietes sowie Rätiens und Noricums, *Bericht der Römisch-Germanischen Kommission* 58, 1977 (1978) 2.Teil, 447–604.

Bibliographie

ALFÖLDY 1968 = G. ALFÖLDY, Epigraphisches aus dem Rheinland III, *Epigraphische Studien* 5, 1968, 1–98.

BARBET/BILLEREY 2004 = G. BARBET/R. BILLEREY, Une plaque de bronze avec dédicace découverte en Franche-Comté, *Gallia* 61, 2004, 281–290.

BAUCHHENSS 1992 = G. BAUCHHENSS, Götterweihungen aus Städten des römischen Deutschland, in: H.-J. SCHALLES/H. VON HESBERG/P. ZANKER (Hg.), Die römische Stadt im 2. Jahrhundert n. Chr. Der Funktionswandel des öffentlichen Raumes: Kolloquium in Xanten vom 2. bis 4. Mai 1990, *Xantener Berichte* 2, 1992, 325–337.

BEHRENS 1941 = G. BEHRENS, Mars-Weihungen im Mainzer Gebiet, *Mainzer Zeitschrift* 36, 1941, 8–21.

BERNHARD 1990 = H. BERNHARD, Die römische Geschichte in Rheinland-Pfalz, in: H. CÜPPERS (Hg.), Die Römer in Rheinland-Pfalz, Stuttgart 1990, 39–167.

BIRKHAN 1999 = H. BIRKHAN, Kelten. Versuch einer Gesamtdarstellung ihrer Kultur, Wien 1999³.

BOGAERS 1955 = J.E. BOGAERS, De gallo-romeinse tempels te Elst in de Over-Betuwe, s-Gravenhage 1955.

BOGAERS/HAALEBOS 1993 = J.E. BOGAERS/J.-K. HAALEBOS, Een armring voor Hercules Magusanus, Westerheem, *Archeologische Werkgemeenschap voor Nederland: Verenigingsnieuws* 42, 1993, 69–71.

BOPPERT 1992 = W. BOPPERT, Militärische Grabdenkmäler aus Mainz und Umgebung, in: CSIR Deutschland, Bd. 2.5, Mainz 1992.

BOSSERT 2001 = M. BOSSERT, Die Skulpturen des gallorömischen Tempelbezirkes von Thun-Allmendingen. Germania superior, civitas Helvetiorum, Thun-Allmendingen/Bern u. a. 2001.

BRUNAUX 1995 = J.-L. BRUNAUX, Die keltischen Heiligtümer Nordfrankreichs, in: A. HAFFNER (Hg.), Heiligtümer und Opferkulte der Kelten, *Archäologie in Deutschland*, Stuttgart 1995, 55–74.

CHASTAGNOL 1995 = A. CHASTAGNOL, La Gaule romaine et le droit latin. Recherches sur l'histoire administrative et sur la romanisation des habitants, Lyon/Paris 1995.

CÜPPERS 1990 = H. CÜPPERS (Hg.), Die Römer in Rheinland-Pfalz, Stuttgart 1990.

DERKS 1998 = T. DERKS, Gods, Temples and Ritual Practices. The Transformation of Religious Ideas and Values in Roman Gaul, Amsterdam 1998.

DERKS/ROYMANS 1994 = T. DERKS/N. ROYMANS, De tempel van Empel. Een Hercules-heiligdom in het woongebied van de Bataven, 's-Hertogenbosch 1994.

DERKS/VAN KERCKHOVE/BAETSEN 2008 = A.M.J. DERKS/J. VAN KERCKHOVE/S. BAETSEN, Nieuw archeologisch onderzoek rond de Grote Kerk van Elst, gemeente Overbetuwe (2002–2003), Amsterdam 2008.

FELLMANN 1988 = R. FELLMANN, Religion, in: W. DRACK/R. FELLMANN (Hg.): Die Römer in der Schweiz. Stuttgart 1988, 220–254

FREI-STOLBA 1985 = R. FREI-STOLBA, Götterkulte in der Schweiz zur römischen Zeit unter besonderer Berücksichtigung der epigraphischen Zeugnisse, *Bulletin des Antiquités Luxembourgeoises* 15, 1985, 75–126.
FRENZ 1992 = H.G. FRENZ, Germania Superior. Denkmäler römischen Götterkultes aus Mainz und Umgebung, in: CSIR. Deutschland, Bd. 2.4, Mainz 1992.
FRÉZOULS 1990 = E. FRÉZOULS, Gallien und römisches Germanien, in: J.H. D'ARMS/F. VITTINGHOFF (Hg.), Europäische Wirtschafts- und Sozialgeschichte in der römischen Kaiserzeit, in: Handbuch der europäischen Wirtschafts- und Sozialgeschichte, Bd. 1, Stuttgart 1990, 429–510.
GABELMANN 1972 = H. GABELMANN, Die Typen der römischen Grabstelen am Rhein, *Bonner Jahrbücher* 172, 65–140.
GALINSKY 1998 = K. GALINSKY, Augustan Culture. An Interpretive Introduction, Princeton, NJ [u. a.], 1998^2.
HAINZMANN 2005 = M. HAINZMANN, Götter(bei)namen – Eine Annäherung, in: W. SPICKERMANN/ R. WIEGELS (Hg.), Keltische Götter im Römischen Reich. Akten des 4. Internationalen Workshops "Fontes Epigraphici Religionis Celticae Antiquae" (F.E.R.C.AN.) vom 4.–6. 10. 2002 an der Universität Osnabrück, Möhnesee 2005, 1–14.
HAYNES 1997 = I. HAYNES, Religion in the Roman Army. Unifying Aspects and Regional Trends, in: H. CANCIK/J. RÜPKE (Hg.), Römische Reichsreligion und Provinzialreligion, Tübingen 1997, 113–128.
HELGELAND 1978 = J. HELGELAND, Roman Army Religion, ANRW II 16.2, 1978, 1470–1505.
HERZ 1978 = P. HERZ, Kaiserfeste der Prinzipatszeit, ANRW II 16.2, 1978, 1135–1200.
HERZ 2001 = P. HERZ, Das römische Heer und der Kaiserkult in Germanien, in: W. SPICKERMANN/ H. CANCIK/J. RÜPKE (Hg.), Religion in den germanischen Provinzen Roms, Tübingen 2001, 91–116.
HERZ 2003 = P. HERZ, Matronenkult und kultische Mahlzeiten, in: P. NOELKE/F. NAUMANN-STECKNER/B. SCHNEIDER (Hg.), Romanisation und Resistenz in Plastik, Architektur und Inschriften der Provinzen des Imperium Romanum. Neue Funde und Forschungen, Mainz 2003, 139–148.
HORNE/KING 1980 = P.D. HORNE/A.C. KING, 17. Romano-Celtic Temples in Continental Europe: A Gazeteer of Those with Known Plans, in: W. RODWELL (Hg.), Temples, Churches and Religion. Recent Research in Roman Britain; with a Gazetteer of Romano-Celtic Temples in Continental Europe, British Archaeological Reports / British Series Bd. 77, Oxford 1980, 369–555.
INSTINSKY 1959 = H.U. INSTINSKY, Kaiser Nero und die Mainzer Jupitersäule, *Jahrbuch des Römisch-Germanischen Zentralmuseums Mainz* 6, 1959, 128–141.
KAUFMANN-HEINIMANN 1998 = A. KAUFMANN-HEINIMANN, Götter und Lararien aus Augusta Raurica. Herstellung, Fundzusammenhänge und sakrale Funktion figurlicher Bronzen in einer romischen Stadt, Augst 1998.
KLEIN 1999 = M.P. KLEIN, Votivwaffen aus einem Mars-Heiligtum bei Mainz, *Journal of Roman Military Equipment Studies* 10, 1999, 87–94.
KLUMBACH 1959 = H. KLUMBACH, Aresaces, in: Limesstudien. Vorträge des 3. Internationalen Limes-Kongresses in Rheinfelden/Basel 1957, Basel 1959, 69–83.
KRECKEL/BERNHARD 2007 = T. KRECKEL/H. BERNHARD, Benefiziarierweihung auf einer Bronzetafel aus Eisenberg/Pfalz, *Osnabrücker Online-Beiträge zu den Altertumswissenschaften* 13. Online verfügbar unter www.varusforschung.de.
KREMER/METZLER/GAENG 2016 = G. KREMER/J. METZLER/C. GAENG, Das öffentliche Zentrum des keltischen Oppidums und das Heiligtum des gallo-römischen Vicus auf dem Titelberg (Luxemburg), in: M. LEHNER/B. SCHRETTLE (Hg.), Tempelberg und Zentralort? Siedlungs- und Kultentwicklung am Frauenberg bei Leibnitz im Vergleich. Akten des Kolloquiums vom 4.–5. Mai 2015 im Schloss Seggauberg/Steiermark, Wien 2016, 123–140.

KRIER 1981 = J. KRIER, Die Treverer ausserhalb ihrer Civitas. Mobilität und Aufstieg, Trier 1981.
LIERTZ 1998 = U.-M. LIERTZ, Kultur und Kaiser. Studien zu Kaiserkult und Kaiser Verehrung in den germanischen Provinzen und Gallia Belgica zur römischen Kaiserzeit, Roma 1998.
MAIER 1994 = B. MAIER, Lexikon der keltischen Religion und Kultur, Stuttgart 1994.
MOITRIEUX 2002 = G. MOITRIEUX, Henri, Hercules in Gallia. Recherches sur la personnalité et le culte d'un dieu romain en Gaule, Paris 2002.
MOREL 1976 = J.-P. MOREL, Circonscription de Franche-Comté, *Gallia* 34, 1976, 413–437.
PETIT/MANGIN 1994 = J.-P. PETIT/M. MANGIN (Hg.), Les Agglomérations secondaires. La Gaule Belgique, les Germanies et l'Occident romain: actes du colloque de Bliesbruck-Reinheim/Bitche, 21–24 octobre 1992, Paris 1994.
RAEPSAET-CHARLIER 1998 = M.-TH. RAEPSAET-CHARLIER, Les Gaules et les Germanies, in: C. LEPELLEY (Hg.), Rome et l'intégration de l'Empire – Tome 2, Paris 1998[2], 143–195.
ROUSSEL 1969 = L. ROUSSEL, Fanum des 'Froidefonds' sur le site de Mediolanum (Mâlain), *Revue Archéologique de l'Est et du Centre-Est* 20, 1969, 179–191.
ROUSSEL 1994 = L. ROUSSEL, Mâlain-Mediolanum (Côte d'Or), in: PETIT/MANGIN 1994, 28
ROYMANS 1990 = N. ROYMANS, Tribal Societies in Northern Gaul. An Anthropological Perspective, Amsterdam 1990.
ROYMANS/DERKS 1993 = N. ROYMANS/T. DERKS, Der Tempel von Empel. Ein Hercules-Heiligtum im Batavergebiet, *Archäologisches Korrespondenzblatt* 23, 1993, 479–492.
RÜGER 1981 = C.B. RÜGER, Vindex cum inermi provincia? Zu einer weiteren Neronischen Marsinschrift vom Rhein, *Zeitschrift für Papyrologie und Epigraphik* 43, 1981, 329–335.
RÜGER 1987 = C. RÜGER, Xanten. Colonia Ulpia Traiana, in: H.G. HORN (Hg.), Die Römer in Nordrhein-Westfalen, Stuttgart 1987, 626–638.
RUPPRECHT 1990 = G. RUPPRECHT, Ober-Olm, in: H. CÜPPERS (Hg.), Die Römer in Rheinland-Pfalz, Stuttgart 1990, 511–512.
SCHÄFER 2001 = A. SCHÄFER, Götter aus dem Rheingebiet in Dakien und Pannonien, in: W.SPICKERMANN/H.CANCIK/J. RÜPKE (Hg.), Religion in den germanischen Provinzen Roms, Tübingen 2001, 259–284.
SCHALLMAYER et al. 1990 = E. SCHALLMAYER et al. (Hg.), Der römische Weihebezirk von Osterburken. 1, Corpus der griechischen und lateinischen Beneficiarier-Inschriften des Römischen Reiches, Stuttgart 1990.
SCHEID 1999 = J. SCHEID, Aspects religieux de la municipalisation. Quelques réflexions générales, in: M. DONDIN PAYRE/M.-TH. RAEPSAET CHARLIER (Hg.), Cités, municipes, colonies. Les processus de municipalisation en Gaule et en Germanie sous le Haut Empire romain, 1999, 381–423.
SCHLEIERMACHER 1933 = W. SCHLEIERMACHER, Studien an Göttertypen der römischen Rheinprovinzen, *Bericht der Römisch-Germanischen Kommission* 23, 1933, 109–143.
SIMEK 2006 = R. SIMEK, Lexikon der germanischen Mythologie, Stuttgart 2006[3].
SPEIDEL 1994 = M.P. SPEIDEL, Die Denkmäler der Kaiserreiter. Equites singulares Augusti, Köln/Bonn 1994.
SPICKERMANN 1989/90 = W. SPICKERMANN, Eine Weihung an Mars Loucetius aus Groß-Gerau, *Mainzer Zeitschrift* 84/85, 1989/1990, 205–208.
SPICKERMANN 1994 = W. SPICKERMANN, Mulieres ex voto. Untersuchungen zur Götterverehrung von Frauen im römischen Gallien, Germanien und Rätien, 1.–3. Jahrundert n. Chr., Bochum 1994.
SPICKERMANN 2001 = W. SPICKERMANN, Die germanischen Provinzen als Feld religionshistorischer Untersuchungen, in: W. SPICKERMANN/H. CANCIK/J. RÜPKE (Hg.), Religion in den germanischen Provinzen Roms, Tübingen 2001, 3–48.
SPICKERMANN 2003 = W. SPICKERMANN, Germania Superior. Religionsgeschichte des römischen Germanien 1, Tübingen 2003.

SPICKERMANN 2007a = W. SPICKERMANN, Gallo-römische Götterpaare in Germanien, in: M. HAINZMANN (Hg.), Auf den Spuren keltischer Götterverehrung. Akten des 5. F.E.R.C.AN.-Workshop, Graz 9.–12. Oktober 2003, Wien 2007, 243–252.

SPICKERMANN 2007b = W. SPICKERMANN, The Sunuci and their Sanctuary at Varnenum (Aachen-Kornelimünster), in: R. HAEUSSLER/A.C KING/P. ANDREWS (Hg.), Continuity and Innovation in Religion in the Roman West, Portsmouth RI 2007, 70–79.

SPICKERMANN 2008 = W. SPICKERMANN, Germania Inferior, Tübingen 2008.

SPICKERMANN 2009 = W. SPICKERMANN, Matronen und Nehalennia. Die Verbreitung von mütterlichen Gottheiten in der Germania Inferior, in: E. OLSHAUSEN/V. SAUER (Hg.), Die Landschaft und die Religion. Stuttgarter Kolloquium zur Historischen Geographie des Altertums 9, 2005, Stuttgart 2009, 353–373.

SPICKERMANN 2013 = W. SPICKERMANN (Hg), Keltische Götternamen als individuelle Option? Celtic Theonyms as an Individual Option? Akten des 11. Internationalen Workshops "Fontes Epigraphici Religionum Celticarum Antiquarum" vom 19.–21. Mai 2011 an der Universität Erfurt, Rahden 2013.

SPICKERMANN 2014 = W. SPICKERMANN, Neue epigraphische Zeugnisse gallo-römischer Götternamen aus den beiden Germanien, in: P. DE BERNARDO STEMPEL/M. HAINZMANN (Hg.), Graekorömische und keltorömische Theonymik und Religion. XII. Workshop F.E.R.C.AN (Berlin 29. 8.2012), Wien 2014, 149–166.

SPICKERMANN 2016 = W. SPICKERMANN, Regionale Zentren und "Stammes"heiligtümer in Nordgallien und Germanien, in: M. LEHNER/B. SCHRETTLE (Hg.), Tempelberg und Zentralort? Siedlungs- und Kultentwicklung am Frauenberg bei Leibnitz im Vergleich. Akten des Kolloquiums vom 4.–5. Mai 2015 im Schloss Seggauberg/Steiermark, Wien 2016, 197–209.

SPICKERMANN/DE BERNARDO STEMPEL 2005 = W. SPICKERMANN/P. DE BERNARDO STEMPEL, Keltische Götter in der Germania Inferior? Mit einem sprachwissenschaftlichen Kommentar von Patrizia de Bernardo Stempel, in: W. SPICKERMANN/R. WIEGELS (Hg.), Keltische Götter im Römischen Reich. Akten des 4. Internationalen Workshops "Fontes Epigraphici Religionis Celticae Antiquae" (F.E.R.C.AN.) vom 4.–6. 10. 2002 an der Universität Osnabrück, Möhnesee 2005, 125–148.

SPICKERMANN/STEENKEN 2003 = W. SPICKERMANN/H.H. STEENKEN, Römische Religion, Reallexikon für Germanische Altertumskunde 25, 2003, 111–127.

STOLTE 1986 = B.H. STOLTE, Die religiösen Verhältnisse in Niedergermanien, ANRW II 18.2, 1986, 591–671.

TOORIANS 2003 = L. TOORIANS, Magusanus and the 'Old Lad': a Case of Germanicised Celtic, *North-Western European Language Evolution: NOWELE* 42, 2003, 13–28.

VAN ANDRINGA 2002 = W. VAN ANDRINGA, La religion en Gaule romaine. Piete et politique, 1.–3. siecle apr. J. C., Paris 2002.

VAN ENCKEVORT/THIJSSEN/MOLS 2005 = H. VAN ENCKEVORT/J. THIJSSEN/R. MOLS, In de schaduw van het noorderlicht. De Gallo-Romeinse tempel van Elst-Westeraam, Abcoude 2005.

WAGNER 1977 = N. WAGNER, Hercules Magusanus, *Bonner Jahrbücher* 177, 1977, 417–422.

WALSER 1979–1980 = G. WALSER, Römische Inschriften in der Schweiz. Für den Schulunterricht ausgewählt, photographiert und erklärt, Bern 1979–1980.

WILMANNS 1981 = J. WILMANNS, Die Doppelurkunde von Rottweil und ihr Beitrag zum Städtewesen in Obergermanien, *Epigraphische Studien* 12, 1979–1980, 1–189.

WOLFF 1976 = H. WOLFF, Kriterien für latinische und römische Städte in Gallien und Germanien und die ‚Verfassung' der gallischen Stammesgemeinden, *Bonner Jahrbücher* 176, 1976, 45–121.

Amina Kropp
Schriftlichkeit in der Schadenzauberpraxis am Beispiel der vulgärlateinischen *defixionum tabellae*

Abstract: As primary sources, the *defixionum tabellae* or curse tablets provide us with valuable evidence allowing the study of ancient literacy. Actually, incantations and other verbal and nonverbal elements are written on small pieces of metal (usually thin sheets of lead), that serve as objects in several ritual operations such as manipulation and deposition. In this particular context, the written formulas can be directed at supernatural forces; at the same time, the physical act of engraving on the tablet constitutes an important ritual operation that stands for the curse's consequences on the victim. Thus, writing does not only involve medial and communicative aspects, but, due to the particular semantics of the ritual operations, also fulfils metaphorical functions.

Zusammenfassung: Als Primärquellen eines spätantiken Schadenzaubers können die sogenannten *defixionum tabellae* oder Fluchtafeln wertvolle Auskunft über eine besondere Form der Schriftlichkeit geben: Im Rahmen eines Rituals werden diese primär aus Blei gefertigten Täfelchen beschriftet, manipuliert und an magischen Orten abgelegt. Dabei können die Täfelchen mit briefartigen Texten an ritualspezifische Gottheiten versehen sein; zugleich stellt die Gravierung der Schreibunterlage eine zentrale rituelle Operation dar, die auf die dem Opfer zugedachten Folgen verweist. Vor diesem Hintergrund kann vermutet werden, dass Schriftlichkeit im Rahmen des *defixio*-Rituals nicht nur medial-kommunikative, sondern auch metaphorische Funktion besitzen kann.

1 Einleitung

Schrift und Verschriftung bilden ein Kernelement zahlreicher magischer Praktiken. Dies lässt sich auch für die (spät)antiken Fluchtafeln bzw. *defixiones* oder *defixionum tabellae* annehmen. Hierbei handelt es sich um primär aus Blei gefertigte Täfelchen, die im Rahmen eines antiken Schadenzauberrituals mit einzelnen Wörtern oder auch längeren Zaubertexten beschriftet, durchbohrt (oder auf andere Weise manipuliert) und an magischen Orten abgelegt wurden. Die Ritualhandlungen können dabei sowohl manuell als auch mittels „performativer" Zauberformeln (z. B. *defigo* oder *describo*) vollzogen werden, die wiederum gesprochen und/oder in die Schreibunterlage graviert werden. Ebenso können die Täfelchen mit briefartigen Texten an ritualspezifische Gottheiten versehen sein, die mit der Realisierung des Schadenzaubers beauftragt werden. Im Rahmen des *defixio*-Rituals fungiert die beschriebene Bleilamelle folglich nicht nur als Ritualobjekt, sondern zugleich auch als Kommunikationsmittel. Diese doppelte Funktion des Schrift- und Textträgers legt nahe, dass Schriftlichkeit im Rahmen des *defixio*-Rituals sich nicht auf medial-kommunikative Aspekte beschränkt, sondern weitergehende „magische" Funktionen besitzen kann, die in einem engen Zusammenhang mit der Semantik der Ritualhandlungen zu sehen sind.

Vor diesem Hintergrund sollen im vorliegenden Beitrag die unterschiedlichen Dimensionen von Schriftmagie anhand der lateinischen *defixionum tabellae* ausgeleuchtet werden. Im Fokus steht dabei nicht nur das Medium Schrift, sondern auch der Vorgang der Verschriftung als zentraler ritueller Operation. Untersuchungsleitend sollen dabei folgende Fragen sein: Welche Rolle spielen sowohl die Schriftform als auch die Verschriftung für die Ritualform *defixio*? Welche Auswirkungen auf das Zauberformular lassen sich dabei beobachten? Welche medialen und kommunikativen Möglichkeiten eröffnet die Schriftform im Umgang mit (katachthonischen) Gottheiten, welche die Mündlichkeit nicht bereithält? Welche Funktionen kommen ihr darüber hinaus im Rahmen eines Schadenzauberrituals zu? Ein besonderes Augenmerk soll dabei zum einen auf die Merkmale schriftlich vermittelter Kommunikation gelegt werden; zum anderen soll der rituelle Verschriftungsvorgang zu Struktur und Semantik der Ritualhandlungen in Bezug gesetzt werden.

2 Die *defixio* – eine Gegenstandssicherung

2.1 Die Inschriftengattung

Als Primärzeugnisse eines (spät)antiken Zwang- und Schadenzauberrituals gehören die sogenannten Fluchtafeln (*defixionum tabellae* oder *defixiones*) zur Gattung der Kleinstinschriften, deren Fundorte sich über die gesamte damalige Welt – von Griechenland bis nach Spanien, von Ägypten bis nach Britannien – erstrecken. Den Ausgangs- und Schwerpunkt bildet der griechische Sprach- und Kulturraum, weswegen die *defixio* in der Forschungsliteratur auch als „uniquely Greek form of cursing"[1] bezeichnet wird; dies zeigt sich nicht zuletzt daran, dass von den über 1.600 bekannten Täfelchen etwa 1.100 in griechischer Sprache abgefasst sind. Der früheste Fundkomplex stammt aus Selinunt (5. Jh. v. Chr.),[2] die erste lateinische *defixio* aus Pompeji (2. Jh. v. Chr.).[3] Ihren Höhepunkt erreicht die magische Praxis im Römischen Reich vom 2. bis zum 4. Jh. n. Chr., danach setzt der Siegeszug des Christentums ihr allmählich ein Ende.[4] Ein Zentrum bleiben in dieser Zeit die Tempelkomplexe von Bath und

---

1 FARAONE 1991, 3.
2 Vgl. LÓPEZ JIMENO 1991.
3 dfx 1.5.4/1. Das Kürzel dfx bezieht sich auf die elektronische Datenbank in KROPP 2008, die insgesamt 537 *defixiones* umfasst; hier finden sich auch die zugehörigen bibliographischen Angaben.
4 Allerdings lassen verschärfte Magiegesetze in den christlichen Gesetzeswerken (z. B. Cod. Theod.

Uley, daneben finden sich noch Häufungen in anderen Randgebieten des Imperiums. Die spätesten in das 4./5. Jh. n. Chr. datierten Inschriften stammen aus den nördlichen gallischen Provinzen, vornehmlich aus dem Amphitheater des antiken Trier.

Entsprechend der *editio princeps* von A. AUDOLLENT 1904 lassen sich die lateinischen *defixiones* nach dem Verwünschungsgrund in vier Gruppen einteilen:[5] (1) Prozess-*defixiones* zur Beeinflussung eines Gerichtsverfahrens zugunsten des *defigens*; (2) agonistische *defixiones* zur Ausschaltung eines Widersachers in Konkurrenzsituationen, insbesondere unter Gladiatoren und Wagenlenkern, weitaus seltener aus wirtschaftlichen und amourösen Gründen; (3) erotische Herbeiführungs-*defixiones* zur Eroberung einer Person; (4) die sogenannten „Gebete für Gerechtigkeit" (engl. *prayers for justice*),[6] eine Sonderform, in der Sühne oder Strafe für ein erlittenes Unrecht verlangt wird.

2.2 Die *defixio* in den Ritualpräskripten

> Defixiones, more commonly known as curse tablets, are inscribed pieces of lead, usually in the form of small, thin sheets, intended to influence, by supernatural means, the actions or the welfare of persons or animals against their will.[7]

Defixiones sind jedoch weitaus mehr als „beschriebene Bleilamellen", kann man doch davon ausgehen, dass die Tafeln das greifbare Resultat eines rituellen Handlungskomplexes darstellen, für dessen Ausführung genaue Anleitungen existiert haben. Hierzu zählen etwa die *Papyri Graecae Magicae*, eine umfangreiche Sammlung magischer Rezepte aus dem kaiserzeitlichen Ägypten des 2. bis 4. nachchristlichen Jahrhunderts. Zubereitung und Ausführung einer *defixio* kann etwa nachfolgendes Ritualpräskript aus Pap.Graec.Mag. 5,304–369 veranschaulichen.

> Nimm [...] ein Bleitäfelchen und einen eisernen Ring [...] schreibe den Namen, die Zauberzeichen [...] und [folgendes]: ‚Gebunden sei seine Vernunft, auf daß er nicht ausführen könne das und das' [...]. Stich ein an den Zauberzeichen mit dem Schreibrohr und vollziehe die Bindung mit den Worten: ‚Ich binde den XY zu dem betr. Zweck: er soll nicht reden, nicht widerstehen, nicht widersprechen, er soll mir nicht entgegenblicken oder entgegenreden können, sondern soll mir unterworfen sein, solange dieser Ring vergraben liegt. Ich binde seinen Sinn und sein Denken, seinen Geist, seine Handlungen, auf daß er unfähig sei gegen jedermann.' Wenn du aber ein Weib bannst, sag auch: ‚Auf daß nicht heirate den XY die XY'. Dann trag [das Bleitäfelchen] weg ans Grab eines vorzeitig Verstorbenen, grab 4 Finger tief, leg es hinein und sprich: ‚Totendämon, wer

---

9,16 und Cod. Iust. 9,18) auch in dieser Zeit auf hohe Vitalität und Verbreitung des Schadenzaubers schließen.
5 Vgl. AUDOLLENT 1904, LXXXVIII: „quattuor defigendi causae". Vgl. hierzu auch FARAONE 1991, 10 f., OGDEN 1999, 31–44.
6 Der Terminus 'prayer for justice' stammt von VERSNEL 1987 und VERSNEL 1991.
7 JORDAN 1985, 151.

du auch bist, ich übergebe dir den XY, auf daß er nicht ausführe das und das.' Dann schütt es zu und geh weg. Am besten agierst du bei abnehmendem Mond [...]. Der Ring kann auch in einen unbenutzten Brunnen gelegt werden oder ins Grab eines vorzeitig Verstorbenen [...].

Genannt sind zunächst die zur Herstellung der Fluchtafel benötigten Ingredienzien. Hierzu zählen einerseits die physischen Schreibutensilien, ein Bleitäfelchen[8] und ein Schreibrohr; andererseits, gewissermaßen als Mustertext, die auf der Schreibunterlage anzubringenden Formeln und Zauberzeichen, denen der Name des Opfers vorangestellt werden muss. Das zentrale Objekt des Rituals bildet somit das bleiernes Täfelchen, das sukzessive mit dem Schreibrohr beschriftet und durchbohrt und anschließend zu nächtlicher Stunde in einem Grab abgelegt werden soll; präzisiert sind dabei auch die Beschaffenheit des Ablageortes sowie Modalität und Zeitpunkt der Deposition. Begleitet werden Manipulation und Ablage überdies durch die Rezitation einer längeren Zauberformel, deren genauer Wortlaut ebenfalls aus dem Rezept zu übernehmen ist. Aufgeführt sind folglich verbale wie non-verbale Ritualelemente und -handlungen, die ihren festen Platz im Ritualablauf haben. Nicht zuletzt finden sich Angaben zu Zweck und Wirkpotential des Rituals. Die Verortung am Rande der sozialen Topographie wie auch die zeitlichen Situierung des Ritualvollzugs legen dabei nahe, dass die *defixio*, im Gegensatz anderen antiken Ritualen, nicht kollektiv vollzogen wird, sondern unter Ausschluss der Öffentlichkeit stattfindet. Als besondere Form des Schadenzaubers, die aus egoistischen Motiven den Einzelnen wie das Kollektiv bedroht, steht die *defixio* zudem außerhalb der Legalität.[9] Zubereitung und Ausführung spielen sich folglich als privat, isoliert und höchstwahrscheinlich heimlich ausgeführtes magisches Ich-Ritual ab.[10]

3 Die rituellen Rahmenbedingungen des Schriftgebrauchs

3.1 Das kommunikative Setting: Achsen der Kommunikation und Mehrfachadressierung

Im Rahmen des *defixio*-Rituals bilden geschriebene und gesprochene Zauberformeln einen konstituierenden Teil des Handlungsablaufs. Dabei zielen diese Texte jedoch nicht primär auf die Rezeption durch menschliche Kommunikationspartner. Ausgeschlossen ist neben anderen Ritualteilnehmern auch das Verwünschungsopfer, nicht

---

8 In zahlreichen Ritualpräskripten heißt es z. B. „nimm eine Bleitafel", so etwa in Pap.Graec.Mag. 4,228 f.; 34,231; 58,5.
9 Schadenzauber wird bereits nach altem römischem Recht als Straftat eingestuft, vgl. etwa die zwei Fragmente des Zwölftafelgesetzes Lex XII tab. 8,8a *(qui fruges excantassit)*, 8,8b *(neve alienam segetem pelleris)*.
10 Vgl. z. B. die Definition magischer Rituale von MAUSS/HUBERT 1966, 16 als „*tout rite qui ne fait pas partie d'un culte organisé*, rite privé, secret, mystérieux et tendant comme limite vers le rite prohibé."

zuletzt um das Risiko eines Gegenzaubers zu minimieren.[11] Hierfür spricht auch die fehlende Adressierung in den *defixiones* ebenso wie die Anweisungen der Zauberpapyri, die nur in seltenen Fällen den Kontakt mit der Zielperson vorsehen.[12] Im Gegenzug ist eine Kontaktaufnahme mit übernatürlichen Mächten intendiert, was etwa die Anrufung des „Totendämons" in besagtem Papyrus zeigen kann. Dies gilt auch für den im Zauberrezept genannten Ablageort, der eine Verbindung zu unterirdischen Mächten eröffnen soll: Neben Gräbern und Totenstätten, denen *per se* unheilvolle Macht zugeschrieben wird, sind dies auch Brunnenschächte und andere möglichst wasserführende Stellen.[13] Das *defixio*-Ritual kann folglich einen Kommunikationsraum mit numinosen Mächten eröffnen.

Dementsprechend stellt F. GRAF fest: „In der rituellen Kommunikation lassen sich zwei Achsen unterscheiden — die horizontale, welche die agierenden und empfangenden Menschen, und die vertikale, welche die Menschen mit den Göttern als Adressaten des Rituals verbindet."[14] Magische Praktiken, die auf die private Initiative des rituell agierenden Laien zurückgehen, sind demzufolge auf vertikaler Ebene angesiedelt. Entsprechendes ist etwa auch einer *defixio* zu entnehmen, in der eine *Dea Ataecina Turibrigensis Proserpina* adressiert wird: 'Göttin Ataecina Turibrigensis Proserpina, bei deiner göttlichen Macht, dich bitte ich, flehe ich an, dass du, was mir an Diebstahl angetan wurde, rächst' (*Dea Ataecina Turibrigensis Proserpina, per tuam maiestatem, te rogo, obsecro, uti vindices quod mihi furti factum est*).[15] In diesem Falle liegt folglich eine Kommunikation auf der vertikalen Achse vor, entlang derer sich die Übermittlung einer Handlungsaufforderung bzw. -anweisung „von unten nach ganz unten"[16] vollziehen kann. Tatsächlich handelt es sich bei den ritualspezifischen Gottheiten der *defixio* überwiegend um katachthonische Götter wie die als 'unterirdisch' (*inferi*) bezeichneten Toten oder auch die Herrscher der Unterwelt *Dis pater* bzw. *Pluto* sowie *Proserpina* bzw. *(A)eracura/Veracura*.[17]

Dieses elementare kommunikative Setting auf der vertikalen Achse kann durch die Beauftragung eines Magiers um eine zusätzliche menschliche Komponente erwei-

---

11 Vgl. hierzu BRODERSEN 2001b, 9; MEYER 2004, 28 f.; 104; RÜPKE 2001b, 171.
12 Vgl. etwa Pap.Graec.Mag. 36,1–3: „Nimm eine bleierne Platte [...] und leg sie nieder in der Nähe, gegenüber (vom NN)." Bisweilen ist im Rahmen des Liebeszaubers die Verbindung zum Opfer vorgeschrieben, z. B. in Pap.Graec.Mag. 13,240 f. durch Berührung des Hauseingangs.
13 Auch das Rezept eines anderen „Bannmittels" (Pap.Graec.Mag. 7,450 f.) schreibt die Ablage „im Brunnen, in der Erde, im Meer, in der Wasserleitung, in einem Sarg oder Brunnen [...]" vor; als Depositionsort genannt ist z. B. auch die „Fußbodenheizung eines Bades" (Pap.Graec.Mag. 7,469). Zu den Totenstätten vgl. z. B. GORDON 1999a, 210; OGDEN 1999, 16, 22.
14 GRAF 1996, 191. Hierzu auch RÜPKE 2001a, 27–29.
15 dfx 2.3.1/1 (Mérida; undatiert).
16 BRODERSEN 2001a, 68.
17 Große römische Götter sind nahezu ausnahmslos auf die Sonderform der Gebete für Gerechtigkeit aus Britannien beschränkt, v. a. *Mercurius* (Schwerpunkt Uley) und die Quellgottheit *Sulis* bzw. *Minerva* (Schwerpunkt Bath); vgl. hierzu WOODWARD/LEACH 1993; TOMLIN 1988.

tert sein. Dabei kann der Auftraggeber auch als passiv-beobachtender Teilnehmer in die professionell vollzogene Ritualhandlung eingebunden und folglich als indirekter Adressat wahrgenommen werden.[18] In dieser Konstellation ist der Ritualvollzug durch den Experten nicht allein an den numinosen Kommunikationspartner gerichtet, vielmehr sind seine verbalen und non-verbalen Handlungen multifunktional: Durch seine Anwesenheit erfährt der Laie unmittelbar von den besonderen Fähigkeiten und Kenntnissen des Spezialisten und schafft zugleich die Kulisse für dessen Selbstdarstellung. Die Exklusivität des magischen Wissensfundus, die sich besonders in der Ausführung komplexer Rituale zeigt, erhöht dabei das Prestige des rituell Agierenden in den Augen des Zuschauers. Derartige mehrfach adressierte kommunikative Vorgänge bestätigen insbesondere Stellung und Autorität des Eingeweihten gegenüber dem Nichteingeweihten und dienen letztlich der sozialen Rollen- und Identitätssicherung. Ausschlaggebend für die Beauftragung einer weiteren Person ist nicht zuletzt die Verschriftung der Verwünschungstexte. Gerade bei ausführlichen Ritualpräskripten, die neben komplexen Handlungsschritten auch elaborierte Textvorlagen umfassen können, zählen Lese- und Schreibfähigkeit zu den notwendigen Kenntnissen des magischen Fachpersonals (s. u. Abschn. 4.2).

3.2 Struktur und Semantik Ritualhandlung

Wie bereits gesagt, stellen Beschriftung, Manipulation und Niederlegung der Tafel feste rituelle Handlungseinheiten dar. Im Sinne einer „persuasiven Analogie"[19] weisen dabei sämtliche an der Tafel ausgeführten manuellen Ritualhandlungen eine besondere Semantik auf, stehen sie doch metaphorisch für die dem Opfer zugedachten Folgen: So wird ein Bezug zwischen der konkreten Manipulation und der gewünschten Einwirkung auf das abwesende Opfer aktualisiert; als Ritualobjekt wird die Bleitafel zugleich semantisch aufgeladen und somit zum Zeichen für das Opfer.[20]

Vollzogen werden die Ritualhandlungen aber nicht nur unmittelbar am Textträger, sondern auch durch die Zaubertexte selbst. Hierbei handelt es sich um sogenannte explizit performative „Manipulationsformeln",[21] wie etwa das „ich binde den XY [...]" aus o.g. Zauberpapyrus. Die Manipulation der Schreibunterlage kann folglich mit wiederkehrenden Textelementen korrespondieren, wodurch die manuell vollzo-

---

18 Vgl. z. B. GRAF 1997, 126 f.; 131 f. Zu den mehrfach adressierten Sprechhandlungen vgl. z. B. KÜHN 1995.
19 TAMBIAH 1978, bes. 265–294. Im Gegensatz zur empirischen Analogie zielt die „persuasive Analogie" nicht auf die Vorhersage erklärungsbedürftiger oder zukünftiger Gegebenheiten ab, sondern auf die Beeinflussung zukünftiger Ereignisse. Hierzu auch KROPP 2008, 175 f.
20 Ganz deutlich zeigt sich dies in den unbeschrifteten, aber manipulierten Täfelchen, wie sie etwa in einem Brunnen in der Nähe des gallischen *Rauranum* (Rom) gefunden wurden (DT 109).
21 Zum Handlungsgehalt der Formeln auf den *defixionum tabellae* vgl. auch KROPP 2008, 144–179.

gene Handlung auf Sprachebene transponiert wird. Die gewünschten Auswirkungen auf das Zielindividuum können ferner auch explizit zu einem geeigneten Moment des Ritualvollzugs in Bezug gesetzt werden; dies geschieht üblicherweise durch Vergleiche innerhalb eines Wunschsatzes: 'Wie dieses Blei nicht auftaucht und untergeht, so soll untergehen seine Jugend, seine Gliedmaßen, sein Leben [...]' (*Quomodo hoc plumbum non paret et decidit, sic decidat aetas, membra, vita [...]*).[22] Durch die Evozierung der Ritualhandlung tritt der „performative" Aspekt der Formeln in den Vordergrund. Dies trifft insbesondere auf die lateinischen *defixiones* zu, wohingegen bei zahlreichen griechischen *defixiones* die Analogie weniger auf den rituellen Operationen basiert als vielmehr auf dem Ritualobjekt Bleitafel und ihren als negativ wahrgenommenen materialimmanenten Eigenschaften, die auf das Opfer übergehen sollen.[23] Nicht zuletzt kann das *defixio*-Ritual einen Kommunikationsraum mit Göttern und Dämonen eröffnen, die per Fluchtafel mit der Realisierung des Schadenzaubers beauftragt werden (s. o., Abschn. 3.1).

Aufgrund der semantischen Vielschichtigkeit der rituellen Handlungen steht der Schrift- und Textträger für die abwesende Zielperson und kann zugleich als Kommunikationsmittel mit den Gottheiten des Rituals eingesetzt werden. Die *defixiones* bilden folglich Hauptgegenstand und Resultat eines rituellen Handlungskomplexes, bei dem nicht nur der gesprochenen Sprache, sondern auch der Verschriftung unterschiedliche Funktionen zukommen.

4 Schriftlichkeit in den *defixiones*: Befunde

4.1 Schriftformen und -bilder

Entsprechend der Anleitung aus Pap.Graec.Mag. 5,304–369 soll der Zaubertext mit einem Schreibrohr auf einem bleiernen Täfelchen angebracht werden. Aufgrund ihrer weichen und elastischen Beschaffenheit bietet sich für die Gravierung der Schreibunterlage ferner auch ein Nagel oder ein anderer spitzer Alltagsgegenstand an. Entsprechend der einfachen Handhabung und der Verbreitung von Blei als herkömmlichem Schreibstoff handelt es sich bei der Schriftart überwiegend um die sogenannte Kursive, die im Alltag gebräuchliche Schreibschrift; selten finden sich kapitale Lettern.[24] Die ältere römische Kursive oder Majuskelkursive steht der kanonisierten Capitalis noch recht nahe. Vergleichbar mit dem Verhältnis moderner Großdruckbuchstaben zu ihrer schreibschriftlichen Ausführung ergeben sich die auffälligsten Unterschiede durch den schnelleren und flüchtigeren Schreibstil, was besonders anhand der 'diagnosti-

---

22 dfx 4.4.1/1 (Montfo; 1. Jh. n. Chr.).
23 Vgl. hierzu z. B. DTA 106 (Nutzlosigkeit); DTA 107 (Kälte). Hierzu auch GRAF 1996, 187.
24 So z. B. dfx 3.22/18 (Uley; 2.–4. Jh.); dfx 11.1.1/34 (Karthago; undatiert).

schen' Buchstaben *B*, *D* und *R* deutlich sichtbar ist.[25] Wie Abb. 1 zeigen kann, ist für die kursiven Buchstabenformen eine große interindividuelle Variationsbreite gegeben.[26] Gerade bei größeren Depositionsorten, wie z.B. dem *Mater-Magna*-Heiligtum in Mainz, verblüfft die große Schriftenvielfalt;[27] gelegentlich weist ein einzelnes Täfelchen auch unterschiedliche Schriften auf.[28] Dabei gibt die individuelle Ausführung der Buchstaben auch Hinweise auf den Schreiber: So lässt ein ungelenker Schriftduktus eine mangelnde Schreibvertrautheit vermuten, während eine geübte oder eine auf unterschiedlichen Tafeln wiederkehrende Handschrift die Mitwirkung eines professionellen Schreibers nahelegt. Häufig korreliert ein gepflegtes Schriftbild mit einer aufwändigen Ausgestaltung der Tafel, was ebenfalls für eine professionelle Anfertigung der Zauberinschrift spricht. Da die Verschriftung überdies einen zentralen rituellen Vorgang darstellt, kann dem Schriftbild auch magische Bedeutung zukommen: Keine Seltenheit sind z.B. retrograde Schriftverläufe oder ungewöhnliche Buchstabenanordnungen, die auf Verschlüsselung und Verfremdung abzielen (s.u., Abschn. 5.5.1).

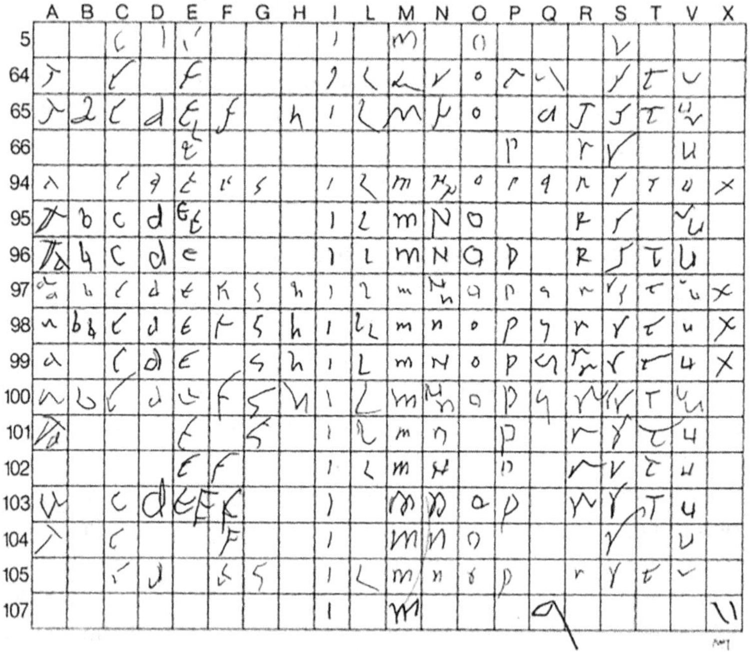

Abb. 1: Alphabet-Tabelle mit jüngerer römischer Kursive, Bath (TOMLIN 2004, Anhang, Abb. 3)

---

25 Zur besonderen Entwicklungslinie der Schrift auf den Bleilamellen vgl. z.B. BARTOLETTI 1990.
26 Verschiedene Einzelpublikationen bieten Tabellen und Listen als Hilfe bei Auswertung und Lesung der Texte. Verwiesen sei insbesondere auf TOMLIN 2004.
27 Vgl. BLÄNSDORF 2012, 26.
28 So z.B. dfx 11.1.1/28 (Karthago; 2. Jh.), das griechisch-lateinisch abgefasst ist.

4.2 Schreibpraxis: abschreiben und schreiben lassen

Wie Pap.Graec.Mag. 5,304–369 verdeutlicht, beschreiben die magischen Anleitungen nicht nur Schritt für Schritt die Ausführung komplexer Zauberhandlungen, sondern fungieren zugleich auch als Kopiervorlagen. Diese Mustertexte, die neben festen Texteinheiten auch Platzhalter umfassen, können dabei an die jeweiligen Bedürfnisse angepasst werden. Entsprechend verweist besagtes Ritualpräskript auf die Veränderbarkeit des Zauberspruches je nach individuellem Bedarf: „Wenn du aber ein Weib bannst, sag auch: 'Auf daß nicht heirate den XY die XY'." Tatsächlich weist eine Vielzahl aggressiv-magischer Rituale ein breites Anwendungsspektrum auf, was in den Rezepten auch explizit hervorgehoben sein kann. So muss der Anwender eines 'Herbeiführungszaubers' „[j]e nach dem Zweck [s]eines Zauberns [...] nur die Formulierung [s]einer Wünsche ändern".[29]

In diesem Kontext kann die Schriftform das Handlungsspektrum des rituell Agierenden über die Optionen der Mündlichkeit hinaus erheblich erweitern: So eröffnen Rezeptarien auch dem wenig oder gar nicht Schreibkundigen die Möglichkeit, Formeln, Zauberzeichen und Bilder aus der Kopiervorlage zu übernehmen und ein magisches Schriftstück abzufassen. Darüber hinaus ist der Schreibvorgang an einen professionellen Schreiber bzw. Magier delegierbar, wenn die Anforderungen des Ritualpräskripts die Kompetenzen des *defigens* übersteigen (s. o. Abschn. 3.1). Hiervon zeugen insbesondere die in Serien vorkommenden Täfelchen aus der antiken nordafrikanischen Stadt *Hadrumetum* (Sousse), die einer „spezialisierten Werkstatt"[30] entstammen. So kann die Zaubertafel als vorgestalteter Lückentext nahezu gebrauchsfertig erworben werden. Die Verwendung partiell fertiggeschriebener Inschriften zeigt sich etwa in mischsprachigen (lateinisch-griechischen) *defixiones* anhand ungrammatischer Übergänge an den jeweiligen sprachlichen Schnittstellen, was nicht zuletzt auch die mangelhaften Sprachkenntnisse des Schreibenden dokumentiert.[31]

Gerade für die Erstellung umfangreicher oder komplizierter Texte kann auf magische Kopiervorlagen zurückgegriffen werden. Hierauf lassen wiederkehrende Formelelemente sowie typische Abschreibfehler, wie das Überspringen von Zeilen, und

---

29 Pap.Graec.Mag. 4,2079 f. Dass gegebenenfalls auch das non-verbale Ritual an die individuellen Bedürfnisse anzupassen ist, zeigt das Beispiel des vielseitig einsetzbaren „Homerischen Dreizeilers" (Pap.Graec.Mag. 4,2145–2240): „Für eine Offenbarung: schreib auf ein Lorbeerblatt [...]. Um Rennwagen zu stürzen, räuchere [...] Knoblauch [...]. Für Bannungen schreib auf eine Meermuschel [...]. Um Gunst zu erwerben [...]: schreib auf ein Goldtäfelchen [...]. Bei herbeizwingenden Liebeszaubereien: räuchere Rose und Sumach [...]" (2205–2232).
30 dfx 11.2.2/1: *ex officina magica* 'aus einer Zauberwerkstatt'. Aus einer seriellen Produktion stammen auch die fünf sogenannten „Johns Hopkins Tabellae Defixionum" (dfx 1.4.4/8–12: Rom; 1. Jh. v. Chr.).
31 z. B. dfx 11.1.1/28 (Karthago; 2./3. Jh. n. Chr.): Hier findet sich als erster Bestandteil einer frei formulierbaren lateinischen Textpassage der Namen des Opfers in einem bezugslosen Nominativ: Z. 49: [τὴν] ψυχὴν τοῦ *Vincentζus*. Vgl. hierzu KROPP 2017.

nachträgliche Korrekturen schließen.³² Ferner dokumentiert sich die Nutzung von Vorbildern auch durch die fälschliche Übernahme der Anleitung. So findet sich auf einem Täfelchen aus dem Quellheiligtum von *Aquae Sulis* (Bath) etwa die Wendung 'das beschriebene Blatt ist abgeschrieben worden' (*charta picta perscripta*),³³ die keinen Bezug zum Inhalt der Verwünschung aufweist, sondern einen Bestandteil des Zauberrezeptes darstellt. In einer *defixio* aus Trier dokumentiert sich der unbeholfene Umgang mit den Ritualpräskripten durch die Übernahme des unveränderten Mustertextes: Im Rahmen der Anrufung wurde der Name der betreffenden Gottheit nicht eingefügt, sondern statt dessen der Platzhalter *nomen* 'Name' von der Vorlage abgeschrieben: 'Gute, heilige NAME, fromme NAME [...]' (*Bona sancta NOMEN pia NOMEN [...]*).³⁴ Diese Lapsus zeugen jedoch nicht nur von fehlerhaften und folglich mehr oder weniger professionellen Kopiervorgängen, sondern lassen auch einen weit verbreiteten Gebrauch von Anleitungen und Formularien vermuten.³⁵

Vor diesem Hintergrund ist die tatsächliche (schrift)sprachliche Kompetenz des Schreibenden kaum einzuschätzen, da er sich an magischen Vorlagen orientieren und die entsprechenden Zaubersprüche gegebenenfalls abschreiben kann. Während Textmängel wie grammatische und inhaltliche Inkongruenzen etc. Hinweise auf unzureichende Sprachkenntnisse geben können, zeigen sprechsprachliche Phänomene eher die Vertrautheit mit der verwendeten Sprache an. Zudem ist zu berücksichtigen, dass durch den mechanischen Kopiervorgang etwa auch Sprachwandel- und Sprachkontaktphänomene aus einem anderen Kontext in die jeweiligen Texte importiert und darin konserviert werden können. Naturgemäß können gesicherte Aussagen zur Verbreitung von Lese- und Schreibkenntnissen in der Antike ohnehin nur schwer getroffen werden, der Alphabetisierungsgrad der römischen Gesellschaft ist aber gerade in der jüngeren Forschungsliteratur zu gering eingeschätzt worden.³⁶

---

32 Vgl. z. B. Gager 1996, 50, Nr. 3; Jordan 2000, 25, Nr. 92 („Evidence of use of formulary"); Nr. 93 („follow formula at PGM IV 336–406").
33 dfx 3.2/8 (Bath; 3. Jh. n. Chr.?). Zu dieser Formel vgl. auch Tomlin 1988, 119.
34 dfx 4.1.3/15 (Trier; 4./5. Jh. n. Chr.?).
35 Vgl. z. B. Graf 1996, 11: „Sie [d. h. die Zaubertexte u. ä.] waren nicht eigentlich geheim – jedenfalls wußte man in der antiken Gesellschaft von ihrer Existenz [...]. " Hierzu auch Kropp 2008, 55–57.
36 Eine minimalistische Position vertritt Harris 1983; Harris 1989. Komplementierend vgl. auch Beard 1991; Ingemark 2000–2001, der für Britannien v. a. auf die *defixiones* aus Bath und Uley eingeht.

5 Die Funktionen von Schrift und Verschriftung im Rahmen des *defixio*-Rituals

5.1 medial-kommunikative und metaphorische Funktionen

Wie o. g. Ritualpräskript zeigt, bildet der Schreibvorgang den Ausgangspunkt des Rituals, wofür präzise Anweisungen gegeben werden: Aufgeführt sind die benötigten Schreibutensilien ebenso wie die zu verschriftenden Bestandteile des Zaubertextes, der neben dem Namen des Opfers Zauberzeichen und -formeln umfasst. An die Gravierung der Schreibunterlage schließt sich ihre Durchbohrung an, die ebenfalls mit dem Schreibrohr vollzogen werden soll. In beide rituelle Operationen werden dieselben Gegenstände einbezogen, Verschriftung und Manipulation sind folglich als miteinander korrespondierende Ritualhandlungen zu verstehen. Diese Parallelität weist nicht nur die Schreibutensilien als zentrale Ritualelemente aus, sondern hebt auch die besondere Rolle des Schreibvorgangs für die Ritualausführung hervor.

Aus dem besonderen Zusammenspiel von schreibbezogenen Ritualelementen und -handlungen tritt nicht nur die Relevanz des Schreibvorgangs zutage; vielmehr ergibt sich hieraus, dass Schrift und Verschriftung unterschiedliche Funktionen zukommen. So hängen die medial-kommunikativen Dimensionen primär mit der Funktion von Schrift als „einem 'sekundären' Trägermedium"[37] zusammen, deren Produktion technischer Unterstützung, etwa den Einsatz eines Schreibinstruments, bedarf; durch die Verschriftung,[38] d. h. die Kodierung ins graphische Medium, wird Schrift auf einem materiellen Schriftträger angebracht, was wiederum mit der Fixierung von Sprache einhergeht. Gegenüber dem gesprochenen Wort besitzt die graphische Form folglich haptische Materialität und „dauerhafte Wahrnehmbarkeit".[39] Zudem ermöglichen die „zwei Dimensionen des Schriftträgers"[40] eine über die (zeitliche) Linearität der Rede hinausgehende Anordnung des Geschriebenen und die Gestaltung des Schriftträgers durch die Anbringung weiterer visuell-simultan wahrnehmbarer informationstragender Elemente. Geschriebene Texte sind folglich multimodal organisiert, d. h. sie können verschiedene semiotische Ressourcen integrieren, indem sie Inhalte nicht nur im Schriftmodus, sondern z. B. auch über Bilder vermitteln.[41] Dabei kann die Integration auf verschiedenen Wegen erfolgen: Bild und Text können ihre Bedeutungen addieren, sie können aber auch komplementär sein. Anders als gesprochene Sprache

---

37 RAIBLE 2006, 12.
38 Die Begriffsverwendung entspricht OESTERREICHER 1993, der 'Verschriftung' (im Gegensatz zu 'Verschriftlichung') als medial zu verstehenden Prozess fasst.
39 GRUBE/KOGGE 2005, 14. Zum Aspekt der medialen Materialität von Zeichen und Zeichenträgern vgl. auch GENZ/GÉVAUDAN 2016, 62–68.
40 RAIBLE 2006, 15, vgl. 114 f.
41 Vgl. hierzu z. B. HESS-LÜTTICH/SCHMAUKS 2004. Ausführlich hierzu auch KLUG/STÖCKL 2016; STÖCKL 2008.

ist die Verwendung von geschriebener Sprache zudem nicht an eine gemeinsame Äußerungssituation von Sender und Empfänger gebunden, auch der Wahrnehmungsraum muss nicht deckungsgleich sein.[42] Im Hinblick auf ihre kommunikative Funktion ermöglicht die schriftliche Fixierung folglich eine raumzeitliche Trennung von Produktion und Rezeption, die, wie etwa im Falle öffentlich angebrachter Inschriften, mit einer Erweiterung des Kommunikationsradius und der Umgestaltung der „kommunikativen Arrangements"[43] einhergehen kann. Über diese medial-kommunikativen Funktionen hinaus weist der Vorgang der Verschriftung im Rahmen des *defixio*-Rituals, aufgrund der besonderen Semantik der manuellen Ritualhandlungen, auch eine metaphorische Dimension auf (s. o., Abschn. 3.2). Zusammenfassend ließe sich somit sagen, dass die mediale Funktion von Schrift die Verschriftung zu einem Prozess der Mediatisierung macht; überdies verleiht die Metaphorik der rituellen Verschriftung im Gegenzug auch der Schrift metaphorische Funktion.[44]

5.2 Die Zauberinschrift als negatives und positives Kommunikationsmedium

Den unmittelbaren Produktionskontext der Zauberinschriften bildet ein höchstwahrscheinlich heimlich ausgeführtes Ich-Ritual. Anders als öffentliche Inschriften oder literarische Texte sind die *defixiones* folglich nicht für die menschliche Rezeption, Überlieferung oder Überarbeitung gedacht; vielmehr ist der Ausschluss menschlicher Adressaten und damit die negative Kommunikation auf horizontaler Achse bewusst intendiert. Vor diesem Hintergrund bietet die Schriftform dem Ausführenden den erheblichen Vorteil, die Handlung unbemerkt von der Öffentlichkeit und dem Opfer zu vollziehen. Durch die rituelle Deposition soll der verschriftete Text dem Zugriff von menschlicher Seite überdies dauerhaft entzogen bleiben. Dieser Umstand reflektiert sich auch an den besonderen Ablagestellen, die z. T. am Rand der sozialen Topographie verortet sind (s. o. Abschn. 2.2).

Im Gegenzug kann das *defixio*-Ritual dem Ausführenden einen Kommunikationsraum mit numinosen Mächten eröffnen, die mit der Realisierung des Verwünschungsinhaltes beauftragt werden. Die Kommunikationsintention auf der vertikalen Achse wird in den Zaubertexten durch adressatenorientierte Formeln angezeigt. Hierzu zählen etwa explizite Aufforderungen oder Bitten an die Gottheiten des Rituals: 'Ich bitte euch, ihr heiligen Namen, die Menschen sollen fallen und die Pferde zerschmettert werden' (*Precor vos, sancta nomina, cadant homines et equi frangantur*).[45] Dabei können die unterschiedlichen Machtverhältnisse zwischen Mensch und Gottheit zutage treten: Auf Seiten des *defigens* findet sich dabei eine Bandbreite von Einstel-

---

42 Vgl. Dürscheid 2016, 26 f.
43 Grube/Kogge 2005, 14.
44 Allgemein zur magischen Bedeutung der Schrift vgl. z. B. Glück 1987, 203–217, 228.
45 dfx 11.2.1/11 (Sousse; 2./3. Jh. n. Chr.?).

lungen gegenüber der involvierten Gottheit, die von devot-protektiv ('ich erlaube mir, den Genius deiner göttlichen Macht zu bitten')[46] bis hin zu nötigend bzw. drohend ('wenn nicht, steige ich in das Heiligtum des Osiris hinab und löse sein Grab auf')[47] reicht.

5.3 Die *defixiones* als „Unterweltsbriefe"

5.3.1 Der Briefcharakter: außertextuelle und textuelle Indikatoren

Aufgrund der semantischen Vielschichtigkeit der rituellen Handlungen dient der Text- bzw. Schriftträger im Rahmen des *defixio*-Rituals als Medium der „vertikalen" Kommunikation zwischen Mensch und Gottheit. Die Funktion als „Unterweltsbrief"[48] kann sich dabei bereits anhand außertextueller Gegebenheiten wie dem Ablageort, der mit ritualspezifischen Göttern und Dämonen in Verbindung gebracht wird, manifestieren (s. o., Abschn. 3.1).[49] Durch die Kombination von Rezitation und Verschriftung kann der kommunikative Kontakt zudem über zwei mediale Kanäle und folglich auch an zwei Kommunikationspartner erfolgen: an den unmittelbar in der Ritualsituation angerufenen Vermittler und Überbringer sowie an den Adressaten der schriftlichen Botschaft. Ferner kann auch die Außenseite des Textträgers wie eine Briefhülle aufgemacht sein.[50] Auch auf Textebene lassen sich Merkmale nachweisen, die nur im Rahmen schriftlich vermittelter Kommunikation sinnvoll und angemessen sind: Neben magischen Schriftanalogien (s. o., Abschn. 5.5.1) zählen hierzu insbesondere „metasprachliche Determinanten"[51] wie etwa ein textphorisches *infrascriptus* bzw. *suprascriptus* 'unten'- bzw. 'obenstehend',[52] die sich ebenfalls explizit auf die Schriftform beziehen und in ihrer Förmlichkeit zudem eine schrift- bzw. distanzsprachliche Konzeption vermuten lassen.[53] Ebenso finden sich Anreden, die dem Haupttext vorangestellt und funktionell mit einleitenden Briefformeln vergleichbar sind.[54] Hieraus wird nicht zuletzt ersichtlich, dass die Schriftform als elementarer Bestandteil der Ritualpraxis verstanden und bewusst reflektiert wird.

---

46 dfx 3.22/29 (Uley; 2./3. Jh. n. Chr.): *rogaverim genium numinis tui*.
47 dfx 11.2.1/8 (Sousse; 2. Jh. n. Chr.): *si minus, descendo in adytus Osyris et dissolvam* τὴν ταφήν.
48 PREISENDANZ 1972, 7. Ebenso schon WÜNSCH 1898, 71, demzufolge die schriftliche *defixio* regelmäßig die „Form eines Briefes an die Unterweltsgötter" aufweist. Vgl. z. B. auch AUDOLLENT 1904, 150 zu dfx 5.1.4/3 (Kreuznach; 1. Jh. n. Chr.): „pars exterior quasi epistulae inscriptio".
49 Eine briefkastenähnliche Zugangsmöglichkeit sind auch Opferröhrchen, vgl. z. B. CESANO 1910, 1588 f.; OGDEN 1999, 18.
50 Vgl. hierzu z. B. PREISENDANZ 1972, 7; 20.
51 SELIG 1989, 103.
52 So z. B. in dfx 4.3.1/1 (Chagnon; 2. Jh. n. Chr.) und dfx 3.1/1 (Mérida; undatiert).
53 Vgl. hierzu auch DÜRSCHEID 2016, 43–53.
54 So z. B. in dfx 2.2.2/1 (Carmona; 1. Jh. v. Chr.).

5.3.2 Textuelle Merkmale schriftlich vermittelter Kommunikation

Ein Kennzeichen schriftvermittelter Kommunikation ist die raumzeitliche Trennung von Sender und Empfänger. Demzufolge ermöglichen die Unterweltsbriefe eine anonyme und heimliche Kontaktaufnahme, bei der die Aufmerksamkeit der angerufenen Gottheit nicht überstrapaziert oder auf den Ausführenden selbst gelenkt wird. Gerade im rituellen Umgang mit katachthonischen und somit als unheilvoll und schadenbringend eingestuften Mächten bildet die beschriftete Fluchtafel somit das ideale Kommunikationsmedium.[55] Im Gegenzug schließt diese Kommunikationsform, anders als etwa die *face-to-face*-Situation, die Möglichkeit einer zeitnahen Rückfrage der Kommunizierenden aus, durch die fehlende oder ungenaue Informationen ergänzt oder präzisiert werden könnten. Aufgrund des fehlenden gemeinsamen Wahrnehmungsraums sind auch keine nonverbalen (körperassoziierten, z. B. Mimik) bzw. paraverbalen (sprechassoziierten, z. B. Intonation) Kanäle aktivierbar, die eine kommunikative Rückkopplung ermöglichen. Um ein adäquates Textverständnis sicherzustellen verlangt schriftvermittelte Kommunikation vom Textproduzenten folglich, sämtliche Kommunikationsinhalte und -ziele im Vorhinein zu reflektieren und möglichst präzise, vollständig und unmissverständlich zu verbalisieren. Dies gilt umso mehr für die Kommunikation mit unheilvollen numinosen Mächten im Rahmen eines Schadenzauberrituals.

Diese Textkonzeption geht einerseits mit dem Rückgriff auf erprobte Formulare und Ritualtexte einher, die bei Bedarf aus einschlägigen Rezeptbüchern übernommen werden können; andererseits äußert sie sich durch sprachliche Kompensationsstrategien, die für größtmögliche Eindeutigkeit und Vollständigkeit sorgen sollen. Zur Vermeidung von Fehlauslegungen oder Versäumnissen von göttlicher Seite werden etwa längere Aufzählungen eingesetzt, die deswegen auch als typisches 'religiös-magisches' Textmuster gelten.[56] Hierzu zählen insbesondere listenartige Kataloge, etwa in Form sogenannter „Glieder-*defixiones*", d. h. katalogartiger anatomischer Listen, sowie Aufzählungen von Krankheiten und Schmerzen.[57] Für eine eindeutige Identifikation des *defixus* wird regelmäßig der sogenannte *quem-peperit*-Ausdruck, der üblicherweise die matrilineare Filiation angibt, dem Opfernamen nachgestellt.[58] Fehlen Informationen zum Verwünschungsopfer, wie dies oftmals auf die Gebete für Gerech-

---

55 Hierzu z. B. SCHEER 2001, 49, Anm. 88, die Burkerts Meinung aufgreift, der „im Fall der Unterweltsgottheiten das stille Gebet für üblich [hält]", um „die Toten und Rachegötter [...] *nicht* auf sich aufmerksam [zu] machen"; hieraus ergibt sich auch, dass man sich der „Anwesenheit der Götter" (36) nicht sicher sein kann. Zu lautem (religiösem) und leisem (magischem) Beten vgl. z. B. auch FYNTIKOGLOU/VOUTIRAS 2005, 165 f.; SUDHAUS 1906; VAN DER HORST 1994.
56 Vgl. die umfassende Darstellung bei GORDON 1999b.
57 Der Terminus „Glieder-Defixion" stammt von PREISENDANZ 1972, 10. Vgl. hierzu auch VERSNEL 1998.
58 Die Verwendung des Metronyms zeigt einerseits die für magische Praktiken typische Umkehrung bestehender sozialer Normen; andererseits auch ihr Streben nach größtmöglicher Eindeutigkeit. Zur matrilinearen Filiation vgl. bereits WÜNSCH 1898, 64; AUDOLLENT 1904, LI f.; GAGER 1992, 14; GRAF

tigkeit zutrifft, stehen ebenfalls kompensatorische sprachliche Verfahren zur Verfügung: Für eine möglichst umfassende Personenangabe wird vielfach die sogenannte „all-inclusive-formula"[59] verwendet, eine mit 'ob – oder' (meist *si – si*) eingeleitete indirekte Doppelfrage. Die Einsetzung dieser Textteile kann dabei abrupt erfolgen, woran sich auch ihre Formelhaftigkeit erkennen lässt: *Templo Sulis dono, si mulier si baro, si servus si liber, si puer si puella.* 'Dem Tempel der Sulis gebe ich, ob Frau oder Mann, ob Sklave oder Freier, ob Knabe oder Mädchen'.[60] Ebenso kennzeichnend für diese Sonderform der *defixio* ist das vertragstechnische Vokabular, das in Anlehnung an den „Rechtsformalismus"[61] juristischer Dokumente, einer möglichst präzisen und unmissverständlichen Darlegung des Sachverhaltes dient. Dies umfasst den Gebrauch explizierender Formeln wie z. B. des feststehenden Glossarausdrucks 'das heißt' (*id est*) oder auch von metasprachlichen Determinanten wie 'obenstehend' (*suprascriptus*) etc. (s. o., Abschn. 5.3.1). Ebenso werden zeitliche Fristen gesetzt, innerhalb derer Strafe oder Wiedergutmachung erfolgen sollen; besonders prominent ist dabei die 'magische' Zeitspanne von 'neun Tagen' (*dies novem*).[62]

In diesen Unterweltsbriefen reflektiert sich der Götteranthropomorphismus der Antike, der den Göttern die Fähigkeit zuschreibt, nicht nur ein gesprochenes Gebet hören, sondern auch eine geschriebene Aufforderung rezipieren zu können; daneben lassen die wiederkehrenden sprachlichen Kompensationsstrategien auch auf andere göttliche Eigenschaften schließen: Die adressierten Gottheiten „sind nicht allmächtig. Sie sind nicht allwissend. [...] Sie sind nicht omnipräsent";[63] vielmehr bedürfen sie der genauen Anleitung durch den Menschen, um tätig werden zu können. Die zunehmende Bedeutung der sprachlichen Ausformulierung zeigt sich auch in der Dynamik von den frühesten wortkargen *defixiones* hin zu den ausführlichen und mitunter redundanten Unterweltsbriefen, in denen die Auswirkungen der Verwünschung überaus detailliert dargestellt werden. Hieraus erklärt sich nicht zuletzt der Eindruck einer expliziten und nachdrücklichen Grausamkeit, den gerade die kaiserzeitlichen *defixiones*, etwa unter Gladiatoren und Wagenlenkern, vermitteln können.

1996, 116. Eine eingehende Analyse des *quem-peperit*-Ausdrucks und seiner Varianten anhand von dfx 11.3.1/1 (Constantine; 4. Jh. n. Chr.?) bietet JORDAN 1976

59 Der Terminus entstammt TOMLINS Kommentar zu dfx 3.14/5. Ebenso TOMLIN 1988 zu diesen „quasi-legal catch-all formulas" (95) und den „mutually exclusive alternatives" (67).

60 dfx 3.2/36 (Bath; 3./4. Jh. n. Chr.).

61 DULCKEIT/SCHWARZ/WALDSTEIN 1995, 74. Zum Einfluss der Gesetzes- und Gerichtssprache auf die *defixiones* vgl. z. B. ADAMS 1992, 2; 7; 25 f.; MÉNARD 2000; TOMLIN 1988, 70 f.; VERSNEL 1987.

62 z. B. dfx 8.3/1 (Petronell; 2. Jh. n. Chr.). Zur Bedeutung der wiederkehrenden Potenzen der Zahl 3 vgl. auch CESANO 1910, 1577; TUPET 1986, 2600.

63 SCHEER 2001, 35.

5.3.3 Multimodalität: Zauberzeichen und -bilder

Aufgrund der „Zweidimensionalität des materiellen Schriftträgers"[64] eröffnet die Verschriftung gegenüber der mündlichen Rezitation die Möglichkeit, die Schreibunterlage mit non-verbalen Elementen zu versehen; wie andere geschriebene Texte sind auch die *defixiones* multimodal organisiert (s. o., Abschn. 5.1). Zu den zusätzlichen semiotischen Ressourcen zählen etwa die sogenannten *charakteres*, buchstabenähnliche Symbole und Zeichen mit wahrscheinlich astrologischer Bedeutung.[65] Auf den rituellen vertikalen Kommunikationsprozess haben sie insofern Einfluss, als sie auf Seiten des Zaubernden von exklusiven Fachkenntnissen und Expertenwissen zeugen.[66] Bisweilen finden sich auch Zeichnungen, die bestimmte Textelemente, wie z. B. Dämonennamen bildlich aufnehmen und somit zur Hervorhebung von Informationen eingesetzt werden können.[67] Vergleichbar mit den Zauberzeichen dienen sie letztlich der Optimierung der rituellen Kommunikationsbedingungen. Wie formelhafte Textpassagen können auch diese graphisch-visuellen Elemente über entsprechende Anleitungen tradiert werden, die eine rein mechanische Reproduktion ermöglichen (s. o., Abschn. 4.2). Nicht zuletzt kann auch ein ungewöhnliches Schriftbild als semiotische Ressource dienen (s. u., Abschn. 5.5). Dies trifft auch auf das Material der Schreibunterlage zu: So wird gerade Blei als unheilvolles und daher insbesondere für den Schadenzauber geeignetes Material bewertet, mit dem sich der Inhalt der Verwünschungsformeln gewissermaßen verstärken lässt.[68]

5.4 Die Schrift als Medium der Konservierung und Verstärkung

Als (sekundäres) Trägermedium ermöglicht Schrift Fixierung und Speicherung. Im rituellen Kontext wird durch die Gravierung des Metallplättchens die dem Wort inhärente Wirkmacht, als *carmen* zunächst nur gesprochen und flüchtig, auf einen Gegenstand gebannt und haltbar gemacht.[69] Die physische Existenz des Wortes wird damit noch greifbarer und seine Wirkdauer 'verewigt'. Diese verstärkende Funktion der Schrift kann auch in den Anleitungen der Zauberpapyri thematisiert sein: „Zur Verstärkung der Worte schreib auf Papyrus [...]."[70] Möglicherweise verbirgt sich dieselbe Vorstellung auch hinter der Gleichzeitigkeit von rituellem Sprechen und Schrei-

---

64 RAIBLE 2006, 115.
65 Zu den astrologischen Anleihen vgl. z. B. CESANO 1910, 1577; VERSNEL 2002, 115.
66 Zum speziellen Wortlaut für die Kommunikation mit Göttern und Dämonen vgl. etwa VERSNEL 2002, 116 f.
67 Zu den magischen Zeichnungen vgl. z. B. GAGER 1992, 6 f.; GORDON 2005.
68 Zur ritualspezifischen Semantik von Blei vgl. KROPP 2008, 80–82.
69 Hierzu stellt RÜPKE (2001a, 30) fest, dass bei Ritualvollzug ohne Öffentlichkeitscharakter Verschriftungen „besonders ausgeprägt" sind. Ebenso GRAF 1996, 190 f.; GRAF 1997, 125–126.
70 Pap.Graec.Mag. 34,167 f. Zu dieser Vorstellung von Schrift vgl. z. B. GRAF 1997, 125; HOPFNER 1938, 131 f.; HUVELIN 1901, 23 (mit zahlreichen Belegen).

ben, wie ein anderes magisches Rezept expliziert: „nimm eine Bleiplatte und schreib den gleichen Spruch darauf und sag ihn her".[71] Auch diesbezüglich spielt die Schriftform eine wichtige Rolle für die Kommunikation mit Göttern und Dämonen: In seiner schriftlichen und damit stabilen Form verhallt das ephemere gesprochene Wort nicht ungehört, sondern kann die Sphäre des numinosen Adressaten auch zu einem späteren Zeitpunkt noch erreichen. Angesichts der anthropomorphen Gottesvorstellungen der Antike, gemäß derer die Gottheiten nicht omnipräsent oder allwissend sind, dient die Verschriftung folglich nicht nur dem Schutz des *defigens*, sondern letztlich auch der Kommunikationssicherung.

5.5 Schriftbild und Schriftwahl

5.5.1 Verschlüsselung und Verkehrung

Im Zusammenhang mit dem rituellen Akt der Verschriftung kann auch das Schriftbild ungewöhnlich ausfallen: So kann zunächst die Schriftgröße auffällig klein und schwer zu lesen sein.[72] Auch die Richtung der Schrift verläuft nicht immer „normal", d. h. von links nach rechts, sondern bisweilen bustrophedon, retrograd oder von unten nach oben.[73] Dies trifft auch auf die ungewöhnliche Ausrichtung der Buchstaben zu, die gespiegelt oder kopfstehend geschrieben sein können. Ferner begegnen Anagramme und ausgefallene Buchstabenanordnungen, wie etwa Spiralen[74] oder Schlangenlinien.

Anders als im Falle der mündlichen Rede kann das Trägermedium Schrift selbst als semiotische Ressource herangezogen werden, indem das Schriftbild zusätzlich zu dem geschriebenen Textinhalt weitere visuell-simultane Informationen transportiert: Tatsächlich erschweren außergewöhnliche Schriftbilder als Strategien der Verschlüsselung nicht nur die Zugänglichkeit der Texte; vielmehr ist insbesondere ein abweichender Schriftverlauf „als Ausdruck und Mittel der verkehrten Welt der Magie"[75] zu sehen. Bisweilen fungiert die verkehrte Schriftrichtung zudem explizit als Analogieträger für die dem Opfer zugedachten Folgen: 'Möge es dir verkehrt (d. h. schlecht) ergehen, wie dies verkehrt geschrieben ist' (*perverse agas, quomodo hoc perverse scriptum est*).[76] Dabei kann das Schriftbild nicht nur der Visualisierung des Verwünschungsinhaltes dienen, sondern auch der Hervorhebung eines bestimmten Wortes, wie eine weitere magische Analogie zwischen Schriftrichtung und Verwün-

---

71 Pap.Graec.Mag. 4,328–330. Vgl. auch GRAF 1997, 125.
72 Vgl. z. B. BLÄNSDORF (2012, 26) für das Mainzer Heiligtum.
73 Vgl. TOMLIN 2004, 26 f.
74 Ein besonders anschauliches Beispiel stellt der Diskus dfx 2.1.2/1 (Barchín del Hoyo; 1. Jh. n. Chr.?) dar, der kreisförmig beschrieben ist. Zur Bedeutung des Schriftverlaufs vgl. z. B. OGDEN 1999, 29 f.
75 BLÄNSDORF 2012, 29.
76 Hierbei handelt es sich um ein unveröffentlichtes Kölner Fluchtäfelchen, vgl. BLÄNSDORF 2012, 30.

schungsinhalt zeigen kann: So stehen in dem retrograd abgefassten Text die beiden letzten Buchstaben des Adjektivs *aversum* 'abgewandt' zusätzlich noch auf dem Kopf (s. Abb. 2 und s. u., Abschn. 5.6).

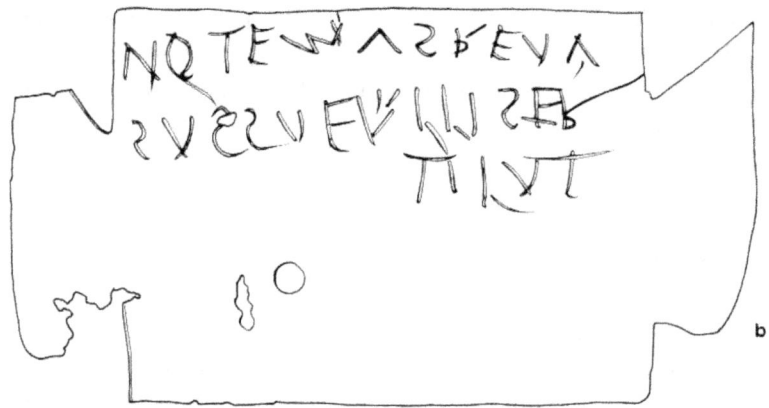

Abb. 2: Fluchtäfelchen aus Rottweil, 1.–3. Jh. n. Chr. (NUBER 1984, 379)

5.5.2 Die Transliteration

Anders als die gesprochene Sprache erlaubt die Schriftform die Wiedergabe eines Textes im Alphabet einer anderen Sprache und folglich einen Sprachwechsel auf einer partiellen, primär optisch-graphischen Ebene.[77] Durch das Zusammenspiel unterschiedlicher Schriftsysteme ergibt sich auch eine besondere Form der Zweisprachigkeit: Im Falle der *defixiones* handelt es sich üblicherweise um nicht-griechische Textelemente, die teilweise oder vollständig in griechische Schriftzeichen transliteriert sein können. Dies betrifft regelmäßig rekurrente Zauberwörter, insbesondere die klassischen *barbara onomata* wie z. B. αβρασαξ, die unmittelbar in das lateinische Formular eingefügt sein können;[78] ebenso kann eine optische Trennung der beiden Sprachen vorliegen.[79] Nicht zuletzt können sich hinter einer einsprachig anmutenden 'monographischen'[80] Inschrift mehrere Sprachen verbergen.[81] Dass gerade auch für

---

77 Zu dieser in der Antike gängigen Verschriftungspraxis vgl. z. B. RADICIOTTI 2013.
78 Vgl. dfx 11.1.1/16 (Karthago; 2./3. Jh.): Καταξιν, *qui es in Aegypto magnus daemon* [...]. Τραβαξιαν, *omnipotens daemon* [...]. Νοχθιριφ, *qui es cogens daemon* [...]. Βιβιριξι, *qui es fortissimus daemon* [...]. Ρικουριθ, *agilissime daemon in Aegypto* [...].
79 Vgl. dfx 4.2.1/1 (Autun; 2. Jh.), wo die Liste der Opfernamen in lateinischen, der rückseitig angebrachte Katalog der *barbara onomata* in griechischen Buchstaben abgefasst ist. Zu Zauberworten und -zeichen vgl. auch KROPP 2008, 140–142.
80 Diese Bezeichnung lehnt sich an den Terminus 'digraphisch' an, d. h. in gleicher Sprache, aber in verschiedenen Schriften abgefasst; vgl. auch KROPP 2017.
81 Dies trifft auf zwei mischsprachige Täfelchen aus Karthago (2./3. Jh. n. Chr.) zu: Auf der Tafel dfx 11.1.1/28 korrespondieren Sprache und Alphabet, so dass sich der Text als Sprach- und Schriftmi-

die Abfassung zweisprachiger *defixiones* mangels sprachlicher Kompetenz auf Mustertexte zurückgegriffen werden musste, legen wiederum typische Abschreibfehler, fehlerhafte Übernahmen von Formelelementen ebenso sowie sehr abrupte Übergänge an den Sprachschnittstellen nahe.

Sprach- und Schriftmischungen finden sich insbesondere in *defixiones* aus zweisprachigen Regionen wie Nordafrika. Die Wahl eines bestimmten Alphabets spiegelt jedoch nicht zwangsläufig eine Situation gesellschaftlicher Mehrsprachigkeit wider, sondern kann auf einer „magischen Diglossie", d.h. auf einem die Zauberwirkung betreffenden Hierarchie- und Prestigegefälle, beruhen:[82] Mit dem Wechsel in ein anderes Alphabet – von J. N. ADAMS in Anlehnung an den linguistischen Begriff des 'Code Switching' als "character switching"[83] bezeichnet – erfolgt zunächst eine besondere Verschlüsselung der Texte, wie dies etwa auch mit einem ungewöhnlichen Schriftverlauf gegeben ist (s.o., Abschn. 5.5.1). Daneben verbirgt sich hinter der Transliteration eines Textes in das Alphabet einer anderen, vorzugsweise älteren Sprache die Vorstellung, dass das Wirkpotential einer Äußerung nicht in jeder Sprache gleich, sondern an ihren ursprünglichen „Dialekt" gebunden sei.[84] Mit der Übertragung in eine andere Sprache würde diese dem ursprünglichen Lautkörper inhärente Macht des Wortes vernichtet. Damit eröffnet die Verschriftung gegenüber der mündlichen Rede die Möglichkeit, diese ursprüngliche und damit prestigereichere Sprache zumindest partiell beizubehalten und mit dem äußeren Anstrich auch ihre magischen Qualitäten zu konservieren. Dabei könnte die Verwendung von griechischen Schriftzeichen mit dem griechischen Ursprung der Ritualgattung wie auch mit ihrer Überzahl und größeren Verbreitung zusammenhängen. Möglicherweise haben auch die einschlägigen griechischen Zauberformulare aus dem kaiserzeitlichen Ägypten zur Konsolidierung dieser magischen Diglossie beigetragen und letztlich die Bedeutungszuweisung als wesentliche Komponente des Rituals bewirkt.[85]

---

schung präsentiert; in dfx 11.1.1/27 hingegen ist auch der lateinischsprachige Text in griechischen *charakteres* verschriftet. In dfx 11.1.1/28 rutscht der Schreiber in die falsche Zeile (Z. 44) und muss nochmals neu ansetzen, vgl. hierzu auch KROPP 2017.

82 Vgl. hierzu bes. die Ausführungen von POCETTI 2002, 37–57.

83 Vgl. ADAMS 2003, 46. Zum Begriff des 'Code Switching' in der Sprachkontaktforschung (als einer Form der transkodischen Markierung im Rahmen mehrsprachiger Rede) vgl. z.B. AUER 2011.

84 Vgl. die Aussage des christlichen Philosophen Origenes (c. Cels. 5,45): „Namen/Wörter, deren Beschaffenheit es ist, in einer bestimmten Sprache wirksam zu sein, die in einen anderen Dialekt überführt werden, bringen nichts mehr zustande, wie sie es mit den ursprünglichen Lauten zustandegebracht haben." Hierzu z.B. GAGER 1992, 34, Anm. 42; GRAF 1996, 70f.; 195–197; GORDON 1999a, 242f. In stoischer Tradition argumentiert Origenes (c. Cels. 1,24), dass sich die verschiedenen Bezeichnungen schließlich naturgegeben (*physei*) und nicht aufgrund von Übereinkunft (*thesei*) ausgebildet hätten und folglich bei Zauberworten und insbesondere bei Götternamen keine arbiträre Beziehung von *signifiant* und *signifié* vorliege.

85 Vgl. hierzu z.B. ZGUSTA 1980, 121–145, bes. 135.

Vor diesem Hintergrund erfüllt die Transliteration ins griechische Alphabet eine doppelte Funktion: Zum einen fungiert sie als Strategie der Verschlüsselung, die sowohl den geheimen Charakter der Verwünschung als auch die exklusiven Kenntnisse des *defigens* unterstreicht. Zum anderen erhöht sie durch die graphische Annäherung an die als potenter wahrgenommene Sprache die Zauberwirkung der Verwünschungsformeln.

5.6 Die Verschriftung als rituelle Operation: Metaphern und Analogien

Wie bereits ausgeführt, stellt die Verschriftung eine zentrale Ritualhandlung dar; eine besondere Bedeutung kommt dabei der Niederschrift des Opfernamens zu. Die namentliche Nennung dient zunächst der Identifizierung des Zielindividuums, wobei Vollständigkeit und Eindeutigkeit durch verschiedene sprachliche Verfahren, wie z. B. den *quem-peperit*-Ausdruck sichergestellt werden können (s. o., Abschn. 5.3.2). Diese besondere Bedeutung des Namens kann sich auch daran zeigen, dass er mitunter das einzige Element der Zauberinschrift bildet; dies trifft zwar vergleichsweise häufig auf die frühen und einfachen *defixiones* zu, bleibt aber bis zu den letzten Zeugnissen der Ritualform nachweisbar.[86]

Aufgrund der besonderen Semantik der Ritualhandlungen kann auch die Gravierung der Bleilamelle als Metapher für die Einwirkungen auf das Opfer verstanden werden, wodurch die manuelle Ritualhandlung gegenüber der verbalen Interaktion in den Vordergrund tritt: Aufgrund der magischen Verbindung zwischen Name und Namensträger wird mit dem Niederschreiben des Namens die „Fixierung" der Zielperson auch unmittelbar auf materieller Ebene vollzogen.[87] Damit ist die Schrift nicht nur auf ihre üblichen medial-kommunikativen Funktionen ausgerichtet, sondern verfügt auch über metaphorische Anteile. Möglicherweise liegt dieselbe Vorstellung auch denjenigen Zauberinschriften zugrunde, die allein aus dem Namen des Opfers bestehen. Mit der Verschriftung korrespondiert auf Textebene die explizit performative Formel 'hiermit schreibe ich nieder' (*describo*), die in einem Täfelchen erscheint und wohl nach dem Muster der geläufigeren Manipulationsformeln *ligo* oder *defigo* gebildet wurde.[88] Daneben kann auch dem Schriftverlauf eine wichtige Rolle zukommen, indem er metaphorisch aufgeladen wird; diese Metaphorik der Schreibhand-

---

86 Hierzu z. B. AUDOLLENT 1904, L, XCI-XCII; OGDEN 1999, 6–10.
87 Zur weitverbreiteten Vorstellung des „bannenden Schriftzaubers" vgl. TIEMANN 1938/1941, bes. 361 f. Zur Verbindung von Name und Namensträger vgl. z. B. PETERSMANN 2002.
88 Die Verbform *describo*, die lateinische Entsprechung zu καταγράφω, erscheint nur in dfx 1.4.2/2 (Mentana; 1. Jh. v. Chr.), parallel zu *defigo* ('ich durchbohre'). Das Verbum *describere* besitzt jedoch, anders als das griechischen Pendant, keine juristische Bedeutungskomponente. In dfx 5.1.5/12 (Mainz; 1./2. Jh. n. Chr.) wird *depono* (*aversum*) synonym zu *describo* verwendet. Vgl. hierzu auch KROPP 2008, 146.

lung kann explizit an Analogien zutage treten, die den ungewöhnlichen Schriftverlauf in Bezug zum Opfer setzen (s. o., Abschn. 5.5.1): So wird in einer *defixio* eine Analogie zwischen der um- bzw. abgekehrten Schriftrichtung und dem Schicksal der verwünschten Person hergestellt: '[...] dass jenen oder jene die Götter (vom Leben) abgewandt machen, so wie dies abgewandt (= retrograd) ist' (*[...] ut illum aut illam aversum faciant dii sicut hoc est aversum*).[89] Die Metaphorik des Rituals, durch welche die konkrete Ritualsituation mit dem Opfer in Bezug gesetzt wird, impliziert dabei die parallele Aktivierung einer zweiten semantischen Ebene desselben Lexems, wonach das Partizip 'abgewandt' im übertragenen Sinne (von 'tot') zu verstehen ist.

Mit Verben wie *describere* 'niederschreiben' wird eine konkrete, physische Handlung bezeichnet, deren Objekt, nach Handlungsvollzug, im Vergleich zu seinem Anfangszustand grundlegend verändert ist. Angesichts der Performativität dieser Manipulationsformel wird die Ritualhandlung nicht nur am Textträger, sondern zugleich auch verbal mittels des darauf eingravierten Textes ausgeführt. Mit den Worten von C. A. FARAONE lässt sich dieser Formeltyp beschreiben als „a performative utterance, that is, a form of incantation by which the *defigens* hopes to manipulate his victim in an automatic way".[90] Dies bedeutet, dass der *defigens* die Handlung vollzieht, die das performative Verb *describere* 'niederschreiben' bezeichnet. Im Gegensatz zu denjenigen Formeln, die einen göttlichen Interaktionspartner erkennen lassen, wie etwa Anrufungen oder Aufforderungen, findet die verbal realisierte Manipulation des Zielindividuums ohne Zwischenschaltung eines numinosen Adressaten oder Empfängers statt. Diese Texte sind folglich nicht zur Rezeption durch Gottheiten und Dämonen bestimmt, vielmehr sollen die Verwünschungen selbst unmittelbar die Beeinträchtigung oder Nötigung des anvisierten Opfers bewirken. An die Stelle eines numinosen Kommunikationspartners, der mit der Erfüllung der Verwünschung beauftragt wird, tritt die Vorstellung einer „mechanischen" bzw. „automatischen" Wirkweise der verbalen und non-verbalen Ritualelemente. „Handlungen und Worte werden als Werkzeuge gedacht."[91] Dieser „einfache götterlose Zauberspruch"[92] kann als Urform der Verwünschung gelten, die erst nach und nach durch die deutlich ausführlicheren Unterweltsbriefe abgelöst wird. Das Verhältnis der späteren Zauberinschriften verschiebt sich dabei zugunsten adressatenorientierter Texte, woran sich zeigt, dass die Kommunikation zwischen *defigens* und übermenschlichen Mächten gegenüber dem

---

[89] dfx 5.1.7/1 (Rottweil; 1.–3. Jh. n. Chr.): Die letzten Buchstaben des Adjektivs *aversum* 'abgewandt' stehen zusätzlich auf dem Kopf. Vgl. hierzu auch FARAONE/KROPP 2010.
[90] FARAONE 1991, 10.
[91] BJÖRCK 1938, 35, Anm. 1.
[92] BJÖRCK 1938, 117. Vgl. hierzu auch LÓPEZ JIMENO 1991, 211: „Las más antiguas carecen por completo de dedicatorias o peticiones a los dioses, lo cual parece apuntar a una incorporación posterior de este elemento religioso a la tradición y rituales mágicos." Ebenso VERSNEL 1991, 61; 94, Anm. 7: „[D]irect instructions to the gods or daemons date from the period of the Roman Empire. Earlier instructions to the gods are the exceptions, not the rule."

als selbstwirksam gedachten Wort zunehmend an Bedeutung gewinnt. Dies hat auch die funktionelle Spezialisierung des Schriftträgers als Mittel der Kommunikation mit Göttern und Dämonen zu Folge.

6 Fazit und Ausblick

Wie im vorliegenden Beitrag ausgeführt, stellen Schrift und Verschriftung Kernelemente des *defixio*-Rituals dar. In diesem Zusammenhang hält der Schriftmodus gegenüber der mündlichen Rede zahlreiche ritualexterne wie auch -interne Vorteile bereit: Zunächst ermöglicht die Schriftform auch dem Unkundigen, das Ritual überhaupt ausführen zu können, weil Texte aus Vorlagen kopiert bzw. der Schreibvorgang teilweise oder ganz an einen Fachmann delegiert werden kann. Darüber hinaus kann das *defixio*-Ritual einen Kommunikationsraum mit numinosen, meist unterirdischen Mächten eröffnen, die in schriftlicher Form zur Umsetzung der Verwünschung aufgefordert werden. Die beschriftete Tafel wird somit zum Unterweltsbrief, der die Handlungsanweisung auf einer vertikale Achse von unten nach ganz unten vermittelt. Hierbei kann die Schrift als besondere Kommunikationsform ebenfalls unterstützend wirken. So kann einerseits aufgrund der asynchron stattfindenden Kommunikation die horizontale Achse von vornherein ausgeschaltet werden; andererseits kann die Schriftvermittlung der Kommunikation auf vertikaler Achse Optionen jenseits der Mündlichkeit eröffnen. Hierzu zählt wiederum die raumzeitliche Trennung von Sender und Empfänger, was vor allem im Umgang mit katachthonen Mächten von Relevanz ist. Zugleich erlaubt die Schriftlichkeit aufgrund ihrer Materialität nicht nur eine Konservierung und Verstärkung der mündlichen Rede, sondern hält auch multimodale Kanäle auf einer visuell-simultanen Ebene bereit, über die die Mündlichkeit nicht verfügt. Auch dieser Umstand dient nicht nur dem Schutz des *defigens*, sondern vor allem der Kommunikationssicherung.

Anders als auf zwischenmenschliche Kommunikation ausgerichtete Verschriftungsprozesse eignet der Verschriftung im Rahmen des *defixio*-Ritual eine besondere Semantik: Die Gravierung der Tafel ist dabei, wie die übrigen rituellen Operationen auch, als Metapher für den Angriff auf das Zielindividuum zu verstehen. Das *defixio*-Ritual ist folglich in hohem Maße auf Schrift und Verschriftung abgestimmt, wobei der Schriftlichkeit in diesem besonderen Kontext mehr als nur mediale Funktion zukommt. Das besondere Wechselspiel von Ritualhandlung und Zauberinschrift zeigt sich wiederum daran, dass die Verschriftung als zentrale Ritualhandlung mit wiederkehrenden Textelementen korrespondiert, d. h. die am Textträger vollzogene Handlung vielfach auf Textebene transponiert wird. Dabei bringt die rituelle Anbringung von Text gegenüber vergleichbaren schriftlosen Ritualen, die lediglich die manuelle Operation des Bindens oder Durchbohrens aufweisen, bestimmte auf die *defixiones* beschränkte Textelemente erst hervor. Die Metaphorik der Schreibhandlung zeigt sich explizit an Analogien, die einen ungewöhnlichen Schriftverlauf (*aversum* 'rückläufig') in Bezug zum Opfer (*aversum* 'tot') setzen. In besonderen Maße trifft dies aber auf performativ verwendete Verben des Schreibens zu, wie 'hiermit schreibe ich nieder' (*describo*). Ab der Kaiserzeit weisen die Täfelchen eine zunehmend detaillierte und durchdachte Komposition auf, was auch anhand von Formelinventar, Zauberworten bzw. Dämonennamen sowie aufwendiger optischer Ausgestaltung greifbar wird. Damit einher geht wiederum eine stärkere Gewichtung der medialen Funktion von Verschriftungsprozessen, deren Performativität im Rahmen eines antiken Schadenzauberrituals die verengte Konzeption von Schrift als Trägermedium kontrastieren kann. Angesichts der Tatsache, dass dies insbesondere auch unserer modernen Auffassung zuwiderläuft, ließe sich somit feststellen: Die Wahrnehmung von Schrift als bloßes Medium ist eine Reduktion, die sich in einer bestimmten Gesellschaftsform entwickelt hat.[93]

Die hier vorgelegte Untersuchung mag als Beitrag zur Erweiterung des Verständnishorizontes im Hinblick auf antike Schriftlichkeit gelesen werden. Um das magische Potential der *defixiones* zu aktivieren, ist nicht allein das richtige Textverständnis, sondern gerade auch die Präsenz und Materialität der Schrift von zentraler Bedeutung. Erst im Prozess der Transformation eines Bleitäfelchens zum Schriftträger, in der weiteren rituellen Behandlung des als Schreibunterlage fungierenden Materials (Bindung bzw. Durchbohrung, Deposition) entfaltet die Fluchtafel ihre Wirksamkeit. In ihrer Rolle als Ritualhandlung, die sowohl über mediale als auch über metaphorische Anteile verfügt, fungieren Schrift und Verschriftung folglich als Katalysator für die Performativität des Rituals.

Bibliographie

ADAMS 1992 = J.N. ADAMS, British Latin: The Text, Interpretation and Language of the Bath Curse Tablets, *Britannia* 23, 1992, 1–26.
ADAMS 2003 = J.N. ADAMS, Bilingualism and the Latin Language, Cambridge u. a. 2003.
AUDOLLENT 1904 = A. AUDOLLENT, Defixionum tabellae quotquot innotuerunt tam in graecis Orientis quam in totius Occidentis partibus praeter Atticas in Corpore Inscriptionum Atticarum editas, Paris 1904. (DT)
AUER 2011 = P. AUER, Code-Switching/Mixing, in: R. WODAK/B. JOHNSTONE/P. KERSWILL (Hg.), The SAGE Handbook of Sociolinguistics, London 2011, 460–478.
BARTOLETTI 1990 = G. BARTOLETTI, La scrittura romana nelle tabellae defixionum (secc. I a.C. – IV d.C.). Note paleografiche, *Scrittura e civiltà* 14, 1990, 7–47, tab. 1–12.
BEARD 1991 = M. BEARD (Hg.), Literacy in the Roman World, Ann Arbor 1991.
BLÄNSDORF 2012 = J. BLÄNSDORF, Die Defixionum tabellae des Mainzer Isis- und Mater-Magna-Heiligtums, Mainz 2012.

---

93 Vgl. ZOLLNA 1985, 72: „Die Wahrnehmung eines Wortes als bloßes Zeichen ist eine Reduktion, die sich in einer bestimmten Gesellschaftsform entwickelt hat."

BRODERSEN 2001a = K. BRODERSEN, Briefe in die Unterwelt. Religiöse Kommunikation auf griechischen Fluchtafeln, in: DERS. (Hg.), Gebet und Fluch, Zeichen und Traum. Aspekte religiöser Kommunikation in der Antike, Münster 2001, 57–68.

BRODERSEN 2001b = K. BRODERSEN (Hg.), Gebet und Fluch, Zeichen und Traum. Aspekte religiöser Kommunikation in der Antike, Münster 2001.

CESANO 1901 = L. CESANO, defixio, Dizionario epigrafico di antichità romane 2.2, 1910, 1558–1591.

DTA = R. WÜNSCH, Defixionum Tabellae Atticae, Berlin 1897.

DT s. AUDOLLENT 1904 (Korpusangabe).

DULCKEIT/SCHWARZ/WALDSTEIN 1995 = G. DULCKEIT/F. SCHWARZ/W. WALDSTEIN, Römische Rechtsgeschichte. Ein Studienbuch, München 1995^9.

DÜRSCHEID 2016 = C. DÜRSCHEID, Einführung in die Schriftlinguistik, Göttingen/Bristol 2016.

FARAONE 1991= C.A. FARAONE, The Agonistic Context of Early Greek Binding Spells, in: C.A. FARAONE/D. OBBINK (Hg.), Magika Hiera, New York/Oxford 1991, 3–32.

FARAONE/KROPP 2010 = C.A. FARAONE/A. KROPP, Inversion, Aversion and Perversion in Imperial Roman Curse-Tablets, in: R.L. GORDON/F. MARCO SIMÓN (Hg.), Magical Practice in the Latin West. Papers from the International Conference held at the University of Zaragoza, 30 Sept. – 1 Oct. 2005, Leiden/Boston 2010, 381–398.

FYNTIKOGLOU/VOUTIRAS 2005 = V. FYNTIKOGLOU/E. VOUTIRAS, Das römische Gebet, *ThesCRA* 3, 2005, 151–179.

GAGER 1992 = J.G. GAGER, Curse Tablets and Binding Spells from the Ancient World, New York 1992.

GENZ/GÉVAUDAN 2016 = J. GENZ/P. GÉVAUDAN, Medialität, Materialität, Kodierung: Grundzüge einer allgemeinen Theorie der Medien, Bielefeld 2016.

GLÜCK 1987 = H. GLÜCK, Schrift und Schriftlichkeit. Eine sprach- und kulturwissenschaftliche Studie, Stuttgart 1987.

GORDON 1999a = R. GORDON, 'What's in a List?' Listing in Greek and Graeco-Roman Malign Magical Text, in: D.R. JORDAN/H. MONTGOMERY/E. THOMASSEN (Hg.), The World of Ancient Magic, Bergen 1999, 239–277.

GORDON 1999b = R. GORDON, Imagining Greek and Roman Magic, in: V. FLINT/R. GORDON/G. LUCK/D. OGDEN (Hg.), Witchcraft and Magic in Europe, Bd. 2, London 1999, 159–275.

GORDON 2005 = R. GORDON, Competence and 'Felicity Conditions' in Two Sets of North African Curse-Tablets (DTAud Nos. 275-85; 286-98), *MHNH* 5, 2005, 61–86.

GRAF 1996 = F. GRAF, Gottesnähe und Schadenzauber. Die Magie in der griechisch-römischen Antike, München 1996.

GRAF 1997 = F. GRAF, Communio loquendi cum dis. Magie und Kommunikation, in: G. BINDER/K. EHLICH (Hg.), Religiöse Kommunikation — Formen und Praxis vor der Neuzeit, Trier 1997, 119–139.

GRUBE/KOGGE 2005 = G. GRUBER/W. KOGGE, Zur Einleitung: Was ist Schrift?, in: G. GRUBE (Hg.), Schrift: Kulturtechnik zwischen Auge, Hand und Maschine, München 2005, 9–23.

HARRIS 1983 = W.V. HARRIS, Literacy and Epigraphy I, *ZPE* 52, 1983, 87–111.

HARRIS 1989 = W.V. HARRIS, Ancient Literacy, Cambridge Mass. u. a. 1989.

HESS-LÜTTICH/SCHMAUKS 2004 = E.W.B. HESS-LÜTTICH/D. SCHMAUKS, Multimediale Kommunikation, in: R. POSNER/K. ROBERING/Th.A. SEBOEK (Hg.), Semiotik. Ein Handbuch zu den zeichentheoretischen Grundlagen von Natur und Kultur, 4. Teilband, Berlin/New York, 2004, 3487-3503.

HOPFNER 1928 = Th. HOPFNER, Mageia, RE 14.1, 1928, 301–393.

HUVELIN 1902 = P. HUVELIN, Les tablettes magiques et le droit romain, *Annales internationales d'histoire. 2e section: Histoire comparée des institutions et du droit* 1902, 15–81.

INGEMARK 2000–2001 = D. INGEMARK, Literacy in Roman Britain: The Epigraphical Evidence, *Opsuscula Romana* 25–26, 2000–2001, 19–30.

Jordan 1976 = D.R. Jordan, CIL VIII 19 525 (B).2QPVVLVA = Q(VEM) P(EPERIT) VVLVA, *Philologus* 120, 1976, 127–132.
Jordan 1985 = D.R. Jordan, A Survey of Greek Defixiones Not Included in the Special Corpora, *GRBS* 26, 1985, 151–197.
Jordan 2000 = D.R. Jordan, New Greek Curse Tablets (1985–2000), *GRBS* 41, 2000, 5–46.
Klug/Stöckl 2016 = N.-M. Klug/H. Stöckl, Handbuch Sprache im multimodalen Kontext, Berlin/Boston 2016.
Kropp 2008 = A. Kropp, Magische Sprachverwendung in vulgärlateinischen Fluchtafeln, Tübingen 2008. Der Monographie ist das elektronische Korpus auf CD beigefügt, abrufbar über http://narr-starter.de/magento/index.php/magische-sprachverwendung-in-vulgarlateinischen-fluchtafeln-defixiones.html.
Kropp 2017 = A. Kropp, Ritualgebundene Sprach- und Schriftwahl am Beispiel zweier griechisch-lateinischer defixiones aus Karthago, in: A. Willi (Hg.), Sprachgeschichte und Epigraphik. Festgaben für Rudolf Wachter zum 60. Geburtstag, Innsbruck 2017, 119–146.
Kühn 1995 = P. Kühn, Mehrfachadressierung. Untersuchungen zur adressatenspezifischen Polyvalenz sprachlichen Handelns, Tübingen 1995.
López Jimeno 1991 = M.d.A. López Jimeno, Las Tabellae defixionis de la Sicilia griega, Amsterdam 1991.
Mauss/Hubert 1966 = M. Mauss/H. Hubert, Esquisses d'une théorie générale de la magie, in: Dies., Anthropologie et Sociologie, Paris 1966, 1–141.
Ménard 2000 = H. Ménard, Le vol dans les tablettes de la Bretagne romaine (Britannia), *Revue historique de droit français et étranger* 78.2, 2000, 289–299.
Meyer 2004 = E.A. Meyer, Legitimacy and Law in the Roman World: Tabulae in Roman Belief and Practice, Cambridge 2004.
Nuber 1984 = H.U. Nuber, Eine Zaubertafel aus Schramberg-Waldmössingen, *FBW* 9, 1984, 377–384.
Oesterreicher 1993 = W. Oesterreicher, Verschriftung und Verschriftlichung im Kontext medialer und konzeptioneller Schriftlichkeit, in: U. Schaefer (Hg.), Schriftlichkeit im frühen Mittelalter, Tübingen 1993, 267–292
Ogden 1999 = D. Ogden, Binding Spells: Curse Tablets and Voodoo Dolls in the Greek and Roman Worlds, in: V.V. Flint/R. Gordon/G. Luck/D. Ogden (Hg.), Witchcraft and Magic in Europe, Bd. 2, London 1999, 1–90.
Pap.Graec.Mag. = Papyri Graecae Magicae, hg. K. Preisendanz. 3 Bde, Leipzig/Berlin 1928, 1931, 1941.
Petersmann 2002 = H. Petersmann, Quam vim nomen in religionibus et superstitionibus gentium habeat, in: B. Hessen, (Hg.), Lingua et Religio. Ausgewählte Kleine Schriften zur antiken Religionsgeschichte auf sprachwissenschaftlicher Grundlage, Göttingen 2002, 29–38.
Pocetti 1995 = P. Pocetti, Lingue speciali e pratiche di magia nelle lingue classiche, in: R. Bombi (Hg.), Lingue speciali e interferenza. Atti del Convegno Seminariale. Udine, 16–17 maggio 1994, Rom 1995, 255–273.
Pocetti 2002 = P. Pocetti, Manipolazione della realtà e manipolazione della lingua: alcuni aspetti dei testi magici dell'antichità, in: R. Morresi (Hg.), 'Linguaggio – Linguaggi. Invenzione – Scoperta'. Atti del Convegno. Macerata-Fermo, 22–23 ottobre 1999, Rom 2002, 11–59.
Preisendanz 1972 = K. Preisendanz, Fluchtafel, RAC 8, 1972, 1–29.
Radiciotti 2013 = P. Radiciotti, Digrafismo nei papyri latini, in: M.-H. Marganne/B. Rochette (Hg.), Bilinguisme et digraphisme dans le monde gréco-romain: l'apport des papyrus latins, Liège 2013, 57–69.
Raible 2006 = W. Raible, Medien-Kulturgeschichte. Mediatisierung als Grundlage unserer kulturellen Entwicklung, Heidelberg 2006.

RÜPKE 2001a = J. RÜPKE, Antike Religionen als Kommunikationssysteme, in: K. BRODERSEN (Hg.), Gebet und Fluch, Zeichen und Traum. Aspekte religiöser Kommunikation in der Antike, Münster 2001, 13–30.

RÜPKE 2001b = J. RÜPKE, Die Religion der Römer, München 2001.

SCHEER 2001 = T.S. SCHEER, Die Götter anrufen: Die Kontaktaufnahme zwischen Mensch und Gottheit in der griechischen Antike, in: K. BRODERSEN (Hg.), Gebet und Fluch, Zeichen und Traum. Aspekte religiöser Kommunikation in der Antike, Münster 2001, 31–56.

SELIG 1989 = M. SELIG, Die Entwicklung des Determinantensystems im Spätlateinischen, in: W. RAIBLE (Hg.), Romanistik, Sprachtypologie und Universalienforschung. Beiträge zum Freiburger Romanistentag 1987, Tübingen 1989, 99–130.

STÖCKL 2008 = H. STÖCKL, Die Sprache im Bild – Das Bild in der Sprache: Zur Verknüpfung von Sprache und Bild im massenmedialen Text. Konzepte. Theorien. Analysemethoden, Berlin/New York 2008.

SUDHAUS 1906 = S. SUDHAUS, Lautes und leises Beten, *ARW* 9, 1906, 185–200.

TAMBIAH 1978 = S.J. TAMBIAH, Form und Bedeutung magischer Akte. Ein Standpunkt (1970), in: H.G. KIPPENBERG/B. LUCHESI (Hg.), Magie. Die sozialwissenschaftliche Kontroverse über das Verstehen fremden Denkens, Frankfurt a.M. 1978, 259–296.

TIEMANN 1938/1941 = K.-A. TIEMANN, Schreiben, Schrift, Geschriebenes, *HDA* 9, 1938/1941, 294–388 (Nachträge).

TOMLIN 1988 = R.S.O. TOMLIN, The Curse Tablets, in: B. CUNLIFFE (Hg.), The Temple of Sulis Minerva at Bath, Bd. 2: The Finds from the Sacred Spring, Oxford 1988, 59–277.

TOMLIN 2004 = R.S.O. TOMLIN, *"carta picta perscripta"*: Anleitung zum Lesen von Fluchtafeln, in: K. BRODERSEN/A. KROPP (Hg.), Fluchtafeln. Neue Funde und neue Deutungen zum antiken Schadenzauber, Frankfurt a.M. 2004, 11–29.

TUPET 1986 = A.-M. TUPET, Rites magiques dans l'Antiquité romaine, ANRW II 16.3, 1986, 2591–2675.

VAN DER HORST 1994 = P.W. VAN DER HORST, Silent Prayer in Antiquity, *Numen* 41.1, 1994, 1–25.

VERSNEL 1987 = H.S. VERSNEL, Les imprécations et le droit, *Revue historique de droit français et étranger* 65, 1987, 5–22.

VERSNEL 1991 = H.S. VERSNEL, Beyond Cursing: The Appeal to Justice in Judicial Prayers, in: C.A. FARAONE/D. OBBINK (Hg.), Magika Hiera, New York/Oxford 1991, 60–106.

VERSNEL 1998 = H.S. VERSNEL, καὶ εἴ τι λ[οιπὸν] τῶν μερ[ῶ]ν [ἔσ]ται τοῦ σώματος ὅλ[ο]υ (... and Any Other Part of the Entire Body there May Be ...). An Essay on Anatomical Curses, in: F. GRAF (Hg.), Ansichten griechischer Rituale. Geburtstags-Symposium für Walter Burkert, Castelen bei Basel, 15. bis 18. März, Stuttgart/Leipzig 1998, 217–267.

VERSNEL 2002 = H.S. VERSNEL, The Poetics of the Magical Charm: An Essay in the Power of Words, in: P. MIRECKI/M. MEYER (Hg.), *Magic and Ritual in the Ancient World*, Leiden/Boston/Köln 2002, 105–158.

WOODWARD/LEACH 1993 = A. WOODWARD/P. LEACH, The Uley Shrines. Excavation of a Ritual Complex on West Hill, Uley, Gloucestershire 1977-9, London 1993.

WÜNSCH 1898 = R. WÜNSCH (Hg.), Sethianische Verfluchungstafeln aus Rom, Leipzig 1898.

ZGUSTA 1980 = L. ZGUSTA, Die Rolle des Griechischen im römischen Kaiserreich, in: G. NEUMANN/J. UNTERMANN (Hg.), Die Sprachen im römischen Reich der Kaiserzeit, Köln/Bonn 1980, 121–145.

ZOLLNA 1985 = I. ZOLLNA, Sprache als Zauber, in: C. BÜTTNER (Hg.), Zauber, Magie und Rituale, München 1985, 67–79.

Administration

A. Caballos Rufino
Monumenta fatiscunt.
Meaning and Fate of Legal Inscriptions on Bronze: the Baetica

Abstract: In Rome, not only private writing but also most public graphic records were regarded as *ephemerae*, and even the proclamation of legal texts on bronze as permanent records is merely a traditional expression of will, later contradicted by historical dynamics. In this work, I shall update the ample catalogue of legal inscriptions on bronze found in Baetica, before moving on to analyse the example posed by this heritage-rich province concerning the elaboration of legal bronzes, the representativeness of the existing catalogue, the administrative function, cultural meaning and ideological impact of these bronzes, and the circumstances surrounding the melting or reuse of *tabulae aheneae*.

Zusammenfassung: Inschriften privater Natur wie auch die meisten öffentlichen Inschriften wurden in römischer Zeit als *ephemerae* betrachtet. Dabei blieb auch die Wahl von Bronze für die dauerhafte Dokumentation von Rechtstexten nur ein traditioneller Willensausdruck, der meist nach kurzer Zeit obsolet wurde. Ziel des vorliegenden Beitrages ist es, den bereits umfangreichen Katalog von Rechtsinschriften auf Bronze aus der Baetica durch Neufunde zu ergänzen. Darauf aufbauend soll das Beispiel der Provinz Baetica im Hinblick auf die Herstellung bronzener Rechtstexte, der Repräsentativität der bekannten Beispiele, ihrer administrativen Funktion, ihrer kulturellen und ideologischen Bedeutung sowie den Umständen ihrer Einschmelzung und Wiederverwendung analysiert werden.

Resumen: Si no sólo la escritura privada, sino la mayoría del registro gráfico público se expresaba en Roma como escritura efímera, también la proclamación oficial de la epigrafía jurídica sobre bronce como registro permanente es mera expresión tradicional de voluntad que la dinámica histórica contradice. Tras la actualización del amplio catálogo de epigrafía jurídica de la Bética romana, analizo en el caso concreto de esta provincia, patrimonialmente tan rica, argumentos en torno a la elaboración de las inscripciones de bronce, la representatividad del repertorio documental, la fun-

---

Anmerkung: This study has been carried out within the framework of "Proyecto de I+D, 'Funciones y vínculos de las elites municipales de la Bética. Marco jurídico, estudio documental y recuperación contextual del patrimonio epigráfico. I' (ORDO V), Reference: HAR2014–55857-P", attached by the Programa Estatal de Fomento de la Investigación Científica y Técnica de Excelencia del Ministerio español de Economía y Competitividad, co-funded by the European Fund for Regional Development. The article has been translated into English by Mr David Govantes Edwards, whom I cordially thank for his work.

cionalidad administrativa, significación cultural e impacto ideológico, así como la casuística de la reutilización y refundición de las *tabulae aheneae*.

The visual graphic experience of the Ancient Romans living in urban communities comprised their relationship with contingent, everyday texts in the private sphere and, collective and open forms of writing conceived, and often, *expressis verbis* conceptualised, to be displayed in public. The impact of these other forms of writing were a result of their greater or lesser visibility, their magnificence, formal and aesthetic features, as well as their contents and the space in which they were displayed.

Little remains of this rich graphic kaleidoscope; what we have is but a pale, unrepresentative reflexion of the whole. The preservation of Roman texts depends on a variety of factors, including whether there is an interest in the preservation of ancient records or, rather, their destruction once they have outlived their purpose; the durability of the material on which the writing is inscribed; whether this material can be reused and/or recycled; and other circumstances and historical variables. As a result, what has survived is inversely proportional to what was, in fact, written at the time. Thus, surviving examples of private and public contingent and ephemeral writing on non-perdurable materials are very rare, and have only withstood the test of time because of unusual environmental conditions, for instance, in Egypt and a few other locations, and in the rest of the Empire, only in very specific and extraordinary circumstances. Among the types classified as private by F. BELTRÁN LLORIS, a small proportion of those written on durable materials survive; the rest has disappeared, except for some exceptional trace that reveals the former presence of what is now lost.[1] Also lost are most of the texts written to be publicly displayed, written by both private citizens, corporations and public institutions: those that were painted either on *tabulae dealbatae*[2] or walls[3], are lost, as are the incidental graffiti[4]. Also lost are a majority of those public texts which, in the Western Empire, following an old and consolidated Roman tradition, were inscribed on bronze. Like with classical sculpture, the stereotypical image of Roman epigraphy in the Western provinces is that of a stone-based form of expression, but this does not represent the reality of writing at the time, when *tabulae aheneae* would have had more of a visual impact. The formal

---

[1] BELTRÁN LLORIS 2015 a; BENEFIEL/KEEGAN 2016.
[2] ECK 1998; ECK 2009, 82: '*Tabulae dealbatae* oder *alba*, oder griechisch λευκώματα, waren in der Verwaltung Roms auf allen Ebenen ein unverzichtbares Mittel zur öffentlichen und schnellen Kommunikation mit der Bevölkerung. Zahllose Edikte und sonstige Anordnungen wurden auf diese Weise bekannt gemacht, nicht nur in Rom, sondern auch in den Provinzen und in allen Städten des Reiches. Die Menge dessen, was so publiziert wurde, kann man sich gar nicht groß genug vorstellen. *Tabulae dealbatae* waren eine allgegenwärtige Erscheinung in der Öffentlichkeit Roms'.
[3] E. g. CABALLOS 2009b, 131–132.
[4] On the abundance of graffiti see CIL IV 2487: *admiro te paries non cecidisse / qui tot scriptorum taedia sustineas*.

grandiloquence of bronze, the intrinsic value of this metallic alloy and its potential for being recycled worked against Horace's famous forecast concerning the durability of bronze inscriptions.[5]

Although, originally, my task for the meeting on 'Literacy in ancient everyday life – Schriftlichkeit im antiken Alltag' was to present a general contribution about legal bronzes, the abundance of recent publications on this topic[6] has encouraged me to be a little more precise. Apart from the edition and publication of documents found in the past few years, recent works have analysed the justification behind the publication of legal texts in bronze, their formal characteristics, their social impact, the reasons behind the large number of examples found in Andalusia, and the reasons behind the significant increase in the number of finds attested in recent times; these issues need not be re-examined here.[7] However, it is necessary to deal with other complementary issues which are very pertinent for the matter at hand.

This contribution, therefore, will focus on Roman legal bronzes in Latin script[8] found in the *Provincia Hispania Ulterior Baetica*. The reasons behind this choice are the large volume of evidence available, our familiarity with the historical dynamics involved, and the constant re-examination and reflexion process of to which the record is subject owing to the frequent addition of new inscriptions. The discovery of the earliest major legal bronzes in the 19th century – the *Lex Coloniae Genetivae Iuliae*[9], the so-called *Leges Flaviae Malacitana*[10] and *Salpensana*[11], or a fragmentary example of the so-called *Oratio de pretiis gladiatorum minuendis*[12] – were a first milestone in the study of legal bronzes. In any case, when they were discovered the interest in these inscriptions was largely restricted to their textual content, so no useful questions concerning their cultural dimension were formulated, for example the meaning of the material upon which they were inscribed, the political-ideological role that they played in their provincial context, and their public impact. Although some minor texts, such as the *Epistula Titi ad Muniguenses*[13] or the hospitality *tabula*

---

5 Hor. Carm. 3,30,1: "*Exegi monumentum aere perennius...*". This passage is often, and rightly, quoted by Eck 2015, 147 to illustrate the importance of bronze epigraphy.
6 The publication of this collective volume coincides with a surge in interest in these topics, as the recent publication of other similar volumes shows. See, for instance Bodel/Dimitrova 2015, Donati 2016 and Kolb 2015; these studies complement classical works such as Corbier 2006.
7 Caballos 1998; Caballos/Fernández 1999; Caballos 2008; Caballos 2009b; Beltrán Lloris 1999 and Eck 2015.
8 For pre-Roman bronzes in the Iberian Peninsula see Simón 2013.
9 CIL II²/5, 1022. Which is still being incorrectly referred to as Lex Ursonensis.
10 CIL II 1964; ILS 6089; Spitzl 1984; Stylow 2001; AE 2001, 1205; HEp 11, 328.
11 CIL II 1963; ILS 6088; D'Ors 1953, 281–309, nº 8.
12 CIL II 6278; ILS 5163; D'Ors 1953, 37–60, nº 3; CILA, Se 339; AE 1952, 51; AE 1962, 403; AE 1965, 137; AE 1967, 221.
13 CILA, Se 1052; AE 1962, 147; AE 1962, 288; AE 1982, 257.

from this same community¹⁴ (*Munigua* = Mulva, Villanueva del Río y Minas, Seville), appeared in the meantime, the revolution in the study of legal bronzes in Andalusia finally took place with the edition of a series of major juridical texts found in Andalusia in the 1980s, with the publication of the so-called *Tabula Siarensis* (owing to the place of discovery)¹⁵ and the so-called *Lex Irnitana*; these were followed by other inscriptions belonging to communities with a similar status, the next in order of size being the so-called *Lex Flavia Villonensis*¹⁶; in 1996, the *S. C. de Cn. Pisone patre*;¹⁷ and in 2006, a new bronze tablet of the *Lex coloniae Genetivae Iuliae*,¹⁸ among others.

The catalogue of legal inscriptions on bronze from the *provincia Hispania Ulterior Baetica* that I published in 2009¹⁹ included 41 examples of municipal or colonial laws, 4 *senatus consulta* or, to be more precise, 3 *senatus consulta* and one extract from the *acta Senatus*,²⁰ 5 imperial letters, 18 decisions adopted by civic communities, which include 8 hospitality and patronage *tabulae*, and 60 other bronze fragments, the content of which, whenever it can be identified, is heterogeneous. This amounts to a total of 128 bronze inscriptions, most of which are but small fragments. Compared with other western provinces, this is a very large number of fragments, but it still remains a very small sample of the total number of inscriptions produced throughout the Roman Empire. Let's compare this figure with the 176 cities that Pliny mentions for *Baetica* and with the wide chronological span of the epigraphical evidence, which comprise the first three centuries of the life of the empire.²¹ Seen from this perspective, it becomes obvious that the evidence represents a very low percentage of all com-

---

14 NESSELHAUF 1960; COLLANTES/FERNÁNDEZ-CHICARRO 1972–1974, 361–362; CILA, Se 1053; AE 1962, 147; AE 1962, 287; AE 1972, 263.
15 GONZÁLEZ/FERNÁNDEZ 1980; GONZÁLEZ/FERNÁNDEZ 1981; SÁNCHEZ-OSTIZ 1999; CILA, Se 927; AE 1983, 515; AE 1984, 508; AE 1986, 275; AE 1986, 308; AE 1988, 703; AE 1989, 358; AE 1989, 408; AE 1991, 20; AE 1999, 31; AE 1999, 891; AE 2001, 33; AE 2001, 39; AE 2001, 87; AE 2002, 43; AE 2002, 44; AE 2002, 45; AE 2002, 46; HEp 5, 734; HEp 9, 524.
16 CILA, Se 1206. None of the beginnings of these documents have survived, so their original title is unknown.
17 CABALLOS/ECK/FERNÁNDEZ 1996; ECK/CABALLOS/FERNÁNDEZ 1996; CIL II²/5, 900; HEp 4, 831z; HEp 5, 727; HEp 6, 881; HEp 7, 927; HEp 8, 479; HEp 9, 525; AE 1993, 21 a; AE 1994, 894 a-b; AE 1996, 885; AE 1997, 29; AE 1998, 27; AE 1998, 28; AE 1998, 29; AE 1998, 30, AE 1998, 31; AE 1998, 32; AE 1998, 33; AE 1998, 34; AE 1998, 35; AE 1998, 36; AE 1999, 32; AE 1999, 33; AE 1999, 34; AE 1999, 35; AE 1999, 36; AE 2000, 37; AE 2000, 38; AE 2000, 39; AE 2000, 72; AE 2001, 33; AE 2001, 40; AE 2001, 41; AE 2001, 42; AE 2001, 87; AE 2002, 43; AE 2002, 44; AE 2002, 45; AE 2002, 46.
18 CABALLOS 2006; HEp 1994, 825 = HEp 2003/04, 646 = HEp 2006, 325 = HEp 2006, 333 = AE 1991, 1020 = AE 2004, 744 = AE 2005, 700 = AE 2006, 645 = AE 2011, 1520.
19 CABALLOS 2009b.
20 This is known as *Oratio de pretiis gladiatorum minuendis* (CIL II 6278 = ILS 5163). COUDRY 1994, 80, citing OLIVER/PALMER 1955, 320–343.
21 Plin. nat. 3,3,7. W. ECK has recently stressed the low rate of survival of inscriptions for the whole of the Empire (ECK 2015).

munities, most of which were of a secondary status, and the apparent homogeneity of the record dissipates.

Moreover, the provisional nature of any catalogue is a direct and happy expression of the constant discovery of new inscriptions, not only in *Baetica*, but in the other Hispanic provinces. For example, in the Ebro Valley, the bronzes of Botorrita, an extraordinary epigraphic assemblage, have been recently joined by the *Lex rivi hiberiensis*, found in Agón, merely 60 km to the northeast.[22] The relevance of the repertoire of Spanish legal bronzes found to date, as well as the impact of the publication of the most significant examples, has triggered the publication of other inscriptions in museum collections that, having been found some time ago, had been overlooked.[23]

A clear example of this is the Museum of Huelva, directed between 1970 and 1985 by MARIANO DEL AMO Y DE LA HERA, who, alongside FERNANDO FERNÁNDEZ GÓMEZ, director at the time of the Seville Archaeological Museum, lead to the rescue of legal inscriptions on bronze from the ravages of clandestine diggers. This resulted in the incorporation to the Museum of Huelva collection of two tablets of the *Lex Irnitana*, along with other bronze fragments. A. U. STYLOW and R. LÓPEZ MELERO have recently edited seven fragments, currently in the Museum of Huelva, found in the outskirts of Arahal (province of Seville).[24] Their alleged place of origin cannot be matched with any known ancient community. *Basilippo* (Cerro del Cincho, Carmona, Seville) is the closest Roman *municipium* to the place of discovery,[25] but it is as yet unclear whether the bronzes come from there or from other unknown community, from which they were brought to their final place of discovery for reuse or recasting, a process which, for unknown reasons, never took place. Finding these legal inscriptions on bronze relatively far from their place of origin is not rare, as shown by the fragments of the *Lex coloniae Genetivae Iuliae* found in a well in El Rubio, 18 km from Osuna.[26] Some of the bronzes from Arahal match the Flavian municipal laws (I: Museo Provincial de Huelva Inv. nº 10605, II: MPH Inv. nº 10608 and IV: MPH Inv. nº 10610),[27] and the editors have assumed that this applies also to the remaining fragments (very likely fragments III: MPH Inv. nº 10607, V: MPH Inv. nº 10604 and VI: MPH Inv. nº 10606, and probably also VII: MPH Inv. nº 10609). Although fragments I and II, and maybe also IV, could have been part of the same copy of the law, the formal characteristics of the rest are different; therefore, should it be confirmed that all of them correspond to the Flavian statute, two possibilities exist: either the different tablets of this law were very different, which seems unlikely, or we are before a compilation of miscellaneous

---

22 BELTRÁN LLORIS 2006; MAGANZANI/BUZZACCHI 2014.
23 E. g. the assemblage published by DEL HOYO/RODRÍGUEZ 2016.
24 STYLOW/LÓPEZ MELERO 2013.
25 Based on the find of inscriptions CIL II 1373 = CILA, Se 907 and CILA, Se 906.
26 CIL II²/5, 1022.
27 Certainly, Fragment I (corresponding to chapter 48 of the Flavian municipal law), and very likely fragments II (chapter 48) and IV (chapter 27).

material brought together for reuse. At any rate, the bronzes were found in a secondary location connected with their unconsummated reuse.

STYLOW and LÓPEZ MELERO successfully completed the fourth line of Fragment VII (MPH Inv. nº 10609) by restoring *[---igno?]miniae [---]*. After this, J. GONZÁLEZ and J. BERMEJO, taking into consideration broader references, changing the reading of the first and last lines of the new bronze, pointed out the coincidence with lines 119–121 of the *Tabula Heracleensis*,[28] although with a different *ordinatio*.[29] The text corresponds to the third of the five main arguments expressed in the *Heraclea* tablet (lines 83–141), which rules access to the decurionate and the exercise of magistracies in any Roman civic community, regardless whether this community is *municipium, colonia, praefectura, forum* or *conciliabulum*, and specifically defining the causes of *indignitas*, which was incompatible with the decurional rank.[30] This is not the place to go into more detail about these authors' arguments concerning *Tabula Heracleensis* and the Augustan or Caesarian municipal legislations, but we can at least reject the notion that this new bronze of the Huelva Museum collection is an exact copy of the Heraclean text.

In a study of the genealogy of Hispano-Roman municipal laws, we divided them into two clearly differentiated groups. A first group was composed of texts which operate as the statutes of newly-created communities, the object of which is to reaffirm the civic community and consolidate its autonomy. As such, their articles mostly deal with political and administrative matters. These laws, which spring from a common legal tradition, include the *Lex osca Tabulae Bantinae* and especially the *Lex municipii Tarentini*, the content of which has significant parallels in the *Lex coloniae Genetivae Iuliae*. This last text was further developed and refined in the Flavian municipal laws. Although continuity with the previous period is clear, the laws enacted during the reign of Domitian, as a result of its more recent chronology and also of its widespread application, which followed the generalisation of the *ius latii* in *Hispania*, are considerably more consistent and systematic. The accumulation of legal and diplomatic experience led to more homogenous and standardised municipal laws, the content of which mostly adhered to a standard model, almost regardless of the community in which it was applied. The second group includes such significant laws as the previously noted *Tabula Heracleensis* or the so-called *Lex de Gallia Cisalpina*. These texts, the function of which is still being debated, are more heterogenous, but their content

---

[28] CIL I 593; ILS 6085; FIRA I 13; AE 1991, 522 = AE 1994, 540 = AE 1995, 34 = AE 1997, 418. See C. NICOLET and M.H. CRAWFORD's critical up-to-date edition in CRAWFORD 1996, 355–391, nº 24. For genealogical references for Roman statutes of Hispania see CABALLOS/COLUBI 2006.

[29] GONZÁLEZ/BERMEJO 2015. The photograph in which they show the piece is substantially better than the one contained in STYLOW/LÓPEZ MELERO 2013.

[30] The Chapter XVI of the new tablet of the *Lex coloniae Genetivae Iuliae* refers to *dignitas* and *idoneitas* as the moral and functional requisites that candidates to magistracies and the decurionate had to possess, CABALLOS 2006, 268–271.

still presents important affinities with the Spanish laws.[31] Considering the fact that the statutes of Roman civic communities, regardless of the category of the community in which they applied, followed the same guidelines, it is misguided to think of the bronze of Huelva as a copy of the Heraclean text. Instead, following STYLOW and LÓPEZ MELERO's initial interpretation, the tablet must be interpreted as corresponding to a fragment of the statute of an unknown provincial *civitas*. It remains to be ascertained whether this text follows Augustan colonial statutes or whether it is another example of Flavian municipal legislation. In any case, the fragments belong to those sections of the first part of the law (either colonial or municipal), which were hitherto unknown; we now know, that this part of the text dealt with the issues covered by lines 83 to 141 of the legal bronze from *Heraclea*.

The collection in the provincial museum of Huelva also includes nine small fragments that belong to as many military diplomas, four of which have been recently published by J. GONZÁLEZ and J. BERMEJO.[32] The relevance of this assemblage is clear, because until recently only six military diplomas were known in *Baetica*.[33] In a first work, GONZÁLEZ and BERMEJO published three of these documents; two were linked to two of Trajan's constitutions, one in 116/117[34] and another in 105/107 or 108[35]. The names of the soldiers and their units have not been preserved. The third of the diplomas was awarded on 22 March 129 to a veteran soldier of unknown identity enrolled in the *cohors I Ulpia Dacorum*, stationed in Syria under *Ti. Claudius Maximinus*.[36] Subsequently, J. GONZÁLEZ and J. BERMEJO edited the largest fragment of these military diplomas in the provincial museum of Huelva.[37] The name and provenance of the veteran to whom it was awarded are, like in the previous example, not known, but it can be dated to the reign of Antoninus Pius. The editors of the inscription date the constitution to which it was related to around 157–159.[38] The piece is of interest because it lists the auxiliary units that benefitted from that constitution, units which were at the time stationed in *Mauritania Tingitana*. GONZÁLEZ and BERMEJO examine these units in detail, and interpret their deployment in the light of the *mauri* rebellions from the reign of Hadrian onwards. It is assumed that these troops had been largely recruited in *Hispania*, and that this was also the origin of the unnamed veteran to whom the diploma had been awarded. While I write these lines, therefore, four of the diplomas

---

31 CABALLOS/COLUBI 2006, 17–18.
32 GONZÁLEZ/BERMEJO 2016a and GONZÁLEZ/BERMEJO 2016b.
33 CABALLOS 2019, 160–161, note 54.
34 Archaeological Museum of Huelva (Museo Arqueológico de Huelva, onwards MPH) Inv. nº 10623, GONZÁLEZ/BERMEJO 2016a, 274–275, nº 1.
35 MPH Inv. nº 10620, GONZÁLEZ/BERMEJO 2016 a, 275–276, nº 2.
36 MPH Inv. nº 10619. The inner face of this tiny fragment partially preserves the name of the military unit and that of its commander, GONZÁLEZ/BERMEJO 2016a, 276–278, nº3.
37 MPH Inv. nº 10615; (2.5) × (3) × 0.1 cm.
38 GONZÁLEZ/BERMEJO 2016b, 520.

in the Huelva museum collection are still waiting to be edited: two are also dated in Antoninus' reign and the other two to unknown emperors.[39]

Prudence is required concerning the origin of bronze inscriptions, especially military diplomas, not found during archaeological excavation and whose transmission process is, therefore, suspicious. This is, for instance, the case with the diploma of the praetorian *M. Aurelius Silvinus*, from *Augusta Vindelicorum*, in *Raetia*, dated in the reign of Severus Alexander, specifically on 7 January 234; the real provenance of this bronze inscription is unknown, even though it was fraudulently reported to have been found on the coast of Almeria.[40]

These are not the only new entries to the repertoire of legal epigraphy in *Baetica* to be added since the publication of my catalogue.[41] A bronze fragment (9) x (11) x 0.5 cm in size with lettering 2.4 cm high, carrying the text MVN V was found in the site of Sierra de Gibalbín, located 20 km to the northeast of Jerez de la Frontera (Cadiz).[42] This same site also yielded a small fragment — (18) × (4) × (0.6) cm — recently edited and carrying the text *[---] / [---]AM[---] / [---]ERIT[---] / [---] · QV[---]*.[43] J. GONZÁLEZ, based on the preserved text and the typology of the letters, speculatively identifies this inscription as a fragment of a municipal law. Such an open sequence, however, precludes any certainty in the identification of the text, even if the preserved text can be matched more or less closely to the those preserved in other documents.[44] In addition, there is a bronze inscription that I listed within the 'Varia' of my catalogue, under the reference V.10, which reads *[---]V[---] / M · DA[---] / [---] S · S · S · O[---] / [---]TORIV[---]*. That the text deals with a tax-related issue is shown by the development of the abbreviation on the third line — e.g. *s(upra) s(cripta) s(umma)* — and the very plausible *[por]toriu[m]* on the fourth. In my catalogue, I followed the editor and described the provenance of the fragment as 'Unknown',[45] but in the catalogue entry in the Seville Archaeological Museum (MAS), the location where the piece was discovered is succinctly given as Gibalbín.[46] Therefore, this site, which is currently abandoned and,

---

39 GONZÁLEZ/BERMEJO 2016a, 274.
40 CABALLOS 2009a; HEp 2009, 523; AE 2009, 1799.
41 CABALLOS 2009b, 147–172.
42 GONZÁLEZ 2014. This author proposed the identification of this site with *Ugia Castrum Iulium*, a *municipium* mentioned by Pliny (nat. 3,3,15). According to J. GONZÁLEZ, Pliny's expression *Caesaris Salutariensis*, which follows the mention of this community, referred to another city of the same name.
43 RUIZ/VEGA/GARCÍA ROMERO 2016, 128. The editors erroneously identify this inscription as a military *diploma*, spuriously repeating the description in their page 124, which corresponds to a military *diploma* found in same location and edited by J. GONZÁLEZ (GONZÁLEZ 1994, 11–16; RMD III 179; HEp 6, 540; AE 1994, 910; CABALLOS 2009b, 161, note 54, nº 3).
44 For instance, merely as an example, and without wishing to suggest further implications, the same sequence of letters may be found in lines 35 *(O: OMNI)*, 36 *(AM: TAMQVAM)*, 37 *(ERIT: CESSERIT)* and 38 *(QV: QVOD)* of Copy A of the *S. C. de Cn. Pisone patre*.
45 FERNÁNDEZ 1991, 131 (AE 1991, 1025; HEp 1994, 830).
46 Archaeological Museum of Seville (Museo Arqueológico de Sevilla, onwards MAS), Inv. nº 1990/100.

sadly, a common haunt of illegal excavators, is associated with a not inconsiderable collection of four epigraphic bronzes.

In this regard, *Baelo Claudia* (Ensenada de Bolonia, Tarifa, Cadiz) stands out even more than Gibalbín. *Baelo Claudia* is being excavated systematically, and new pleasing discoveries are a common occurrence.[47] To date, the catalogue of bronze inscriptions from *Baelo Claudia* included seven pieces: a possible imperial *epistula* by Vespasian or Titus,[48] a military diploma dated to AD 161,[49] as well as five other unidentified public documents.[50] In the excavation campaigns undertaken in the south-eastern corner of the city in 2014, 2015, 2016 and 2017, up to forty-two bronze tablet fragments were found. All of these fragments are small and a good number carry inscribed letters, but in most cases the text is too succinct to enable identification of the larger document to which they belonged. However, one fragment may well be identified as a fragment of the city's municipal statutes. The importance of the assemblage, rather than in the textual content of the tablets, lies in the number and variety of the fragments and, especially, the circumstances of their discovery, in a secure archaeological and chronological context, of which more shortly.[51]

RUIZ/VEGA/GARCÍA 2016, 134–135, nº 52. The complexity of studying fragmentary legal inscriptions on bronze, especially when only a few letters survive, and the usual difficulties in establishing the provenance of these fragments, propitiate that the databases in use, for example the extraordinary and by now indispensable EDCS, often include two entries for a single inscription – for this case EDCS-05000454 and EDCS-21700488; the first entry marks the provenance with a question mark, while the second indicates a provenance in Seville/*Hispalis*, which in reality is nothing but the current location of the piece, which is held by the Seville Archaeological Museum.

47 The excavating team is under the direction of L. BRASSOUS, X. DERU and O. RODRÍGUEZ, after the sad loss of B. GOFFAUX (see https://www.casadevelazquez.org/fileadmin/fichiers/publicaciones/Cahiers_archeologie/Baelo_2011–2015.pdf; consulted on 15. 02. 17).

48 Currently in the National Archaeological Museum (Inv. nº 342925). D'ORS 1959, 367–370; AE 1960, 158; BONNEVILLE/DARDAINE/LE ROUX 1988, 33–34, nº 8; GONZÁLEZ 1990, 211, nº 24; CABALLOS 2009b, 162, III.3.

49 Currently in the Cadiz Museum (Inv. nº 17092). See JACOB 1984a; JACOB 1984b; AE 1984, 529; RMD II 107; HEp 1, 214; LÓPEZ PARDO 1986; AE 1987, 500; BONNEVILLE/DARDAINE/LE ROUX 1988, 31–33, nº 7; CABALLOS 2009b, 161, note 54, nº 2.

50 Inv. nº 79/2398 (BONNEVILLE/DARDAINE 1980, 417 s.; BONNEVILLE/DARDAINE/LE ROUX 1988, 34, nº 9; CABALLOS 2009b, 167–168); Inv. nº 72/1573 (BONNEVILLE/DARDAINE/LE ROUX 1988, 35, nº 11; CABALLOS 2009b, 171, nº V.20); Inv. nº 73/703 (BONNEVILLE/DARDAINE/LE ROUX 1988, 34–35, nº 10; CABALLOS 2009b, 166, nº IV.13); Inv. nº 75/2086b (BONNEVILLE/DARDAINE/LE ROUX 1988, 35, nº 12; CABALLOS 2009b, 171, nº V.21); Inv. nº 75/2086a (BONNEVILLE/DARDAINE/LE ROUX 1988, 36, nº 13; CABALLOS 2009b, 172, nº V.22).

51 CABALLOS/RODRÍGUEZ/BRASSOUS 2018.

Another fragment of a legal inscription on bronze, larger this time,[52] was found in La Veguilla[53] or Las Torrecillas,[54] 1.8 km to the east of the town of Maguilla (Badajoz), in the territory of *Baeturia Turdulorum*, part of the *Conventus Cordubensis*, in the northwest of the province of *Baetica*. This inscription has posed new questions and has thus rekindled the debate about the institutional implications of these legal bronzes. The inscription carries twelve lines of text,[55] which the original editors identified as part of two unknown chapters of the Flavian municipal statute, which deal with the celebration of *comitiae*.[56] The most controversial part of the text is the reference to *IIIIviri* in the ninth line, followed by the letters *co[...]*, where the preserved text comes to an end. SAQUETE and IÑESTA developed these last letters as referring to *comitia*, suggesting that these *quattuorviri* were magistrates elected collectively in the initial steps of the constitution of a Flavian municipality, this magistracy being later replaced by *IIviri*.[57]

P. LE ROUX[58] and J. GONZÁLEZ[59] are of a very different opinion: they suggest that the ninth line concludes with a mention to an unidentified *colonia latina*, the statutes of which the new bronze was part of. Should that be the case, this bronze would be the only one of its kind known to us. For LE ROUX, the magistrates cited would be *quattuorviri iure dicundo*, associated to the old colonial Latin status, and the community to which the bronze belonged would be, according to Pliny, one of the 27 communities *Latio antiquitus donata* in the province.[60] J. GONZÁLEZ dates the granting of this status to the Augustan or the Caesarian period.

---

52 (9'2) x (7'8) x 0'7/0'85. The fragment was clipped from a larger tablet; to the left, the cut has severed the text.
53 In SAQUETE/IÑESTA 2009, 293.
54 In LE ROUX 2014, 254.
55 ...... / [supra] scriptae [sunt ...] / [...]unto quiq(ue) m[...] / [...]t erunt ita uti +[...] / [...]erisq(ue) eorum qui e+[...] / [... c]uria una libertino[rum ...] / [...]t erit in ea curia li[bertin ...] / [...]qui eorum pubes e+[...] / ...]
Comitia ex h(ac) l(ege) habere [...] / [...] quam is IIIIvir co[...] / [...]+et satisdare op[ortebit (?) ...] / [...] ve ex h(ac) l(ege) de[...] / [...] quam [......
56 SAQUETE/IÑESTA 2009 suggest that the inscription refers to the curia in which *libertini* must vote, and also, among other things, the caution or guarantee which magistrates must provide, which draws a link between this inscription and *Lex Malacitana* 52–60.
57 The authors refer to the mention made of *IIIIviri*, (supra note 14) in Titus' *epistula* to the *municipia* of *Munigua*, where *IIviri* are epigraphically attested at a later date, and *Sabora*, where Vespasian's letter addresses the *IIIIviri*, although the publication of the imperial *epistula* is entrusted to the *IIviri* (CIL II 1423; CIL II²/5, 871; ILS 6092. Furthermore, cases similar to these can be attested in other municipalities, such as *Carmo*, where the office *IIIIvir* is also attested (CIL II 1380; ILS 5080a; CILA, Se 842). What the first editors have not taken into account is that, should this be a temporary magistracy, it would not feature in the municipal statutes, which consolidated the political-administrative model based on the duovirs, as reflected in the preserved Flavian municipal laws, where the *IIIIviri* are never mentioned.
58 LE ROUX 2014, 254–259.
59 GONZÁLEZ 2015.
60 Plin. nat. 3,3,7.

The archaeological materials found on the surface of the site are described as 'poor' by Saquete and Iñesta, which thus interpret the site as a rural settlement. No archaeological excavation has, however, been undertaken, so this characterisation is unconfirmed. Le Roux's more detailed description, based on J.-G. Gorges's information, refers to 10 archaeologically 'fertile' hectares, including *tegulae*, disperse construction materials and ceramic fragments, which date the settlement between the late 1st and the late 3rd, if not early 4th centuries.[61] With this information, and considering the inscriptions recently found in Maguilla and its surroundings, the presence of a larger settlement in this location cannot be ruled out.[62] One thing on which all authors agree is the abundance of smelting slags on the surface of the site,[63] which indicates metallurgical activity. This means that bronze inscriptions could well have been carried there from elsewhere for melting. Although previous evidence shows how far bronzes could travel in this way, making certainty concerning provenance impossible, the closest privileged communities are the *municipium Flavium V(...)*, which has been identified with Azuaga (Badajoz), 16 km to the southeast,[64] and *Regina* (Casas de Reina, Badajoz), approximately 20 km to the southwest.[65] If we assume that the document refers to a colony, the first option must be rejected. Not so with *Regina*, which both Saquete and Iñesta and P. Le Roux explicitly consider the foremost candidate, although for different reasons.[66]

The extreme mobility of bronzes during antiquity and the criminal activity of clandestine excavators are not the only factors adding complexity to the study of legal inscriptions on bronze; the uncontrolled trade in archaeological pieces, for example, does little to clarify the picture. I have already referred to the case posed by the military diploma of *M. Aurelius Silvinus* and its problematic recovery. Another example of the bizarre routes followed by bronze inscriptions in antiquity and, even more so, in recent times, is the adventure undergone by one of the missing fragments of Copy A of the *Senatus consultum de Cn. Pisone patre*, specifically a small triangular piece from

---

61 Le Roux 2014, 254.
62 De Maguilla CIL II²/7, 897; CIL II²/7, 898 y CIL II²/7, 899. Near Maguilla CIL II²/7, 901; and 10 km from the village CIL II²/7, 900. A.U. Stylow (CIL II²/7, ad loc.) ascribes Maguilla and Campillo de Llerena to the *Municipium Flavium V(---)* of Azuaga (Badajoz).
63 A similar case is attested in *Munigua* (Mulva, Villanueva del Río y Minas, Seville). Maguilla has also yielded a circular bronze seal (CIL II²/7, 901).
64 CIL II²/7, p. 202.
65 CIL II²/7, p. 222.
66 Saquete/Iñesta 2009, 297; Le Roux 2014, 258. The inscription dedicated to the genie of the *oppidum* of *Regina* by a *Xvir max(imus)* has been dated by A.U. Stylow to between the reign of Nero and little earlier than AD 73/74 (CIL II²/7, 974). This suggests a peregrine status, and promotion to *municipium* at a later date. We do not know the office held by the persons entrusted to supervise the restoration of the *Templum Pietatis* commissioned by the *r(es) p(ublica) R(eginensium)* (CIL II²/7, 976), name that this community used to designate itself (also in CIL II²/7, 979 y CIL II²/7, 980). For A.U. Stylow the *[---]Ivir* de CIL II²/7, 977 would be a *[III]Ivir* rather than a *[I]Ivir*.

the middle of the first column, between lines 25 and 29. It is clear that this fragment, along with another one, even smaller and devoid of any writing, between the 'P' and the 'I' of 'Pisone' in the *titulus*, were lost in the process of illegal extraction of the piece, on the site of Las Herrizas (El Saucejo, Seville), where *Irni* appears to have been located. An informant in Osuna told me that a person in El Saucejo was in possession of a small fragment. At the time, our attempts to recover it were fruitless. Finally, a colleague managed to find an inscription fragment on the international market, which was later identified as none other but the piece that was missing from Copy A. The fragment was, at last, handed over to the Seville Archaeological Museum, and, although the proceedings of the deposit are still ongoing, in this way this exceptional document is finally complete[67].

The new discoveries listed above should, as far as I am aware, complete the catalogue of legal bronzes found in the province of *Baetica* to date.[68] I shall not elaborate upon arguments that I and others have abundantly discussed elsewhere.[69] Instead, I shall henceforth be focusing on the production, display, functionality and impact of legal bronzes, as well as on their reuse and recycling.

Concerning the production of legal bronze inscriptions, I think it is important to separate metallurgical activity on the one hand and the engraving of the text on the other; with epigraphy on stone, the preparation of the medium and the engraving of the texts are most connected operations, at least in comparison to epigraphy on bronze. The former began with the casting of bronze sheets, which demanded a more substantial infrastructure. For health reasons, the casting workshops would be situated in suburban areas. The final preparation of the bronze, the *ordinatio* of the text and the engraving of the letters by percussion with *scalprum* and *malleum* would be a more delicate craft that relied more on the skill of the engraver than in a complex combination of infrastructure and tools.

The evidence fully supports the separation of both processes. The reverse of several of the tablets of the *Lex Coloniae Genetivae Iuliae* presents identical irregularities, owing to the use of the same mould. This is clear evidence that the tablets were produced in series. The case of the hospitality and patronage tablets is particularly significant. These must have been produced in great numbers, not only because of the large number of patrons that communities accumulated over time — *Canusium*'s album, which lists 39 patrons, is particularly remarkable in this regard[70] —, but because, owing to an old tradition, those patronages were recorded not on one but on

---

67 GRADEL 2014.
68 A.U. STYLOW is studying a new set of seven fragments of epigraphic bronzes found near *Contributa Iulia Ugultunia*, a *municipium* located in Los Cercos de los Castillejos, Medina de las Torres, Badajoz (STYLOW/LÓPEZ MELERO 2013, 387 note 10).
69 Supra note 9.
70 CIL IX 338; SALWAY 2000. In contrast with *Canusium*'s large number of patrons, *Thamugadi*'s album only contains six names (CIL VIII 2403; CIL VIII 17824; CIL VIII 17903; ILS 6122; CHASTAGNOL 1978).

two tablets, one to be displayed in the patron's *domus* and the other in the patronised community.⁷¹

Díaz Ariño and Cimarosti's recent catalogue lists 26 surviving hispanic hospitality tablets found in the Iberian Peninsula. This is a very large number in relative terms, for it amounts to 23 % of the total number of hospitality tablets found in the whole of the empire (111 in total), but once more it reminds us of the poor representativeness of the epigraphic record, one of historiography's capital questions. Given the small size of the record, it is particularly significant that four of these tablets are formally identical. One of these four tablets, found in *Munigua* (Mulva, Villanueva del Río y Minas, Seville) and dated in the early 1st century BC, records the *hospitium* of *Sex. Curvius Silvinus* with the city;⁷² two more, from the *castrum* of Monte Murado (Pedroso, Vilanova de Gaia, Portugal) and dated to AD 7 and AD 9 respectively, record pacts between two *D. Iulii Cilones*, one of whom is cited as *D. f.* and the other as *M. f.*, with members of the *Turduli Veteres*;⁷³ the last one, dated to AD 38, is the *hospitium* of *Q. Lucius Fenestella* with *Aratispi*. The provenance of this last tablet must be somewhere in *Baetica*,⁷⁴ probably Cauche el Viejo (Villanueva del Cauche, Antequera, Málaga),⁷⁵ which at the time was a *civitas stipendiaria*, being promoted to *municipium* in the Flavian period.

All four tablets are formally identical. They have quadrangular epigraphic fields, with neither frame nor drill holes for hanging on a surface. The top side projects in a triangular shape framed by three riveted listels. The resulting gable presents no internal decoration. This temple-like shape gives the document sacred connotations, reinforced by the complex laced acroteria with which the bottom corners and the top of the gable are decorated. They are all dated within a short time span, little more than three decades. Also, the three communities involved were at the time small stipendiary cities, and it is thus reasonable to assume that they did not need to set up bronze inscriptions particularly often. This, along with the fact that the cities are relatively distant from one another — *Munigua* is 450 km to the southeast of Monte Murado, and *Aratispi* is 150 km further to the southeast of *Munigua* — suggests that all four inscriptions were produced in a single workshop, the production of which would have spread far and wide.

---

71 Díaz Ariño/Cimarosti 2016, 334–335.
72 While Grünhagen 1961, 214–216 only indicated that the inscription must have been produced before AD 40, D'Ors 1961, 203–205 dated it to AD 5/6, and Alföldy 1969, 182–183 to the Augustan or the Tiberian period. See also Balbín Chamorro 2006, 243–244, nº 72; Díaz Ariño/Cimarosti 2016, nº 46; AE 1962, 287.
73 Balbín Chamorro 2006, 192–195, nº 46a y 46b; Díaz Ariño/Cimarosti 2016, nº 45; AE 1994, 923.
74 Balbín Chamorro 2006, 244–245, nº 73; Díaz Ariño/Cimarosti 2016, nº 52 y 53; AE 1983, 476 y 477.
75 CIL II²/5, 732. P. Balbín Chamorro, however, believes that the preserved copy was the one given to *Lucio Fenestella* (Balbín Chamorro 2006, 244–245, nº 73).

The two tablets from Monte Murado present diplomatic and linguistic differences,[76] as well as some dissimilarities in the lettering, despite being nearly contemporary. This suggests that the engraving of the texts did not take place in this city in the *conventus Bracaraugustanus*. If we compare the tablets from *Munigua* and *Aratispi*, the formal differences are, again, small. The surviving acroterion from *Munigua* is better executed than that from *Aratispi*, which is approximately 30 years later. The formula is also similar — the one from *Munigua* does not record the consular date — but the lettering suggests that they were executed by different hands. It is, therefore, reasonable to assume that the tablets, including the standard decorative elements and epigraphic fields, were executed and commercialised blank, to be filled, using a similar formula,[77] with the specific text required in each case.

If, on the other hand, we compare the inscription from *Munigua* with other two coetaneous hospitality tablets, the one from the colony of *Emerita Augusta*, dated to AD 6,[78] and that found in Peñón de Audita (Cortijo de Clavijo, Grazalema, Cadiz), dating to AD 5 and probably corresponding to the, at the time, stipendiary city of *Lacidula*,[79] both of which are incomplete,[80] the similarities are such that, if not by the same hand, they must have been engraved by the same workshop or, at the very least,

---

[76] The formulas used in the earliest is simpler, while the latest one presents certain archaisms.

[77] All but two of the tablets found in the Iberian Peninsula use the older 'provincial formula', in the words of Díaz Ariño/Cimarosti 2016.

[78] Balbín Chamoro 2006, 234–235, nº 66; Díaz Ariño/Cimarosti 2016, nº 51; AE 1952, 49.

[79] Balbín Chamorro 2006, 237–238, nº 68; Díaz Ariño/Cimarosti 2016, nº 45; CIL II 1343. The ancient city was also known as *Lacilbula*, although the correct denomination seems to have been *Lacidula* or even *Lacidulum*. One inscription, of which only a literary record remains, referred to *Lacilbulensium* or *Lacidulemium* (CIL II 1342). It could be that the last of these formulas was a misreading of *Lacidulensium* (Correa 2016, 358). *Lacidula* was located in Cortijo de Clavijo, as demonstrated by CIL II 1342 and CIL II 5409 and the archaeological remains found in association with this site, the *hospitium* included. E. Balbín Chamorro suggested that the tablet was the copy handed over to Q. Marius Balbus, beneficiary of the *hospitium*, which would indicate that the site was a property of his. Balbín Chamorro's argument is based on the fact that Q. Marius Balbus's name appears first, considering that the other copy, which has not been found, would mention the host community first. We do not preserve both tablets from any of the hospitality pacts attested in Hispania; the chances of that happening are astronomical. However, Balbín Chamorro's argument can be rejected with the evidence offered by the hospitality tablet from Mérida (Balbín Chamorro 2006, 234–235, nº 66). This inscription was found in the peristyle of the theatre, so there is little doubt that it was the colony's copy, despite which the name of the city appears second.

[80] The hospitality tablet from Mérida is missing the top part, so we do not know whether it was also decorated with a gable, acroteria and upper decorative motif. This tablet presents boring holes on the edges, which are not present in the tablet from *Munigua*. It is not clear, in any case, whether these holes were bored during the production of the tablet or at a later date; in fact, while the left side presents three holes, the right one has only one (a second one, near the fracture point, is also possible). Only the left part of the text is preserved in the case of *Lacidula*'s hospitality tablet, which is also missing the top. This makes it impossible to ascertain whether the inscription was decorated by a gable.

following the same technical and graphic tradition. Another fragmentary hospitality tablet was found in Cabeza de Hortales (Prado del Rey, Cadiz), formerly *Iptuci*, which in the early years of the empire was also a *civitas stipendiaria*. Given the fragmentary state of the tablet, which records the hospitality pact subscribed by this city and the colonists of *Ucubi* in AD 31, some formal aspects are uncertain.[81] In any case, the *ordinatio* of the text, the graphic model and the formula[82] are very similar to those presented by the inscription from *Lacidula*, which is barely 20 km away. This, and other evidence, points towards the existence, at least in the Early Empire, of regional workshops engaged in the engraving of bronze inscriptions. These workshops would either serve orders to different communities from a stable location,[83] or its craftsmen would travel to the city in question to engrave the tablet *in situ* when the scale of the commission so required.

There is epigraphic evidence of concentrated metallurgical activity and the operation of *societates* for the production of, and work in, bronze in *Baetica*:[84] *e.g.* the funerary inscription of a freedman who belonged to a *societas aerariorum* on *Corduba*[85] and the inscription that a group of *confectores aeris* erected in *Hispalis* to an imperial freedman who was *procurator montis Mariani*,[86] a mining district in Sierra Morena.[87] It is not a coincidence that the inscriptions were found in these two cities: *Corduba* was the provincial capital and seat of the provincial administration, as well as the place where political documents and laws, both coming from Rome and enacted by the proconsul, had to be displayed;[88] and *Hispalis* was seat of a *conventus* and a central point of reference at the regional level, and base of the provincial procurator and his office, and thus of the financial administration of the province, as well as of other procurators and their agents.[89]

---

[81] BALBÍN CHAMORRO 2006, 238–239, nº 69; DÍAZ ARIÑO/CIMAROSTI 2016, nº 31; AE 1955, 21.
[82] With due allowances to the fact that the *Lacidula* tablet records a pact between an individual and a city, not a pact between two communities.
[83] One of the functions of the embassies of civic communities, as regulated by municipal laws (*Lex Irnit*. F-I) was to negotiate and supervise the engraving of bronze inscriptions commissioned by their communities when that involved contacting a workshop located in a different community.
[84] Naturally, their work was not limited to the production of tablets and other epigraphic media, but also included statues, ornaments, weapons, tools and the wide array of artefacts included under the general category of *instrumenta*.
[85] *M(arcus) Aerarius soc(ietatis) aerar(iorum) l(ibertus) / Telemac(h)us medicus / hic quiescit vale* (CIL II²/7, 334; HEp 1994, 286; AE 1971, 181).
[86] *T(ito) Flavio Aug(usti) / lib(erto) Polychryso / proc(uratori) montis / Mariani prae/stantissimo / confectores aeris* (CIL II 1179; ILS 1591; CILA, Se 25).
[87] See DOMERGUE 1990, for the exploitation of copper in Sierra Morena 47–48, in the southwest 49–62, and especially the administration of mines in *Baetica* 282–283 and 292–307.
[88] HAENSCH 1997, 178–183.
[89] HAENSCH 1997, 180, note 141; and OJEDA 1993, 43–86 and 211–216.

The engraving on bronze of certain types of widespread, small-format documents, such as hospitality and patronage *tabulae*[90] or military diplomas, was habitual practice.[91] Political statements and legal dispositions pose an entirely different case. On the one hand, legal documents were not displayed in Rome as a result of an administrative demand, because they did not come into effect with their public display but with their file in the *tabularium*;[92] on the other hand, should the publication of the norm be decided, they did not have necessarily to be displayed in bronze, and in fact the most common procedure was to display the text on *tabulae dealbatae*.[93] The same applies to the administrative measures undertaken by proconsuls in the province, owing to his *imperium*, or for the instructions sent to Baetica by the imperial government. In this regard, we must distinguish between two different circumstances.

On the one hand are the municipal statutes, which had to be systematically engraved on bronze and publicly displayed in their communities, following the traditional Republican model.[94] This is stated by Pliny[95] and is also clearly reflected in chapter 95 of *Irni*'s statute, which has survived: *R(ubrica) De lege in aes incidenda. / Qui IIvir{i} in eo municipio iure d(icundo) p(raerit) facito uti haec lex primo quo/que tempore in aes incidatur et in loco celeberrimo eius mu/nicipii figatur ita ut d(e) p(lano) r(ecte) l(egi) p(ossit)*. Domitian's attached *epistula*, which is dated to AD 91, refers to the celebration of marriages in defiance to the law, and the Emperor requests obedience for the norm. This circumstance suggests that the rule that demanded laws to be published promptly was being broken (*primo quoque tempore*).

---

90 In the case of patronage agreements, whenever possible the subscription of the pact was also accompanied with the erection of a statue (Díaz Ariño/Cimarosti 2016, 323–324, as shown in *Aquincum* (CIL X 5426, ll. 2–9: *huic universus populus Aquinatium tabulam aeneam patronatus traditum, sed et statuam perpetuabilem cum picturam similitudinis eius hoc in loco ad perennem testimonium censuer(it) constituendam*) and *Leptis Magna* (IRT 558, ll. 3–9: *Lepcimagnensis ordo et populus, ut incomparabilium beneficiorum eius memoria, etiam ad posteros mitteretur, praeter hospitalem tesseram etiam statuam marmoream constituendam esse duxeretur*).
91 Díaz Ariño/Cimarosti 2016, 338.
92 Hence the formula *referre in tabulas publicas*, of the, originally hand-written, *susbcriptio* which closes the *S. C. de Cn. Pisone patre*. For the archive and publication of public documents, see Coudry 1994; Ferrary 2009, 59–74 and Eck 2009.
93 Eck 2009, 79, refers to a set of instructions contained in the *Tabula Siarensis* (fragm. II b, ll. 21–27); after the document had been displayed in the temple of Apollo, the consuls had to publish the text in Rome in order to make it available to the magistrates and emissaries of Italian and provincial colonies and municipalities so they could order copies to be made and sent to their cities. He thinks that this means that the publication of the text was not necessarily understood as permanent, but only temporary —they were in all certainty inscribed on wood— a habit developed already during the Republican period.
94 Crawford 1996, I 25–26.
95 Plin. nat. 34,99: *usus aeris ad perpetuitatem monumentorum iam pridem tralatus est tabullis aereis, in quibus publicae constitutiones inciduntur*.

The consequence of this obligation to engrave and display municipal statutes on bronze tablets in the province is that, despite the fact that the vast majority of *tabulae aheneae* have been lost, we have remains of up to 47 local statutes. It needs to be taken into account that most of this evidence is fragmentary, and that its survival depends on random factors, such as the abandonment of the settlement to which the tablets belonged in combination with exceptional post-depositional circumstances. For this reason, the importance of the extraordinary survival of more complete examples, especially the *Lex coloniae Genetivae Iuliae* and the so-called *Lex Irnitana* (or *Lex municipii Irnitani*), cannot be overstated. The written evidence attests to the existence of twelve *civium Romanorum* colonies in *Baetica*,[96] but we have found the statutes of only one of them, *colonia Genetiva Iulia*, established in *Urso* (Osuna, Seville), and this was possible owing to the relocation of Osuna's urban nucleus during the Modern Age. Concerning *municipia*, only five of the preserved texts mention the name of the city to which they belong (*Irni, Malaca, Salpensa, Villo* and *Ostippo*), while in three cases the identification can be deduced from the location of the find (*Carruca, Conobaria* and *Iliturgicola*); we may tentatively add *Baelo* to this list, based on one of the recently found fragments to which I made an earlier reference. Except for *Malaca* (Málaga) and *Conobaria* (Las Cabezas de San Juan, Seville), the other municipalities mentioned were abandoned and are currently uninhabited. The catalogue includes another 32 fragments which has been impossible to assign to any known city. Assuming that the fragments found in Arahal[97] correspond to five different *municipia*, the number of unidentified statutes ascends to 37.

On the other hand, aside from municipal statutes, which had to be publicly displayed in bronze in the province, other kinds of document were inscribed on *tabulae aheneae* and were given a public projection only rarely, and not for legal-administrative reasons but for political and ideological motivations, as these publications aimed at achieving maximum public impact. This is the reason behind the publication in bronze of the so-called *tabula Siarensis* and the *S. C. de Cn. Pisone patre*. It is important to point out that the communities in which these documents were displayed were, at the time of the publication, a *municipium*, in the case of *Siarum*, and a *civitas stipendiaria*, in that of *Irni*, so they were excluded from Rome's orders concerning dissemination; their publication in these communities, as explicitly stated in the *titulus* of Copy A of the *Senatus consultum de Cn. Pisone patre*, was an initiative of the proconsul of *Baetica*.[98]

---

[96] The nine cited by Pliny (Plin. nat. 3,3: *Patricia Corduba, Hasta Regia, Romula Hispalis, Claritas Iulia Ucubi, Genetiva Iulia Urso, Caesarina Augusta Asido, Augusta Firma Astigi, Virtus Iulia Ituci, Augusta Gemella Tucci*), plus *Iulia Gemella Acci*, which at its foundation was included in the *Ulterior, Iulia Traducta* and the later *Aelia Augusta Italica*.
[97] Vide supra.
[98] *S · C · DE · CN · PISONE · PATRE · PROPOSITVM · N · VIBIO · SERENO · PRO · COS.*

Municipal laws, political documents arrived from Rome and decrees enacted by provincial governors that had to be engraved in bronze and publicly displayed, as well as hospitality and patronage pacts,[99] and all documents significant enough for public display, must be installed in the most visited, conspicuous and noble areas of the city.[100] This was a ritual reproduction of the prescriptions contained in such venerable documents as the Law of the Twelve Tables[101] and the *S. C. de Bacchanalibus*.[102] We have already seen that this obligation was likewise expressed in chapter 95 of the *Lex Irnitana*, and that, before that, it was also mentioned in lines 170–172 of Copy A of the *S. C. de Cn. Pisone patre*: *item hoc s(enatus) c(onsultum) {hic} in cuiusque provinciae celeberruma{e} urbe eiusque i<n> urbis ipsius celeberrimo loco in aere incisum figeretur...*, although in this case no mention is made to the need to place the inscription at eye level.[103]

Despite the large number of public documents in bronze that have been preserved in the Roman province of *Baetica*, the circumstances in which they were found yield no precise evidence with regard to their public display. For one, the original place of display of most of them is uncertain. Even when the location in which they were found is known, this is, as a rule, not where they were originally displayed, but a secondary position related to the piece's storage or reuse. At best, the tablets can be found in association with the forensic area of the city, for instance with what Mallon refers to as tablets A-E of *Lex coloniae Genetivae Iuliae*, although in this case, owing to the circumstances of the find, it has been impossible to associate the inscriptions to a specific building. Hübner states that the *Oratio de pretiis gladiatorum minuendis* was found '*prope Italicam*'.[104] Currently, a copy is displayed in one of the side-rooms of the perimeter gallery of the *ima cavea*, in the amphitheatre of *Italica*; however the only argument for this location, and a very weak one at that, is its alleged coherence with the content of the text. *Italica*'s other bronze[105] was indeed found in the amphitheatre, specifically in the excavation of the *arena*, near the *podium*, but, once again, it is impossible to associate the inscription with a specific building, or even know whether it was conceived to be displayed in the amphitheatre or was there merely in a secondary position.

---

99 Díaz Ariño/Cimarosti 2016, 338.
100 Eck 2009, 75–96.
101 This document, exceptionally engraved on ivory, is absolutely plain in this regard: *Quas in tabulas eboreas perscriptas pro rostris composuerunt, ut possint leges apertius percipi* (Dig. 1,2,2,4).
102 CIL I² 581, vv. 25–27; CIL X 104; ILS 18; ILLRP 511 (*Atque utei / hoce in tabolam ahenam inceideretis ita senatus aiquom censuit / uteique eam figier ioubeatis ubei facilumed gnoscier potisit*).
103 For this matter, see our edition of the document, *supra* note 17.
104 Also Luzón 1999, 101–103 has been unable to add anything more precise concerning the provenance of the inscription.
105 CIL II 5368; Mommsen, EE II, 149–150; HAE 4–5, 11; HAE 8–11, 26; Rodríguez de Berlanga 1891, 210–211; D'Ors 1953, 357–360, nº 14; CILA, Se 341; Arcaria 2000, 155–174; AE 2000, 721; HEp 2000, 574.

Owing to the incompleteness of our evidence, we can only assume that in *Baetica* the display of public documents followed the Roman model. This, especially considering the large number of bronze tablets needed to convey the long colonial and municipal statutes, limits the potential location of these displays to a few possibilities: the *podia* of temples and public places such as the porticos in the forum.[106] These places meet the legal requirement of ensuring a display *in loco celeberrimo eius municipii figatur*,[107] and before in the *tabula Siarensis* (*...eos quoque qui in provinci(i)s prae(e) ssent recte atque ordine facturos si hoc s(enatus) c(onsultum) dedisse(n)t operam ut quam celeberrumo loco figeretur*)[108] and the *senatus consultum de Cn. Pisone patre* (*in cuiusque provinciae celeberruma{e} urbe eiusque i<n> urbis ipsius celeberrimo loco in aere incisum figeretur*).[109] In any case, it is worth noting again that when the senate entrusted the provincial governors with disseminating these documents throughout the province, they were not referring to the sort of city to which these specific inscriptions belonged, for *Siarum* was a *municipium* and *Irni* was a *civitas stipendiaria* at the time of the publication of these documents,[110] and they were, therefore, excluded from Rome's orders concerning dissemination.

The engraving of laws on bronze had no effect on the validity of the laws in question, but their public display aimed to make their contents as widely known as possible.[111] What was, then, the impact of the publication of these long texts in provincial cities? That would, to a large extent, depend on the qualifications of the audience and, concerning documents other than the statutes of the community, on their ability to comprehend the arguments contained therein; it seems fair to draw a line between the inhabitants of colonies and *municipia* and the citizens of stipendiary cities. We

---

106 Merida's hospitality *tabula* (AE 1952, 49) was found in the peristyle of the theatre, in association to a head of Augustus *capite velato*, and several toga-clad statues belonging to a *sacellum* (BALBÍN CHAMORRO 2006, 234–235, nº 66).
107 Lex Irnit. 95.
108 TabSiar. II b, ll. 26–28 (CILA, Se 927; SÁNCHEZ-OSTIZ 1999; HEp 1995, 734; HEp 1999, 524; HEp 2011, 447; AE 1984, 508; AE 1986, 275; AE 1986, 308; AE 1988, 703; AE 1989, 408; AE 1991, 20; AE 1999, 31; AE 1999, 891).
109 *S. c. de Cn. Pisone patre*, copy A, ll. 170–172.
110 ECK 2001 has recreated the dissemination of the events surrounding the death of *Germanicus*, the process in Rome against *Gnaeus Calpurnius Piso* and the subsequent decisions by the senate and the emperor, as well as the customary publication in bronze in the provincial cities of political decisions and ideological statements issued by the imperial government.
111 The *Tabula Siarensis* explains that the text was published because (TabSiar II b, ll. 22–23), '*item senatum velle atque aequom censere quo facilius pietas omnium ordinum erga domum Augustam et consensus universorum civium memoria honoranda Germanici Caesaris appareret*"; concerning the *S. C. de Cn. Pisone patre* the reasons behind its publication were (copy A, ll. 165–167) '*Et quo facilius totius actae rei ordo posterorum memoriae tradi posset atque hi scire<nt>, quid et de singulari moderatione Germ(anici) Caesa(ris) et de sceleribus Cn. Pisonis patris*'. See CORBIER 2006, 53–75. A fragment from the *Lex Valeria Aurelia* was found in *Carissa* (Cortijo de Carija, Bornos, Cadiz; Plin. nat. 3,3,13: *Carissa cognomine Aurelia*) (GONZÁLEZ 2000; HEp 7, 273).

can reasonably question the informative efficacy of the publication of these bronze tablets; it seems unlikely that the majority of the population was capable of fully and accurately understanding the historical and institutional arguments involved. For example, in our edition of the *S. C. de Cn. Pisone patre* we dealt extensively with the textual differences between copies A and B; some of these are mere grammatical errors, or engraving mishaps,[112] but in some cases Copy B directly does not tally with what is expressed in Copy A, for example concerning the gradation of *imperium*.[113] A. Eich has also examined this issue in detail.[114] These disparities stress the fact that even the scribes found it difficult to fully understand the texts with which they were working, so it can easily be inferred how much harder it must have been for the general public. In addition to this, I want to insist upon another fact, which I deem to be enormously relevant concerning how the message that Rome was trying to convey was understood: although Copy B inverted the understanding of the notion of *imperium*, leading to a legal interpretation that contradicted the law and the foundations of imperial policy — a lèse-majesté offence —, no authority, either provincial or imperial, appears to have given instructions for the text to be corrected.

This underlines the idea that the role played by these bronze documents was ideological rather than functional.[115] Their impact derives merely from their public display. Their presence was a grandiloquent reminder of the ubiquity of power and the organizational prowess of the Roman state. A.E. Cooley has authoritatively extended this idea not only to documents the dissemination of which was political-ideological in nature, such as the *Senatus consultum de Cn. Pisone patre* or the *Tabula Siarensis*, but also to those that conveyed administrative provisions, such as municipal statutes: 'Many legal inscriptions were far too unwieldy to have been designed with a reader in mind, even if their use of paragraphing and punctuation might appear to imply a concern with legibility. It has been calculated, for example, that the Flavian municipal law as displayed at *Irni* consisted of some ten tablet, with thirty columns of text in roughly 1500 lines. Each tablet was 57–8 cm high and 90–1 cm wide, and the whole inscription must have extended over some 9 metres; the text was inscribed in lettering 4–6 mm high. Even though the town's magistrates were instructed to ensure that the law was inscribed so as to be clearly legible from ground level, this must have reflected an ideological concern that the law should be publicly available rather than an expectation that anyone would in fact have read the text from the inscription'.[116]

---

112 In most cases, these mistakes are due to confusions in the transcription of the minute (in cursive lettering) to the tablet (in capital letters) or to the engraving technique, which propitiates the confusion between similar signs.
113 Caballos/Eck/Fernández 1996, 108–114; and Eck/Caballos/Fernández 1996, 67–70.
114 Eich 2009, 267–299; concerning the differences between the two main copies of the *Senatus consultum de Cn. Pisone patre*, see Eich 2009, 273–275.
115 For a characterisation of 'Symbolic Epigraphy' see Schmidt 2004, 33.
116 Cooley 2012, 170–171.

It is a common place, often even explicitly stated in the inscription, that the engraving of a document on bronze revealed a will to preserve its contents for posterity. Thus, in major bronze tablets, such as the *Senatus consultum de Cn. Pisone patre* '...*ordo posterorum tradi posset*';[117] but likewise in relation to patronage *tabulae*, the public display of which aimed at the permanent remembrance — *ad perennem testimonium* — of the pact.[118] This determination, however, clashed with harsh reality, but not only because the destruction of documents from Late Antiquity onwards but, indeed, already during the Roman period.[119] The accumulation of bronze documents must have saturated public spaces, not only in Rome but also in Italian and provincial cities, and *tabulae aheneae* had to be removed after a reasonable time had elapsed and once their validity had expired and the personal and legal arguments contained therein had gone out of date. The first to disappear would be the most contingent among them, those related to transient and changing historical circumstances; those that survived the longest were those which individualised civic communities, especially their statutes. But even these were bound to disappear at some point.

After being removed, the tablets were either filed in the *tabularium* or in other storage space. Storage was only one step away from recasting, and this step was, except in extraordinary circumstances, taken sooner or later. Only exceptional circumstances can, therefore, explain the lucky recovery of the extant documents, rare survivors in what can be regarded as a catastrophic shipwreck.

As previously noted, most surviving bronzes were found in secondary contexts. Let us now use several examples to illustrate the various circumstances that can be encountered in this regard. The *Epistula Titi ad Muniguenses* and the hospitality tablet of *Munigua* were found piled up together by W. Grünhagen, carefully protected by *tegulae*, on the floor of one of the rooms of the north-western side of the forum,[120] which may be plausibly interpreted as the local *tabularium*,.[121] They were placed there for storage and preservation, and miraculously escaped recasting and reuse.

The bronzes discovered in the site variously known as Las Herrizas, Los Baldíos or El Diente de la Vieja, in El Saucejo (Seville),[122] the *Lex Irnitana* and the Copy A of

---

117 *S. C. de Cn. Pisone patre*, Copy A, l. 166; Copy B, l. 121.
118 See Díaz Ariño/Cimarosti 2016, 323–324 y 330–331, who cite several examples: CIL X 5426 (ll. 2–9: *huic universus populus Aquinatium tabulam aeneam patronatus traditum, sed et statuam perpetuabilem cum picturam similitudinis eius hoc in loco ad perennem testimonium censuer(it) constituendam*); IRT 558 (ll. 3–9: *Lepcimagnensis ordo et populus, ut incomparabilium beneficiorum eius memoria, etiam ad posteros mitteretur, praeter hospitalem tesseram etiam statuam marmoream constituendam esse duxeretur*; and, CIL XI 1354 (ll. 17–19: *tabulamq(ue) aeneam huius decreti n(ostri) scriptura adfigi pracecipiat, ubinam iusserit, testem futurum in aevo huius consensus nostri*).
119 Eck 2015, 131.
120 Nesselhauf 1960, 142–154.
121 For provincial archives see Rodríguez Neila 1991–1992; Rodríguez Neila 2003 and Rodríguez Neila 2005.
122 Caballos/Eck/Fernández 1996, 15–16.

the *Senatus consultum de Cn. Pisone patre*, were also located in, and illegally extracted from, a secondary context. Although the *Lex Irnitana* and Copy A of the *Senatus consultum de Cn. Pisone patre* could be rescued from the antiquities market, the excavations carried out in the site by F. FERNÁNDEZ and M. DEL AMO in 1982 led to the recovery of more tablets and also confirmed the provenance of the remaining inscriptions[123] as well as the identification of the site with the hitherto unidentified *municipium* of *Irni*. Both bronzes — the former is dated to soon after AD 20 and the latter to after AD 91 — had been eventually taken down from display and stored together in a small room built with naked stone walls. Other finds included an un-engraved bronze tablet, several sheets with clippings and small rectangular plates of the kind used to repair the surface of the large tablets before engraving, and other bronze materials. Owing to the modest characteristics of the room and the materials found within it, archaeologists have interpreted this room as 'a bronzesmith's workshop, as the presence of bronze clippings (used as "grafts") seems to confirm, although the absence of tools also needs to be noted. It is, therefore, possible, that the room was nothing more than the storeroom of a scrap dealer'.[124] All we can say, it follows, is that the room was used for storing bronze, but nothing can be said about its ownership, which could well be public. In any case, it is beyond doubt that the bronzes were there in a secondary position concerning their primitive function. Once again, the survival of these inscriptions is due to exceptional circumstances. The tablets were found underneath a layer of ash and debris, indicating that the building where they were kept burned and collapsed. The rest of the site remains unexcavated, and nothing can be said about its urban layout[125] and the role of the storeroom within it. Archaeologists have been unable to date the destruction of the building with precision, and the archaeological remains only offer a date between AD 90 and AD 140.[126] The possibility that the fire was related to the invasion of the *mauri* during Marcus Aurelius' reign (in AD 171 and AD 177) is suggestive,[127] because *Irni* was in the route that links the coast with the heart of the province. The inscription dedicated to the *liberator C. Vallius Maxumianus* in the nearby *Singilia Barba* bears witness to the level of devastation brought about by these incursions.[128]

Reuse was a given fate for bronze inscriptions after they had played their original role. The nature of this reuse largely depends on the shape and size of the available surface and the new use for which the bronze tablet has been earmarked. Hospi-

---

[123] FERNÁNDEZ/DEL AMO 1990, 15–28.
[124] FERNÁNDEZ/DEL AMO 1990, 21.
[125] However, different domestic structures built using the same technique as the storeroom where the bronzes were found can be appreciated near the canyon excavated by the Corbones River.
[126] FERNÁNDEZ/DEL AMO 1990, 23.
[127] ALFÖLDY 1985.
[128] CIL II²/5, 783; CIL II 2015; ILS 1354 a; HEp 1989, 469; AE 1961, 340.

tality and patronage tablets are particularly well suited for this purpose.[129] We have a good example of this in the small opistographic bronze tablet found around 1940 in Cortijo de los Alamillos, approximately 3 km to the northeast of Cañete de las Torres (Córdoba), and currently kept in the local municipal history museum. Originally, the tablet, dated to AD 34, was engraved with the *hospitium* that linked the *Baxonenses* and *Ucubi*;[130] over two centuries later, in AD 247, the reverse was reused to engrave a patronage pact between one *Bellus Licinianus* and the *Collegium corporis fabrorum subaedianorum Patriciensium Cordubensium*.[131] The engraving of this new inscription on the reverse of this tablet illustrates the intense circulation and reuse to which these bronzes were subject. Remarkably, this reuse coexists with the expressed will to keep the contents of these inscriptions for posterity, which thus becomes little more than a *pio desiderio*. An even more extreme case was presented by B. Díaz Ariño and E. Cimarosti:[132] the *tabula patronatus* engraved in honour of *Aurelius Gentianus* was reused barely ten years later to pay homage to *Aquilius Nestorius*.[133]

The intrinsic value of bronze, and their usefulness for the engraving of new inscriptions once their original purpose had been fulfilled led, to its reuse or, sooner or later, its recasting.[134] There was a specific market for this activity, which explains the wide circulation of the pieces, as shown by the large number of examples, like the paradigmatic case of the statute of *Salpensa*, found alongside the *Lex Malacitana* in the outskirts of Malaga, which is over 115 km away.

In any case, recasting seems to have been merely a matter of time. Some inscriptions have been recast only recently, for instance for the production of false Classical statuettes made with ancient bronze, but often this took place in the past, for instance with the tablet that contains part of chapters XIII to XX of the *Lex coloniae Genetivae Iuliae* which narrowly escaped being recast in the late 18th century;[135] it must be stressed, however, that most of these tablets had already been recast in Antiquity.

The multiple epigraphic fragments on bronze found in *Baelo Claudia* were discovered in the course of archaeological excavation, and accordingly we can partially outline the events surrounding their final fate. Until recently, our evidence was limited to an undetermined public document found in the north end of the *decumanus*,[136]

---

129 Large bronze tablets were also cut for engraving military diplomas on the reverse (Eck 2015, 130 and note 14).
130 CIL II²/7, 187; AE 1983, 530 a; AE 1985, 564 a; Balbín Chamorro 2006, 239–241, nº70 and Díaz Ariño 2004.
131 CIL II²/7, 188; AE 1983, 530 b and AE 1985, 564 b.
132 Díaz Ariño/Cimarosti 2016, 331–332.
133 CIL X 476 and 477; Mello/Voza 1968, nº 106.
134 Eck 2009, 84.
135 Caballos 2006, 36–41.
136 Inv. nº 79/2398 (Bonneville/Dardaine 1980, 417–418; Bonneville/Dardaine/Le Roux 1988, 34, nº 9; Caballos 2009 b, 167–168).

another one from the *basilica*,[137] and, three from the western sector of the *forum*.[138] Most of the new tiny bronze fragments to which I made an earlier reference were recovered during the 2014–2017 excavation campaigns from the north-eastern corner of the structures located to the southeast of the *forum*, near the so-called *cardo* nº4. The bronzes were found in the earliest abandonment layer of the building, directly sitting on top of the pavement of *opus signinum*, which suggests a date for their deposition between the late 4th and the 5th century. By that time, the city and its civic institutions were in full decadence, and the *tabulae aheneae* with official texts had lost all function. Accordingly, the context and state in which the fragments of bronze were found —clipped, bent and twisted— also indicates that they were in the process of being reused or recycled.

The classical texts also offer supporting evidence for the reuse of bronze tablets after they had become obsolete, contradicting the expressed desire for permanence or, in Tacitus's words, *aera sacrandam ad memoriam*.[139] A beautiful text by Pliny the Elder, including the only recorded instance of the use of the adjective *collectaneus*, to refer to bronze, talks about this issue in the following terms: *Sequens temperatura statuaria est eademque tabularis hoc modo: massa proflatur in primis, mox in proflatum additur tertia portio aeris collectanei, hoc est ex usu coempti. Peculiare in eo condimentum attritu domiti et consuetudine nitoris veluti mansuefacti. Miscentur et plumbi argentarii pondo duodena ac selibrae centenis proflati*.[140] Therefore, we owe Pliny the knowledge that the procedure followed in the casting of both bronze statues and epigraphic tablets consisted of the addition of a third of bronze scraps to two thirds of bronze alloy, presumably in order to expedite the procedure and because the addition of used bronze fragments facilitated the melting process. The last step of the process involved adding twelve and a half pounds of argenteous lead per hundred pounds of bronze.

Most of the bronze fragments recently found in *Baelo Claudia* were located in the same area and in association with a single archaeological stratum. The location corresponded to a former public, or perhaps semi-public, building dated to the Early Imperial Period, a building that was later reused, plausibly, as a domestic space. However, they were not found together, as would be expected should they have been intentionally stored or even put together as a unit for further transport, instead of for recasting. Furthermore, the bronzes recently excavated in *Baelo Claudia* (Tarifa, Cadiz) are not the large fragments that would result from violently extracting great bronze tablets from the walls in which they were displayed, but only small pieces. These either went

---

137 Inv. nº 72/1573 (BONNEVILLE/DARDAINE/LE ROUX 1988, 35, nº 11; CABALLOS 2009b, 171, nº V.20).
138 Inv. nº 73/703 (BONNEVILLE/DARDAINE/LE ROUX 1988, 34–35, nº 10; CABALLOS 2009b, 166, nº IV.13); Inv. nº 75/2086b (BONNEVILLE/DARDAINE/LE ROUX 1988, 35, nº 12; CABALLOS 2009b, 171, nº V.21); Inv. nº 75/2086a (BONNEVILLE/DARDAINE/LE ROUX 1988, 36, nº 13; CABALLOS 2009b, 172, nº V.22).
139 Tac. ann. 3,63,4.
140 Plin. nat. 34,20,97.

unnoticed and were lost already in antiquity, or may have been destined for recasting —as *aes tabularis*— or for reuse cold-working, although this operation, for whatever reason, never took place.

Regardless of how they were meant to be reused, the fragmentary inscriptions found in *Baelo Claudia* and elsewhere are the small and humble fossils of the majestic bronze tablets that once conveyed the legal principles and the ideological and political foundations of the formerly flourishing urban communities of *Baetica*, saved *in extremis* and for purely fortuitous circumstances from the sad fate that befell most of these documents, dispossessing us of the precious information that they carried. Thus, Ausonius' ominous forecast of the fate of inscriptions in stone becomes also especially of application concerning bronze inscriptions: *Miremur periisse homines? Monumenta fatiscunt: mors etiam saxis nominibusque venit.*[141]

Bibliography

ALFÖLDY 1969 = G. ALFÖLDY, Fasti Hispanienses. Senatorische Reichsbeamte und Offiziere in den spanischen Provinzen des Römischen Reiches von Augustus bis Diokletian, Wiesbaden 1969.

ALFÖLDY 1985 = G. ALFÖLDY, Bellum mauricum, *Chiron* 15, 1985, 87–105.

ARCARIA 2000 = F. ARCARIA, Il bronzo di Italica: una testimonianza sulla competenza dei magistrati municipali in materia di operis novi nuntiatio, *Minima Epigraphica et Papyrologica* 3, 2000, 3, 155–174.

BALBÍN CHAMORRO 2006 = P. BALBÍN CHAMORRO, Hospitalidad y Patronato en la Península Ibérica durante la Antigüedad, Salamanca 2006.

BELTRÁN LLORIS 1999 = F. BELTRÁN LLORIS, Inscripciones sobre bronce: ¿un rasgo característico de la cultura epigráfica de las ciudades hispanas?, in: AAVV., XI Congresso Internazionale di Epigrafia Greca e Latina (Roma, 18–24 settembre 1997), Atti, vol. II, Roma 1999, 21–37.

BELTRÁN LLORIS 2006 = F. BELTRÁN LLORIS, An Irrigation Decree from Roman Spain: the *Lex riui Hiberiensis*, *JRS* 96, 2006, 147–197.

BELTRÁN LLORIS 2015a = F. BELTRÁN LLORIS, Latin Epigraphy: the Main Types of Inscriptions, in: C. BRUUN/J. EDMONSON (ed.), The Oxford Handbook of Roman Epigraphy, Oxford 2015, 89–110.

BELTRÁN LLORIS 2015b = F. BELTRÁN LLORIS, The 'Epigraphic Habit' in the Roman World, in: C. BRUUN/J. EDMONSON (ed.), The Oxford Handbook of Roman Epigraphy, Oxford 2015, 131–148.

BENEFIEL/KEEGAN 2016 = R. BENEFIEL/P. KEEGAN (ed.), Inscriptions in the Private Sphere in the Greco-Roman World, Leiden/Boston 2016.

BODEL/DIMITROVA 2015 = J. BODEL/N. DIMITROVA, Ancient Documents and their Contexts. First North American Congress of Greek and Latin Epigraphy 2011, Leiden/Boston 2015.

BONNEVILLE/DARDAINE 1980 = J.-N. BONNEVILLE/S. DARDAINE, La campagne de fouilles d'octobre 1979 à Belo, *MCV* 16, 1980, 375–420.

BONNEVILLE/DARDAINE/LE ROUX 1988 = J.-N. BONNEVILLE/S. DARDAINE/P. LE ROUX, Belo V. L´épigraphie. Les inscriptions romaines de Baelo Claudia, Madrid 1988.

---

[141] Ausonius, *Epitaphia* 31, 9–10. Verses pertinently collected by my admired friend BELTRÁN LLORIS 2015 b, 146.

Caballos 1998 = A. Caballos Rufino, Las fuentes del Derecho: La Epigrafía en bronce, in: M. Almagro-Gorbea (ed.), Hispania. El legado de Roma. En el año de Trajano, Zaragoza 1998, 181–195 (= Zaragoza 1999, 205–221).

Caballos 2006 = A. Caballos Rufino, El nuevo bronce de Osuna y la política colonizadora romana, Sevilla 2006.

Caballos 2008 = A. Caballos Rufino, ¿Típicamente romano? Publicación de documentos en tablas de bronce, *Gerión* 26.1, 2008, 439–452.

Caballos 2009a = A. Caballos Rufino, Diploma militar en beneficio de M. Aurelio Silvino (7.1.234), in: Espacios, usos y formas de la Epigrafía Hispana en Épocas Antigua y Tardoantigua. Homenaje al Dr. A.U. Stylow, *Anejos de AEspA* vol. 48, Madrid 2009, 77–84.

Caballos 2009b = A. Caballos Rufino, Publicación de documentos públicos en las ciudades del Occidente romano: el ejemplo de la Bética, in: R. Haensch (ed.), Selbstdarstellung und Kommunikation. Die Veröffentlichung staatlicher Urkunden auf Stein und Bronze in der römischen Welt, München 2009, 131–172.

Caballos/Colubi 2006 = A. Caballos Rufino/J.M. Colubi Falcó, Referentes genéticos de los estatutos municipales hispanorromanos: la *Lex municipii Tarentini* y la *Tabula Heracleensis*, in: J.F. Rodríguez Neila/E. Melchor Gil (ed.), Poder central y autonomía municipal: la proyección pública de las élites romanas de Occidente, Córdoba 2006, 17–54.

Caballos/Eck/Fernández 1996 = A. Caballos/W. Eck/F. Fernández, El senadoconsulto de Gneo Pisón padre, Sevilla 1996.

Caballos/Fernández 1999 = A. Caballos Rufino/F. Fernández Gómez, Novedades, estado de la cuestión y expectativas de la Epigrafía en bronce en Andalucía, in: AAVV., XI Congresso Internazionale di Epigrafia Greca e Latina, Atti, Roma 1999, 653–660.

Caballos/Rodríguez/Brassous 2018 = A. Caballos Rufino/O. Rodríguez Gutiérrez/L. Brassous, Aes collectaneus: fragmentos de bronces jurídicos procedentes del foro de *Baelo Claudia*, *AEspA* 91, 2018, forthcoming.

Chastagnol 1978 = A. Chastagnol, L'album municipal de Timgad, Bonn 1978.

CILA, Se = J. González Fernández, Corpus de Inscripciones latinas de Andalucía, vol. 2: Sevilla, Sevilla 1991–1996.

Collantes/Fernández-Chicarro 1972–1974 = F. Collantes de Terán/C. Fernández-Chicarro, Epigrafía de Munigua (Mulva, Sevilla), *AEspA* 45–47, 1972–1974, 337–410.

Cooley 2012 = A.E. Cooley, The Cambridge Manual of Latin Epigraphy, Cambridge 2012.

Corbier 1987 = M. Corbier, L'écriture dans l'espace public romain, in: L'Urbs: espace urbain et histoire (Ier siècle av. J.-C. – IIIe siècle ap. J.-C.), Actes du colloque international de Rome, 8–12 mai 1985, Roma 1987, 27–60.

Corbier 2006 = M. Corbier, Donner à voir, donner à lire. Mémoire et communication dans la Rome ancienne, Paris 2006.

Correa 2016 = J.A. Correa Rodríguez, Toponimia antigua de Andalucía, Sevilla 2016.

Coudry 1994 = M. Coudry, Sénatus-consultes et *acta senatus*: rédaction, conservation et archivage des documents émanant du sénat, de l'époque de César à celle des Sévères, in: J. Andreau (ed.), La mémoire perdue. À la recherche des archives oubliées, publiques et privées de la Rome antique, Paris 1994, 65–102.

Crawford 1996 = M.H. Crawford (ed.), Roman Statutes, London 1996.

Del Hoyo/Rodríguez 2016 = J. Del Hoyo/M. Rodríguez Ceballos, Bronces epigráficos inéditos del Museo de Burgos, *Veleia* 33, 2016, 279–287.

Díaz Ariño 2004 = B. Díaz Ariño, Pactos entre ciudades, un rasgo peculiar del hospitium hispánico, in: F. Beltrán Lloris (ed.), Antiqua Iuniora, en torno al Mediterráneo en la Antigüedad, Zaragoza 2004, 97–108.

Díaz Ariño/Cimarosti 2016 = B. Díaz Ariño/E. Cimarosti, Las tábulas de hospitalidad y patronato, Chiron 46, 2016, 319–360.
Domergue 1990 = C. Domergue, Les mines de la péninsule Ibérique dans l'Antiquité romaine, Roma 1990.
Donati 2016 = A. Donati (ed.), L'Iscrizione esposta. Atti del Convegno Borghesi 2015, Faenza 2016.
D'Ors 1953 = Á. d'Ors, Epigrafía Jurídica de la España Romana, Madrid 1953.
D'Ors 1959 = Á. d'Ors, Miscelánea epigráfica: I. El bronce de Belo, Emerita 27, 1959, 367–370.
D'Ors 1961 = Á. d'Ors, Miscelánea epigráfica. Los bronces de Mulva, Emerita 29, 1961, 203–218.
Eck 1998 = W. Eck, Inschriften auf Holz. Ein unterschätztes Phänomen der epigraphischen Kultur Roms, in: P. Kneissl/V. Losemann (ed.), Imperium Romanum. Studien zu Geschichte und Rezeption. Festschrift für Karl Christ zum 75. Geburtstag, Stuttgart 1998, 203–217.
Eck 2001 = W. Eck, Der Blick nach Rom. Die Affäre um den Tod des Germanicus und ihr Reflex in der Baetica, in: A. Caballos Rufino (ed.), Carmona Romana. Actas del II Congreso de Historia de Carmona, Carmona 2001, 543–557; Translation of A. Caballos Rufino, La mirada a Roma. Asuntos en torno a la muerte de Germánico y su repercusión en la Bética, in: A. Caballos Rufino, a.a.O., 559–570 (2nd. ed., Carmona 2012, 751–773 and Translation 775–791).
Eck 2009 = W. Eck, Öffentlichkeit, Politik und Administration. Epigraphische Dokumente von Kaisern, Senat und Amtsträgern in Rom, in: R. Haensch (ed.), Selbstdarstellung und Kommunikation: die Veröffentlichung staatlicher Urkunden auf Stein und Bronze in der römischen Welt, München 2009, 75–96.
Eck 2015 = W. Eck, Documents on Bronze: A Phenomen of the Roman West?, in: J. Bodel/N. Dimitrova (ed.), Ancient Documents and their Contexts. First North American Congress of Greek and Latin Epigraphy (2011), Leiden/Boston 2015, 127–151.
Eck/Caballos/Fernández 1996 = W. Eck/A. Caballos/F. Fernández, Das senatus consultum de Cn. Pisone patre, München 1996.
Eich 2009 = A. Eich, Diplomatische Genauigkeit oder inhaltliche Richtigkeit? Das Verhältnis von Original und Abschrift, in: R. Haensch (ed.), Selbstdarstellung und Kommunikation: die Veröffentlichung staatlicher Urkunden auf Stein und Bronze in der römischen Welt, München 2009, 267–299.
Fernández 1991 = F. Fernández Gómez, Nuevos fragmentos de leyes municipales y otros bronces epigráficos de la Bética en el Museo Arqueológico de Sevilla, ZPE 86, 1991, 121–136.
Fernández/Del Amo 1990 = F. Fernández Gómez/M. del Amo y de la Hera, La Lex Irnitana y su contexto arqueológico, Sevilla 1990.
Ferrary 2009 = J.L. Ferrary, La gravure de documents publics de la Rome républicaine et ses motivations, in: R. Haensch (ed.), Selbstdarstellung und Kommunikation: die Veröffentlichung staatlicher Urkunden auf Stein und Bronze in der römischen Welt, München 2009, 59–74.
González 1990 = J. González Fernández, Bronces jurídicos romanos de Andalucía, Sevilla 1990.
González 1994 = J. González Fernández, Epigrafía jurídica de la Bética, in: J. González Fernández (ed.), Roma y las provincias. Realidad administrativa e ideología imperial, Madrid 1994, 1–16.
González 2000 = J. González, Un nuevo fragmento de la Tabula Hebana, AEspA 73, 2000, 253–257.
González 2014 = J. González Fernández, Inscripción romana del yacimiento de Gibalbín (Cádiz) con indicación de su condición de municipio, Spal 23, 2014, 191–196.
González 2015 = J. González Fernández, Texto legal epigráfico de una colonia latina de César o Augusto en la Hispania Ulterior Baetica, SDHI 81, 2015, 307–321.
González/Bermejo 2015 = J. González Fernández/J. Bermejo Meléndez, Fragmento de un texto legal encontrado en la Betica con parte de un capítulo de la Tabula Heracleensis, Athenaeum 103.2, 2015, 477–491.

González/Bermejo 2016a = J. González Fernández/J. Bermejo Meléndez, Diplomata Militaria del Museo de Huelva, *Onoba* 4, 2016, 275–279.

González/Bermejo 2016b = J. González Fernández/J. Bermejo Meléndez, Un nuevo diploma militar de *Mauretania Tingitana*, *Epigraphica* 78, 2016, 516–525.

González/Fernández 1980 = J. González Fernández/F. Fernández Gómez, Tabulae Siarenses, *Iura* 31, 1980, 135–137.

González/Fernández 1981 = J. González Fernández/F. Fernández Gómez, Tabula Siarensis, *Iura* 32, 1981, 1–36.

Gradel 2014 = I. Gradel, A New Fragment of Copy A of the Senatus Consultum de Cn. Pisone Patre, *ZPE* 192, 2014, 284–286.

Grünhagen 1961 = W. Grünhagen, Hallazgos epigráficos de la excavación de Munigua, in: Secretaría General de los Congresos Arqueológicos Nacionales (ed.), Actas del VI Congreso Arqueológico Nacional (Oviedo 1959), Zaragoza 1961, 214–216.

Haensch 1997 = R. Haensch, Capita provinciarum. Statthaltersitze und Provinzialverwaltung in der römischen Kaiserzeit, Mainz 1997.

Jacob 1984a = P. Jacob, Un diplôme militaire romain à *Baelo Claudia* (Tarifa, province de Cadix), *MCV* 20, 1984, 7–16.

Jacob 1984b = P. Jacob, Un diploma militar romano en *Baelo Claudia*, *Gerión* 2, 1984, 325–332.

Kolb 2015 = A. Kolb, Bronze in Epigraphy, in: E. Deschler/P. Della Casa (ed.), New Research on Ancient Bronzes. Acta of the XVIIIth International Congress on Ancient Bronzes, Zürich 2015, 11–16.

Le Roux 2014 = P. Le Roux, Fragments épigraphiques d'Estrémadure, in: C. Zaccaria (ed.), L'epigrafia dei porti. Atti della XVIIe Rencontre sur l'Épigraphie du Monde Romain, Trieste 2014, 251–260.

López Pardo 1986 = F. López Pardo, A propósito de un diploma militar hallado en *Baelo*, *Gerión* 4, 1986, 319–324.

Luzón 1999 = J.M. Luzón Nogué, Sevilla la vieja. Un paseo histórico por las ruinas de Itálica, Sevilla 1999.

Maganzani/Buzzacchi 2014 = L. Maganzani/C. Buzzacchi (ed.), *Lex rivi hiberiensis*. Diritto e tecnica in una comunità di irrigazione della Spagna Romana, Milano 2014.

Mello/Voza 1968 = M. Mello/G. Voza, Le iscrizioni latine di Paestum, Napoli 1968.

Nesselhauf 1960 = H. Nesselhauf, Zwei Bronzeurkunden aus Munigua, *MM* 1, 1960, 142–154.

Ojeda 1993 = J.M. Ojeda Torres, El servicio administrativo imperial ecuestre en la Hispania romana durante el Alto Imperio, Sevilla 1993.

Oliver/Palmer 1955 = J.H. Oliver/R.E.A. Palmer, Minutes of an Act of the Roman Senate, *Hesperia* 24, 1955, 320–349.

Rodríguez de Berlanga 1891 = M. Rodríguez de Berlanga, El nuevo bronce de Itálica, Málaga 1891.

Rodríguez Neila 1991–1992 = J.F. Rodríguez Neila, Archivos municipales en las provincias occidentales del imperio romano, *Veleia* 8–9, 1991–1992, 144–174.

Rodríguez Neila 2003 = J.F. Rodríguez Neila, Administración financiera y documentación de archivo en las leyes municipales de Hispania, *Cahiers du Centre G. Glotz* 14, 2003, 115–129.

Rodríguez Neila 2005 = J.F. Rodríguez Neila, Tabulae Publicae: Archivos municipales y documentación financiera en las ciudades de la Bética, Madrid 2005.

Ruiz/Vega/García 2016 = A. Ruiz Castellanos/E.J. Vega Geán/F.A. García Romero, Inscripciones latinas de Jerez de la Frontera, Cádiz 2016.

Salway 2000 = B. Salway, Prefects, *Patroni*, and Decurions: a New Perspective on the Album of *Canusium*, in: A.E. Cooley (ed.), The Epigraphic Landscape of Roman Italy, London 2000, 115–171.

Sánchez-Ostiz 1999 = Á. Sánchez-Ostiz, Tabula Siarensis: edición, traducción y comentario, Pamplona 1999.

Saquete/Iñesta 2009 = J.C. Saquete Chamizo/J. Iñesta Mena, Un fragmento de Ley municipal hallado en la *Baeturia Turdulorum* (Conventus *Cordubensis*, Provincia *Baetica*), *ZPE* 168, 2009, 293–297.

Schmidt 2004 = M.G. Schmidt, Einführung in die lateinische Epigraphik, Darmstadt 2004.

Simón 2013 = I. Simón Cornago, Los soportes de la epigrafía paleohispánica. Inscripciones sobre piedra, bronce y cerámica, Zaragoza/Sevilla 2013.

Spitzl 1984 = T. Spitzl, *Lex municipii Malacitani*, München 1984.

Stylow 2001 = A.U. Stylow, La lex malacitana. Descripción y texto, *Mainake* 23, 2001, 39–50.

Stylow/López Melero 2013 = A.U. Stylow/R. López Melero, Un grupo de bronces jurídicos de Arahal (Sevilla), in: R.Mª Cid López/E.B. García Fernández (ed.), Debita verba: estudios en homenaje al profesor Julio Mangas Manjarrés, Vol. 1, Madrid 2013, 385–396.

W. Graham Claytor
The Municipalization of Writing in Roman Egypt

Abstract: Municipalization in the Roman Empire was a multifaceted process that entailed not only the development of civic self-governance but also the cultural promotion of a governing elite. This paper examines the process of municipalization in the province of Egypt and from the point of view of village society, with a particular focus on Greek literacy and notarial institutions. The main argument is that there was a measurable shift in the writing landscape of Egypt between the second and fourth centuries, which involved the concentration of literate men and notarial services in the nome capitals.

Zusammenfassung: Die (sogenannte) Munizipalisierung im römischen Reich war ein vielgestaltiger Prozess und betraf nicht nur den Aufbau einer zivilen Selbstverwaltung, sondern auch die kulturelle Förderung einer Herrschaftselite. Der vorliegende Beitrag untersucht diesen Prozess in der Provinz Ägypten aus der Perspektive der dörflichen Gesellschaft mit einem besonderen Schwerpunkt auf griechische Schriftlichkeit und notarielle Institutionen. Es zeigt sich, dass die Schriftlichkeit in der ägyptischen Provinz zwischen dem zweiten und vierten Jahrhundert einem signifikanten Wandel unterworfen war, der etwa die Konzentration von Schreibkundigen und notariellen Dienstleistungen in den Gaumetropolen umfasste.

Municipalization is a well-known feature of Roman provincial development. In Egypt, the grant of autonomous city councils in the year 199/200 CE is the most important milestone, but the process was well underway in the preceding centuries, and later reforms further tightened the urban grip on the countryside.[1] This process was marked by the development of a class of Hellenic elites whose privileges and prestige came at the cost of corporate responsibility for the administration of the city and, later, the surrounding territory. The move towards civic self-governance is well in line with Rome's efforts in the rest of the empire, even if the process was more drawn out in Egypt.

This paper explores the process of municipalization through the lens of Greek literacy and from the point of view of Egyptian villages. To what extent was the municipalization of the Egyptian countryside a cultural process, in addition to its admin-

---

[1] See BOWMAN 1971 for the city councils (*boulai*) of Roman Egypt, BOWMAN/RATHBONE 1992 on the process of municipalization before the formal creation of the councils, and BAGNALL 1993, 59–62 for the consolidation that begins under Diocletian. The author wishes to express his thanks to Susan Rahyab for proofreading this chapter.

istrative, fiscal, and economic aspects? In particular, did this process entail the concentration of writing institutions and literate men in the nome capitals, with a corresponding drain of cultural capital from the villages? No one doubts, of course, that urban centers of the Roman Empire had a higher degree of literacy than villages, but the Egyptian evidence allows for some insight into how this balance changed over time.

On the institutional level, one can trace a clear move toward the municipalization of writing in the case of the village *grapheion*, or writing office, and this chapter will focus on the type of writing generated by these offices, Greek contracts and petitions in particular. The *grapheion* was a holdover from the Ptolemaic period that had a long history in the Roman province before succumbing to centralization efforts in the late second and early third century CE.[2] The social and economic importance of the village *grapheia* during their heyday cannot be overstated. Along with the temples, they were among the few institutions run by and for villagers in Roman Egypt. Accordingly, I will first establish the nature and scope of the *grapheion*'s activities, before turning to the evidence for their absorption by central offices located in the nome *metropoleis* and the reasons behind this measure. We will then shift our focus to the fourth century and attempt to determine how the writing landscape of Egyptian villages had changed in the meantime.

Two caveats before proceeding. One, the focus here is on Greek documentary writing, with only a nod towards Greek literature and Egyptian language material. The finds of Greek literature in the towns and villages are important markers of advanced literacy and the educational process, and more attention should be given to their geographic spread and diachronic patterns.[3] As for Egyptian material, the Roman period encompasses both the demise of Demotic and the rise of Coptic, important phenomena that are tied to my subject, but which will not be considered here in detail. The second caveat is that our knowledge of village life in Roman Egypt is dominated by evidence from a single region, the Fayum, or Arsinoite nome. The famous rubbish dumps of Oxyrhynchus offer an almost exclusively urban perspective, while the other main sources of Roman-period documents, namely Antinoopolis, Hermopolis, Panopolis, and Thebes, were likewise urban centers. But the Arsinoite evidence is at least spread across some dozen villages of different sizes and cultural profiles: Soknopaiou Nesos, Karanis, Bakchias, Philadelphia, Tebtynis, Theadelphia, Dionysias, and others provide a wealth of evidence from the first three centuries of Roman rule. In the fourth century, however, the scene narrows. Only Karanis, Philadelphia, and Theadelphia offer much of anything, and of these Karanis towers above the others. Fortunately,

---

2 There is no monograph on this institution, but key studies include PIERCE 1968, HUSSELMAN 1970, COCKLE 1984, and BURKHALTER 1990. WOLFF 1978 should also be consulted (see discussion below). See below, n. 8, for literature on the Ptolemaic *grapheion*. A number of my articles have explored different aspects of the *grapheion* in Ptolemaic and Roman Egypt: CLAYTOR 2013, 2014a and b, and 2015.
3 An important foundational study is VAN MINNEN 1998.

excavations over the past thirty years at the village of Kellis in the Dakhleh Oasis have provided a welcome comparandum for village activity in this period.[4] Kellis and Karanis will therefore play a significant role in our story.

We will return to the fourth century, but let us first look at the village in earlier centuries, when the local *grapheion* was the center of writing activities (notwithstanding the continued importance of the native temples). The *grapheion* was part of an extensive notarial system that the Romans took over from the Ptolemies in 30 BCE. This system also included offices called *agoranomeia*, located in the *metropoleis*, which were established early in the Ptolemaic period on the basis of classical precedent and theory,[5] as well as regional archives located in these same *metropoleis* and central archives located in Alexandria.[6]

The *grapheion*, on the other hand, appears to have been established only in 146 BCE and its original purpose would have been foreign to the practices of the classical polis – namely, the registration of Egyptian language contracts drawn up through temple scribes.[7] A few decades later, however, Greek private instruments known as double documents were also brought under the purview of the *grapheion*. This measure dramatically affected the form of such documents.[8] Whereas previously both the inner, sealed copy and the outer copy of the double document were written out in full, afterwards the inner script became simply an abstract, with subscriptions, and the notary's registration docket added at the bottom. While nominally still private instruments, double documents were now often being composed in public writing offices, and their registration meant that the contract details were being stored in some kind of archive, though whether in the village, *metropolis*, or even Alexandria, we simply do not know. Further insight on the late Ptolemaic *grapheion* can be expected from the complete publication of a bilingual notarial archive from Tebtunis that is being studied by Francisca Hoogendijk and Brian Muhs.[9] In any case, the Romans institutionalized this development, and from Augustus on contracts written in the *grapheion* were officially *demosioi chrematismoi*, public instruments on the same level as those composed in the *agoranomeia*.

---

4 See P.Kell. I-VII.
5 Aristotle, for instance, recommended that the *agoranomos* "oversee contracts and good order" in the marketplace (Pol. 1321b13–15; cf. 1321b29–31), and the recent publication of a slave sale dating to 270 BCE (P. Sorb. III 70) shows that from the earliest period from which we have good evidence, the Ptolemaic *agoranomos* was endowed with notarial functions. See FARAGUNA 2000 for an examination of theoretical and practical methods of monitoring and recording private transactions in the fourth-century Greek world.
6 See generally COCKLE 1984, where on p. 111 one finds a schematic representation of this system in the Roman period.
7 PESTMAN 1985.
8 YIFTACH-FIRANKO 2008a.
9 MUHS 2010 and HOOGENDIJK 2013.

The extent of this Ptolemaic network of writing offices is unknown. It is often stated that the real boom in the number of *grapheia* only occurred under the Romans,[10] but we need to be wary of the uneven survival of evidence. The end of the Ptolemaic period is poorly documented compared to the first few centuries of Roman rule, which in my view is enough to explain why so many *grapheia* seem to have been established later. An unpublished scrap of a Demotic contract with a Greek registration, for instance, is the only evidence that Karanis' *grapheion* was operational already under the Ptolemies, even though it is one of the best attested writing offices of the Roman period.[11] Other unpublished contracts show that the *grapheion* of Bakchias can now also be firmly traced back to the Ptolemaic period,[12] and further discoveries will probably add to the list. To the extent that the Roman peace brought an increase in population, I am open to the idea of new *grapheia*, but I do not think the evidence warrants the idea of a concerted expansion of village writing offices.

Most attestations of these offices come from the Arsinoite nome, which is unsurprising given the rich finds from rural settlements in this region mentioned above. In the Oxyrhynchite nome, we find evidence of 11 village *grapheia* and three that covered entire toparchies, or subdivisions of the nome.[13] Rural writing offices are known from a number of other nomes, and even the distant oases were equipped with these institutions. Recently published second century documents related to the village of Mesobe in the eastern part of the Dakhleh Oasis show that its notarial procedure was much like the rest of Egypt, despite some local variation.[14]

This is enough to establish that *grapheia* were widespread institutions, most likely found in all the larger villages of the Roman province. But who was making use of these offices and why? Hundreds of individual contracts survive from the villages of Roman Egypt, but even so the picture they present is impressionistic. Fortunately, we possess some "thick" data from the well-known archive of Kronion, notary of Teb-

---

10 E. g., WOLFF 1978, 18–19 and YIFTACH-FIRANKO 2011, 549.
11 P.Mich. inv. 5665 (29-B166*-D). Based on a print held in the University of Michigan Papyrology Collection, the registration docket can be read as follows: ἔτους κα Μεσορὴ ιᾱ ἐν Καρα(νίδι) π[έπτωκεν εἰς ἀναγραφὴν (?)]. Wolfgang Wegner reports that the 21st year is that of Ptolemy X Alexander; the document was accordingly registered on 22 August, 93 BCE.
12 P.Mich. inv. 5739, a Demotic contract found in Karanis (29-C137A¹-C), but registered in Bakchias on 3 September, 71 BCE. P.Köln inv. 7807 can likewise be attributed to Ptolemaic Bakchias and is registered through a *synallagmatographos*. I thank Wolfgang Wegner for discussing the date of the former document and bringing the latter to my attention.
13 WOLFF 1978, 18, n. 51 lists *grapheia* of the middle, upper, and western toparchies of the Oxyrhynchite nome, along with those in the villages of Sinary, Nemerai, Talao, Sephtha, Pakerke, Senepta, and Peenno, to which can be added the villages found in P.Oxy. IV 808 descr. (65–68 CE): Palosis, Sepho, Kesmouchis, and Teis.
14 HEILPORN/WORP 2007 and BAGNALL/WORP 2011. Nearby Trimithis also had a *grapheion*: P.Oxy. LX 4058,19–20 (158/159 CE).

tunis,[15] which can be complemented by a lengthy account from Karanis' *grapheion*, which I edited as part of my dissertation (see Fig. 1).[16] These accounts and registers give us a sense how many documents the local notary and his staff could produce on behalf of their fellow villagers.

The following table offers a comparison of notarial activity over the same four month period.

Registered Contracts by Month in Tebtunis and Karanis[17]

Source	Hathyr	Choiak	Tybi	Mecheir
P.Mich. II 123 (Tebtunis), 45 CE	61	37	53	50
P.Mich. V 238 (Tebtunis), 46 CE	65	39	–	–
Karanis Account, early II CE	72 (estimated)	80 (actual)	101 (est.)	83 (est.)

The Karanis office was producing an average of roughly 84 registered contracts a month, which, extrapolated over the course of the year, comes to just over 1,000 contracts. This is about 40 % more than the ca. 700 registered contracts recorded in the complete Tebtunis account P.Mich. II 123 recto. These figures only include notarial contracts, since other documents are not itemized in the Karanis account and are thus less susceptible to quantification and comparison with the Tebtunis material. But even within the category of notarial contracts the variety of transactions is immense: loans, receipts, leases, cessions, rental agreements and rent payments, wills, sales, property divisions, nursing contracts, marriage contracts, and more are all found in the fragmentary Karanis account alone.

Of the non-registered documents written in the *grapheion*, the most important were private contracts (*hypomnemeta* and *cheirographa*), written oaths, and petitions. Such documents could in theory be written by anyone, but it is no wonder that villagers frequently turned to the local institution specifically geared toward writing to have them drawn up. The writing of petitions in *grapheia* is particularly interesting, although it cannot be quantified in the same way as notarial contracts. As Benjamin KELLY has noted, *grapheion* staff were well positioned to put the complaints of their fellow villagers into proper form, particularly since the majority of complaints revolved around property and contracts – the bread and butter of the village notary – as well as the violence that could ensue when agreements were broken.[18] Given the institutional "thinness" of the villages of Roman Egypt, the *grapheion* must have been one of the few sources of practical legal knowledge in the village beyond one's friends and family.

---

15 For an overview of this archive see VAN BEEK 2013.
16 CLAYTOR 2014c.
17 The figures for P.Mich. II 123 and P.Mich. V 238 come from TOEPEL 1973, 92.
18 KELLY 2011, 43–44.

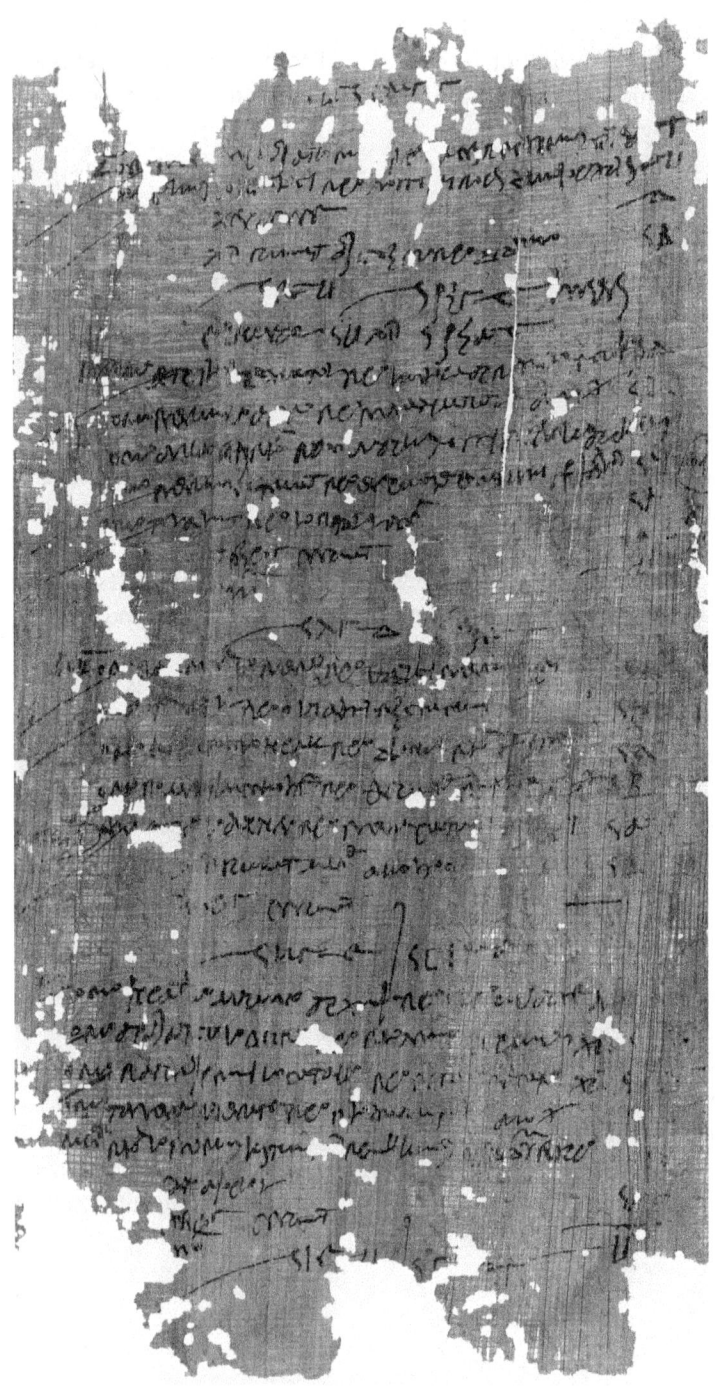

Fig. 1: P.Mich. inv. 4384 verso: col. 22 of the Karanis Grapheion Account (image courtesy of the University of Michigan Papyrology Collection).

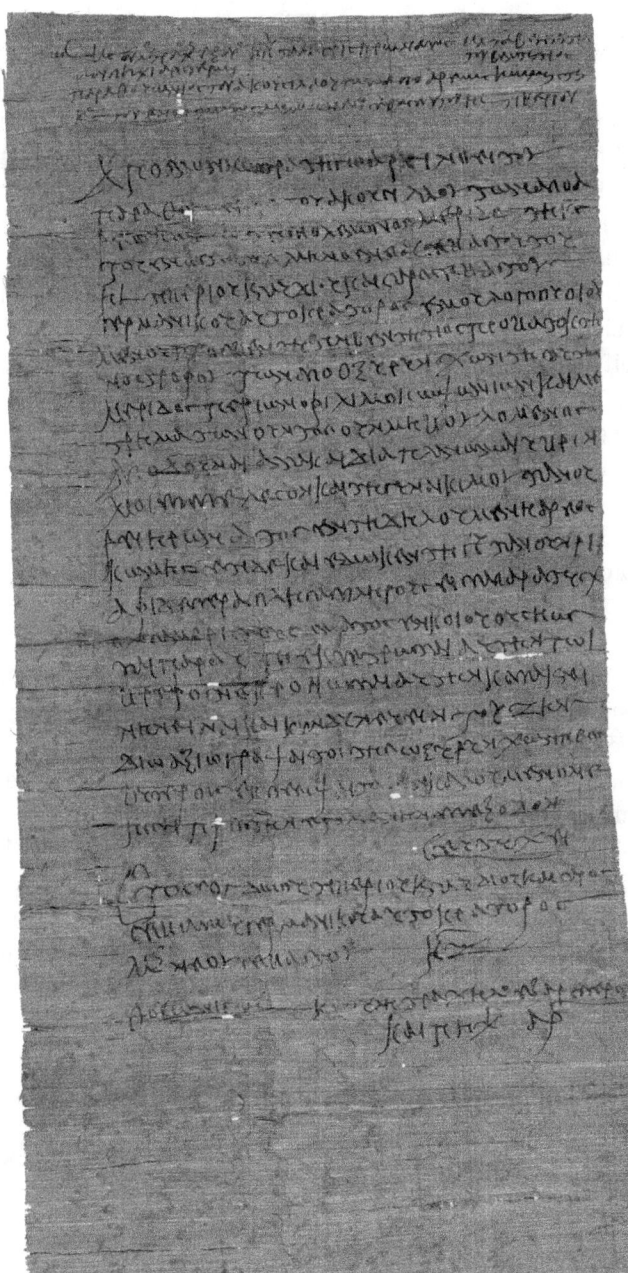

Fig. 2: P.Mich. V 228 (Image courtesy of the University of Michigan Papyrology Collection). This petition, in which a man narrates a trip to collect a debt that ended in assault against his pregnant wife, demonstrates the *grapheion*'s mediating role in the petitioning process. At the top of the document, the *grapheion* scribe added notes about the parties to the complaint; this particular copy was retained in the Tebtunis *grapheion* as a draft, rather than being submitted to the authorities.

The *grapheion* was run as a concession from the Roman state. Would-be notaries had to pay a license fee for the exclusive rights to notarial business in a certain area. Beside drawing up individual contracts and other documents for their clients, duties included sending copies and registers of contracts to state archives in the *metropoleis* and Alexandria. Besides the Tebtunis archive, which includes drafts of such registers that were never sent, and the Karanis account, which was the notary's private account of income and expenditures, fragments of numerous registers survive, largely because the rolls were eventually pulled from the archives and reused for other purposes.[19]

Notaries could stay in office for decades at a time and were assisted by a small team of scribes. Some of these assistants may be the professional writers who were paid to write subscriptions on behalf of illiterates. One such figure was Heron, son of Satyros, who was active in the Karanis *grapheion* over a 35 year period, while another scribe in Tebtunis can be traced over the same period of time.[20] But, perhaps surprisingly, plenty of individuals coming into the *grapheion* could write for themselves, some 40 % in Tebtunis, including the so-called slow writers, whose crude capital letters sufficed only for a short subscription.[21] Many individuals simply turned to family members or associates, but in a pinch professional writers like Heron were always available with pen in hand.

The scant evidence on the background of these village notaries and professional writers indicates that in the first century CE they were connected to the Egyptian priestly elite and well-off landowners who formed the upper-crust of village society. In the second century, however, there are clues that metropolites were encroaching on these village writing offices. The family of Apollonios alias Lourios, for instance, who is attested as the notary of Tebtunis in nine contracts dating between 101 and 135 CE, belonged to the Arsinoite gymnasial class, the highest social group to which Egyptians could attain and the basis for the later class of city councilors.[22] Isolated evidence supports this picture of well-off notaries in the second century. A list of men suitable for nome-wide liturgical service includes the notary of the village of Pharbaithos, whose estate is valued at 4,000 drachmas,[23] while a letter from Oxyrhynchos shows a *nomographos* (a usual term for village notary) travelling in the company of a gymnasiarch-elect.[24]

This encroachment of metropolite interests perhaps portends the demise of village *grapheia* and the concentration of notarial services in the metropolis. The last attestations of many village *grapheia* in the Arsinoite nome are in the 160s and 170s

---

19 P.Fay. 344 descr. = CLAYTOR 2013, for example, is a sheet cut from such a register, which was then re-used for a private letter.
20 CLAYTOR 2014a.
21 YIFTACH-FIRANKO 2016.
22 On this figure and his family see SMOLDERS 2013.
23 W.Chr. 298 (169 CE).
24 P.Oxy. LIX 3992 (II CE).

CE.²⁵ In the Oxyrhynchite nome, rural *grapheia* lasted into the early third century, but no later. So, what happened?

An important intermediate step, at least in the Arsinoite nome, was the subordination of the village *grapheia* to one authority in the metropolis. There are three references in the years 188–190 to a figure called "the representative of the *grapheia* of both the metropolis and the villages of the three *merides*."²⁶ The title and its narrow timeframe suggest that this was a temporary measure. Such a centralized position, moreover, raises conceptual problems, as Dieter HAGEDORN and Fabian REITER note in their recent reedition of P.Berl.Cohen 8.²⁷ Did this manager of all the nome's *grapheia* personally make the rounds to each office in order to make his services available? This would be conceivable only if there were few village *grapheia* left, a situation suggested by the paucity of attestations after the 170s. But P.Berl.Cohen 8 stands squarely in the unique diplomatic tradition of Kerkesoucha's *grapheion* that I analyzed in a recent article.²⁸ Either our nome-wide *grapheion* manager was particularly sensitive to local scribal traditions – which I find highly unlikely – or Kerkesoucha's local scribes were going on as before, though now operating under the umbrella of a nome-wide notarial official. In any case, by the time of the next extant sale written in the village, 219 CE, this diplomatic tradition had given way to a new style of contract that was not unique to Kerkesoucha. The era of the local *grapheion* had come to an end.

The eventual concentration of all notarial services in the nome metropolis puzzled legal historian Hans-Julius WOLFF, who considered this measure "a departure from the decentralized policies marking the previous century and a half."²⁹ He was influenced by the view that the network of *grapheia* dramatically expanded under the Romans,³⁰ a problematic assumption, as already indicated. This centralization of notarial activity, moreover, fits in nicely with Rome's long-term municipalization of the nomes and occurs around the same time as the granting of autonomous city councils to the nome capitals, as Rodney AST has observed.³¹ The disappearance of local writing offices is, in my view, just another sign of the subordination of the countryside to metropolite interests.

---

25 A late holdout appears to be the *grapheion* of Ptolemais Arabon, through which a contract was drawn up in the year 208 (referred to at P.Col. X 274,9–10).
26 διέπων or διαδεχόμενος τὰ γραφεῖα τῆς τε μητροπόλεως καὶ κωμῶν τῶν τριῶν μερίδων. See REITER 2013; HAGEDORN/REITER 2015.
27 HAGEDORN/REITER 2015.
28 CLAYTOR 2015.
29 WOLFF 1978, 22. The full quote is: "Über den Grund der von der Provinzialregierung wohl nicht schlagartig verordneten, aber vermutlich immerhin geförderten Zusammenfassung, die eine Abkehr von der von ihr anderthalb Jahrhunderte vorher eingeschlagenen Dezentralisationspolitik bedeutete, ist beim gegenwärtigen Stand der Quellen noch keine Aussage möglich."
30 Cf. WOLFF 1978, 18–19.
31 AST 2015.

By the middle of the third century CE, all evidence for notarial offices is found in the nome capitals, now run by city councils consisting of the wealthiest local landowners. Even these notarial offices, however, would disappear by the end of the fourth century in a process that Uri YIFTACH-FIRANKO has called the "'privatization' of scribal activity:"[32] objective notarial contracts were fully replaced by private *cheirographa*, or notes of hand, written in the form of a letter. This relaxation of state control, however, should not be confused with an amateurization of writing; on the contrary, most *cheirographa*, although nominally written in the first party's own hand, were actually written by professional scribes. The great drawback of such documents for the social historian is that, unlike their notarial counterparts, they generally do not state where they were written, which impedes analysis of the balance between urban and rural writing in this period.[33]

They do, however, generally contain subscriptions and in some cases the name of the scribe who drew up the main contract, so a combined prosopographical and palaeographical approach offers one way forward. Rodney AST is currently examining the networks of known writers in the fourth century Arsinoite nome, and his preliminary findings point to city councilors and their assistants as the main circle of writers for much of the documentation from this region, despite the fact that most of this evidence was actually found in villages.[34]

For an example of the new dynamics of writing, we can examine a group of four contracts that were found bundled together and form part of the well-known archive of Aurelius Isidorus.[35] Isidorus was an illiterate but well-off farmer from Karanis whose papers span the late third to early fourth centuries and give us our best look at the late Roman village liturgical class. The four contracts are all advance sales of beans made by Isidorus and his partners in a village farming association over a short period of time, perhaps made out to the same buyer in all cases. These types of sales involve the immediate payment of cash in exchange for the later delivery of the crop after the harvest, with the amount of produce delivered calculated to include interest.[36] In two of these contracts, a certain Aurelius Theodorus signs on behalf of the associated farmers, all of whose members are illiterate, but nothing more is known of this Theodoros.[37] Another contract, however, is signed by one Demetrios, son of Besarion, who reappears as a subscriber in the Sakaon archive of Theadelphia and in an unpublished documents from the Michigan collection, where he subscribes on behalf of the grain

---

32 YIFTACH-FIRANKO 2008b, 338.
33 Many fourth-century *cheirographa*, moreover, are not signed by the notary, in contrast to the later practice documented in DIETHART/WORP 1986.
34 AST 2015.
35 P.Cair.Isid. 87–89 and 97.
36 See BAGNALL 1977a, RUPPRECHT 1984, 279–280, and JÖRDENS, P.Heid. V pp. 333–335.
37 P.Cair.Isid. 88 and 89.

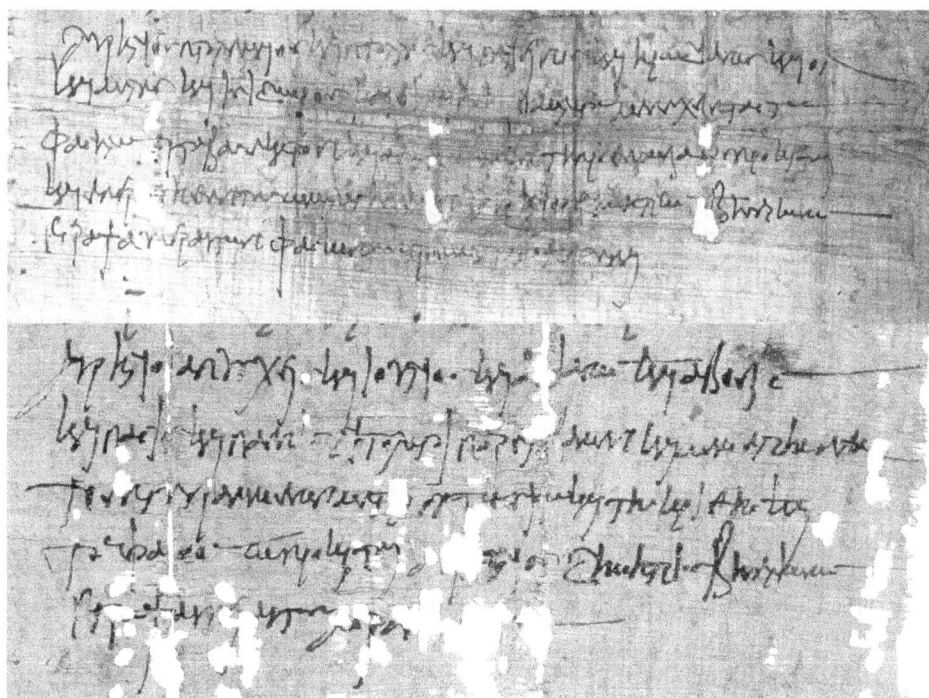

Fig. 3: Comparison of the subscriptions of P.Cair.Isid. 97 and P.Mich. inv. 397b, both written by Demetrios, son of Besarion. Images courtesy of the University of Michigan Papyrology Collection.

collectors of Philadelphia (see fig. 3).[38] Given that he writes on behalf of groups from three different villages, it is most economical to place Demetrios in the metropolis, offering his pen to the steady stream of village officials, rural landholders, and tenant farmers coming to the city for business.

In another of these contracts, we find a rare statement about the author of the contract itself, since it says "it was executed through Aninos, *nomikos*."[39] Such notarial signatures are not common in fourth century Arsinoite contracts, and even more rarely do we get the scribe's title. *Nomikoi* were legal experts who assisted advocates in the preparation of cases and advised judges during proceedings.[40] Such advisors, whose main haunts would be the tribunals of magistrates and the offices of advocates, are unlikely to have been found in the villages, and we may accordingly suggest that this contract was also drawn up in nome capital.

---

38 P.Cair.Isid. 97, P.Sakaon 5,64–66, and P.Mich. inv. 397b and c. The identification of Demetrios' hand in the Sakaon text is due to Fred JENKINS, who is also editing the Philadelphia documents for publication in a future volume of Michigan Papyri.
39 P.Cair.Isid. 88.
40 P.Col. VII 174.

Finally, there is one indication as to why Isidorus and his partners were disposing of their future bean crop in exchange for ready cash. In P.Cair.Isid. 89, the 15 talents received are said to have been expended on "the purchase of gold and silver bullion to satisfy the imperial assessment on their estate."[41] We can thus reconstruct the series of events as follows: Isidorus and his partners were hit with a series of demands for cash from the state. With insufficient funds on hand, the partners turned to mortgaging the future yield of their bean crop and went to the city to find buyers. When an agreement was reached, they secured the services of one of the city's many professional writers to draw up the contract, and found other metropolite writers to pen the required subscription in their names. This narrative, if correctly reconstructed, suggests that it was not necessarily a lack of writers or writing institutions in the village, but rather the centrifugal economic and administrative forces at play in fourth century Egypt that focused writing activities in the metropolis.

This of course is just one story, and we should not push the argument too far. Contracts and other documents were still produced in the villages. Karanis, though much reduced in population in this period, was home to a number of proficient writers, including Aurelius Kasios, who signs multiple rent receipts in his own proficient hand. BAGNALL sees him as a "family writer, called upon whenever serious writing was needed."[42]

The evidence from the ongoing excavations of Kellis in the Dakhleh Oasis, on the other hand, seems to offer a brighter picture. One fortunate quirk of the Kellis documentation is that subscribers almost always identify themselves by their domicile, which allows for a comparison between the balance of city and village writers.

Subscribers in P.Kell. I

Domicile	Subscribers
Village	19
Metropolis	8
Other (cavalryman)	1

The village writers include the son of a "village scribe," who offers his services as a subscriber[43] and a komarch, or village headman, who signs his own petition and claims to have posted it publically.[44] Finding someone called a village scribe in this period is interesting because his role as chief village official had long given way to the komarch; perhaps this reference and similar ones from Karanis and Magdola in the

---

41 On these purchases see BAGNALL 1977b.
42 BAGNALL 1993, 242–243.
43 P.Kell. I 14 (356).
44 P.Kell. I 23 (353).

Hermopolite nome[45] simply mean that these men made their living from writing, like our earlier professional writers.

Other village writers in Kellis include a church reader, a Christian priest, and a priest of a pagan cult.[46] When we get a peek into other rural writing environments, we can find a similar set of writers. Three early fifth century contracts from Alabastrine in the Hermopolite nome, for example, concern only village affairs and were no doubt written there.[47] The subscribers in the three documents are a local priest, a village official, and a man from a neighboring village.

The appearance of priests and church readers and, in other texts, literate monks involved in villager affairs,[48] points to Christian institutions as a new pole of rural writing activity. Intimately connected with the establishment of the church in Egypt is the rise of a new script for the Egyptian language. The development of Coptic in the bilingual milieux of the Egyptian countryside meant that for the first time in centuries Egyptians could express in writing something resembling their everyday speech.[49] Yet, for the types of official writing that we have been looking at here, Greek remained mandatory until at least the sixth century.

Our foray into the fourth century villages has given us mixed signals. On the one hand, the Karanis evidence gives the distinct impression of a village with a small group of mostly functional writers. We are far from the bustling activity of the second century *grapheion*. Part of this is surely attributable to the great reduction in population, but my impression is that fourth century Karanis is not just a smaller version of its previous self, but a fundamentally different type of village.

Kellis so far has not provided enough earlier evidence to make a diachronic assessment of its development. When lined up next to fourth century Karanis, however, it gives the appearance of a wider and more varied writing class. Village and church officials along with a number of others contribute to the pool of local writers, though residents of the Oasis cities also make an appearance, as expected. Greek literature also makes up a fair amount of the fourth century material from Kellis. The most famous example is the wooden codex containing speeches of Isocrates,[50] but there is also an amusing 15 line Homeric parody written either by a local schoolmaster or student, since it was found with teaching material and school exercises.[51] Karanis is again lacking in comparison, with few Greek literary texts dated to the fourth century, although much was found from earlier periods. School texts are also rare.

---

45 P.Cair.Isid. 68 and CPR VII 18 (with note): cf. BAGNALL 1993, 134.
46 P.Kell. I 13, 32 and 58.
47 SB XXII 15618–20.
48 E. g. M.Chr. 363 and P.Würzb. 16. In the latter the monk is the son of a former *prytanis*: cf. BAGNALL 1993, 249.
49 See CHOAT 2010 and BAGNALL 2011, 75–95.
50 WORP/RIJKSBARON 1997.
51 HOPE/WORP 2006.

But let us try to take a step back and consider village writing more abstractly. In all periods, the villages of Greco-Roman Egypt required a basic level of literacy to function. Village landholdings needed to be tracked and tax accounts drawn up. Someone needed to be able to read instructions, both routine and urgent, from nome administrators: find this fugitive, send so-and-so to the city to meet his creditor, prepare for the arrival of this official, and so forth. A few literate individuals could fulfill these demands, and we can consider this baseline village literacy.

Wherever we have evidence, however, villagers are found not only responding to the demands of the state, but creating their own paper trail: contracts, petitions, private accounts, letters, school exercise, etc. Add a few more people for these activities and I think you have reached the extent of proficient writers in a village like Karanis in the fourth century, whereas Kellis I would classify as a step above. But this is still a far cry from the era of the *grapheion*, when the large villages had dedicated writing offices churning out contracts, petitions, written oaths, and more, all while a good number of their clients could actually write for themselves, and not a few indulged in Greek literature.

I am inclined to accept, then, the idea of a municipalization of writing over the first four centuries of Roman rule. But there has been a glaring chronical gap in the evidence I have covered: what is happening in the third century? This is where neither Karanis nor Kellis offers much help: the Oasis evidence is almost non-existent and Karanis is lightly attested. The great archive of Heroninos from Theadelphia, the second largest we have, tells us much about estate administration in village territory, but little about the villages themselves.

The next step, then, is to gather the scattered evidence from third century villages in order to try to connect the dots. What can we find between the village *grapheion* of the second century and the village scribes of fourth century Karanis and Kellis?

Bibliography

Ast 2015 = R. Ast, Writing and the City in Later Roman Egypt. Towards a Social History of the Ancient 'Scribe,' *CHS Research Bulletin* 4.1, 2015. http://nrs.harvard.edu/urn3:hlnc.essay:AstR. Writing_in_the_City_in_Later_Roman_Egypt.2016

Bagnall 1977a = R.S. Bagnall, Price in 'Sales on Delivery,' *GRBS* 18, 1977, 85–96.

Bagnall 1977b = R.S. Bagnall, Bullion Purchases and Landholding in the Fourth Century, *CE* 52, 1977, 322–336.

Bagnall 1993 = R.S. Bagnall, Egypt in Late Antiquity, Princeton 1993.

Bagnall 2011 = R.S. Bagnall, Everyday Writing in the Graeco-Roman East, Berkeley 2011.

Bagnall/Worp 2011 = R.S. Bagnall/K.A. Worp, Family Papers from Second-Century A.D. Kellis, *CE* 86, 2011, 228–253.

Bowman 1971 = A.K. Bowman, The Town Councils of Roman Egypt, Toronto 1971.

Bowman/Rathbone 1992 = A.K. Bowman/D.W. Rathbone, Cities and Administration in Roman Egypt, *JRS* 82, 1992, 107–127.

BURKHALTER 1990 = F. BURKHALTER, Archives locales et archives centrales en Égypte romaine, *Chiron* 20, 1990, 191–216.
CHOAT 2010 = M. CHOAT, Early Coptic Epistolography, in: A. PAPACONSTANTINOU (ed.), The Multilingual Experience in Egypt, from the Ptolemies to the Abbasids, Surrey/Burlington 2010, 153–178.
CLAYTOR 2013 = W.G. CLAYTOR, A Schedule of Contracts and a Private Letter: P. Fay. 344, *BASP* 50, 2013, 77–121.
CLAYTOR 2014a = W.G. CLAYTOR, Heron, Son of Satyros: a Scribe in the Grapheion of Karanis, *ZPE* 190, 2014, 199–202.
CLAYTOR 2014b = W.G. CLAYTOR, Rogue Notaries? Two Unusual Double Documents from the Late Ptolemaic Fayum, *JJP* 44, 2014, 93–115.
CLAYTOR 2014c = W.G. CLAYTOR, Mechanics of Empire: the Karanis Register and the Writing Offices of Roman Egypt, Ann Arbor (Dissertation), 2014.
CLAYTOR 2015 = W.G. CLAYTOR, Donkey Sales from the Grapheion of Kerkesoucha, *ZPE* 194, 2015, 201–208.
COCKLE 1984 = W.E.H. COCKLE, State Archives in Graeco-Roman Egypt from 30 B.C. to the Reign of Septimius Severus, *JEA* 70, 1984, 106–122.
DIETHART/WORP 1986 = J.M. DIETHART/K.A. WORP, Notarsunterschriften im byzantinischen Ägypten, Vienna 1986.
FARAGUNA 2000 = M. FARAGUNA, A proposito degli archivi nel mondo greco: terra e registrazioni fondiarie, *Chiron* 30, 2000, 65–115.
HAGEDORN/REITER 2015 = D. HAGEDORN/F. REITER, Eine Neuedition von P.Berl. Cohen 8, *APF* 61.2, 2015, 317–322.
HEILPORN/WORP 2007 = P. HEILPORN/K.A. WORP, A Wet Nurse Contract with an Unusual Provenance, *CE* 82, 2007, 218–226.
HOOGENDIJK 2013 = F.A.J. HOOGENDIJK, Greek Contracts Belonging to the Late Ptolemaic Tebtynis Grapheion Archive, in: C. ARLT/M.A. STADLER (ed.), Das Fayyûm in Hellenismus und Kaiserzeit. Fallstudien zu multikulturellem Leben in der Antike, Wiesbaden 2013, 63–74.
HOPE/WORP 2006 = C.A. HOPE/K.A. WORP, Miniature Codices from Kellis, *Mnemosyne* 59.2, 2006, 226–258.
HUSSELMAN 1970 = E.M. HUSSELMAN, Procedures of the Record Office of Tebtunis in the First Century A.D, in: D.H. HOBSON (ed.), Proceedings of the Twelfth International Congress of Papyrology, Toronto 1970, 223–238.
KELLY 2010 = B. KELLY, Petitions, Litigation, and Social Control in Roman Egypt, Oxford 2010.
MUHS 2010 = B.P. MUHS, A Late Ptolemaic Grapheion Archive in Berkeley, in: T. GAGOS (ed.) Proceedings of the Twenty-Fifth International Congress of Papyrology, Ann Arbor 2010, 581–588.
PESTMAN 1985 = P.W. PESTMAN, Registration of Demotic Contracts in Egypt. P. Par. 65; 2nd Cent. B.C., in: J.A. ANKUM/J.E. SPRUIT/F.B.J. WUBBE (ed.), Satura Roberto Feenstra sexagesimum quintum annum aetatis complenti ab alumnis collegis amicis oblata, Fribourg 1985, 17–25.
PIERCE 1968 = R.H. PIERCE, Grapheion, Catalogue, and Library in Roman Egypt, *SO* 43, 1968, 68–83.
REITER 2013 = F. REITER, Ein Neuer Blick auf SPP XXII 78 und das Schicksal der Dorfgrapheia im 2. Jh. n. Chr., in: C. ARLT/M.A. STADLER (ed.), Das Fayyûm in Hellenismus und Kaiserzeit. Fallstudien zu multikulturellem Leben in der Antike, Wiesbaden 2013, 159–167.
RUPPRECHT 1984 = H.-A. RUPPRECHT, Vertragliche Mischtypen in den Papyri, in: P. DIMAKIS (ed.), Μνήμη Γεωργίου Πετροπούλου 2, Athens 1984, 271–283.
SMOLDERS 2013 = R. SMOLDERS, Apollonios Alias Lurius, Head of the Grapheion of Tebtynis (Version 2), Leuven Homepage of Papyrus Collections, http://www.trismegistos.org/arch/archives/pdf/351.pdf.

Toepel 1973 = L.R. Toepel, Studies in the Administrative and Economic History of Tebtunis in the First Century A. D. Dissertation: Duke University, 1973.

Van Minnen 1998 = P. Van Minnen, Boorish or Bookish? Literature in Egyptian Villages in the Fayum in the Graeco-Roman Period, *JJP* 28, 1998, 99–184.

Van Beek 2013 = B. Van Beek, Kronion Son of Apion, Head of the *grapheion* of Tebtynis, Leuven 2013. Homepage of Papyrus Collections, http://www.trismegistos.org/arch/archives/pdf/93.pdf.

Wolff 1978 = H.J. Wolff, Das Recht der griechischen Papyri Ägyptens in der Zeit der Ptolemäer und des Prinzipats II, München 1978.

Worp/Rijksbaron 1997 = K.A. Worp/A. Rijksbaron, The Kellis Isocrates Codex, Oxford 1997.

Yiftach-Firanko 2008a = U. Yiftach-Firanko, Who Killed the Double Document in Ptolemaic Egypt? *APF* 54, 2008, 203–218.

Yiftach-Firanko 2008b = U. Yiftach-Firanko The *Cheirographon* and the Privatization of Scribal Activity in Early Roman Oxyrhynchus, in: E. Harris/G. Thür (ed.), Symposion 2007: Vorträge zur griechischen und hellenistischen Rechtsgeschichte (Durham, 2.–6. September 2007), Wien 2008, 325–340.

Yiftach 2016 = U. Yiftach, Quantifying and Qualifying Literacy in Early Roman Egypt, in: D. Schaps/U. Yiftach/D. Dueck (ed.), When West Met East: The Encounter of Greece and Rome with the Jews, Egyptians, and Others. Studies Presented to Ranon Katzoff in Honor of his 75th Birthday, Trieste 2016, 269–281.

Paul Schubert
Who Needed Writing in Graeco-Roman Egypt, and for What Purpose? Document Layout as a Tool of Literacy

Abstract: Numerous aspects in the life of the inhabitants of Graeco-Roman Egypt were determined by actions that required writing, even in the countryside. The level of literacy, however, was very uneven among individuals and officials. The layout of documents was devised in such a way that it helped those with a moderate level of literacy to follow intricate administrative procedures. The specific case of blank windows is used to illustrate this phenomenon.

Zusammenfassung: Die Schrift übte einen gewissen Einfluss in vielen Angelenheiten im Leben der Einwohner im griechisch-römischen Ägypten aus, sogar auf dem Lande. Die Tätigkeit des Schreibens und Lesens war allerdings unter einzelnen Personen und Beamten ungleich verbreitet. Der Umbruch der Urkunden half Leuten mit einer beschränkten Fähigkeit des Lesens, damit sie komplexe Verfahren verfolgen konnten. Der bestimmte Fall von leeren Fenstern wird verwendet, um dieses Phänomen zu veranschaulichen.

Introduction

On October 21st, 137 CE, two peasants from the village of Soknopaiou Nesos, Stotoetis and Panouphis, submit a complaint to the strategos of the Arsinoite nome, district of Herakleides, in Middle Egypt: they are the victims of a fraud and have lost three hundred drachmas to a man called Horion. Horion came from the capital of the nome, and the two peasants apparently went there, made a payment, only to discover that Horion had disappeared with the money. The alleged transaction was for a purchase of wheat from Horion's father, but the said father was apparently not aware of the arrangement made by his son.[1]

---

[1] See P.Gen. I² 28 (= M.Chr. 109) < http://www.ville-ge.ch/musinfo/imageZoom/?iip=bgeiip/papyrus/pgen4-ri.ptif> Trismegistos # 11223. For a similar case elsewhere in the same area, see P.Grenf. II 61 (Psenyris [Arsinoite nome], 197/198 CE), where a woman declares that she has been cheated of 800 dr. by a wine merchant. On money theft, see DREXHAGE 1988, 986–991. Many papyri quoted in this paper can be viewed online; when a digital image is available, it is usually recorded on <www.papyri.info>. When appropriate, reference is also given to a stable Trismegistos number; see <www.trismegistos.org>.

A look at an image of the papyrus shows that the petition submitted by Stotoetis and Panouphis was written by a trained professional: the elegant writing, the neat layout and the spelling all suggest a level of competence far above that of an Egyptian peasant from Soknopaiou Nesos. Nonetheless, Stotoetis and Panouphis found a way to file a complaint, and we can assume that this was no hopeless endeavour, or else they would not have wasted time and money hiring a professional scribe. We find ourselves in a complex network of people who write, are written about, also people who can read and others who need the help of others to do so.

To this should be added that we possess a second copy of this petition, with almost the same wording.[2] The most salient difference lies in the fact that one of the two plaintiffs adds that Horion also stole a box containing a girdle.[3] The two copies are not by the same hand, but the second document too was produced by a skilled scribe with a trained hand. The size of the papyrus sheet is comparable to the other copy, which suggests that the two sheets were cut off from a roll of standard size in use in a professional scribal office.[4] Since these papyri were found in Soknopaiou Nesos, they must have been copies kept by the plaintiffs – and not stored in a nome archive in the capital.

The issue of literacy in Graeco-Roman Egypt has already been subjected to intense scrutiny. Here I intend to provide a brief survey of the process of writing in Egypt at the time of the Roman Empire, with the aim of better understanding what the purpose of writing was in that part of the world. We shall then focus our attention on two kinds of documents that should illustrate more precisely how writing was put into use in a very concrete fashion. I shall adduce the example of the certificates of pagan sacrifice, putting emphasis on the layout of the documents; I shall also recall the case of business notes in the context of large agricultural estates.

Those Who Write, Those Who are Written about, Those Who Read: a Brief Survey

The sands of Egypt have yielded a huge amount of written texts, dating mostly from the period between the arrival of Alexander the Great (332 BCE) and the Arab conquest (642 CE). More than sixty thousand documents have been published to this day, to which we should add a few thousand fragments of literary texts of various kinds.[5] Under the Ptolemies, and also during the Roman Empire, Greek was the main lan-

---

2 P.Brook. 3; Trismegistos # 10291.
3 13–15: βαστ[ά]|ξας μου καὶ χείλωμα [ἐν] ᾧ νέ[α] | ζωνή.
4 P.Gen. I² 28: H 21 × W 8.8 cm; P.Brook. 3: H 21 × W 10 cm.
5 For an access to those texts, see <www.trismegistos.org>.

guage of written communication in Egypt, but we also have many texts written in Egyptian (hieratic, demotic and coptic scripts), in Latin, as well as in a few other more exotic languages. Let us try to figure out who wrote, who was written about, and who read all this material.

The competence of writing is – by far – not shared equally by all individuals in Egypt.[6] It should be said from the outset that the available testimonies give us only a partial view of the oral and written skills of the population. Although the Greek language took precedence in written communication for almost a millenium, the resurgence of Egyptian in the coptic script during the Empire shows that it was probably the common language of oral communication in the countryside during that whole period. Stotoetis, the villager from Soknopaiou Nesos, presumably spoke Egyptian. When he filed his complaint against Horion, he resorted to the help of a scribe who could write in Greek to the strategos. It has also been suggested that the prevalence of Egyptian was even stronger among women, with the consequence that the home language in most households would have been Egyptian.[7]

Since we encounter people from all social backgrounds in our papyri, our written testimonies could impress on us the idea that we are dealing with a population where the skill of writing is shared almost universally, from villagers to the members of the social elite in the nome capitals. Such is probably not the case. There were various degrees of skill in writing, from those who could barely sign a contract to those who knew – with unequal degrees of success – how to craft complex sentences.[8] We should therefore make a distinction between those who actually wrote and those who needed writing but required help from someone else.

Nonetheless, writing was pervasive in the existence of virtually all inhabitants of Graeco-Roman Egypt. It could take many forms, the most current being letters and *memoranda* (ὑπομνήματα). Other formats can be found too. Based on the testimony of our papyri, we could establish a rough list of domains where writing was requested from individuals, in one form or another.[9]

Individuals who
- learned and taught writing as well as other school activities.
- needed to stay in touch with relatives, or who had to coordinate their business with partners at a distance.
- entered any kind of legal business, like contracts for sale, lease, hire, marriage etc.
- owned property, housing, land or cattle.

---

6 A summary of the topic can be found in HARRIS 1989, 276–281; see also 10, 116–146 and 201–203.
7 See BAGNALL/CRIBIORE 2006, 21.
8 See YOUTIE 1971.
9 Here I shall leave aside the copying of books for literary purposes, which would be yet another vast domain to explore. On this point, see JOHNSON/PARKER 2009; on literacy in Greek and Roman literature, HOUSTON 2009.

- were liable to any kind of tax, starting with the poll tax.
- had any special civic status and needed to ascertain their rights.
- needed to submit a petition to an official.
- had to interact with the officials of the province, at all levels of the hierarchy.

Officials also wrote quite a lot. They had to:
- coordinate their various activities at all levels, which implies an abundant correspondance.
- submit reports.
- inform the population of orders received from above.
- keep detailed registers of people and property.
- assess taxes to be paid and submit accounts to the higher levels of administration.
- issue receipts for payments of taxes in kind and in cash.
- designate individuals for public service (liturgies).
- accomplish police duties.
- summon individuals to appear in court.
- keep minutes of meetings and court proceedings.

This very complex network of correspondance and recording becomes interesting when we observe the interaction between people through their writing. To come back to the case of Stotoetis and Panouphis, who filed their complaint to the strategos after having been cheated of three hundred drachmas, it would of course be desirable to follow the whole string of writing that this affair may have produced: once the strategos received the complaint, he would have written to a subordinate, asking him to check whether this accusation was credible and requesting that Horion be summoned in his presence. He must have informed Horion in writing about the nature of the complaint; Horion could thus oppose the accusation in writing, or challenge the summons. If he did not, the strategos would issue a decision and instruct subordinates to take proper action. Horion could be fined or sentenced to hard labour, which would produce even more red tape, from the issuance of the sentence to the order of liberation once the sentence was served.[10]

We cannot examine here all the links in this chain of possible paperwork. Let us nonetheless stop at one stage, namely the challenge to the summons, where we have a newly published parallel dating from the same period, but found in Oxyrhynchos.[11]

---

10 On this last element of the procedure, see SB XX 14631, 4–7 (= ChLA X 421 = CEL I 151; unknown provenance, 139 CE [under the Praefect C. Avidius Heliodorus]); SB I 4639, 3–6 (Alexandria, 209 CE [under the Praefect Ti. Claudius Subatianus Aquila]).
11 P.Oxy. LXXXII 5316 (11 Nov. 133 – 26 May 137), published in 2016. The editor cites several cases where an accused person challenged not the summons, but the whole accusation, claiming that it had no grounding: P.Oxy. I 68 (131 CE), BGU VII 1574 (176/177 CE) and PSI Com. 14 (mid- to late second cent. CE).

Here, the accused person sends a *memorandum* to the strategos, summarizing the accusation and stating that the case is void. Unfortunately, the papyrus breaks off precisely at this point. Parallels to this document show that the accused person could react by hiring a person not only skilled in writing, but with a precise command of the legal phrasing.[12] Writing is therefore not a straightforward matter: as soon as things became serious, the ordinary Egyptian had to resort to the help of more qualified people, be it to file a complaint or to oppose an accusation. As for the strategos, he relied on a competent staff to settle such cases as efficiently as possible.

Writing is essential for the structure of the whole province of Egypt: its economy, administration and social networks cannot be envisaged without a very intricate web of correspondance and recording. The Romans did not innovate inasmuch as there was already a rather complex network of written communication in the Ptolemaic period; but they were masters at casting a wide net over the population, with as few loopholes as possible. Living in a paperless – or, as it were, papyrus-less – environment was almost impossible.

We should also remember that the exceptional documentation which we can use in the case of Roman Egypt was preserved due to special circumstances: a very ancient tradition of writing on papyrus in Egypt, a dry climate, and also settlements turned into ghost towns due to social changes and fiscal pressure. In other words, in spite of the long-held view that Egypt was a particular case within the Roman Empire, we have reached in the past decades a growing consensus that the elements of homogeneity are more significant than the differences. The culture of writing which we observe so clearly in Egypt was presumably present in most parts of the Empire; it so happens that, in other regions, the documents were not preserved in the same way. Our image of northern provinces, for instance, is fashioned for the most part after inscriptions, the purpose of which was very different from texts written on papyrus with a short to medium preservation expectancy.

A Focus on the Layout of Some Papyri

After this admittedly broad overview of the situation, let us focus on a specific aspect of the layout of these documents. My starting hypothesis is that writing and reading belong to a dynamic process, and that a skilled writer will be able to produce a standard layout that does not only allow for reading, but that guides the reader in the actions that are expected from him. In an administrative context, a well-designed layout should accompany the process that is under way. We take this for granted in our age of computing and design; but would this also be the case in Roman Egypt? By

---

[12] See e.g., among texts quoted in the preceding note, P.Oxy. I 68, where the intricate syntax indicates the presence of a person with legal training.

testing this hypothesis against two specific cases, I intend to show that the training of scribes in Roman Egypt went well beyond the mere process of writing: they knew how to create a layout that constitued an essential part of a given procedure.

In both cases, the papyri we shall examine were not produced by scribes working for the administration of the province: in the first case, we shall be dealing with documents copied by people working in private offices, who provided service for any individual requiring help in the preparation of an application to be submitted to the authorities; the second case pertains to messages produced by scribes in the service of an agricultural estate, in other words a private business with a well-oiled organization and staff.

The specific element which I would like to examine in the layout of these documents is made of 'windows': by windows, I mean spaces left purposely blank for someone else to fill at a definite stage of the procedure. They are to be found everywhere in our modern administrative forms; in Greek papyri from Egypt, they are less prevalent, but some definite categories of documents display such windows in a systematic way. I intend to show that these windows constituted an essential element in some given procedures.

Windows in Certificates

The first case I shall adduce is that of the well-known certificates of pagan sacrifice.[13] Those certificates were produced during the so-called 'persecution of Decius' in the summer of AD 250. Following an edict from the emperor, every person in the Empire was required to perform several acts:
- declare that he/she had always performed sacrifices and libations for the gods;
- declare that he/she had repeated this act before a control commission;
- declare that he/she had actually ingested a share of the sacrifice;
- obtain from the control commission a certificate confirming that the act had been performed.

Our sources on this peculiar procedure are both literary (Christian apologetic writings) and documentary, the latter consisting of a group of 47 such certificates, in a diverse state of preservation. Of the 47, 35 (perhaps up to 39) were found together in the village of Theadelphia in the Fayum. Without going into much detail, it is worth recalling a few useful points about this small archive from Theadelphia.[14]

---

[13] On the certificates of pagan sacrifice, see esp. KNIPFING 1923; RIVES 1999; SCHUBERT 2016.
[14] A list of certificates for sacrifice is provided in SCHUBERT 2016, 192–194. To this should now be added a further example of a certificate from Theadelphia, which came out too late to be included in this list: see CLAYTOR 2015.

Since those documents were found together, they were presumably copies that had been assembled by the control commission, and not certificates in the hands of individuals. One can compare the format, phrasing and writing: a) most of the certificates were cut from standard-size rolls (21 cm in height, comparable to P.Gen. 1² 28 and P.Brook. 3, discussed above); b) the phrasing is very consistent, with small variations depending on the model used by the scribe, a model based on a master version at the level of the nome; c) the certificates were all produced by scribes of professional skill, albeit not always with the most elegant hand.

Those documents indicate that the inhabitants of the village, when they were forced to appear before the control commission for pagan sacrifice, first had to seek assistance from a scribe who prepared a certificate following a model provided to him. The only major variation was the name of the applicant. One must insist on the word 'applicant', for the procedure was devised in such a way that every individual had to apply for certification: the authorities asked for nothing, they simply issued an order. It must have been hard to escape getting involved in the procedure, because it entailed the specific act of tasting the offering from the sacrifice.

The control commission was probably established next to the altar for sacrifice. Applicants showed up, perhaps swore an oath about past performance of sacrifice, repeated the action in the presence of the commission and handed in the pre-filled form for the commissioners to sign. This is where our windows become relevant.

All certificates from the Arsinoite nome (not only Theadelphia, but also a few from other places) display a layout where the scribe wrote the main text of the application, then inscribed a date at the bottom of the sheet, leaving a blank window between the two. The window served a double purpose. First, we can observe that a moderately trained hand states that the control commissioners have witnessed the sacrifice: Αὐρήλιοι Σερῆνος καὶ Ἑρμᾶς εἴδαμέ(ν) σε θυσιάσοντα « We, the Aurelii Serenus and Hermas, have seen you perform the sacrifice. »[15] Second, the window allows room for the actual signature of one of the two commissioners, Hermas, written in a very clumsy hand. Hermas abbreviates his name to EPM, followed by another abbreviation, ΣΕΣΗΜ for σεσημείωμαι.

What does this tell us on the writers and their actions? The commissioners received help from an assistant who knew how to write, although he always wrote the same sentence on the certificates. Of the commissioners Serenus and Hermas, we have no clue indicating that Serenus could write at all; and Hermas, who was next to illiterate, could barely sketch a rough signature. In other words, the level of writing

---

15 See e.g. SB I 5943, 14–15 <http://ww2.smb.museum/berlpap/index.php/00318> Trismegistos # 14001; Theadelphia (Arsinoite nome), June 16, 250 CE. The scribe, using a standard model, did not adapt it to the fact that this certificate was issued for a woman named Aurelia Charis. He should have written θυσιάζουσαν instead of the masculine θυσιασοντα (i. e. θυσιάζοντα). SB I 4440 is a duplicate of this document.

skill is – in this case – inversely proportional to the position in the administrative hierarchy. The commissioners, and also to a certain extent their assistant, need some guidance, which is provided by the window left blank by a trained scribe.

As mentioned before, the model was presumably devised at the nome level, by an official with some degree of competence in preparing such forms. It should be said at this point that certificates of sacrifice have been compared, for their content, with other declarations that displayed a close structure, namely census declarations and declarations of death. Census declarations were no more than a declaration and required no signature from an official, which explains why the model does not include a window. Declarations of death are more interesting for our purpose because they also display, in a somewhat different way, another sort of window.

In P.Petaus 7, we find a declaration of death.[16] It is adresssed to the royal secretary (βασιλικὸς γραμματεύς) of the nome. The certificate was produced by a scribe who must have been working, on behalf of the applicant, in an environment similar to that of the Theadelphia certificates of sacrifice: the size of the papyrus sheet is comparable, the skill of the hand too, and the wording offers many similarities.[17] In this case, however, the window left by the scribe consisted of a blank space at the bottom of the sheet of papyrus, separated from the main text by a horizontal stroke. Inside this window, a member of the royal secretary's staff, in a fast and cursive hand, wrote a subscription on behalf of his superior, giving instructions to the village secretary (κωμογραμματεύς).

We know from other documents that the latter man's skill in writing was about the same as that of Hermas: he could barely sign a document, and left mistakes when doing so.[18] In the case of the declaration of death, however, his lack of skill does not show because he is only the recipient of the document. He is told to check whether the person declared as deceased is actually dead, and is held responsible for this control.

This is not the end of the story: for the staff member has placed, between the instructions and a date, yet another window, leaving some space for the royal secretary to sign. In other words, he has created a window within a window. This man, however, is either very busy or unskilled in writing, and the royal secretary's personal assistant signs in his name and stead: 'I, Hermophilos, royal secretary, have signed through Horos my assistant.' This signature is dreadfully difficult to decipher, not because the assistant did not know how to write, but because his hand was very fast and he used abbreviations.

---

16 <http://www.uni-koeln.de/phil-fak/ifa/NRWakademie/papyrologie/PPetaus/bilder/PK358r.jpg> Trismegistos # 8801; Ptolemaïs Hormou (Arsinoite nome), 185 CE.
17 Size: H 21 × W 10.3 cm.
18 This is the famous village secretary Petaus, 'le scribe qui ne savait pas écrire', in the words of Youtie 1966. See P.Petaus 121 < http://www.uni-koeln.de/phil-fak/ifa/NRWakademie/papyrologie/PPetaus/bilder/PK328r.jpg> Trismegistos # 12630; Ptolemaïs Hormou (Arsinoite nome), ca 182–187 CE.

Let us summarize the result achieved by looking at those windows. In a fashion similar to what we find nowadays in many administrative forms, scribes in Roman Egypt knew how to provide blank spaces that guided implicitly the hand of the person whose next action was required. Here, the succession of a window inside a window illustrates the process quite neatly: first, a staff member fills in the available window, but he leaves a smaller window within for the royal secretary's signature.

Other such boxes appear elsewhere in the Petaus archive. To name only two instances, one could consider P.Petaus 60, a list of proposed tax collectors, written in two columns, where the scribe left some space between the bottom of the text and the date so that Petaus himself could, in his clumsy hand, indicate that he had transmitted the document.[19] P.Petaus 56 has an elongated shape.[20] This document was prepared in advance by a scribe for Petaus, who had to designate someone to accompany a shipload of wheat. This time, Petaus' assistant left a rather sizeable window, which was actually far too large for the name that was inscribed at a second stage of the procedure.

This descriptive approach based on the observation of a few *specimina* leaves open a fundamental question: are these windows an illusion projected by a modern scholar used to filling forms in his daily life? Although I am offering here a plausible interpretation, we still need a proof that these windows were really what our ancient scribes had in mind. In order to achieve this, we must add one more detail to the concept of window: that of window-filling. Whereas the second scribe of P.Petaus 56 filled in his window and simply left the blank spaces – as it were – open to the wind, in another case the scribe took care to close the remaining space after he had used the window. In P.Gen. 1² 18, a declaration for the control of the civic status of a young man, we witness the work of an exquisitely elegant hand: the man knew his trade better than most of his colleagues.[21] This document was submitted to an official in the capital of the Arsinoite nome, who inserted – in a trained but much more cursive hand – his signature in the window. Once this was done, he added a string of crosses in the remaining space, effectively filling the window. He probably wanted to avoid any addition by an unwanted third hand. This case therefore indicates without a doubt the intention of the scribes when they designed their windows.

---

19 P.Petaus 60 <http://www.uni-koeln.de/phil-fak/ifa/NRWakademie/papyrologie/PPetaus/bilder/PK312r.jpg> Trismegistos # 8762; Syron Kome (Arsinoite nome), May 26, 185 CE.
20 P.Petaus 56 <http://quod.lib.umich.edu/a/apis/x-3005> Trismegistos # 8824 Ptolemaïs Hormou (Arsinoite nome), 186/187 CE.
21 P.Gen. I² 18 <http://www.ville-ge.ch/musinfo/imageZoom/?iip=bgeiip/papyrus/pgen4-ri.ptif> Trismegistos # 11216; Ptolemaïs Euergetis (Arsinoite nome), Jan. 25, 187 CE.

An Estate and its Business Notes

The windows we have been looking at are but one element in a more complex design by which skilled scribes could guide their readers and prompt them to take appropriate action. There were other aspects of the layout that could help the reader.

For instance, the heading was structured in a highly recognizeable fashion. Most of the certificates and applications we have seen so far are *memoranda* – as opposed to letters – where the writer indicates first the name of the adressee (in the dative), then the name of the sender (with the preposition παρά followed by the name in the genitive). Between the first and the second element, the scribe regularly jumps to the next line, and the letter π of παρά becomes immediately recognizeable. Often, the scribe sets off the line so as to make it even more conspicuous. Thus whoever receives the document knows at once that he is dealing with a *memorandum*, and where to look for the name of the sender.

This traditional layout undergoes a metamorphosis in the hands of scribes employed by the owners of large agricultural estates in the third century. We know of several such estates, the best documented being that of Appianos, who had hired a manager called Heroninos, hence the name of the large 'Heroninos archive'.[22] In this huge lot of papyri, consisting of almost five hundred published texts (there are more awaiting publication), we find many business notes sent by various members of Appianos' staff. Most of them are written by skilled scribes with a rather elegant hand; these men follow a standard format in their notes, allowing for great efficiency. We shall observe both similarities and changes in comparison with the certificates issued a century earlier, but the relation between the two seems unmistakeable.

A sample of images taken from the papyrus collection at the Geneva Library, and comparable to the material mentioned above, will immediately show that the structure of the *memorandum* (ὑπόμνημα) has undergone a change:

---

22 See RATHBONE 1991.

Who Needed Writing in Graeco-Roman Egypt, and for What Purpose — 345

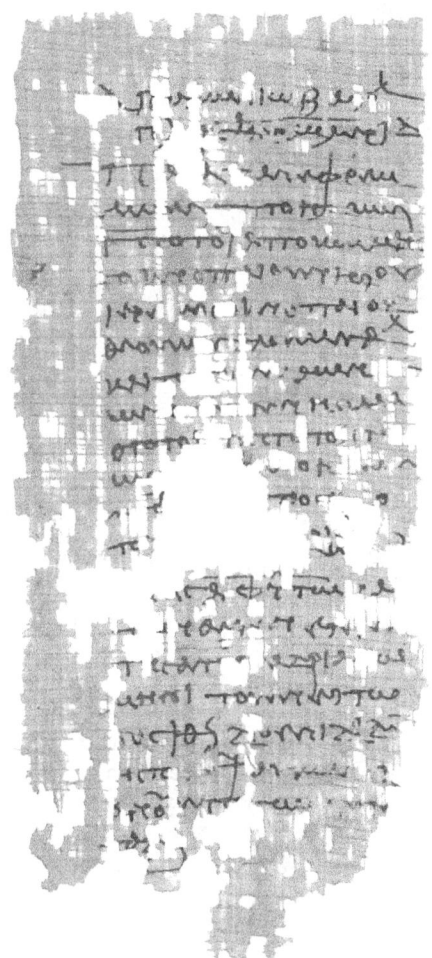

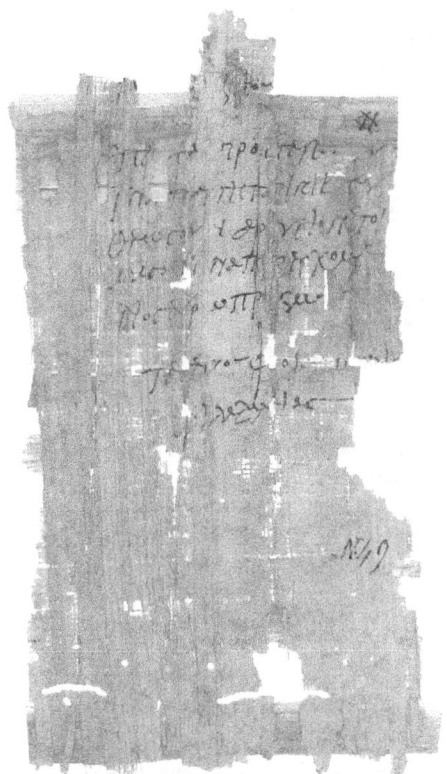

Fig. 2: P.Gen. I² 72 = Trismegistos # 32143
Note about a wine delivery
Ptolemaïs Euergetis (?), 211 CE (?)
< http://www.ville-ge.ch/musinfo/image-Zoom/?iip=bgeiip/papyrus/pnic49-vi.ptif>
© Bibliothèque de Genève / Viviane Siffert

Fig. 1: P.Gen. III 139 = Trismegistos # 11627
Notification of death
Soknopaiou Nesos, Nov. 27 – Dec. 26, 178 CE
< http://www.ville-ge.ch/musinfo/image-Zoom/?iip=bgeiip/papyrus/pgen46-ri.ptif>
© Bibliothèque de Genève / Viviane Siffert

Ἀπολλωνίῳ βασιλ(ικῷ)
γρα(μματεῖ) Ἀρσι(νοίτου) Ἡρακ(λείδου)
μερίδ(ος)
  πα[ρ]ὰ Πανεφρέμ-
μεως Στοτοήτεως
(τρίτου) Στοτοή(τεως) ἀπὸ κώμης
Σοκνοπαίου Νήσου
ἱερέως Σοκνοπαίου
θεοῦ μεγάλου μεγάλ(ου)
καὶ τῷ[ν συ]γνάων [θ]ε-
ῶν. ὁ συγγενής μου
Στοτοῆτις Στοτοήτε-
ως [τοῦ Στ]ο[τ]οήτεως
μητ(ρὸς) [. . . .]τιος καὶ ὁ
τού[του υἱὸς .] . .[. .]ς
[ἱερ]εῖς α φυλ(ῆς) τῶν αὐτῶν θεῶν ἐτελεύ-
τησαν τ[ῷ] Ἁδριανῷ
μηνὶ τοῦ ἐνεστῶ-
τος ιθ (ἔτους). διὸ ἐπιδίδω(μι)
εἰς τὸ ταγῆ(ναι) αὐτῶν τ[ὰ]
ὀνό(ματα) [ἐ]ν τῇ τῶν τετελ(ευτηκότων)
τάξει.

π(αρὰ) [Φ]ι[λο]ξ[έ]νου.
ἔπε[μ]ψα πρός σὲ παι[δ]ί[ο]ν,
ἵνα ἀπαιτῇ τὰ οἰνικ[ά]. εὐ-
θέως οὖν ἀρ[γ]ύριον ἑτοί-
μασον ε[ἵ]να π[α]ρερχόμε-
νος εὕρω πρ[ὸ] ἐμοῦ.

(2nd hand) Τεσενούφ[ι] οἰν[ο]πώλῃ
Φιλαδελφίας.

To Apollonios, royal scribe of the Arsinoite nome, district of Herakleides,
from Panephremmis son of Statoetis the third, grandson of Stotoetis, from the village of Soknopaiou Nesos, priest of Soknopaios, the very great god and of the gods that share his temple.
My relative Stotoetis son of Stotoetis, whose mother is (...), and his son (...), both priests of the first tribe of the same gods, died in the month of Hadrianos of the current 19th year. Therefore I submit (this declaration) in order that their names be placed in the register of deceased persons.

From Philoxenos.
I have sent you a slave who should collect the price for the wine. Therefore, hasten to prepare some silver so that I find it upon my arrival.
To Tesenouphis, wine merchant.

memorandum (second cent. AD)	*business note (third cent. AD)*
recipient (dat.)	
from sender (παρά + gen.)	from sender (π′ + gen.)
main text	main text (short)
greetings (εὐτύχει)	(optional) greetings (ἐρρῶσθαί σε εὔχομαι), sometimes with an additional remark
	recipient (dat.)
date	(optional) date

The main differences are:
a) The recipient's name was moved from the top to the bottom of the document.
b) Before the sender's name, the preposition παρά is replaced by the single letter π.
c) The sender adds greetings in his own hand and sometimes inserts an additional remark.

There is also a fundamental difference in content and intent that may explain the evolution of the layout: whereas a *memorandum* is a note addressed by an individual to a representative of the authorities (strategos, secretary etc.), expressing due respect, a business notes is sent by a manager to a subordinate in a private estate, conveying an order. Let us now examine more closely the three differences listed above.

a) Recipient's name: in the *memorandum*, putting the name of the recipient first in the heading constitutes a mark of respect, similar to putting the recipient's name first in the heading of a letter. In the business note, the hierarchic relationship is inverted; therefore, the sender take precedence. It is in fact not necessary to see the recipient's name at once during transmission: the business note is folded while it is being carried to the recipient, with an address written on the back of the sheet, as in a letter.

b) Sender's name preceded by letter π′: already in *memoranda*, the π of παρά was highly recognizeable and enabled the reader to immediately locate the sender. There were two shapes of π, either in three straight strokes or in a continuous arched shape. In business notes, the arched shape is used for the abbreviation, which works like a modern logo, i. e. a symbol.

c) Greetings and additional remark: this point brings us back to the notion of windows in documents. The business notes, which emanate from managers, are not written by the managers: the task is left to skilled scribes. Those scribes, however, regularly leave a window between the main text and the name of the recipient so that the manager can first add his greetings, which would be the equivalent of our present-day signature. Whereas in *memoranda* the sender would end with a formal wish for well-being (εὐτύχει 'farewell', written by the same hand that copied the whole text), in business notes we find the traditional greetings found at the end of letters, not *memoranda* (ἐρρῶσθαί σε εὔχομαι 'I pray for your health'). Sometimes, the sender adds a personal remark in his own hand. On the notes, such remarks stand out because the writing is usually much less elegant than in the rest of the document.

In short, the evolution between the *memorandum* and the business note sent by managers in large estates seems to reflect a desire for enhanced efficiency in the process of communication. The use of a standard form means that both the actual sender and the recipient know at once where to find the relevant information. Once the scribe has prepared the note, the sender is presented a document with a blank window, which

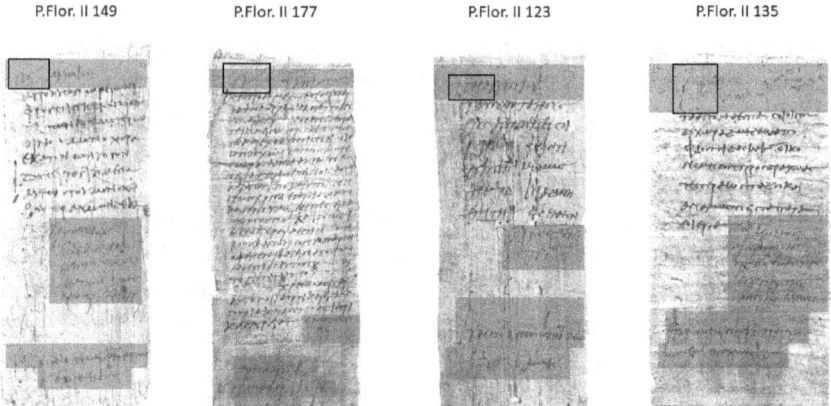

Fig. 3: Four business notes from the Heroninos Archive (outline). Images assembled from P.Flor. II (Comparetti 1911, no longer under copyright).

helps him to perform his own work: in the window, he can add his personal touch, first a greeting and perhaps also a personal comment.

The recipient's work is also made easier because the origin of the note is pinpointed by the symbol π'. The rest of the document is clearly structured so that the reader immediately knows where to find the relevant information. At the bottom, clearly separated from the rest, he can check the recipient's name as well as the date of expedition. Then, the actual order is placed in the center, together with any personal comment by the manager.

Conclusion

The evolution from the *memorandum* to the business note paves the way for some more substantial changes in the format of documents, notably letters, in the fourth century, a topic which we cannot address here.[23] I can simply mention the fact that the windows, which are used in *memoranda* and business notes to guide subsequent writers in complex procedures where several individuals insert their own contribution to the document, remain blank spaces in letters of the fourth century: as Jean-Luc Fournet shows convincingly, their purpose is to separate different parts of a letter's structure.

We should nonetheless ask how those observations on the layout of documents impress on our perception of writers and readers. We have been aware for a long time of the fact that literacy is not a matter of black or white: there are varying degrees of competence in writing and reading. What we have seen here is that the relation-

---

23 See FOURNET 2013.

ship between reader and writer is even more dynamic than one would suspect at first glance. A skilled scribe does not only provide a grammatically sound text with a legible writing: he can also adapt his document to an architecture that will guide his reader, who may himself constitute a link in a chain of writing and reading; for this reader will himself become a writer for the next reader. At the end of the chain, the ultimate reader thus receives a multi-layered document that should, if it is well made, allow more than a linear reading.

This takes us back to the initial story, that of Stotoetis and Panouphis. To the question 'do they need writing?', the answer is clearly 'yes': without the help of writing, they cannot file their complaint against the crook Horion, and there are many other areas of their existence where some kind of writing will be required. Since they are presumably unskilled in writing, they need the help of someone who will, at a cost, do the job in their stead. We have seen that these scribes do not satisfy themselves with copying the words uttered by an angry plaintiff: they know the standard phrasing; they can use models; and the models are sometimes structured so as to ensure that the layout will mirror the envisaged procedure. In this respect, symbols preceding the name of a sender, or windows indicating where a subsequent user should add his greetings or a remark, are helpful tools that improve the efficiency of the whole writing and reading process. When it comes to paperwork, we owe a considerable debt to the Roman Empire.

Bibliography

BAGNALL/CRIBIORE 2006 = R.S. BAGNALL/R. CRIBIORE, Women's Letters from Ancient Egypt 300 BC – AD 800, Ann Arbor 2006.
CLAYTOR 2015 = W.G. CLAYTOR, A Decian libellus at Luther College (Iowa), *Tyche* 30, 2015, 13–18.
COMPARETTI 1911 = D. COMPARETTI, Papiri letterari ed epistolari (P.Flor. II), Firenze 1911.
DREXHAGE 1988 = H.-J. DREXHAGE, Eigentumsdelikte im römischen Ägypten, ANRW II 10.1, 1988, 952–1004.
FOURNET 2013 = J.-L. FOURNET, Culture grecque et document dans l'Égypte de l'Antiquité tardive, *JJP* 43, 2013, 135–162.
HARRIS 1989 = W.V. HARRIS, Ancient Literacy, Cambridge Mass./London 1989.
HOUSTON 2009 = G.W. Houston, Papyrological Evidence for Book Collections and Libraries in the Roman Empire, in: JOHNSON/PARKER 2009, 233–267.
JOHNSON/PARKER 2009 = W.A. JOHNSON/H.N. PARKER (ed.), Ancient Literacies. The Culture of Reading in Greece and Rome, Oxford 2009.
KNIPFING 1923 = J.R. KNIPFING, The Libelli of the Decian Persecution, *Harvard Theological Review* 16, 1923, 345–390.
RATHBONE 1991 = D. RATHBONE, Economic Rationalism and Rural Society in Third-Century A. D. Egypt, Cambridge 1991.
RIVES 1999 = J.B. RIVES, The Decree of Decius and the Religion of Empire, *JRS* 89, 1999, 135–154.
SCHUBERT 2016 = P. SCHUBERT, On the Form and Contents of the Certificates of Sacrifice, *JRS* 106, 2016, 172–198.

Youtie 1966 = H.C. Youtie, Pétaus, fils de Pétaus, ou le scribe qui ne savait pas écrire, *CE* 81, 1966, 127–143 (repr. in H.C. Youtie, Scriptiunculae 2, chap. 34, Amsterdam 1973, 677–695).
Youtie 1971 = H.C. Youtie, 'Bradeos graphon': Between Literacy and Illiteracy, *GRBS* 12 1971, 239–261 (repr. in H.C. Youtie, Scriptiunculae 2, chap. 30, Amsterdam, 1973, 629–651).

Benjamin Hartmann
Schreiben im Dienste des Staates. Prolegomena zu einer Kulturgeschichte der römischen *scribae*

Abstract: The Roman *scribae*, in their official function as paid *apparitores* of the Roman *res publica*, were responsible for the documentary needs of the magistrates as well as the administration of the public archives. It was their role as experts of literate practice at the centre of the Roman polity, which earned them new social and financial opportunities. Their close connection to the *tabulae publicae* provided the basis for their social prestige. Their position as guardians of the public documentation eventually attained symbolic significance.

Zusammenfassung: Als bezahlte *apparitores* im Dienste der römischen *res publica* kümmerten sich die römischen *scribae* um die schriftliche Dokumentation der Magistrate und bewirtschafteten die staatlichen Archive. Es war diese Rolle als Experten der Schriftlichkeit im Zentrum des republikanischen Staates, die den römischen *scribae* soziale und monetäre Möglichkeiten eröffnete. Die enge – nicht zuletzt materielle – Verbindung zwischen den *scribae* und den *tabulae publicae* bildete die Basis ihres sozialen Prestiges. Als Hüter des staatlichen Schriftgutes erlangten die *scribae* schließlich symbolische Bedeutung.

Der historischen Bedeutung der römischen *scribae* nähert man sich am besten über einen ihrer Helden: Cn. Flavius. In seiner Person hat die republikanische Annalistik in fast schon legendärer Form den Prototypen des römischen *scriba* gezeichnet. Livius, der sich sowohl auf C. Licinius Macer als auch auf L. Calpurnius Piso Frugi stützt[1], überliefert für das Jahr 304 v. Chr. eine Vignette unvergleichlichen sozialen Aufstiegs als Symptom der römischen Ständekämpfe.[2] Flavius, der Sohn eines Freigelassenen, ist *scriba* der curulischen Ädile, als er vom Volk selbst zum Ädil gewählt wird. Demonstrativ legt er sein Schreibgerät nieder, um das Amt antreten zu können – ganz zum Ärger der senatorischen Aristokratie, die dem Emporkömmling voller Missgunst und Verachtung entgegentritt und sich weigert, ihn in ihre Reihen aufzunehmen. Flavius wird so zur Personifizierung der Ständekämpfe. Der starke Mann hinter Flavius ist mit App. Claudius Caecus schnell identifiziert; der *scriba* gehört, wie auch sein Patron, zur plebejischen Partei – oder wie sie Livius herablassend nennt, der „*forensis factio*". Wohl noch als *scriba* veröffentlicht Flavius in einer heimlichen Aktion die von der

---

[1] Zur Überlieferungstradition WOLF 1980.
[2] Liv. 9,46,1–12.

Priesterschaft unter Verschluss gehaltenen *fasti* und *legis actiones*, den rechtlichen Kalender und die Spruchformeln. Er wird damit zum Helden der *plebs*. Sein Zugang zu den Schriftdokumenten wie auch seine Fähigkeit, lesen und schreiben zu können, befähigen den *scriba* überhaupt erst zu einer solchen Aktion. Nicht von ungefähr lässt Cicero Flavius in seiner Version der Geschehnisse die unter Verschluss gehaltenen Rechtsmittel Stück für Stück auswendig lernen und anschließend publizieren.[3] Mit dieser annalistischen Episode sind die Leitthemen aufgestellt, die die Geschichte der römischen *scribae* wie einen roten Faden durchziehen. Charakteristisch waren auf der einen Seite das Stigma der niederen Herkunft wie auch der Lohnarbeit; auf der anderen Seite die enge Verbindung mit der schriftlichen Dokumentation der *res publica* und der unmittelbare Kontakt zu den aristokratischen Eliten und damit die Nähe zur Macht.

Die *scribae* bildeten im republikanischen römischen Staat die höchste Klasse der so genannten *apparitores*, der Hilfsbeamten der römischen Magistrate. Als solche bezogen sie einen Lohn, waren *mercenarii*. Wie ihr Name vermuten lässt, waren die *scribae* primär mit Schreibaufgaben betraut, die sie zur Unterstützung der Magistrate tätigten. Schreiben bedeutete in diesem Sinne nicht zuletzt auch Rechnen. Die angesehensten der *scribae*, diejenigen der Quästoren, waren sogar fast ausschließlich als Buchhalter tätig. Sie unterhielten entweder im Gefolge eines Quästors die Provinzialkasse oder in Rom selbst – im *aerarium* – die Staatskasse. Den übrigen Magistraten, die entweder selbst über ein Archiv verfügten oder aber Schreib- und Buchhaltungsarbeiten zu tätigen hatten, waren ebenfalls *scribae* beigegeben. So unter anderem den Ädilen, den Volkstribunen oder etwa den Wasserkuratoren und den Präfekten der *annona*. Das System fand schließlich in anderen Städten des Reiches wie auch in anderen gesellschaftlichen Vereinigungen, wie beispielsweise *collegia*, Anwendung. Die Arbeit der *scribae* brachte es mit sich, dass sie über Fertigkeiten und ein Wissen verfügten, welche in einer Gesellschaft, die nur zu einem geringen Teil alphabetisiert war[4], Möglichkeiten und Einfluss bedeuten konnten. In ihrer Rolle als Buchhalter und Sekretäre der Magistrate wie auch als Bewirtschafter der staatlichen Archive hatten sie exklusiven Zugang und damit bis zu einem gewissen Grad auch Macht über die schriftliche Dokumentation der römischen res publica. Es verwundert deshalb nicht, dass uns in der Republik *scribae* vor allem dann begegnen, wenn es um Machtmissbrauch oder Unterschlagung von öffentlichen Geldern geht. Am bekanntesten dürfte Maevius sein, der mit seiner Buchführung Verres tatkräftig bei der Plünderung der Provinz Sizilien in den späten 70er Jahren des 1. Jahrhunderts v. Chr. unterstützte.[5] Cato der Jüngere sah sich kurze Zeit später gezwungen, die *scribae quaestorii* in die Schranken zu weisen, da sie seinen Vorgängern im *aerarium* aufgrund ihrer größeren Expertise

---

3 Cic. Mur. 25.
4 Noch immer grundlegend HARRIS 1989, 149–322; für einen Überblick über die spätere Forschung WERNER 2009; für eine fruchtbare methodische Neubetrachtung der Fragestellung WOOLF 2015.
5 Cic. Verr. 2,3,171–187.

im Umgang mit den Archivalien den Gehorsam verweigert hatten.[6] Cicero schließlich stellt in *de legibus* wohl mit einiger Übertreibung resigniert fest, dass die Römer nur diejenigen Gesetze besäßen, welche die *scribae* wollten, da diese die betreffenden Dokumente verwalteten.[7] Diese Mischung aus Expertise, Kontrolle über die staatliche Dokumentation und Nähe zur Macht – IVAN DI STEFFANO MANZELLA hat im Zusammenhang mit den *accensi* dafür den Begriff der Kollateralmacht geprägt[8] – resultierte für die *scribae* in hoher sozialer Mobilität.[9] Viele *scribae* schafften aus bescheidenen Verhältnissen den Aufstieg in den Ritterstand oder blieben nur knapp darunter. Cicero zählte die *scribae* am Ende der römischen Republik selbstverständlich zu den Rittern.[10] Und in der Tat bestätigen die epigraphischen Zeugnisse der Kaiserzeit diese Tendenz. Rund ein Drittel der *scribae quaestorii* und ein Viertel der *scribae aedilicii* begegnen als *equites romani*.

Die römischen *scribae* haben in der altertumswissenschaftlichen Forschung wenig Beachtung gefunden. THEODOR MOMMSEN hatte sie in seinem "Staatsrecht" zum Ende des 19. Jahrhunderts als Teil der "Dienerschaft der Magistrate" mit Blick auf staatspolitische Überlegungen in seiner gewohnt gründlichen Art umfassend behandelt.[11] MOMMSENS monumentales Werk hatte Maßstäbe gesetzt. Die *scribae* waren für die nächsten fünfzig Jahre außerhalb von Überblicken über die systematische Verwaltungsgeschichte kaum eine Erwähnung wert. Als sich ARNOLD HUGH MARTIN JONES 1949 den *scribae* im Rahmen einer Betrachtung der römischen *apparitores* annahm, interessierte er sich neben verwaltungsgeschichtlichen Fragen erstmals auch für sozialhistorische Überlegungen.[12] Es sollte allerdings bis zum Beginn der 80er Jahre dauern, bis sich die Forschung eingehender und mit neuen Fragestellungen den *scribae* widmete. Es ist neben anderen vor allem NICHOLAS PURCELL zu verdanken, dass die *scribae* sozialgeschichtlich und in einem weiteren Schritt auch erstmals kulturgeschichtlich eingeordnet werden konnten, womit die eingangs gezeichnete Charakterisierung überhaupt erst möglich wurde.[13] Meine eigenen Arbeiten zur Geschichte der römischen *scribae* im Rahmen meiner Dissertation setzen an dieser Stelle an und legen den Fokus auf die kulturellen Implikationen von Schreiberamt und Amtsträger. Es waren insbesondere die Fertigkeiten im Umgang mit Schrift und Schriftgut, die es den *scribae* ermöglichte, eine einflussreiche Position im Zentrum der römischen Staatsordnung einzunehmen. Als Experten der Schriftlichkeit besorgten sie

---

6 Plut. Cato minor 16,2–3.
7 Cic. leg. 3,46.
8 DI STEFANO MANZELLA 2000, „*poteri collaterali*".
9 Bereits PURCELL 1983, 136 hat das Apparitorenwesen, gerade auch mit Blick auf die *scribae*, als „the world of the social climber" bezeichnet.
10 Cic. Verr. 2,3,185; cf. Cic. dom. 74; Cic. Catil. 4,15.
11 MOMMSEN 1887, 320–371.
12 JONES 1949.
13 PURCELL 1983; Purcell 2001; daneben Cohen 1984; Badian 1989.

die schriftliche Dokumentation der Magistrate und führten die staatlichen Archive. Es war diese verantwortungsvolle Stellung als Hüter der schriftlichen Arcana des Staates, die den *scribae* nicht nur Prestige, sondern auch Nähe zu den politischen Entscheidungsträgern und daraus resultierend neue (nicht immer gänzlich legale) monetäre Möglichkeiten und soziale Beziehungen ermöglichte. Die Fähigkeit, lesen, schreiben und rechnen zu können, bedeutete für die Inhaber dieser höchsten Apparitorenposten in diesem Sinne Zugang zu sozialer Mobilität. Dies war der Grund, weshalb die *scribae* letztlich als soziale Aufsteiger in die Geschichte eingehen konnten. Geprägt waren die *scribae* also in erster Linie durch ihre Rolle als Experten der Schriftlichkeit, sowohl in der Eigen- als auch in der Fremdwahrnehmung. Dabei kam ihnen nicht zuletzt auch symbolische Bedeutung als Hüter der öffentlichen schriftlichen Dokumentation und dem darin gespeicherten Wissen zu.[14]

Die Welt der römischen *scribae* war die Welt der dokumentarischen Schriftlichkeit. Eine wissenschaftliche Beschäftigung mit dieser Welt stößt jedoch sehr schnell an Grenzen. Romreisende können heute zwar noch immer die Substruktionen des imposanten Bauwerks auf dem Kapitolhügel bewundern, welches das Forum Romanum überblickt und wohl einst das wichtigste staatliche Archiv und damit den Arbeitsplatz eines Teils der *scribae* beherbergte.[15] Die hohen Arkaden des sogenannten „Tabularium" sind heute jedoch leer, sämtliches Verwaltungsschriftgut ist in seiner materiellen Form gänzlich verloren. Ein von CLAUDE NICOLET Anfang der 90er Jahre initiiertes Forschungsunternehmen zu den römischen Archiven hat die Problematik mit dem Titel „*la mémoire perdue*" treffend auf den Punkt gebracht.[16] Dass das Verwaltungsschriftgut heute verloren ist, ist eng mit der Materialität desselben verbunden. Das Archiv trug bereits in der Antike den Namen *tabularium*, nach den darin aufbewahrten hölzernen Wachstafeln, den *tabulae ceratae*.[17] Wir haben das Medium bereits in der Episode des Cn. Flavius kennengelernt: Flavius entledigte sich seines Schreiberamtes, indem er seine Schreibutensilien, eine Wachstafel, niederlegte – „*tabulam ponere*". Haben antike Wachstafeln bis heute überlebt, so nur unter spezifischen Bedingungen. Anaerobe Konditionen in bleibender Nässe oder aber dauerhafter Trockenheit sind Voraussetzung dafür. Das Klima auf der italischen Halbinsel ist dafür leider gänzlich ungeeignet. Einzig der Ausbruch des Vesuv im Jahre 79 n. Chr. hat in *Pompeii* und *Herculaneum* gleichbleibende Bedingungen geschaffen und uns prompt span-

---

[14] Die Dissertation mit dem Titel „Guardians of the Written. A Cultural and Social History of the Roman *scribae*", betreut von Prof. Dr. ANNE KOLB, wurde Anfang 2018 an der Universität Zürich angenommen.
[15] Dazu GROS 2001, 110–112. Zur Forschungsgeschichte und den umstrittenen Deutungen des „Tabularium" zusammenfassend MAZZEI 2009.
[16] NICOLET 1994; MOATTI et al. 1998; MOATTI et al. 2000; MOATTI et al. 2001.
[17] Zur Verwendung und Archivierung von Wachstafeln als offizielle Dokumente und die daraus resultierenden Probleme bei CULHAM 1996.

nende Bestände von (privatem) Verwaltungsschriftgut überliefert.[18] Selbst wenn die klimatischen Bedingungen vorteilhafter gewesen wären, dürften wir heute dennoch kaum mit einer Überlieferung der alltäglichen Schreibarbeiten der *scribae* rechnen. Ganz abgesehen von einem fehlenden Überlieferungsinteresse der nachrömischen Gesellschaften an fremdem Verwaltungsschriftgut brennt mit Wachs bestrichenes Holz schlicht zu gut; vor allem dann, wenn absichtlich nachgeholfen wird. Cicero überliefert den Fall des Q. Sosius, der das stadtrömische *tabularium* in Brand steckte.[19] Seine Motive dürften zwar weniger gut gemeint, aber dennoch grundsätzlich ähnlicher Natur gewesen sein wie diejenigen des Hadrian, der 118 n. Chr. einen allgemeinen Schuldenerlass mit der Verbrennung der Schuldbücher vollzog.[20] Die Reliefs der sogenannten „Plutei Traiani" überliefern dieses Ereignis auch in bildlicher Form. Als Soldaten identifizierbare Personen tragen aus dem *tabularium* bzw. *aerarium* großformatige, zu mehreren zu *codices* zusammengebundene Wachstafeln auf dem Forum Romanum zusammen.[21] Das Schriftgut, welches hier zur Erleichterung vieler in Flammen aufging, bezeichneten die Zeitgenossen mit dem Begriff *tabulae publicae*. Ein Blick in die literarische Überlieferung zeigt, dass diese *tabulae publicae* in der Vorstellung der Römer aufs engste mit den *scribae* verbunden waren. Ciceros Charakterisierung des *ordo scribarum* in seiner Anklage gegen Verres ist diesbezüglich aufschlussreich:

> „'Ordo [scil. scribarum] est honestus.' Quis negat, aut quid ea res ad hanc rem pertinet? Est vero honestus, quod eorum hominum fidei tabulae publicae periculaque magistratuum committuntur."[22]

Die *tabulae publicae* wie auch die offiziellen Aufzeichnungen der Magistrate – letztere quasi die Vorstufe ersterer – waren der Zuverlässigkeit und Gewissenhaftigkeit (*fides*) der *scribae* anvertraut. Die *scribae* hafteten mit ihrem persönlichen Ansehen für einen gewissenhaften und redlichen Umgang mit den *tabulae publicae* und dem darin gespeicherten Wissen, worauf sie per Eid (*iusiurandum*) verpflichtet wurden.[23] Es war diese verantwortungsvolle Position, die ihnen das von Cicero angesprochene soziale Prestige sicherte. Die religiös-rechtliche Sanktionierung machte aus dem Verhältnis zwischen *scribae* und *tabulae publicae* gleichzeitig ein enge, ja exklusive Verbindung. *Scribae* und *tabulae publicae* stellten sozusagen zwei Elemente einer Gleichung dar. Festus (bzw. seine augusteische Vorlage Verrius Flaccus) bestätigt dies in seiner Definition des Begriffes *scriba*:

---

18 Eine Übersicht über die erhaltenen hölzernen Schreibtafeln bei HARTMANN 2015a.
19 Cic. nat. deor. 3,74.
20 CIL VI 967; cf. SHA Hadr. 7,6; Cass. Dio 69,8,1,2.
21 KOEPPEL 1986, 21–23, Nr. 2.
22 Cic. Verr. 2,3,183: „Der Stand der *scribae* ist ehrenwert. Wer leugnet's, oder was hat das hiermit zu tun? Er ist jedoch ehrenwert, weil der Zuverlässigkeit dieser Leute die amtlichen Rechnungen und die Protokolle der Behörden anvertraut sind." (Übers. M. FUHRMANN).
23 Das *iusiurandum* der *scribae* überliefert in Lex. Urson. 81,17–23; cf. Lex Irnit. 73,39–42.

„*Scribas proprio nomine antiqui et librarios et poetas vocabant; at nunc dicuntur scribae equidem librarii, qui rationes publicas scribunt in tabulis.*"[24]

Einen *scriba* erkannte man daran, dass er auf *tabulae* schrieb. Hatte man es mit *tabulae* zu tun, konnten *scribae* nicht weit sein. Die Verbindung des *scriba* mit den Wachstafeln wurde als geradezu emblematisch wahrgenommen. Festus' „*scribunt in tabulis*" stellt sowohl einen materiellen Bezug zu Schreibtafeln im Allgemeinen als auch mit dem Hinweis auf die „*rationes publicae*" eine Verbindung zu den *tabulae publicae* her.

Diese Verbindung von Person und Material, die die literarischen Quellen herausstreichen, auf bildlichen Zeugnissen der römischen Zeit nachzuvollziehen und zu verifizieren ist schwierig. Schreibende oder mit Schreibmaterialien ausgestattete Personen sind zwar nicht selten bildlich oder plastisch dargestellt. Man denke beispielsweise an die populären Darstellungen von Privatpersonen mit Schreibutensilien aus den Städten Kampaniens.[25] Die eindeutige Identifizierung von Personen auf Senatorensarkophagen oder anderen Denkmälern, die potenziell *scribae* darstellen könnten, ist jedoch meist nur schwierig möglich und nicht selten umstritten.[26] Glücklicherweise verfügen wir seit dem Jahre 2000 über ein Selbstzeugnis zweier stadtrömischer *scribae* aus spätaugusteisch-tiberischer Zeit.[27] Der wunderschöne Grabaltar für die Gebrüder Fulvius, Priscus und Faustus, zeigt an seiner Front eine Reliefdarstellung der *scribae* bei der Arbeit. Der Blick in eine staatliche Schreibstube des frühen 1. Jhs. n. Chr. zeigt zwei Togati auf *subsellia* sitzend, die eine großformatige Holztafel konsultieren, die zusammen mit anderen Tafeln in einem Stapel auf einem Tisch lagern. Assistiert werden sie von drei Personen in *tunica*. Es dürfte die einzige derartige „Beamtenszene" sein, die uns aus der Antike überliefert ist. Freilich ist auch hier die Identifikation der beteiligten Personen nicht gänzlich geklärt. Wie die Inschriften erläutern, waren beide Brüder *scribae* der curulischen Ädile. Die Forschung hat sich deshalb darauf geeinigt, in den sitzenden Personen die *scribae* zu erkennen. Bei der Person, die als einzige den Betrachter direkt anblickt, dürfte es sich wohl um Priscus handeln, für den der Altar ursprünglich gedacht war. Wie auch immer man die Darstellung interpretieren mag: Ins Auge fällt primär der Stapel an großformatigen *tabulae*, der prominent das Zentrum der Darstellung einnimmt und das Hauptidentifikationsmerk-

---

24 Fest. 446,26–29 (L): „The ancients used the formal appellation *scriba* for both *poetae* and *librarii*; but now those who write down the financial accounts of the state on tablets are known as *scribae librarii.*" (Übers. Purcell 2001, 644).
25 Meyer 2009.
26 Siehe für mögliche Abbildungen von *scribae* im Allgemeinen Wrede 1981; für Senatorensarkophage Himmelmann 1973; Wrede 2001; für die *ara* des Ahenobarbus Meyer 1993.
27 Zevi 2012: *Dis Manibus / Q(uinto) Fulvio Q(uinti) f(ilio) Qui(rina tribu) / Fausto scribae et / scribae librario aedilium / curulium vix(it) an(nis) XXXII // Dis Manibus / Q(uinto) Fulvio Q(uinti) f(ilio) Qui(rina) Prisco / scr(ibae) aed(ilium) cur(ulium) vixit an(nos) XXVII / Q(uintus) Fulvius Eunus pater / fecit*; für den archäologischen Kontext Rotondi 2010.

mal für die Szenerie darstellt. Wir finden die *scribae* beschäftigt mit den ihnen anvertrauten *tabulae publicae*. Die Fremdwahrnehmung entspricht also tatsächlich auch der Selbstwahrnehmung von *scribae* und ihrer Arbeit: *scribae* und *tabulae* gehörten zusammen.

Die Wachstafel war in der römischen Antike freilich nicht das einzige zur Verfügung stehende Schreibmaterial. Wir kennen aus dem religiösen Bereich etwa Bücher aus Leinen, die *libri lintei*. Ansonsten schrieb man auf Stein, Metall, Holz in unterschiedlichen Formen und nicht zuletzt Papyrus als Rolle (*volumen*) oder in einzelnen Blättern (*charta*). Ab dem Ende des 1. Jhs. n. Chr. begann schließlich der Pergamentcodex, wie er uns erstmals bei Martial überliefert ist, seinen Siegeszug.[28] So sind auch im Zusammenhang mit *scribae* andere Medien überliefert. Ein *senatus consultum* aus dem Jahre 11 v. Chr., welches Frontin erwähnt, spricht bezüglich der Ausrüstung der *scribae* der *curatores aquarum* nicht nur von *tabulae* sondern auch von *chartae*.[29] Papyrus spielte in der Verwaltung offensichtlich eine Rolle.[30] Diese Rolle war jedoch in Republik und Kaiserzeit eine untergeordnete. Das Zeugnis bleibt für die Zeit im Zusammenhang mit dem Archiv ein Einzelfall. Die Außenwahrnehmung der *scribae* blieb fest mit der hölzernen Wachstafel, der *tabula cerata*, verbunden.

Wenn wir die *scribae* nicht nur als Schreibende, sondern auch als Lesende zu fassen versuchen, stoßen wir wiederum auf die enge Verbindung zwischen Person und Materialität. Gleichzeitig wird erneut klar, dass sich die Verbindung von *scriba* und *tabulae publicae* nicht auf das Materielle beschränkte. Ein Überblick über die erhaltenen Quellen zu lesenden *scribae* zeigt, dass das mittlerweile überholte Dogma der älteren Leseforschung, dass die griechisch-römische Antike eine vornehmlich laut lesende gewesen sei, für einmal dennoch zutrifft.[31] Sicherlich haben *scribae* bei der täglichen Arbeit auch leise und zu sich selbst gelesen; nur fehlen uns dafür die Quellen. Ein in der Öffentlichkeit auftretender *scriba* las grundsätzlich immer laut; er las vor. Cicero ist mit seinen Verrinen auch hier wieder unser Kronzeuge:

> „*Ego enim, cum hoc tota Sicilia diceret, tamen adfirmare non auderem, si haec edicta non ex ipsius tabulis totidem verbis recitare possem, sicuti faciam. Da, quaeso, scribae, recitet ex codice professionem. Recita. Edictum de professione.*"[32]

Der *scriba* rezitiert; und zwar „*ex tabulis*", „*ex codice*". Interessanterweise liest der *scriba* hier nicht etwa vor, weil er der einzige Anwesende gewesen wäre, der überhaupt lesen konnte. Cicero hätte selbst vorlesen können, für seine Zwecke vielleicht sogar effektvoller. Mit Sicherheit war auch ein weiterer *apparitor*, ein *praeco*, anwe-

---

28 Mart. 1,2; cf. ROBERTS 1983.
29 Frontin. aqu. 2,100.
30 Siehe Cassiod. var. 12,21, *chartae* als Dokumente; cf. den Fokus auf Briefe bei Fest. 359,8–10 (L).
31 Ein Überblick bei HARTMANN 2015b; cf. JOHNSON 2000.
32 Cic. Verr. 2,3,26.

send, der explizit als Herold für diese Aufgabe vom Staat bezahlt war. Dass der *scriba* vorlas, dürfte mit Material und Materie zusammenhängen. Der *scriba* kümmerte sich von Berufes wegen um die *tabulae publicae*, er war als ihr Archivar und Bewirtschafter mit Ordnung, Form und Funktion wie auch mit dem Inhalt am besten vertraut. Deutlich wird dieser Zusammenhang aus weiteren Zeugnissen von vorlesenden *scribae*. Mehrere Quellen zeugen von unterschiedlichen Episoden der späten Republik, in welchen Volkstribune sich um Gesetzesanträge zanken.[33] Dabei werden immer *scribae* damit beauftragt, aus den *tabulae publicae* zu rezitieren. Die Episoden enden jeweils damit, dass der feindlich gesinnte Tribunenkollege dem *scriba* Schweigen befiehlt, sodass der Volkstribun sein Gesetz schließlich selbst vorliest, um das Anliegen doch noch durchzuboxen. Aufschlussreich ist schließlich die von Asconius in einem Kommentar zu Ciceros verlorener Rede *pro Cornelio de maiestate* geschilderte Vorgehensweise.

> „Is [scil. tribunus plebis], ubi legis ferundae dies venit et praeco subiciente scriba verba legis recitare populo coepit, et scribam subicere et praeconem pronuntiare passus non est. Tum Cornelius ipse codicem recitavit."[34]

Obwohl hier der *praeco*, seines Amtes gemäß, spricht, liest trotzdem der *scriba* aus dem *codex*, indem er dem *praeco* souffliert („*subiciente scriba*"). Dasselbe Prinzip finden wir auch an anderer Stelle für einen *scriba*, der dem *censor* das *carmen* für die Suovetaurilia „*ex publicis tabulis*" vorspricht („*praeire*").[35] Es wird klar, dass der *scriba* hier nicht nur aus Gründen seiner professionellen Expertise und Erfahrung mit dem Medium und dem Inhalt der *tabulae* den Text vorspricht. Vielmehr kam seiner Aufgabe hier symbolische Bedeutung zu. Der *scriba* bürgte mit seiner *fides* für die korrekte Wiedergabe des in den *tabulae publicae* bewahrten Wissens, welches autoritativen Charakter besaß.[36] Er amtete als die unvoreingenommene Stimme der *tabulae*.

Diese symbolische Verbindung zwischen *scriba* und geschriebenem Dokument war fest etabliert. Wir finden sie schließlich mehrere Jahrhunderte später wieder. In einem bemerkenswerten Rückgriff auf römische Tradition bediente sich Cassiodor, *praefectus praetorio* im Ostgothischen Reich in den 30er-Jahren des 6. Jhs. n. Chr., dem Bild des treuen und zuverlässigen Beschützers der staatlichen Dokumentation, um Deusdedit, seines Zeichens s*criba Ravennas*, seiner eminenten Position zu erinnern.[37]

---

33 Ascon. Corn. 58; Plut. Cato minor 28,1; Cass. Dio 37,43,2; App. civ. 1,1,11–12.
34 Ascon. Corn. 58.
35 Val. Max. 4,1,10: „*qui censor, cum lustrum conderet inque solitaurilium sacrificio scriba ex publicis tabulis sollemne ei precationis carmen praeiret [...]*".
36 MEYER 2004, 88.
37 Cassiod. var. 12,21,1–4: „*Deusdedit scribae Ravennati Senator praefectus praetorio. Scribarum officium securitas solet esse cunctorum, quando ius omnium eius sollicitudine custoditur. [...] vide quod tibi committitur antiqua fides et cotidiana diligentia. [...] hoc honorabile decus, indisputabile testimonium: vox antiqua chartarum cum de tuis adytis incorrupta processerit, cognitores reverenter excipiunt: litigan-*

Cassiodors Ziel war die Bündelung der Kräfte des Reiches im Angesicht des drohenden Krieges mit dem Ostreich unter Justinian. Sein Appell an den *scriba* war sodann primär auf die Verhinderung von Korruption und Bestechlichkeit ausgelegt, welcher der *scriba* in seiner Rolle als Archivar und Hüter althergebrachter Besitzrechte und Rechtsnormen naturgemäß ausgesetzt war. Neben der Pflege einer „*cotidiana diligentia*" sollte sich Deusdedit auch die „*antiqua fides*" vor Augen halten. Denn es war letztlich die autoritative „*vox antiqua chartarum*" die erst durch ihn als Sprachrohr zu Geltung gelangte. Es wird offenbar, dass der *scriba* damit zum unparteilichen Garant von Recht und Wahrheit wurde. Von seiner Unbestechlichkeit und Unbefangenheit hingen rechtsstaatliche Prinzipien ab. Die vielfach festgestellte Mittlerrolle des *scriba* zwischen Dokument und Außenwelt wird so verständlich. Der *scriba* garantierte die unbefangene Vermittlung der in Schrift gefassten Wahrheit – ohne Abänderung oder Zusatz. Es ist dasselbe Prinzip, welches für die vorlesenden *scribae*, die bei religiösen Zeremonien, vor Volksversammlungen oder im Gericht auftreten, festgestellt werden konnte. Der *scriba* war vor allem deshalb untrennbar mit dem materiellen Zeugnis verbunden, weil nur damit eine Vereinnahmung der im Dokument beinhalteten Wahrheit durch Parteiungen ausgeschlossen werden konnte. *Scriba*, materielles Dokument (*tabula*, *charta*) und staatliche bzw. bürokratische Autorität waren drei Parameter derselben Gleichung.

Bibliographie

BADIAN 1989 = E. BADIAN, The scribae of the Roman Republic, *Klio* 71.2, 1989, 582–603.
COHEN 1984 = B. COHEN, Some Neglected ordines: the Apparitorial Status-Groups, in: C. NICOLET (Hg.), Des Ordres à Rome, Paris 1984, 24–60.
CULHAM 1996 = PH. CULHAM, Fraud, Fakery and Forgery: The Limits of Roman Information Technology, *The Ancient World* 27.2, 1996, 172–183.
DI STEFANO MANZELLA 2000 = I. DI STEFANO MANZELLA, Accensi: profilo di una ricerca in corso (a proposito dei "poteri collaterali" nella società romana), *Cahiers du Centre Gustave Glotz* 11, 2000, 223–257.
GROS 2001 = P. GROS, Les édifices de la bureaucratie impériale: administration, archives et services publics dans le centre monumental de Rome, *Pallas* 55, 2001, 107–126.
HARRIS 1989 = W.V. HARRIS, Ancient Literacy, Cambridge 1989.
HARTMANN 2015a = B. HARTMANN, Die hölzernen Schreibtafeln im Imperium Romanum – ein Inventar, in: M. SCHOLZ/M. HORSTER (Hg.), Lesen und Schreiben in den römischen Provinzen. Schriftliche Kommunikation im Alltagsleben. Akten des 2. Internationalen Kolloquiums von DUCTUS – Association international pour l'étude des inscriptions mineures, RGZM Mainz, 15.–17. Juni 2011, Mainz 2015, 43–58.

---

tes quamvis improbi coacti tamen oboediunt. [...] pascat te editio decora veritatis: facultas tua habeatur integritas. da petentibus quae olim facta sunt. translator est, non conditor antiquorum gestorum. exemplar velut anulum ceris imprime, ut sicut vultus expressa non possunt signa refugere, ita manus tua ab authentico nequeat discrepare".

HARTMANN 2015b = B. HARTMANN, Geschichte des Lesers. Antike und Spätantike, in: U. RAUTENBERG/U. SCHNEIDER (Hg.), Lesen. Ein interdisziplinäres Handbuch, Berlin/Boston 2015, 703–718.

JONES 1949 = A.H.M. JONES, The Roman Civil Service (Clerical and Sub-Clerical Grades), *The Journal of Roman Studies* 39, 1949, 38–55.

KOEPPEL 1986 = G.M. KOEPPEL, Die historischen Reliefs der römischen Kaiserzeit IV, *Bonner Jahrbücher* 186, 1986, 1–90.

MAZZEI 2009 = P. MAZZEI, Tabularium – Aerarium nelle fonti letterarie ed epigrafiche, *Rendiconti della Classe di Scienze morali, storiche e filologiche dell'Academia die Lincei* 20 (s. 9), 2009, 275–378.

MEYER 2004 = E.A. MEYER, Legitimacy and Law in the Roman World. Tabulae in Roman Belief and Practice, Cambridge 2004.

MEYER 2009 = E.A. MEYER, Writing Paraphernalia, Tablets, and Muses in Campanian Wall Painting, *American Journal of Archaeology* 113.4, 2009, 569–597.

MOATTI et al. 1998 = C. MOATTI et al., La mémoire perdue. Recherches sur l'administration romaine (Collection de l'École Française de Rome 243), Rom 1998.

MOATTI et al. 2000 = C. MOATTI et al., La mémoire perdue III, *Mélanges de l'École française de Rome, Antiquité* 112.2, 2000, 647–779.

MOATTI et al. 2001 = C. MOATTI et al., Les archives du census: le contrôle des hommes. Actes de la table ronde, Rome, 1er décembre 1997, *Mélanges de l'École française de Rome, Antiquité* 113.2, 2001, 559–764.

MOMMSEN 1887 = TH. MOMMSEN, Römisches Staatsrecht. Leipzig 1887³.

NICOLET 1994 = C. NICOLET, La mémoire perdue. À la recherche des archives oubliées, publiques et privées, de la Rome antique, Rom 1994.

PURCELL 1983 = N. PURCELL, The Apparitores: A Study in Social Mobility, *Papers of the British School at Rome* 51, 1983, 125–173.

PURCELL 2001 = N. PURCELL, The Ordo Scribarum: A Study in the Loss of Memory, *Mélanges de l'École française de Rome, Antiquité* 113.2, 2001, 633–674.

ROBERTS 1983 = C.H. ROBERTS/T.C. SKEAT, The Birth of the Codex, Oxford 1983.

ROTONDI 2010 = A. ROTONDI, L'ara degli scribi e i colombari di via di porta S. Sebastiano, in: D. MANACORDA/R. SANTANGELI VALENZIANI (Hg.), Il primo miglio della via Appia a Roma. Atti della Giornata di Studio Roma – Museo Nazionale Romano 16 giugno 2009, Rom 2010, 137–152.

WERNER 2009 = S. WERNER, Literacy Studies in Classics. The Last Twenty Years, in: W.A. JOHNSON/H.N. PARKER (Hg.), Ancient Literacies. The Culture of Reading in Greece and Rome, Oxford 2009, 333–382.

WOLF 1980 = J.G. WOLF, Die literarische Überlieferung der Publikation der Fasten und Legisaktionen durch Gnaeus Flavius, *Nachrichten der Akademie der Wissenschaften in Göttingen. I. Philologisch-historische Klasse* 2, 1980, 11–29.

WOOLF 2015 = G. WOOLF, Ancient Illiteracy, *Bulletin of the Institute of Classical Studies* 58.2, 2015, 31–42.

ZEVI 2012 = F. ZEVI/R. FRIGGERI, Ara degli scribi, in: R. FRIGGERI/M.G. GRANINO CECERE/G.L. GREGORI (Hg.), Terme di Diocleziano. La collezione epigrafica, Mailand 2012, 355–362.

Education

Marietta Horster
Geschichte und Geschichten im Alltag

Abstract: In the life of the educated and well-off citizens of the Hellenistic and Roman world, well told stories and well written history were part of the universe of letters, rhetoric and art. Notwithstanding the high methodological demands and thorough investigations of historiographers like Thukydides, Polybios or Tacitus, it is far from clear that the readers of their work appreciated high-standard historiography more than other genres of literature and technical writings. This paper addresses various methodological ways of approaches how to explore the esteem in which historiographical writing and history-telling was held outside the "inner circle" of historiography and its self-referential appreciation.

Zusammenfassung: Ohne Frage spielten gut erzählte Geschichten und sehr gut geschriebene Geschichte eine wichtige Rolle im Leben eines jeden Gebildeten. Unabhängig davon, wie sehr sich einzelne Historiographen bemühten, mit ihren hohen methodischen Ansprüchen und großem Rechercheaufwand neue Standards für die Geschichtsschreibung zu etablieren, so ist es dennoch keineswegs gesichert, ob diese und andere Texte gerade deswegen geschätzt wurden. Um die Leserkreise von Historiographie aufzuspüren und deren Präferenzen nachzuvollziehen, reicht es nicht, den selbstreferentiellen Hinweisen und Zitaten der Kollegen in den Werken der Geschichtsschreiber zu folgen. Der Beitrag versucht daher, die verschiedenen methodischen Möglichkeiten auszuloten, mit denen man die Wertschätzung von Geschichtsschreibung in mehr oder weniger breiten Leserschaften identifizieren, qualifizieren, möglicherweise auch quantifizieren kann.

Einleitung

Viele Medien weisen auf die Omnipräsenz der Vergangenheit in der Gegenwart: Von den Bauwerken, die „älter" sind, vielleicht sogar verfallen, über Bildnis- und Statuenreihen wichtiger Persönlichkeiten der Geschichte, bis hin zu Erinnerungsdenkmälern, die durch ihre Gestaltung, aber auch durch In- und Aufschriften im öffentlichen Raum, die Wirkung und Größe des Vergangenen präsentieren. In den Epochen und Jahrhunderten, in denen Eliten sich unter anderem über Bildung definieren, galten und gelten Geschichtskenntnisse als selbstverständlich, und in Zeiten massiver gesellschaftlicher und politischer Umbrüche ist zumindest im politischen Diskurs der Verweis auf die Geschichte Bestandteil der Identitätsbehauptung und wird entsprechend für anspruchsbezogene Aushandlungsprozesse instrumentalisiert.[1] In den

---
1 Vgl. bspw. zum politischen Gewicht des Geschichtsbezugs in hellenistischer Zeit CHANIOTIS 2016.

letzten beiden Jahrzehnten jedoch ist die Klage über eine so bisher nie dagewesene Geschichtslosigkeit und über eine mangelnde Wertschätzung historischer Kenntnisse ein Dauerbrenner nicht nur der Literaten, Politiker und Publizisten. Das Thema dieses Beitrags ist aus diesem durchaus aktuellen Kontext der Frage nach dem Wert von Geschichte und dem Umfang von Geschichtskenntnissen heraus entwickelt und fragt entsprechend nach historischen Interessen und Kenntnissen in der griechisch-römischen Antike.[2]

War Geschichte als das Wissen und das Interesse an der Vergangenheit so omnipräsent und von so großer Bedeutung, wie wir, die wir uns mit antiker Geschichte befassen, es annehmen? Wie können wir methodisch erfassen, was jenseits einer gebildeten Insidergruppe von Geschichten und Biographien verfassenden Autoren, die sich aufeinander berufen oder sich unter Umständen vehement voneinander abgrenzen, an Geschichte bekannt, an Geschichte vermittelt, gelesen, erzählt wurde? Studien zum kulturellen Gedächtnis, zur Bildersprache oder auch zum Kommunikationswert öffentlich auf- und ausgestellter Texte machen oftmals nicht explizit, wer die sozialen Gruppen waren, die an diesen von uns aufgespürten öffentlichen Diskursen an einem gegebenen Ort und zu einer bestimmten Zeit teilnahmen beziehungsweise teilnehmen konnten. Ähnliches gilt für die Frage nach Leserschichten, zu denen sicher die sozio-politischen Eliten gehörten, aber wohl in vielen städtisch geprägten Regionen auch diejenigen, die man heute als „Mittelschicht" bezeichnen würde. Daneben gab es eine hohe Bildung auch bei einer kleinen Gruppe besonders ausgebildeter Sklaven, die damit „quer" zu den durch personenrechtlichen Status und ökonomische Basis definierten gebildeten Eliten lagen. Darüber hinaus verdeutlicht der vorliegende Band mit seiner Vielfalt an Zugängen zum Thema der Alltagsbildung, ebenso wie viele frühere Studien, dass für Bildung und deren Basis mit Schreib- und Lesefähigkeit nicht nur regionale und zeitbezogene Unterschiede für das römische Reich gelten, sondern dass es insbesondere methodisch schwierig ist, diese präzise zu benennen.

Die folgenden Überlegungen werden daher keinen Beitrag zur Diskussion um die Lese- und Schreibfähigkeit breiter Bevölkerungsschichten bieten, sondern einen methodischen Weg aufzeigen, um dem Umgang mit Geschichte im römischen Ägypten auf die Spur zu kommen.

Geschichte(n) erzählen

Textzeugnisse und zahlreiche Gaben an die Götter in Heiligtümern zeugen davon, dass nicht nur eine kleine Elite, sondern viele Bürger und Fremde, Männer und Frauen,

---

[2] Mit dieser Fragestellung für die Materialgruppe der Münzen in Bezug auf die Verweise auf Augustus in späteren Prägungen vgl. HORSTER 2017.

nicht nur tagaus, tagein arbeiteten und sich um persönliche und familiäre Angelegenheiten kümmerten, sondern auch Anteil an der Gemeinschaft nahmen sowie an gemeinsamen Festen und Feiern in einer Stadt oder größeren Siedlung.³ Eine literarische Anekdote, die allerdings nicht in den römischen Kontext gehört, sondern von Herondas im 3. Jh. v. Chr. für Leser im griechischsprachigen Raum konzipiert wurde, dürfte dennoch einen guten Einstieg in die Themen des Wissens um Geschichte und des Erzählens von Geschichte(n) bieten. Dabei geht es um Personen, die vom Autor als nicht zur Elite gehörig skizziert werden. Von zwei Frauen ist in der 4. Mimiambe die Rede. Diese weiblichen Charaktere besitzen die Neugier, das Interesse und zum Teil sogar die Kenntnisse, durch die sie zu dem von modernen Wissenschaftlern „benötigten" Personal gehören, das ein kulturelles Gedächtnis mitgetragen haben dürfte. Herondas' beide Damen besuchen das Asklepiosheiligtum von Kos, um dort ein Hühnchen zu opfern (4,27–29): „Sieh meine Liebe", lässt er die eine zur anderen sagen, während sie umhergehen und die Bildwerke betrachten, „das Mädchen dort, das zu dem Apfel aufguckt. Meinst du nicht, wenn es den Apfel nicht kriegt, dass es meint, es müsste sterben vor Sehnsucht?"⁴

Die Begeisterung gilt der Kunst und nicht dem Inhalt; es spielt keine Rolle, welche Szene dargestellt wird: Ist hier vielleicht vom Urteil des Paris die Rede oder vielleicht von den goldenen Äpfeln der Hesperiden? Was die beiden Damen interessiert, ist einzig die Lebendigkeit der Darstellung. Herondas hat eine seiner Alltagsheldinnen mit Lesefähigkeit ausgestattet, die andere aber nicht, fragt doch Kokkale ihre Begleiterin, wer wohl dieses hervorragende und lebensnahe Werk geschaffen habe, woraufhin die andere sagt, „siehst Du das denn nicht, da, die Inschrift unter der Statue". Sie liest dann die Namen der Künstler vor: Hier die Söhne des Praxiteles, dort Apelles. Diese fiktive, aber lebensnahe Darstellung, sollte davor warnen, immer zu vermuten, dass „die" antiken Bewohner, welche die Muße zur Betrachtung hatten, alles (oder zumindest den Kern der Geschichte) verstanden haben und einordnen konnten – oder auch nur ein solches Bedürfnis hatten.

Welche Kriterien gibt es aber, um zu erfahren, was zu einer bestimmten Zeit an einem bestimmten Ort gängige und verbreitete Kenntnis war: Etwa dass ein durchschnittlicher Römer wusste, dass noch vor Romulus und Remus der aus Troia zurückgekehrte Aeneas am Anfang der römischen Geschichte stand? War jedem Besucher des Augustusforums bekannt, dass hinter dem Helden, der einen alten Mann auf dem Rücken trug, das brennende Troja zurückgeblieben war (und an dem dortigen Krieg ein Agamemnon, Paris, Achill usw. Anteil hatten), und dass vor diesem Aeneas und seinem kleinen Sohn eine lange Reise nach Latium lag, an deren Ende die Gründung

---

3 Die Beteiligung am gemeinschaftlich organisierten Kult (kleinerer Verbände ebenso wie der gesamten Bürgerschaft) ist jedoch nicht notwendigerweise korreliert mit politischem Engagement wie der Teilnahme an (Volks-)Versammlungen; vgl. etwa die Weihungen und Aktivitäten der verschiedenen sozialen Gruppen im Athener Asklepieion hellenistischer und römischer Zeit, ALESHIRE 1989, 54–60.
4 Übersetzung nach O. CRUSIUS, Leipzig 1926 (mit Nachdrucken).

Roms stand?⁵ Oder war einem Legionär der *XXI rapax*, der in Vindonissa stationiert war, verständlich, welche Bauten der Stadt Rom auf Münzen abgebildet waren, auf welche Priesterämter angespielt und auf welche früheren Siege referiert wurde?⁶

Wir gehen davon aus, dass der größte Teil der Bevölkerung vormoderner Gesellschaften, so auch der römischen, weder lesen noch schreiben konnte, wenig Anteil am öffentlichen Leben hatte und äußerst selten an Festen und Märkten in einer Stadt teilnehmen konnte, da er nicht nur täglich hart arbeiten musste, sondern außerdem noch auf dem Lande wohnte. Andererseits rechnen wir damit, dass jeder auch nur einigermaßen in das gemeinsame Leben integrierte Bürger einen Grundstock an Geschichten kannte, Bilder verstand, die monumentalen Buchstaben auf kurzen Inschriften entziffern und die Herstellerstempel der für ihn interessanten Waren als Bilder mit Schriftzeichen wiedererkennen konnte. Ähnlich folgen wir PAUL ZANKER und anderen Autoren in deren Annahme, dass die statuarische Ausstattung auf dem Augustusforum in seiner Auswahl und Komposition verstanden wurde und eine wichtige Botschaft transportierte: Für die Existenz von Rom musste immer wieder gekämpft werden, so dass alles, was die Römer jetzt haben und mit Stolz erfüllt, auf dem richtigen Tun vieler und heldenhaften Taten einzelner aufbaut.

Agrippa und seine Berater für den Ausbau der neuen Kolonie Emerita Augusta (Merida) waren zumindest der Meinung, dass genau diese *Summi viri*-Aufstellung zum Export geeignet sei, um römischen Bürgern in der Ferne nicht nur Gemeinsinn und das Bewusstsein von Überlegenheit gegenüber der Umwelt zu vermitteln, sondern auch um die enge Verbindung zur Stadt Rom durch eine ganz bestimmte Geschichtserzählung und ganz bestimmte Helden zu visualisieren.⁷

An wen also adressierten ein Augustus und ein Agrippa mit ihren Entscheidungen für Statuendekor ihre Botschaften, an wen ein Münzmeister bzw. der Kaiser und seine Berater die Entscheidung, welches Bauwerk auf dem Revers eines Dupondius dargestellt wurde? Bei den Konkretisierungen der Rezeption der Bilder, Monumente und der dazugehörigen Geschichten wird auch im vorliegenden Band mehr oder weniger explizit vom durchschnittlich gebildeten Römer ausgegangen, auf den die „Macht der Bilder" wirkt, der die Ikonographie auf Münzen versteht, der Kenntnis einiger römischer Heldengeschichten, großer Kriege und Siege hat, und der die propagierten Wohltaten von Senatoren und später vor allem von Kaisern gebührend zu schätzen weiß. Wie dieses Wissen vermittelt wurde und welchen Anteil zufällig aufgeschnappte

---

5 Zum Augustusforum und der Konzeption der aufgestellten *summi viri*, ZANKER 1990, 213–217.
6 E. g. RIC I² Nero 111 = BMC 197, ein im Jahr 63 geprägter Dupondius, der eine Büste des Kaisers Nero auf der Vorderseite trägt. Das Porträt ist durch eine Umschrift mit Namen und Titeln gekennzeichnet; die Münze trägt auf der Rückseite eine Abbildung des neronischen Macellums, wenn auch ohne erläuternde Umschrift. Zur umfangreichen Diskussion um die Rezeption und das Verständnis von Münzikonographie vgl. etwa METCALF 1993, NOREÑA 2002, HEKSTER 2005.
7 Zu Merida siehe TRILLMICH 1996; NOGALES 2008. Eine 3D-Rekonstruktion bietet MERCHAN/SALAMANCA/ADÁN 2011.

Erzählungen hatten, welchen mündliche, allerdings gezielte Vermittlung hatte und schließlich welchen die schriftliche Überlieferung an der Kenntnis von Geschichte und Geschichten besaß, ist unklar. Am Ende geht es doch immer wieder darum, wie hoch der Alphabetisierungsgrad in einem bestimmten Raum und zu einer bestimmten Zeit war, denn anders als in der zeitgenössisch forschenden Ethnologie ist mündliche Überlieferung für die Antike methodisch nicht zu greifen. ASSMANNS „cultural memory"-Konzept[8] ist ein gutes Erklärungsmodell, kann aber keinen Ersatz für wissenschaftliche Nachweise im Detail bieten. Indirekt wird es daher im Folgenden um die Möglichkeiten der modernen Validierung der antiken Verbreitung von Geschichtskenntnissen einerseits und des Lektüreverhaltens andererseits gehen, und darum, ob es Wege gibt, das Interesse an Geschichte bei antiken Lesern und Zuhörern nachzuweisen.

Methoden und Wege zu Kenntnissen und Interesse an Geschichte(n)

Verschiedene Medien außerhalb der antiken Geschichtsschreibung geben Hinweise auf deren Leserschaften bzw. auf diejenigen, die Interesse an der durch Gespräche, Texte und Bilder vermittelten Geschichte im engeren und Geschichten im weiteren Sinne hatten, inklusive der mythischen Geschichte, der Skandalgeschichten oder auch der Viten edler Männer. Zwar belegen Graffiti aus Pompei und anderen Orten nichts Vergleichbares für die lateinische Sprache,[9] während in den Schulpapyri und Schulostraka aus Ägypten ebenfalls kein Zitat oder Halbzitat aus einem Geschichtswerk überliefert ist, dafür aber zahllose Geschichten, Mythen und Geschichtsfetzen durch Homerzitate, durch Euripides und andere Autoren, in verschiedenen Erzählformen und Versmaßen präsent sind. Die Trennung zwischen Geschichte und Mythos, wie sie ein Historiograph Thukydides betonte, hatte kaum Wirksamkeit in der breiten Rezeption; sie stieß aber nicht einmal bei der Historikerzunft immer auf Gegenliebe.[10] Ätiologie und Mythographie waren in der Antike durchaus Teil der Geschichte, so dass man behaupten könnte, dass mit der alles dominierenden homerischen Ilias

---

8 Vgl. e.g. ASSMANN 2007.
9 Vergils *arma virumque* findet sich in dieser ‚sinnfreien' Zitatform als Graffito 17mal in Pompei, vgl. mit Nachweisen und weiteren Beispielen SUERBAUM 2012, 203–206; MILNOR 2014, 238–272 mit umfassender Diskussion der Vergilzitate. Dabei wird zwar der Schulkontext als Bildungshintergrund evoziert, es handelt sich allerdings nicht um Übungsaufgaben, so wie sie aus ägyptischen Papyrusabrissen bzw. Fetzen oder Ostraka bekannt sind, zu diesen CRIBIORE 2001, 160–184; HORSTER 2015.
10 Einen Überblick über das *genos historikon* und den historisierenden Stil gibt NICOLAI 1992, 108–176. Vgl. auch MITCHELL 2010 mit Bemerkungen zu modernen Versuchen der klaren Grenzziehung für ein Genos „Historiographie". Die Spannung zwischen thukydideischen oder auch polybianischen historiographischen Idealen (und deren moderner Wertschätzung) einerseits und die antike Kritik an Autoren wie Herodot wird unter anderem von MARINCOLA 2016 thematisiert.

als Schultext die Kinder in der Regel einen Zugang zur Schrift über eine Geschichte, ja über „die" Geschichte erhalten haben. Die Werke eines Diodor oder eines Livius, in denen die mythische Vorgeschichte organisch mit der dann folgenden, „realen" Geschichte verbunden ist, verdeutlichen diese enge Verbindung von Geschichte und „Mythos" (im modernen Sinn). Davon zeugen auch Vorwürfe wie *mythizisein* und Homernähe, die Thukydides seinen Vorgängern macht — Vorhaltungen, die wir später in einem anderen Kontext ebenfalls bei Lukian finden. Dem entspricht, wenn auch im Gegenteil dazu positiv markiert in der „Salmakis Inschrift", einem Städtelob für Halikarnassos aus späthellenistischer Zeit (Mitte 2./1. Jh. v. Chr.), die knappe Charakterisierung des berühmten Sohns der Stadt, Herodot, als Homer der historischen Prosa.[11] Nicht nur in der Schule dominieren einzelne Passagen und Wortgruppen Homers, auch in privaten Briefen finden sich Homerzitate, insbesondere aus der Ilias.[12] Darüber hinaus sind neben weiteren wichtigen Schulautoren wie Euripides wenige andere Autoren in privaten Zeugnissen mit Zitaten und Anspielungen vertreten. Dagegen sind in außerliterarischen Kontexten Referenzen auf Geschichtsschreibung im engeren Sinn nur äußerst selten zu finden, was beispielsweise gleichermaßen für Reden eines Demosthenes, Isokrates oder Lysias gilt, die konkrete historische Kontexte behandeln, obwohl auf diese Rhetoren in spätantiker und byzantinischer Zeit häufig rekurriert wird und von ihnen größere Mengen an Paraphrasen und Zitaten überliefert sind als von Thukydides oder Herodot.[13]

Zu den wenigen erhaltenen kaiserzeitlichen Kontexten mit Historiographie-Nutzung, jenseits eines literarischen Elaborats, gehört eine rhetorische Übung mit Beispielen für Deklamationsthemen aus dem 3 Jh. n. Chr., die auf Thukydides Bezug nimmt (P.Oxy. XXIV 2400). Thukydides ist im Übrigen auch der einzige griechischsprachige Historiograph, den Quintilian in seinen *Institutiones* (10,2,1) explizit als geeigneten Schulautor benennt, der benutzt werden könne, vornehmlich wegen seines virtuosen Einsatzes von Stilfiguren (*varietas figurarum*) in Verbindung mit einer

---

[11] SEG 48, 1998, 1838 col. II Z. 43: Ἡρόδοτον τὸν πεζὸν ἐν ἱστορίαισιν Ὅμηρον mit ISAGER/PEDERSEN 2004 mit Text, Übersetzung und zahlreichen Kommentaren. Vgl. PRIESTLEY 2014, 188–219 nicht nur zur Inschrift und zum Einzeiler-Lob des „Prose Homer of History", sondern auch zu weiteren Zeugnissen hellenistischer Wertschätzung bzw. Kritik an poetischen Aspekten des ionischen Dialekts (nicht nur der Herodots) und des poetisch, fiktionalen Erzählstils von Historikern und anderen Fachschriftstellern. Vgl. auch CAREY 2016 gegen PELLING 2006, der die betonte Homer-Distanz Herodots mit dessen teilweise homerisch anmutenden Figuren kontrastiert, um darin eine Lesart und Weiterentwicklung Homers zu finden, die dann allerdings so wohl nicht weiterverfolgt (oder verstanden?) wurde.
[12] OTRANTO 2000, 9–15 zu P.Vindob. G inv. 39966 Col. 1 (Mitte 1. Jh. n. Chr.), bspw. zu Homerzitaten in aus Ägypten überlieferten Privatbriefen. In diesem Privatbrief wird neben zahlreichen anderen Büchern als Empfehlung auch Homers' Ilias genannt. Historische Werke oder auch Biographien sind in den von OTRANTO bearbeiteten Briefen nicht genannt. SCHWERDTNER 2015, 59–61 zur deutlichen Dominanz von Vergil- und Homerzitaten in Pliniusbriefen.
[13] Vgl. CAVALLO 1986, 86; STENGER 2009.

überzeugenden Gesamtkomposition (*componendi ratio*), schließlich aber auch wegen seines Ziels, historische Vorbilder (*exemplum virtutum*) zu hinterlassen.[14]

Auch in den überlieferten Lese- und Kauflisten von Werken und Autoren, die ROSA OTRANTO zusammenstellte, sind die Historiker rar. Die sogenannte historische Bibliothek in Tauromenion (2. Jh. v. Chr.?) weist durch pinaxähnliche, zusammenfassende Beschreibungsfragmente in ihrem Bestand zumindest die Autoren Kallisthenes von Olynth, Quintus Fabius Pictor und Philistos von Syrakus nach.[15]

Methodisch wenig hilfreich ist es, Autoren zu glauben, die sich bei ihren Vorgängern an Thema und Methode reiben. Auch die Kritik an einer vermeintlich ungerechtfertigten Beliebtheit eines Autors, der schließlich mit seiner effektvollen Art zu schreiben und mit seinen Inhalten billig und primitiv auf Leserfang gehe, lässt sich quantifizierend nicht nachweisen. Im Gegenteil, es finden sich kaum Spuren der von Polybios so heftig kritisierten, aber angeblich viel gelesenen Autoren.[16] Das gilt ebenso für den Alexanderroman Kleitarchs, der nach Curtius Rufus und Arrian doch enorm verbreitet gewesen sein soll.[17]

---

14 Vielleicht weist Thuk. 3,38,4–5 indirekt darauf hin, dass er selbst schon eine solche Rezeption seines Werkes befürchtet: An dieser Stelle geht es ihm allerdings konkret darum, davor zu warnen, dass ein breites Publikum in der Volksversammlung laut Kleon zwar kenntnisreich die Kunst der Redner bewundere, darüber aber das Ziel und den Inhalt der Rede aus den Augen verliere. Etwas anders MALITZ 1990, 330–31, der von einem „an Feinfühligkeit unübertroffenen" Publikum des späten 5. Jhs. ausgeht, das sich von allen späteren Leserschaften positiv unterschieden habe (so auch S. 348 zum qualitätvollen Publikum des 5. Jhs.). Dabei verweist MALITZ 1990, 332 auf Thuk. 1,21,1, der einen Herodot und damit auch implizit dessen avisiertes „Durchschnittspublikum" (1990, 333) historischer Lektüre und Vortrags kritisiert, welches lediglich kurzfristige Unterhaltung suche. MALITZ 1990, 334–35 zieht weitreichenden Folgerungen aus einem möglichen Zusammenhang politischer Unselbstständigkeit und entsprechender Lust an Unterhaltung (statt Information), was das Publikum späterer Zeiten geprägt habe. Diese Behauptung scheint m.E. jedoch eher einer persönlichen Zeitkritik zu entspringen, die allerdings ihre Analogie durchaus in der schon seit dem 6. Jh. v. Chr. bekannten und über die Jahrhunderte und Epochen hinweg bis heute existierenden Vorstellung hat, dass jeweils zeitgenössisch der Verfall von Werten, Verantwortung und Ernsthaftigkeit begonnen habe.
15 MANGANARO 1974 und OTRANTO 2000, XIV datieren ins 2. Jh. v. Chr, vgl. BLANCK 1997. Allerdings wird in der leider nur aus zwei Namen bestehenden fragmentarischen Liste der Bibliotheksstiftung von 100 Büchern für die Athener Epheben in den 40er Jahren des 1. Jhs. v. Chr. nur Euripides und die Ilias erwähnt. Dass trotz des stark fragmentarischen Erhaltungszustands diese wenig überraschende Liste der „Klassiker" zu finden ist, könnte darauf weisen, dass andere Namen auch kaum eine Rolle gespielt haben, vgl. PLATTHY 1968, e. g. 110–112 zu den Testimonia Nr. 29–35 (IG II² 1041, inter 47/6–43/2, Z. 23.24); die anderen Epheben inschriften erwähnen nur die Zahl der 100 Bücher ohne mit Autoren oder Werken konkret zu werden, IG II² 1009 (116/5 v. Chr.); 1029 (96/5 v. Chr.) Z. 24–25 usw.
16 Auch Diodor mit seiner einen Teil dieser Autoren integrierenden bzw. exzerpierenden Schrift ist hierfür kein Gegenbeispiel. Vgl. zur lediglich auf Stofffülle und Zuverlässigkeit reduzierten Rezeption des Polybios die Angaben bei MALITZ 1990, 337–8, wenn auch erneut nur mit einem literaturinternen Referenzhinweis der Aussagen in Cic. rep. 1,54; 2,27, Liv. 33,100,10 und wenigen mehr.
17 MALITZ 1990, 336 Anm. 50 führt drei Belege für die Beliebtheit Kleitarchs als Alexanderbiograph an: Curt. 9,5;11; Arr. an. 6,11,8 und letztlich noch den Hinweis auf die Lektüre eines Caelius Rufus, Cic. fam. 2,10,3. Ähnlich der Hinweis S. 338 auf den „meistgelesenen Autor über die Geschichte des III.

Allerdings wurde der „Oberkritiker" Polybios selbst offenbar extrem selten in Ägypten rezipiert. Aus seiner Feder ist nicht mehr an kurzen Fragmenten überliefert als von Ps.-Kallisthenes' Alexanderbiographie.[18] Das ist im Verhältnis zu anderen Historiographen sehr wenig, dennoch ist es ein ausgezeichnetes Beispiel dafür, dass unsere innerliterarischen und intratextuellen Bezüge der intellektuellen Autoren keineswegs Realitäten der Verbreitung und Lektüre abbilden müssen und man ihren Qualifikationen im Hinblick auf Beliebtheit und Leserschaft nicht glauben muss. Allerdings sei hier als Einwand bemerkt, dass die erhaltenen Papyri zwar einen Einblick in die Schreibkultur geben und in ihrer Gesamtheit durchaus Proportionen widerspiegeln, aber keine Detailargumente auf ihrem Überlieferungszufall aufgebaut werden können.

Mit der entsprechenden Zurückhaltung kann man dennoch festhalten, dass nicht nur die geringe Präsenz in der Papyrusüberlieferung, sondern auch die im Verhältnis zu anderen Autoren eher wenigen Exzerpte und Zitate bei späteren Autoren,[19] und die fast völlige Abwesenheit in den (wenigen bekannten) Bibliothekslisten und Kaufhinweisen, auf weniger Resonanz *in concreto* hinweisen, als es die Übertreffens- und Konkurrenztopik der Autorenkollegen glauben machen will. Diese methodische Problematik ist, ebenso wie die Überlieferungszufälle, keineswegs historiographie-spezifisch, wie man beispielsweise an der Neueren Komödie nachvollziehen kann. Zwar bietet für zahlreiche Komödienschreiber ein Athenaeus ‚bits and peaces' und die byzantinischen Lexika präsentieren zahlreiche Namen und noch mehr Titel: Aber wie will man diese Texte bzw. deren Zitate in den Papyri wiederfinden, wie ihren Stil eindeutig charakterisieren? Die Schwierigkeit aufgrund so schlechter Überlieferung mögliche Zitate zu identifizieren, macht auf das gleiche Dilemma aufmerksam, das auch für die vielen historiographischen Werke gilt, die wegen ihrer Unbekanntheit nicht im erhaltenen Material der Papyri entdeckt werden können bzw. bei welchen entsprechende Zuweisungen hypothetisch bleiben müssen.[20]

Jahrhunderts" Phylarch, der sich nur auf das Testimonium Pol. 2,56 beruft, eine wenig zuverlässige Aussage im Rahmen der Historikerkritik des Polybios. So problematisch die MALITZsche Argumentation ist, die mehr oder wenige Abwesenheit beider Autoren, Kleitarch und Phylarch, in den Papyri ist kein Gegenargument, denn wie sollten sie auch eindeutig identifiziert werden. Nichtsdestotrotz ist zumindest sicher, dass die fragmentarischen Alexanderbezüge in den Papyri unabhängig davon, ob man sie einem Autor zuweisen kann oder nicht, nur gering sind. Allerdings ist deren Aufspüren wegen der mangelnden Klassifizierung in den Indices der Papyruseditionen und Datenbanken entsprechend schwierig.

18 Polybios: P.Oxy. LXXXII 5300 kaiserzeitlich; BKT IX 30 (P.Berol.inv. 21129,2) 1. Jh. v. Chr. (?); P.Ryl I 60 mit P.Berol.inv. 9570, Ende 1. Jh. n. Chr.; Ps.-Kallisthenes: BKT IX 170 (P.Berol.inv. 21266v) 2./3. Jh. n. Chr.; P.Hal.inv. 31, 1. Jh. v. Chr.; P.Mich. XVIII 761 (inv. 6021) Ende 1./Anfang 2. Jh. n. Chr.
19 Vgl. zu Athenaeus, Anm. 37.
20 Auf diese zirkuläre Problematik weist NESSELRATH 2011 anhand zweier Beispiele der Neueren Komödie hin.

Inschriften als Zeugnisse der Wertschätzung von Historiographie und Historiographen

Die Präsenz der Geschichte und von Historikern in der Öffentlichkeit durch deren Existenz in inschriftlicher Fixierung zeugt zunächst vor allem von einem Referenzrahmen der Elitenkommunikation.[21] Das belegt beispielsweise die knappe Erwähnung Herodots im Rahmen des Städtelobs für Halikarnassos in späthellenistischer Zeit (s. oben). Die Menge der durch Grab- und Ehreninschriften belegten, durch die Lande wandernden Historiker, die ihre Geschichtserzählungen öffentlich in Theatern und an anderen Plätzen zur Schau gestellt bzw. vorgetragen hatten, ist sehr gering. ANGELOS CHANIOTIS hat insgesamt 33 solcher Historiographen oder Historiker-Rhetoren für einen Zeitraum von 650 Jahren und den gesamten griechischsprachigen Osten zusammengestellt, die durch gerade einmal 29 Inschriften aus Delphi, Athen und einigen anderen Orten nachgewiesen sind. Schwerpunkte in der Überlieferung gibt es im 3. (7 Personen) und 2. Jh. v. Chr. (7–8 Personen) und erneut im 2. Jh. n. Chr. (5 Personen), wobei einige der Geehrten auch Bürger der sie ehrenden Stadt waren und keineswegs herumzogen. Diese wenigen Inschriften bieten sicher kein für Differenzierungen belastbares Material, selbst wenn die zeitliche und räumliche Verteilung durchaus grob repräsentativ sein mag. Was zumindest deutlich wird, ist, dass die Menge der Autoren und Redner, die sich explizit als Geschichtsschreiber bezeichnen bzw. die von anderen als solche bezeichnet werden, im Verhältnis zu denen gering ist, die Begriffe wie Sophisten, Philosophen und Rhetoren zur Selbst- und Fremdrepräsentation wählen.[22]

Zwar gibt es einige literarische Hinweise in den byzantinischen Lexika und in den Sophistenviten Philostrats auf derartige Auftritte, doch insgesamt geht es mehr um Rhetorik, öfter sogar um die Varianten von Geschichtsereignissen und virtuellen Geschichtsfolgen unter anderen Voraussetzungen, zum Beispiel wie es gewesen wäre, wenn bei Salamis die Perser gesiegt hätten.[23] Zumindest ist wahrscheinlich, dass

---

21 CHANIOTIS 1984.
22 Vgl. e. g. die Untersuchungen von HAHN 1989 zu den Philosophen sowie die Sammlung und Analyse von Inschriften zu Rhetoren und Sophisten der Kaiserzeit durch PUECH 2002, in denen sich auch einige der von HAHN aufgeführten Personen finden, deren „Berufs"-Bezeichnung ganz offensichtlich zwischen Philosoph, Rhetor und Sophist schwanken kann. Die meisten der Dokumente konzentrieren sich, ebenso wie die von CHANIOTIS zu den Historikern untersuchten, auf die Orte Athen und Delphi, gefolgt von Ephesos, wie die Übersicht bei PUECH 2002, 17 verdeutlicht.
23 NICOLAI 1992, 83–88 zu historischen Themen in Deklamationen; SPAWFORTH 2012, 127 zur kaiserzeitlichen Deklamationspraxis über das Sujet der Perserkriege und die Veränderung in Einsatz und Wahrnehmung historischer Themen unter den veränderten Rahmenbedingungen römischer Autoritätsbehauptung. Die Bandbreite „historischer" Kontexte in rhetorischer Umsetzung im 2. Jh. n. Chr. wird beispielsweise an Pollux' von Naukratis berühmtester Rede über die bedeutendsten und bewundernswertesten Dinge Griechenlands deutlich, in der wichtige historische Ereignisse, die treffsicheren Orakelsprüche Delphis, berühmte Monumente Athens und anderen Ortes sowie spektakuläre Feste zusammengeführt wurden (Philostr. soph. 2,12[593]).

sowohl die Virtuosität des Redners (oder Sophisten bzw. Historikers) goutiert, als auch seine fundierten Kenntnisse in Geschichte vom Publikum durchaus bemerkt wurden, vor allem wenn es sich um Vorträge im Rahmen eines Redewettbewerbs handelte. Dass ein solches Publikum nicht nur aus Elite bestand, ist nachweisbar, wenn auch der Geschmack der verschiedenen Gruppen unterschiedlich gewesen sein mag. Wie weit die Publikumsbreite jedoch ging, ist fraglich, schließlich mussten die Teilnehmer Zeit erübrigen können und sollte die Anreise nicht zu weit und kostspielig gewesen sein. So wäre man dann bei der Identifizierung der möglichen Zuhörergruppen eines solchen Wettbewerbs am innerstädtischen Veranstaltungsort wohl bei so etwas wie einer (diffusen) Mittelschicht, vielleicht aber bei Tagelöhnern ohne Arbeit. Bei dem ein oder anderen Zuhörer mag jedoch die Kenntnis von Geschichte und Geschichten auf dem Umweg der Rhetorik vielleicht entfacht, im Einzelfall auch vertieft worden sein. Über die Lektüren und Leseinteressen des Einzelnen und den Besitz von ausgewählten Schriften aber sagt die zuhörende Teilnahme an solchen Rededuellen und das Schätzen von mündlich vorgetragenen rhetorischen Feuerwerken „historischen" Inhalts nichts aus.

Fragmente und ihre Überlieferungskontexte

Kaum vielversprechender sind andere methodische Wege, um die Rolle der Historiographie im Lektüre- und Bildungskanon im Verhältnis zu anderen Formen und Inhalten wie Philosophie, Grammatik oder Tragödie zu konkretisieren oder auch den Umfang von Geschichtskenntnissen einer breiteren Masse für einen bestimmten Raum und eine bestimmte Zeit nachzuweisen.

Ein solcher Zugang könnte sein zu überprüfen, in welchen Kontexten historiographische Texte physisch vorkommen – ein Ergebnis, das man dann mit anderen Textgruppen in Relation stellen müsste. Jedoch bieten selbst Kenntnisse über den Fundkontext in der Regel keinen Hinweis darauf, wer die Erst-Besitzer waren, welchen Status sie hatten und ob genau diese oder andere Personen den Papyrus weiter- und wiederbenutzt haben. Trotz dieser Schwierigkeiten hat WILLY CLARYSSE mit seinen Literary Papyri in „documentary archives" (1983) diesen Weg beschritten, ebenso wie beispielsweise JEAN-LUC FOURNET mit der Untersuchung der Zitate und Hinweise auf Homer in nichtliterarischen Kontexten und den Vorderseiten dokumentarischer Papyri.[24] Dabei kann CLARYSSE zumindest zeigen, dass die Auswahl der literarischen Papyri in Archiven weniger antiken literarischen Ansprüchen folgte, sondern mehr den konkreten (lebensweltlichen) Bedürfnissen: Im einen Fall sind es eben Konjugationstabellen, im anderen medizinische Texte. Es finden sich aber auch einzelne

---

24 CLARYSSE 1983; FOURNET 2012.

Gedichte, Gnomologien oder Astronomie, möglicherweise zur Orientierung und als weniger konkrete denn geistige Lebenshilfe zu interpretieren.

Zwar gibt es keine größeren geschlossenen Archiv-Kontexte mit historiographischen Texten, an denen man zumindest exemplarisch untersuchen könnte, ob und, wenn ja, wie sozialer Status, geographische Verortung usw. Einfluss auf den „historischen" Geschmack eines Individuums hatten. Dennoch ist es ein vielversprechender Weg, wie die bisherigen Ergebnisse solcher Untersuchungen zu dokumentarischen Papyri und Archiven zeigen. Wenn in Zukunft Neufunde oder Editionen schon gefundener Archive bzw. Kartonagen auch historiographische Texte beinhalten, dann sollte zumindest im Vergleich mit anderen so erhaltenen literarischen Texten der Versuch der Identifizierung der Auswahlkriterien unternommen werden.

Im Einzelfall jedoch kann ein solcher Weg in eine Sackgasse führen, wie das folgende Beispiel zeigt. Dabei wird genau dieses Exemplum in der Literatur zur Erörterung der Frage von Belesenheit und Literaturinteressen von Subeliten benutzt: Aus dem Serapeion von Memphis stammt aus der Mitte des 2. Jhs. v. Chr. das sogenannte „Archiv des Ptolemaios". Dabei handelt es sich um Texte des Ptolemaios, Sohn eines makedonischen Soldaten namens Glaukias, und um wenige Texte, die Ptolemaios jüngeren Bruder Apollonios betreffen. Ptolemaios ist Dauergast (von *katoche* ist die Rede) im Serapeion und arbeitet dort als eine Art Kultdiener mit Aufgaben in der Verwaltung und Beschaffung von Nahrungsmitteln. Dadurch hat er bescheidene Einkünfte. Unter Einbezug seines Bruders bemüht er sich darüber hinaus einen Kleinhandel von Tuchen und Kleidern außerhalb des Heiligtums in Gang zu bringen.[25] Die Briefe und Dokumente von Behörden, die in Ptolemaios' Archiv versammelt sind, zeugen in ihrer Gesamtheit von seinen persönlichen Schwierigkeiten, denen des Heiligtums, der etwas ungelenken Rechnungslegung des Ptolemaios, dem Finanzgebaren der Heiligtumsverwaltung, sowie der, wenn auch geringen staatlichen bzw. königlichen, Förderung des Tempels. Einige wenige literarische Texte haben in dieses Dossier Eingang gefunden, ob daraus allerdings eine Vorliebe des Besitzers Ptolemaios zur griechischen Komödie einer eher deftigen Art[26] und zu Traumbüchern und Traumdeutung[27] deutlich wird, ist nicht nur wegen der geringen Zahl, sondern auch wegen unserer Unkenntnis der Herkunft dieser Texte und ihres Weges in Ptolemaios' Besitz keineswegs eindeutig. Unter seinen Papryri fand sich ein illustrierter Text, der eine an die Theorien des Eudoxos von Knidos (4. Jh. v. Chr.) angelehnte astronomischen Kurzfassung bietet. Dabei ist völlig unklar, wie diese schöne Abschrift in die Hände der Söhne des Glaukos gelangte, denn die Rückseite des illustrierten Papyrus wurde

---

25 THOMPSON 1988, 212–265 zum Serapeion-Archiv, den Strukturen und wirtschaftlichen Vorgängen im Heiligtum und den konkreten Aufgaben Ptolemaios'.
26 UPZ I 56 (P.Didot 1), vgl. THOMPSON 1988, 259.
27 Einen Überblick über die literarischen Texte aus dem Serapeion-Archiv gibt THOMPSON 1988, 252–262 darunter als astronomische Texte die *Eudoxou Techne* und eine *Didaskalea Ouranios*.

nicht nur von Ptolemaios genutzt.[28] Folgt man DOROTHY THOMPSONs Einschätzung, dann war es wohl weniger der reizvoll illustrierte astronomische Text, als vielmehr die leere Rückseite, die für Ptolemaios von Relevanz war. Ansonsten deutet der gesamte Kontext zwar auf einen Mann hin, der lesen und schreiben konnte, der aber nicht besonders gebildet war.[29] Dieses kurze Beispiel dürfte verdeutlichen, dass selbst bei Eindeutigkeit der Besitzverhältnisse und mit näheren Kenntnissen über den Status und die Familie des Besitzers die Identifizierung von Leseinteressen sowie von Funktion und Wert eines literarischen Textes auf einem Papyrus für den konkreten Besitzer schwierig ist.

Diese Problematik wird ähnlich am schon mehrfach untersuchten Beispiel der Überlieferung von Herodotzitaten und von längeren Passagen des herodoteischen Werkes deutlich: Die meisten der Texte sind zwar auf der für den Schreibvorgang qualitativ schlechteren, in der Regel sekundär beschriebenen Rückseite überliefert, allerdings ist die Bandbreite der Texte auf den Vorderseiten groß. Besitzergruppen oder Nutzerverhalten daraus feststellen zu wollen, ist schlechterdings unmöglich.[30] Die zum Teil ungelenken Handschriften und die Auswahl der kurzen Zitate und Wörter weisen darauf hin, so STEPHANIE R. WEST, dass schon in hellenistischer Zeit eine eher fragmentierende Wahrnehmung und fragmentierte Nutzung des herodoteischen Textes gegenüber einer zusammenhängenden Lektüre des gesamten Werkes dominierte.[31]

Es wird diskutiert, ob möglicherweise die optische Gestaltung der Texte, die dem Leser im Einzelfall durch Eingriffe verschiedene Hilfestellungen geben, uns als Hinweis auf einen weniger geübten Leser als Auftraggeber oder Käufer dienen könnte. Gliederungskennzeichen sind allerdings ein spätes Phänomen, das kaum für die Analyse von Texten aus Hellenismus und früher Kaiserzeit zu nutzen ist und im Kontext von Historiographie zunächst gar nicht belegt ist. Dagegen ist die Kategorisierung von Schreiberhänden als professionell, geübt oder weniger geübt ein solides Kriterium für die Identifizierung von Besitzern und Lesern von literarischen Texten

---

28 Die eigentliche Zusammenfassung soll auf den im Text genannten Leptines zurückgehen, der diese Arbeit für die Ptolemäer angefertigt habe, vgl.THOMPSON 1988, 253.
29 THOMPSON 1988, 259: Dabei findet sich in seinem Archiv unter anderem das Fragment eines durchaus anspruchsvollen Werks über Negation mit zahlreichen Zitaten aus Euripides und wenigen anderen Autoren. Auch hier vermutet THOMPSON, die Besitzer hätten den Text vielleicht nicht einmal gelesen, denn genutzt wurde die Rückseite des anonymen philosophischen Traktats durch Ptolemaios, indem er darauf mit eigener Hand die Träume seines Freundes Nektembes verzeichnete. THOMPSON 1988, 259–60 zu einem Menanderpapyrus, bei dem allerdings Ptolemaios auf der Rückseite, wie bei einem Schulpapyrus, einen Teil des Textes als Schriftübung abschreibt. Ob er am Inhalt besonderen Gefallen gefunden hatte und dieses Zitat durch Abschrift lediglich besser memorieren wollte, ist nicht bekannt.
30 BANDIERA 1997.
31 WEST 2011, 75–77.

auch für die frühe Zeit, wie dies MARIA ROSARIA FALIVENE für die literarischen Papyri aus El-Hibeh aufgezeigt hat.[32]

Geschichte und ihre „Historiographie"

Die Überlieferung von Geschichten als methodischen Hinweis für die Verbreitung und Kenntnisse von Historiographie zu benennen, ist unter anderem begründet in einem Analogieschluss von modernen Präferenzen des historischen Romans und der Biographie bei einem Massenpublikum. Diese populäre Geschichtsschreibung begleite die wenig gelesene Geschichtsschreibung mit wissenschaftlichem Anspruch, die eher sperrig sei und sich dem „normalen" Leser verweigere. Entsprechend seien "such transparent and accessible charmers as Herodotus and Xenophon ... widely read and known in the fourth century and early Hellenistic periods, in a way that ... Thucydides was surely not."[33] Der Hintergrund für diese Behauptung sind Bezüge auf diese Autoren in anderen Texten, nicht aber die Papyri (s. unten für die konkreten Zahlen). In der Sache der „angenehmen" Lektüren dürften der zitierte SIMON HORNBLOWER und andere wohl recht haben, denn biographische Geschichten, auch Mirabilia und anderes, spielen neben den omnipräsenten Mythen eine wichtigere Rolle in den Papyri als die Schilderung eines Krieges und die distanzierte beschreibende Darstellung einer Herrschaft. Selbst ein Kaiser Tiberius soll, so Sueton, bei der Lektüreauswahl die Präsentation des mythischen Teils der Geschichte jeder anderen Art von Historiographie vorgezogen haben.[34] Das ist kaum repräsentativ, wird es doch bei Sueton als unangenehme Marotte dieses gebildeten Kaisers dargestellt, der mit seinen Spezialkenntnissen die ihn umgebenden Grammatiker aufs Unangenehmste vorzuführen sucht. Auch wenn ein Kaiser Claudius dagegen die Kenntnis der Geschichte ganz offensichtlich vielem anderen vorgezogen hat, macht selbst ein kurzer Blick auf die in der biographischen Überlieferung benannten literarischen Vorlieben der Kaiser von Augustus bis Hadrian die Bandbreite der Schwerpunktsetzung deutlich, unter der Geschichte doch eher selten genannt wird.[35]

Andererseits erscheint wahrscheinlich, dass die gebildeten Vielleser sich nicht nur auf eine Gattung und ein Thema beschränkten und die Geschichte dazugehörte, ob nun romanhaft, biographisch oder eher „wissenschaftlich" dargestellt. Die persönlichen Vorlieben steuerten Auswahl und Menge im Detail. Wer (sprachlich) anspruchsvolle Historiographie und längere biographische Darstellungen las, kannte

---

32 FALIVENE 1997.
33 HORNBLOWER 1995, 46. Er benennt dabei auch grundsätzliche methodische Schwächen der MALITZ'schen Argumentation.
34 Suet. Tib. 70: *Maxime tamen curavit notitiam historiae fabularis ...*, vgl. LEVICK 1999, 16–18, KLOOSTER 2017.
35 Einen Überblick bietet die Arbeit von BARDON 1940.

neben Homer, Euripides und den Menandersentenzen auch viele andere Autoren bzw. deren Texte. Die gebildeten Reichen, auch ein Tiberius, lasen sicher vieles.

Nicht-literarische Kontexte

Man könnte meinen, dass häufige literarische Referenzen auf Historiographie außerhalb ihrer selbst einen Nachweis für breite Lektüren bildet, benötigen doch die Leser für das genussvolle Wiedererkennen von Zitaten und die Anspielungen in Texten wie den Tischgesprächen eines Plutarchs oder Athenios genau diesen Lese-Hintergrund.[36] Vielleicht sind aber zumindest die komplexen Geschichtswerke, die keinem biographischen Leitstern folgen, in ihren Details literarisch zu geschlossen, als dass sie ein spezifisch historisches Referenzsystem anbieten. Neben beinah geschichtsphilosophischen Anknüpfungspunkten, die auf das Gewicht eines Ereignisses und die Dramatik von Konsequenzen, beispielsweise für den sittlichen Niedergang oder die Etablierung einer tyrannischen Herrschaft, Bezug nehmen, bieten diese Texte für gelehrte Gespräche und literarische Werke einen ebenso reichen Fundus, wie der anderer literarischer, nicht-historiographischer Texte. Zwar übertreffen beispielsweise im Referenzrahmen der spätantiken lateinischen Autoren die „historischen" Hinweise auf die Republik die auf die Kaiserzeit deutlich, dennoch umspannen die gewählten Namen und Zitate die Helden von Romulus über die frühe bis in die späte Republik.

Die identitätsstiftende Funktion von Geschichte und Geschichten ist daher ein literarischer Kontext, der das Römische an sich an *exempla* präsentiert, anhand derer die Berechtigung des Selbstbewusstseins der Überlegenheit des einzelnen Römers ebenso wie die Größe und Stärke des Reiches und seiner Bürgerschaft insgesamt mit wenigen Worten und mit wenigen Begriffen und Namen aufgezeigt wird.[37] Auch wenn es Ansätze hierzu schon in der Kaiserzeit gibt, so erscheinen sie doch weniger prägnant zu sein als in der Spätantike. Geschichte und Historiographie spielen dementsprechend auch keine besonders herausgehobene Rolle im Verhältnis zu anderen Themen und Autoren bzw. Genres in den literarischen Tischgesprächen eines Plutarchs und Athenaeus in der griechischen oder eines Schriftstellers wie Aulus Gellius in der lateinischen Tradition.[38] Bis auf Vokabulareinsatz und grammatische Verweise auf

---

[36] Vgl. zur spezifischen Elitenbildung als Voraussetzung für den literarischen Umgang mit Geschichte: HOSE 2015, hier angewendet auf die Spätantike.
[37] Zur Dominanz republikanischer Exempla und historischen Ereignisbezügen in spätantiken lateinischen Texte unter Vernachlässigung kaiserzeitlicher Beispiele, vgl. SEHLMEYER 2009 passim; ähnlich HORSTER 2017 am Bespiel der Livius-Epitome zu den Veränderungen von Botschaften historiographischer Traditionen in der Spätantike durch eine leicht verschobene Komposition und veränderte Gestaltung.
[38] Zur Präsenz griechischer Historiographie in verschiedenen kaiserzeitlichen Autoren mit einem Schwerpunkt auf Plutarch, vgl. CANDAU 2013, 39–57.

die frühen Autoren Ennius und seltener Naevius gibt es beispielsweise in der Lesewelt eines Gellius kaum Geschichtsschreiber. Wenn ein Athenaeus Historiker zitiert, dann wenig von den von uns Modernen so gepriesenen Autoren Herodot, Thukydides oder auch Polybios. Vielmehr wählt er Zitate und Paraphrasen aus Autoren, die er möglicherweise gerade wegen ihrer Rarität, ihrer Unbekanntheit auswählt, um damit seine Bildung umso mehr zu demonstrieren. Vor allem müssen diese Autoren etwas zu seinen Themen der Gastmahle, Nahrungsmittel und Tischgefäße liefern, um sie in seine Gesprächssituation einbinden zu können.[39] Die Auswahl zeugt also, abgesehen vom inhaltlichen Kontext des Gastmahls, vor allem vom Spiel von Autor und Leser, wozu das Präsentieren seltener Autoren gehört. Sie zu erkennen ist Aufgabe des Lesers. Die Mischung aus prägnantem Beispiel und Attraktivität für den Leser hat auch den Umgang der Grammatiker mit Historiographie geprägt.[40]

Will man also die Mittelschichten und lokalen Eliten ebenso wie die weniger Gebildeten greifen, die vielleicht den Hörgenuss gegenüber der Lektüre bevorzugten, den ihnen solche (bei CHANIOTIS in den Inschriften identifizierten) Historiker-Rhetoren vermittelten,[41] kommen wir daher mit den Selbstaussagen der historischen Autoren nicht weiter, genauso wenig wie mit dem, was andere Autoren über sie sagten und wie diese sie (be-)nutzten.

Diejenigen, die überhaupt Texte besaßen, ihre persönliche Korrespondenz archiviert und die Dokumente zu Steuern und Besitz aufgehoben haben, hatten im Einzelfall vielleicht den einen oder anderen literarischen Text darunter, den sie dann zwar für die Zweitverwendung der Rückseite (verso) erhielten und schätzten, vielleicht aber auch an- oder sogar durchgelesen haben. Dies dürfte für den Besitzer der Eudoxos-Techne gelten, bei der von Ptolemaios' Hand auf der Rückseite dieser schön bebilderten Handschrift oben noch vor der Beschriftung durch weitere Dokumente

---

[39] Athenaeus ist ein gutes Beispiel des schwierigen Geschäfts von Quantifizierungen, sind doch beispielsweise Anzahl und Umfang der Komikerfragmente und die der Historikerfragmente kaum zu vergleichen, weil die Identifizierung der 108 von ihm zitierten Komiker den strengen Klassifizierungsregeln von AUSTIN/KASSEL 1983–2001 folgen; dagegen sind die 191 „Historiker", die von Athenaeus zitiert werden, im Wesentlichen das Ergebnis der deutlich großzügigeren Kategorisierungen in der Felix Jacoby-Tradition und umfasst die (historische) Geographie und Geologie ebenso wie eine Vielfalt von kulturhistorischen und ethnographischen Schriften, vgl. SCHEPENS 1997 zu Jacobys Kriterien und GRAFTON 1997 zu nachantiken Genre-Grenzen. Das ist insofern sicher zielführend, da der antike „Geschichts"-Begriff genau diese Offenheit hatte. Zum Ärger eines Thukydides und Polybios konnte die Vielfalt historischen Schreibens eben nicht auf deren Vorstellungen „seriöser" Historiographie reduziert werden. Dafür allerdings kassieren die beiden die „Rezeptionsquittung", wenn man das so sagen darf, denn anders als für Herodot mit 60 Verweisen bei Athenaeus, finden sich lediglich 13 Zitate von Thukydides. Und ein Polybios ist bei Athenaeus nicht öfter zitiert bzw. genannt als ein Kallisthenes von Rhodos oder Hegesander aus Delphi und wird von den so gescholtenen Autoren Theopomp und Phylarch zumindest in den Deipnosophisten überholt. Vgl. die auf der Basis der Indices von OLSON 2012 zur Verfügung gestellte Onlinedatenbank www.digitalathenaeus.org.
[40] Zur Auswahl der Historiographie-Zitate vgl. MONTANARI 2013.
[41] Zu CHANIOTIS 1991.

die Überschrift "die Kunst/die Fertigkeiten des Eudoxos" geschrieben wurde. Ob es jedoch eher die Bilder oder vielleicht doch der Inhalt waren, welcher die Rolle für ihn so besonders attraktiv machte, ist uns trotz dieser persönlichen Notiz nicht bekannt.

Andererseits lassen gerade die seltenen, listenartigen Chroniken der hellenistischen und römischen Zeit daran zweifeln, dass ein originäres Interesse an einer klaren Differenzierung einzelner Handlungsabläufe oder auch regionaler Entwicklungen in der Zeit bestand. Die meisten solcher Text bedienen einen engen lokalen Kontext. Für das Verständnis der weiter verbreiteten Epen, Tragödien, Komödien, einzelnen Reden, medizinischen Texte, geographischen Fachtexte und Philosophieexzerpte war es nicht notwendig, eine konkrete Zeitschiene zu besitzen, in die man die Generationen und Ereignisse, die in den Texten erwähnt werden, in die Weltgeschichte einordnen konnte.

(Ver-)Kürzungen

Einen weiteren methodischen Zugang zur Text- und Geschichtsrezeption könnte die Nutzung von Geschichtswerken durch Zusammenfassungen und Exzerpte sein. In dieser Art der Verwertung und Tradierung könnte sich das Bedürfnis spiegeln, lediglich den Kern der Dinge zu erfassen und literarisch weniger anspruchsvolle, aber wichtige und nützliche Informationen zu erhalten. Allerdings ist dies wohl ein methodischer Irrweg, denn es sind nur wenige, oft fragmentarische „Kompendien" historiographischen Inhalts aus Ägypten überliefert. Auch die geringe Präsenz von Texten historiographischen Kontextes in den Anthologien weist in die gleiche Richtung. Inzwischen sind gut 70 Papyri mit Anthologien und Exzerpt-Präsentationen von Dichterfragmenten ediert, Texte, für die MONIQUE VAN ROSSUM-STEENBEEK den Begriff "Greek Readers' Digests" im Hinblick auf Anspruch und Nutzerverhalten diskutiert. Nicht zuletzt wegen der Häufigkeit des Versmaßes solcher Texte, steht sie jedoch diesem modernen Verständnis und Begriff von geradezu vorverdauter Information und Auswahl von Sinnsprüchen und nützlicher Information kritisch gegenüber.[42] Dagegen gibt es einen deutlichen Schwerpunkt an zusammengefassten Prosatexten in der Kaiserzeit, selbst wenn es am Ende nur wenige Demosthenesreden und vier, vielleicht fünf weitere Autoren sind, die identifizierbar so vermittelt wurden.[43] Es ist eine spätantik-christliche Idee, Geschichte knapp vermittelt als kulturelles Gerüst zu nutzen, um durch eine dadurch mögliche Parallelisierung mit der Heilsgeschichte

---

42 Vgl. VAN ROSSUM-STEENBEEK 1998 ergänzt durch PORDOMINGO 2013, der davon fünf Anthologien als „antologías scolares" klassifiziert.
43 So das Ergebnis auf der Basis von PACK[3] und Ergänzungen aus ROSSUM-STEENBEEK 1998 bspw. zu den Paraphrasen und Hypotheseis, aber auch zu Epitomai mit historischen oder historisierenden Argumenten und Anspielungen wie bspw. Ps.-Plutarchs Placita Philosophorum oder Hermippus' Philosophenviten.

die solide Basis einer gemeinschaftsstiftenden und die Vielfalt der kulturellen Erzeugnisse einbindenden Vergangenheit zu nutzen. Vergleichbare Chroniken hatten zumindest, so das Bild der jetzigen Überlieferung, keine große Tradition in der Zeit vor dem 3. Jh. n. Chr.

Wenn man es auf der Basis der geringen Menge an Hypotheseis, Kompendien und Epitomae überhaupt wagt Schlüsse zu ziehen, dann sollte dieser eher lauten, dass für viele der Papyrusbesitzer umfassende und leicht zu generierende Bildung und Kenntnisse der Geschichte als eine Abfolge in der Zeit keinen besonders hohen Stellenwert hatten! Nur wenige Leser scheinen die Möglichkeit genutzt zu haben, mittels eines Sets an knapp präsentierten „Informationen" verschiedener Themen (nicht nur der „Geschichte") und Textgattungen ihre vorhandenen Kenntnisse und präferierten Lektüren zu kontextualisieren und zu vertiefen.

Dagegen ist die Menge der Texte in der Kaiserzeit, in denen entweder historiographische Texte kurz zitiert werden, und solcher, in denen längere Passagen oder gar ganze Rollen/Bücher abgeschrieben wurden, in absoluten Zahlen durchaus hoch, wenn auch im Verhältnis zur epischen und dramatischen Dichtung gering. Es ist allerdings durch den oft schlechten Erhaltungszustand der Texte nicht immer klar, ob ein kurzes Zitat nicht möglicherweise Teil eines größeren zusammenhängenden historiographischen Textes war bzw. ob das Zitat nicht vielleicht doch in einen neuen Zusammenhang eingebettet wurde, was dann wieder für eine größere Selbstständigkeit im Umgang mit historischen Texten sprechen würde, als es die Abschriften langer Passagen oder Bücher nahelegen.

Die Problematik, den Zweck und Nutzungskontext eines Papyrus mit historiographischem Zitat zu identifizieren, mag ein Thukydidesfragment verdeutlichen.[44] Die Herkunft dieses 2005 publizierten Papyrus der Sammlung in Yale ist unbekannt. Ein Fragment kann nicht zugeordnet werden, die anderen beiden geben Teile von Buch 8 des Peloponnesischen Krieges wieder. Die Paläographie weist in die Zeit von der Mitte des 3. bis in die 1. Hälfte des 2. Jhs. Wegen der Platzierung der Fragmente am Anfang bzw. Ende der Kolumnen, konnte der Editor, KEVIN WILKINSON, das wahrscheinliche Gesamtvolumen der Rolle berechnen, die er mit 153 Kolumnen je 653 Buchstaben für Buch 8 des Thukydides auf neun Meter Länge und etwa 24cm Höhe ansetzt (p. 71), eine durchaus durchschnittliche Größe qualitätsvoller, ptolemäischer Rollen.[45] Die vorhandenen kleinen Textteile würden in einer modernen Edition gerade einmal zehn Zeilen darstellen. Nicht nur einige orthographische Varianten sind vorhanden, sondern das zweite Fragment mit knapp vierzig Wörtern weicht außerdem bei sechs von allen bisherigen Überlieferungsvarianten ab. Interessanterweise hat selbst der ptolemäische Hamburger Papyrus (P.Hamb. II 163) mit einem längeren Thukydideszitat von weniger als achtzig Wörtern eine derart überdurchschnittlich hohe

---

44 WILKINSON 2005 für P.Yale (P.CtYBR inv. 4601).
45 JOHNSON 2004, 130–143; WILKINSON 2005, 71.

Abweichung von der Überlieferung durch spätere Manuskripte.[46] Offenbar bestand kein dringender Bedarf nach einer Standardisierung des Thukydidestextes vor dem Ende der ptolemäischen Epoche, was zusammen mit den wenigen Zeugnissen seiner Bücher für eine verhältnismäßig geringe Verbreitung und kleine Leserschaft vor der Kaiserzeit sprechen könnte.[47] Allerdings entspricht die kleine Zahl historiographischer Textfragmente und identifizierter Zitate in ptolemäischer Zeit durchaus proportional der übrigen ptolemäischen Überlieferung aller datierten Papyri, auch denen der literarischen Papyri, und bildet keinen besonderen Ausreißer, der Aussagen über Vorlieben oder Vernachlässigung historischer Texte zuließe.[48]

Nicht einmal mögliche Ägypten-spezifische Themen, wie bspw. die Vita Alexanders oder das zweite Buch Herodots, sind im überlieferten Material aus Ägypten zu identifizieren. Weder Menge noch Inhalt dieser zufällig überlieferten Textausschnitte bieten daher eine Basis um über Lesegeschmack oder Bildungsstand der ersten Besitzer dieser Abschriften historiographischer und biographischer Texte zu spekulieren, geschweige denn derjenigen, die dann diese Papyrusrollen erbten und/oder weiternutzten.[49]

Trotz des Vorbehalts des Zufalls und der immer noch geringen Zahl, ergibt die Gesamtmenge kaiserzeitlicher Überlieferung doch zumindest Tendenzen für inhaltliche Schwerpunkte und damit auch für Leseinteressen und Bildungsvorstellungen. So steigt zumindest ab dem 2. Jh. n. Chr. nachweislich das Interesse an Thukydides und Herodot, nicht nur in absoluten Zahlen, sondern ebenso im Verhältnis zur Gesamtmenge der Texte. Die große Vergangenheit der Griechen mit ihrem Sieg über die Perser, die perikleische Zeit Athens, die lange Geschichte Thebens und die der siegreichen Spartaner im 2. und frühen 3. Jh., die oft Thema und Lehrstück für die Rhetorik und den Rhetorikunterricht der Zeit waren, könnten für diese Schwerpunktsetzung den Hintergrund bilden.[50] Die Begründungsstrategien der Redner der zweiten Sophistik

---

46 Zum Hamburger Papyrus TURNER 1956 und WILKINSON 2005, 72.
47 Die Rezeption schließt allerdings seine Nutzung durch andere Autoren ein, auch wenn diese oft ohne Namensnennung erfolgt, wobei die Bezüge und Anspielungen für den Kenner wohl ersichtlich gewesen sein dürften, vgl. HORNBLOWER 1995. Er diskutiert die Thukydides-Anspielungen in Autoren des 4. Jhs. und setzt damit implizit ein entsprechend an der Thukydides-Lektüre gebildetes Publikum voraus, wohingegen MORRISON 2007, 221–226 explizit argumentiert, dass ein kleines Zielpublikum in der Plato-Lektüre die mehr oder weniger versteckten Hinweise auf Thukydides Werk erkannt habe.
48 Vgl. die Zahlen und Tabellen bei HABERMANN 1998, die trotz der vielen, seither erfolgten Papyruseditionen die chronologische Überlieferung in ihrer Grundtendenz und Proportion abbilden.
49 Aus der kleinen Menge an Fragmenten zur Alexandergeschichte bzw. zur frühhellenistischen Zeit auf ein größeres Interesse an der eigenen, unmittelbaren ägyptisch-griechischen Vergangenheit (im Gegensatz zu der „großen" der Griechen außerhalb Ägyptens) zu schließen, wie dies MALITZ 1990, e. g. 340 und 344–345 macht, ist nicht nachvollziehbar, ganz unabhängig davon, dass die Gesamtmenge der inhaltlich die klassische Zeit betreffenden Fragmente und Zitate nicht geringer ist als die zur hellenistischen Zeit.
50 Vgl. BOUQUIAUX-SIMON/MERTENS 1991 zur Verteilung der bis dahin bekannten Thukydides-Papyri. BANDIERA 1997 gruppiert die Herodotüberlieferung in Papyri nach Büchern und Jahrhunderten: Die

und die damit verbundenen literarischen Moden scheinen an Ägypten nicht vorbeigegangen zu sein. So ließe sich zumindest die wachsende Zahl der erhaltenen umfangreichen Fragmente und längeren Passagen attischer Redner erklären – ein Phänomen, das sich beispielsweise ähnlich bei den in den Sophistenviten genannten Themen der Auftritte und schriftlichen Schaustücke abbildet.[51] Abgesehen von Thukydides und Herodot kann man für einen großen Teil der überlieferten „historischen" Papyrus-Fragmente sagen, dass ein deutlicher Fokus des kaiserzeitlichen Interesses auf der Biographie von Königen und anderen berühmten Persönlichkeiten lag.[52]

Die Vorlieben und Auswahl der Texte ab dem 2. Jh. wurden allerdings auch von einem gänzlich anderen, nicht inhaltsbezogenen Aspekt mitgeprägt: der Sprache. Diese dürfte für die mehr und die weniger Gebildeten, aber doch immerhin Lektüre-, Vortrags- und Performanz-Interessierten, eine wichtige Rolle gespielt haben. Schon STRASBURGER hat darauf hingewiesen, dass in der römischen Zeit literarische Texte in Koiné und ionischem Griechisch immer mehr zurückgedrängt werden. Am Ende dominieren die Abschriften von in attischem Griechisch geschriebenen Werken.[53] Diese Beobachtung sollte davor warnen, das Vorhandensein und Verschwinden von Autoren, die nicht zum Schulkanon gehören, ausschließlich über die inhaltliche Ebene erklären zu wollen – nicht nur bei den Papyri, sondern auch im Zitierverhalten der über spätere Manuskripte erhaltenen Autoren und ihrer Werke.

Fazit

„Geschichtsschreibung ist nach antiker Vorstellung in erster Linie Kunst, der epischen Dichtung benachbart."[54] Neben Informationsdichte und Qualität sind mehr noch Unterhaltung und sprachliche Gestaltung zentrale Kriterien. Die Salmakis-Inschrift macht explizit, was die außer-„historiographische" Literatur in ihren oft nicht nachvollziehbaren Vorlieben unterstreicht und was auch die doch zufällig erhaltenen und

---

Bücher 6 und 9 sind in den bisher publizierten mehr als 40 Textfragmenten nicht vertreten (S. 51). Deutlich dominiert das Buch 1 und die meisten aller Herodot-Texte wurden im 2. Jh. n. Chr. abgeschrieben (S. 52).
[51] SCHMITZ 1999 mit einem darüber hinaus gehenden Textcorpus zur Attraktivität der Autoren des 5. Jhs. in der zweiten Sophistik.
[52] Überliefert sind fragmentarisch etwa Arrians Biographie des Eumenes, Gründer der attalidischen Dynastie; vielleicht eine Lebensgeschichte von Tilliborus, berühmter bithynischer Räuber der Mitte des 2. Jhs. n. Chr.; Hieronymus oder Ps.-Hieronymus von Cardias Brief an den König von Makedonien, Ps.-Callisthenes' Fragmente seines Alexanderromans. Zu Xenophons Kyropädie in den Papyri, vgl. mit einem Überblick über den Gesamtbestand, PELLÉ 2007.
[53] DIHLE 1999 über die Rolle der attischen Sprache seit dem 2. Jh. n. Chr.; STRASBURGER 1977, 18–19 zum in der Kaiserzeit beginnenden Verdrängungsprozess von nicht-attischen Texten. Den Aspekt der ionischen Sprache für die Herodotrezeption in der Kaiserzeit diskutiert TRIBULATO 2016.
[54] STRASBURGER 1977, 23.

nicht dem streng historiographischen Kanon-Rang eines Polybios folgenden erhaltenen Papyri belegen.

So ist es im Einzelfall zwar durchaus möglich, in den erhaltenen Papyri Ägyptens Schwerpunkte auszumachen, dennoch ist die Gesamtmenge der literarischen Papyri mit historiographischem Text so gering, dass wenige Neufunde den Eindruck über Autor-Präferenzen und inhaltliche Interessen in einer bestimmten Zeit durchaus verändern können.

Einige Debatten erledigen sich bei genauerem Hinsehen von selbst. Dazu gehört die Frage nach den Vorlieben in ptolemäischer Zeit, bei denen die geringe Zahl literarischer Papyri bis auf die Grundaussage über ein möglicherweise geringeres Interesse an Historiographie und anderen Prosatexten im Verhältnis zu Werken im Versmaß, wohl nichts weiter zulässt. Wenig sinnvoll erscheint es daher beispielsweise, die Diskussion um die Beliebtheit der von Polybios so getadelten schlechten Historiographen für bare Münze zu nehmen und deren Abwesenheit in Ägypten mit bewusster Auswahl der (gebildeten und pro-polybischen) Leserschaft zu verbinden. Diese innerliterarische Debatte basiert auf dem Werben des Autors für seine pragmatische Geschichtsschreibung durch die Abwertung aller anderen. So kann er seinem Publikum nicht nur durch den Stoff und seine Durchdringung als überlegen erscheinen, sondern auch durch die sprachliche Gestaltung seines Sujets.

Wichtiger für das Thema der Alltagsbildung ist jedoch, ob und, wenn ja, wie geschichtliche Texte und Biographielektüren mit dem Alltag zumindest der Lesefähigen zu tun hatten und wer nun konkret diese Gruppe war, die solche Texte vollständig oder in kleinen Auszügen las.

Mit den in diesem Beitrag aufgezeigten Wegen kommt man aber für diese Frage kaum weiter. In den Papyri, aber selbst bei den Autoren wie Athenaeus, die Historiker nennen und deren Texte nutzen, ist zumindest in der Quantität „die Geschichte" nicht zentral. In der heutigen Überlieferungslage könnte man vielleicht sogar von einem lediglich am Rande liegenden Bildungsgut sprechen. Für die Untersuchung der Rolle der Geschichte und des Geschichte-Erzählens (oder in Reden Präsentierens) jedoch lässt die Konzentration auf die griechische Sprache im Kontext einer Bildungsdiskussion für die griechisch-römische Antike darüber hinaus eine sprachbezogene Lücke, denn in demotischen Texten finden sich beispielsweise Reflexe des griechischen Alexanderromans.[55] Der Ansatz über die Papyri einen Weg zur Kenntnis der Geschichte und der Beliebtheit von Geschichten jenseits Homers und der Dramen zu finden, führt nicht zuletzt wegen der Beliebigkeit der Überlieferung und der kleinen Zahlen für die hellenistische Zeit über Anekdotisches kaum heraus. Die Menge der Papyri lässt aber selbst für die Kaiserzeit nur Weniges an Aussagen zum Leseverhalten durch die An- und Abwesenheit von Texten und Inhalten zu. Vielleicht führte die rhetorische Praxis der zweiten Sophistik, die unter anderem die Auseinandersetzung der griechi-

---

55 JASNOW 1997.

schen Städte und Regionen widerspiegelt, mit dem Ziel vom Kuchen der Vorteile und Privilegien, die die Römer verteilten, mit Verweis auf große Vergangenheit ein Stück zu erhalten, zu einem Rezeptionsaufschwung historiographischer und die Vergangenheit behandelnder Texte – auch in Ägypten.

Aber selbst für diese Zeit und diesen Kontext kann man wie so oft zwar Unterstützendes in den Papyri finden, aber ebenso gut eine andere „Geschichte" erzählen. Mangels Vergleichsmaterials ist es nicht einmal möglich festzustellen, ob die griechischen Leserschichten in Ägypten eine etwas andere Sozialisation hatten, ob sie (daher?) andere Lektüren bevorzugten, ob die viel beschworene „civic identity" der bürgerlichen Identität und Tugenden und die Rolle der griechischen Vergangenheit in Ägypten von etwas weniger Relevanz war als in anderen, städtisch geprägten Regionen der griechischen Welt: Nicht einmal das können wir mit Sicherheit sagen.

Bibliographie

ALESHIRE 1989 = S.B. ALESHIRE, The Athenian Asklepieion. The People, their Dedications, and the Inventories, Amsterdam 1989.

ASSMANN 2007 = J. ASSMANN, Das kulturelle Gedächtnis. Schrift, Erinnerung und politische Identität in frühen Hochkulturen, München 2007.

AUSTIN/KASSEL 1983–2001 = C. AUSTIN/R. KASSEL (Hg.), Poetae Comici Graeci, Berlin 1983–2001.

BANDIERA 1997 = A. BANDIERA, Per un bilancio della tradizione papiracea delle Storie di Erodoto, in: B. KRAMER et al. (Hg.), Akten des 21. Internationalen Papyrologenkongresses Berlin, 13.–19. 8. 1995, Stuttgart/Leipzig 1997, 49–56.

BARDON 1940 = H. BARDON, *Les Empereurs et les lettres latines d'Auguste à Hadrien,* Paris 1940 (ND 1968).

BLANCK 1997 = H. BLANCK, Un nuovo frammento del ‚Catalogo' della Biblioteca di Tauromenion, *PP* 52, 1997, 241–255.

BOUQUIAUX-SIMON/MERTENS 1991 = O. BOUQUIAUX-SIMON/P. MERTENS, Les papyrus de Thucydide, *Chronique d'Égypte* 66, 1991, 198–210.

CAVALLO 1986 = G. CAVALLO, Conservazione e perdita dei testi greci. Gattori materiali, sociali, culturali, in: A. GIARDINA (Hg.), Tradizione dei classici, trasformazioni della cultura, Bari 1986, 83–172.

CANDAU 2013 = J.M. CANDAU, Le coordinate letterarie dei trasmissori. La storiografia greca frammentaria negli autori di età imperiale, in: F. GAZZANO/G. OTTONE (Hg.), Le età della trasmissione. Alessandria, Roma, Bisanzio. Atti delle giornate dei studio sulla storiografia greca frammentaria, Tivoli 2013, 33–59.

CAREY 2016 = C. CAREY, Homer and Epic in Herodotus' Book 7, in: A. EFSTATHIOU/I. KARAMANOU (Hg.), Homeric Receptions across Generic and Cultural Contexts, Berlin/Boston 2016, 71–89.

CHANIOTIS 1984 = A. CHANIOTIS, Historie und Historiker in den griechischen Inschriften. Epigraphische Beiträge zur griechischen Historiographie, Stuttgart 1984.

CHANIOTIS 2016 = A. CHANIOTIS, History as an Argument in Hellenistic Oratory: The Evidence of Hellenistic Decrees, in: P. DERRON/M. EDWARDS/P. DUCREY (Hg.), La rhétorique du pouvoir: une exploration de l'art oratoire délibératif Grec. Neuf exposés suivis de discussions. Entretiens sur l'Antiquité classique, Vandœuvres 2016, 129–174.

Clarysse 1983 = W. Clarysse, Literary Papyri in Documentary "Archives", in: E. Van't Dack (Hg.), Egypt and the Hellenistic World, Leuven 1983, 43–61.

Cribiore 2001 = R. Cribiore, Gymnastics of the Mind. Greek Education in Hellenistic and Roman Egypt, Princeton/Oxford 2001.

Dihle 1999 = A. Dihle, Literaturkanon und Schriftsprache, in: J. Dummer/M. Vielberg (Hg.), Leitbilder der Spätantike – Eliten und Leitbilder, Stuttgart 1999, 9–30.

Falivene 1997 = M.R. Falivene, The Literary Papyri from Al-Ḥība. A New Approach, in: B. Kramer et al. (Hg.), Akten des 21. Internationalen Papyrologenkongresses Berlin, 13.–19. 8. 1995, Stuttgart/Leipzig 1997, 273–280.

Fournet 2012 = J.-L. Fournet, Homère et les papyrus non littéraires. Le Poète dans le contexte de ses lecteurs, in: G. Bastianini/A. Casanova (Hg.), I papiri Omerici. Atti del convegno internazionale di studi Firenze, 9–10 giugno 2011, Florenz 2012, 125–157.

Grafton 1997 = A. Grafton, Fragmenta historicorum Graecorum: Fragments of Some Lost Enterprises, in: G.W. Most (Hg.), Collecting Gragments – Fragmente sammeln, Göttingen 1997, 124–143.

Habermann 1998 = W. Habermann, Zur chronologischen Verteilung der papyrologischen Zeugnisse, *ZPE* 122, 1998, 144–160.

Hahn 1989 = J. Hahn, Der Philosoph und die Gesellschaft. Selbstverständnis, öffentliches Auftreten und populäre Erwartungen in der hohen Kaiserzeit, Stuttgart 1989.

Hekster 2005 = O. Hekster, Coins and Messages. Audience Targeting on Coins of Different Denominations?, in: L. De Blois et al. (Hg.) The Representation and Perception of Roman Imperial Power, Amsterdam 2005, 20–35.

Hornblower 1995 = S. Hornblower, The Fourth-Century and Hellenistic Reception of Thucydides, *JHS* 115, 1995, 46–68.

Horster 2015 = M. Horster, Learning by Doing. Schreibübungen auf Ostraka, in: M. Horster/M. Scholz (Hg.), Ductus. Kleininschriften römischer Zeit, Mainz 2015, 1–14.

Horster 2017 = M. Horster, Livius-Epitome. Ein spätantiker Blick auf die (kurzgefasste) Römische Republik, in: S. Dusil/G. Schwedler/R. Schwitter (Hg.), Exzerpieren – Kompilieren – Tradieren. Entwicklungen und Strategien im Umgang mit der Komplexität von Wissen in Spätantike und Frühmittelalter, Berlin 2016, 25–48.

Isager/Pedersen 2004 = S. Isager/P. Pedersen (Hg.), The *Salmakis* Inscription and Hellenistic Halikarnassos, Odense 2004.

Johnson 2004 = W. Johnson, Bookrolls and Scribes in Oxyrhynchus, Toronto 2004.

Jasnow 1997 = R. Jasnow, The Greek Alexander Romance and Demotic Egyptian Literature, *JNES* 56, 1997, 95–103.

Klooster 2017 = J. Klooster, Tiberius and Hellenistic Poetry, *aitia* 7, 2017 (http://aitia.revues.org/1766).

Levick 1999 = B. Levick, Tiberius the Politician, London 1999².

Malitz 1990 = J. Malitz, Das Interesse an der Geschichte. Die griechischen Historiker und ihr Publikum, in: H. Verdin/G. Schepens/E. De Keyser (Hg.), Purposes of History. Studies in Greek Historiography from the 4th to the 2nd Centuries B.C., Leuven 1990, 323–349.

Manganaro 1974 = G. Manganaro, Una biblioteca storica nel ginnasio di Tauromenion e il P. Oxy. 1241, *PP* 29, 1974, 389–409.

Marincola 2016 = J. Marincola, History without Malice: Plutarch Rewrites the Battle of Plataea, in: J. Priestley/V. Zali (Hg.), Brill's Companion to the Reception of Herodotus in Antiquity and Beyond, Leiden/Boston 2016, 101–119.

Merchan/Salamanca/Adán 2011 = P. Merchan/S. Salamanca/A. Adán, Restitution of Sculptural Groups Using 3D Scanners, Sensors 11, 2011, 8497–8518 (http://www.mdpi.com/1424-8220/11/9/8497/htm).

METCALF 1993 = W.E. METCALF, Whose Liberalitas? Propaganda and Audience in the Early Roman Empire, *RIN 95*, 1993, 337–346.

MILNOR 2014 = K. MILNOR, Graffiti and the Literary Landscape in Roman Pompeii, Oxford 2014.

MITCHELL 2010 = L. MITCHELL, Rezension von: L. PITCHER, Writing Ancient History: An Introduction to Classical Historiography, London/New York 2009, (http://bmcr.brynmawr.edu/2010/2010-07-12.html).

MONTANARI 2013 = F. MONTANARI, Gli storici greci e la filologia di età ellenistico-romana, in: F. GAZZANO/G. OTTONE (Hg.), Le età della trasmissione. Alessandria, Roma, Bisanzio. Atti delle giornate die studio sulla storiografia greca frammentaria, Tivoli 2013, 1–32.

MORRISON 2007 = J.V. MORRISON, Thucydides' History Live. Reception and Politics, in: C. COOPER (Hg.), Politics and Orality, Boston 2007, 217–233.

NESSELRATH 2011 = H.-G. NESSELRATH, Menander and his Rivals. New Light from the Comic Adespota?, in: D. OBBINK/R. RUTHERFORD (Hg.), Culture in Pieces. Essays on Ancient Texts in Honour of Peter Parsons, Oxford 2011, 119–137.

NICOLAI 1992 = R. NICOLAI, La storiografia nell'educazione antica, Pisa 1992.

NOGALES 2008 = T. NOGALES BASARRATE, "Rómulo en el Augusteum del foro colonial emeritense", in: E. LA ROCCA/P. LEÓN/C. PARISI PRESICCE (Hg.), Le Due Patrie Acquisite. Studi di archeologia dedicati a Walter Trillmich, Roma 2008, 301–312.

NOREÑA 2002 = C.F. NOREÑA, Emperor's Virtues, *JRS* 91, 2001, 146–168.

OTRANTO 2000 = R. OTRANTO, Antiche liste di libri su papiro, Rom 2000.

PACK³ = CEDOPAL: The Mertens-Pack² database project (www.ulg.ac.be/facphl/services/cedopal/pages/mp3).

PELLÉ 2007 = N. PELLÉ, Ricerche sui papiri di Senofonte, in: B. PALME (Hg.), Akten des 23. Internationalen Papyrologenkongresses, Wien 22.–28. Juli 2001, Wien 2007, 525–534.

PELLING 2006 = C. PELLING, Homer and Herodotus, in: M.J. CLARKE/B.G.F. CURRIE/R.O.A.M. LYNE (Hg.), Epic Interactions: Perspectives on Homer, Virgil, and the Epic Tradition Presented to Jasper Griffin by Former Pupils, Oxford 2006, 75–104.

PLATTHY 1968 = J. PLATTHY, Sources on the Earliest Greek Libraries. With the Testimonia, Amsterdam 1968.

PORDOMINGO 2013 = F. PORDOMINGO, Antologías de época helenística en papiro, Florenz 2013.

PRIESTLEY 2014 = J. PRIESTLEY, Herodotus and Hellenstic Culture. Literary Studies in the Reception of the Histories, Oxford 2014.

PUECH 2002 = B. PUECH, Orateurs et Sophistes grecs dans les inscriptions d'époque impériale, Paris 2002.

OLSON 2012 = S.D. OLSON, Athenaeus, The Learned Banqueters, Vol. 8/15, Cambridge, Mass. 2012.

VAN ROSSUM-STEENBEEK 1998 = M. VAN ROSSUM-STEENBEEK, Greek Readers' Digests? Studies on a Selection of Sub-literary Papyri, Leiden 1997.

SCHEPENS 1997 = G. SCHEPENS, Jacoby's FGrHist: Problems, Methods, Prospects, in: G.W. MOST (Hg.), Collecting Fragments – Fragmente sammeln, Göttingen 1997, 144–172.

SCHMITZ 1999 = T. SCHMITZ, Performing History in the Second Sophistic, in: M. ZIMMERMANN (Hg.) Geschichtsschreibung und politischer Wandel im 3. Jh. n. Chr., Stuttgart 1999, 72–92.

SCHWERDTNER 2015 = K. SCHWERDTNER, Plinius und seine Klassiker. Studien zur literarischen Zitation in den Pliniusbriefen, Berlin/Boston, 2015.

SPAWFORTH 2012 = A.J.S. SPAWFORTH, Greece and the Augustan Cultural Revolution, Cambridge 2012.

STENGER 2009 = J. STENGER, Hellenistische Identität in der Spätantike. Pagane Autoren und ihr Unbehagen an der eigenen Zeit, Berlin 2009.

STRASBURGER 1977 = H. STRASBURGER, Umblick im Trümmerfeld der griechischen Geschichtsschreibung, in: Historiographia Antiqua. Commentationes Lovanienses in honorem W. Peremans septuagenarii editae, Leuven 1977, 3–52.

SUERBAUM 2012 = W. SUERBAUM, Der Anfangsprozess der ‚Kanonisierung' Vergils, in: E.M. BECKER/S. SCHOLZ (Hg.), Kanon in Konstruktion und Dekonstruktion. Kanonisierungsprozesse religiöser Texte von der Antike bis zur Gegenwart: Ein Handbuch, Berlin 2012, 171–219.

THOMPSON 1988 = D.J. THOMPSON, Memphis under the Ptolemies, Princeton 1988.

TRIBULATO 2016 = O. TRIBULATO, Herodotus' Reception in Ancient Greek Lexicography and Grammar: From the Hellenistic to the Imperial Age, in: J. PRIESTLEY/V. ZALI (Hg.), Brill's Companion to the Reception of Herodotus in Antiquity and Beyond, Leiden/Boston 2016, 169–192.

TRILLMICH 1996 = W. TRILLMICH, Eine Wiederholung der Aeneas-Gruppe vom Forum Augustum samt ihrer Inschrift in Mérida (Spanien), *RM 103*, 1996, 119–138.

TURNER 1956 = E.G. TURNER, Two Unrecognised Ptolemaic Papyri, *JHS* 76, 1956, 95–98.

HOSE 2015 = M. HOSE, Intertextualität als hermeneutisches Instrument in spätantiker Literatur. Das Beispiel Ammianus Marcellinus, in: J. STENGER (Hg.), Spätantike Konzeptionen von Literatur, Heidelberg 2015, 81–96.

WEST 2011 = S.R. WEST, The Papyri of Herodotus, in: D. OBBINK/R. RUTHERFORD (Hg.), Culture in Pieces. Essays on Ancient Texts in Honour of Peter Parsons, Oxford 2011, 69–83.

WILKINSON 2005 = K.W. WILKINSON, Fragments of a Ptolemaic Thucydides Roll in the Beinecke Library, *ZPE* 153, 2005, 69–74.

ZANKER 1990 = P. ZANKER, Augustus und die Macht der Bilder, München 1990².

Winfried Schmitz
Bedrohte Latinitas. Sprachliche Veränderungen auf spätantik-frühmittelalterlichen Grabinschriften aus dem Rhein-Mosel-Gebiet

Abstract: The late Roman and early medieval funerary inscriptions (4.–7. c.) from the Rhine and Moselle area help us understand the process of linguistic change from Classical Latin to a late antique, Moselle provincial Latin and to an early Romanic language. The inscriptions show that Latin had been a spoken language in the cities and fort towns along the Rhine and the Moselle well into what is usually considered to be the Middle Ages. In comparison, funerary inscriptions from rural areas of the same region and period show a marked decline in latinity.

Zusammenfassung: Die spätantik-frühmittelalterlichen Grabinschriften des 4. bis 7. Jahrhunderts aus dem Gebiet von Rhein und Mosel lassen den Prozess sprachlicher Veränderungen vom Hochlatein über ein spätantik mosselländisches Provinziallatein zu einer frühromanischen Sprache nachvollziehen. Die Inschriften zeigen, dass in den Städten und Kastellorten an Rhein und Mosel Latein über die Epochengrenze zum Mittelalter gesprochen wurde und eine lebendige Sprache war. Im ländlichen Bereich ist demgegenüber auf den Grabsteinen ein deutlicher Rückgang von Latinität festzustellen.

Die Grabinschriften des 4. bis 7. Jahrhunderts n. Chr. bilden eine eigenständige und in sich relativ geschlossene Inschriftengruppe. Voraus geht ein deutlicher Rückgang in der Zahl der Inschriften während des 3. Jahrhunderts. Dem entspricht ein ebenso deutlicher Rückgang im 8. Jahrhundert, was seinen Grund auch darin hat, dass die Friedhöfe direkt an die Kirchen verlagert wurden, so dass die Erhaltungsbedingungen andere sind.[1] Die Inschriften des 4. bis 7. Jahrhunderts unterscheiden sich auch durch die äußere Form und das Material von den früh- und mittelkaiserzeitlichen Inschrif-

---

[1] SPICKERMANN 2015, 75 setzt den drastischen Rückgang der Inschriften ab etwa 250 n. Chr. an, bedingt durch den Verlust des Dekumatlandes und den Zusammenbruch des Gallischen Sonderreichs. Zur regionalen und zeitlichen Verbreitung in der frühen und hohen Kaiserzeit ebd. 75–79. – In Köln bilden die beiden für Kölner Erzbischöfe angefertigten Grabinschriften von 762 und 819 den Abschluss dieser Inschriftengruppe (SCHMITZ 1995, 645 Anm. 9). In Trier und in Mainz lässt sich eine stärkere Kontinuität feststellen; dennoch ist die Zahl der Inschriften aus dem 8., 9. und 10. Jahrhundert geringer als im 4.–7. Jahrhundert; FUCHS 2015, 63 schätzt für Trier nicht einmal 30 Inschriften des 7. und 8. Jh. statt über 1000 in den drei Jahrhunderten zuvor. Die Trierer Inschriften sind publiziert in RICG I; MERTEN 1990; FUCHS 2006 und 2012; MERTEN [in Vorber.], die Mainzer Inschriften in BEHRENS 1950 und BOPPERT 1971. Zur Verlegung der Friedhöfe an die Kirchen NIKITSCH 2015, 124 mit Anm. 59.

ten: Vielfach wurden Steine, darunter auch Architekturteile, wiederverwendet oder wenig geeignete Steinarten wie Granit- oder Tuffsteine mit Inschriften versehen.[2] Statt des in den ersten drei Jahrhunderten verbreiteten *hic situs est* finden sich auf den Inschriften der Spätantike und des frühen Mittelalters – nun zu Beginn des Grabtextes – Formulare wie *hic iacet, hic quiescit in pace* oder *hic pausat*, die die Hinwendung zum Christentum anklingen lassen. Statt der tria nomina herrscht nun Einnamigkeit vor, wobei zu den aus der lateinischen oder griechischen Sprache abgeleiteten Namen auch germanische treten. Namenssysteme sind in der Regel sehr langlebig – es sind Phänomene der longue durée –, und so verdeutlicht der Übergang zur Einnamigkeit einmal mehr den tiefgreifenden Wandel von der hohen zur späten Kaiserzeit.[3] Neben Inschriften, die ein korrektes Latein bieten oder die Verstorbenen mit einem Grabgedicht ehren, treten solche, die zahlreiche, für die Spätantike typische Vulgärformen aufweisen.[4] Die Inschriftengattungen schließlich reduzieren sich in der Spätantike weitgehend auf Grabinschriften; Weihesteine fehlen fast vollständig, Bauinschriften sind nur in sehr kleiner Zahl erhalten geblieben.[5] Die meisten Inschriften des 4. bis 7. Jahrhunderts sind christliche Grabinschriften, so dass man – etwas überspitzt formuliert – sagen kann, dass Weiheinschriften und Grabinschriften in eine Inschriftengattung zusammenfallen.[6] Die Grabinschriften der Spätantike und des frühen Mittelalters bleiben weitgehend stereotyp, trotzdem lassen sich an ihnen wichtige Beobachtungen zur Schriftlichkeit im Alltag der Spätantike ablesen.

Die Inschriften aus dem Gebiet von Rhein, Mosel und Maas der Zeit des 4. bis 7. Jahrhunderts bilden auch räumlich eine relativ geschlossene Gruppe. Insgesamt kennen wir aus diesem Gebiet etwa 1500 Inschriften und Inschriftenfragmente, wovon allein auf die kaiserliche Residenzstadt Trier ca. 1300 Inschriften entfallen, die in Formular und Schrift zwar eine Entwicklung durchlaufen, alles in allem aber ohne erkennbaren Bruch bis in karolingische Zeit hineinreichen.[7] Jeweils etwa 50 Inschrif-

---

2 ENGEMANN/RÜGER 1991, Nr. 16 (Tuffstein); Nr. 35 (Trachyt); Nr. 38 (Hälfte einer Säulentrommel); Nr. 39 (Gesims); SCHMITZ 1995, Nr. 5 (Granit).
3 Die Reduzierung allein auf das Cognomen weisen auch die Inschriften Südgalliens und auch Roms und Italiens auf (RICG XV; ICUR I-X). Bei den insgesamt 13 Belegen für Zweinamigkeit in Trier, die durchweg in das 4. Jh. zu datieren sind, handelt es sich um hochgestellte Personen (MERTEN 2015, 32).
4 KRAMER 2007, 13: „Unter dem Begriff Vulgärlatein faßt man die zwischen dem 3. Jahrhundert v. Chr. und dem 7. Jahrhundert n. Chr. überall im römischen Reich und in seinen Nachfolgestaaten auftretenden schriftsprachlichen Varianten der lateinischen Umgangssprache zusammen, also die Varianten, die nur in geringem Umfang von schulischer Bildung und Anlehnung an literarische Muster geprägt sind. Diese Form des Lateinischen fungierte als Sprache des vertrauten Umgangs, als Nähesprache, während die literarisch-offizielle Form des Lateinischen als Distanzsprache in Situationen formeller Prägung angewendet wurde". Zu den charakteristischen Veränderungen des Vulgärlateinischen ebd. 23–36.
5 Zu den spätantiken Weiheinschriften siehe SPICKERMANN 2003, 485–489; SPICKERMANN 2008, 246; SPICKERMANN 2015, 81–85; Bauinschriften: IKöln² 259; 261.
6 Singulär sind zwei Märtyreranrufungen auf Trierer Steinen, die in das 4. Jh. zu datieren sind (MERTEN 2015, 34).
7 MERTEN 2015.

ten sind es in den alten Provinzhauptstädten Köln und Mainz, zwei bis fünfzehn Inschriften in den Kastellorten am Rhein und an der unteren Mosel, also in Bonn, Remagen, Andernach, Koblenz, Boppard und Bingen sowie in Kobern-Gondorf.[8] Die Fundorte von Inschriften reichen im Norden bis zu einem vereinzelten Exemplar in Xanten, im Westen bis Jülich, Aachen und Maastricht, an der oberen Mosel bis Metz und am Rhein südwärts bis Worms (Abb. 1). Noch deutlicher wird die Konzentration spätantiker Latinitas im Rhein-Mosel-Gebiet, wenn man sich die Verteilung der Inschriften in größerem Maßstab ansieht; spätantik-frühmittelalterliche Inschriften fehlen nämlich am Oberrhein vollständig – die ersten Funde stammen erst wieder aus Kaiseraugst, vom Neuenburger und Genfer See und aus Chur.[9] Auch im Innern Galliens ist die Verbreitung solcher Inschriften deutlich geringer; allein in Südfrankreich, vor allem in Lyon und Vienne, finden sie sich wieder in hoher Zahl und räumlicher Dichte.[10] Die Gebiete von Rhein und Mosel und von Rhône und Saône sind also über die Epochengrenze und das Ende der römischen Herrschaft hinaus Regionen intensiver romanischer Siedlungs-, Bevölkerungs- und Sprachkontinuität.[11] Durch eine genauere Untersuchung der Inschriften lassen sich aber noch weitreichendere Aussagen über den Grad dieser Kontinuität gewinnen.

Viele der in Trier, Köln und Mainz aufgestellten Grabinschriften zeigen noch bis weit ins 5. und 6. Jahrhundert hinein ein korrektes Latein; die Kölner Inschriften zeichnen sich dadurch aus, dass viele von ihnen Grabgedichte sind oder Bestandteile von solchen aufgenommen haben.[12] Ohne große Sorgfalt eingeschlagen ist ein

---

8 Verbreitungskarten wurden vorgelegt in: BOPPERT 1988, 123; ENGEMANN/RÜGER 1991, XXII-XXIII; RISTOW 2007, Tafel 3; SCHMITZ 2001, 294–305 und SCHMITZ 2015, 88 Abb. 1; 102 Abb. 9; 103–111 (jeweils mit Fundangaben und Publikationsnachweis). Zur regionalen Verbreitung der Grabinschriften im Gebiet von Rhein, Maas und Mosel MERTEN 2015, 29; zu den Inschriften von Metz siehe jetzt VIPARD 2015.
9 Siehe die Verbreitungskarte SCHMITZ 2001, 295 mit den Nachweisen S. 296–305. Zu den spätantik-frühmittelalterlichen Inschriften der Schweiz CIMAH I-V.
10 RICG XV. Zu den Inschriften Aquitaniens siehe RICG VIII.
11 Zu diesen Indikatoren kultureller Kontinuität siehe WOLFF 1991. Die starke Kontinuität im Neuwieder Becken lässt sich auch an Hand der Mayener Keramik und der Basaltmühlsteine dokumentieren, die ohne Bruch von spätrömischer Zeit in das frühe Mittelalter reicht, so dass „ein Technik-, Wissens- und Produktionstransfer über das 5. Jahrhundert in das Frühmittelalter hinein zu vermuten" ist (GRUNWALD 2015, 193). Diese Kontinuität wird von LUTZ GRUNWALD auf die relative Sicherheit in diesem Raum bis in die Mitte des 5. Jh. zurückgeführt (ebd. 201–203). Vgl. auch GLAUBEN 2012, bes. 92–95.
12 So die Grabinschrift von dem Kölner Friedhof um die spätere Kirche St. Gereon (SCHMITZ 1995, Nr. 7; IKöln² 763; 2. Hälfte 4./Anfang 5. Jh.): *Hic iacet Martinianus qui laeta iuventae perdidit et patribus lacrimas dimisit in aevo. Hic vixit annos XXVI dies XVI m(inus/ensem). In d(eo/eum) ivit.* – „Hier liegt Martinianus, der um die Blüten der Jugend kam und den Eltern für alle Zeiten (nur) Tränen ließ. Hier lebte er an Jahren 26, abzüglich 16 Tage (oder: einen Monat und 16 Tage). Zu Gott ist er gegangen." Der von Mars abgeleitete Name Martinianus ist in der Spätantike häufiger belegt, wobei die Aneinanderreihung von Suffixen typisch für diese Zeit ist. Auf den Namen des Verstorbenen folgen einige Textbestandteile, die sehr häufig auf Grabgedichten zu finden sind. Allerdings sind Beginn und Schluss des Grabtextes nicht in das Versmaß eingepasst, so dass der Verfasser vermutlich Teile eines älteren Epigramms übernommen hat.

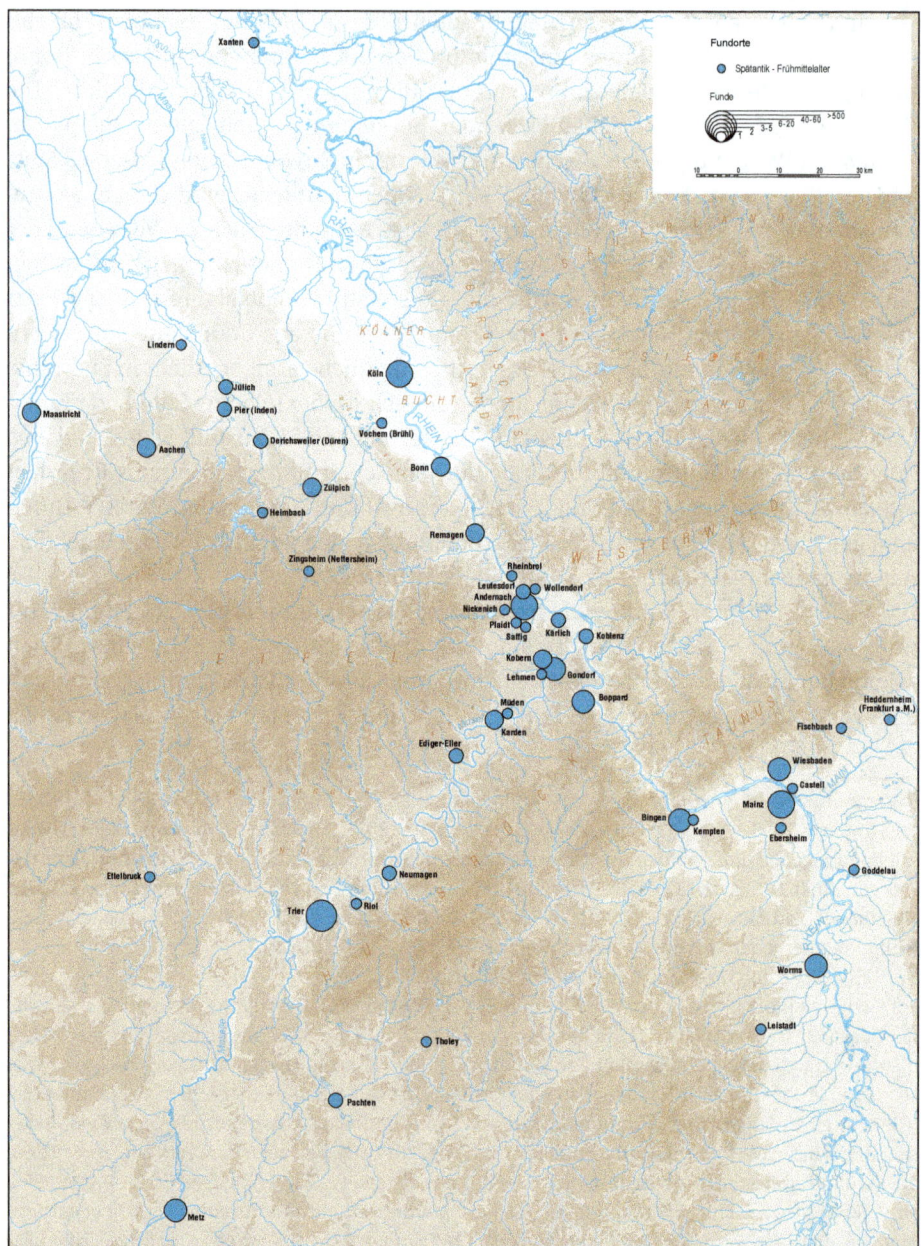

Abb. 1: Fundorte spätantik-frühmittelalterlicher Grabinschriften im Gebiet von Rhein, Mosel und Maas (Karte: Stefan Zoeldi, Geographisches Institut der Universität Bonn)

sprachlich ansprechendes und von Trauer und einer emotionalen Nähe gekennzeichnetes Grabgedicht, dass die Eltern dem früh verstorbenen Catulus aufgestellt haben: „Ach, der Vater reicht als Überlebender seinem Sohn traurige Gaben / und erweist ihm die Ehren, von denen er hoffte, sie würden ihm selbst erwiesen. / Oh Mutter, des Jungen Spiel und Lachen stets im Herzen tragend, / klagt sie und vermisst sein Ringen um süße Worte. / Catulus, dies ist sein Name, im Lichte (hier) weilte er dreimal zehn Monate".[13] Inschriften dieser sprachlichen Qualität setzen voraus, dass in den städtischen Zentren und auch in den größeren Kastellorten am Rhein die lateinische Sprache gepflegt und unterrichtet wurde.[14]

Eine Sprachkontinuität in den Rückzugsgebieten der römischen Bevölkerung lässt sich auch an solchen Inschriften nachweisen, die typisch spätantike Vulgärformen aufweisen, denn sie zeigen, dass Latein, wenn auch nicht mehr in der Aussprache des klassischen Latein, in diesen Regionen lebendig blieb. Die Steinmetze – wenn es denn noch professionelle Steinmetze gab – meißelten den Text häufig in der Form der gewandelten Aussprache ein. Ein schönes Beispiel dafür ist der Grabstein des Leo von dem Friedhof um St. Gereon in Köln, der aufgrund der langen Eingangsformel und der Verwendung von *transire* im Sinne von ‚sterben' in das späte 5. oder in das 6. Jahrhundert zu datieren ist und damit in die nachrömische Zeit gehört: *In oh tumolo reqiescet in pace bone memorie Leo. Vixet annus XXXXXII. Transiet nono Id(u)s Ohtuberes.* – „In diesem Grab ruht in Frieden seligen Angedenkens Leo. Er lebte 52 Jahre. Er schied dahin am 9. Tag vor den Iden des Oktober (7. Oktober)". Der kurze Grabtext enthält insgesamt zwölf Vulgärformen, wie sie für die Spätantike charakteristisch sind. Sie beruhen eindeutig nicht auf mangelnden Sprachkenntnissen, sondern sind ein Beleg für die Fortexistenz, ja für die Fortentwicklung des Lateinischen hin zu einer frühromanischen Sprache. Der Grabtext verweist auf eine gesprochene Sprache, die noch in Kontakt mit anderen romanischen Sprachgebieten stand.

Die Grabinschriften für Catulus und Leo zeigen auch, dass für die Angehörigen nicht der soziale Status der Familie durch die Angabe eines Berufs oder eines städ-

---

13 Schmitz 1995, Nr. 2; IKöln² 755: *Heu, genitor nato dat tristi{ti}a dona supestis*
quosque sibi solvi sperabat reddit honores.
O, mater lusus pueri risusque recordans
ingemi⟨t⟩ et dulcis recolit luctamina lingue.
Catulus huic nomen ter deni in lumine menses.
Lebek 1982 hatte sich aus metrischen Gründen für die Lesung *heu, genitor nato* in Zeile 1 und *recolit* in Zeile 4 ausgesprochen. Das Gedicht lasse einen Autor erkennen, der die Dichtersprache gut beherrschte und in Metrik und Prosodie zu Hause war. Vgl. auch das in Hexameterform gefasste Grabgedicht für Dessideratus aus Kobern-Gondorf (Schulze-Dörlamm 1990, 2, 254 f. Nr. 2725; Engemann/Rüger 1991, Nr. 23; Matijević 2010, 378–382 Nr. 102).
14 Die Grabinschriften Triers weisen auf eine sehr starke Kontinuität hin; dafür sprechen die weit überwiegend romanischen Namen, die korrekten Formulierungen und die gute Sprachbeherrschung auf hohem Niveau. In Trier fand die für die Spätantike typische Sprachentwicklung erst sehr spät ihren Niederschlag in den Inschriften (RICG I S. 75–77 § 96–97; Merten 2015, 33, 35).

tischen Amtes demonstriert werden sollte, sondern die Trauer der Familie und die Hinwendung zum Jenseits, eines in christlichem Sinne verstandenen Paradieses, im Vordergrund standen.[15] Der Name der oder des Verstorbenen ‚verbirgt sich' hinter der Eingangsformel oder ist darin eingebunden, ist nicht mehr in hervorgehobenen Lettern an den Anfang der Inschrift gesetzt. Die Grabmäler waren in der Regel auch keine großformatigen Steine oder Grabbauten mehr, sondern vielfach dünne Steintafeln, die durch einen Steinrahmen gefasst auf dem Grab lagen oder in einen Sarkophagdeckel eingelassen waren,[16] zu sehen und zu lesen nur, wenn man an das Grab herantrat. Textformeln wie „er ruhe in Frieden", „gläubig schied er in Frieden dahin", „in der Hoffnung auf ein ewiges Paradies" oder die Einbeziehung eines Psalmverses sind Ausdruck der Trauer und der Wünsche, wie sie die Hinterbliebenen dem Verstorbenen mitgeben und in denen sie selbst Trost zu finden hoffen.

Anhand des Formulars lassen sich indes deutliche habituelle Unterschiede zwischen den Bevölkerungsgruppen nachweisen. Auf den Grabsteinen von Romanen, also den Angehörigen der römischen Restbevölkerung, ist der Text ganz von christlichem Gedankengut geprägt: „In diesem Grab ruht in Frieden seligen Angedenkens Leo"[17].

Auf dem Kölner Grabstein des mit 3 Jahren verstorbenen Valentinianus wurde vermerkt, dass er im Taufgewand in Frieden hinschied (Abb. 2: *in albis cum pace recessit*).[18] Ein Grabstein des 5. Jahrhunderts aus dem Kastell Remagen endet mit dem Psalmvers: „Der Herr, unser Gott Jesus Christus, möge geruhen, mir seine Wege zu weisen, denen ich folgen kann".[19] Diese Grabinschriften, die zum Teil in die nachrömische Zeit gehören und alle aus Rückzugsgebieten der romanischen Bevölkerung

---

15 Berufsangaben finden sich nur auf wenigen spätantik-frühmittelalterlichen Grabinschriften: CIL XIII 3704; RICG I 56 (Trier; *negotiator*); ENGEMANN/RÜGER 1991, Nr. 19 (Gondorf; *medica*); EGGER 1954, Nr. 4; BOPPERT 1988, 134 (Andernach: *notarius*); FUCHS 2006, Nr. 7 (Trier: *arcarius ex cive Gabaletana* – „Schatzmeister, aus der Stadt Javals"). Eine Herkunftsangabe in SCHMITZ 1995, Nr. 3 (*civis Afer*). Für Trier sind Verstorbene in kaiserlichen Ämtern nachgewiesen (*a veste sacra*); ein cursus honorum ist allein für Masclinius Maternus auf einer Inschrift aus Zülpich belegt (CIL XIII 7918 von 352 n. Chr.). Häufiger begegnen nach wie vor Grabinschriften von Militärangehörigen und von Klerikern (zur Selbstdarstellung von Klerikern auf den Grabinschriften BINSFELD 2015; ebd. 57: vom 7./8. Jh. an tragen sie vielfach germanische Namen). Eine Zusammenstellung aller inschriftlich belegten Berufsangaben einschließlich der klerikalen und der Hofämter in Trier sowie militärischer Funktionen hat KRÄMER 1978 vorgelegt. Dabei arbeitet auch er heraus, dass die Nennung eines zivilen Berufs nur äußerst selten nachzuweisen ist. Deutlich häufiger seien Kleriker belegt (ebd. 26 f.).
16 So ließen sich auch Teile von Wandinkrustationen als Grabsteine wiederverwenden (z. B. SCHMITZ 1995, Nr. 37; 41). Grabstein in Steinfassung: RICG I 35, 38, 62; ENGEMANN/RÜGER 1991, Nr. 34; vgl. Nr. 31; in einen Sarkophagdeckel eingelassen war vermutlich der Stein ENGEMANN/RÜGER 1991, Nr. 23.
17 SCHMITZ 1995, Nr. 6; IKöln² 760.
18 SCHMITZ 1995, Nr. 10; IKöln² 765.
19 ENGEMANN/RÜGER 1991, Nr. 35; HEMGESBERG 1986. Vgl. auch FUCHS 2006, Nr. 16: „... Aus dem Leben scheidend ist ihr ein besseres zuteil geworden. Sie verdiente mit Christi Hilfe die ewige Krone. Ihr ist erlaubt, daß ihre Ruhe ehrenhalber (den Heiligen) beigesellt ist. ..." (Übersetzung R. FUCHS).

Abb. 2: Grabstein des Valentinianus aus Köln (Köln, St. Gereon; RGM Köln Foto-Nr. 20937)

stammen, geben Ausdruck von einer bereits einhundert bis zweihundert Jahre währenden christlichen Tradition in diesen romanisch geprägten Gebieten an Mosel und Rhein. Über die soziale Stellung des Verstorbenen im Diesseits erfahren wir nichts mehr. Die Hinwendung zu Gott steht im Vordergrund.

Von diesen christlich geprägten Inschriften sind solche zu unterscheiden, die sich von den Namen als solche von Franken bzw. Angehörigen anderer germanischer Gruppen zu erkennen geben.[20] Diese fränkischen Herren und adeligen Damen weisen in den Grabinschriften durchaus auf ihre hohe soziale Stellung hin. Der Grabstein des Flodericus (oder Hlodericus) aus Trier zeichnet sich nicht durch christliche Grabformeln aus (nur ein an den Anfang gesetztes Kreuz zeugt von seinem christlichen Glauben) und weist mit keinem Wort auf das Leben nach dem Tod hin. Ihm war es wichtiger festzuhalten, dass „er im Volke beliebt und in seinem Geschlecht der Vornehmste war". Seine Frau, eine *uxor nobelis*, hat ihm den Grabstein aufgestellt.[21] Aus

---

20 Auf den lateinischen Inschriften weisen viele dieser germanischen Namen romanisierte Elemente auf, z. B. die romanische Ersatzlautung [oa] für [wa]. Siehe z. B. FUCHS 2006, Nr. 4, 6, 10, 12, 19, 20, 23.
21 FUCHS 2006, Nr. 1 (Ende 6.–Anfang 8. Jh.): +*Hic requies data Hloderici* (oder: *Floderici*) *membra sepu[l]crum, qui capus in nomero vicarii nomine sumsit. Fuit in pupulo gratus et in suo genere pr[i]mus, cui uxor nobelis pro amore tetolum fie[ri] iussit, qui vixit in saeculo annus plus menus [..]L, cui deposicio fuit in saeculo VII [Kal(endas) Aug]ustas.* Als *vicarius* war Flodericus Stellvertreter des Grafen und übte

Abb. 3: Grabinschrift des Rainovaldus aus Leutesdorf
(Bonn, LVR-Landesmuseum; Inv. Nr. 2422; Neg. Nr. 608)

adeligem Geschlecht (*de nobile [g]enere*) ist auch Ludubertus, der vermutlich dem geistlichen Stand angehörte und im 8. Jh. bei St. Matthias beigesetzt wurde.[22] Der Grabstein des Rainovaldus aus Leutesdorf am Rhein (Abb. 3) beginnt zwar ebenfalls mit einem Kreuz und endet mit dem Wort *Amen*. Im Grabtext aber heben seine Eltern

---

unter anderem Gerichtsgewalt aus (Fuchs 2006, 4; vgl. Krämer 1978, 21 f.). Es gibt daneben allerdings auch Grabsteine mit germanischen Namen, deren Text ganz christlich gehalten ist, so z. B. der Grabstein des Hari[...] (Fuchs 2006, Nr. 11).

22 Fuchs 2006, Nr. 22; Binsfeld 2015, 53: auf den geistlichen Stand verweist die Bezeichnung *vir venerabiles*; er hat sein ganzes Vermögen dem hl. Petrus vermacht und wurde Kleriker. Vgl. Krämer 1978, 22 f.

hervor, dass ihn der „neidische Tod" aus dieser Welt entrissen hat, was einer christlichen Vorstellung vom Paradies eher entgegensteht.[23] Der in den Grabtext eingefügte Satz *puerum* (oder: *pueram*) *nubelem produxit in gentem* verweist auch hier auf die hohe soziale Stellung des Verstorbenen.[24]

In Inden-Pier (zwischen Köln und Aachen) wurde der Grabstein für die *domina* Cheldofrida gefunden, deren „Name erstrahlte und deren Nachkommen sich hohen Ansehens erfreuen".[25] Es ist sicher kein Zufall, dass alle diese Grabsteine germanische Namen aufweisen. Wir erkennen, dass sich hier zwei unterschiedliche Formen des Selbstverständnisses gegenüberstehen, ein römisch bzw. romanisch geprägtes, dem ein Bekenntnis zum christlichen Glauben ausreichte und bei dem die soziale Stellung weitgehend ausgeblendet wurde, und eines der romanisierten Germanen, die ihre soziale Stellung nach außen kenntlich machten, so wie dies die städtische Oberschicht in der frühen und mittleren Kaiserzeit auch praktiziert hatte.

Die spätantik-frühmittelalterlichen Inschriften, die in Trier, an der unteren Mosel und in Köln gefunden wurden, tragen fast ausschließlich römisch-griechische Namen, was als Ausweis einer starken Kontinuität gewertet werden kann (Abb. 4).

Auf den Mainzer Inschriften ist der Anteil von römischen Namen zwar noch bemerkenswert hoch, doch überwiegen dort, ebenso wie in Andernach und Koblenz, in Boppard und Worms germanische Namen, wenn auch in romanisierten Formen. Die Inschriften mit germanischen Namen gehören dabei vor allem in das ausgehende 6., 7. und 8. Jahrhundert. Möglicherweise war der Einfall der Sueben, Alanen und Vandalen am Mittelrhein an der Wende des Jahres von 406 auf 407 die Ursache dafür, dass das Mittelrheingebiet eine stärkere germanische Prägung aufweist. Die germanischen Namen zeugen jedenfalls davon, dass sich am Mittelrhein Germanen angesiedelt hatten, deren Oberschicht die römische Sitte übernahm, einen Grabstein mit lateinischer Inschrift aufzustellen. Die Grabsteine sind damit Zeugnisse einer Akkulturation von Romanen und Germanen in diesem Raum.[26]

Veränderungen in der Besiedlung des Rhein-Mosel-Gebietes lassen sich auch durch archäologische Surveys, archäobotanische Funde und Reliktwörter nachweisen. Alle drei Indikatoren lassen erkennen, dass in den ländlichen Gebieten, vor allem in Eifel und Hunsrück, die Bevölkerung das offene Land verlassen und Zuflucht in den Städten Trier, Köln und Mainz und dem geographisch günstig gelegenen Rhei-

---

23 ENGEMANN/RÜGER 1991, Nr. 32: *Inveda mors abstrait di secolum*.
24 Zu verstehen ist der Satz im Sinne von: „er führte ein adeliges Mädchen in die *gens*" (heiratete sie) oder „er führte einen adeligen Jungen als Unfreien in die *gens*".
25 ENGEMANN/RÜGER 1991, Nr. 42: *nomen eius refuls[it et pro]les clara*. Vgl. auch den Grabstein für einen *nobilis puer*, einen „adeligen Jungen", aus Köln (SCHMITZ 1995, Nr. 13).
26 Eine Auswertung des Namensmaterials hat HAUBRICHS 2014 vorgelegt. Den Übergang zu einer Dominanz germanischer Namen setzt FUCHS 2015, 63 für Trier in die Zeit zwischen ca. 650 und 800. Auch an den Bopparder Inschriften lässt sich der Wandel in der Dominanz der Namen feststellen. Dazu NIKITSCH 2015.

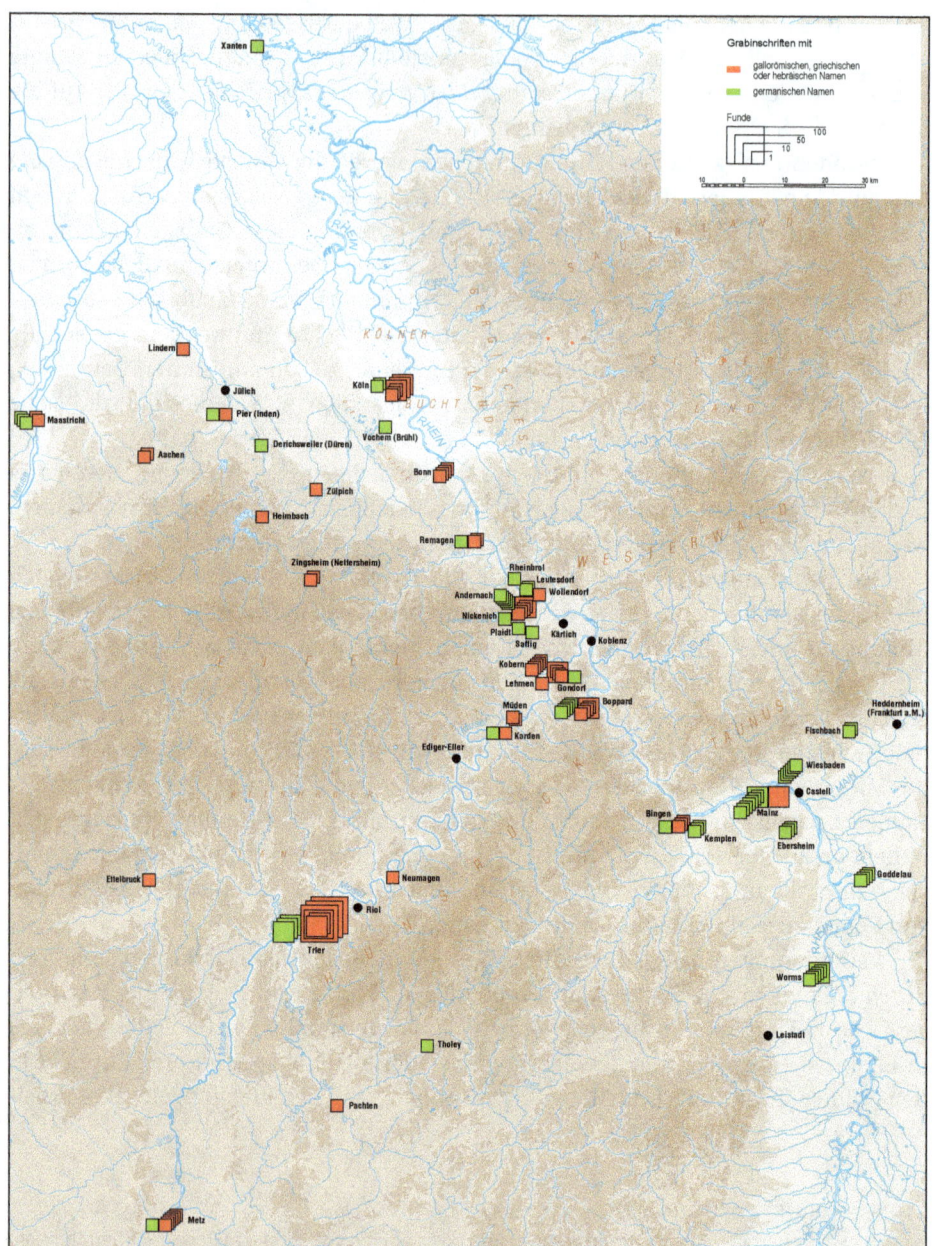

Abb. 4: Römische bzw. romanische und germanische Namen auf den spätantik-frühmittelalterlichen Grabinschriften im Gebiet von Rhein, Mosel und Maas (Karte: Stefan Zoeldi, Geographisches Institut der Universität Bonn)

Abb. 5: Grabinschrift des Dessideratus aus Kobern-Gondorf
(Bonn, LVR-Landesmuseum; Inv. Nr. 3100)

nengtal zwischen Bonn und Bingen mit stark bewehrten Kastellen gesucht hat.[27] Dieser Prozess wird durch die Grabinschriften bestätigt, nicht nur durch die Fundorte, sondern auch durch die Sprache, die seit der Spätantike in zunehmendem Maße vulgärlateinische Formen aufweist.

Vergleicht man die Sprache der Inschriften in den Kernzonen römischer Kontinuität bis in das frühe Mittelalter hinein mit den Inschriften des ländlichen Raums, zeigen sich unterschiedliche Entwicklungen. Ich möchte dies in einer Gegenüberstellung von Inschriften aus den Städten und Kastellen im Rhein- und Moseltal einerseits und solchen aus dem ländlichen Raum andererseits demonstrieren. Sehen wir uns dazu zunächst zwei Inschriften aus Kobern-Gondorf an der unteren Mosel an.[28] Von dort stammt die Grabinschrift, die die trauernden Eltern ihrem mit 9 Jahren verstorbenen Sohn auf das Grab setzten (Abb. 5):[29]

---

27 Zu den Siedlungsveränderungen in diesem Zeitraum AMENT 1992; MÜLLER-WILLE/OLDENSTEIN 1981; GECHTER/KUNOW 1986; STEIN 1989; SCHMITZ 2001. Zu den Reliktwörtern und Toponymen: BUCHMÜLLER-PFAFF 1990; KLEIBER/PFISTER 1992. Zur Besiedlungsgeschichte des Schweizer Mittellandes MARTIN 1979.
28 Zu den Inschriften von Kobern-Gondorf MATIJEVIĆ 2015.
29 CIL XIII 7642; ILCV 3450; ENGEMANN/RÜGER 1991, Nr. 23; MATIJEVIĆ 2010, 378–382 Nr. 102; DERS. 2015, 128 f.

Dura quidem frangit parvorum morte parentes
condicio rapido pr‹u›aecipitata gradu.
Spes aeterna tame‹n› trebuet solacia luctus
aetates teneras qu(o)d paradisus abet.
Sex super adiectis ad nonum mensebus a[n]n[um]
conditus hoc tumolo Dessideratus iaces.

„Mit dem bitteren Tod der Kleinen trifft die Eltern zwar
das schnellen Schrittes jäh hereinbrechende Schicksal.
Ewige Hoffnung jedoch spendet Trost in der Trauer;
ewige Jugend verheißt uns ja das Paradies.
Sechs Monate fügten sich nur zu den neun Jahren hinzu.
Geborgen im Grab, Dessideratus, liegst du hier."

Das Christusmonogramm, die beiden Tauben oder Pfaue unter dem Text und der Grabtext selbst geben Zeugnis vom christlichen Glauben der Familie. Der eher heidnischen Vorstellung vom schlimmen, jäh hereinbrechenden Schicksal wird die Hoffnung auf das Paradies entgegengestellt.[30] Es handelt sich bei diesem Grabstein um ein in Hexametern abgefasstes Grabgedicht. Solche Grabgedichte finden sich besonders häufig in den Gebieten mit einer starken römischen Tradition, in Köln und in Trier, aber auch im Rheinengtal und an der unteren Mosel.

Auch der Grabstein des Mauricius aus Gondorf weist sich durch die Symbole als christlicher Grabstein aus (Abb. 6):[31]

Hoc tetolo fecet Montana coniux sua Mauricio qui visit con elo annus dodece et portavit annus qarranta. Trasit die VIII K(a)l(endas) Iunias. – „Dieses Grab errichtete Montana, seine Frau, dem Mauricius, die mit ihm zwölf Jahre lebte und der vierzig Jahre alt wurde. Er starb am 8. Tag vor den Kalenden des Juni (25. Mai)". Diese Inschrift weist deutlich auf den Wandel in der gesprochenen Sprache, der spätlateinischen Umgangssprache hin, mit Indizien für den Quantitätenkollaps, Aussprachevereinfachungen, Schnellsprechformen und der Aufgabe der morphologischen Differenzierung:[32] Statt wie im klassischen Latein *cum illo* heißt es *con elo*, was näher

---

30 Zu den Jenseitsvorstellungen auf frühchristlichen Grabinschriften CLAUSS 2015.
31 CIL XIII 7645; ILCV 2917; SCHULZE-DÖRLAMM 1990, 2, 53 f. Nr. 457; ENGEMANN/RÜGER 1991, Nr. 18; KRAMER 2007, 115–120 (mit ausführlichem sprachwissenschaftlichen Kommentar); MATIJEVIĆ 2010, 335–340 Nr. 85. Dazu MATIJEVIĆ 2015, 131 f.; KRAMER 1997. BARME 2008, 15 f. fordert erstmals eine aus romanischer Perspektive unternommene sprachwissenschaftliche Auswertung der spätantiken und frühmittelalterlichen Inschriften.
32 KRAMER 1997, 285: Aussprachevereinfachungen lassen sich beim Wandel von -x- > -s- und -ns- zu -s- und dem Wegfall des auslautenden -m feststellen; Schnellsprechformen sind *dodece* und *qarranta*; *qui* statt *quae* zeigt die mangelnde morphologische Differenzierung an. Ebenso KRAMER 2007, 116 zum Quantitätenkollaps bei *tetolo*, *fecet*, *elo*, *annus* und *dodece*, Aussprachevereinfachungen, Schnellsprechformen und fehlender Genusdifferenzierung (vgl. ebd. 119 zu *dodece* und *qarranta*).

Abb. 6: Grabinschrift des Mauricius aus Kobern-Gondorf
(Bonn, LVR-Landesmuseum; Inv. Nr. 3513; Neg. Nr. 1941)

am Italienischen *con lei* ist,[33] statt des klassischen *duodecim* heißt es *dodece* (italienisch *dodici*) und statt *quadraginta* gibt der Text *qarranta*, als direkte Vorgängerform des romanischen Zahlwortes *douze* (<altfrz. *doze*) bzw. des italienischen *quaranta* und des französischen *quarente*.[34] An dem einleitenden *hoc tetolo* statt *hunc titulum* zeigen sich die Auswirkungen des sog. Quantitätenkollapses; es kam also nicht mehr primär auf die Quantität der Vokale (Länge oder Kürze), sondern auf die Qualität (geöffnete oder geschlossene Aussprache) an. Dieser Wandel hatte zur Folge, dass in betonten Silben langes ē und kurzes ĭ sowie langes ō und kurzes ŭ in eine Lautung zusammenfielen, was in den unbetonten Silben noch weiterreichte. Zudem ging das schwache

---

[33] KRAMER 1997, 284 f. plädiert mit gutem Grund dafür, *con elo* als *cum illo* zu deuten, mit einleitendem genusneutralen *qui* und Subjektwechsel im zweiten Nebensatz.
[34] KRAMER 1997, 285. BARME 2008 stellt folgende Merkmale des spätantiken moselländischen Provinziallateins an der Mosel, einer Vorstufe des Moselromanischen, zusammen: die Reduktion des stimmlosen Labiovelarlautes [kʷ] zu [k] vor den Vokalen i, a und ae, sodann xs, cs, sx und xx für den Doppelkonsonanten [ks] (x), also die Reduzierung von [ks] zu [s] (z. B. x > ss > s wie in vixit > visit) sowie die Ersetzung des finalen -m durch -n. Diese Verschiebung von x zu s könnte auch der Grund für die eigentümliche Schreibweise des S in manchen Inschriften sein, das einem X angenähert ist (z. B. bei dem *milix Florentius* in Mainz, dem *hic quiexcit* in Wiesbaden oder dem *hic requiixcit* und *annux* auf der Inschrift der Audulpia aus Boppard).

Auslaut-m verloren, so dass aus *hunc titulum* ein *hoc tetolo* wurde.³⁵ Auch der merkwürdige Satzbau zeugt von deutlich zu beobachtenden Veränderungen der gesprochenen Sprache. Aber: Die Inschrift, die in das 6. Jahrhundert datiert wird, ist ein Zeugnis der im Moseltal verbliebenen und Latein sprechenden Bevölkerung, wobei die gesprochene Alltagssprache die geschriebene Sprachform beeinflusst hat.³⁶ Die Namen Montana und Mauricius folgen römischer Tradition.³⁷ STEFAN BARME hat aus den Belegen für die Reduktion des stimmlosen Labiovelarlautes [kʷ] zu [k] einen sozialen Unterschied in der romanischen Restbevölkerung herausgelesen. Innerhalb der Oberschicht sei die korrekte Aussprache [kʷ] üblich geblieben, da viele der Inschriften die Reduktion zu [k] nicht aufweisen, während von den sozial niedrigeren Schichten – vielleicht allein im nähesprachlichen Bereich – [kʷ] häufig zu [k] reduziert wurde. Hinsichtlich der Übernahme von Ortsnamen hätten sich die Franken nach ihrer Eroberung des Mosellandes an der Aussprache der sozial höherstehenden Gruppe orientiert und daher auch bei den Ortsnamen das [kʷ] beibehalten.³⁸

Stellen wir diesen Inschriften aus dem Moseltal andere aus dem ländlichen Raum, also aus Eifel und Voreifel, gegenüber. Aus Nettersheim-Zingsheim stammt der Grabstein, den Villatius seiner Frau aufgestellt hat:³⁹ *Vi[l]latius et nati nostri kari coiugi mei So[l/i]e t[it]lum ponet. Anorum XXX[--].* – „Villatius und unsere Kinder setzt meines liebes Gattin Sola/Soia (diesen) Grabstein. ...unddreißig Jahre alt". Die Namen sind römisch, oder eher pseudorömisch („der von der Villa"), aber: das Verb steht im Singular statt im Plural, und *kari* und *mei* sind *coiugi* angeglichen (statt des korrekten *carae coniugi meae*). Folgen wir weiteren Inschriften, die an der Rur gefunden wurden: ein neuerer Fund aus Heimbach beginnt mit *D(is) M(anibus) Innocentius* und wird in den Zeilen 4 und 5 korrekt weitergeführt mit *qui vixsit annos XXV*, also „Den Totengöttern. Innocentius ..., der 25 Jahre gelebt hat" (Abb. 7).⁴⁰ In Zeile 3 hingegen findet sich eine – durchaus gut lesbare – Buchstabenkombination (ENDNNIT[---]), in die kein Sinn zu bringen ist.

In Inden-Pier bei Düren setzte Ru[--- (vielleicht Rufinus oder Rufina) dem Ehepartner einen Grabstein (Abb. 8): *Ru[---] R[---] coiux karisimus memoria facere qui*

---

35 KRAMER 1997, 283. Zu den sprachlichen Veränderungen, die die Inschrift für Mauricius aufweist, siehe im Einzelnen KRAMER 1997 und BARME 2008, 18.
36 KRAMER 1997, 286.
37 Vgl. auch die Grabinschrift des Presbyters Aetherius aus Bingen: *[A]etherius pres[bi]ter tegitur hoc tomulo carus omnibus moribus et gratia sed ma(xime) Chr(ist)o* [oder: *max(ime) p<r>o*] *fede et relegione probatus*, sowie die Inschrift des Lektors Leupadus aus Koblenz: *Hic requiscet Leupa[r]dus lector amatus gratus in fede provatus qui vixit annus XVIIII cui pater Leuninus [---* (BINSFELD 2015, 58 f.).
38 BARME 2008, 20. Vgl. auch KRAMER 2007, 118 zu *coniux sua*: Bei Verwandtschaftsbezeichnungen vermeide man im literarischen Latein die besitzanzeigenden Fürwörter, wohingegen die Umgangssprache mit Vorliebe die Possessivpronomina verwende, um die persönlichen Beziehungen zum Ausdruck zu bringen.
39 CLAUSS 1976, 2 f. Nr. 1; ENGEMANN/RÜGER 1991, Nr. 40.
40 MEIER/SCHMITZ 1999, 296–298 Nr. 3.

Abb. 7: Grabinschrift des Innocentius aus Heimbach an der Rur (Bonn, LVR-Landesmuseum; Inv. Nr. E 58/93)

vixit anos XXVI. – „Für Ru[---] hat R[---], liebster Gatte, Grabmal zu machen, der/die 26 Jahre gelebt hat".[41]

Voran geht möglicherweise ein nach links gesetztes D für *Dis Manibus*. Eine wirkliche Satzstruktur weist der Inschrifttext kaum mehr auf. Den Endpunkt in dieser Reihe bildet ein Inschriftenstein aus Geilenkirchen-Lindern, bei dem nur noch zu erkennen ist, dass es sich um eine Grabinschrift handeln sollte; man erkennt am Anfang *hic*, dann in Zeile 2–3 *et co(niux) tetulum pater vix(it)* und weitere, nicht sicher zu deutende Zeichen. Von einer sinnvollen Satzstruktur ist auch dort nicht viel zu erkennen.[42] Vor

---

41 ENGEMANN/RÜGER 1991, Nr. 43.
42 ENGEMANN/RÜGER 1991, Nr. 44.

Abb. 8: Grabinschrift aus Inden-Pier (Bonn, LVR-Landesmuseum; Inv. Nr. 78/85; Neg. Nr. 1829/87; Foto: H. Lilienthal)

wenigen Jahren ist ein weiterer Neufund aus einem Gräberfeld in Zülpich hinzugekommen, der offenbar den Wunsch zeigt, einen Grabstein mit Inschrift zu setzen, dessen Dedikant aber nicht in der Lage war, überhaupt einen lateinischen Text zu formulieren, ja der nicht einmal der lateinischen Schrift mächtig war (Abb. 9).[43]

---

[43] Schmitz 2012.

Abb. 9: Grabinschrift aus Zülpich
(Bonn, LVR-Landesmuseum;
Inv. Nr. E_2012_1_99_210)

Also: je weiter man in den ländlichen Bereich hineingeht, desto mehr lässt die Kenntnis der lateinischen Sprache nach. Es handelt sich in diesen Fällen eindeutig um einen Rückgang von Latinität und nicht um Veränderungen einer gesprochenen Sprache.[44] Auffällig ist außerdem, dass keine dieser Grabinschriften ein Zeichen christlichen Bekenntnisses trägt, weder in den Textformeln noch in Form eines Christogramms. Wir haben also auf der einen Seite romanisch und christlich geprägte Inschriften im Rhein- und Moseltal, auf der anderen Seite Inschriften aus dem ländlichen Raum, die sprachlich deutlich abfallen und noch pagan ausgerichtet sind, wie das *Dis Manibus* zeigt.

Herangezogen werden sollten für den Aspekt bedrohter oder inzwischen verlorener Latinität auch die Grabsteine ohne Inschrift, die von Angehörigen aufgestellt wurden, die wie die Romanen ein steinernes Grabmal wünschten, aber offensichtlich der lateinischen Sprache und der Schrift nicht mächtig waren und die den Grabstein daher mit geometrischen Verzierungen und Symbolen füllten. Solche anepigraphen

---

[44] Zur Verbreitung der Schriftlichkeit in den Provinzen des Römischen Reichs siehe auch die Beiträge in: SCHOLZ/HORSTER 2015. In einem der Beiträge dieses Sammelbandes arbeitet Markus Scholz heraus, dass in der hohen Kaiserzeit die Schriftlichkeit im ländlichen Raum kaum hinter der in den Städten und *vici* nachstand (SCHOLZ 2015).

Grabmäler finden sich vor allem im Neuwieder Becken, aber auch im Trierer Raum (Abb. 10–13).[45]

Die mit ornamentalen Mustern und Symbolen verzierten Grabsteine und die Grabinschriften aus dem ländlichen Raum dokumentieren einen Rückgang, wenn nicht die Unkenntnis lateinischer Sprache. Eine Bestätigung findet dies in einer Passage eines um 475 n. Chr. verfassten Briefs an den in Trier residierenden *comes* Arbogast. Sidonius Apollinaris dankt Arbogast für seinen „wohlformulierten Brief" (*litterae litteratae*) und feiert ihn, der aus einer romanisierten fränkischen, inzwischen zum Christentum übergetretenen Familie entstammt, als Verteidiger antiker Bildung und Rhetorik.[46] Sein Brief sei mit großer Hochschätzung und großem Respekt vor den römischen Tugenden und einer Weltläufigkeit verfasst, die aus dem Quell römischer Beredsamkeit gespeist seien:[47]

„Der Du aus der Mosel trinkst und doch die Sprache des Tibers von Dir gibst, der Du, auch wenn Du unter Barbaren lebst, keine Barbarismen kennst und so durch Deine Zunge und Deinen Arm den alten Führern gleichst, deren Rechte nicht weniger den Schreibgriffel zu führen wusste als das Schwert. So hat die Pracht römischer Rede, wenn es sie noch irgendwo gibt, nachdem sie in den belgischen und rheinischen Landen längst verschwunden ist, in Dir ihre Zuflucht gefunden, und solange Du lebst und die Rede pflegst, kommen, obwohl an der Grenze die lateinische Herrschaft gefallen ist, die lateinischen Worte nicht ins Wanken".[48] Hält man sich die lateinischen Grabinschriften aus dem ländlichen Gebiet des Rhein-Mosel-Raums vor Augen, kann man wohl nur bestätigen, dass in großen Teilen der „belgischen und rheinischen Lande" die Pracht römischer Rede vergangen ist und „die lateinischen Worte ins Wanken geraten sind" (*Latina verba titubant*).

An den Inschriften lässt sich also der Prozess einer allmählichen Siedlungsveränderung nachvollziehen, der auch durch die archäologische Forschung zu belegen ist.

---

45 Eine umfassende Zusammenstellung dieser der nachrömischen Zeit angehörenden Grabsteine ohne Inschrift vom Niederrhein bietet NISTERS-WEISBECKER 1983; zum Mittelrheingebiet ENGEMANN/ RÜGER 1991, 7–19 (Verbreitungskarte ebd. 8 f.) und Nr. 48–72; zum Trierer Land BÖHNER 1958.
46 Arbogasts Vater Arigius war als *comes* sein Vorgänger im Amt, seine Mutter stammte aus einer vornehmen galloromanischen Familie.
47 Sidonius Apollinaris epist. 4,17,1: *quarum utique virtutum caritas prima est, ...; tum verecundia, ...; tertia urbanitas, ...*
48 Sidonius Apollinaris epist. 4,17,1: *... et Quirinalis impletus fonte facundiae potor Mosellae Tiberim ructas, sic barbarorum familiaris, quod tamen nescius barbarismorum, par ducibus antiquis lingua manuque, sed quorum dextera solebat non stilum minus tractare quam gladium. (2) quocirca sermonis pompa Romani, si qua adhuc uspiam est, Belgicis olim sive Rhenanis abolita terries in te resedit, quo vel incolumi vel perorante, etsi apud limitem [ipsum] Latina iura ceciderunt, verba non titubant* (Übersetzung BOTERMANN 2005, 403). Zu Arbogast in Trier: ANTON 1984; ANTON 1987, 50–59; HEINEN 1996, 267–269; NONN 2010, 103–107. Zum Rückgang von lateinischer Sprache und Bildung in den spätantiken nordwestlichen Provinzen BOTERMANN ebd. 403–404; vgl. KRAMER 1999, 19: „Politisch-kulturelle Einheit bringt sprachliche Einheit mit sich, politisch-kulturelle Zersplitterung bewirkt sprachliche Zersplitterung".

Abb. 10–13: Anepigraphe Grabsteine aus Andernach und Kobern (Bonn, LVR-Landesmuseum; Inv. Nr. 2206; 2421; 4823; 10147; Neg. Nr. 237; 2280/91; Foto: H. Lilienthal)

Die Einfälle von Germanen seit der Mitte des 3. Jahrhunderts n. Chr. führten im ländlichen Bereich der römischen Nordwestprovinzen zu sehr unsicheren Verhältnissen, die viele bäuerliche Höfe zur Aufgabe zwangen; die Bewohner zogen sich in Städte oder in weiter südlich gelegene Gebiete des römischen Reiches zurück. Im 4. Jahrhundert leisteten die römischen Kaiser nochmals gewaltige Anstrengungen, um den Schutz der germanischen und gallischen Provinzen zu gewährleisten: Kaiser Constantin ließ in Köln eine feste Rheinbrücke und einen stark befestigten Brückenkopf, das Kastell in Köln-Deutz, anlegen.[49] Kastellbauten in Remagen, Andernach, Koblenz, Boppard und Bingen schützten die Rheingrenze, und in Eifel und Hunsrück wurden zahlreiche Höhenbefestigungen und befestigte Straßenposten errichtet.[50] Aber nach dieser Konsolidierung im 4. Jahrhundert sank die Bevölkerungsdichte, bedingt durch neue Einbrüche germanischer Gruppen ins Rheinland, drastisch.[51] Eine Auswertung von Landschaftsbegehungen hat ergeben, dass verschiedene Landschaftsräume vollständig verlassen wurden, andere wie die in römischer Zeit landwirtschaftlich intensiv bebauten fruchtbaren Lößplatten zwischen Aachen und Köln weitgehend aufgegeben und allein Güter am Rande der Lößterrasse weiterhin bewirtschaftet wurden. Die fränkischen Bestattungsplätze setzen im Rheinland vielfach erst im 6. und im 7. Jahrhundert ein, so dass es im ländlichen Raum nach den archäologischen Funden nur an wenigen Orten eine Besiedlungskontinuität gegeben hat. Belegt ist außerdem, dass vom 3. Jahrhundert an die Wälder zunahmen und die Feuchtwiesen in den Talauen verbuschten. Die fortschreitende Bewaldung erreichte um 500 n. Chr. ihren Höhepunkt. Die in römischer Zeit intensiv betriebene Landwirtschaft war in diesem Raum zum Erliegen gekommen. Erst zu Beginn des 6. Jh. begannen wieder ackerbauliche Aktivitäten, wie Anzeichen von Brandrodungen belegen. Die waldfreien Flächen nahmen wieder zu, die teils als Grünland, teils zum Anbau von Getreide genutzt wurden.[52]

Weitere Hinweise für eine römische Siedlungs- und Sprachkontinuität im Rhein- und Moseltal und für eine fehlende Kontinuität im ländlichen Bereich bietet die historische Sprachwissenschaft. Sie hat sich intensiv mit dem Namen- und Sprachgut im Rheinland und speziell mit dem Problem der gegenseitigen Beeinflussung von romanischer und germanischer Sprache, der Interferenz, auseinandergesetzt und versucht, mit Hilfe sprachlicher Nachweise die Frage zu klären, in welchen Gebieten und wie lange romanische Bevölkerungsgruppen einer Germanisierung standgehalten haben

---

49 Dazu SCHMITZ 1995, 754–761.
50 Dazu HUNOLD 2012.
51 Zum Bevölkerungsrückgang in ländlichen Gebieten WIGHTMAN 1985, 243–266, die zu Recht darauf hinweist, dass die Entwicklung von Ort zu Ort und von Gebiet zu Gebiet sehr unterschiedlich verlief. Vgl. dazu auch KAISER 1993, 94. Den Aspekt der Rückwanderung in das Innere des Reiches betont WIERSCHOWSKI 1998, 124 f.
52 GECHTER/KUNOW 1986; vgl. dazu BRIDGER 1994. Zum Mittelrheingebiet siehe des weiteren ZELLER 1992, 212–235; NEUMAYER 1993. – Zu den sprachwissenschaftlichen und paläobotanischen Befunden siehe die bei SCHMITZ 1997, 199–201 Anm. 19 und 23–32 angegebene Literatur, zur Gallia Belgica WIGHTMAN 1985, 262–263.; vgl. PRINZ 1994, 181.

bzw. eine Zweisprachigkeit festzustellen ist. Anhand von Orts- und Flurnamen, von Relikt- und Lehnwörtern kann die Sprachwissenschaft die Besiedlungsgebiete der romanischen Restbevölkerung ermitteln und das sukzessive Aufgehen romanischer Reliktareale in das germanische Sprachgebiet nachzeichnen. Einer dieser Gradmesser ist z. B. die Häufigkeit von Orts- und Flurnamen mit romanischer Endbetonung wie Tawern, Tarnehrs und Riol, Ortsnamen, bei denen die Umsetzung ins Fränkisch-Deutsche nie erfolgt ist. Auch bei den romanischen Reliktwörtern zeigt sich eine deutlich zu erkennende Konzentration auf das Moseltal, so dass davon auszugehen ist, dass dort bis in das 10. Jahrhundert hinein noch eine Zweisprachigkeit bestand.[53] Romanische Sprachrelikte sind umso häufiger, je später sich die Germanisierung in den betreffenden Gebieten durchgesetzt hat. Endbetonte Orts- und Flurnamen sind im Moseltal sehr häufig. Neuere sprachwissenschaftliche Untersuchungen haben gezeigt, dass auch am Mittelrhein zwischen Bonn und Bingen auf römische Zeit zurückgehende Orts- und Flurnamen zu belegen sind, so dass die Existenz eines ursprünglichen romanischen Bevölkerungssubstrats auch im Rheinengtal nicht zu bezweifeln ist. Auch das Rheinengtal bildete eine romanische Sprachinsel, doch der Sprachenwechsel ist dort deutlich früher anzusetzen als im Moseltal.[54] Die spätantiken und frühmittelalterlichen Grabinschriften bestätigen, dass nicht nur das Moseltal, sondern auch das Rheintal zwischen Worms und Köln ein Gebiet war, in dem eine starke römische Restbevölkerung auch nach dem Abzug von römischem Militär und römischer Verwaltung geblieben war, inzwischen weitgehend den christlichen Glauben angenommen hatte und ein spätrömisches mosselländisches Provinziallatein, schließlich eine frühromanische Sprache gesprochen hat. In das ländliche Gebiet war in der Spätantike das Christentum noch nicht vorgedrungen; die lateinische Sprache konnte sich dort nicht kontinuierlich bis ins Mittelalter halten.

---

53 Die sprachwissenschaftlich nachzuweisende Zweisprachigkeit zeugt von regionaler Kontinuität galloromanischer Bevölkerungsreste. Dazu mit Verweis auf frühere Literatur und regionale Einzelstudien PFISTER 1992; PFISTER 1995. „Vermutlich erfolgte die germanische Siedlungstätigkeit zuerst im Bereich der siedlungsgünstigeren Böden (Bliesgau, Saargau, Seillegau, Nahetal) und war vom Erschließungsgrad des Landes und der Romanendichte abhängig. ... Gebiete, die außerhalb dieser germanischen Kerngebiete liegen, z. B. das Moseltal östlich von Neumagen oder die Reliktgebiete um Prüm, Mayen, im Hochwald, im Hunsrück, im Raum Saint-Avold und im Westricher Raum, konnten ihr Romanentum länger bewahren" (PFISTER 1992, 90). Ähnlich PFISTER 1995, 76–77.: „Die höchste Reliktwortfrequenz weist das Moselgebiet auf, es entspricht in dieser Hinsicht dem Befund der Toponomastik. Sie kann nur durch den besonders intensiven romanisch-germanischen Sprachkontakt erklärt werden, durch das lange Fortdauern des moselromanischen Substrats bis ins Hochmittelalter. Wenn die Reliktwortzahl an der Mittelmosel am höchsten ist (Trier, Schweich, Graach, Cochemer Krampen) und an der Untermosel und am Mittelrhein sowie an der Obermosel und an der Saar sich um die Hälfte vermindert, so sehen wir an dieser staffelförmigen Abnahme ein Spiegelbild der Entromanisierung im Moselbereich". Vgl. ebd. 78.
54 Zu den sprachwissenschaftlichen Forschungen im Rhein- und Moselgebiet siehe die bei SCHMITZ 1997, 199–201 Anm. 23–32 genannte Literatur, außerdem BUCHMÜLLER-PFAFF 1990. Ein anderes Bild ergibt sich für den Oberrhein. Die Rückzugsräume, angezeigt durch Reliktwörter, lagen dort im Schwarzwald (KLEIBER/PFISTER 1992).

Literaturverzeichnis

CIL XIII	Corpus Inscriptionum Latinarum XIII. Inscriptiones trium Galliarum et Germaniarum Latinae. Ed. O. Hirschfeld u. C. Zangemeister, Berlin 1899–1943.
CIMAH I–V	Corpus inscriptionum medii aevi Helvetiae. Die frühchristlichen und mittelalterlichen Inschriften der Schweiz, I-V. Ed. C. Pfaff, Freiburg/Schweiz 1977–1997.
IKöln[2]	B. und H. Galsterer, Die römischen Steininschriften aus Köln (Kölner Forschungen Bd. 10), Mainz 2010.
ICUR I–X	Inscriptiones Christianae urbis Romae septimo saeculo antiquiores N.S., Rom 1922–1992.
ILCV	E. Diehl, Inscriptiones latinae christianae veteres 1–3, Berlin 1925–1931.
RICG I	N. Gauthier, Recueil des inscriptions chrétiennes de la Gaule antérieures à la renaissance carolingienne I. Première Belgique, Paris 1975.
RICG VIII	F. Prévot, Recueil des inscriptions chrétiennes de la Gaule antérieures à la renaissance carolingienne VIII. Aquitaine Première, Paris 1997.
RICG XV	F. Descombes, Recueil des inscriptions chrétiennes de la Gaule antérieures à la renaissance carolingienne XV. Viennoise du nord, Paris 1985.

AMENT 1992 = H. AMENT, Romanen an Rhein und Mosel im frühen Mittelalter, *BJ* 192, 1992, 261–271.
ANTON 1984 = H.H. ANTON, Trier im Übergang von der römischen zur fränkischen Herrschaft, *Francia* 12, 1984, 1–52.
ANTON 1987 = H.H. ANTON, Trier im frühen Mittelalter, Paderborn 1987.
BARME 2008 = S. BARME, Latein – Vulgärlatein – Moselromanisch. Zur Sprache der frühchristlichen Grabinschriften im Raum Trier, *Zeitschrift für romanische Philologie* 124, 2008, 15–30.
BEHRENS 1950 = G. BEHRENS, Das frühchristliche und merowingische Mainz, *Wegweiser RGZM* 20, Mainz 1950.
BINSFELD 2015 = A. BINSFELD, Kirchliche Würdenträger in Trierer Inschriften, in: L. CLEMENS/H. MERTEN/C. SCHÄFER (Hg.), Frühchristliche Grabinschriften im Westen des Römischen Reiches. Beiträge zur Internationalen Konferenz „Frühchristliche Grabinschriften im Westen des Römischen Reiches", Trier, 13.–15. Juni 2013, Trier 2015, 37–60.
BÖHNER 1958 = K. BÖHNER, Die fränkischen Altertümer des Trierer Landes, Berlin 1958.
BOPPERT 1971 = W. BOPPERT, Die frühchristlichen Inschriften des Mittelrheingebietes, Mainz 1971.
BOPPERT 1988 = W. BOPPERT, Die frühchristlichen Grabinschriften von Andernach, in: K. SCHÄFER (Hg.), Andernach im Frühmittelalter – Venantius Fortunatus, Andernach 1988, 121–144.
BOTERMANN 2005 = H. BOTERMANN, Wie aus Galliern Römer wurden. Leben im Römischen Reich, Stuttgart 2005.
BRIDGER 1994 = C. BRIDGER, Die römerzeitliche Besiedlung der Kempener Lehmplatte, *BJ* 194, 1994, 61–164.
BUCHMÜLLER-PFAFF 1990 = M. BUCHMÜLLER-PFAFF, Siedlungsnamen zwischen Spätantike und frühem Mittelalter. Die -(i)acum-Namen der römischen Provinz Belgica Prima, *Beihefte zur Zeitschrift für romanische Philologie*, Tübingen 1990.
CLAUSS 1976 = M. CLAUSS, Neue Inschriften im Rheinischen Landesmuseum Bonn, *Epigraphische Studien* 11, 1976, 1–39.
CLAUSS 2015 = M. CLAUSS, Jenseitsvorstellungen in frühchristlichen Grabinschriften, in: L. CLEMENS/H. MERTEN/C. SCHÄFER (Hg.), Frühchristliche Grabinschriften im Westen des Römischen Reiches. Beiträge zur Internationalen Konferenz „Frühchristliche Grabinschriften im Westen des Römischen Reiches", Trier, 13.–15. Juni 2013, Trier 2015, 17–27.
EGGER 1954 = R. EGGER, Römische Grabsteine der Merowingerzeit, *BJ* 154, 1954, 146–158.

ENGEMANN/RÜGER 1991 = J. ENGEMANN/C.B. RÜGER (Hg.), Spätantike und frühes Mittelalter. Ausgewählte Denkmäler im Rheinischen Landesmuseum Bonn. *Führer des Rheinischen Landesmuseums Bonn und des Rheinischen Amtes für Bodendenkmalpflege Bd. 134*, Köln/Bonn 1991.

ENGEMANN 1995 = J. ENGEMANN, Epigraphik und Archäologie des spätantiken Rheinlands, in: H. GIERSIEPEN/R. KOTTJE (Hg.), Inschriften bis 1300. Probleme und Aufgaben ihrer Erforschung, Opladen 1995, 11–45.

FUCHS 2006 = R. FUCHS, Die Inschriften der Stadt Trier I (bis 1500), Wiesbaden 2006.

FUCHS 2012 = R. FUCHS, Die Inschriften der Stadt Trier II (1500–1674), Wiesbaden 2012.

FUCHS 2015 = R. FUCHS, Epigraphische Zeugnisse des frühen Mittelalters in Trier. Einige methodische Überlegungen, in: L. CLEMENS/H. MERTEN/C. SCHÄFER (Hg.), Frühchristliche Grabinschriften im Westen des Römischen Reiches. Beiträge zur Internationalen Konferenz „Frühchristliche Grabinschriften im Westen des Römischen Reiches", Trier, 13.–15. Juni 2013, Trier 2015, 61–74.

GECHTER/KUNOW 1986 = M. GECHTER/J. KUNOW, Zur ländlichen Besiedlung des Rheinlandes in römischer Zeit, *BJ* 186, 377–396 (wiederabgedruckt in: R.F.J. JONES [Hg.], First Millenium Papers. Western Europe in the First Millenium, A. D., Oxford, 1986, 109–128).

GLAUBEN 2012 = A.M. GLAUBEN, Der vicus von Mayen (Lkr. Mayen Koblenz). Alte Grabungen und neue Forschungen, in: M. GRÜNEWALD/S. WENZEL (Hg.), Römische Landnutzung in der Eifel. Neue Ausgrabungen und Forschungen, Mainz 2012, 87–98.

GRUNWALD 2015 = L. GRUNWALD, Produktion und Warendistribution der Mayener Ware in spätrömischer und frühmittelalterlicher Zeit, in: C. LATER/M. HELMBRECHT/U. JECKLIN-TISCHHAUSER (Hg.), Infrastruktur und Distribution zwischen Antike und Mittelalter, Hamburg 2015, 191–207.

HAUBRICHS 2014 = W. HAUBRICHS, Vitalis, Remico, Audulpia. Romanische, germanische und romanisierte Personennamen in frühen Inschriften der Rhein- und Mosellande, *Rheinische Vierteljahrsblätter* 78, 2014, 1–37.

HEINEN 1996 = H. HEINEN, Frühchristliches Trier. Von den Anfängen bis zur Völkerwanderung, Trier 1996.

HEMGESBERG 1986 = H. HEMGESBERG, Die frühchristliche Meteriola-Inschrift aus Remagen, *BJ* 186, 1986, 299–314, Abb. 1.

HUNOLD 2012 = A. HUNOLD, Mayen und der Katzenberg (Lkr. Mayen-Koblenz). Spätrömische Höhenbefestigungen als Elemente der Landnutzung, in: M. GRÜNEWALD/S. WENZEL (Hg.), Römische Landnutzung in der Eifel. Neue Ausgrabungen und Forschungen, Mainz 2012, 99–110.

KAISER 1993 = R. KAISER, Das römische Erbe und das Merowingerreich, München 1993.

KLEIBER/PFISTER 1992 = W. KLEIBER/M. PFISTER, Aspekte und Probleme der römisch-germanischen Kontinuität. Sprachkontinuität an Mosel, Mittel- und Oberrhein sowie im Schwarzwald, Stuttgart 1992.

KRÄMER 1978 = K. KRÄMER, Titel und Berufsbezeichnungen auf Frühchristlichen Inschriften der Rheinlande, *Kurtrierisches Jahrbuch* 18, 1978, 8–27.

KRAMER 1997 = J. KRAMER, Zwischen Latein und Moselromanisch: die Gondorfer Grabinschrift für Mauricius, *ZPE* 118, 1997, 281–286.

KRAMER 1999 = J. KRAMER, Sind die romanischen Sprachen kreolisiertes Latein?, *Zeitschrift für romanische Philologie* 115, 1999, 1–19.

KRAMER 2007 = J. KRAMER, Vulgärlateinische Alltagsdokumente auf Papyri, Ostraka, Täfelchen und Inschriften, Berlin/New York 2007.

LEBEK 1982 = W.D. LEBEK, Ein neues lateinisches Versepitaph aus Köln, *ZPE* 45, 1982, 88–90.

MARTIN 1979 = M. MARTIN, Die spätrömisch-frühmittelalterliche Besiedlung am Hochrhein und im schweizerischen Jura und Mittelland, in: J. WERNER /E. EWIG, Von der Spätantike zum frühen Mittelalter. Aktuelle Probleme in historischer und archäologischer Sicht, Sigmaringen 1979, 411–446.

MATIJEVIĆ 2010 = K. MATIJEVIĆ, Römische und frühchristliche Zeugnisse im Norden Obergermaniens. Epigraphische Studien zu unterer Mosel und östlicher Eifel, Rahden in Westfalen 2010.

MATIJEVIĆ 2015 = K. MATIJEVIĆ, Frühchristliche Grabinschriften von der Untermosel: Kobern-Gondorf und Umgebung, in: L. CLEMENS/H. MERTEN/C. SCHÄFER (Hg.), Frühchristliche Grabinschriften im Westen des Römischen Reiches. Beiträge zur Internationalen Konferenz „Frühchristliche Grabinschriften im Westen des Römischen Reiches", Trier, 13.–15. Juni 2013, Trier 2015, 125–135.

MEIER/SCHMITZ 1999 = M. MEIER/W. SCHMITZ, Zu einigen spätantiken und frühmittelalterlichen Inschriften aus dem Rheinland, ZPE 124, 1999, 293–299.

MERTEN 1990 = H. MERTEN, Katalog der frühchristlichen Inschriften des Bischöflichen Dom- und Diözesanmuseums Trier, Trier 1990.

MERTEN 2015 = H. MERTEN, Frühchristliche Grabinschriften in Trier. Stand der Bearbeitung, in: L. CLEMENS/H. MERTEN/C. SCHÄFER (Hg.), Frühchristliche Grabinschriften im Westen des Römischen Reiches. Beiträge zur Internationalen Konferenz „Frühchristliche Grabinschriften im Westen des Römischen Reiches", Trier, 13.–15. Juni 2013, Trier 2015, 29–36.

MERTEN [in Vorber.] = H. MERTEN, Katalog der frühchristlichen Inschriften aus St. Maximin in Trier [in Vorber.].

MÜLLER-WILLE/OLDENSTEIN 1981 = M. MÜLLER-WILLE/J. OLDENSTEIN, Die ländliche Besiedlung des Umlandes von Mainz in spätrömischer und frühmittelalterlicher Zeit, BerRGK 62, 1981, 261–316.

NEUMAYER 1993 = H. NEUMAYER, Merowingerzeitliche Grabfunde des Mittelrheingebietes zwischen Nahe- und Moselmündung, Mainz 1993.

NIKITSCH 2015 = E.J. NIKITSCH, Frühchristliche Grabinschriften am Mittelrhein, in: L.CLEMENS/H. MERTEN/C. SCHÄFER (Hg.), Frühchristliche Grabinschriften im Westen des Römischen Reiches. Beiträge zur Internationalen Konferenz „Frühchristliche Grabinschriften im Westen des Römischen Reiches", Trier, 13.–15. Juni 2013, Trier 2015, 113–124.

NISTERS-WEISBECKER 1983 = A. NISTERS-WEISBECKER, Grabsteine des 7.–11. Jahrhunderts am Niederrhein, BJ 183, 1983, 175–326.

NONN 2010 = U. NONN, Die Franken, Stuttgart 2010.

PFISTER 1992 = M. PFISTER, Die Moselromania aus romanistischer Sicht, in: W. KLEIBER/M. PFISTER, Aspekte und Probleme der römisch-germanischen Kontinuität: Sprachkontinuität an Mosel, Mittel- und Oberrhein sowie im Schwarzwald, Stuttgart 1992, 71–97.

PFISTER 1995 = M. PFISTER, Die sprachliche Situation zwischen Maas und Rhein im Frühmittelalter, in: K. GÄRTNER/G. HOLTUS (Hg.), Beiträge zum Sprachkontakt und zu den Urkundensprachen zwischen Maas und Rhein, Trier 1995, 61–96.

PRINZ 1994 = F. PRINZ, Formen, Phasen und Regionen des Übergangs von der Spätantike zum Frühmittelalter: Reliktkultur – neue Ethnica – interkulturelle Synthese im Frankenreich, in: F. STAAB (Hg.), Zur Kontinuität zwischen Antike und Mittelalter am Oberrhein, Sigmaringen 1994, 171–192.

RISTOW 2007 = S. RISTOW, Frühes Christentum im Rheinland. Die Zeugnisse der archäologischen und historischen Quellen an Rhein, Maas und Mosel, Münster 2007.

SCHMITZ 1995 = W. SCHMITZ, Die spätantiken und frühmittelalterlichen Grabinschriften in Köln (4.–7. Jahrhundert), Kölner Jahrbücher 28, 1995, 643–776.

SCHMITZ 1997 = W. SCHMITZ, Zur Akkulturation von Romanen und Germanen im Rheinland. Eine Auswertung des inschriftlichen Materials, Das Altertum 43, 1997, 177–202.

SCHMITZ 2001 = W. SCHMITZ, Spätantike und frühmittelalterliche Grabinschriften als Zeugnisse der Besiedlungs- und Sprachkontinuität in den germanischen und gallischen Provinzen, in: T. GRÜNEWALD (Hg.), Germania inferior. Besiedlung, Gesellschaft und Wirtschaft an der Grenze der römisch-germanischen Welt, Berlin/New York 2001, 261–305.

Schmitz 2012 = W. Schmitz, Zwei neue spätantik-frühmittelalterliche Grabsteine aus Zülpich, in: 25 Jahre Archäologie im Rheinland 1987–2011, Stuttgart 2012, 135–137.
Schmitz 2015 = W. Schmitz, Neue spätantik-frühmittelalterliche Grabinschriften in der Provinz Germania secunda, in: L. Clemens/H. Merten/C. Schäfer (Hg.), Frühchristliche Grabinschriften im Westen des Römischen Reiches. Beiträge zur Internationalen Konferenz „Frühchristliche Grabinschriften im Westen des Römischen Reiches", Trier, 13.–15. Juni 2013, Trier 2015, 87–111.
Scholz/Horster 2015 = M. Scholz/M. Horster (Hg.), Lesen und Schreiben in den römischen Provinzen. Schriftliche Kommunikation im Alltagsleben, Mainz 2015.
Scholz 2015 = M. Scholz, Tumbe Bauern? Zur Schriftlichkeit in ländlichen Siedlungen in den germanischen Provinzen und Raetien, in: M. Scholz/M. Horster (Hg.), Lesen und Schreiben in den römischen Provinzen. Schriftliche Kommunikation im Alltagsleben, Mainz 2015, 67–89.
Schulze-Dörrlamm 1990 = M. Schulze-Dörrlamm, Die spätrömischen und frühmittelalterlichen Gräberfelder von Gondorf, Berlin 1990.
Spickermann 2003 = W. Spickermann, Germania Superior. Religionsgeschichte des römischen Germanien I, Tübingen 2003.
Spickermann 2008 = W. Spickermann, Germania Inferior. Religionsgeschichte des römischen Germanien II, Tübingen 2008.
Spickermann 2015 = W. Spickermann, Das Ende der Weihinschriftenkultur in den beiden Germanien, in: L. Clemens/H. Merten/C. Schäfer (Hg.), Frühchristliche Grabinschriften im Westen des Römischen Reiches. Beiträge zur Internationalen Konferenz „Frühchristliche Grabinschriften im Westen des Römischen Reiches", Trier, 13.–15. Juni 2013, Trier 2015, 75–85.
Stein 1989 = F. Stein, Die Bevölkerung des Saar-Mosel-Raumes am Übergang von der Antike zum Mittelalter, *Archaeologia Mosellana* 1, 1989, 89–195.
Vipard 2015 = P. Vipard, Les inscriptions chrétiennes de Metz: une mise à jour du corpus, in: L. Clemens/H. Merten/C. Schäfer (Hg.), Frühchristliche Grabinschriften im Westen des Römischen Reiches. Beiträge zur Internationalen Konferenz Frühchristliche Grabinschriften im Westen des Römischen Reiches, Trier 2015, 13.–15. Juni 2013, Trier 2015, 137–150.
Wierschowski 1998 = L. Wierschowski, Grenzverläufe und Migrationsverhalten im Nordwesten des Römischen Reiches, in: A. Gestrich/M. Krauss (Hg.), Migration und Grenze, Stuttgart 1998, 124–140.
Wightman 1985 = E.M. Wightman, Gallia Belgica, London 1985.
Wolff 1991 = H. Wolff, Die Kontinuität städtischen Lebens in den nördlichen Grenzprovinzen des römischen Reiches und das Ende der Antike, in: W. Eck/H. Galsterer (Hg.), Die Stadt in Oberitalien und in den nordwestlichen Provinzen des Römischen Reiches, Mainz 1991, 287–318.
Zeller 1992 = G. Zeller, Die fränkischen Altertümer des nördlichen Rheinhessen, 2 Bde., Stuttgart 1992.

List of Authors

1. **Prof. Dr. Antonio Caballos**, Universidad de Sevilla, Departamento de Historia Antigua, caballos@us.es
2. **Asst. Prof. Dr. W. Graham Claytor**, Hunter College of the City University of New York, Department of Classical and Oriental Studies, graham.claytor@hunter.cuny.edu
3. **Prof. em. Dr. Harry Falk**, Freie Universität Berlin, ehem. Institut für die Sprachen und Kulturen Südasiens, falk@zedat.fu-berlin.de
4. **Prof. Dr. William V. Harris**, Columbia University New York, History Department, wvh1@columbia.edu
5. **Benjamin Hartmann**, lic. phil., Historisches Seminar, Universität Zürich, hartmann.bj@gmail.com
6. **Prof. Dr. Marietta Horster**, Johannes Gutenberg-Universität Mainz, Lehrstuhl Alte Geschichte, horster@uni-mainz.de
7. **Prof. Dr. Sabine Huebner**, Universität Basel, Fachbereich Alte Geschichte, sabine.huebner@unibas.ch
8. **Prof. Dr. Anne Kolb**, Universität Zürich, Historisches Seminar, kolb@hist.uzh.ch
9. **Dr. Amina Kropp**, Universität Mannheim, Romanisches Seminar, kropp@phil.uni-mannheim.de
10. **Prof. Dr. Feng Li**, Columbia University New York, Early Chinese History and Archaeology, fl123@columbia.edu
11. **Asst. Prof. Dr. Irene Madreiter**, Universität Innsbruck, Institut für Alte Geschichte und Altorientalistik, Zentrum für Alte Kulturen, Irene.Madreiter@uibk.ac.at
12. **Prof. Dr. Kai Ruffing**, Universität Kassel, Alte Geschichte, kai.ruffing@uni-kassel.de
13. **Prof. Dr. Winfried Schmitz**, Universität Bonn, Alte Geschichte, wschmitz@uni-bonn.de
14. **Prof. Dr. Paul Schubert**, Université de Genève, Unité de Grec Ancien, paul.schubert@unige.ch
15. **Prof. Dr. Michael A. Speidel**, Universität Warschau / Universität Bern / Universität Zürich, mspeidel@sunrise.ch
16. **Prof. Dr. Wolfgang Spickermann**, Universität Graz, Institut für Alte Geschichte und Altertumskunde, wolfgang.spickermann@uni-graz.at
17. **Dr. Roger Tomlin**, University of Oxford, Roman History and Epigraphy, roger.tomlin@wolfson.ox.ac.uk
18. **Prof. em. Dr. Josef Wiesehöfer**, Christian-Albrechts-Universität zu Kiel, Institut für Klassische Altertumskunde, Alte Geschichte, jwiesehoefer@email.uni-kiel.de
19. **Dr. Katharina Zinn**, University of Wales Trinity Saint David, Lampeter, Egyptian Archaeology and Heritage, k.zinn@uwtsd.ac.uk

Fotograph of the Participants during the Conference

Index

Literary Sources

Anon. De mul.
  7   133 n. 143
App. civ.
  1,1,11–12   358 n. 33
Apul. met.
  9,17   145
Aristot. mund.
  398a30–35   116 n. 10
Aristot. pol.
  1321b13–31   321 n. 5
  1337a33–34   147
  1337b24–26   147
Arr. an.
  6,11,8   369 n. 16
  6,30,2 f.   104
  10   45 n. 4
Ascon. Corn.
  58   358 n. 33, 34
Athen.
  14, 652f-653a   56 n. 29
  14, 633d-e   138 n. 161
Auson. Epitaphia
  31, 9–10   313 n. 141
Caes. Gall.
  6,14   44
Cass. Dio
  37,43,2   358 n. 33
  54,5,4–5   179 n. 1
  57,2,3   182 n. 15
  69,8,1,2   355 n. 20
Cassiod. var.
  12,21   357 n. 30,
                                358–359 n. 37
Cic. Att.
  4,18,5   201 n. 1
Cic. Catil.
  4,15   353 n. 10
Cic. dom.
  74   353 n. 10
Cic. fam.
  2,10,3.   369 n. 17
Cic. leg.
  3,46   353 n. 7
Cic. Mur.
  25   352 n. 3
Cic. nat. deor.
  3,74   355 n. 19
Cic. rep.
  1,54   369 n. 16
  2,27   369 n. 16
Cic. Verr.
  2,3,26   357 n. 32
  2,3,171–187   352 n. 5, 353 n. 10,
                                355 n. 22
Clem. strom.
  1,16,76,10   133 n. 143
Cod. Iust.
  9,18   263 n. 4
Cod. Theod.
  9,16   262–263 n. 5
Curt.
  3,3,9   138 n. 161
  5,1,22   138 n. 161
  5,4,4.10   104
  5,13,6–7   122 n. 53
  7,5,28 f.   104
  9,5,11   369 n. 17
Demetr. de eloc.
  213–215   113 n. 1
Dig.
  1.2.2.4   306 n. 101
  50,6,7 (Tarrutienus
    Paternus)   189 n. 43
Diod.
  12,12,4   146
  17,109,3–5   104
Diog. Laert.
  10,6   148 n. 17
Gal
  3,28   216 n. 61
Esr
  4,17–22; 6,6–12; 7,
    12–26   114 n. 2
Est
  1,22   119 n. 32
  3,12   114 n. 2
  8,9   119 n. 32

Eus. HE
- 6,23 — 167 n. 16

Fest.
- 359,8–10 — 357 n. 30
- 446,26–29 — 356 n. 24

FGrHist
- 70 F149 — 147

Frontin. aqu.
- 2,100 — 357 n. 29

Gildas, De Excidio
- 85.2 — 215 n. 57

Hdt.
- 1,123,3–124,3. — 114 n. 2
- 1,132 — 138 n. 161
- 1,136 — 123 n. 67
- 3,68,4–5 — 134 n. 146
- 3,119,3–5 — 134 n. 147
- 5,14,2 — 114 n. 2
- 7,239 — 115 n. 8
- 8,8,1–2 — 116 n. 10

Herondas
- 4,27–29 — 365

Hor. Carm.
- 3,30,1 — 291 n. 5

Iust.
- 1,2,1ff. — 133 n. 143

Lex XII tab.
- 8,8a-b — 264 n. 9

Liv.
- 9,46,1–12 — 351 n. 2
- 33,100,10 — 369 n. 16

Mart.
- 1,2 — 357 n. 28

Menander
- F 702 (Körte) — 133 n. 144

Nik. v. Damask. de virt.
- 1 p.335,20 — 113 n. 1

Origenes c. Cels.
- 1,24 — 279 n. 84
- 5,45 — 279 n. 84

Patricius, Confessio
- 9–12 — 216 n. 58

Paus.
- 5,27,5–6 — 138 n. 161

Petron. Sat.
- 58,7 — 8

Philostr. soph.
- 2,12[593] — 371 n. 23

Plat. leg.
- 7,804c-e — 147

Plat. Phaidr.
- 275c-279b — 99

Plin. nat.
- 3,3 — 305 n. 96
- 3,3,7 — 292 n. 21, 298 n. 60
- 3,3,13 — 307 n. 111
- 3,3,15 — 296 n. 42
- 3,6,3f. — 106 n. 27
- 6,35,181–182 — 179 n. 1
- 34,20,97 — 312 n. 140
- 34,21,99 — 304 n. 95

Plut. Alex.
- 37,1 — 104

Plut. Cato minor
- 16,2–3 — 353 n. 6
- 28,1 — 358 n. 33

Plut. Them.
- 6,3 — 105 n. 25, 122 n. 53

Pol.
- 2,56 — 370 n. 17
- 31,31 — 146

Quint. inst.
- 10,2,1 — 368
- 12,2,24 — 148 n. 17

R. Gest. div. Aug.
- 26,5 — 180 n. 1

SHA Hadr.
- 7,6 — 355 n. 20

Sidonius Apollinaris epist.
- 4,17,1 — 404 n. 46 und 47

Strab.
- 2,5,8 — 154
- 4,5,3 — 154
- 10,4,20 — 147 n. 14
- 15,2,9 — 57 n. 31
- 15,3,14 — 138 n. 161
- 15,3,18 — 123 n. 67
- 16,4,22–24 — 180 n. 1
- 17,1,54 — 179 n. 1

Suet. Tib.
- 70 — 375 n. 34

Tac. Agr.
- 21,1 — 205 n. 18

Tac. ann.		Xen. an.	
3,63,4	312 n. 139	1,2,17.	105 n. 25, 122 n. 53
14,33	205 n. 13, 17	1,9,2–6	123 n. 67
Theophrast		4,4,5	105 n. 25, 122 n. 53
(Stob. 4, p. 193 Nr. 31 Meineke)	133 n. 144	8,12	105 n. 25
Thuk.		Xen. hell.	
1,21,1	369 n. 14	7,1,36–37; 5,1,31	114 n. 2
1,29,3	114 n. 2	7,1,37	105 n. 25
1,137,2. 138,1	104	Xen. Kyr.	
3,38,4–5	369 n. 14	1,2,2–12	123 n. 67
4,15	114 n. 2	4,5,26–34	114 n. 2
8,85,1–2	105 n. 25, 122 n. 53	7,5,86	123 n. 67
Val. Max.		8,1,23	138 n. 161
4,1,10	358 n. 35	8,6,10	123 n. 67
Verg. Aen.		8,6,17–18	116 n. 10
6,851–853	106		

Inscriptions

AE		2002, 192	182 n. 15
1919, 60	182 n. 15	2003, 2040	190 n. 50
1930, 57	196 n. 70	2004, 998	246 n. 39
1940, 82	196 n. 70	2004, 1223	196 n. 70
1952, 49	302 n. 78, 307 n. 106	2007, 1044	248 n. 55
		2009, 1799	296 n. 40
1955, 21	303 n. 81	Binsfeld 2015	
1955, 238	196 n. 70, 197 n. 72	58 f.	400 n. 36
		Britannia	
1960, 158	297 n. 48	17, 1986, 450, No. 84	207 n. 28
1962, 287	301 n. 72	20, 1989, 329, No. 3	218 n. 67
1969/70, 633	196 n. 70, 197 n. 72	26, 1995, 387, No. 28	212 n. 45
		28, 1997, 461, No. 20	207 n. 29, 208
1981, 134	192 n. 61	40, 2009, 321, No. 14	213 n. 48
1981, 690	244 n. 20, 28	CIL	
1983, 476–477	301 n. 74	I 593	294 n. 28
1984, 508	182 n. 15	I^2 581	306 n. 102
1984, 650	244 n. 20, 28	I^2 709	195 n. 68
1987, 500	297 n. 49	II^2/5, 732	301 n. 75
1989, 63	192 n. 61	II^2/5, 783	310 n. 128
1990, 740	251 n. 72	II^2/5, 900	292 n. 17
1991, 1025	296 n.45	II^2/5, 1022	182 n. 15, 291 n. 9, 293 n. 26
1994, 910	296 n. 43		
1994, 923	301 n. 73	II^2/7, 187	311 n. 130
1994, 1282	251 n. 72	II^2/7, 188	311 n. 131
1994, 1284	251 n. 74	II^2/7, 334	303 n. 85
1999, 891	182 n. 15	II^2/7, 897	299 n. 62
2001, 555	196 n. 70	II^2/7, 898	299 n. 62

II²/7, 899	299 n. 62	VI 37045	195 n. 68
II²/7, 900	299 n. 62	VIII 1090	251 n. 73
II²/7, 901	299 n. 62, 63	VIII 18065	196 n. 70
II²/7, 974	299 n. 66	VIII 18067–8	196 n. 70
II²/7, 976	299 n. 66	VIII 18084	196 n. 70
II²/7, 977	299 n. 66	IX 338	300 n. 70
II²/7, 979	299 n. 66	X 104	306 n. 102
II²/7, 980	299 n. 66	X 5426	304 n. 90, 309 n. 118
II 1179	303 n. 86		
II 1342	302 n. 79	XI 1354	309 n. 118
II 1343	302 n. 79	XIII 2887	244 n. 22
II 1373	293 n. 25	XIII 3592	253 n. 86
II 1380	298 n. 57	XIII 3704	392 n. 15
II 1423	298 n. 57	XIII 5035–5037	250 n. 69
II 1963	291 n. 11	XIII 5035–5041	250 n. 70
II 1964	291 n. 10	XIII 5046	249 n. 63
II 2015	310 n. 128	XIII 5054	249 n. 61, 250 n. 64
II 5368	306 n. 105		
II 5409	302 n. 79	XIII 5315	254 n. 93
II 6278	225 n. 12, 13, 291 n. 12, 292 n. 20	XIII 5479	243 n. 19
		XIII 5597–5604	243 n. 16
III 6178–79	196 n. 70	XIII 5688	246 n. 41
III 6580	196 n. 70	XIII 6131	249 n. 58
III 6627	196 n. 70–71	XIII 6145	249 n. 57
III 7106	225 n. 12	XIII 6474	250 n. 66
III 8110	196 n. 70	XIII 6562	254 n. 93
III 10307	192 n. 62	XIII 6681	196 n. 70
III 14214	196 n. 70	XIII 6801	196 n. 70
III 14507	196 n. 70	XIII 7252	248 n. 49
IV 1904	1 n. 3; 151	XIII 7253	248 n. 53
IV 1906	1 n. 3	XIII 7642	397 n. 28, 398
IV 2461	1 n. 3	XIII 7645	398 n. 30
IV 2487	1 n. 1, 151, 290 n. 4	XIII 7918	392 n. 15
IV 5380	229	XIII 8010	251 n. 74
VI 793	192 n. 61	XIII 8492	251 n. 74
VI 967	355 n. 20	XIII 8610	251 n. 74
VI 1057	196 n. 70	XIII 8646	242 n. 13
VI 31140–47	196 n. 70	XIII 8701	244 n. 28
VI 31149–52	196 n. 70	XIII 8705	251 n. 74
VI 31162	251 n. 73	XIII 8771	251 n. 72, 251 n. 78
VI 31234	196 n. 70		
VI 32323	182 n. 15	XIII 8777	251 n. 74
VI 32515–23	196 n. 70	XIII 10027.212a	251 n. 74
VI 32525–31	196 n. 70	XIII 10027.212b	251 n. 74
VI 32533	196 n. 70	XIII 10027.212d	251 n. 74
VI 32536	196 n. 70	XIII 11473	249 n. 61, 250 n. 64
VI 32542–44	196 n. 70		
VI 32547	196 n. 70	XIII 11605	247 n. 43
VI 32623–40	196 n. 70	XIV 2258	192 n. 61

XIV 4301	182 n. 15	Nr. 23	389 n. 13, 392
XIV 4303	182 n. 15		n. 16
XVI, app. 12	189 n. 48	Nr. 32	395 n. 22
CILA, Se		Nr. 35	388 n. 2, 392
927	292 n. 15, 307		n. 18
	n. 108	Nr. 38	388 n. 2
1052	291 n. 13	Nr. 39	388 n. 2
1053	292 n. 14	Nr. 40	400 n. 38
Clauss 1976		Nr. 42	395 n. 24
Nr. 60	251 n. 74	Nr. 43	401 n. 40
dfx		Nr. 44	401 n. 41
1.4.2/2	280 n. 88	Fuchs 2006	
1.4.4/8–12	269 n. 30	Nr. 1	393 n. 20
1.5.4/1	262 n. 3	Nr. 4	393 n. 19
2.1.2/1	277 n. 74	Nr. 6	393 n. 19
2.2.2/1	273 n. 54	Nr. 7	392 n. 15
2.3.1/1	265 n. 15	Nr. 10	393 n. 19
3.1/1	273 n. 52	Nr. 11	394 n. 20
3.2/8	270 n. 33	Nr. 12	393 n. 19
3.2/36	275 n. 60	Nr. 19	393 n. 19
3.14/5	275 n. 59	Nr. 20	393 n. 19
3.22/18	267 n. 24	Nr. 22	394 n. 21
3.22/29	273 n.46	Nr. 23	393 n. 19
4.1.3/15	270 n. 34	González/Bermejo 2016 a	
4.2.1/1	278 n. 79	274–275, n. 1	295 n. 34
4.3.1/1	273 n. 52	275–276, n. 2	295 n. 35
4.4.1/1	267 n. 22	276–278, n. 3	295 n. 36
5.1.4/3	273 n. 48	HEp 1994	
5.1.5/12	280 n. 88	825	292 n. 18
5.1.7/1	281 n. 89	IG	
8.3/1	275 n. 62	II^2 1009	369 n. 15
11.1.1/16	278 n. 78	II^2 1009	369 n. 15
11.1.1/27	279 n. 81	II^2 1041	369 n. 15
11.1.1/28	268 n. 28, 269	IKöln^2	
	n. 31, 278 n. 81,	259; 261	388 n. 5
	279 n. 82	755	389 n. 13
11.1.1/34	267 n. 24	763	389 n. 12
11.2.1/8	273 n. 47	765	392 n. 17
11.2.1/11	272 n. 45	ILB	
11.2.2/1	269 F n. 30	29	253 n. 86
11.3.1/1	275 n. 58	ILS	
DTA		18	306 n. 102
106	267 n. 23	505	192 n. 61
107	267 n. 23	1010	248 n. 53
Egger 1954		2157	196 n. 70
Nr. 4	392 n. 15	1591	303 n. 86
Engemann/Rüger 1991		4552	249 n. 63
Nr. 16	388 n. 2	5050	182 n. 15
Nr. 19	392 n. 15	5163	225 n. 12

6085	294 n. 28	I 1647	211 n. 42
6088	291 n. 11	I 1668	210 n. 39
6089	291 n. 10	I 1669	210 n. 38
8888	195 n. 68	I 1674	211 n. 41
9059	189 n. 48	I 1679	210 n. 39, 211 n. 43
9340	225 n. 12		
IRT		I 1758	210 n. 38
558	304 n. 90, 309 n. 118	I 1761	210 n. 39
		I 1770	210 n. 39
Lex Irnit.		I 1821	207 n. 29
73, 39–42	355 n. 23	I 1849	211 n. 42
95	307	I 1853	210 n. 39
F-I	303	I 1854	210 n. 39, 211 n. 43
Lex. Urson.			
81, 17–23	355 n. 23	I 1855	210 n. 39
Meier/Schmitz 1999		I 1857	211 n. 42
296–298, Nr. 3	400 n. 39	I 1860	210 n. 38
Morel 1976		I 1862	210 n. 38
426	250 n. 66	I 1972	210 n. 38
Nesselhauf 1937		I 1973	210 n. 38
71	254 n. 93	I 2081	210 n. 39, 211 n. 44
88	254 n. 93		
Nesselhauf/Lieb 1959,		I 2083	210 n. 39
40	250 n. 65	II.4, 2443.13	217 n. 65
54	244 n. 21	II.4, 2457.2	214 n. 50
RIB		II.5, 2491.96	213 n. 49
I 6	214 n. 51	II.5, 2491.124	207 n. 29
I 7	214 n. 51	II.5, 2491.148	202 n. 6–7
I 712	203 n. 10	II.8, 2502.51	202 n. 6
I 1007–1015	208 n. 31	III 3113	209 n. 34
I 1008	209 n. 32	III 3294	209 n. 33
I 1009	209 n. 32	III 3296	210 n. 39
I 1010	109 n. 32	III 3297	210 n. 39
I 1014	209 n. 32	III 3308	210 n.39
I 1345	210 n. 38	III 3379	210 n. 39, 211 n. 43
I 1346	210 n. 38		
I 1362	210 n. 38	III 3382	211 n. 42, 211 n. 43
I 1363	210 n. 38		
I 1402	210 n. 38	III 3385	210 n. 39
I 1440	210 n. 39, 212 n. 44	III 3401	210 n. 37
		III 3402	210 n. 38
I 1447	210 n. 39	III 3411	211 n. 42
I 1515	210 n. 39	III 3512	208 n. 30
I 1564	210 n. 39	RICG	
I 1565	210 n. 39	I 35, 38, 62	292 n. 16
I 1572	210 n. 39	RIU	
I 1632	210 n. 40	185	189 n. 44
I 1640	209 n. 35	RMD	
I 1646	211 n. 41	4, app. 1, 1–3	191 n. 55

Schillinger-Häfele		78	205 n. 20, 206
161	251 n. 74, n. 77	79	205 n. 19
167	251 n. 74, n. 77	Tab. Luguval.	
Schmitz 1995		1	207 n. 27
Nr. 5	388 n. 2	14	207 n. 26
Nr. 13	395 n. 24	Tab. Sulis	
Nr. 37; 41	392 n. 16	10, 30 and 1	214 n. 53
SEG		97	215 n. 56
7, 1934, 381–430	230	98	216 n. 59
7, 1934, 417	231	Tomlin 1993	
8, 1937, 860	179 n. 1	121 (Tablet 2)	217 n. 66
48, 1998, 1838	368 n. 11	129 (Tablet 52)	218 n. 68
49, 1999, 1481–1485	229	T. Vindol.	
56, 2006, 1359	224 n. 10	II 186	232
Tab. Lond. Bloomberg		II 250	184 n. 28
7	206 n. 21	II 291	215 Fn 55
33	206 n. 22	II 346	189 n. 45
44	204 n. 12	III 581	232
45	205 n. 16	III 628	232
50	204 n. 11	III 643	188 n. 38
55	213 n. 47	Urk.	
62	213 n. 46	IV, 662	90 n. 187
70	232	Weiss 2015	189 n. 48, 190
72	232	Zevi 2012	356 n. 27

Papyri

BGU		O.Krok.	
II 362	226 n. 18, 20	94	189 n. 45
II 423	192 n. 60	P.Alex.Giss.	
IV 1083	192 n. 63, 195 n. 69, 196	59	172 n. 34
		P.Berl.Cohen	
VII 1574	338 n. 11	8	327
Ch.L.A.		P.Berol.inv.	
VI-IX	181	9570	370 n. 18
CPR		21266v	370 n. 18
VII 18	331 n. 45	21129,2	370 n. 18
Derda/Łajtar/Płóciennik		P.Brem.	
2014/15	185 n. 31	63	173 n. 37, 44, 45
Derda/Łajtar/Płóciennik		P.Brook.	
2015,		3	336 n. 2, 4, 341
49–55	193 n. 64, 194	P.Cair.Isid.	
M.Chr.		68	331 n. 45
363	331 n. 48	P.Cair.Isid. 87–89	328 n. 35, 37, 329 n. 39, 330
O.Did.			
383	188 n. 38	97	328 n. 35, 329 n. 38
417	186 n. 37, 187–188		
418–420	186 n. 37, 188 n. 39–40	P.Col.	
		VII 174	329 n. 40

X 274,9–10	327 n. 25	VII 400	174 n. 46
P.CtYBR inv.		P.Heid.	
4601	379 n. 44	V pp. 333–335	328 n. 36
P.Didot		P.Kell.	
1	373 n. 26	I–VII	321 n. 4
P.Dura		I 13	331 n. 46
122	192 n. 63	I 14	330 n. 43
P.Fay.		I 23	331 n. 46
344	326 n. 19	I 32	331 n. 46
P.Flor.		I 58	330 n. 44
II 123	348	P.KRU	
II 135	348	68,95–99	171 n. 32
II 149	348	P.Louvre	
II 177	348	I 4	227 n. 28, 29
III 332	173 n. 38	P.Mich.	
P.Gen.		II 123	323
I² 18	343	III 206, 209	174 n.46
I² 28	335 n. 1, 336 n. 4, 341	V 228	325
		V 238	323
I² 72	345–346	VIII 464	168 n. 22, 23
III 139	345–346	VIII 468	184 n. 28
P.Giss.		IX 549	192 n. 60
19–20	173 n. 40	XV 751–752	174 n. 46
21	173 n. 37	XV 752, 27–42	175 n. 51
22–24	173 n. 39	XVIII 761	370 n. 18
78	173 n. 40, 41	inv. 397b-c	329 n. 38
79	173 n. 39	inv. 4384	324
80	173 n. 41, 42	inv. 5665	322 n. 11
85	173 n. 41, 43	inv. 5739	322 n. 12
Pap.Graec.Mag.		P.Oslo	
4,228 f.	264 n. 8	III 122	192 n. 63
4,328–330	277 n. 71	P.Oxy.	
4,2079 f.	269 n. 29	I 68	338 n. 11, 339 n. 12
4,2145–2240	269 n. 29		
5,304–369	269	IV 808	322 n. 13
7,450 f.	265 n. 13	XXII 2330	113 n. 1
7,469	265 n. 13	XXII 2349	192 n. 60
13,240 f.	265 n. 12	XXII 2349	193 n. 64
34,167 f.	276 n. 70	XXIV 2400	368
34,231	264 n. 8	XXXXI 2978	192 n. 60
36,1–3	265 n. 12	L 3555	168 n. 22
58,5	264 n. 8	LIX 3992	326 n. 24
P.Grenf.		LX 4058,19–20	322 n. 14
II 61	335 n. 1	LXXXII 5300	370 n. 18
P.Hal.inv.		LXXXII 5316	338 n. 11
31	370 n. 18	P.Petaus	
P.Hamb.		7	342
II 163	379	56	343 n. 20
P.Heid.Gr.		60	343 n. 19

121	342 n. 18	24	192 n. 63
P.Ryl		32	192 n. 63
I 60	370 n. 18	36	192 n. 63, 195
II 79	192 n. 63		n. 69, 196
P.Sakaon		SB	
5,64–66	329 n. 38	I 4440	341 n. 15
P.Sorb.		I 4639, 3–6	338 n. 10
III 70	321 n. 5	I 5943	341 n. 15
P.Sot.		III 6263	174 n. 46, 49, 188
19–21	165 n. 7		n. 38
P.Tebt.		V 7944	179 n. 1
II 315	227 n. 26	X 10652C	172 n. 34
II 416	188 n. 38	XX 14631, 4–7	338 n. 10
P.Vindob.		XXII 15618–20	331 n. 47
G inv. 39966 Col. 1	368 n. 12	XXVI 16578	174 n. 46
P.Wisc.		XXVI 16652	225 n. 14
II 84	174 n. 46, 175	W.Chr.	
	n. 50	71	227 n. 26
II 84a	175 n. 51	298	326 n. 23
P.Würzb.			
16	331 n. 48	**Coins**	
PSI Com.		BMC	
14	338 n. 11	197	366 n. 6
RMR		RIC	
10	191 n. 52	I² Nero 111	366 n. 6

Sources of Other Ancient Cultures: Egypt, Persia, India, China

A1Pa		688 F 8b	113 n. 1
11–12	114 n. 4	CT	
AO		22, 225	131 n. 130
8821	131 n. 131	CTN	
Arthaśāstra	59	3,39	130 n. 122
Assurbanipal		3,40	130 n. 122
Prisma A I 23–34		Cylinder seal of Peribsen	75 n. 63
Borger	120 n. 36	Daiva-inscription	60
Prisma F I 18–32		DE	
Borger	120 n. 36	15–16	114 n. 4
BE		DNb	
10, 102: 7	122 n. 54	A–G	123 n. 67
Bisutun-Inschrift		40–45	123 n. 67
IV 52–57. 57–59.		Frahm/Jursa 2011	
88–92	107, 115, 119 n. 32,	47 Nr. 140	125 n. 82
	120 n. 35	Hackl/Jursa/Schmidl 2014	
BM		Nr. 7	125 n. 78
84943	131 n. 130	Nr. 31	125 n. 78
BNJ		Nr. 39	125 n. 78
4 F 178b	133 n. 143	Nr. 77	125 n.78
90 F 5	113 n. 1	Nr. 210	125 n. 80

Nr. 216, 8–9	131	Pap. Sallier	
	n. 130	II, column XI, lines 1–4	67 n. 1
Nr. 224	125 n. 81	PBS	
Nr. 235	125 n. 78	2/1 34: 4, 9	122 n. 54
Nr. 240	131 n. 129	PF	
Nr. 241, 4–11	131 n. 131	323	115 n. 6
Instruction of Ani	73 n. 48	871: 4–5	120 n. 40
JC		1137: 5–6	120 n. 40
2706	28	1808	115 n. 6
2809	32	1810	115 n. 6, 121 n. 43
2829	30	1828	121 n. 43
2835	28	1947	115 n. 6, 121 n. 43, 122 n. 54
3747	30		
3748	30	1986	115 n. 6
3827	28	PFa	
4031	26	27	115 n. 6, 134 n. 150
4112	28	PFNN	
4140	26	0061	115 n. 6
4160	28	1040	115 n. 6
4241	26	1255	115 n. 6
4262	26, 32	1369	115 n. 6
4293	32	1485: 5–6	120 n. 40
4300	28	1511	115 n. 6
10176	30	1588: 4	120 n. 40
Jedaniah-Archiv	127 n. 91	1747	115 n. 7
Kamb.		1752	115 n. 6
384: 15–16	122 n. 54	1775	115 n. 6
Khalili		2356: 12–15	122 n. 54
IA 1	123 n. 62	2394	115 n. 6, 121 n. 43
IA 15	123 n. 63	2486	115 n. 6
Law book of Yājñavalkya	59	2493	115 n. 6
Memphite Theology (Shabaka Stone)		2529	115 n. 6, 121 n. 43
48–56	72	PFS	
MRE	45	0038	134 n. 149
NA		Porten 1996	
0709	32	Texte B 1–4	128 n. 100
Oracle-bone inscriptions	15 n. 6, 16–17, 20–25	Texte B 1–7	127 n. 98
		Texte B 1,12–13	128 n. 103
P.Beatty		Text B 2	132 n. 132
IV	70 n. 19, 87	Texte B 2,17	128 n. 103
Pap. Berlin		Text B 3	132 n. 135, 133 n. 142
3033, 8,3–4	88 n. 159		
Pap. Bibliothèque Nationale		Text B 3,2–3	132 n. 134
196, III	77 n. 92	Text B 3,4–5, 6–8	132 n. 139
Pap. Mallet	77 n. 91	Text B 3,6–8	132 n. 132
Pap. Louvre		Texte B 3,11–12	128 n. 102
1050 (E11006), V, 1–5	77 n. 91	Texte B 3,12–13	128 n. 103
Pap. Ramesseum		Texte B 4,7–8	128 n. 104
II, vso ii,5	72 n. 40	Texte B 4,13	128 n. 103

Texte B 5	133 n. 142	A 3.3	128 n. 105
Texte B 5–6	128 n. 100	A 4.1	127 n. 92
Text B 5,2–3	128 n. 101	A 4.7–8	127 n. 93
Text B 5,7–8	132 n. 137	A 6.1:1, 6	122 n. 54
Text B 5,7–9	132 n.138	A 6.1–15	126 n. 90
Texte B 5,14–15	128 n. 103	B 3.1–13	127 n. 96
Text B 7,2–3	132 n. 133	B 4.4:12	122 n. 54
Text B 8	128 n. 105	C 1.1	126 n. 89
Texte B 13–22	127 n. 91	C 2.1	126 n. 89
Texte B 19–20	127 n. 93	D 7–10	128 n. 106
Texte B 23–33	127 n. 94	D 7.1	128 n. 108
Texte B 34–46	127 n. 96	D 7.2	128 n. 108
Texte C 10 und C 20	132 n. 137	D 7.3	128 n. 108
PTS		D 7.6	129 n. 110, 133 n. 140
2357	131 n. 129		
Pyramid texts	71	D 7.8	128 n. 109
Rock Edict		D 7.20	128 n. 109
2	56, 57	D 7.24	128 n. 109
12	52 Abb. 2	D 7.48	128 n. 108
13	57	D 8.1–2	129 n. 111
13(Q)	57	D 9.1–2	129 n. 111
SAA		D 13.1	126 n. 86
7,24	130 n. 121	D 15.1	126 n. 85
16,28	130 n. 123	D 15.2	126 n. 85
16,49	130 n. 122	D 15.3	126 n. 85
SF		D 15.4	126 n. 85
1399	122 n. 57	TCL	
1400	122 n. 57	9, 141	131 n. 131
Shaked/Naveh 2012		Teaching of Khety	76 n. 76
94–99, Text A 4	123 n. 62	Tomb of pharaoh	
30, 122–125, Text A 9	123 n. 63	Horemheb (KV 57)	89 n. 175
Stela of Jkj	88	Tomb of Rawer	70, 73 n. 44
Stela MMA		Tomb U-j in Abydos	74 n. 52, 84
1. 4. 93	85	Tombs in Deir el-Medina	76
Sūtras of Pāṇini		XE	
3.2,21	60	15–16	114 n. 4
TAD		XPa	
A.2.1– 4	128 n. 100	7	114 n. 4
A 2.1–7	127 n. 98	XPc	
A 2.2	128 n. 102	10	114 n. 4
A 2.2:4–7	132 n. 132	XPd	
A 2.4	128 n. 104	11	114 n. 4
A 2.5	132 n. 132, 134, 135, 137, 138; 133 n. 142	XPh	
		6	114 n. 4
		XPl	
A 2.5,2–3	128 n. 101	9 A–J	123 n. 67
A 2.5–6	128 n. 100	XV	
A 2.7	132 n. 133	12	114 n. 4

www.ingramcontent.com/pod-product-compliance
Lightning Source LLC
Chambersburg PA
CBHW081822230426
43668CB00017B/2350